GUN TRADER'S GUIDE TO SHOTGUNS

© 2015

A Comprehensive, Fully Illustrated Reference for Modern Shotguns with Current Market Values

Edited by Robert A. Sadowski

Skyhorse Publishing

A version of "Short Hairs, Long Barrels and Fast Feathers" is reprinted from the November 2011 issue of *GunHunter Magazine* courtesy of Buckmasters LTD.
A version of "Spring Turkey Circa 1887" is reprinted from the October 2012 issue of *GunHunter Magazine* courtesy of Buckmasters LTD.
A version of "Stoeger Condor" is reprinted from the November 2012 issue of *GunHunter Magazine* courtesy of Buckmasters LTD.
A version of "Inertia Driven Operator: Benelli M2 Tactical" is reprinted from the July 2013 issue of *Tactical Weapons* magazine courtesy of Harris Tactical Group.

Skyhorse Publishing books may be purchased in bulk at special discounts for sales promotion, corporate gifts, fund-raising, or educational purposes. Special editions can also be created to specifications. For details, contact the Special Sales Department, Skyhorse Publishing, 307 West 36th Street, 11th Floor, New York, NY 10018 or info@skyhorsepublishing.com.

Skyhorse® and Skyhorse Publishing® are registered trademarks of Skyhorse Publishing, Inc.®, a Delaware corporation.

Visit our website at www.skyhorsepublishing.com.

10 9 8 7 6 5 4 3 2 1

Library of Congress Cataloging-in-Publication Data is available on file.

Cover design by Brian Peterson
Cover photographs courtesy Beretta and Caesar Guerini.

Print ISBN: 978-1-63450-586-4
Ebook ISBN: 978-1-63450-965-7

Printed in China

Contents

©2015

Shotgun Testing & Evaluation

Shotgun Provenance

Appendix

Introduction

This is the first edition of the *Gun Trader's Guide to Shotguns* or *GTG Shotguns* for short. In the tradition of the *Gun Trader's Guide*, *GTG Shotguns* gives professional and private shotgun collectors a complete reference guide to identifying and determining the value of modern shotguns made between the late nineteenth through to the the twenty-first century.

SPECS AND PHOTOS

Included are specifications and illustrations or photographs for thousands of different shotguns. The easy-to-use format is simple and straightforward. All shotguns are listed in alphabetical order by manufacturer or importer name, and the models are also in alpha-numeric order so you can find a specific model fast. The index also makes it easy to find a specific model by a manufacturer. Entries are alphabetized by manufacturer and model and further divided by action type if applicable. Full specifications include:

- Manufacturer
- Model Name
- Model Number
- Gauge
- Barrel Length
- Overall Length
- Weight
- Distinguishing Features
- Variations of Different Models
- Grades
- Dates of Manufacture (when they can be accurately determined)
- Date of Discontinuation (if applicable)
- Current Value (by condition)

PHOTOS OR ILLUSTRATIONS

A full-color section, Featured Shotguns, with detailed information on more than thirty collectible shotguns contains detailed photos to help aid in identifying shotguns. Also included in *GTG Shotguns* is information on how to grade firearms, buying and selling shotguns in online auctions, what to expect at gun shows, the AFT definition of curios and relics, state by state firearm purchase permit requirements, how to identify old and new shotgun types, shotgun collector organizations, online auctions, and more.

ACCURATE SHOTGUN VALUES

We have made every effort to ensure the information listed here is current and up to date. Not every shotgun ever manufactured can be listed in a reference book of this size, but we have made every effort to include the makes and models most popular with American owners and collectors. Please note *GTG Shotguns* does not include antique or recently manufactured black powder firearms. Values shown are based on national averages obtained by conferring with knowledgeable gun dealers, traders, collectors, and auctioneers around the country. The values listed accurately reflect the nationwide average at the time of publication. Keep in mind that the stated values are averages based on a wide spectrum of variables. No price given in any such reference book should be considered the only value for a particular shotgun. Value is ultimately determined by the buyer and seller.

In the case of rare or one-of-a-kind items, such as the Parker Brothers Invincible or the Parker Brother AA1 Special shotgun in 28 gauge, where very little trading takes place, active gun collectors were consulted to obtain current market values. In researching data, some manufacturers' records were unavailable, and at times information was unobtainable. Some early firearms manufacturers' production records have been destroyed in fires, lost, or were simply not accurately maintained. These circumstances resulted in minor deviations in the presentation format of certain model listings. For example, production dates may not be listed when manufacturing records are unclear or unavailable.

As an alternative, approximate dates of manufacture may be listed to reflect the availability of guns from a manufacturer or distributor. These figures may represent disposition dates indicating when that particular model was shipped to a distributor or importer. Frequently, and especially with foreign manufacturers, production records are unavailable. Therefore, availability information is often based on importation records that reflect domestic distribution only. This is meant to explain the procedures and policies used for these published dates and to establish the distinction between production dates, which are based on manufacturers' records, and availability dates, which are based on distribution records in the absence of recorded production data.

To ensure *GTG Shotguns* has the most accurate information available, we encourage users to contact the research staff at Skyhorse Publishing to forward any verifiable information they may have, especially about older out-of-production models.

In addition to shotgun identification and values, *GTG Shotguns* features Shotgun Testing & Evaluation, a testing and evaluation section with a hands-on review of a variety of shotguns from a pair of reproductions (CZ Hammer Classic Side-By-Side and Puma M-87) to an inexpensive over-and-under (Stoeger Condor) and a best-in-class tactical shotgun (Benelli M2 Tactical).

The Shotgun Provenance section looks in detail at one of John M. Browning's personal shotguns, a Model 1893 pump. Browning's influence on firearm design was wide and far-reaching. By 1900, more than 75 percent of the repeating sporting arms in the United States were John Browning's designs. Even today, many firearms manufacturers use a modified version of a John Browning design.

Finally, all shotgunners—from die-hard collectors to hunters to competitive shooters—have a bucket list. Let us know if we've included your must-do items in the Shotgun Collector's Bucket List.

ACKNOWLEDGMENTS
The editor and publisher wish to express special thanks to the many collectors, dealers, manufacturers, shooting editors, firearm firms, distributors' public relations and production personnel, research personnel, and other industry professionals who provided us with specifications and updates throughout the year. We are especially grateful for assistance and cooperation in compiling information for *GTG Shotguns* and to reproduce photographs and illustrations of collectible firearms. Special thanks to Mike Bishop of Bishop's Fine Guns in Fitzgerald, Georgia, (bishopsfineguns.com) for many of the detailed color photographs; the Union Station for access to the John Browning collection in the John M. Browning Firearms Museum (theunionstation.org); the John F. Kennedy Library (jfklibrary.org); and the help received from J. David Williamson, Journal Editor and Technical Advisor at the L.C. Smith Collectors Association.

Finally, *GTG Shotguns* thanks all the dedicated shotgunners who collect, hunt, compete, or defend their home with a shotgun. We welcome your comments. Please send comments or suggestions to:

Robert A. Sadowski, Editor
Gun Trader's Guide to Shotguns
Skyhorse Publishing, Inc.
307 West 36th Street, 11th Floor
New York, NY 10018
info@skyhorsepublishing.com

How to Use *GTG Shotguns*: Shotgun Buying and Selling Strategies

The price of shotguns fluctuates just like the prices of gasoline, smart phones, and real estate. Shotgun prices are not as volatile, but there are yearly changes in prices due to the seasonality or popularity of certain models. The number one question asked by gun owners, collectors, hunters, competition shooters, or those who have inherited a shotgun: What is it worth?

To know what a shotgun is worth, you must start by knowing exactly what it is. The first questions to answer: Who is the manufacturer? What is the action type? Model? Gauge? Barrel length? Grade? Are there any markings other than model?

Another question that could mean the difference between a junker and a firearm worth more than the normal price: Who owned it? Famous and infamous people having owned a shotgun give that shotgun provenance. A Winchester Model 12 owned by Ernest Hemingway will fetch much more than a Model 12 owned by an avid bird hunter in Wisconsin.

Know what it is to know what it is worth. This is where *GTG Shotguns* is a valuable resource. In this book, we identify models, include specifications and dates the model was produced or imported in the United States, and provide photographs.

They say a photo is worth a thousand words, and images are extremely helpful when trying to identify a specific model. In this way, *GTG Shotguns* is unique in providing hundreds of photos to help aid identification. Providing an image of each shotgun would be impossible—and it would create a book that would require a hand truck to tote around. The images in *GTG Shotguns* are carefully chosen to provide a representative image of a model. The text helps to narrow down the model to a specific variant.

POPULARITY

Some shotguns are always going to be popular and in demand. Parker Brothers, L.C. Smith, and A.H Fox side-by-side shotguns will always fetch a high price. Many of these grand old American shotguns have die-hard followings and organizations where members gather to talk shotguns in person or online in forums. Many of these fans know how many of a certain model were made, who has which model, which models have been refurbished, and which ones to stay away from. If you are interested in any of these shotguns, consult with some of these enthusiasts. You will not be disappointed. They have encyclopedic knowledge of the guns and are more than happy to share their knowledge. But be aware, once you start collecting old guns from America's golden age of shotguns, you may be afflicted for life.

SEASONALITY FLUCTUATION

You may be less a collector of fine shotguns and more of a hunter in need of a goose gun. Or your neighbor is selling a worn pump that might be a good starter gun for a novice bird hunter. First, don't buy a shotgun a week before hunting season opens, as prices are high and you will have less negotiating power because shotguns are in demand. Buy that goose gun after hunting season when a hunter may trade in a nearly new gun because he or she didn't like the way the gun fit them.

I recently came across a Beretta trap shotgun made in the late 1980s that was literally used by a little old lady only on Sundays. Really. She shot trap with her late husband on Sundays at their club. The asking price was a fraction of what a new model would cost. Yes, it was old and used, but that Beretta had plenty of use left in it. Trap season was well over when the Beretta came on the market, so demand was low and so was the price.

NOT SO NEW
Those who must have the latest and greatest shotgun immediately may trade in or want to sell those nearly new guns because they are tired of them and want to move onto the next new, shiny shotgun. Yes, those may be slightly used, but they're still almost new—and not even close to the manufacturer's suggested retail price. That tickles the frugal Yankee in me.

Shotguns are versatile firearms and can easily be used to shoot backyard clays, hunt birds, and defend your home. Understanding what types of shotguns are available in your budget can literally make you sleep more soundly and safely at night.

WHAT'S IT WORTH?
Many times instead of a buyer or seller searching for a specific shotgun, one is placed in their lap. A relative or a neighbor may have passed away, and the surviving spouse wants to get rid of the guns in the house. Or a friend or acquaintance may need to weed out their collection and make room in their gun safe for other guns. Many times these opportunities are unexpected, and a quick decision needs to be made.

Now the task is to determine the value. Do not assume that the newly acquired side-by-side shotgun from your late Uncle Harry's estate is worth a bucket load of money—but then again, don't instantly think you should surrender the firearm to the local police station for a minor reward. Your buddy who wants to buy a brand new semiauto for 3-Gun competition might want to sell you his old one.

Firearms Grading

THE RESEARCH BEGINS

Do not think of the research process as a laborious time suck, but instead consider it a journey of discovery. Let's walk through the steps to identify and determine the value of a shotgun to see whether you have a junker suitable for a wall hanging at best or a valuable piece desired by a collector and to be treasured. Going through our checklist, we were quickly able to determine our example shotgun is a 28-gauge over-and-under manufactured by Gebr. Adamy. The barrels measured about 28 inches in length. Here is the process we went through to identify the shotgun in detail.

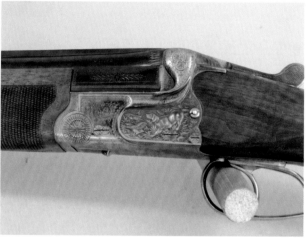

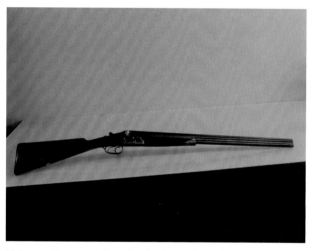

This small over-and-under looks at first glance like it was built in Germany due to the tell-tale Teutonic design aesthetic of the receiver and forend.

Note the lines of the forend—thin and flat—like many shotgun forends of German manufacture. The checkering pattern also is reminiscent of a German manufacturer.

The engraving on the sides of the receiver are hand-engraved, not etched by a machine or a laser. Though the engraving is not typical German engraving with oak leaf clusters, the scrollwork still leads us to believe it is of German descent. The over-and-under uses a Blitz-style action, which is recognizable from the outside due to the extra-wide trigger plate.

Under the receiver were engraved the manufacturer's name and the grade of the shotgun: "Gebr. Adamy/Suhl, Germany/Diamond Grade." So it is confirmed the shotgun was manufactured in Germany—Suhl, Germany, in fact—an area known for gun makers. A quick Internet search showed that Gebr. Adamy has been in the gun making business since 1820 and today produces custom-built side-by-side and over-and-under shotguns, as well as single shot rifles, drillings, vierlings, and hammer guns. All are handmade with the finest wood and custom engravings.

Many times, a manufacturer's website allows you to look up a serial number to date the man-ufacture of your gun. The Gebr. Adamy website does not have that option, so an email will suffice—we hope they are fluent in English. In the meantime, we looked up the Adamy in *GTG SHOTGUNS* and find the Gebr. Adamy is a custom gun maker—all guns are custom made to order, so there is no way to easily determine value or to categorize them except by action type.

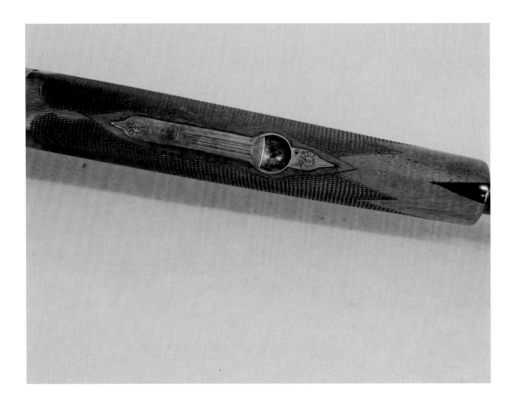

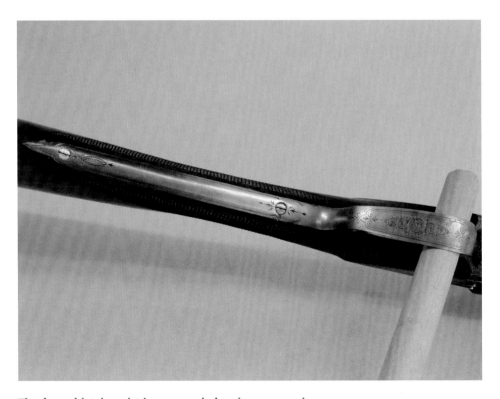

The forend latch and trigger guard also show engraving.

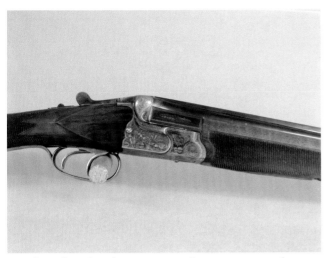

Another clue the shotgun was of German manufacture: the way the receiver is fitted to the stock.

The leather recoil pad led us to believe that the original stock was modified, which could decrease the value of the shotgun. Regardless, the recoil pad was expertly fitted.

The Adamy had fixed chokes, which led us to believe the shotgun was manufactured in the twentieth century prior to the 1950s. We thought initially even earlier.

We assumed the 28-gauge would fetch a higher value than the typical 12-, 16-, or 20-gauges, which are more common. The condition of the shotgun was 95 percent with the case-hardened receiver having nearly all its color. The blued barrel were also in fine condition, and the wood showed some handling marks. No doubt the shotgun was used but not extensively. From our initial research and our gut instinct, we thought the Adamy was valued at anywhere between $5,000 and $10,000. Since the Adamy was so unique, we brought the gun to an appraiser who deals in German guns. Our appraiser said the shotgun was manufactured before WWII in the late 1920s or early 1930s. The estimated value of the Adamy Diamond Grade is about $7,500.

Online Auctions

There is not a facet of our lives that isn't touched by technology. Today, auction websites, such as gunbroker.com and gunsamerica.com, and online dealers, such as impactguns.com and galleryofguns.com, offer gun buyers a vast selection of firearms. You can buy and sell guns using your computer.

Buyers can easily search for that one rare gun to complete their collection or look for a new shotgun for next dove season. The Internet allows buyers to search for new and used firearms, as well as curios and relics, surplus guns, gun parts, ammunition, reloading equipment, and just about anything firearm related.

Online auction websites enable sellers to reach buyers they might not have reached otherwise. A small one-room gun store in Maine can now sell to buyers across the country, or if you are a private individual with a gun to sell, all you need to do is create an account, type in a description, take a few digital pictures of the item, and list it. It's that simple and that easy.

Remember: all the same federal, state, and local gun laws apply when selling and purchasing a gun online as when purchasing a gun at a brick-and-mortar retailer. In fact, the transfer of the firearm is the same. When a buyer purchases a firearm from gunsamerica.com, for example, the buyer must provide the seller with a copy of their gun shop's Federal Firearms Licenses (FFLs) or arrange to have the seller ship the firearm to one of the FFLs near the buyer. The seller then ships the gun to the gun shop with the FFL holder—not directly to the buyer—and the buyer then fills out the necessary state and local paperwork to take transfer of the gun. Gun shops usually charge the buyer a fee to transfer the gun, which is typically $45 to $65.

It is up to the buyer to be aware of state and local laws. For example, a buyer in Connecticut cannot take ownership of a Bushmaster AR-15 M4 style carbine that is offered by a seller in, say, Georgia or Texas. The gun laws in Connecticut forbid sales of any assault-style rifles. Know your local and state laws before buying. If you bid on it and win, you own it.

Auction sites charge a fee, usually a small percentage of the sale, to all sellers. The fee is only charged if the seller actually sells the gun through an auction. There is no charge to list a firearm.

When setting up an account with online auction websites, a seller needs to provide a credit card. Once an auction closes with a sale, the fee is automatically charged to the seller's credit card.

Online gun dealers, such as gallery of guns.com, are not auction sites, but these sites allow users to purchase guns that are then shipped to an FFL-holding retailer in or near the buyer's zip code.

TYPES OF ONLINE AUCTIONS

Basic: In a basic auction, the seller's staring price is the amount the seller is willing to sell the item for.

Dutch: In a Dutch auction, a seller is auctioning two or more identical items, and a buyer bids on the per-item cost for all the items the seller is auctioning. If you bid $1.00 and there are ten items, the total price is $10.

Absolute or Penny: An absolute or penny auction starts out at $.01 with no reserve. The item sells for the last bid after the auction closes.

Reserve: In a reserve auction, a seller has a minimum reserve price set for the item. This amount is hidden from buyers.

Finding a specific firearm is easy for buyers because of search functionality built into the auction websites. Once users have an account, they can zero in on a specific manufacturer, model, caliber, barrel length, magazine capacity, and other criteria. Users can save the search and receive email alerts with search results.

Many online auctions also offer services for after the sale with shipping profiles, FFL look-up, and other tools to smoothly complete the transaction.

Most sellers and buyers online do business fairly and ensure all parties are satisfied. Like with any business, some unscrupulous sellers try to take advantage of you. Do your due diligence and contact the seller prior to making a bid, get as much information as you can about the item, and check the seller's rating. Most sellers do their best to keep their rating high, and most will be willing to go the distance to make a customer satisfied. The auction websites have a system in place to deal with buyer and seller protection. Like anything, the old dictum "buyer beware" applies. If the deal seems too good to be true, it probably is.

I have used online gun auctions to bid on and purchase firearms I would never have seen at my local gun dealer. Online auctions generate excitement about bidding against other buyers, but remember your budget, and remember what the firearm is worth. You do not want to get caught up in a bidding war and overpay. On the other hand, you may be inclined to pay more for an item that is less popular in your geographic area or for an item that is no longer manufactured. Technology has opened up gun trading 24/7/365.

ONLINE AUCTION GLOSSARY

10- or 15-Minute Rule: After the last bid activity or an auction is ready to close, a time interval of 10 to 15 minutes must pass to allow any last bids to be entered. Think of it as the "going, going, gone" statement made by an auctioneer. If a bid is entered during the last 10 or 15 minutes, the 10- or 15-minute interval resets. Only when the entire 10 or 15 minutes have passed with no bids is the auction considered closed.

Auto Bid or Proxy Bid: A buyer bids the maximum amount they are willing to pay for an item, and auto bid automatically enters the least amount to win and continues to automatically bid to the specified maximum. For example, Buyer 1 sets up an auto bid for $500, yet the current bid on the item is $450. Buyer 2 bids $475, and Buyer 1's auto bid bids according to the bid increment of the auction and the maximum amount specified Buyer 1. Once auto bid hits the maximum amount, it stops bidding.

Bid: The amount a buyer is willing to pay for an item.

Bid History: Shows the bids of buyers and time and date of bid. During a live auction, the bid amounts are hidden. After the auction closes, bid amounts per shown.

Bid Increment: The amount the bid is increased as specified by the seller.

Buy Now: Displayed price the seller is willing to accept to end the auction.

FFL: Federal Firearms License; a holder of an FFL is required in order to transfer a firearm from a seller to a buyer.

Feedback: Buyers and sellers can leave feedback on the auction transaction for public viewing. Typically, both sellers and buyers are rated.

Fixed Price: An item that sells at a set price with no bidding.

Inspection Period: Some auction websites require the seller to give the buyer a time limit, usually three days, to inspect the item. If the buyer declines the item, the buyer is entitled to a full refund on the auction price. Return shipping is paid by the buyer.

Minimum Bid: The total amount of the current high bid plus the bid increment.

Reserve Price: The lowest price the seller is willing to accept; typically the reserve price is hidden.

Reserve Price Not Met/Reserve Price Met: In a reserve auction, the indication of whether bidding met the reserve price.

Starting Bid: Least amount a bidder is allowed to bid; this is set by the seller.

Watch List: A buyer can use a watch list to track items they are interested in. Items stay in a user's watch list until deleted by a user even if the item's auction has closed.

Gun Shows

Nearly every weekend, organized gun shows take place around the country. These events are places for shotgun collectors of all types to converge and buy and sell firearms of all types—shotguns, handguns, rifles—as well as accessories and related items from gun cases and holsters to military surplus and other accoutrements. Depending on the size of the show, hundreds of dealer booths can be set up for miles with firearms ranging in value from junkers for less than $20 to luxurious, pristine examples that can cost $100,000 or more.

DO YOUR HOMEWORK
Gun shows are places to buy and sell, so make sure you have done your homework on a firearm model you're interested in. You could be paying too much or selling for too little, so try to know the value of the guns you are interested in before attending a show. Use *GTG Shotguns* to help determine the value of your gun so you have a benchmark. Also look online to see what your particular gun is selling for. Depending on the area of the country, some guns sell better than others. Also, a dealer may purchase your gun at a low price only to sell it for more online. If you are fine with that, know the rock bottom price you will take for your item. Likewise, know the top dollar you will pay for an item.

WHO ATTENDS GUN SHOWS?
Dealers from the region and sometimes from across the country will rent a booth to show, sell, buy, trade, and talk about new and used guns of every make and model. Some dealers specialize in firearms made by a specific manufacturer—Beretta, Benelli, Winchester, Remington, Savage, Ruger, or Stevens, for example—while some deal in just one model of firearm, such as pre-1964

Winchester Model 70s. Others may offer custom guns or firearms made by European or Asian manufacturers, while others have a variety of collectibles including swords, knives, military surplus, gun art, and ancient weaponry. Gun buyers, collectors, and dealers benefit from attending gun shows by seeing a wide variety of firearms, their condition, and their value.

Dealers are experts in firearms value, and while some know a specific make or a type, most can explain the nuances of a firearm's condition, why perfectly refurbished guns are worth so much less than a rusted or beat-up original, and what makes one gun worth so much while another seemingly similar model is worth so much less. It's their business to know.

Many gun show attendees are pure collectors who also concentrate on one area or type of firearms, such as Winchester Model 12s or L.C. Smith side-by-sides. Hunters and shooters also attend to purchase a new goose gun for the upcoming hunting season or perhaps trade in an entry-level trap gun for an intermediate model.

GUN SHOW BASICS
Unless otherwise noted, all gun shows in the United States are open to the public. Typically there is a small admission charge, usually about $10. Larger shows have higher admission fees. Many times parking is free. Security requirements must be met and procedures must be followed when attending a show. In general, anyone attending a gun show may bring guns for appraisal, sale, or trade. Typically no loaded guns in any form are allowed in the show. If you are bringing a gun for appraisal, it's a good idea to have it zip-tied. This lets everyone know that the firearm is not loaded. Carry some extra zip ties, as you will probably need to cut off the tie

to allow a prospective buyer to check the firearm's mechanism.

Remember to market your gun by placing a FOR SALE sign on it. A dealer or someone in the crowd may see your sign as you walk the show floor and want to examine and discuss your gun. There's no need to be subtle—you have a gun and you want to sell it, so advertise.

Many shows do not allow concealed carry, so leave your personal defense weapon at home or in your vehicle. Laws vary from state to state, so be sure to check with show promoters or local law enforcement personnel before bringing a gun to a show. Many shows have websites with details on show rules, as well as dates, times, and locations. It is also a good idea to understand out-of-state laws if you choose to attend an out-of-state show. Contact the show organizer or ask a dealer.

WORKING THE FLOOR

Most guns shows are well attended and often crowded. Be patient while moving through the crowd between booths. If a particular dealer or booth is five customers deep, come back later to talk when the booth is less crowded. There are always slow periods at gun shows. Early in the day, lunchtime, and just before closing are typically slow, so schedule your visits to dealers and make the most of your time.

Do not expect to get top dollar for your shotgun unless you have a rare model. Since many dealers at shows often work in volume sales, they may have a dozen or more of your model on the table for sale. This is especially true of inexpensive imports and popular shotguns, such as a Remington Model 870 or Mossberg Model 500. Millions of these guns have been produced over the years. Specialty guns, however, will draw a dealer's attention, and once in a while you will get far more than you expected for a particular firearm. Many times a dealer has customers back home that are looking for a specific model, gauge, or some other feature.

If your gun is in the rare category—or even if it isn't—it is best to bring your gun in for appraisal only. See what the dealer is willing to give you for it and compare that to the prices listed in the *GTG Shotgun* and other collectible gun books, as well as online. If a dealer is offering you a much higher price than you expected, tell him you'll think about it and then do some more research because you may have a unique model with a higher value. Maybe you have a shotgun Ernest Hemingway traded in or a gun with a few models manufactured. In most cases there will be too much hubbub, conversation, and diversion at gun show booths to allow you to make a serious sale or trade. If you are feeling rushed or pressured, move on but ask the dealer for a business card with email or telephone information. This is a smart and easy way to get a lot of face time with multiple dealers. Besides, you don't want to waste the dealers' time or your time. You can always follow up later when you are ready to negotiate. Don't be rushed into a sale. You may not make a sale that day, but you may make a valuable contact for the future.

On the flip side, also remember that when you buy a gun at a show, you may pay slightly more. Do you really want to risk missing that perfect piece for your collection because a dealer wanted $50 more than the typical price? Sometimes it comes down to immediate satisfaction and adding that desired piece to your collection. A buyer who needs a particular piece to complete his or her collection could easily offer you more than the gun is listed for, more than the dealer offered, and more than you ever expected to get for it.

Gun shows are ongoing events that occur weekly, monthly, or annually around the country. For a complete, updated schedule of gun shows near you and around the country, go to gunshows-usa.com.

Shotgun Action Types

The shotgun is one of the most common and, in a sense, more complicated firearms developed. Not only do shotguns come in different action types, shotguns also come with a number of barrels and barrel configurations. The operating mechanism or action for a shotgun can generally be classified into five types.

BREAK ACTION

When modern, self-contained shells were invented, the break action was the most common shotgun action. As the name implies, the action of the shotgun is broken open via a lever or button. The top lever is the most common opening device today. As the action is opened by moving the lever, the barrel or barrels pivot away from the receiver to allow the user to load and unload the shotgun. The barrels are attached to the receiver by a hinge.

Break-action shotguns come in three main variants: single barrel, double barrel, and triple barrel. Single- and double-barrel variants are the most common. The double-barrel shotgun is also divided into two subvariants, the side-by-side and over-and-under. The side-by-side shotgun has the barrels configured horizontally, hence the name side-by-side. Purdey, A.H. Fox, L.C. Smith, Beretta, Parker Brothers, Stoeger, Winchester, and a long list of other manufacturers have built side-by-side shotguns that range from the mere utilitarian to the outright luxurious. Side-by-sides these days range from inexpensive imports to true works of the gun maker's art. The over-and-under shotgun is distinguished from the side-by-side by the barrels being stacked on top of each other. Again the name is a clue. These stacked-barrel shotguns are the most common double-barrel shotguns built today by most major American, German, and Italian shotgun makers that produce a variety of models in all price points.

Single-barrel shotguns, as the names implies, have only one barrel. At one time, these single-barrel, single-shot shotguns were a common tool on farms. Today, H&R is one of the few manufactures that still manufactures an economy workhorse of a shotgun called the Pardner. On the other end of the single-barrel shotgun spectrum are competitive trap shotguns, such as the Browning BT-99, Perazzi TM9, and MX15, as well as others built to take the rigors of word-class trap competition shooting.

Triple-barrel shotguns are a bit of an anomaly, and though three-barrel smoothbore shotguns have been manufactured over the centuries, these are quite rare. Chiappa Firearms recently introduced a shotgun line of triple-barrel shotguns built with two horizontal barrels and the third barrel on top and in between the bottom two.

More common yet also rare are drillings and combination guns. Drillings and combination guns both use a break action and differ in barrel configuration. A combination gun, such as the Savage M24, the M6 survival rifle, Baikal M94, and Valmet 412, are a few examples of combination guns that pair a rifle and shotgun barrel in a stacked over-and-under configuration. A drilling features a pair of shotgun barrels and a rifle barrel or one shotgun barrel and two rifle barrels. Numerous configurations are available from custom gun makers. JP Sauer & Sohn was a major manufacturer of drillings at the turn of the twentieth century. Blaser is currently one of the few gun makers that produces a drilling. The Blaser D99 drilling can be custom made with two side-by-side shotgun barrels and a rifle barrel over them. Another variation on the multiple barrel shotgun is the vierling, which is the German word for quadruplet. A vierling has four barrels in a variety of configurations. The Johann Fanzoj Firm in Austria is one of the few custom gun makers that will make a vierling to order.

The Chiappa Triple Barrel fires the right barrel first, the left barrel second, then the top barrel.

The Russian-made Baikal M94 is a combination gun with a shotgun barrel over a rifle barrel.

The H&R Pardner is an example of a single-barrel break action.

A classic American over-and-under break action is the Winchester Model 101.

The inexpensive Stoeger Uplander Supreme; a rugged side-by-side break action.

Cross section of the barrels from a drilling; two shotgun barrels side by side over a rifle barrel.

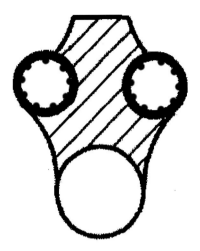

And the inverse: two rifles side by side over a shotgun.

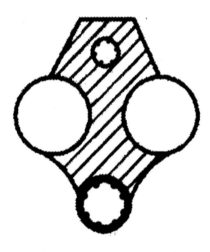

This cross section of a vierling's barrels uses two side by side shotgun barrels with a big bore rifle barrel underneath and a small bore rifle barrel above.

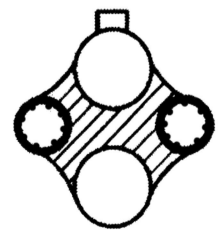

An example of a vierling with over-and-under shotgun barrels with two big bore rifle barrels on the sides.

PUMP ACTION

Pump- or slide-action shotguns require the operator to manually slide the forend rearward to operate the mechanism. As the operator slides the forend rearward, the empty shell is ejected and the hammer is cocked. On the forward stroke, a fresh shell is pushed into the chamber, which makes the shotgun ready to fire. The forend slides along a tubular magazine located under the barrel. Shells are loaded into the tubular magazine through a loading port located at the bottom of the receiver. Pump-action shotguns are common and popular. Mossberg is the world's largest pump-action shotgun manufacturer. The Mossberg Model 500 alone has had more than ten million units produced. The first successful pump-action shotgun was the Spencer Arms 1882 shotgun, the same manufacturer that made the Spencer Repeating rifle. It could be argued, however, that the first truly successful pump gun was the Winchester Model 1897. More than a million Model 1897s were built by Winchester up until 1957.

In the late twentieth century, the Chinese manufacturer Norinco reproduced the famed shotgun as Cowboy Action Shooting (CAS) became popular. The Remington Model 31 and Model 870, the Winchester Model 12, and the Ithaca Model 37 are some of the more iconic and popular models. Companies such as Browning, Savage, Marlin, High Standard, Ithaca, and other American makers also built and continue to build pump guns used by hunters, competitive shooters, the military, and law enforcement. Since WWI, short-barrel pumps have been sometimes referred to as Trench Sweepers. Short-barreled, maneuverable pump guns were effectively used to clear enemy trenches in the Great War. Some sounds send a shiver down your spine: the sound of a twisting tornado, low flying F-16s, and the sound of a pump-action shotgun being cycled. Modern pump-action shotguns are known for durability and reliability. Experienced shooters can operate a pump at a fast rate of fire. For hunting, tactical use, and home defense, a pump shotgun is hard to beat.

Popular for more than sixty years, the Remington Model 870 pump action comes in a variety of finishes and stocks.

Made for home defense and tactical applications is the Mossberg Model 500 Cruiser pump action; this model has a built-in tactical light in the forend.

SEMIAUTOMATIC ACTION

Similar to semiautomatic pistols and rifles, a semiautomatic shotgun fires with each pull of the trigger. The three main semiautomatic action variants are gas operated, inertia operated, and recoil operated.

Gas-operated models, such as the Remington Model 1100, Bereatta Model A-390, and Browning Gold to mention just a few, siphon gas from a fired shell through a small hole or port in the barrel. The gas then pushes rearward a piston attached to a connection rod that is connected to the bolt assembly. Recoil springs pull the bolt carrier group forward and chamber a shell, which makes the shotgun ready for the next shot.

The Benelli M2 and the late model Browning A5 are two inertia-operated shotguns. When a round is fired, the shotgun moves rearward while the bolt body stays in position due to the inertia spring, which is a short, thick spring inside the bolt body. Almost the entire shotgun is a recoiling component; only the bolt remains stationary during firing.

Recoil-operated shotguns, such as the Franchi 48/AL and the older Browning Auto-5, use the force of the recoil from a fired round to cycle the action. The barrel literally moves rearward and pushes on the bolt to eject and chamber a shell.

In operation, all three actions work the same—with each pull of the trigger, the action cycles and becomes ready for the next pull of the trigger. Semiautomatic actions reduce felt recoil more than any other action types since some of the energy from the fired shell is used to operate the mechanism. The felt recoil of a gas-operated actions is usually less pronounced than that of an inertia- or recoil-operated action. Inertia- and recoil-operated actions, however, run cleaner and cooler since all the burning powder is contained in the barrel. Gas-operated actions require more diligent cleaning of the piston and the rest of the system. Older gas-operated guns, such as the Remington Model 58 and others made in the 1950s, required the user to adjust the piston to suit the shell load. Some newer guns manufactured in Turkey also require the user to match the load to the piston. Recoil-operated guns also need to be user adjusted; bronze friction rings in older Browning Auto-5s need to be configured to ensure proper functioning.

The semiautomatic Remington Model 1100 has been a favorite with hunters and clay shooters due to the light recoiling gas-operating system.

The original Browning Auto-5 was a recoil-operated semiautomatic. This newer A5 uses an inertia-operated system.

Last of the recoil-operated action, the Franchi 48AL Deluxe with Prince of Wales grip is a lithe 20-gauge.

The Puma M-87 is a reproduction of the Winchester 1882 lever-action shotgun.

BOLT ACTION

Less common but nonetheless useful in some hunting situations are bolt-action shotguns. A generation or two ago, the Marlin Model 55 Goose Gun with a 36-inch barrel could take down high flying honkers with regularity, depending on the skill of the operator. Today, the Savage Model 212 and Browning A-Bolt are bolt-action shotguns designed to fire slugs for those hunters required by law to hunt deer with a shotgun. The bolt-action shotgun is similar to a bolt-action rifle, where an operator must manually cycle the bolt to eject and chamber a fresh shell. Most use a detachable box magazine.

LEVER ACTION

Lever-action shotguns are even less common, and if it weren't for Cowboy Action Shooting competition guns—such as the Winchester 1887 designed by John Browning—most would have faded from memory. Reproductions of the Model 1887 are offered by Italian and Chinese companies and are popular with CAS competitors. The Ithaca Model 66 series offered hunters a single-shot lever-action shotgun during the 1960s and '70s. In 2001, Winchester Repeating Firearms offered a lever action .410 shotgun, a Model 9410, that was similar to their Model 94 lever-action rifle.

This Savage 212 bolt-action shotgun is made to accurately shoot slugs when a scope is mounted.

Cyborg, played by Arnold Schwarzenegger, carried a cut-down version of the Winchester 1882 in the *Terminator 2* movie. More than likely, it was a Chiappa 1887 T-Series.

Stock Styles

Shotgun stock styles come in numerous configurations and really depend on the end use of the shotgun. A hunter with a break-action shotgun may prefer a straight English grip over a pistol grip, while an operator needing a shotgun to maneuver in cramped quarters may opt for an adjustable stock. Competition shooters know that a stock properly fitted to their stature makes a shotgun easier to shoot and break clays.

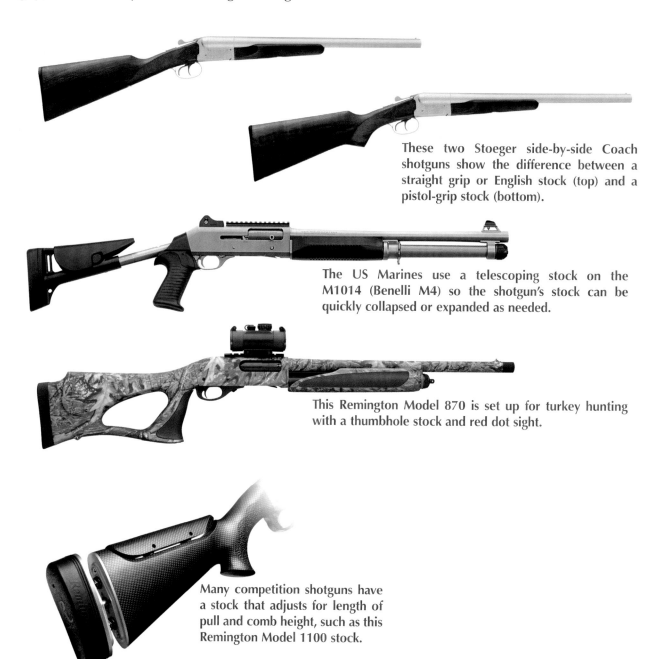

These two Stoeger side-by-side Coach shotguns show the difference between a straight grip or English stock (top) and a pistol-grip stock (bottom).

The US Marines use a telescoping stock on the M1014 (Benelli M4) so the shotgun's stock can be quickly collapsed or expanded as needed.

This Remington Model 870 is set up for turkey hunting with a thumbhole stock and red dot sight.

Many competition shotguns have a stock that adjusts for length of pull and comb height, such as this Remington Model 1100 stock.

Shotgun Testing & Evaluation

SHORT HAIRS, LONG BARRELS, AND FAST FEATHERS: CZ HAMMER CLASSIC SIDE-BY-SIDE AND A RESCUED POINTER

In the fall, I prefer the company of pointers, especially dogs that are slightly independent and feverish to hunt every niche of the woods. Years ago, before I knew I was becoming a grouser, an old hunter and I would cross paths coming and going from coverts we both haunted. I don't remember the breed of his dog, but I do recall him carrying a side-by-side. On occasion he'd impart bits of wisdom, such as loading barrels with #6s during the early season when the leaves were still on the trees. He'd give his ancient dog a drink of water, nod, and off he went. The CZ Hammer Classic reminds me of that old-timer's gun, and Bella reminds me of his dog. Hammer shotguns in a world of semiautos and pumps seems eccentric, especially when it is an affordable CZ and not a custom gun that costs a king's ransom. When the CZ and Bella came into my life, there was no doubt in my mind the days of hammer guns were not over.

Bella admires her rooster while Cooper wonders when it will be his turn to hunt.

A timeless picture of a frosty fall morning and Bella on scent.

The CZ Hammer Classic is a 12-gauge side-by-side shotgun with long 30-inch barrels and exposed hammers. It's about as old-school as you can get with a shotgun. Most hunters these days are used to looking over one barrel or stacked barrels, but this CZ allows you to hunt birds the way your great-grandfathers did. The CZ Classic Hammer has been catalogued by

The CZ Hammer Classic carried well and came up to the shoulder easily.

CZ since 2009, and the 2010 Vintage World Championship was won with the CZ Hammer Classic.

The Hammer Classic weighs a hair more than seven pounds. The wood is rather plain Turkish walnut with a pistol grip stock and a length of pull at 14½ inches. It is utilitarian yet classically elegant with frothy casehardening colors on the sideplates and receiver. The barrels and steel buttplate are blued. The lock up is typical for a side-by-side. The barrels pivot on a hinge pin. Two bolts at the bottom of the receiver engage two lugs milled into the bottom of the monobloc when the barrels are closed. Another lug built into the base of the monobloc fits into a notch in the base of the receiver. The Classic Hammer closed tight and looked like it would give good, long service.

The barrels sport a solid raised rib and accept choke tubes. Five choke tubes are provided: full, improved modified, modified, improved cylinder, and cylinder. Empties are extracted and pulled out by hand, which prohibits quick reloads but does allow a hunter to easily save empty hulls for reloading. The rebounding hammers are fully functioning and work in conjunction with a sliding safety located on the top tang. Double triggers allow the shooter to quickly

The front trigger fires the right barrel, and the rear trigger fires the left barrel.

The CZ may look a few centuries old, but those choke tubes make the shotgun a modern hunter.

The CZ's forearm latch is casehardened; the forearm checkering was well executed.

choose what barrel to fire when a bird flushes. The front trigger fires the right barrel; the rear fires the left barrel. The front trigger has a pull that averages nine pounds, fourteen ounces; the rear is less at seven pounds, five ounces. The old-timer, I recall, especially liked double triggers. He could load different shells in either barrel depending on the conditions.

I put the CZ through what I call the Davies-Foster test—that is, a round or two of skeet shot with the stock unshouldered. Davies and Foster invented and refined the game of skeet, respectively. It was and still is good practice for grouse and pheasant hunting. At the skeet field, 2¾-inch Hevi-Shot shotshells were employed. The Hevi-Shot Pheasant load in 12-gauge in #6s provides a 1⅛-ounce payload at 1200 fps (feet per second). Hevi-Shot Classic Doubles had the same load of #6s at a velocity of 1150 fps.

The Hammer Classic was quick to shoulder and allowed me to pull through and hit targets I normally have issues with using an over-and-under or semiautomatic. It was a bit odd to have to cock back the hammers. It was another step in the process, but I acclimated and began to enjoy the extra effort.

The true test, though, is in the field, and that's where the other old dog in this story appears. Bella was about to have her subscription can-celed at a shelter when we intervened. She is a brindle German Shorthaired Pointer whom my wife and I rescued with hope of giving Cooper, our year-old liver-colored male German Shorthair Pointer, companionship. Bella's soulful brown eyes show wisdom, and her paws are one size too big for her body. Her coat is mink smooth. We have no idea of her real age, but we and our vet think she is pushing ten.

For all of us, having another dog in the house was difficult at first. Bella's history is sketchy, but from the pieces we've heard, she was bounced from family member to family member with no one really committed to caring for her. She shows

The long barrels do not add length to the CZ as they would with a pump or semiautomatic.

The CZ Hammer Classic is a handsome shotgun that is at home in chopped corn fields after pheasant or in hardwood coverts for grouse.

The CZ with two mouthfuls of 12-gauge Hevi-Shot.

scars that are evident emotionally and physically. She was tense and edgy, and she asserted her dominance over Cooper as most females will. We were told she liked to play ball. She did not. She lived to hunt, we were told, yet no one from the former owner's hunt club would have her. Physically, she bears scars from a fire and a terrible ordeal. Errant fireworks caused her to chew through a wire kennel and pull her body through the wires, which shredded her abdomen at the same time. She needed numerous surgeries. If the gun club members didn't want her, I was sure she wasn't a hunter, and that would be OK.

Early on a frosty fall morning, I took Bella on our first hunt to a public hunting area. I hoped to flush a put-and-take pheasant or native grouse. It was in those fields we connected and where she learned to trust me and I her. In the ruff at the edge of field, she locked up and shook with excitement. Her front paw was up, her back straight, and her tail out. Not a ribbon-winning field trial point but a beautiful point just the same.

"Whoa."

She stood in place quivering with anticipation. Before I could kick it up, the rooster took off in a flash of feathers and clucks. The CZ shouldered easily. With the flying rooster over those side-by-side barrels, I touched off a right barrel, and the Hevi-Shot took care of business

and crumpled him in a heap. Bella ferreted out the rooster and dropped him at my feet. I extracted the empty from the fired barrel and dropped it in my pocket. It seemed like old

CZ markets the Hammer Classic, but the firearm is manufactured in Turkey.

The tang safety is a modern enhancement to a hammer gun.

The CZ Hammer Classic is a handsome shotgun with side-by-side barrels that are practical.

times.

With the cost of new and older hammer side-by-sides prohibitively expensive, the CZ Hammer Classic is one way to experience bird hunting as it was practiced by your great-great-great-grandfather. If you are looking to walk the fields less traveled, the CZ Classic Hammer is a perfect companion—as is an old dog that no one wanted.

The CZ Classic Hammer recreates a bygone era of shotgunning.

SPECIFICATIONS:
CZ Classic Hammer
PRODUCED: 2009-present
GAUGE: 12
CHAMBER: 3 in.
BARREL: 30 in.
CHOKE: Screw-in choke tubes; F, IM, M, IC, C
OA LENGTH: 47.4 in.
WEIGHT: 6.7 lbs.
STOCK: Turkish walnut with pistol grip
LENGTH OF PULL: 14.5 in.
COMB: 1.5 in.
HEEL: 2.25 in.

FOREND: Splinter
SIGHTS: Brass bead front
ACTION: Break action, side-by-side
RECEIVER FINISH: Color case hardened
BARREL FINISH: Gloss black chrome
EJECTOR/EXTRACTOR: Extractor
RIB: 8mm flat
CAPACITY: 2
TRIGGER: Dual triggers, mechanical
SAFETY: Manual tang safety, rebounding hammers
NiB: $963
Ex: $500
Gd: $300

STOEGER CONDOR: ARE INEXPENSIVE OVER-AND-UNDERS A GOOD INVESTMENT?

There's something luxurious about shooting an over-and-under. It is in the way they balance and swing on a clay target or bird, the ability to use two barrels choked differently for a given situation, and the pure ease in their use. Rotate the thumb lever to the right, and the barrels break to load or unload. The Stoeger Condor exudes that type of luxury and at a reasonable cost.

The Stoeger Condor Field grade is imported from Brazil by Stoeger and is available in .410, 28, 20, and 12-gauge and, depending on the gauge, in barrel lengths from 24 inches to 28 inches. Our 12-gauge sported 28-inch barrels with screw-in choke barrels. Chambers allowed for 2¾- and 3-inch shells. A vent rib with a single brass bead topped the stacked barrels. A nice touch was a vent rib between the barrels. Two choke tubes were provided: IC (Improved Cylinder) and M (Modified). Optional tubes are available in C (Cylinder), IM (Improved Modified), and F (Full) for those who like to tweak their choke constrictions to their quarry. The stock was a dark piece of A-grade American walnut. The checkering was not sharp. It didn't

The two screw-in choke tubes provided were IM and M.

bite into my hand, but it did provide a good grip. The metalwork was a matte blue finish. The monobloc was nicely jeweled.

Out of the box, the Condor felt rugged and able to handle anything from pheasant and ducks to skeet and sporting clays. On average, the weight of the trigger pull measured 5.5 pounds, which suited me just fine for a gun born to hunt and to crossover on the skeet field.

The Condor action is opened like most over-and-unders: rotate the lever to the right and the action opens. As with many new over-and-unders, the barrel needed to be levered down to fully expose the chamber for loading and unloading.

Extractors are featured on the Condor. I like being able to pluck and save my empties for two reasons: to reload the shells and to help me keep track of how many shells I fired during the day in the field. A feature some shooters may need to get used to is the automatic safety. Every time the Condor action is opened,

The Stoeger Condor is a workhorse of an over-and-under at home and best in the field but can moonlight on the skeet field.

A meaty recoil pad and the Condor's weight of 7.4 pounds helped reduce felt recoil with heavy loads.

The Condor's single trigger is nonselective—the bottom barrel fires first.

the safety automatically goes to the safe position, which I needed to remind myself of when I fired the Condor on the skeet field. It was a minor bruise to my ego to call "pull" then miss the bird because I forgot to slide the thumb safety to the fire position.

The single trigger was not selective. (On the Condor Supreme model, though, the trigger is selective.) The lower barrel fired first on the Condor, which helps a shooter who may shoot too high on a feathered or clay bird. The lower barrel helps send the shot slightly below the target as the target descends.

Assorted 2¾-inch loads were used: Remington Gun Club Target Loads with #7½ shot at 1200 fps, Remington Premier Target Loads with #7½ shot at 1235 fps, and Hevi-Shot with #6 shot at 1200 fps. At my favorite stations, I was equally good with all loads in the Condor; at my not-so-favorite stations, the Condor gave me good service.

The Stoeger Condor shoulders easily when tested on the skeet field with a variety of target and hunting loads.

The Condor did what I told it to do, and at a price of less than $500, I think the Condor will find itself in the hands of many hunters who shoot targets on occasion or prior to opening day.

The inexpensive Condor is a good investment for those shooters wanting the experience of an over-and-under without the cost and who want a shotgun that works as hard as they do.

The Stoeger Condor is an economical over-and-under that performs.

SPECIFICATIONS:
Stoeger Condor Field
PRODUCED: 2009-Present
GAUGE: 12 (tested), 20, 28, .410
CHAMBER: 2¾ and 3 in.
BARREL: 26 in. or 28 in. (tested)
CHOKE: Screw-in choke tubes; F, IM, M, IC, C
OA LENGTH: 44 in.
WEIGHT: 7.4 lbs.
STOCK: A-grade American walnut, satin
LENGTH OF PULL: 14.5 in.
COMB: 1.5 in.
HEEL: 2.5 in.
SIGHTS: Brass bead front
ACTION: Break action, over-and-under
RECEIVER FINISH: Matte blue
BARREL FINISH: Matte blue
EJECTOR/EXTRACTOR: Extractor
CAPACITY: 2
TRIGGER: Single trigger
SAFETY: Manual tang safety
NiB: $499
Ex: $441
Gd: $350

SPRING TURKEY CIRCA 1887: OLD SCHOOL RUNNIN' AND GUNNIN' WITH A PUMA M-87

Calling a tom in close is a thrill and a challenge. A lot of turkey hunters brag about the distance they have killed a tom from, and I have done my share of boasting, but the Puma M-87 had me thinking about why I started turkey hunting in the first place—the challenge of calling in birds close.

The Puma M-87 is a clone of Winchester's Model 1887, which was the first truly successful repeating shotgun. It was designed by John Browning in response to Winchester's desire for branding (not cattle branding but the marketing concept of brand recognition). Winchester rifles were lever actions, so their shotguns should be lever actions, too—or so went the reasoning of the Winchester executives. Back in the day, the 1887 shotgun was chambered in 10- and 12-gauge black powder loads. An under-barrel tubular magazine held five rounds, and the lever cycled a breech block that rotated. Originals had a fixed choke. The lever-action shotgun was really shelved when Browning designed and Winchester built the 1897 pump-action shotgun, but the lever action still had a toehold through 1920, when Winchester dropped the Model 1901 (a revised version of the 1887) from their catalog.

Cowboy Action Shooting resurrected many Old West and turn-of-the-century firearms, and that is the intended audience for the Puma M-87. The M-87 is manufactured in Italy by Chiappa and copies the Winchester's nineteenth-century design while incorporating subtle improvements,

The Puma M-87 liked the Federal Premium loads best, which placed a good percentage of pellets in the kill zone.

Old-time shotgun and box calls work just fine with modern loads.

Shells are loaded through the top of the receiver and pushed into the magazine tube.

Empties are efficiently ejected with a sturdy cycling of the lever.

such as stronger steel and screw-in choke tubes. Models are available with a 22-, 24- or 28-inch barrel. A fast-load model is best suited for Cowboy Action Shooting due to its two-round capacity.

The model I used could have been bought from a Sears and Roebuck catalog in the early 1900s. It sported a 22-inch barrel that was deeply blued. The receiver was a frothy case color, and the stock was a smooth deep brown walnut with a pistol grip. The forearm is more like two slabs of wood held to the barrel and magazine tube via screws and nuts. The finish was well executed, and the wood-to-metal fit was nice. Those Winchester execs of yore would be proud.

The magazine tube holds five shells and has a modern touch—a plug device to limit the number of shells per hunting regulations. The barrel sported a single brass bead at the muzzle. A shallow groove in the receiver served as a rear sight. The barrel also employed interchangeable choke tubes. For all intents and purposes, this was a shotgun capable of keeping up with modern guns—even if it did look like a late nineteenth century gun.

A hunter's view of the M-87; the checkered nub is the hammer.

The lever and breech bolt are one piece, and all loading, firing, and ejecting is accomplished by operating the lever. On pushing the lever forward, the breech rotates back to expose the chamber and the loading tube follower. A shell is loaded by placing it on two guides and pressing it down and into the magazine tube. Pull back the lever and the shotgun will be cocked; cycle the lever again to chamber a shell and start talking turkey—2¾-inch turkey loads, that is. The barrel is chambered for 2¾-inch 12-gauge shells. The M-87, like originals, has an exposed hammer that is a checkered nub, which took getting used to in order to safely decock the hammer, but I soon became accustomed to its late-nineteenth-century ways.

At times, a fast follow-up shot is needed for turkeys, and the M-87 was quite capable of fast shooting. No wonder Cowboy Action Shooters like the lever-action shotgun.

During a recent trip, I chose three types of shell loads for hunting: Remington Premier Duplex Magnum, Winchester Supreme, and Federal Premium. The Federal and Winchester were loaded with #5 shot, and the Remington used a combination of #4 and #6 shot. All were

1½-ounce payloads delivered at about 1300 fps. I broke in the gun with Remington Gun Club Target loads and soon realized the advantages of modern technology. The M-87 has a steel buttplate that was more than happy to relay the recoil into my shoulder. The amount of drop in the stock and the height of the bore made the M-87 a brute to shoot, especially with the turkey loads. There are no soft, spongy recoil pads or synthetic stocks to absorb recoil. I cowboyed up and took to it, and I learned to enjoy the jolt.

The M-87 may be circa 1887, but it fits right in with modern camo and turkey hunting techniques.

The Puma pattern with Federal turkey loads.

The M-87 was fast on follow-up shots and felt perfectly natural pointing over a decoy layout.

The M-87 efficiently spit empties out as fast as I loaded them in the tube, fired, and ejected. At first it felt slightly awkward levering a shotgun, but soon it felt natural. Next, turkey shells were loaded into the tube. The recoil was noticeable, but the results on the target made me grin. The M-87 definitely liked the Federal Premium loads and placed a high percentage of pellets in the kill zone. This was the load I would use, and I was fully confident on a spring day in May that I could call in a turkey and bag him just like they did all those years ago.

Reproduction shotguns, such as the Puma M-87, are a good alternative to shooting a prized collector's item. The M-87 is not inexpensive, but it's well made and updated for modern ammunition. It does not use larger shells that offer longer range, but that's fine with me. These days, the challenge is getting a tom to strut in close, and with the M-87 I can close the deal.

SPECIFICATIONS:
Puma M-87
PRODUCED: 2009-Present
GAUGE: 12
CHAMBER: 2¾ in.
BARREL: 22 in. (tested), 24 in., or 28 in.
CHOKE: Screw-in choke tube; C
OA LENGTH: 39 in.
WEIGHT: 9 lbs.
STOCK: Walnut, satin

LENGTH OF PULL: 13 in.
SIGHTS: Brass bead front
ACTION: Lever action
RECEIVER FINISH: Case hardened
BARREL FINISH: Blue
CAPACITY: 5+1
SAFETY: Half cock
NiB: $1180
Ex: $830
Gd: $555

INERTIA-DRIVEN OPERATOR: BENELLI M2 TACTICAL

The shotgun is the consummate defense weapon, as it has the ability and versatility to be loaded up or down depending on the situation—down for close range work with buckshot, up for longer range with slugs. Shotguns can also be loaded with less lethal loads—polymer or rubber shot—that can incapacitate an intruder or get the attention of a spring black bear in the bird feeder. The Benelli M2 Tactical is specifically designed for defensive and tactical use and is at home with law enforcement, as well as civilians. Unlike a pistol or rifle, which typically uses only one type of round, the shotgun can be loaded for the situation. For nearly twenty years, Benelli's inertia system shotguns have been on the front lines with law enforcement, starting with the M1 and evolving into the M2. The M1 and M2 shotguns use an identical inertia operating system, but the M2 has cosmetic and ergonomic modifications that make it more friendly to use. The Indiana and New Jersey State Police both use Benelli's inertia shotguns, and they have become known as reliable fight stoppers.

There are only three primary parts in the inertia-operated action system: the bolt body, the inertia spring, and the rotating bolt head. Inertia is the tendency for an object at rest to remain at rest, so when a round is fired, the weapon moves rearward while the bolt body stays in position due to the inertia spring, which is a short, thick spring inside the bolt body. Nearly the entire weapon is a recoiling component; only the bolt remains stationary during firing.

Benelli's inertia system is often compared to gas-operated systems, such as those found in Mossberg, Remington, and other semiautomatic shotguns. The Benelli does not divert burning gases to operate the mechanism, though. Burning powder and gas is contained in the barrel with the Benelli, so the action stays cleaner and cooler than a gas-operated action. The M2 also uses fewer moving parts than gas-operated shotguns do. These characteristics mean the M2 is very reliable.

Len Lucas with Beretta Law Enforcement and Defense (Beretta owns Benelli) trains end users with all types of Benelli models—pump-action Novas, gas-assisted inertia-operated M4s, combination pump and semiautomatic M3s, and inertia-operated M2s. "The reason the shotgun is such a versatile tool is because it can be loaded up or down from fifteen meters with buckshot or out to one hundred meters with slugs," Lucas told me.

There are two types of gunfights, Lucas explains: those where you come as you are and those

A typical three-shot group at fifty yards are a cluster of huge slugsholes.

Slugs, buckshot, and birdshot all cycled flawlessly through the M2 Tactical.

The M2 Tactical is quick to shoulder and hang on to even when shooting rapid fire.

where you are invited. In the come-as-you-are scenario, the user has only the tools immediately available. In the second scenario, a user can gear up for the encounter using their known intelligence and modifying their setup for the expected encounter. In either scenario, the shotgun is the most versatile weapon because it can easily be loaded up or down depending on the circumstances.

Lucas mentions the LAPD trains out to one hundred meters with shotguns. The combat ghost-ring sights on the M2 make this close and long-distance shooting easy. For first responders and home defenders, understanding the tool and

how it works with different ammo is critical, and that is where training comes in—training for real world situations.

One of the most versatile features of the M2—and the M4, for that matter—is a free carrier. No round leaves the magazine—the end user controls the shotgun and when the round chambers. For instance, the M2's magazine tube is loaded. To chamber a round, the user must press the cartridge round release—the small silver button on the right side of the receiver—and a round will be moved to the carrier. The user then smartly manipulates the bolt to chamber a round. When the round is moved to the carrier, it can be heard, seen, and felt by the operator. If there is no threat, the round can be ejected and either pocketed or reloaded into the magazine. If the threat is real and the weapon is fired, the

After a few hundred rounds, the interior of the M2 was still clean.

The large triangular ambidextrous safety button of the M2 is located behind the trigger in the rear of the trigger guard on the right side of the M2, which is a natural and common place for it to be. It was easy to manipulate with and without gloved hands. The red dot shows on the cartridge drop lever located on the right side of the receiver just forward of the trigger guard, which indicates the M2 is cocked.

The rubber butt pad comes in a variety of thicknesses so the user can adjust the length of pull.

act of firing the M2 causes a fresh round to be placed on the carrier and loaded into the chamber. The next round is held in the magazine tube ready for a shot to be fired again or for the operator to clear the chamber and insert a round or to press the cartridge release button. This feature is useful, as it allows the operator to quickly chamber a round in the M2 while still having rounds in the magazine. The weapon can be made ready in an instant.

Another feature of the M2 is the scalloped receiver. When a left- or right-handed operator is in the ready position—hand on the pistol grip and trigger finger along the receiver—the trigger finger can easily swipe downward to disengage the safety button and get on the trigger. This may seem like a subtle modification, but it gives the operator a slight edge in speed and is more comfortable to hold even when wearing gloves. Also the M2's safety is ambidextrous and can be set up for either a left- or right-handed operator.

Lucas goes on to say that many law enforcement personnel are setting up their rifles and shotguns with similar accessories—light vertical handles and the like. The M2, because it is inertia operated, relies on the user as a backstop and the weight of the weapon to operate properly. Therefore, the rule of thumb is that up to one pound of extra weight can be added to the M2. The receiver of the M2 is drilled and tapped so a red dot optic can be a viable accessory on the weapon if the operator should so choose.

The M2 also incorporates a barrel stop so the user knows the barrel is fully seated during reassembly. At times with all types and brands of shotguns, if the barrel is not fully seated and the retaining nut fully engaged, the weapon can shoot loose and the retaining nut can loosen. The M2 mitigates this situation with the barrel

A solid rubber recoil pad helped absorb some of the recoil, as did the rubber insert in the backstrap of the pistol grip. The lip on the front strap of the pistol grip helps keep your shooting hand in position during recoil and rapid fire.

The Benelli M2 Tactical uses an inertia operating mechanism that makes the shotgun run cleaner than a gas-operated shotgun.

The extended magazine tube increased capacity to a total of six rounds—five rounds in the tube plus one in the chamber.

seat.

Making the M2 suitable for all operator statures was a design criteria. The length of pull on the M2 can be modified by swapping out recoil pads of various thicknesses. Three recoil pads are available, so the weapon can be modified to most body types and for equipment. For instance, in the case of body armor, the thinner recoil pad can be used. The forend is also thinner and easier to hold, especially for small-stature operators with small hands. The forend allows the operator good purchase.

The features and the real-world use of the M2 make it a viable, reliable, consistent brute for law enforcement and home defense.

The inertia operating system in the M2 offers clean reliability in a shotgun. One of the amazing things about Benellis is how well they are manufactured. Strip one down, and you'll see that the parts and interior of the M2 are as beautiful as the exterior.

The fit, finish, and performance of the Benelli were tops—and for a stiff price. It is a good investment, though. Aftermarket parts are available, so you can change the stock or add a magazine extension if 3-Gun shooting is on your agenda. Some of you might even be inclined to use one

The rear sight could be adjusted for windage and elevation using a coin, shell rim, or flat blade screw driver with the clicks of the elevation screw felt. Small lines keep track of windage adjustments. The receiver was drilled and tapped with a Picatinny-style rail, which allowed a low-power scope or red dot sight to be mounted. I tested using open sights.

for turkey or deer hunting.

The ability to mount a tactical light and other accessories is limited; other brands of shotguns offer more accessories. The real trade off for the M2 is its cleaner running mechanism and the ability to top off the magazine without running it empty. On the down side, recoil was slightly more pronounced than that of gas-operated shotguns.

SPECIFICATIONS
Benelli M2 Tactical
PRODUCED: 2004-Present
GAUGE: 12
CHAMBER: 2¾ in., 3 in.
BARREL: 18.5 in.
CHOKE: Screw-in choke tubes; F, M, IC
OA LENGTH: 39.8 in.
WEIGHT: 6.7 lbs. (unloaded)
STOCK: Black synthetic pistol grip, solid rubber butt-pad, checkered synthetic forend
LENGTH OF PULL: 14.4 in.
COMB: 1.4 in.
HEEL: 2.0 in.
SIGHTS: Adjustable ghost ring rear, post front, Picatinny rail mount
ACTION: Semiauto, inertia-operated
RECEIVER FINISH: Matte black
BARREL FINISH: Matte black
CAPACITY: 5+1
SAFETY: Manual trigger block
NiB: $1249
Ex: $900
Gd: $510

PERFORMANCE

Benelli M2 Tactical

BUCKSHOT	PATTERN
Federal Personal Defense 00 Buck – 9 pellets	6.875
BIRDSHOT	PATTERN
Fiocchi Golden Pheasant #6 shot	30
SLUGS	ACCURACY
Winchester Super X Rifled Slugs	3.5

Buckshot and birdshot patterns in inches at twenty-five yards; slug accuracy in inches for five three-shot groups at fifty yards.

Shotgun Provenance

provenance [prov-uh-nuh-ns, -nahns]—noun: place or source of origin; the beginning of something's existence; something's origin; a record of ownership of a work of art or an antique, used as a guide to authenticity or quality (dictionary.com)

JOHN M. BROWNING'S WINCHESTER MODEL 1893 PUMP SHOTGUN

One of twenty-two children, John Moses Browning was born on January 23, 1855, in Ogden, Utah. Browning's father, Jonathan Browning, was a gunsmith, so John followed his father into the trade. Though his father was an accomplished gunsmith, it was John who would go on to become the father of modern firearms. What Thomas Edison is to the light bulb John Browning is to firearms.

At the age of twenty-four, he received a patent for his first firearm, a single-shot rifle. Winchester Repeating Arms Co. purchased the design from Browning for $8,000 and began manufacturing the Winchester Model 1885 rifle. It would be the start of a long relationship between the Winchester company and John Browning. In total, Browning held one hundred and twenty-eight US patents and designed ten different long arms for Winchester, including lever-action rifles and shotguns, as well as pump- or slide-action rifles and shotguns and rimfire bolt-action rifles. Browning also designed firearms for Colt, Remington, Savage, and Stevens in the United States, as well as Fabrique Nationale de Herstal (FN) in Belgium. Browning Arms Company was formed a year after Browning's death. Browning died in 1926.

There is not an aspect of firearms that Browning did not touch, from pistols and rifles to shotguns and machine guns. He built firearms for sports-men, as well as for the military. It is hard to believe, but by 1900 more than 75 percent of the repeating sporting arms in the US were Browning's designs. To this day, many firearm manufacturers use a modified version of a Browning design. Not only was Browning prolific in inventing firearm mechanisms, his designs are also renowned for their reliability and effectiveness.

The Model 1893 was Browning's first pump-action shotgun design, and it was the first of its kind that Winchester manufactured. The Model 1893 was the forerunner of one of the more prolifically produced shotguns to come out of the Browning/Winchester relationship, the Model 1897.

The Model 1893 was introduced in 1893—hence the model name—and was manufactured until 1897, when Winchester introduced the Model 1897 pump-action, a reengineered version of the Model 1893 built to take the pressure of smokeless powder, as well as improve some Model 1893 features. The Model 1893 was made in 12-gauge black powder loads only with a 2 5/8-inch chamber. Barrels were steel and available in 30- or 32-inch lengths. A full choke was standard. Some 34,000 Model 1893s were produced, which is a small number compared with the 1,024,000 Model 1897 shotguns produced. The Model 1893 was a victim of the change from black powder to smokeless powder shells. In the early twentieth century, Winchester advertisements encouraged owners of Model 1893 shotguns to return them to the factory in exchange

John Browning's personal Model 1893 trap gun is the second from the top. (Ogden Union Station Collection)

Browning's pump has a relief engraving of two sporting dogs on point on the receiver.

Browning was a proficient trap shooter and liked to hunt duck.

for the new Model 1897. Winchester feared that owners of Model 1893 shotguns would accidentally use smokeless shells and potentially cause injury.

The Model 1893 is a pump-action or slide-action shotgun with an exposed hammer and was the first successful pump-action shotgun produced, though the Model 1897 is usually given the credit since it used smokeless shells. Many more were produced until 1957. Shells are loaded into the Model 1893 through the bottom of the receiver and into a tubular magazine located under the barrel. The magazine holds five shells. The Model 1893 lacks a trigger disconnector, which means the shotguns can be slam fired by the user pressing the trigger rearward while pumping the forend. On the forward movement of the forend by the user, the shotgun will fire. This feature allowed the shotgun to be rapidly fired. Standard models were given a blued finish with a smooth walnut buttstock and a metal butt-plate. The wood forend was typically grooved. Custom models were available from Winchester by special order.

Markings include a two-line roll mark on the top of the barrel that reads: "Manufactured by the Winchester Repeating Arms Co. / New Haven, Conn. U.S.A. Model 1893. Pat. Nov. 25 1890 & Dec. 6, 1892." A "12" appears on the top of barrel where it fits into the receiver, which indicates the shotgun is chambered for 12-gauge shells. Note that the black powder 12-gauge shell is 2⅝-inches long; 12-gauge smokeless shells, such as those used today, have a minimum chambered length of 2¾-inches. On the left side of the shotgun on the action bar appears a two-line roll mark: "Winchester/Model 1893." Browning's personal trap gun was a Winchester Model 1893 shotgun in 12-gauge and is on display at the Union Station John M. Browning Firearms Museum in Ogden, Utah. The model 1893 is not the standard model most shooters purchased. Browning's pump has a relief engraving of two sporting dogs on point on the left side of the receiver. The forend is slender and features fine checkering. The buttstock has a straight grip or English-style grip; standard models had a pistol grip stock. A leather cheek piece was added by Browning to raise the comb slightly higher. The leather cheek rest is laced onto the buttstock.

Not only was Browning a firearm designer, but he also had a passion for shooting and was a proficient trap shooter, which was as popular a sport then as it is today. Browning was also a duck hunter with a love for fishing and the outdoors.

The Model 1893s that were returned to Winchester in exchange for a Model 1897 were destroyed by Winchester, which makes Model 1893s rare. A Model 1893 that grades 90% to 80% and was not modified by previous owners could fetch as much as $1,900, and the average value of a standard Model 1893 would be about $1,100. When determining the value of John Browning's personal Model 1893, one must take into consideration the person and the person's notoriety. John Browning is considered by many firearm enthusiasts to be a demigod. To an enthusiast, Browning's shotgun might be valued the same as Steve Jobs's original Apple computer. As with all celebrities, fame waxes and wanes. If this shotgun was in someone's possession, it would be best to have the sale conducted by an auction house.

ERNEST HEMINGWAY'S BROWNING SUPERPOSED OVER-AND-UNDER SHOTGUN

Ernest Hemingway was one of the most important American authors in the early twentieth century. His novels—*For Whom the Bell Tolls*, *The Sun Also Rises*, and *A Farewell to Arms* to name just a few—have influenced later generations of writers. He won the Nobel Prize in Literature in 1954 for the *The Old Man and the Sea*.

On the personal side, Hemingway was a man's man. Men wanted to be like him, and women wanted to be with him. Papa, as he liked to be called, manifested an image of an outdoorsman. Having grown up in Michigan, Hemingway loved to hunt and fish at an early age. As his fame and success brought wealth, he would travel to his house in Key West, Florida, to fish for blue marlin or shoot box pigeon at a local club. He would stay for months on end at his other home in Idaho to fish for trout and hunt pheasant and other beasts in the West.

With him on many a pheasant hunt was a Browning Superposed Over-and-Under (O/U) shotgun. Next to his Winchester Model 12, the Browning was one of Hemingway's favorite shotguns. According to authors Silvio Calabi, Steve Helsley, and Roger Sanger, who together wrote *Hemingway's Guns,* Hemingway amassed a collection of sporting guns—and a Thompson machine gun, too—mostly for hunting and clay shooting. Actually, in Hemingway's day, live pigeons were still used.

The Browning Superposed was the last patent John Browning received for a firearm design. He was seventy-one years old. In 1931, the design was finished and production began. The Superposed was revolutionary at the time: it was an American-designed O/U that was rugged, reliable, and affordable even for the average working-class guy. The Superposed debuted during the Great Depression at the

This is an example of a later model Browning Superposed, which is similar to the type Hemingway won in a shooting competition.

Hemingway (second from left) with his Browning Superposed and his pheasant hunting pals in Idaho circa 1939. (John F. Kennedy Library)

reasonable sum of a little more than $100. The United States was in the throes of the Great Depression, but $100 was still a manageable price compared to the prices of European guns. Other O/U shotguns were available at the time—those built by Boss and Purdey in England, for example—but these were custom guns that came with an extremely high price. The Superposed brought the O/U to the common man, and ever since, the O/U shotgun has become the most popular double-barrel shotgun in America and around the world.

Hemingway's Superposed was his go-to gun, according to the authors mentioned previously. Hemingway used it to hunt duck, pheasant, and snipe in Idaho, as well as at competitive shooting clubs in the US, Europe, and Cuba. Papa's Browning ". . . is clearly a first-generation Grade I B25 [the Superposed was called the B25 in Europe] produced between 1931 and 1935, and it may be that Hemingway won it in 1934 or later."

As the story goes, Hemingway won the Superposed in a live bird shooting competition in France against Ben Gallagher, a wealthy sportsman "synonymous with top shotgunning" and a shooter on the live-pigeon shooting circuit in the 1920s and '30s. The gun was probably won in 1934. If the way Hemingway came into possession of the Superposed is true, then the fate of shotguns leaves more to the imagination. The whereabouts of the Superposed is unknown, as is the serial number to the gun. The distinguishing features of Hemingway's Superposed is that it was a pre-1936 Grade I with no engraving, and more than likely it had two triggers (Browning's son Val perfected a single trigger with barrel selector in 1939) a low-step rib, a Jostam Hy-gun vented recoil pad, and a longer squared-off target forend.

A Superposed Grade I that rates 95 percent to 90 percent currently fetches $2,200 to $1,800. The one that Papa owned?

A Shotgun Collector's Bucket List

☐ Shoot a matched pair of Purdey Best guns on driven pheasant at an estate in the UK. Using a loader and wearing tweed is mandatory.

Courtesy of Browning.

☐ Break in some really good pants, such as Filson's Double Tin pants made of waxed cloth, which keep out briars and thorns and repel water when you bust brush looking for grouse. Your son may inherit these pants.

☐ Introduce someone—your child, neighbor, niece, significant other, or anyone, really—to the outdoors and shotgun shooting. Share your passion.

☐ Score a wild turkey grand slam. Harvest an Eastern, Rio Grande, Oscelo, and Merriam. Extra points if you do it in one year. Add a Gould and Ocellated subspecies and you've accomplished a World Slam.

☐ Hunt pheasant with a side-by-side hammer gun just like old-timers did five generations ago. Even better, use a muzzle-loading shotgun.

☐ Shoot doves in Argentina. Correction: shoot a lot of doves in Argentina. Correction: shoot your weight in empty hulls at doves in Argentina.

☐ Go on a green timber mallard hunt.

☐ Shoot a round of trap at the Camp Fire Club in Chappaqua, New York, then have lunch in the club house. Please note that you'll need to be invited by member.

☐ Experience Maryland's Eastern Shore water fowling history by limiting out on canvasbacks.

☐ Visit any of the states in the Prairie Pothole Region. Think Big Sky filled with mallards.

☐ Introduce yourself to the teal population in South Carolina's ACE Basin (Ashepoo, Combahee, Edisto).

☐ Gaze lustfully on at least one of the three Parker Invincible guns. Remember to bring a paper towel to wipe the drool off the glass case.

Courtesy of Browning.

- [ ] Shoot a perfect score at sskeet, trap, sporting clays and 5 stand.
- [ ] Buy a better gun and have it fitted to your stature, then proceed to shoot the dickens out of it in an effort to try and wear it out.
- [ ] Take a sporting clays road trip. The East Coast route has you starting at Orvis Sandanona in Millbrook, New York, where you can take a lesson so you'll be prepared, then jog over to Nemacolin Woodlands in Pennsylvania. You could stop at M&M in Pennsville, New Jersey, before heading south. Go to the Homestead in Virginia, and after a round, you might want a massage in their spa. Head west to The Greenbriar in West Virginia. Then head south to North Carolina and Rose Hill Plantation in Nash County. Stay at the eighteenth-century Manor House overnight before going deeper into South Carolina to Myrtle Grove in Myrtle Beach. Stay a few days here to play some golf and give the O/Us a rest. In Georgia, go to Forest City, the oldest continually operated gun club in America. Finish the East Coast road trip at Quail Creek in Okeechobee, Florida.
- [ ] Hunt wild turkey in Florida with a Winchester 1887 lever-action shotgun, then hunt sea ducks off the coast of Maine with the same gun.
- [ ] Shoot sporting clays with an L.C. Smith or Lefever double.
- [ ] Shave a half-second off your load time in 3-Gun.
- [ ] Follow the woodcock migration from Mississippi to Maine.
- [ ] In honor of Tom Knapp, make coleslaw with a head of cabbage using a full choke Benelli.
- [ ] Hunt quail from horseback or mule-drawn wagon on a south Georgia plantation.

Courtesy of Browning.

Courtesy of Browning.

Classic American Shotgun Manufacturer: L.C. Smith

When talking about classic American shotguns, we are really talking about four major manufacturers: Parker Brothers Gun Company; A.H. Fox; D. M. Lefever, Sons & Company; and L.C. Smith Shotgun Company. I am sure there are some who would say Ithaca and perhaps Winchester belong on the list, but that could be debated—preferably with a finger of single malt while sitting in front of a crackling fireplace on a cold November night.

When I speak of classic American shotguns, I refer specifically to American doubles manufactured during the so-called golden age of American shotguns from the 1930s to '40s. It could be argued that pump-action—and lever-action shotguns, for that matter—are classic American shotguns, and they are. But in terms of elegance, none can match a side-by-side shotgun. The four manufacturers mentioned above built guns that were magnificent and tried to rival their European competitors, but the American golden age of shotguns came well after the established English firms, such as Boss, Purdey, and Holland & Holland, and Italian makers, such as Famars and Fabbri, had perfected the side-by-side as a hunting and competition gun, as well as a work of art. American double guns stand out from their English and Italian counterparts. They are not as refined and are more rugged. Like with most anything, from clothing and automobiles to food and sports, it is easy to spot the American. So, too, is it easy to spot the American double in a rack of multinational guns.

THE BEGINNINGS IN UPSTATE NEW YORK
Lyman Cornelius (L.C.) Smith was an American industrialist who opened his first business, a livestock commission, in New York City in 1873. It failed. Like most entrepreneurs, Smith was undeterred and opened a lumber business. It, too, failed. In 1877, L.C. Smith and his brother Leroy partnered with William H. Baker, who was an established gun maker and designer. The company was named W.H. Baker & Co., and from 1877 through 1880, it manufactured the Baker Three-Barrel Gun in Syracuse in upstate New York. Baker and Leroy left that company in 1880 to form their own venture and eventually founded the Ithaca Gun Company. L.C., always the consummate businessman, was focused on the business at hand even though his brother broke family ties and left to work at another firearm company. So L.C. Smith took over the W.H. Baker & Co. and renamed it L.C. Smith Shotgun Company, Maker of the Baker Gun.

Early on, Smith advertised itself as "The Baker Guns, L.C. Smith Maker, Syracuse, N.Y."

Smith hired his younger brother Wilbert and

An example of a Quality AA hammer gun circa 1885. (Courtesy of J. David Williamson.)

Alexander T. Brown, an inventor and engineer, to help him run the company. From this point on, the company flourished and produced a number of popular breech-loading hammer shotgun models. The company manufactured their first hammerless shotgun in 1886, which also went on to become extremely popular.

Smith sold the manufacturing rights to all the shotguns bearing the L.C. Smith name to the Hunter Arms Company in 1889. Hunter Arms Company went on to produce shotguns until 1945, when they in turn sold the rights to the Marlin Firearms Company. Marlin ceased production of L.C. Smith shotguns in 1950 and has tried to revive the brand several times—first from 1968 to 1971 and again from 2005 to 2009. But the newer L.C. Smiths, manufactured after 1968, do not hold a candle to the guns manufactured in the late nineteenth century through the early twentieth century.

L.C. Smith went on to be quite successful. His legacy and namesake are on one of the most cherished classic American shotguns, as well as one of the most important business tools of the early the twentieth century: the typewriter. The "Smith" in the Smith-Corona Typewriter Company is L.C Smith.

ELSIE COLLECTORS

To their exuberant brethren, they are referred to as an Elsie, an affectionate nickname for the L.C. Smith shotgun. The L.C. Smith is known for its simplicity of design and as America's only sidelock double. The models, particularly the high-grade models produced by the Hunter Arms Company up until about 1913, are some of the most elegant looking American shotguns ever made. The hand engraving is some of the finest executed at the time. After 1913, production fell victim to cost-cutting manufacturing techniques that eroded the pleasing lines of the Elsie. As with most sought after and collectable

firearms, there have been numerous iterations of the company with specific models built during specific periods.

W.H. BAKER COMPANY (1877–1880)

This was the period when W.H. Baker started building guns—notably the three-barrel gun or drilling. In 1879, the Smith brothers joined Baker in a partnership, and by 1880, L.C. Smith had sole ownership in the company.

L.C. SMITH, MAKER OF THE BAKER GUN (1880–1888)

During this period, shotguns had the inscription "L.C. Smith Maker of Baker Guns Syracuse, N.Y. 1880-1883" engraved on the top of the barrels. These are known as Syracuse guns by avid collectors, as the guns were manufactured in Syracuse, New York. Syracuse guns were built on three different frames: medium, heavy, and extra heavy. The difference between them is the breech ball diameter, which is also reflected in the thickness of the barrels. Catalogs of the period only list 10 or 12 gauge available, but two 8-gauge hammer guns and three hammerless guns have surfaced in recent years. One of these hammer guns is privately owned; the other is in the Cody Museum. Two of the hammerless ones are also privately owned. Models included both double-barrel and three-barrel shotguns and were chambered in 10 and 12 gauge. All shotguns and drillings will have "W.H. Baker" on the locks.

When L.C. Smith started the L.C. Smith Gun Company in 1884, all shotguns had "L.C. Smith" engraved on the locks, and on the barrels was engraved "L.C. Smith Maker, Syracuse, N.Y." The drillings have "L.C. Smith" engraved in script on the locks.

L.C. Smith double-barrel hammer models were introduced in 1884 and were graded from Quality A to Quality F, although most records do not have anything higher than a Quality D. Grades of hammer guns went from Quality F priced at $55 in 1886 to Quality AA priced at $300. Only

This hammer gun was manufactured in about 1885 and is an example of a Quality F grade. (Courtesy of J. David Williamson)

three Quality AA guns are known to exist.

Hammerless models went into production in 1886 and were graded from Quality 1 to Quality 7. A Quality 1 could be bought new for $75 in 1886 and a Quality 5 for $200. A Quality 7 hammerless was priced at $450 in 1886. Only five Quality 7 guns are known to exist. From No. 4 up, these guns were made special order.

By 1888, the three-barrel guns were no longer being manufactured, and owner L.C. Smith sold the company to Hunter Arms Company owner John Hunter Sr. from Fulton, New York.

To contrast the price of some L.C. Smiths, take a three-barrel presentation grade. Of notable importance is a Presentation Grade three-barrel drilling given to Leroy H. Smith from L.C. Smith upon his joint venture with W.H. Baker, George Livermore, and L.H. Smith—the Ithaca Gun Company. On top of the barrels is the engraving "Presented to L.H. Smith from L.C. Smith Maker of the Baker Gun Syracuse." The particular shotgun was on display at Ithaca headquarters for a few years and was sold at auction by James D. Julia, Inc., on October 13, 2013, for a realized price of $63,250.

HUNTER ARMS COMPANY (1889–1929)

After the sale from L.C. Smith to to John Hunter Sr., manufacturing was moved to Fulton, New

Syracuse Quality 7 left side (top left) shows a gold inlay of a setter and grouse, the right side lock (top right) shows a gold pointer and a woodcock, and the trigger bow (above) shows another setter. This gun would rate about 85 to 80 percent even with the cracked pistol grip, which would give it a value between $21,000 and $17,000. (Courtesy of J. David Williamson)

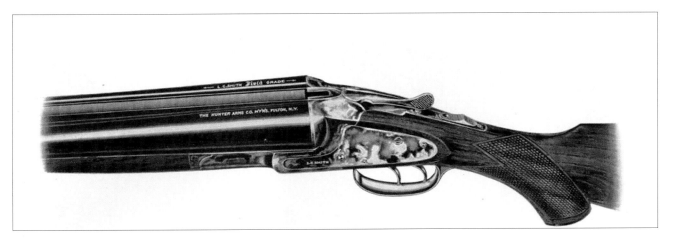

From a Hunter Arms catalog, this is an example of a Field Grade model.

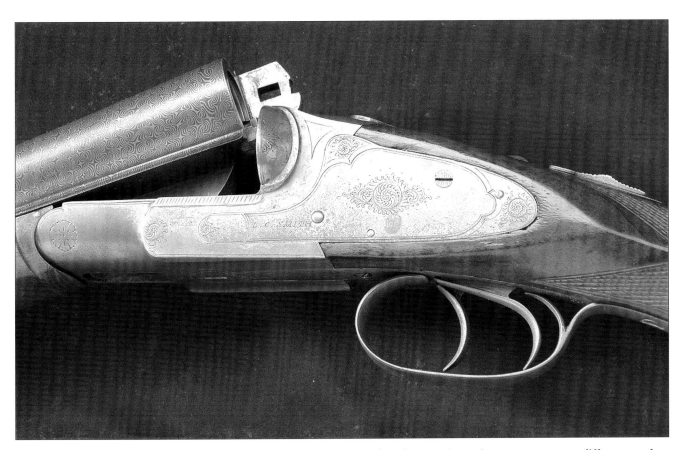

Serial number 1047 is a Grade 2E and shows the second style of engraving. There were seven different styles of engraving on the Grade 2s. After 1896, grades were changed to No. grades and would be No.2 or 2E if it had ejectors. Price new was $102.50 with ejectors, and today's value is $2,200 to $2,900. Some 12,483 were made. (Courtesy of J. David Williamson)

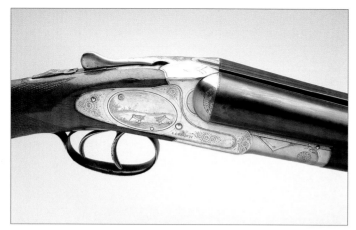

Made in 1897, this No. 3E shows the engraving of two quail on left lock and two woodcock or snipe on the right lock. A few examples have two ducks in a larger circle. Price new was $122.50 with ejectors; 3,042 were manufactured. The value today is in the $3,200 to $3,800 range. (Courtesy of J. David Williamson)

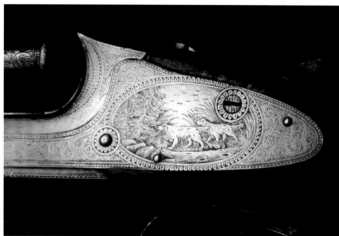

This model from 1898–99 shows No. 5 engraving with setters on the left lock and pointers on the right lock. Its current value is $9,500 to $11,500; the price new was $225. Only 523 were produced. (Courtesy of J. David Williamson)

This A2 shows the second style of engraving of which there were four styles. Price new with ejectors was $400—with a Hunter One–Trigger add $25—only 213 were made. The current value is $17,000 to $20,000. (Courtesy of J. David Williamson)

York. Hunter Arms enhanced the design and offered new features, such as automatic ejectors (1892), a single-trigger option called the Hunter One-Trigger (1904), and featherweight guns (1908). Pigeon grade guns were also added.

Pre-1912, the highest grade made was an A3. This model came with ejectors, and in 1906 it was listed for $750, which made it the highest priced shotgun in the United States or abroad. Only nineteen were ever made. By 1913, manufacturing efficiencies were put in place to cut costs. Guns that were a number grade—except De Luxe, Monogram, and Pigeon—were now known as grades. For example, Field Grade pre-1912 was known as 00, Ideal Grade pre-1912 was 0 grade, Grade 1 discontinued after 1912, Specialty Grade pre-1912 was Grade 2, and so on. Grade 3 was discontinued after 1912. The full list of new model names were changed to Field, Ideal, Trap, Specialty, Eagle, Crown, Monogram, Premier, and De Luxe. Field was the least expensive, and De Luxe cost the most.

During 1915 to 1945, model names changed again to seven models: Fulton, Fulton Special, Hunter Special, Ranger, Gladiator Field, Gladiator Tournament, and Gladiator Diamond. These have less collector value than the Syracuse guns and are often referred to as cheap Elsie boxlocks even though the manufacturing of these gun was top-notch, including machined forgings.

Ownership of the company changed hands, but the company was still producing new models, such as a One-Barrel Trap gun introduced in 1917, a Long-Range Wild Fowl gun debuted in 1924, and a new Skeet Grade in 1929. By 1945, the company was purchased by Marlin Firearms Company.

MARLIN FIREARMS COMPANY (1945–1950, 1968–1971, 2005–2009)

The L.C. Smith Gun Company became a subsid-

This is the cover from the 1905 L.C. Smith catalog during the Hunter Arms era.

iary of Marlin Firearms, and L.C. Smith shotguns continued to be produced. In 1949, the factory in Fulton, New York, collapsed, which ended production, and by 1950 the factory was closed.

In 1968, Marlin began manufacturing L.C. Smith guns in the Marlin factory in North Haven, Connecticut. There were two models produced: a Field Grade Model and a Deluxe Model. The prefix FWM is found on the serial numbers of these Marlin-manufactured Elsies. Some 2,038 Field Grades were produced, plus 189 Deluxe Models. Both models were chambered only in 12 gauge. By 1971, production ceased.

Marlin brushed off the L.C. Smith brand name in 2005 and offered an over-and-under—heresy if there ever was—and a side-by-side. Both of these models were manufactured for Marlin in either Italy or Spain. These lines were discontinued in 2009.

With guns manufactured over centuries, such as L.C. Smith shotguns, information is scarce. Records were handwritten in ledgers, and at times these valuable books were lost or destroyed. Deciphering older L.C. Smith shotgun models was not easy until some devoted individuals wrote some excellent reference books with great information and insight for the Elsie collector. For L.C. Smith descriptions and numbers, refer to *The L.C. Smith Production Records* by Jim Stubbendieck. A quote from Stubbendieck's book states, "Owners of L.C. Smith shotguns will forever be thankful to Lt. Col. William R. Brophy (US Army, Retired) of the Marlin Firearms Company for preventing the destruction of the 1890 to 1950 L.C. Smith shotgun production ledgers." Some individuals know what to keep and what is valuable. William Brophy himself wrote two books on L.C. Smith shotguns*: L.C. Smith Shotguns* and *Plans and Specifications of the L.C. Smith Shotgun*. These two books were produced from the records and drawings that Brophy rescued.

Another book for the Elsie collector is *L.C. Smith — The Legend Lives* by John Houchins, which details grades from the L.C. Smith Syracuse guns and L.C. Smith guns manufactured by Hunter Arms Company to the L.C. Smith Gun Company, a subsidiary of Marlin Firearms Company. In the words of one member of the L.C. Smith Collector's Association, and *L.C. Smith Journal* editor and technical advisor, J. David Williamson, "Without these records nobody would have known anything about these guns."

REFERENCES

Brophy, William S. *L.C. Smith Shotguns*. Sherman Oaks, CA: Beinfeld Publications, Inc.,1977.

Brophy, William S. *Plans and Specifications of the L.C. Smith Shotgun*. Montezuma, IA: F. Brownell & Son, Publishers, 1981.

Houchins, John. *L.C. Smith — The Legend Lives*. Winston-Salem, NC: Walker Houchins, 2007.

Stubbendieck, Jim. *The L.C. Smith Production Records*. Minneapolis, MN: Blue Book Publications, Inc., 2013.

Featured Shotguns:
A Close Look at Common and Rare Shotguns

Beretta USA Corp.
Model 682 Sporting

This particular Beretta is one of the 680 series of O/Us and is a uppercase Sporting model. These shotguns were imported into the US from 1984 to 2000. "Sporting" is etched on the trigger guard. This cased set will bring a slightly higher price than just the gun. (See page 88 for specifications and grading values.)

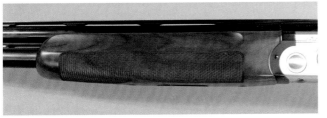

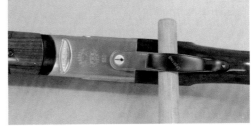

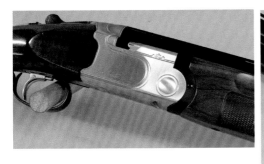

Beretta USA Corp.
Model 686 Silver Pigeon S

During 1996, Beretta changed the nomenclature from Silver Perdiz to Silver Pigeon. This Silver Pigeon S is in near-mint condition. The Silver Pigeon S came with a lovely nickel finish receiver and scroll engraving, gold trigger, and either a pistol grip or straight high-gloss stock. (See page 89 for specifications and grading values.)

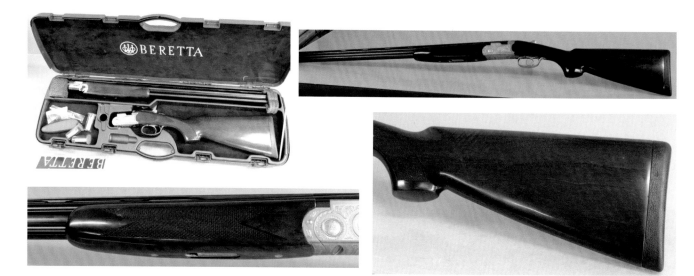

Beretta USA Corp.
Model Silver Snipe

The Silver Snipe is an older boxlock imported from 1955 to 1967. Models can be found in 12-, 20-, and 28-gauge. The smaller bores, such as this 20-gauge, will command a higher price. (See page 94 for specifications and grading values.)

Beretta USA Corp.
Model SO-6

The SO series of shotguns are all custom built to the customer's specifications. This example, like others, shows the rich engraving and luxurious wood. Features include a low-profile sidelock action. (See page 94 for specifications and grading values.)

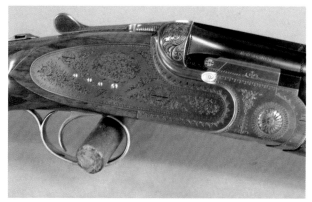

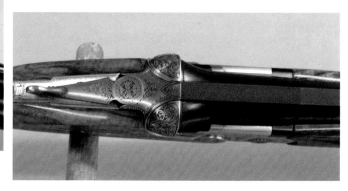

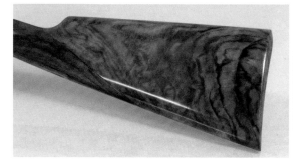

Beretta USA Corp.
Model SV10 Perennia III

The SV10 Perennia III model was introduced in 2008 with satin finish laser engraving and a checkered walnut wood stock with the Q-Stock feature that offers quick take down.

These models are offered in 12 gauge (which was discontinued in 2010) and 20 gauge only and feature either a standard or Kick-Off recoil pad.

Browning
Auto-5 Light 20

This is a Japanese-manufactured Auto-5 in 20-gauge and is similar to the Belgium-made Auto-5s. Browning had these manufactured from 1987 through 1997. The Invector choke tube system became standard starting in 1993 and Invector Plus sateen in 1994. "Light Twenty" in script is engraved on left side of receiver. (See page 101 for specifications and grading values.)

Browning
B-SS Side-By-Side
This boxlock was manufactured by Miroku in Japan from 1972 through 1988. Early model guns had a nonselective single trigger. This example rates 98 percent or better. (See page 103 for specifications and grading values.)

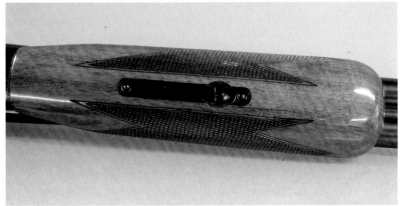

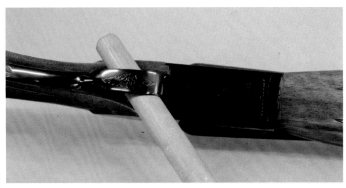

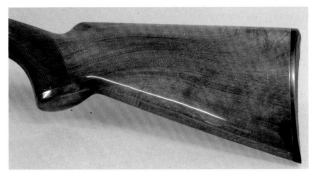

Browning
Citori Quail Unlimited Edition

The Citori has been made into a number of comparative guns. This specimen is a Quail Unlimited Fifth Edition. The serial number is 003 of 100, which makes this an early model with a desirable serial number.

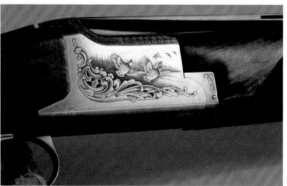

Browning
Model 42 Grade I

The Model 42 was a limited edition run of reproduction Winchester Model 42 pump-action shotguns that were made from 1991 through 1993. About 6,000 of these .410 guns were manufactured. (See page 99 for specifications and grading values.)

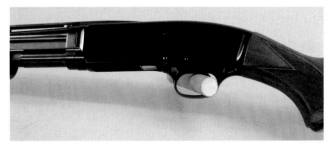

GUN TRADER'S GUIDE TO SHOTGUNS

Browning
Model 42 Grade V

This is a Grade V Model 42 also a limited edition run of reproduction Winchester Model 42 pump-action shotguns. This model was engraved with gold inlay and produced from 1991 through 1993. About 6,000 of these ornate .410 guns were built. (See page 99 for specifications and grading values.)

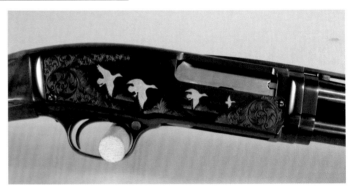

Caesar Guerini, s.r.l.
Tempio

Caesar Guerini, located in Marcheno, Italy, builds some excellent O/Us for hunting and competition use. Importation into the United States began in 2003. This is a Tempio model that wears ornate engraving with gold inlays. These guns come from the factory in a velvet-lined case with five choke tubes. (See page 110 for specifications and grading values.)

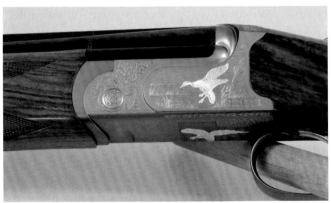
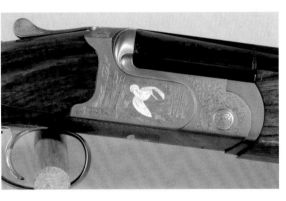
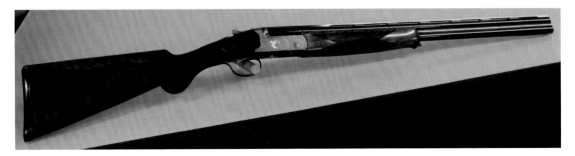

Auguste Francotte & Cie. S.A.
Boxlock Hammerless Double

Francotte boxlocks are some of the finest doubles made in Belgium. They are all custom made, and this particular model uses an Anson & Deely-type lockwork. Some features include double triggers, straight English stock, and splinter forend. (See page 126 for specifications and grading values.)

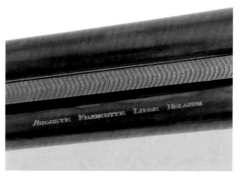

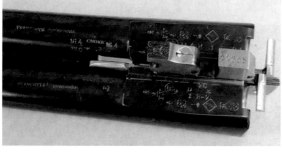

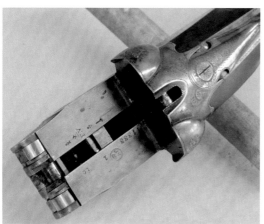

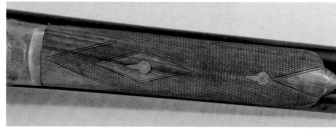

Parker Brothers
DH Grade

This DH shows Parker's attention to detail. It is a fine specimen of a side-by-side double from one of America's classic double makers of a bygone era. About 9,400 DH grades were manufactured in 12, 16, 20, 28 and .410. (See page 180 for specifications and grading values.)

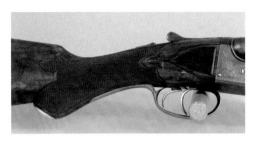

Parker Reproductions
DHE Grade

From about 1983 to 1989, reproduction Parker shotguns were manufactured in Tochigi, Japan, to original Parker specifications. This DHE is a fine example of a cloned American double. Some 12,268 were produced, and these versions are almost as collectible as original Parkers. (See page 181 for specifications and grading values.)

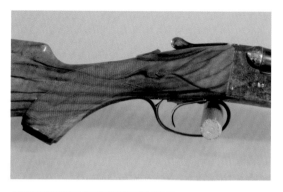

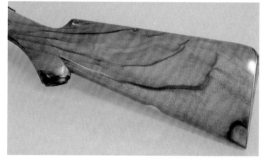

Fratelli Piotti
Piuma (BSEE) Double

Fratelli Piotti is one of the world's premier shotgun makers. This Piuma model features an Anson & Deely-style boxlock with a scalloped frame. (See page 185 for specifications and grading values.)

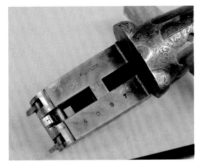

Remington Arms Company
Model 11-48

The 11-48 was produced by Remington shortly after WWII and replaced the Model 11. It uses a recoil-operated semiautomatic action. (See page 197 for specifications and grading values.)

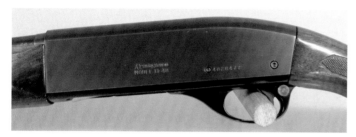

**Remington Arms Company
Model 1100 Sporting 28**
The 1100 has been configured in a multitude of variations, and this Sporting 28 is no exception.

Chambered in 28-gauge, it came with extended Briley choke tubes. (See page 193 for specifications and grading values.)

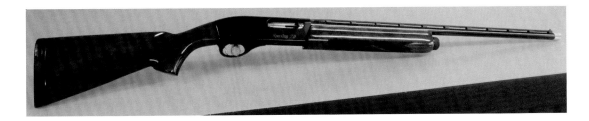

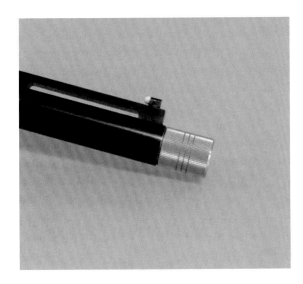

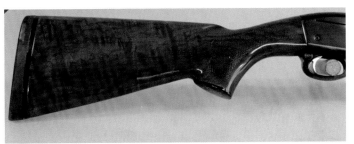

Savage Arms
Model 24C Camper's Companion

All Savage Model 24s are combination guns with a rifle barrel over a shotgun barrel. The 24C Camper's Companion was manufactured from 1972 to 1988 and features a .22 LR barrel over a 20-gauge barrel. This specimen has the original carry case. (See page 204 for specifications and grading values.)

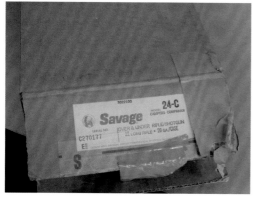

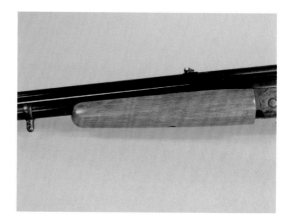

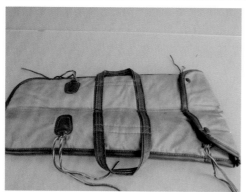

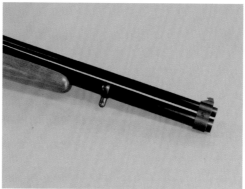

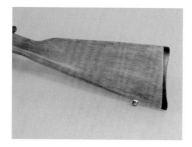

Winchester
Model 21 Grand American Small Gauge

Original production of Model 21s was from 1931 to 1959. Winchester's Custom Shop then began manufacture in 1960 and ceased in 1991. This is a Grand American Small Gauge, which were offered starting in 1982 and shipped with 28-gauge and .410 bore barrel sets and matching forends. (See pages 228-9 for specifications and grading values.)

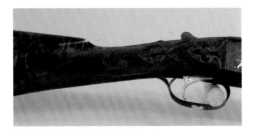

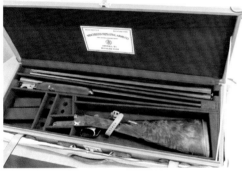

Winchester
Model 101 Pigeon Grade

This is a recently manufactured 101 with select checkered wood, deluxe engraved receiver, and WinChoke tubes. (See page 232 for specifications and grading values.)

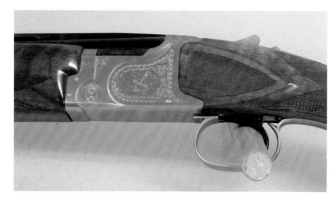

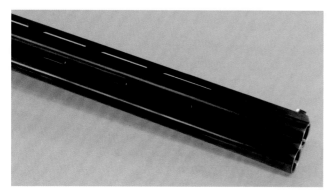

Winchester
Model 9410

The Model 94 lever-action rifle has been chambered in numerous calibers and in .410 bore. The 9410 was produced from 2001 through 2006 and was offered in either cylinder bore choke or Standard Invector choke tubes.

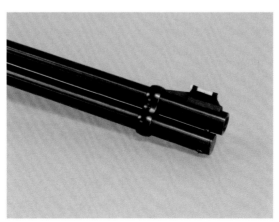

GUN TRADER'S GUIDE to

Shotguns

Abbreviations:

adj.	=	adjustable	IC	=	Improved Cylinder	S/S	=	side-by-side
bbl.	=	barrel			choke	O/U	=	over-and-under
C	=	Cylinder choke	ga.	=	gauge	w/	=	with
c.	=	circa	M	=	Modified choke			
F	=	Full choke	mfg.	=	manufactured			

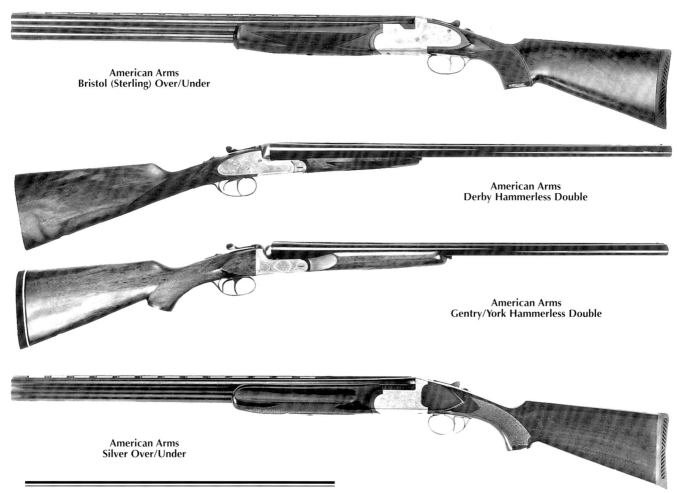

American Arms
Bristol (Sterling) Over/Under

American Arms
Derby Hammerless Double

American Arms
Gentry/York Hammerless Double

American Arms
Silver Over/Under

ADAMY, GEBR. JAGDWAFFEN — Suhl, Germany

Custom gunmaker established 1820; currently from 1921. Previously imported by New England Custom Gun service, Claremont, NH. Specializes in custom break-action shotguns (S/S, O/U) drillings, vierlings, single-shot rifles. Models and grades are numerous, contact factory for specific information .

ALDENS SHOTGUN — Chicago, Illinois

MODEL 670 CHIEFTAIN SLIDE ACTION .. NiB $331 EX $239 GD $190
Hammerless. Gauges: 12, 20, and others. 3-round tubular magazine. Bbl.: 26- to 30-inch; various chokes. Weight: 6.25 to 7.5 lbs. depending on bbl. length and ga. Walnut-finished hardwood stock.

AMERICAN ARMS — N. Kansas City, Missouri

See also Franchi Shotguns.

BRISTOL (STERLING) O/U . . . . NiB $853 Ex $621 Gd $500
Boxlock w/Greener crossbolt and engraved sideplates. Single selective trigger. Selective automatic ejectors. Gauges: 12, 20; 3-inch chambers. 26-, 28-, 30-, or 32-inch vent-rib bbls. w/screw-in choke tubes (IC/M/F). Weight: 7 lbs. Antique silver receiver w/game scene or scroll engraving. Checkered full pistol-grip-style buttstock and forearm w/high-gloss finish. Imported 1986-88 designated Bristol; redesignated Sterling 1989 to 1990.

BRITTANY HAMMERLESS DOUBLE. . . . .NiB $863 Ex $744 Gd $508
Boxlock w/engraved case-colored receiver. Single selective trigger. Selective automatic ejectors. Gauges: 12, 20. 3-inch chambers. Bbls.: 25- or 27-inch w/screw-in choke tubes (IC/M/F). Weight: 6.5 lbs. (20 ga.). Checkered English-style walnut stock w/semi-beavertail forearm or pistol-grip stock w/high-gloss finish. Imported 1989 to 2000.

CAMPER SPECIAL . . . . NiB $217 Ex $166 Gd $90
Similar to the Single Barrel except takedown model w/21-inch bbl., M choke, and pistol-grip stock. Made in 1989.

COMBO . . . . NiB $292 Ex $200 Gd $156
Similar to the Single Barrel except available w/interchangeable rifle and shotgun bbls. .22 LR/20-ga. shotgun or .22 Hornet/12-ga. shotgun. Rifle bbl. has adj. rear sights; blade-type front sight. Made in 1989.

DERBY HAMMERLESS DOUBLE
Sidelock w/engraved sideplates. Single nonselective or double triggers. Selective automatic ejectors. Gauges: 12, 20, 28, and .410. 3-inch chambers. Bbls.: 26-inch (IC/M) or 28-inch (M/F). Weight: 6 lbs. (20 ga.). Checkered English-style walnut stock and splinter forearm w/hand-rubbed oil finish. Engraved frame/sideplates w/ antique silver finish. Imported 1986 to 1994.
12 or 20 ga. . . . . NiB $1254 Ex $907 Gd $677
28 ga. or .410 (disc. 1991) . . . . . NiB $1377 Ex $979 Gd $855

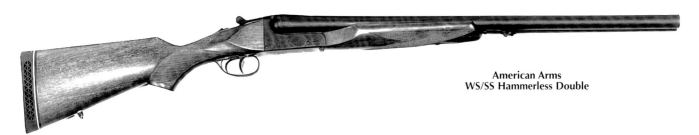

**American Arms
WS/SS Hammerless Double**

F.S. SERIES O/U

Greener crossbolt in Trap and Skeet configuration. Single selective trigger. Selective automatic ejectors. 12-gauge only. 26-, 28-, 30-, or 32-inch separated bbls. Weight: 6.5 to 7.25 lbs. Black or chrome receiver. Checkered walnut buttstock and forearm. Imported 1986 to 1987.

Model F.S. 200 Boxlock	NiB $867	Ex $677	Gd $490
Model F.S. 300 Boxlock	NiB $1099	Ex $827	Gd $568
Model F.S. 400 Sidelock	NiB $1386	Ex $1197	Gd $871
Model F.S. 500 Sidelock	NiB $1386	Ex $1197	Gd $871

GENTRY/YORK HAMMERLESS DOUBLE

Chrome, coin-silver, or color casehardened boxlock receiver w/ scroll engraving. Double triggers. Extractors. Gauges: 12, 16, 20, 28, .410. 3-inch chambers (16 and 28 have 2.75-inch). Bbls.: 26-inch (IC/M) or 28-inch (M/F, 12, 16, and 20). Weight: 6.75 lbs. (12 ga.). Checkered walnut buttstock w/pistol-grip and beavertail forearm; both w/semi-gloss oil finish. Imported as York from 1986 to 1988, redesignated Gentry 1989 to 2000.

Gentry 12, 16, or 20 ga.	NiB $733	Ex $577	Gd $428
Gentry 28 ga. or .410	NiB $755	Ex $590	Gd $488
York 12, 16, or 20 ga. (disc. 1988)	NiB $690	Ex $577	Gd $433
York 20 ga. or .410	NiB $690	Ex $577	Gd $433

GRULLA #2 HAMMERLESS DOUBLE

True sidelock w/engraved detachable sideplates. Double triggers. Extractors and cocking indicators. Gauges: 12, 20, .410. 3-inch chambers; 28 w/2.75-inch. 26-inch bbl. Imported 1989 to 2000.

Standard model	NiB $3798	Ex $2886	Gd $2166
Two-bbl. set (disc. 1995)	NiB $3876	Ex $3688	Gd $2544

SILVER I O/U

Boxlock. Single selective trigger. Extractors. Gauges: 12, 20, and .410. 3-inch chambers; 28 w/2.75 inch. Bbls.: 26-inch (IC/M), 28-inch (M/F, 12 and 20 ga. only). Weight: 6.75 lbs. (12 ga.). Checkered walnut stock and forearm. Antique silver receiver w/ scroll engraving. Imported 1987 to 2000.

12 or 20 ga.	NiB $622	Ex $535	Gd $368
28 ga. or .410	NiB $663	Ex $590	Gd $477

SILVER II O/U

Similar to Model Silver I except w/selective automatic ejectors and 26-inch bbls. w/screw-in tubes (12 and 20 ga.). Fixed chokes (28 and .410). Made 1987 to 2000.

12 or 20 ga.	NiB $735	Ex $600	Gd $489
28 ga or .410	NiB $730	Ex $652	Gd $464
Upland Lite II	NiB $1254	Ex $1066	Gd $855
Two-bbl. set	NiB $1293	Ex $1088	Gd $867

SILVER LITE O/U

Similar to Model Silver II except w/blued, engraved alloy receiver. Available in 12 and 20 ga. only. Imported from 1990 to 1992.

Standard Model	NiB $922	Ex $655	Gd $477
Two-bbl. set	NiB $1169	Ex $908	Gd $733

SILVER SKEET/TRAP .... NiB $855 Ex $640 Gd $569

Similar to the Silver II Model except has 28-inch (Skeet) or 30-inch (Trap) ported bbls. w/target-style rib and mid-bead sight. Imported 1992 to 1994.

SILVER SPORTING O/U .... NiB $966 Ex $768 Gd $633

Boxlock. Single selective trigger. Selective automatic ejectors. Gauge: 12. 2.75-inch chambers. 28-inch bbls. w/Franchoke tubes (SK/IC/M/F). Weight: 7.5 lbs. Checkered walnut stock and forearm. Special broadway rib and vented side ribs. Engraved receiver w/ chrome-nickel finish. Imported from 1990 to 2000.

SINGLE-SHOT SHOTGUN

Break-open action. Gauges: 10 (3.5), 12, 20, .410. 3-inch chamber. Weight: about 6.5 lbs. Bead front sight. Walnut-finished hardwood stock w/checkered grip and forend. Made from 1988 to 1990.

10 ga. (3.5-inch)	NiB $198	Ex $117	Gd $75
12, 20 ga., .410	NiB $200	Ex $99	Gd $66
Multi-choke bbl., add			$50

SLUGGER SINGLE-SHOT SHOTGUN..... NiB $190 Ex $100 Gd $79

Similar to the Single-Shot model except in 12 and 20 ga. only w/24-inch slug bbl. Rifle-type sights and recoil pad. Made 1989 to 1990.

TS/OU 12 SHOTGUN .... NiB $744 Ex $555 Gd $490

Turkey Special. Boxlock. Single selective trigger. Selective automatic ejectors. Gauge: 12. 3.5-inch chambers. Bbls.: 24-inch O/U w/screw-in choke tubes (IC/M/F). Weight: 6 lbs., 15 oz. Checkered European walnut stock and beavertail forearm. Matte blue metal finish. Imported 1987 to 2000.

TS/SS 10 HAMMERLESS DOUBLE ...... NiB $700 Ex $533 Gd $400

Turkey Special. Same general specifications as Model WS/SS 10 except w/26-inch side-by-side bbls., screw-in choke tubes (F/F), and chambered for 10-ga. 3.5-inch shells. Weight: 10 lbs., 13 oz. Imported 1987 to 1993.

TS/SS 12 HAMMERLESS DOUBLE ...... NiB $766 Ex $533 Gd $421

Same general specifications as Model WS/SS 10 except in 12 ga. w/26-inch side-by-side bbls. and 3 screw-in choke tubes (IC/M/F). Weight: 7 lbs., 6 oz. Imported 1987 to 2000.

WS O/U 12 SHOTGUN .... NiB $644 Ex $538 Gd $377

Waterfowl Special. Boxlock. Single selective trigger. Selective automatic ejectors. Gauge: 12. 3.5-inch chambers. Bbls.: 28-inch O/U w/screw-in tubes (IC/M/F). Weight: 7 lbs. Checkered European walnut stock and beavertail forearm. Matte blue metal finish. Imported 1987–2000.

WS/SS 10 HAMMERLESS DOUBLE ..... NiB $883 Ex $671 Gd $428

Waterfowl Special. Boxlock. Double triggers. Extractors. Gauge: 10. 3.5-inch chambers. Bbls.: 32-inch side/side choked F/F. Weight: About 11 lbs. Checkered walnut stock and beavertail forearm w/ satin finish. Parkerized metal finish. Imported from 1987 to 1995.

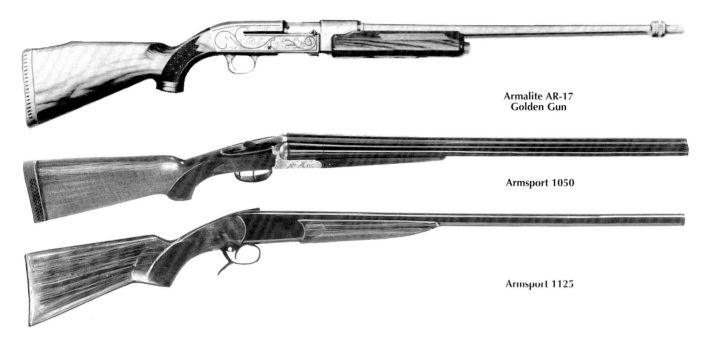

Armalite AR-17
Golden Gun

Armsport 1050

Armsport 1125

WT O/U SHOTGUN. . . . . NiB $844 Ex $657 Gd $533
Same general specifications as Model WS/OU 12 except chambered for 10-ga. 3.5-inch shells. Extractors. Satin wood finish and
matte blue metal. Imported 1987 to 2000.

ARMALITE, INC. — Costa Mesa, California

AR-17 GOLDEN GUN . . . . NiB $863 Ex $643 Gd $559
Recoil-operated semiautomatic. High-test aluminum bbl. and receiver
housing. 12 ga. only. Two-round capacity. 24-inch bbl. w/interchange-
able choke tubes (IC/M/F). Weight: 5.6 lbs. Polycarbonate stock and
forearm recoil pad. Gold-anodized finish standard, also made w/black
finish. Made 1964 to 1965. Fewer than 2,000 produced.

ARMSCOR (Arms Corp.) — Manila, Philippines

*Imported until 1991 by Armsco Precision, San Mateo,
CA; 1991–95 by Ruko Products, Inc., Buffalo NY*

MODEL M-30 FIELD PUMP SHOTGUN
Double slide-action bars w/damascened bolt. Gauge: 12 only.
3-inch chamber. Bbl.: 28-inch w/fixed chokes or choke tubes.
Weight: 7.6 lbs. Walnut or walnut finished hardwood stock.
Model M-30F (w/hardwood
    stock, fixed choke). . . . . NiB $288 Ex $212 Gd $149
Model M-30F (w/hardwood
    stock and choke tubes) . . . . NiB $288 Ex $212 Gd $149
Model M-30F/IC (w/walnut
    stock and choke tubes) . . . . NiB $366 Ex $247 Gd $169

MODEL M-30 RIOT PUMP
Double-action slide bar w/damascened bolt. Gauge: 12 only.
3-inch chamber. Bbls: 18.5- and 20-inch (IC). 5- or 7-round maga-
zine. Weight: 7 lbs., 2 oz. Walnut finished hardwood stock.
Model M-30R6 (5-round magazine) . . . . . . NiB $190 Ex $121 Gd $90
Model M-30R8 (7-round magazine) . . . . . NiB $219 Ex $135 Gd $100

MODEL M-30 SPECIAL COMBO
Simlar to Special Purpose Model except has detachable synthetic
stock that removes to convert to pistol-grip configuration.
Model M-30C (disc. 1995) . . . . . . NiB $249 Ex $200 Gd $155
Model M-30RP (disc. 1995) . . . .NiB $249 Ex $200 Gd $155

MODEL M-30 SPECIAL PURPOSE
Double-action slide bar w/damascened bolt. 7-round magazine.
Gauge: 12 only. 3-inch chamber. 20-inch bbl. w/cylinder choke.
Iron sights (DG Model) or venter handguard (SAS Model). Weight:
7.5 lbs. Walnut finished hardwood stock.
Model M-30DG (Deer Gun) . . . . NiB $266 Ex $198 Gd $137
Model M-30SAS (Special Air Services) . . . . . NiB $277 Ex $218 Gd $125

ARMSPORT, INC. — Miami, Florida

1000 SERIES HAMMERLESS DOUBLES
Side-by-side w/engraved receiver, double triggers, and extractors.
Gauges: 10 (3.5), 12, 20, .410. 3-inch chambers. Model 1033: 10
ga., 32-inch bbl. Model 1050/51: 12 ga., 28-inch bbl., M/F choke.
Model 1052/53: 20 ga., 26-inch bbl., I/M choke. Model 1054/57:
.410 ga., 26-inch bbl., I/M choke. Model 1055: 28 ga. Weight:
5.75 to 7.25 lbs. European walnut buttstock and forend. Made in
Italy. Importation disc. 1993.
Model 1033 (10 ga., disc. 1989). . . . . NiB $844 Ex $690 Gd $497
Model 1050 (12 ga., disc. 1993). . . . . NiB $766 Ex $692 Gd $477
Model 1051 (12 ga., disc. 1985). . . . . NiB $503 Ex $412 Gd $326
Model 1052 (20 ga., disc. 1985). . . . . NiB $477 Ex $390 Gd $288
Model 1053 (20 ga., disc. 1993). . . . . NiB $790 Ex $666 Gd $459
Model 1054 (.410, disc. 1992) . . . . . . NiB $888 Ex $739 Gd $522
Model 1055 (28 ga., disc. 1992). . . . . NiB $554 Ex $448 Gd $336
Model 1057 (.410, disc. 1985) . . . . . . NiB $569 Ex $481 Gd $357

MODEL 1125 SINGLE-SHOT SHOTGUN . . . . . NiB $196 Ex $139 Gd $98
Bottom-opening lever. Gauges: 12, 20. 3-inch chambers. Bead
front sight. Plain stock and forend. Imported 1987–89.

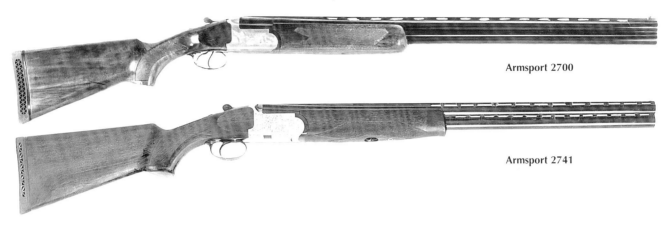

Armsport 2700

Armsport 2741

MODEL 2700 GOOSE GUN

Similar to the 2700 Standard Model except 10 ga. 3.5-inch chambers. Double triggers w/28-inch bbl. choked IC/M or 32-inch bbl., F/F. 12mm wide vent rib. Weight: 9.5 lbs. Canada geese engraved on receiver. Antiqued silver finished action. Checkered European walnut stock w/rubber recoil pad. Imported from Italy 1986 to 1993.

w/fixed choke . . . . NiB $1167 Ex $933 Gd $676
w/choke tubes . . . . NiB $1433 Ex $979 Gd $724

MODEL 2700 OVER/UNDER SERIES

Hammerless, takedown shotgun w/engraved receiver. Selective single or double triggers. Gauges: 10, 12, 20, 28, and .410. Bbl.: 26- or 28-inch w/fixed chokes or choke tubes. Weight: 8 lbs. Checkered European walnut buttstock and forend. Made in Italy. Importation disc. 1993.

Model 2701 12 ga. (disc. 1985) . . . . NiB $613 Ex $500 Gd $357
Model 2702 12 ga. . . . . NiB $635 Ex $525 Gd $378
Model 2703 20 ga. (disc. 1985) . . . . NiB $668 Ex $544 Gd $365
Model 2704 20 ga. . . . . NiB $655 Ex $548 Gd $400
Model 2705 (.410, DT, fixed chokes) . . . . NiB $775 Ex $638 Gd $454
Model 2730/31 (Boss-style action,
    SST Choke tubes) . . . . NiB $868 Ex $733 Gd $538
Model 2733/35 (Boss-style
    action, extractors) . . . . NiB $790 Ex $644 Gd $466
Model 2741 (Boss-style
    action, ejectors) . . . . NiB $678 Ex $566 Gd $412
Model 2742 Sporting Clays
    (12 ga./choke tubes) . . . . NiB $835 Ex $679 Gd $555
Model 2744 Sporting Clays
    (20 ga./choke tubes) . . . . NiB $855 Ex $677 Gd $499
Model 2750 Sporting Clays
    (12 ga./sideplates) . . . . NiB $955 Ex $723 Gd $528
Model 2751 Sporting Clays
    (20 ga./sideplates) . . . . NiB $943 Ex $759 Gd $544

MODEL 2755 SLIDE-ACTION SHOTGUN

Gauge: 12. 3-inch chamber. Tubular magazine. Bbls.: 28- or 30-inch w/fixed choke or choke tubes. Weight: 7 lbs. European walnut stock. Made in Italy 1986 to 1987.

Standard model, fixed choke . . . . NiB $444 Ex $366 Gd $270
Standard model, choke tubes . . . . NiB $579 Ex $489 Gd $355
Police model, 20-inch bbl . . . . NiB $390 Ex $333 Gd $244

MODEL 2900 TRI-BARREL (TRILLING) SHOTGUN

Boxlock. Double triggers w/top-tang bbl. selector. Extractors. Gauge: 12. 3-inch chambers. Bbls.: 28-inch (IC/M/F). Weight: 7.75 lbs. Checkered European walnut stock and forearm. Engraved silver receiver. Imported 1986 to 1987 and 1990 to 1993.

Model 2900 (w/fixed chokes) . . . . NiB $2288 Ex $1844 Gd $1307
Model 2900 (choke tubes) . . . NiB $2945 Ex $2385 Gd $1669
Deluxe grades, add $600

ARRIETA, S.L. — Elgoibar, Spain

Imported by New England Arms Corp., Wingshooting Adventures Quality Arms, Griffin & Howe, and Orvis

Custom double-barreled shotguns with frames scaled to individual gauges. Standard gauges are 12 and 16. Add 5% for small gauges (20, 24, 28, 32, and .410 bore) on currently manufactured models. $900 for single trigger (most actions); 5% for matched pairs; 10% for rounded action on standard models; extra bbls., add $1375 to $2000 per set.

MODEL 557 STANDARD . . . . . . .NiB $4428 Ex $3966 Gd $2044
Gauges: 12, 16, or 20. Demi-Bloc steel barrels, detachable engraved sidelocks, double triggers, ejectors.

MODEL 570 LIEJA . . . . NiB $4949 Ex $4210 Gd $2588
Gauges: 12, 16, or 20. Nondetachable sidelocks.

MODEL 578 VICTORIA . . . . NiB $6280 Ex $4366 Gd $2290
Gauges: 12, 16, or 20. Similar to Model 570 but with fine English scrollwork.

LIGERA MODEL . . . . NiB $5634 Ex $4247 Gd $3270
Available in all gauges. Lightweight 12 ga. has 2-inch chambers, lightweight or standard action. Includes unique frame engraving and Turkish wood upgrade. Weight: appox. 6 lbs.

MODEL 590 REGINA . . . . NiB $3589 Ex $3177 Gd $2229
Gauges: 12, 16, or 20. Similar to Model 570 but has more elaborate engraving.

MODEL 595 PRINCIPE . . . . NiB $5579 Ex $4367 Gd $3410
Available in all gauges, sidelock, engraved hunting scenes, ejectors,double triggers.

MODEL 600 IMPERIAL . . . . NiB $9115 Ex $5910 Gd $3588
Gauges: 12, 16, or 20. Self-opening action, ornate engraving throughout.

MODEL 601 IMPERIAL TYRO . . . NiB $9350 Ex $6005 Gd $4337
Available in all gauges, sidelock, nickel plating, ejectors,single selective trigger, border engraving.

MODEL 801 . . . . NiB $12,870 Ex $11,665 Gd $10,644
All gauges, detachable sidelocks, ejectors, coin-wash finish, Churchill-style engraving.

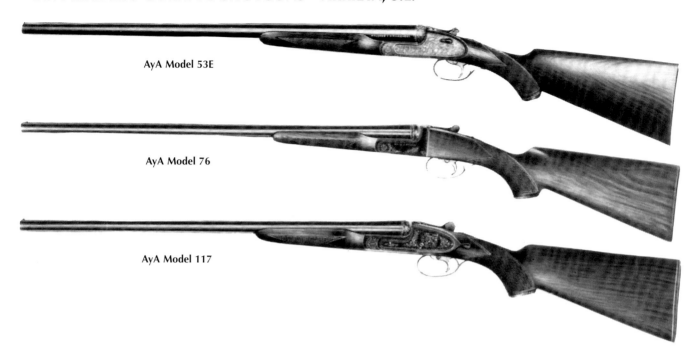

AyA Model 53E

AyA Model 76

AyA Model 117

MODEL 802 . . . . NiB $13,669 Ex $11,544 Gd $8534
Gauges: 12, 16, or 20. Similar to Model 801 except with non-detachable sidelocks, finest Holland-style engraving.

BOSS ROUND BODY . . . . NiB $8799 Ex $7733 Gd $6477
Available in all gauges, Boss pattern best quality engraving, wood upgrade.

MODEL 803 . . . . NiB $11,333 Ex $9121 Gd $6344
Available in all gauges. Similar to Model 801 except finest Purdey-style engraving.

MODEL 871 . . . . .NiB $7333 Ex $4144 Gd $2608
Available in all gauges. Rounded frame sidelock action with Demi-Bloc barrels, scroll engraving, ejectors, double trigger.

MODEL 871 EXTRA FINISH . . NiB $7555 Ex $4759 Gd $3977
Similar to Model 871 except with standard game scene engraving with woodcock and ruffed grouse.

MODEL 872 . . . . NiB $16,788 Ex $13,690 Gd $11,550
Available in all gauges, rounded frame sidelock action, Demi-Bloc barrels, elaborate scroll engraving with third lever fastener.

MODEL 873 . . . . NiB $17,228 Ex $14,788 Gd $11,766
Available in all gauges. Sidelock, gold line engraved action, ejectors, single selective trigger.

MODEL 874 . . . . NiB $12,980 Ex $11,887 Gd $6,777
Available in all gauges. Sidelock, gold line engraved action, Demi-Bloc barrels.

MODEL 875 . . . . NiB $18,960 Ex $14,449 Gd $11,733
Available in all gauges. Custom model built to individual specifications only, elaborate engraving, gold inlays.

MODEL 931 . . . . NiB $26,877 Ex $19,785 Gd $15,860
Available in all gauges. Self-opening action, elaborate engraving, H&H selective ejectors.

ASTRA SHOTGUNS — Guernica, Spain
Manufactured by Unceta y Compania

MODEL 650 O/U SHOTGUN
Hammerless, takedown w/double triggers. 12 ga. .75-inch chambers. Bbls.: 28-inch (M/F or SK/SK), 30-inch (M/F). Weight: 6.75 lbs. Checkered European walnut buttstock and forend. Disc. 1987.
w/extractors . . . . NiB $733 Ex $579 Gd $454
w/ejectors . . . . NiB $844 Ex $685 Gd $477

MODEL 750 O/U SHOTGUN
Similar to the Model 650 except w/selective single trigger and ejectors. Made in field, skeet, and trap configurations from 1980. Disc. 1987.
Field model w/extractors . . . . NiB $779 Ex $637 Gd $500
Field model w/ejectors . . . . NiB $888 Ex $755 Gd $566
Trap or Skeet model . . . . NiB $1099 Ex $867 Gd $559

AYA (Aguirre Y Aranzabal) — Eibar, Spain
Previously manufactured by Diarm, imported by Armes De Chasse, Hertford, NC

MODEL 1 HAMMERLESS DOUBLE
A Holland & Holland sidelock similar to the Model 2 except in 12 and 20 ga. only, w/special engraving and exhibition-grade wood. Weight: 5-8 lbs. depending on ga. Imported by Diarm until 1987, since 1992 by Armes de Chasse.
Model 1 Standard . . . . NiB $9177 Ex $5448 Gd $3229
Model 1 Deluxe . . . . NiB $13,110 Ex $10,077 Gd $7470
Extra set of bbls., add $750

AyA Matador II

AyA Model XXV Boxlock

MODEL 2 HAMMERLESS DOUBLE
Sidelock action w/selective single or double triggers, automatic ejectors, and safety. Gauges: 12, 20, 28, .410 (3-inch chambers). 2.75-inch chambers. Bbls.: 26- or 28-inch w/various fixed choke combinations. Weight: 7 lbs. (12 ga.). English-style straight walnut buttstock and splinter forend. Imported by Diarm until 1987, since 1992 by Armes de Chasse.

12 or 20 ga. w/double triggers . . . . .NiB $4777
  Ex $3178 Gd $2090
12 or 20 ga. w/single trigger . . . . NiB $4777
  Ex $3178 Gd $2090
28 ga. or .410 w/double triggers . . . . .NiB $4777
  Ex $3178 Gd $2090
28 ga. or .410 w/single trigger . . . ..NiB $3533 Ex $2970 Gd $2135
Extra set of bbls., add $1450

MODEL 4 HAMMERLESS DOUBLE
Lightweight Anson & Deely boxlock, scalloped frame. Gauges: 12, 16, 20, 28, and .410. Bbls.: 25- to 28-inch w/concave rib. Importation disc. 1987 and resumed in 1992 by Armes de Chasse.

12 ga. . . . . NiB $2098 Ex $1376 Gd $1099
16 ga. (early importation). . . . ..NiB $2098 Ex $1376 Gd $1099
20 ga. . . . . NiB $2098 Ex $1376 Gd $1099
28 ga. . . . . NiB $2098 Ex $1376 Gd $1099
.410 ga. . . . . NiB $2098 Ex $1376 Gd $1099
Deluxe grades, add. $700

MODEL 37 SUPER
O/U SHOTGUN . . . . NiB $3266 Ex $2279 Gd $2099
Sidelock. automatic ejectors. Selective single trigger. Made in all gauges, bbl. lengths, and chokes. Vent rib bbls. Elaborately engraved. Checkered stock w/straight or pistol grip and forend. Disc. 1995.

MODEL 37 SUPER A
O/U SHOTGUN . . . . NiB $14,879 Ex $12,776 Gd $11,340
Similar to the Standard Model 37 Super except has nickel-steel frame and is fitted w/detachable sidelocks engraved w/game scenes. Importation disc. 1987 and resumed 1992 by Armes de Chasse. Disc.

MODEL 53E . . . . NiB $6860 Ex $4950 Gd $2910
Same general specifications as Model 117 except more elaborate engraving and select figured wood. Importation disc. 1987 and resumed in 1992 by Armes de Chasse.

MODEL 56 HAMMERLESS DOUBLE
Pigeon weight Holland & Holland sidelock w/Purdey-style third lug and sideclips. Gauges: 12, 16, 20. Receiver has fine-line scroll and rosette engraving; gold-plated locks. Importation disc. 1987 and resumed 1992 by Armes de Chasse.

12 ga. . . . . NiB $10,477 Ex $7880 Gd $4610
16 ga. (early importation), add 20%
20 ga. (early importation), add. 20%

MODEL 76 HAMMERLESS
DOUBLE . . . . .NiB $955 Ex $838 Gd $529
Anson & Deeley boxlock. Auto ejectors. Selective single trigger. Gauges: 12, 20 (3-inch). Bbls.: 26-, 28-, 30-inch (in 12 ga. only), any standard choke combination. Checkered pistol-grip stock/ beavertail forend. Disc.

MODEL 76 .410. . . . . NiB $1099 Ex $877 Gd $669
Same general specifications as 12 and 20 ga. Model 76 except chambered for 3-inch shells in .410, has extractors, double triggers, 26-inch bbls. only, English-style stock w/straight grip, and small forend. Disc.

MODEL 117 HAMMERLESS
DOUBLE . . . . NiB $1887 Ex $1077 Gd $868
Holland & Holland-type sidelocks, hand-detachable. Engraved action. Automatic ejectors. Selective single trigger. Gauges: 12, 20 (3-inch). Bbls.: 26-, 27-, 28-, 30-inch; 27- and 30-inch in 12 ga. only. Any standard choke combination. Checkered pistol-grip stock and beavertail forend of select walnut. Manufactured in 1985.

BOLERO . . . . NiB $556 Ex $479 Gd $357
Same general specifications as Matador except nonselective single trigger and extractors. Gauges: 12, 16, 20, 20 Magnum (3-inch), .410 (3-inch). This model, prior to 1956, was designated F. I. Model 400 by the importer. Made from 1955 to 63.

CONTENTO OVER/UNDER SHOTGUN
Boxlock w/Woodward side lugs and double internal bolts. Gauge: 12. 2.75-inch chambers. Bbls.: 26-, 28-inch field; 30-, 32-inch trap; fixed chokes as required or screw-in choke tubes. Hand-checkered European walnut stock and forend. Single selective trigger and automatic ejectors.

M.K.2 . . . . NiB $1155 Ex $897 Gd $655
M.K.3 . . . . NiB $1887 Ex $1533 Gd $1095
Extra bbl., add. $500

MATADOR HAMMERLESS
DOUBLE . . . . NiB $619 Ex $490 Gd $339
Anson & Deeley boxlock. Selective automatic ejectors. Selective single trigger. Gauges: 12, 16, 20, 20 Magnum (3-inch). Bbls: 26-, 28-, 30-inches; any standard choke combination. Weight: 6.5 to 7.5 lbs. depending on ga. and bbl. length. Checkered pistol-grip stock and beavertail forend. This model, prior to 1956, was designated F. I. Model 400E by the importer, Firearms Int'l. Corp. of Washington, D.C. Made from 1955 to 1963.

MATADOR II. . . . . **NiB $754 Ex $567 Gd $421**
Improved version of Matador w/same general specifications except has vent-rib bbls. Made 1964 to 1969.

MATADOR III . . . . **NiB $859 Ex $744 Gd $590**
Same general specifications as AyA Matador II. Made 1970 to 1985.

MODEL XXV BOXLOCK
Anson & Deeley boxlock w/double locking lugs. Gauges: 12 and 20. 25-inch chopper lump, satin blued bbls. w/Churchill rib. Weight: 5 to 7 lbs. Double triggers. Automatic safety and ejectors. Color case-hardened receiver w/Continental-style scroll and floral engraving. European walnut stock. Imported 1979 to 1986 and 1991.
12 or 20 ga. . . . . **NiB $3190 Ex $2688 Gd $2100**
Extra set of bbls., add $1250

MODEL XXV SIDELOCK
Holland & Holland-type sidelock. Gauges: 12, 20, 28, and .410; 25-, 26-, 27-, 28-, 29-, and 32-inch bbls. Chopper lump, satin blued bbls. w/Churchill rib. Weight: 5 to 7 lbs. Double triggers standard or selective or nonselective single trigger optional Automatic safety and ejectors. Cocking indicators. Color casehardened or coin-silver finished receiver w/Continental-style scroll and floral engraving. Select European walnut stock w/hand-cut checkering and oil finish. Imported 1979 to 1986 and 1991.
12 or 20 ga. . . . . **NiB $5975 Ex $4220 Gd $3188**
28 ga. (disc. 1997) . . . . **NiB $6177 Ex $5063 Gd $3580**
.410 bore (disc. 1997) . . . . . . **NiB $6177 Ex $5063 Gd $3580**
w/single trigger, add $100
w/single-selective trigger, add. $200
Extra set of bbls., add $2250

BAIKAL SHOTGUNS — Izhevsk and Tula, Russia

MODEL IZH-18M SINGLE SHOT. . . . . . .**NiB $110 Ex $80 Gd $65**
Hammerless w/cocking indicator. Automatic ejector. Manual safety. Gauges: 12 , 20, 16 w/2.75-inch chamber or .410 w/3-inch chamber. Bbls.: 26-, 28-inch w/fixed chokes (IC/M/F). Weight: 5.5 to 6 lbs. Made in Russia.

MODEL IZH-27 O/U
Boxlock. Single selective trigger w/automatic ejectors or double triggers w/extractors. Gauges: 12 or 20. 2.75-inch chambers. Bbls.: 26- or 28-inch w/fixed chokes. Weight: 7 lbs. Checkered European hardwood stock and forearm. Made in Russia.
**Model IJ-27 (w/double
triggers and extractors.)** . . . . **NiB $400 Ex $334 Gd $171**
**Model IJ-27 (single selective
trigger and ejectors)** . . . . **NiB $400 Ex $334 Gd $171**

MODEL IZH-27 FIELD O/U . . . . **NiB $400 Ex $341 Gd $244**
Boxlock. Double triggers w/extractors. 12 ga. 2.75-inch chambers. Bbls.: 26-inch, IC/M; 28-inch, M/F w/fixed chokes. Weight: 6.75 lbs. Made in Russia.

MODEL IZH-43 FIELD SIDE-BY-SIDE
Side-by-side; boxlock. Double triggers, extractors. 12 or 20 ga. 2.75-inch chambers. Bbls: 20-inch cylinder bbl and 26- or 28-inch modified full bbl. Weight: 6.75 to 7 lbs. Checkered walnut stock, forend. Blued, engraved receiver. Imported 1994 to 1996.
Field model w/20-inch bbl. . . . . **NiB $425 Ex $275 Gd $200**
**Model IJ-43 Field
model w/26- or 28-inch bbls.** . . . . **NiB $425 Ex $275 Gd $200**

IZH-43 SERIES SIDE-BY-SIDE
Boxlock. Gauges: 12, 16, 20, or .410. 2.75- or 3-inch chambers. Bbls.: 20-, 24-, 26- or 28-inch w/fixed chokes or choke tubes. Single selective or double triggers. Weight: 6.75 lbs. Checkered hardwood (standard on Hunter II Model) or walnut stock and forend (standard on Hunter Model). Blued, engraved receiver. Imported 1994 to 1996.

Model IZH-43 Hunter
Hunter model (20, 16 ga., .410) . . . . **NiB $457 Ex $366 Gd $255**
Model IZH-43 Hunter II
Hunter II model (12 ga. w/internal hammers) . .**NiB $477 Ex $366 Gd$257**
Hunter II model (12 ga. hammerless) . . . . . . **NiB $477 Ex $366 Gd $257**
Hunter II model (12, 16, or 20 ga.) . . . .**NiB $477 Ex $366 Gd$257**
Hunter II model w/walnut stock, add. $60
Hunter II model w/single-selective trigger, add $75
**Model IZH-43 Hunter model
w/12 ga. w/walnut stock** . . . .**NiB $544 Ex $335 Gd $260**

MODEL MP94 (IZH-94) . . . . **NiB $560 Ex $350 Gd $220**
O/U combination shotgun over rifle. Boxlock. Gauges/calibers: 12 or 20 ga./.223 Rem., .30-06, .308 Win., or 7.62x39mm. Double triggers w/extractors. Bbls.: 19.5- or 23.5-inch w/ choke tubes or fixed choke. Weight: 8.5 lbs. Blued. Checkered walnut stock and forearm. Made in Russia. Made 2009 to date. Also sold as Model SPR94.
.410/.22 LR or .22 Mag. . . . . **NiB $562 Ex $300 Gd $170**

BAKER SHOTGUNS — Batavia, New York
Made 1903–1933 by Baker Gun Company

BATAVIA EJECTOR . . . . **NiB $1258 Ex $1178 Gd $798**
Same general specifications as the Batavia Leader except higher quality and finer finish throughout. Damascus or homotensile steel bbls., checkered pistol-grip stock, and forearm of select walnut; automatic ejectors standard. 12 and 16 ga. only. Deduct 60% for Damascus bbls.

BATAVIA LEADER HAMMERLESS DOUBLE
Sidelock. Plain extractors or automatic ejectors. Double triggers. Gauges: 12, 16, 20. Bbls.: 26- to 32-inch; any standard boring. Weight: About 7.75 lbs. (12 ga. w/30-inch bbls.). Checkered pistol-grip stock and forearm.
w/extractors . . . . **NiB $1465 Ex $944 Gd $500**
w/ejectors. . . . . **NiB $1600 Ex $1100 Gd $400**

BATAVIA SPECIAL. . . . . **NiB $2000 Ex $1230 Gd $500**
Same general specifications as the Batavia Leader except 12 and 16 ga. only; extractors; Homotensile steel bbls.

BLACK BEAUTY
Same general specifications as the Batavia Leader except higher quality and finer finish throughout; line engraving, special steel bbls., select walnut stock w/straight, full, or half-pistol grip.
w/extractors . . . . **NiB $2000 Ex $1200 Gd $444**
**Black Beauty Special
w/extractors** . . . . **NiB $2166 Ex $1790 Gd $577**
**Black Beauty Special
w/ejectors.** . . . . **NiB $2208 Ex $1834 Gd $544**

GRADE R . . . . **NiB $4000 Ex $2833 Gd $1106**
High-grade gun w/same general specifications as the Batavia Leader except has fine Damascus or Krupp fluid steel bbls., engraving in line, scroll and game scene designs, checkered stock, and forearm of fancy European walnut; 12 and 16 ga. only. Deduct 60% for Damascus bbls.

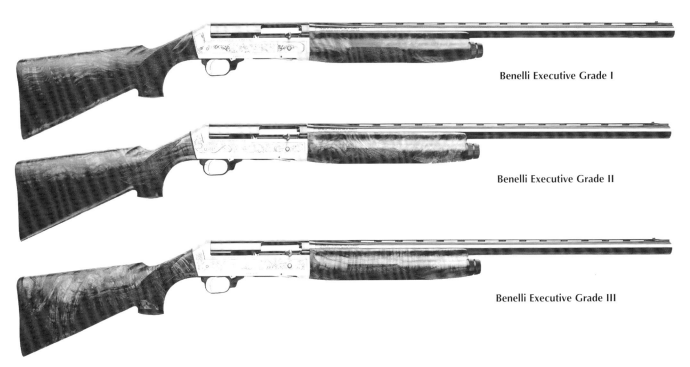

Benelli Executive Grade I

Benelli Executive Grade II

Benelli Executive Grade III

GRADE S
Same general specifications as the Batavia Leader except higher quality and finer finish throughout; has Flui-tempered steel bbls., line and scroll engraving, checkered stock w/half-pistol grip, and forearm of semi-fancy imported walnut; 10, 12, and 16 ga.
Non-ejector. . . . . NiB $3886 Ex $2013 Gd $1077
w/ejectors. . . . . NiB $4100 Ex $2315 Gd $1366

PARAGON, EXPERT, AND DELUXE GRADES
Made to order only, these are the higher grades of Baker hammerless sidelock double-bbl. shotguns. After 1909, the Paragon Grade, as well as the Expert and Deluxe intro. that year, had a crossbolt in addition to the regular Baker system taper wedge fastening. There are early Paragon guns w/Damascus bbls. and some are non-ejector, but this grade was also produced w/automatic ejectors and w/the finest fluid steel bbls. in lengths to 34 inches, standard on Expert and Deluxe guns. Differences among the three models are in overall quality, finish, engraving, and grade of fancy-figured walnut in the stock and forearm; Expert and Deluxe wood may be carved, as well as checkered. Choice of straight, full, or half-pistol grip was offered. A single trigger was available in the two higher grades. The Paragon was available in 10 ga. (Damascus bbls. only), and the other two models were regularly produced in 12, 16, and 20 ga.
Paragon grade, no ejector. . . . NiB $4277 Ex $2660 Gd $2033
Paragon grade w/auto ejector. . . . NiB $4455 Ex $2978 Gd $2270
Expert grade . . . . NiB $6177 Ex $4588 Gd $2844
Deluxe grade . . . . .NiB $11,477 Ex $9968 Gd $7133
w/ejectors, add. $350

BELKNAP SHOTGUNS — Louisville, Kentucky

MODEL B-63 SINGLE-SHOT . . . . .NiB $229 Ex $135 Gd $105
Takedown. Visible hammer. Automatic ejector. Gauges: 12, 20, and .410. Bbls.: 26- to 36-inch, F choke. Weight: Average 6 lbs. Plain pistol-grip stock and forearm.

MODEL B-63E SINGLE-SHOT . . . . .NiB $209 Ex $133 Gd $95
Same general specifications as Model B-68 except has side-lever opening instead of top lever.

MODEL B-64 SLIDE-ACTION SHOTGUN . . . . .NiB $339 Ex $244 Gd $225
Hammerless. Gauges: 12, 16, 20, and .410. 3-round tubular magazine. Various bbl. lengths and chokes from 26- to 30-inch. Weight: 6.25 to 7.5 lbs. Walnut-finished hardwood stock.

MODEL B-65C
AUTOLOADING SHOTGUN . . . . NiB $533 Ex $400 Gd $290
Browning-type lightweight alloy receiver. 12 ga. only. 4-round tubular magazine. Bbl.: plain, 28-inch. Weight: About 8.25 lbs. Disc. 1949.

MODEL B-68 SINGLE-SHOT . . . . .NiB $199 Ex $144 Gd $100
Takedown. Visible hammer. Automatic ejector. Gauges: 12, 16, 20, and .410. Bbls.: 26 to 36-inch; F choke. Weight: 6 lbs. Plain pistol-grip stock and forearm.

BENELLI SHOTGUNS — Urbino, Italy
Imported by Benelli USA, Accokeek, MD

MODEL 121 M1 MILITARY/POLICE. . . . . . . .NiB $656 Ex $432 Gd $335
Semiautomatic. Gauge: 12. 7-round magazine. 19.75-inch bbl. 39.75 inches overall. C choke, 2.75-inch chamber. Weight: 7.4 lbs. Matte black finish and European hardwood stock. Post front sight, fixed buckhorn rear sight. Imported in 1985. Disc.

BLACK EAGLE
Semiautomatic. Two-piece aluminum and steel receiver. Gauge: 12. 3-inch chamber. 4-round magazine. Screw-in choke tubes (SK/IC/M/IM/F). Bbls.: Ventilated rib; 21, 24, 26, or 28 inches w/bead front sight; 24-inch rifled slug. 42.5 to 49.5 inches overall. Weight: 7.25 lbs. (28-inch bbl.). Matte black lower receiver w/blued upper receiver and bbl. Checkered walnut stock w/high-gloss finish and drop adjustment. Imported from 1989 to 1990 and 1997 to 1998.
Limited edition. . . . . NiB $1587 Ex $1090 Gd $965
Competition model . . . . NiB $953 Ex $755 Gd $523
Slug model (disc. 1992) . . . . NiB $815 Ex $608 Gd $466
Standard model (disc. 1990) . . . . NiB $879 Ex $770 Gd $505

Benelli Legacy
Limited Edition (Only 250 Made)

Benelli M1 – Super 90 w/Pistol Grip

BLACK EAGLE EXECUTIVE

Semiautomatic. Custom Black Eagle Series. Montefeltro-style rotating bolt w/three locking lugs. All-steel lower receiver engraved, gold inlay by Bottega Incisione di Cesare Giovanelli. 12 ga. only. 21-, 24-, 26-, or 28-inch vent-rib bbl. w/5 screw-in choke tubes (Type I) or fixed chokes. Custom deluxe walnut stock and forend. Built to customer specifications on special order.

Grade I . . . . NiB $4190 Ex $3295 Gd $2293
Grade II . . . . NiB $4378 Ex $3566 Gd $2500
Grade III . . . . NiB $5690 Ex $4177 Gd $2960

LEGACY

Semiautomatic. Gauges: 12 and 20. 3-inch chambers. 24-, 26-, or 28-inch bbl. 47.63 to 49.62 inches overall. Weight: 5.8 to 7.5 lbs. 4- round magazine. 5 screw-in choke tubes. Lower alloy receiver and upper steel reciever cover. Benelli's inertia recoil operating system. Imported 1998 to date.

Legacy model . . . . NiB $1292 Ex $977 Gd $877
Limited Edition . . . . NiB $1944 Ex $1620 Gd $1010

M1 FIELD . . . . NiB $867 Ex $767 Gd $671
Interia-operated semiautomatic. Gauge: 20. 2.75- or 3-inch chambers. Bbl.: 24 or 26 inches, stepped ventilated rib and red bar sights. Stock: Synthetic, black, or camo. Weight: 5.7 to 5.8 lbs. Includes set of 5 choke tubes. Imported from Italy.

M1 SUPER 90 . . . . NiB $955 Ex $836 Gd $554
Interia-operated semiautomatic. Gauge: 12. 7-round magazine. C choke. 19.75-inch bbl. 39.75 inches overall. Weight: 7 lbs., 4 oz. to 7 lbs., 10 oz. Matte black finish. Stock and forend made of fiberglass-reinforced polymer. Sights: Post front, fixed buckhorn rear, drift adj. Introduced 1985; when the model line expanded in 1989, this configuration was disc.

M1 SUPER 90 DEFENSE . . . . . . NiB $1093 Ex $966 Gd $509
Same general specifications as Model Super 90 except w/pistol-grip stock. Available w/ghost-ring sight option. Imported 1986 to 1998.

M1 SUPER 90 FIELD

Inertia-recoil semiautomatic shotgun. Gauge: 12. 3-inch chamber. 3-round magazine. Bbl.: 21, 24, 26, or 28 inches (SK/IC/M/IM/F). 42.5 to 49.5 inches overall. Matte receiver. Standard polymer stock or satin walnut (26- or 28-inch bbl. only). Bead front sight. Imported from 1990 to 2006.

w/Realtree camo stock . . . . NiB $1066 Ex $743 Gd $488
w/polymer stock . . . . NiB $766 Ex $563 Gd $447
w/walnut stock . . . . NiB $1031 Ex $660 Gd $458

M1 SUPER 90 SLUG

Same general specifications as M1 Super 90 Field except w/5-round magazine. 18.5-inch bbl. C bore. 39.75 inches overall. Weight: 6.5 lbs. Polymer standard stock. Rifle or ghost-ring sights. Imported 1986 to 1998.

w/rifle sights . . . . NiB $988 Ex $677 Gd $549
w/ghost-ring sights . . . . NiB $1096 Ex $786 Gd $659
Realtree camo finish, add $150

M1 SUPER 90 SPECIAL

SPORTING AUTOLOADER . . . . . . NiB $877 Ex $655 Gd $589
Same general specifications as M1 Super 90 Field except w/18.5-inch bbl. 39.75 inches overall. Weight: 6.5 lbs. Ghost-ring sights. Polymer stock. Imported from 1994 to 1998.

M2

Redesign of M1w/new receiver, trigger guard, safety. Interia-operated semiautomatic. Imported 2004 to date.

Three Gun . . . . NiB $2350 Ex $1800 Gd $1000
Practical . . . . NiB $1196 Ex $970 Gd $480
Tactical . . . . NiB $1249 Ex $900 Gd $510

M3 SUPER 90 PUMP/AUTOLOADER

Inertia-recoil semiautomatic and/or pump action. Gauge: 12. 7-round magazine. C choke. 19.75-inch bbl. 41 inches overall (31 inches folded). Weight: 7 to 7.5 lbs. Matte black finish. Stock: standard synthetic, pistol-grip, or folding tubular steel. Standard rifle or ghost-ring sights. Imported 1989 to date. Caution: Increasing the magazine capacity to more than 5 rounds in M3 shotguns w/pistol-grip stocks violates provisions of the 1994 Crime Bill. This model may be used legally only by the military and law-enforcement agencies.

Standard model. . . . . NiB $1477 Ex $1067 Gd $799
Pistol-grip model . . . . NiB $1644 Ex $1133 Gd $990
w/folding stock . . . . NiB $1190 Ex $955 Gd $944
w/laser sight . . . . NiB $1766 Ex $1388 Gd $1100
Ghost-ring sights, add $100

Benelli Montefeltro
Super 90 Left-Handed
Model

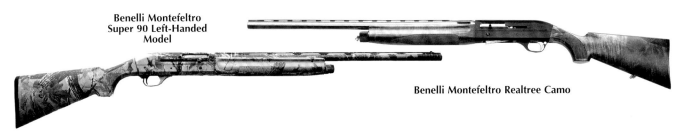

Benelli Montefeltro Realtree Camo

M4 TACTICAL . . . . NiB $1680 Ex $1230 Gd $870
Gas-operated semiautomatic. Civilian version of US military M4, gas regulating system. Gauge: 12. 3-inch chamber. 4- round magazine. Bbl.: 18.5 inches (M). 40 inches overall. Matte receiver. Standard and pistol-grip sythetic stock. Ghost ring rear, post front sights. Imported from 2003 to date.
M1040 Limited Edition . . . . . . NiB $1380 Ex $960 Gd $660

MONTEFELTRO/SUPER 90
Semiautomatic. Gauges: 12 or 20. 3-inch chamber. 21-, 24-, 26-, or 28-inch bbl. 43.7 to 49.5 inches overall. Weight: 5.3 to 7.5 lbs. 4- round magazine. Five screw-in choke tubes (C/IC/M/IM/F). High gloss, satin walnut, or Realtree camo stock. Blued metal finish. Imported 1987 to 1992.
Standard Hunter model . . . . NiB $1155 Ex $865 Gd $490
Slug model (disc. 1992) . . . . NiB $744 Ex $639 Gd $440
Turkey model . . . . NiB $744 Ex $639 Gd $440
Uplander model . . . . NiB $744 Ex $639 Gd $440
Limited Edition (1995-96) . . . . NiB $2077 Ex $1688 Gd $1176
20 ga. w/Realtree camo . . . . NiB $1269 Ex $988 Gd $775
20 ga. Youth Model w/short stock, add $75
Left-hand model, add $50

NOVA . . . . NiB $466 Ex $368 Gd $256
Pump action. Gauge: 12 or 20. 2.75- or 3-inch chambers; 3.5-inch in 12 gauge only. 4-round magazine. Bbl. 24, 26, or 28 inches; red bar sights. Stock: Synthetic (Xtra Brown in 12 gauge or Timber HD in 20 gauge). Montefeltro rotating bolt, magazine cutoff, synthetic trigger assembly. Introduced 1999. Imported from Italy.

SL 121V (SL-80 SERIES) . . . . NiB $466 Ex $359 Gd $270
Recoil-operated semiautomatic w/split receiver design. Gauge: 12. 5-round capacity. 26-, 28-, or 30-inch ventilated-rib bbl. 26-inch choked M, IM, IC; 28-inch, F, M, IM; 30-inch, F choke - Mag. Straight walnut stock w/hand-checkered pistol grip and forend. Importation disc. in 1985.

SL 121V SLUG (SL-80 SERIES) . . . . .NiB $578 Ex $376 Gd $305
Same general specifications as Benelli SL 121V except designed for rifled slugs and equipped w/rifle sights. Disc. in 1985.

SL 123V (SL-80 SERIES) . . . . NiB $500 Ex $378 Gd $297
Semiautomatic. Gauge: 12. 26- and 28-inch bbls. 26-inch choked IM, M, IC; 28-inch choked F, IM, M. Disc. in 1985.

SL 201 (SL-80 SERIES) . . . . NiB $459 Ex $365 Gd $300
Semiautomatic. Gauge: 20. 26-inch bbl. M choke. Weight: 5 lbs., 10 oz. Ventilated rib. Disc. in 1985.

SPORT . . . . NiB $1266 Ex $999 Gd $654
Similar to the Black Eagle Competition model except has one-piece matte-finished alloy receiver w/inscribed red Benelli logo. 26- or 28- inch bbl. w/2 interchangeable carbon fiber vent ribs. Oil-finished checkered walnut stock w/adjustable buttpad and buttstock. Imported 1997 to 2002.

SUPER BLACK EAGLE
Interia-operated semiautomatic. Same general specifications as Black Eagle except w/3.5-inch chamber that accepts 2.75-, 3-, and 3.5-inch shells. 2-round magazine (3.5-inch), 3-round magazine (2.75- or 3-inch). High-gloss, satin finish, or camo stock. Realtree camo, matte black, or blued metal finish. Imported 1991 to 2005.
Standard model . . . . NiB $1096 Ex $933 Gd $766
Realtree camo model . . . . NiB $1221 Ex $1099 Gd $866
Custom slug model . . . . NiB $1254 Ex $958 Gd $744
Limited edition . . . . NiB $1979 Ex $1654 Gd $1177
Wood stock, add $40
Left-hand model, add $100

ULTRA LIGHT . . . . NiB $1480 Ex $1010 Gd $610
Interia-operated semiautomatic. Gauges: 12, 20, or 28 gauge. 3-inch chamber. 24- or 26-inch bbl. 45.5 to 47.5 inches overall. Weight: 5.0 to 6.1 lbs. 2-round magazine. Five screw-in choke tubes (C/IC/M/IM/F). High gloss WeatherCoat stock. Blued metal finish. Imported 2006 to date.

CORDOBA . . . . .NiB $1800 Ex $1230 Gd $760
Interia-operated semiautomatic. Gauges: 12 or 20 gauge. 3-inch chamber. 28- or 30-inch bbl. 49.7 to 51.7 inches overall. Weight: 6.3 to 7.3 lbs. 4-round magazine. Five screw-in choke tubes (C/IC/M/IM/F). ComfortTech stock. Matte black finish. Imported 2005 to date.

VINCI . . . . NiB $1300 Ex $930 Gd $560
Interia-operated semiautomatic. Modular construction. Gauges: 12. 3-inch chamber. 26- or 28-inch bbl. 45.7 to 49.7 inches overall. Weight: 6.7 to 6.9 lbs. 3-round magazine. Five screw-in choke tubes (C/IC/M/IM/F). ComfortTech stock. Matte black finish. Imported 2009 to date.

BERETTA USA CORP. — Accokeek, Maryland
Manufactured by Fabbrica D'Armi Pietro Beretta S.P.A. in Gardone Val Trompia (Brescia), Italy, Imported by Beretta USA (previously by Garcia Corp.)

MODEL 409PB
HAMMERLESS DOUBLE . . . . NiB $966 Ex $733 Gd $545
Boxlock. Double triggers. Plain extractors. Gauges: 12, 16, 20, 28. Bbls.: 27.5-, 28.5-, and 30-inch, IC/M choke or M/F choke. Weight: from 5.5 to 7.75 lbs. depending on ga. and bbl. length. Straight or pistol-grip stock and beavertail forearm, checkered. Imported 1934 to 1964.

MODEL 410E
Same general specifications as Model 409PB except has automatic ejectors and is of higher quality throughout. Imported 1934 to 1964.
12 ga. . . . . NiB $1367 Ex $1144 Gd $922
20 ga. . . . . NiB $2882 Ex $2096 Gd $1377
28 ga. . . . . NiB $3881 Ex $3036 Gd $2456

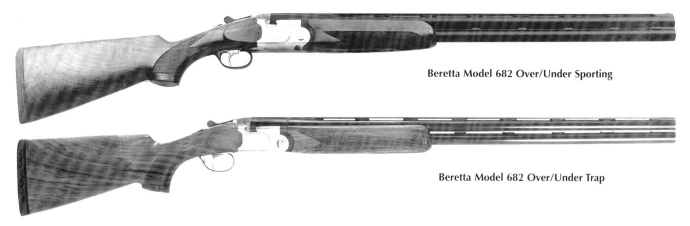

Beretta Model 682 Over/Under Sporting

Beretta Model 682 Over/Under Trap

MODEL 410 10-GA. MAGNUM ..... **NiB $1269 Ex $945 Gd $700**
Same as Model 410E except heavier construction. Plain extractors. Double triggers. 10-ga. Magnum. 3.5-inch chambers. 32-inch bbls., both F choke. Weight: About 10 lbs. Checkered pistol-grip stock and forearm, recoil pad. Imported 1934 to 1984.

MODEL 411E
Same general specifications as Model 409PB except has sideplates, automatic ejectors, and is of higher quality throughout. Imported 1934 to 1964.
12 ga. .... **NiB $2077 Ex $1700 Gd $1179**
20 ga. .... **NiB $2866 Ex $2234 Gd $1590**
28 ga. .... **NiB $4339 Ex $3977 Gd $2766**

MODEL 424 HAMMERLESS
DOUBLE .... **NiB $1288 Ex $1292 Gd $957**
Boxlock. Light border engraving. Plain extractors. Gauges: 12, 20; chambers 2.75-inch in former, 3-inch in latter. Bbls.: 28-inch M/F choke, 26-inch IC/M choke. Weight: 5 lbs., 14 oz. to 6 lbs., 10 oz. depending on ga. and bbl. length. English-style straight-grip stock and forearm, checkered. Imported 1977 to 1984.

MODEL 426E .... **NiB $1588 Ex $1233 Gd $1067**
Same as Model 424 except action body is finely engraved, silver pigeon inlaid in top lever; has selective automatic ejectors and selective single trigger. Stock and forearm of select European walnut. Imported 1977-84.

MODEL 450 SERIES HAMMERLESS DOUBLES
Custom English-style sidelock. Single nonselective trigger or double triggers. Manual safety. Selective automatic ejectors. Gauge: 12. 2.75- or 3-inch chambers. Bbls.: 26, 28, or 30 inches choked to customer specifications. Weight: 6.75 lbs. Checkered high-grade walnut stock. Receiver w/coin-silver finish. Imported 1948. Disc.
Model 450 EL (disc. 1982)...... **NiB $8334 Ex $6688 Gd $4731**
Model 450 EELL (disc. 1982) .... **NiB $10,655 Ex $6798 Gd $4880**
Model 451 (disc. 1987)...... **NiB $6443 Ex $5670 Gd $3990**
Model 451 E (disc. 1989) .... **NiB $7125 Ex $6225 Gd $4350**
Model 451 EL (disc. 1985) .... **NiB $17,787 Ex $14,866 Gd $11,700**
Model 451 EELL (disc. 1990) ...... **NiB $15,788 Ex $12,877 Gd $10,777**
Model 452 (Intro. 1990).... **NiB $29,988 Ex $21,980 Gd $18,799**
Model 452 EELL (intro. 1992) ...... **NiB $41,665 Ex $35,000 Gd $27,889**
Extra bbls, add 30%

MODEL 470 SERIES HAMMERLESS DOUBLE
Gauge: 12 and 20. 3-inch chambers. 26- or 28-inch bbl. Weight: 5.9 to 6.5 lbs. Low profile, improved boxlock action w/single selective trigger. Selected walnut, checkered stock and forend. Metal front bead sight. Scroll-engraved receiver w/gold inlay and silver-chrome finish. Imported 1999 to date.

Silver Hawk 12 ga. ....NiB $9332 Ex $6880 Gd $5440
Silver Hawk 20 ga. ....NiB $9566 Ex $6465 Gd $5566
EL Silver Hawk 12 ga. .... NiB $8310 Ex $7223 Gd $5600
EL Silver Hawk 20 ga. .... NiB $8554 Ex $6133 Gd $5477
EELL (Jubilee II) 12 ga. .... NiB $8366 Ex $6328 Gd $4790
EELL (Jubilee II) 20 ga. .... NiB $9000 Ex $7231 Gd $4889
Extra bbls., add...................................30%

MODEL 625 S/S HAMMERLESS DOUBLE
Boxlock. Gauges: 12 or 20. Bbls.: 26-, 28-, or 30-inch w/fixed choke combinations. Single selective or double triggers w/extractors. Checkered English-style buttstock and forend. Imported 1984 to 1987.
w/double triggers .... **NiB $1591 Ex $900 Gd $667**
w/single selective trigger ..... **NiB $1880 Ex $1067 Gd $700**
20 ga., add $200

MODEL 626 S/S HAMMERLESS DOUBLE
Field Grade side-by-side. Boxlock action w/single selective trigger, extractors, and automatic safety. Gauges: 12 (2.75-inch chambers), 20 (3-inch chambers). Bbls.: 26- or 28-inch w/Mobilchoke or various fixed-choke combinations. Weight: 6.75 lbs. (12 ga.). Bright chrome finish. Checkered European walnut buttstock and forend in straight English style. Imported 1985 to 1994.
Model 626 Field (disc. 1988) ....NiB $1345 Ex $1190 Gd $700
Model 626 Onyx .... **NiB $1779 Ex $1288 Gd $1006**
Model 626 Onyx (3.5-inch
  magnum, disc. 1993) ...... **NiB $1798 Ex $1388 Gd $1098**
20 ga., add 50%

MODEL 627 S/S HAMMERLESS DOUBLE
Same as Model 626 S/S except w/engraved sideplates and pistol-grip or straight English-style stock. Imported 1985 to 1994.
Model 627 EL Field......... **NiB $2370 Ex $2090 Gd $1550**
Model 627 EL Sport .... **NiB $2592 Ex $2210 Gd $1776**
Model 627 EELL .... **NiB $4460 Ex $3978 Gd $2666**

MODEL 682 O/U SHOTGUN
Hammerless takedown w/single selective trigger. Gauges: 12, 20, 28, .410. Bbls.: 26- to 34-inch w/fixed chokes or Mobilchoke tubes. Checkered European walnut buttstock and forend in various grades and configurations. Imported 1984 to 2000.
Comp Skeet model .... **NiB $1566 Ex $1160 Gd $1004**
Comp Skeet Deluxe model....... **NiB $1789 Ex $1440 Gd $1166**
Comp Super Skeet ....NiB $2599 Ex $2055 Gd $1490
Comp Skeet model, 2-bbl.
  set (disc. 1989)..............NiB $5100 Ex $4256 Gd $2920
Comp Skeet, 4 bbl.
  set (disc. 1996) ....NiB $5786 Ex $4670 Gd $3241
Sporting Continental.............NiB $1589 Ex $1170 Gd $1097
Sporting Combo ....NiB $1778 Ex $1566 Gd $1180

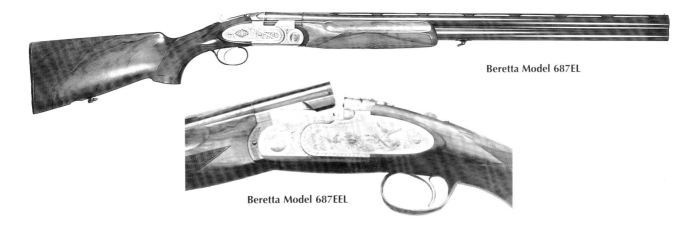

Beretta Model 687EL

Beretta Model 687EEL

Gold Sporting . . . . NiB $1788 Ex $1266 Gd $1011
Super Sporting .NiB $1566 Ex $1365 Gd $1291
Comp Trap Gold X . . . . NiB $2269 Ex $1775 Gd $1231
Comp Trap Top Single (1986-95). . . . . . . NiB $2177 Ex $1688 Gd $1166
Comp Trap Live Pigeon (1990-98). . . . . . NiB $2769 Ex $2255 Gd $1568
Comp Mono/Combo Trap Gold X . . . . . . NiB $2977 Ex $2510 Gd $1765
Comp Mono Trap (1985-88) . . . . NiB $1867 Ex $1588 Gd $1100
Super Trap Gold X (1991-95) . . . . NiB $2267 Ex $1880 Gd $1266
Super Trap Combo Gold X (1991-97) . . . . NiB $3166 Ex $2478 Gd $1776
Super Trap Top Single Gold X (1991-95). . . . . .NiB $2265 Ex $2099 Gd $1369
Super Trap Unsingle (1992-94) . . . . NiB $2210 Ex $2050 Gd $1319

MODEL 686 O/U SHOTGUN
Low profile improved boxlock action. Single selective trigger. Selective automatic ejectors. Gauges: 12, 20, 28. 3.5-, 3-, or 2.75-inch chambers depending upon ga. Bbls.: 26-, 28-, 30-inch w/fixed chokes or Mobilchoke tubes. Weight: 5.75 to 7.5 lbs. Checkered American walnut stock and forearm of various qualities depending upon model. Receiver finishes vary, but all have blued bbls. Sideplates to simulate sidelock action on EL models. Imported 1988 to 1995.
Field Onyx . . . . .NiB $1335 Ex $1108 Gd $733
(3.5-inch Mag., disc.
  1993 & reintro.1996) . . . . .NiB $4370 Ex $2888 Gd $2280
EL Gold Perdiz (1992-97). . . . . .NiB $2077 Ex $1576 Gd $1200
Essential (1994-96) . . . . NiB $1009 Ex $808 Gd $635
Silver Essential (1997-98) . . . . NiB $1180 Ex $966 Gd $680
Silver Pigeon Onyx (intro. 1996) . . . . NiB $1566 Ex $1254 Gd $870
Silver Perdiz Onyx (disc. 1996) . . . . .NiB $1488 Ex $1155 Gd $866
Silver Pigeon/Perdiz Onyx Combo . . . . NiB $1133 Ex $866 Gd $633
L Silver Perdiz (disc. 1994) . . . . .NiB $1288 Ex $1007 Gd $766
Skeet Silver Pigeon (1996-98) . . . . .NiB $1276 Ex $988 Gd $766
Skeet Silver Perdiz (1994-96) . . . . NiB $1570 Ex $1288 Gd $944
Skeet Silver Pigeon/Perdiz Combo . . . . .NiB $1570 Ex $1288 Gd $944
Sporting Special (1987-93) . . . . .NiB $1798 Ex $1369 Gd $1100
Sporting English (1991-92). . . . . .NiB $1820 Ex $1400 Gd $1188
Sporting Onyx
  w/fixed chokes (1991-92) . . . . .NiB $1743 Ex $1388 Gd $1014
Sporting Onyx
  w/choke tubes (intro. 1992) . . . . .NiB $1344 Ex $1130 Gd $966
Sporting Onyx Gold (disc. 1993) . . . . .NiB $1879 Ex $1577 Gd $1188
Sporting Silver Pigeon (intro. 1996) . . . . . .NiB $1598 Ex $1266 Gd $1005
Sporting Silver Perdiz (1993-96) . . . . .NiB $1612 Ex $1288 Gd $1130
Sporting Collection Sport (1996-97) . . . . . .NiB $1188 Ex $1033 Gd $892
Sporting Combo . . . . .NiB $2667 Ex $2174 Gd $1545
Trap International (1994-95) . . . . .NiB $1144 Ex $967 Gd $755
Trap Silver Pigeon (intro. 1997) . . . . .NiB $1266 Ex $1057 Gd $798
Trap Top Mono (intro. 1998) . . . . .NiB $1279 Ex $1088 Gd $800

Ultralight Onyx (intro. 1992) . . . . .NiB $1599 Ex $1366 Gd $968
Ultralight Del. Onyx (intro. 1998) . . . . NiB $2056 Ex $1665 Gd $1156

MODEL 687 O/U SHOTGUN
Same as Model 686 except w/decorative sideplates and varying grades of engraving and game scene motifs.
L Onyx (disc. 1991) . . . . NiB $1460 Ex $1233 Gd $865
L Onyx Gold Field (1988-89). . . . . NiB $1688 Ex $1344 Gd $966
L Onyx Silver Pigeon . . . . NiB $1288 Ex $1668 Gd $1208
EL Onyx (disc. 1990) . . . . NiB $2855 Ex $2344 Gd $1629
EL Gold Pigeon . . . . NiB $3266 Ex $2688 Gd $1863
EL Gold Pigeon small frame . . . . NiB $3090 Ex $2451 Gd $1761
EL Gold Pigeon Sporting (intro 1993) . . . . .NiB $4388 Ex $3571 Gd $2510
EELL Diamond Pigeon . . . . NiB $4416 Ex $3620 Gd $2560
EELL Diamond Pigeon Skeet . . . . NiB $4233 Ex $3548 Gd $2480
EELL Diamond Pigeon Sporting . . . . NiB $4416 Ex $3578 Gd $2560
EELL Diamond Pigeon X Trap . . . . NiB $3966 Ex $3133 Gd $2190
EELL Diamond Pigeon Mono Trap . . . . . NiB $4088 Ex $3310 Gd $2366
EELL Diamond Pigeon Trap Combo . . . . NiB $5480 Ex $4766 Gd $3266
EELL Field Combo. . . . . NiB $4570 Ex $3775 Gd $2760
EELL Skeet 4-bbl. set . . . . NiB $7588 Ex $5977 Gd $3554
EELL Gallery Special. . . . . NiB $7233 Ex $5610 Gd $3798
EELL Gallery Special Combo . . . . NiB $8235 Ex $6799 Gd $4571
EELL Gallery Special pairs . . . . NiB $17,844 Ex $14,560 Gd $10,134
Sporting English (1991-92). . . . . NiB $2247 Ex $1867 Gd $1359
Sporting Silver Pigeon (intro. 1996). . . . . . NiB $2079 Ex $1677 Gd $1261
Sporting Silver Perdiz (1993-96) . . . . . . NiB $2255 Ex $1767 Gd $1388

MODEL 1200 SERIES SEMIAUTOLOADING SHOTGUN
Short recoil action. Gauge: 12. 2.75- or 3-inch chamber. 6- round magazine. 24-, 26-, or 28-inch vent-rib bbl. w/fixed chokes or Mobilchoke tubes. Weight: 7.25 lbs. Matte black finish. Adj. technopolymer stock and forend. Imported 1988 to 1990.
w/fixed choke (disc. 1989) . . . . NiB $466 Ex $359 Gd $266
Riot (disc. 1994) . . . . NiB $476 Ex $368 Gd $277
w/Mobilchoke (disc. 1994). . . . . NiB $741 Ex $577 Gd $400
Riot model . . . . NiB $805 Ex $633 Gd $451
Pistol-grip stock, add $65
Tritium sights, add $100

MODEL A-301
AUTOLOADING SHOTGUN . . . . NiB $644 Ex $470 Gd $356
Field Gun. Gas-operated. Scroll-decorated receiver. Gauge: 12 or 20; 2.75-inch chamber in former, 3-inch in latter. 3-round magazine. Bbl.: Ventilated rib; 28-inch F or M choke, 26-inch IC. Weight: 6 lbs., 5 oz. to 6 lbs., 14 oz. depending on gauge and bbl. length. Checkered pistol-grip stock and forearm. Imported 1977 to 1982.

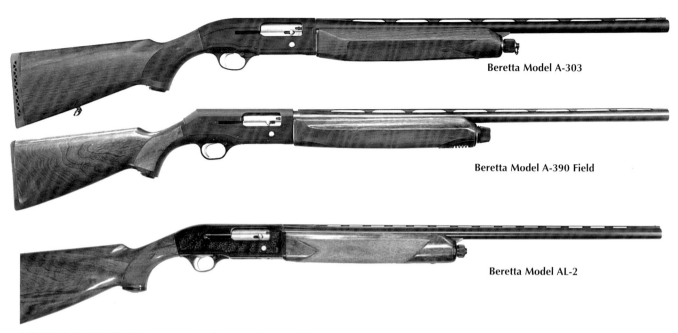

Beretta Model A-303

Beretta Model A-390 Field

Beretta Model AL-2

MODEL A-301 MAGNUM . . . . . . NiB $455 Ex $277 Gd $200
Same as Model A-301 Field Gun except chambered for 12 ga. 3-inch Magnum shells, 30-inch F choke bbl. only, stock w/recoil pad. Weight: 7.25 lbs.

MODEL A-301 SKEET GUN . . . . . NiB $466 Ex $300 Gd $210
Same as Model A-301 Field Gun except 26-inch bbl. SK choke only, skeet-style stock, gold-plated trigger.

MODEL A-301 SLUG GUN . . . . . NiB $488 Ex $287 Gd $217
Same as Model A-301 Field Gun except has plain 22-inch bbl., slug choke w/rifle sights. Weight: 6 lbs., 14 oz.

MODEL A-301 TRAP GUN . . . . . NiB $466 Ex $287 Gd $233
Same as Model A-301 Field Gun except has 30-inch bbl. in F choke only, checkered Monte Carlo stock w/recoil pad, gold-plated trigger. Blued bbl. and receiver. Weight: 7 lbs., 10 oz. Imported 1978 to 1982.

MODEL A-302 SEMIAUTOLOADING SHOTGUN
Similar to gas-operated Model 301. Hammerless, takedown shotgun w/tubular magazine and Mag-Action that handles both 2.75- and 3-inch Magnum shells. Gauge: 12 or 20. 2.75- or 3-inch Mag. chambers. Bbl.: Vent or plain; 22-inch/Slug (12 ga.), 26-inch/IC (12 or 20), 28-inch/M (20 ga.), 28-inch/Multi-choke (12 or 20 ga.), 30-inch/F (12 ga.). Weight: 6.5 lbs., 20 ga.; 7.25.lbs., 12 ga. Blued or black finish. Checkered European walnut, pistol-grip stock and forend. Imported from 1983 to c. 1987.
Standard model w/fixed choke . . . . . NiB $466 Ex $338 Gd $254
Standard model w/multi-choke . . . . . . NiB $490 Ex $345 Gd $258

MODEL A-302 SUPER LUSSO . . . . . . NiB $1844 Ex $1452 Gd $1166
A custom A-302 in presentation grade w/hand-engraved receiver and custom select walnut stock.

MODEL A-303 SEMIAUTOLOADER
Similar to Model 302 except w/target specifications in Trap, Skeet, and Youth configurations, and weighs 6.5 to 8 lbs. Imported from 1983 to 1996.
Field and Upland models . . . . NiB $523 Ex $400 Gd $288
Skeet and Trap (disc. 1994) . . . . . . NiB $488 Ex $366 Gd $257
Slug model (disc. 1992) . . . . NiB $453 Ex $377 Gd $260
Sporting Clays . . . . NiB $600 Ex $453 Gd $279

Super Skeet . . . . NiB $500 Ex $433 Gd $318
Super Trap . . . . NiB $643 Ex $494 Gd $388
Waterfowl/Turkey model
 (disc. 1992) . . . . NiB $525 Ex $460 Gd $354
Mobilchoke, add $75

MODEL A-303 YOUTH GUN . . . . . . NiB $498 Ex $376 Gd $277
Locked-breech, gas-operated action. Ga: 12 and 20; 2-round magazine. Bbls.: 24, 26, 28, 30, or 32-inches, vent rib. Weight: 7 lbs. (12 ga.), 6 lbs. (20 ga.). Crossbolt safety. Length of pull shortened to 12.5 inches. Imported 1988-96.

MODEL AL-390 SEMIAUTOMATIC SHOTGUN
Gas-operated, self-regulating action designed to handle any size load. Gauges: 12 or 20. 3-inch chamber. 3-round magazine. Bbl.: 24, 26, 28, or 30 inches w/vent rib and Mobilchoke tubes. Weight: 7.5 lbs. Select walnut stock w/adj. comb. Blued or matte black finish. Imported 1992-96. Superseded by AL-390 series.
Standard/Slug models . . . . NiB $525 Ex $377 Gd $296
Field/Silver Mallard models . . . . . NiB $525 Ex $377 Gd $296
Deluxe/Gold Mallard models . . . . ..NiB $485 Ex $335 Gd $250
Turkey/Waterfowl model
 w/matte finish . . . . NiB $577 Ex $366 Gd $300
20 ga., add $75

MODEL AL-390 TARGET
Similar to the Model 390 Field except w/2.75-inch chamber. Skeet: 28-inch ported bbl. w/wide vent rib and fixed choke (SK). Trap: 30- or 32-inch w/Mobilchoke tubes. Weight: 7.5 lbs. Fully adj. buttstock. Imported from 1993 to 1996.
Sport Trap model. . . . . NiB $599 Ex $367 Gd $290
Sport Skeet model. . . . . NiB $479 Ex $345 Gd $266
Sporting Clays model (unported) . . . . . . NiB $700 Ex $579 Gd $421
Super Trap model (ported) . . . . . . NiB $577 Ex $367 Gd $292
Super Skeet model (ported) . . . . . NiB $569 Ex $355 Gd $307
Ported bbl., add $100
20 ga., add $75

MODEL AL-1 FIELD GUN . . . . . . NiB $566 Ex $349 Gd $279
Same as Model AL-2 gas-operated Field Gun except has bbl. w/o rib, no engraving on receiver. Imported from 1971 to 1973.

Beretta Model AL-391
Urika Gold Sporting

Beretta Model AL-391
Urika Gold Trap

MODEL AL-2 AUTOLOADING SHOTGUN
Field Gun. Gas-operated. Engraved receiver (1968 version, 12 ga. only, had no engraving). Gauge: 12 or 20. 2.75-inch chamber. 3-round magazine. Bbls.: Vent rib; 30-inch F choke, 28-inch F/M choke, 26-inch IC. Weight: 6.5 to 7.25 lbs. depending on ga. and bbl. length. Checkered pistol-grip stock and forearm. Imported from 1968 to 1975.
w/plain receiver . . . . NiB $435 Ex $315 Gd $229
w/engraved receiver . . . . NiB $633 Ex $500 Gd $378

MODEL AL-2 MAGNUM . . . . NiB $515 Ex $377 Gd $255
Same as Model AL-2 Field Gun except chambered for 12 ga. 3-inch Magnum shells; 30-inch F or 28-inch M choke bbl. only. Weight: About 8 lbs. Imported from 1973 to 1975.

MODEL AL-2 SKEET GUN . . . . . . NiB $466 Ex $321 Gd $234
Same as Model AL-2 Field Gun except has wide rib, 26-inch bbl. in SK choke only, checkered pistol-grip stock and beavertail forearm. Imported 1973 to 1975.

MODEL AL-2 TRAP GUN . . . . NiB $445 Ex $341 Gd $246
Same as Model AL-2 Field Gun except has wide rib, 30-inch bbl. in F choke only, beavertail forearm. Monte Carlo stock w/recoil pad. Weight: About 7.75 lbs. Imported from 1973 to 1975.

MODEL AL-3
Similar to corresponding AL-2 models in design and general specifications. Imported from 1975 to 1976.
Field model . . . . NiB $466 Ex $331 Gd $244
Magnum model . . . . NiB $475 Ex $350 Gd $266
Skeet model . . . . NiB $486 Ex $351 Gd $264
Trap model . . . . NiB $453 Ex $335 Gd $266

MODEL AL-3 DELUXE TRAP GUN NiB $700 Ex $566 Gd $339
Same as standard Model AL-3 Trap Gun except has fully-engraved receiver, gold-plated trigger and safety, stock and forearm of premium-grade European walnut, gold monogram escutcheon inlaid in buttstock. Imported 1975 to 1976.

AL390 FIELD SHOTGUN
Lightweight version of A-390 series. Gauges: 12 or 20 ga. 22-, 24-, 26-, 28-, or 30-inch bbl., 41.7 to 47.6 inches overall. Weight: 6.4 to 7.5 lbs. Imported 1992 to 1999.
Field/Silver Mallard model (12 or 20 ga.) . . . NiB $655 Ex $465 Gd $300
Field/Silver Mallard Youth model (20 ga.) . . NiB $500 Ex $355 Gd $245
Field/Slug (12 ga. only) . . . . NiB $525 Ex $433 Gd $266
Silver Mallard camo model . . . . NiB $533 Ex $379 Gd $295
Silver Mallard model, synthetic stock . . . . NiB $566 Ex $430 Gd $349
Gold Mallard (12 or 20 ga.) . . . . NiB $800 Ex $656 Gd $445
NWTF Special model, camo . . . . NiB $645 Ex $355 Gd $339
NTWF Special model, synthetic . . . . . NiB $600 Ex $440 Gd $322
NWTF Special Youth model. . . . . NiB $590 Ex $367 Gd $292

AL390 SPORT SKEET SHOTGUN
Gauges: 12 ga. only. X26- or 28-inch bbl. 3-round mqagazine. Weight: 7.6 to 8 lbs. Matte finish wood and metal. Imported 1995 to 1999.
Sport Skeet . . . . NiB $498 Ex $366 Gd $279
Sport Super Skeet . . . . NiB $576 Ex $377 Gd $301
Ported bbl., add $125

AL390 SPORT SPORTING SHOTGUN
Similar to Model AL390 Sport Skeet. Gauges: 12 or 20 ga., 28- or 30-inch bbls. Weight: 6.8 to 8 lbs. Imported from 1995-1999.
Sport Sporting . . . . NiB $566 Ex $396 Gd $300
Sport Sporting Collection . . . . . . NiB $590 Ex $433 Gd $335
Sport Sporting
  Youth (20 ga. only). . . . . NiB $590 Ex $454 Gd $397
Sport Gold Sporting . . . . NiB $823 Ex $577 Gd $446
EELL Sport
  Diamond Sporting . . . . NiB $2166 Ex $1488 Gd $1094
Ported bbl., add $100

AL390 SPORT TRAP SHOTGUN
Gauges: 12 ga. only. 30- or 32-inch bbl. 3-round chamber. Weight: 7.8 to 8.25 lbs. Matte finish wood and metal. Black recoil rubber pad. Imported from 1995 to 1999.
Sport Trap . . . . NiB $564 Ex $379 Gd $288
Sport Super Trap . . . . NiB $688 Ex $512 Gd $360
Multi-choke bbl. (30-inch only), add $65
Ported bbl., add $125

AL391 URIKA AUTOLOADING SHOTGUN
Gauge: 12 and 20 ga. 3-inch chambers. 28-, 30-, or 32-inch bbl. Weight: 6.6 to 7.7 lbs. Self-compensating gas valve. Adj. synthetic and walnut stocks w/five interchangeable chokes. Imported from 2001 to 2006.
Urika . . . . NiB $923 Ex $800 Gd $655
Urika synthetic . . . . NiB $865 Ex $758 Gd $600
Urika camo
  w/Realtree Hardwoods . . . . NiB $977 Ex $844 Gd $654
Urika
  Gold w/black receiver . . . . NiB $896 Ex $588 Gd $464
Urika Gold
  w/silver receiver . . . . NiB $1196 Ex $974 Gd $799
Urika Youth . . . . NiB $900 Ex $779 Gd $698
Urika Sporting . . . . NiB $1088 Ex $965 Gd $600
Urika Gold
  Sporting w/black receiver . . . . . NiB $859 Ex $655 Gd $488
Urika Gold Sporting
  w/silver receiver . . . . NiB $1256 Ex $1011 Gd $733
Urika Trap . . . . NiB $1047 Ex $798 Gd $633
Urika Gold Trap . . . . NiB $1066 Ex $881 Gd $700
Parallel Target . . . . NiB $1066 Ex $881 Gd $700

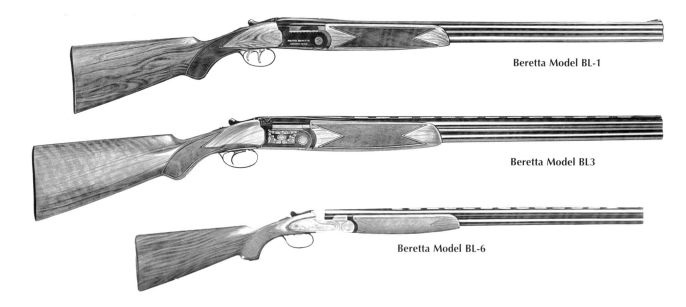

Beretta Model BL-1

Beretta Model BL3

Beretta Model BL-6

MODEL ASE 90 O/U SHOTGUN
Competition-style receiver w/coin-silver finish and gold inlay featuring drop-out trigger group. Gauge: 12. 2.75-inch chamber. Bbls.: 28- or 30-inch w/fixed or Mobilchoke tubes; vent rib. Weight: 8.5 lbs. (30-inch bbl.). Checkered high-grade walnut stock. Imported 1992 to 1994.

Pigeon, Skeet, Trap models . . . . NiB $3719 Ex $2466 Gd $1967
Sporting Clays model . . . . NiB $8171 Ex $6559 Gd $4577
Trap Combo model . . . . . . NiB $13,878 Ex $10,798 Gd $8657
Deluxe model (introduced 1996) . . . NiB $17,366 Ex $12,988 Gd $9853

MODEL ASE SERIES O/U SHOTGUN
Boxlock. Single nonselective trigger. Selective automatic ejectors. Gauges: 12 and 20. Bbls.: 26-, 28-, 30-inch; IC/M choke or M/F choke. Weight: About 5.75 to 7 lbs. Checkered pistol-grip stock and forearm. Receiver w/various grades of engraving. Imported 1947 to 1964.

Model ASE (light scroll engraving) . . . NiB $2366 Ex $1971 Gd $1388
Model ASEL (half coverage engraving) . . . NiB $3341 Ex $2679 Gd $1882
Model ASEELL (full coverage engraving) . . . NiB $4966 Ex $4054 Gd $2866
20 ga., add 95%

MODEL BL-1/BL-2 O/U
Boxlock. Plain extractors. Double triggers. 12 gauge. 2.75-inch chambers only. Bbls.: 30 and 28-inch M/F choke, 26-inch IC/M choke. Weight: 6.75 to 7 lbs. depending on bbl. length. Checkered pistol-grip stock and forearm. Imported 1968 to 1973.

Model BL-1 . . . . NiB $478 Ex $339 Gd $227
Model BL-2 (single selective trigger) . . . NiB $596 Ex $487 Gd $356

MODEL BL-2/S . . . . NiB $554 Ex $451 Gd $307
Similar to Model BL-1 except has selective Speed-Trigger, vent-rib bbls., 2.75- or 3-inch chambers. Weight: 7 to 7.5 lbs. Imported 1974 to 1976.

MODEL BL-3 . . . . NiB $690 Ex $579 Gd $491
Same as Model BL-1 except has deluxe engraved receiver, selective single trigger, vent-rib bbls. 12 or 20 ga. 2.75- or 3-inch chambers in former, 3-inch in latter. Weight: 6 to 7.5 lbs. depending on ga. and bbl. length. Imported 1968 to 1976.

MODELS BL-4/BL-5/BL-6
Higher grade versions of Model BL-3 w/more elaborate engraving and fancier wood; Model BL-6 has sideplates. Selective automatic ejectors standard. Imported 1968-76.

Model BL-4 . . . . NiB $966 Ex $779 Gd $633
Model BL-5 . . . . NiB $996 Ex $800 Gd $671
Model BL-6 (1973-76) . . . . NiB $1287 Ex $1108 Gd $977

SERIES BL SKEET GUNS
Models BL-3, BL-4, BL-5, and BL-6 w/standard features of their respective grades plus wider rib and skeet-style stock, 26-inch bbls. SK choked. Weight: 6 to 7.25 lbs. depending on ga.

Model BL-3 skeet gun . . . . NiB $1166 Ex $877 Gd $588
Model BL-4 skeet gun . . . . NiB $822 Ex $658 Gd $433
Model BL-5 skeet gun . . . . NiB $966 Ex $700 Gd $582
Model BL-6 skeet gun . . . . NiB $1139 Ex $1076 Gd $755

SERIES BL TRAP GUNS
Models BL-3, BL-4, BL-5, and BL-6 w/standard features of their respective grades plus wider rib and Monte Carlo stock w/recoil pad; 30-inch bbls., IM/F or F/F choke. Weight: About 7.5 lbs.

Model BL-3 . . . . NiB $679 Ex $466 Gd $388
Model BL-4 . . . . NiB $733 Ex $566 Gd $452
Model BL-5 . . . . NiB $966 Ex $753 Gd $521
Model BL-6 . . . . NiB $1166 Ex $893 Gd $600

D10 TRIDENT TRAP
GUNS . . . . NiB $7520 Ex $5000 Gd $2510
Removeable trigger group. 12 gauge. 3-inch chambers. Bbls.: 30 and 32-inch Optima choke tubes. Weight: 8.8 lbs. depending on bbl. length. Wlanut stock and forearm. Imported 2000 to 2008.

Top Single . . . . NiB $7520 Ex $5000 Gd $2510
Bottom Single . . . . NiB $7520 Ex $5000 Gd $2510
Combo . . . . NiB $9060 Ex $7200 Gd $4000
Model BL-6 . . . . NiB $1166 Ex $893 Gd $600

MODEL FS-1
FOLDING SINGLE . . . . NiB $238 Ex $167 Gd $95
Formerly Companion. Folds to length of bbl. Hammerless. Underlever. Gauge: 12, 16, 20, 28, or .410. Bbl.: 30-inch in 12 ga.; 28-inch in 16 and 20 ga.; 26-inch in 28 and .410 ga.; all F choke. Checkered semi-pistol grip stock and forearm. Weight: 4.5-5.5 lbs. depending on ga. Disc. 1971.

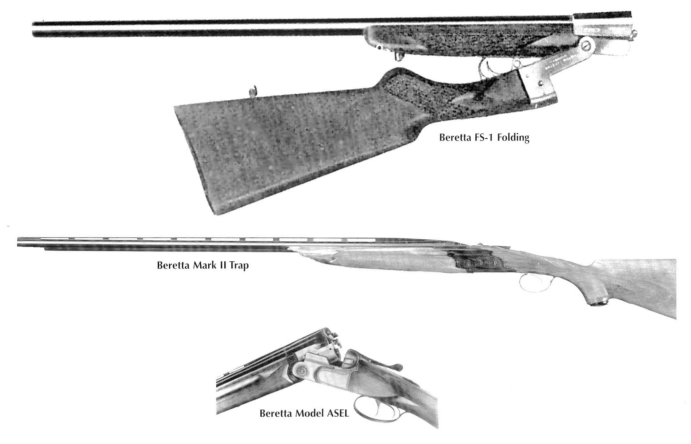

Beretta FS-1 Folding

Beretta Mark II Trap

Beretta Model ASEL

MODEL GR-2 HAMMERLESS DOUBLE.......NiB $956 Ex $788 Gd $641
Boxlock. Plain extractors. Double triggers. Gauges: 12, 20; 2.75-inch chambers in former, 3-inch in latter. Bbls.: Vent rib. 30-inch M/F choke (12 ga. only); 28-inch M/F choke, 26-inch IC/M choke. Weight: 6.5 to 7.5 lbs. depending on ga. and bbl. length. Checkered pistol-grip stock and forearm. Imported 1968 to 1976.

MODEL GR-3 . . . . NiB $1174 Ex $1021 Gd $751
Same as Model GR-2 except has selective single trigger chambered for 12-ga. 3-inch or 2.75-inch shells. Magnum model has 30-inch M/F choke bbl., recoil pad. Weight: About 8 lbs. Imported 1968 to 1976.

MODEL GR-4 . . . . NiB $1359 Ex $1165 Gd $943
Same as Model GR-2 except has automatic ejectors and selective single trigger, higher grade engraving and wood. 12 ga. 2.75-inch chambers only. Imported 1968 to 1976.

GRADE 100 O/U
SHOTGUN . . . . NiB $2134 Ex $1741 Gd $1288
Sidelock. Double triggers. Automatic ejectors. 12 ga. only. Bbls.: 26-, 28-, 30-inch; any standard boring. Weight: About 7.5 lbs. Checkered stock and forend, straight or pistol grip. Disc.

GRADE 200 . . . . NiB $2780 Ex $2284 Gd $1633
Same general specifications as Grade 00 except higher quality; bores and action parts hard chrome plated. Disc.

MARK II SINGLE-BARREL TRAP GUN . . . . . . NiB $774 Ex $623 Gd $441
Boxlock action similar to that of Series BL over/unders. Engraved receiver. Automatic ejector. 12 ga. only. 32- or 34-inch bbl. w/wide vent rib. Weight: About 8.5 lbs. Monte Carlo stock w/pistol grip and recoil pad, beavertail forearm. Imported 1972 to 1976.

MODEL S55B O/U
SHOTGUN . . . . NiB $672 Ex $490 Gd $336
Boxlock. Plain extractors. Selective single trigger. Gauges: 12, 20; 2.75- or 3-inch chambers in former, 3-inch in latter. Bbls.: vent rib; 30-inch M/F choke or both F choke in 12-ga. 3-inch Magnum only; 28-inch M/F choke; 26-inch IC/M choke. Weight: 6.5 to 7.5 lbs. depending on ga. and bbl. length. Checkered pistol-grip stock and forearm. Introduced in 1977. Disc.

MODEL S56E . . . . NiB $853 Ex $567 Gd $356
Same as Model S55B except has scroll-engraved receiver selective automatic ejectors. Introduced in 1977. Disc.

MODEL S58 SKEET GUN . . . . NiB $855 Ex $621 Gd $443
Same as Model S56E except has 26-inch bbls. of Boehler Antinit Anticorro steel, SK choked, w/wide vent rib; skeet-style stock and forearm. Weight: 7.5 lbs. Introduced in 1977.

MODEL S58 TRAP GUN . . . . NiB $620 Ex $494 Gd $368
Same as Model S58 Skeet Gun except has 30-inch bbls., bored IM/F Trap, Monte Carlo stock w/recoil pad. Weight: 7 lbs., 10 oz. Introduced in 1977. Disc.

SILVER HAWK FEATHERWEIGHT
HAMMERLESS DOUBLE-BARREL SHOTGUN
Boxlock. Double triggers or nonselective single trigger. Plain extractor. Gauges: 12, 16, 20, 28, 12 Mag. Bbls.: 26- to 32-inch w/high matted rib; all standard choke combinations. Weight: 7 lbs. (12 ga. w/26-inch bbls.). Checkered walnut stock w/beavertail forearm. Disc. 1967.
w/double triggers . . . . NiB $1133 Ex $844 Gd $521
Single trigger, add $200

Beretta S682 Gold E Trap

Beretta S682 Gold E Double
Trap

SILVER SNIPE O/U SHOTGUN
Boxlock. Nonselective or selective single trigger. Plain extractor. Gauges: 12, 20, 12 Mag., 20 Mag. Bbls.: 26-, 28-, 30-inch; plain or vent rib; chokes IC/M, M/F, SK number 1 and number 2, F/F. Weight· From about 6 lbs. in 20 ga. to 8.5 lbs. in 12 ga. (Trap gun). Checkered walnut pistol-grip stock, forearm. Imported 1955 to 1967.
w/plain bbl., nonselective trigger . . . . NiB $779 Ex $643 Gd $448
w/vent rib bbl., nonselective
single trigger . . . . NiB $779 Ex $643 Gd $448
Selective single trigger, add $100

GOLDEN SNIPE O/U
Same as Silver Snipe except has automatic ejectors; vent rib is standard feature. Imported 1959 to 1967.
w/nonselective single trigger . . . . NiB $1256 Ex $1065 Gd $645

MODEL 57E O/U
Same general specifications as Golden Snipe but higher quality throughout. Imported 1955 to 1967.
w/nonselective single trigger . . . . NiB $977 Ex $765 Gd $545
w/selective single trigger . . . . . . NiB $1165 Ex $996 Gd $703

MODEL SL-2 PIGEON SERIES SHOTGUN
Hammerless. Takedown. 12 ga. only. 3- round magazine. Bbls.: Vent rib; 30-inch F choke, 28-inch M, 26-inch IC. Weight: 7 to 7.25 lbs. depending on bbl. length. Receiver w/various grades of engraving. Checkered pistol-grip stock and forearm. Imported 1968 to 1971.
Pump shotgun . . . . NiB $553 Ex $442 Gd $308
Silver Pigeon . . . . NiB $466 Ex $367 Gd $377
Gold Pigeon . . . . NiB $663 Ex $507 Gd $464
Ruby Pigeon . . . . NiB $863 Ex $638 Gd $477

SO SERIES SHOTGUNS
Jubilee Series was introduced in 1998. The Beretta Boxlock is made with mechanical works from a single block of hot forged, high- resistance steel. The gun is richly engraved in scroll and game scenes. All engraving is signed by master engravers. High-quality finishing on the inside with high polishing of all internal points. Sidelock. Selective automatic ejectors. Selective single trigger or double triggers. 12 ga. only. 2.75- or 3-inch chambers. Bbls.: Vent rib (wide type on skeet and trap guns); 26-, 27-, 29-, 30-inch; any combination of standard chokes. Weight: 7 to 7.75 lbs., depending on bbl. length, style of stock, and density of wood. Stock and forearm of select walnut, finely checkered; straight or pistol-grip, field, skeet, and trap guns have appropriate styles of stock and forearm. Models differ chiefly in quality of wood and grade of engraving. Models SO-3EL, SO-3EELL, SO-4, and SO-5 have hand-detachable locks. SO-4 is used to designate skeet and trap models derived from Model SO-3EL but with less elaborate engraving. Models SO-3EL and SO-3EELL are similar to the earlier

SO-4 and SO-5, respectively. Imported 1933 to date.
Jubilee O/U (.410, 12, 16,
   20, 28 ga.) . . . . NiB $18,766 Ex $15,580 Gd $12,654
Jubilee II Side-by-Side . . . . NiB $20,888 Ex $16,876 Gd $13,777
Model SO-2 . . . . NiB $9121 Ex $4760 Gd $3231
Model SO-3 . . . . NiB $7786 Ex $6988 Gd $4766
Model SO-3EL. . . . . .NiB $10,573 Ex $8227 Gd $5470
Model SO-3EELL . . . . .NiB $12,098 Ex $10,866 Gd $8977
Model SO-4 Field, Skeet, or Trap gun. . . . . NiB $10,677 Ex $9154 Gd $7110
Model SO-5 Sporting,
   Skeet, or Trap model . . . . NiB $12,779 Ex $10,870 Gd $8965
Extra bbl. set, add. 25%

MODELS SO-6 AND SO-9 PREMIUM GRADE SHOTGUNS
High-grade over/unders in the SO series. Gauges: 12 ga. only (SO-6); 12, 20, 28, and .410 (SO-9). Fixed or Mobilchoke (12 ga. only). Sidelock action. Silver or casehardened receiver (SO-6); English custom hand-engraved scroll or game scenes (SO-9). Supplied w/ leather case and accessories. Imported 1990 to date.
SO-6 O/U . . . . NiB $9044 Ex $6987 Gd $4733
Model SO-6EELL O/U . . . . .NiB $8343 Ex $6865 Gd $6577
Model SO-9 O/U . . . . NiB $50,000 Ex $47,750 Gd $45,000
Model SO-9EELL w/custom
   engraving . . . . NiB $110,000 Ex $95,000 Gd $80,000
Extra bbl. set, add. 25%

MODEL SO-6 AND SO-7 S/S SHOTGUNS
Side-by-side shotgun w/same general specifications as SO Series over/unders except higher grade w/more elaborate engraving, fancier wood.
Model SO-6
   (imported 1948-93) . .NiB $7254 Ex $6144 Gd $4988
Model SO-7
   (imported 1948-90) . .NiB $8977 Ex $7238 Gd $6144

SV10 PREVAIL I . . . . NiB $2900 Ex $1830 Gd$1400
O/U. Boxlock. Gauges: 12 or 20 ga. only. Bbls.: 26- or 28-in. w/VR and Optima choke tubes. Satin finish receiver. Imported 2012-present

SV10 PREVAIL III . . . . NiB $3950 Ex $2250 Gd$1580
Similar to SV10 Prevail I except w/26-, 28-, 30-, or 32-in. bbl.; laser engraved receiver. Quick takedown stock. Imported 2008-present.

MODEL TR-1 SINGLE-SHOT
TRAP GUN . . . . NiB $355 Ex $279 Gd $125
Hammerless. Underlever action. Engraved frame. 12 ga. only. 32-inch bbl. w/vent rib. Weight: About 8.25 lbs. Monte Carlo stock w/pistol grip and recoil pad, beavertail forearm. Imported 1968 to 1971.

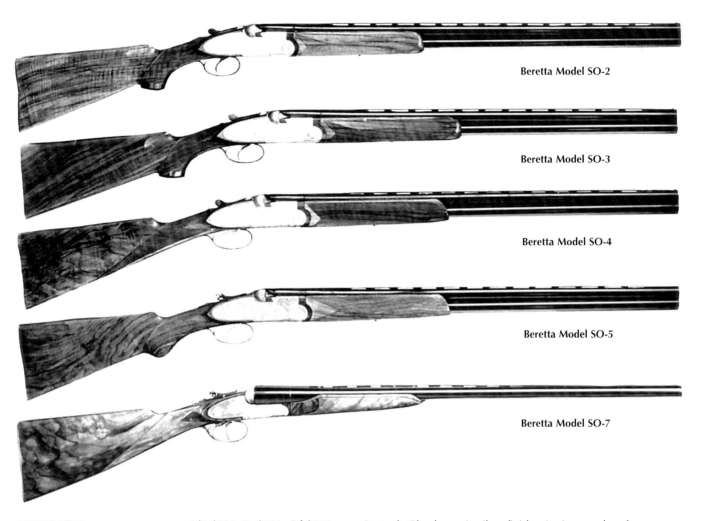

Beretta Model SO-2

Beretta Model SO-3

Beretta Model SO-4

Beretta Model SO-5

Beretta Model SO-7

MODEL TR-2 . . . . **NiB $364 Ex $231 Gd $156**
Same as Model TR-1 except has extended ventilated rib. Imported 1969-73.

VICTORIA PINTAIL (ES100) SEMIAUTOLOADER
Short Montefeltro-type recoil action. Gauge: 12. 3-inch chamber. Bbl.: 24-inch slug, 24-, 26-, or 28-inch vent rib w/Mobilchoke tubes. Weight: 7 to 7 lbs., 5 oz. Checkered synthetic or walnut buttstock and forend. Matte finish on both metal and stock. Imported 1993 and 2005.
Field model w/synthetic
  stock (intro. 1998) . . . . NiB $522 Ex $320 Gd $244
Field model w/walnut stock (disc. 1998) . . . . . . NiB $733 Ex $535 Gd $431
Rifled slug model w/synthetic
  stock (intro. 1998) . . . . NiB $544 Ex $378 Gd $296
Standard slug model
  w/walnut stock (disc. 1998). . . . NiB $544 Ex $378 Gd $296
Wetland Camo model (intro. 2000) . . . . . NiB $677 Ex $460 Gd $339

VINCENZO BERNARDELLI —
Gardone V.T. (Brescia), Italy
Previously imported by Armsport, Miami, FL (formerly by Magnum Research, Inc., Quality Arms, Stoeger Industries, Inc, and Action Arms, LTD)

115 SERIES O/U SHOTGUNS
Boxlock w/single trigger and ejectors. 12 ga. only. 25.5-, 26.75-, and 29.5-inch bbls. Concave top and vented middle rib. Anatomical grip stock. Blued or coin-silver finish w/various grades of engraving. Imported 1985 to 1997.

Standard Model .NiB $1844 Ex $1532 Gd $1176
Hunting Model 115E (disc. 1990) . . . . . . NiB $2247 Ex $1993 Gd $1612
Hunting Model 115L (disc. 1990) . . . . . NiB $2788 Ex $2391 Gd $2095
Hunting Model 115S (disc. 1990) . . . . NiB $3712 Ex $3122 Gd $2210
Target Model 115 (disc. 1992) . . . . .NiB $1977 Ex $1678 Gd $1440
Target Model 115E (disc. 1992) . . . . NiB $6108 Ex $5388 Gd $3789
Target Model 115L (disc. 1992) . . . . NiB $3855 Ex $3410 Gd $2377
Target Model 115S (disc. 1992) . . . . NiB $6077 Ex $4129 Gd $3755
Trap/Skeet Model 115S
  (imported 1996-97) . . . . . . NiB $3366 Ex $2581 Gd $1786
Sporting Clays Model 115S
  (imported 1995-97) . . . . NiB $3944 Ex $3216 Gd $2533

BRESCIA
HAMMER DOUBLE . . . . NiB $1564 Ex $1096 Gd $839
Back-action sidelock. Plain extractors. Double triggers. Gauges: 12, 20. Bbls.: 27.5 or 29.5-inch. M/F choke in 12 ga., 25.5-inch IC/M choke in 20 ga. Weight: 5.75 to 7 lbs. depending on ga. and bbl. length. English-style stock and forearm, checkered. No longer imported.

ELIO . . . . **NiB $1232 Ex $1006 Gd $781**
Lightweight game gun, 12 ga. only, w/same general specifications as Standard Gamecock (S. Uberto 1) except weight: About 6 to 6.25 lbs. Has automatic ejectors, fine English-pattern scroll engraving. No longer imported.

Bernardelli Gamecock

Bernardelli Standard Gamecock

Bernardelli Gardone

Bernardelli Italia

Bernardelli Roma 6

GAMECOCK, PREMIER (ROMA 3)

Same general specifications as Standard Gamecock (S. Uberto 1) except has sideplates, auto ejectors, single trigger. No longer imported.

Roma 3 (disc. 1989,
   Reintroduced 1993-97) .... NiB $1790 Ex $1435 Gd $1108
Roma 3E (disc. 1950) .... NiB $1956 Ex $1600 Gd $1119
Roma 3M
   w/single trigger (disc. 1997) .... NiB $1956 Ex $1600 Gd $1119

GAMECOCK, STANDARD (S. UBERTO 1) HAMMERLESS

DOUBLE-BARREL SHOTGUN...... NiB $900 Ex $766 Gd $563
Boxlock. Plain extractors. Double triggers. Gauges: 12, 16, 20. 2.75-inch chambers in 12 and 16, 3-inch in 20 ga. Bbls.: 25.5-inch IC/M choke; 27.5-inch M/F choke. Weight: 5.75 to 6.5 lbs. depending on ga. and bbl. length. English-style straight-grip stock and forearm, checkered. No longer imported.

GARDONE HAMMER DOUBLE....... NiB $2766 Ex $2261 Gd $1600
Same general specifications as Brescia except for higher grade engraving and wood but not as high as the Italia Half-cock safety. Disc. 1956.

HEMINGWAY HAMMERLESS DOUBLE

Boxlock. Single or double triggers w/hinged front. Selective automatic ejectors. Gauges: 12 and 20 w/2.75- or 3-inch chambers, 16 and 28 w/2.75-inch. Bbls.: 23.5- to 28-inch w/fixed chokes. Weight: 6.25 lbs. Checkered English-style European walnut stock. Silvered and engraved receiver.

Standard model .... NiB $2288 Ex $1866 Gd $1383
Deluxe model
w/sideplates (disc. 1993) ...... NiB $2698 Ex $2210 Gd $1679
Single trigger, add................................ $125

ITALIA................... NiB $1866 Ex $1044 Gd $623
Same general specifications as Brescia except higher grade engraving and wood. Disc. 1986.

ROMA 4 AND ROMA 6

Same as Premier Gamecock (Roma 3) except higher grade engraving and wood, double triggers. Disc. 1997.

Roma 4 (disc. 1989) .... NiB $1847 Ex $1412 Gd $1095
Roma 4E (disc. 1997) .... NiB $1796 Ex $1370 Gd $1060
Roma 6 (disc. 1989) .... NiB $1488 Ex $1233 Gd $1000
Roma 6E (disc. 1997) .... NiB $2533 Ex $2000 Gd $1277

ROMA 7, 8, AND 9

Side-by-side. Anson & Deeley boxlock; hammerless. Ejectors, double triggers. 12 ga. Bbls. 27.5- or 29.5-inch. M/F chokes. Fancy hand-checkered European walnut straight or pistol-grip stock, forearm. Elaborately engraved silver-finished sideplates. Imported 1994 to 1997.

Roma 7 .... NiB $3366 Ex $2160 Gd $1500
Roma 8 .... NiB $3866 Ex $2571 Gd $1880
Roma 9 .... NiB $4665 Ex $3748 Gd $2977

S. UBERTO 2.............. NiB $1460 Ex $1277 Gd $898
Same as Standard Gamecock (S. Uberto 1) except higher grade engraving and wood. Currently imported.

S. UBERTO F.S.

Same as Standard Gamecock except w/higher grade engraving, wood and has auto-ejectors. Disc. 1989, reintro. 1993 to 1997.

Model FS................ NiB $1746 Ex $1544 Gd $1100
Model V.B. Incisio.......... NiB $2169 Ex $1754 Gd $1239
Single trigger, add................................. $100

HOLLAND V.B. SERIES SHOTGUNS
Holland & Holland-type sidelock action. Auto-ejectors. Double triggers. 12 ga. only. Bbl. length or choke to custom specification. Silver-finish receiver (Liscio) or engraved coin-finished receiver (Incisio). Extra-select wood and game scene engraving (Lusso). Checkered stock, straight or pistol-grip. Imported 1992 to 1997.
Model V.B. Liscio. . . . . NiB $11,650 Ex $10,500 Gd $8675
Model V.B. Incisio. . . . . NiB $12,200 Ex $9779 Gd $6755
Model V.B. Lusso. . . . . NiB $9465 Ex $8119 Gd $5231
Model V.B. Extra . . . . NiB $14,766 Ex $10,877 Gd $8669
Model V.B. Gold . . . . NiB $49,600 Ex $44,688 Gd $37,789
Engraving Pattern
   No. 4, add $1250
Engraving Pattern
   No. 12, add $5000
Engraving Pattern No. 20, add $9500
Single trigger, add. $700

BOSS & COMPANY — London, England

HAMMERLESS DOUBLE-BARREL
SHOTGUN . . . . NiB $64,887 Ex $57,955 Gd $35,898
Sidelock. Automatic ejectors. Double triggers, nonselective or selective single trigger. Made in all gauges, bbl. lengths, and chokes. Checkered stock and forend, straight or pistol-grip.

HAMMERLESS O/U
SHOTGUN . . . . NiB $117,650 Ex $94,800 Gd $45,000
Sidelock. Automatic ejectors. Selective single trigger. Made in all gauges, bbl. lengths, and chokes. Checkered stock and forend, straight or pistol-grip. Disc.

BREDA MECCANICA BRESCIANA — Brescia, Italy
Formerly ERNESTO BREDA, Milan, Italy, previously imported by Tristar (Kansas City, MO), Gryphon International (Kansas City, MO) and Diana Imports Co. (San Francisco, CA)

VEGA SPECIAL O/U SHOTGUN. . . ....NiB $676 Ex $543 Gd $410
12 or 20 ga. Boxlock action. Bbl.: 26 or 28 inches; single trigger; ejectors. Blue only.

VEGA SPECIAL TRAP . . . . .NiB $966 Ex $733 Gd $590
12 or 20 ga. Boxlock action. Competition triggers and lock. Bbl.: 30 or 32 inches; single trigger; ejectors. Blue only.

VEGA LUSSO . . . . .NiB $1765 Ex $1430 Gd $1100
12 ga. only. 3-inch chambers. Scalloped boxlock action, single selective trigger, ejectors. Bbl.: 26 or 28 inches, ventilated rib. Coin-finished receiver with light engraving. Deluxe checkered Circassian walnut stock and forearm. Imported 2001 to 2002.

SIRIO STANDARD . . . . .NiB $2176 Ex $1788 Gd $1354
12 or 20 ga. Engraved boxlock action. Bbl.: 26 or 28 inches; single trigger; ejectors. Blue only. Also available in skeet model.

ANDROMEDA SPECIAL . . . . NiB $755 Ex $665 Gd $525
Side-by-side.12 ga., single trigger; ejectors, select checkered walnut stock; satin finish on receiver with elaborate engraving.

GOLD SERIES SEMIAUTOMATIC SHOTGUN
12 or lightweight 20 ga. 2.75-inch chamber. Bbl.: 25 or 27 inches; ventilated rib standard. Recoil operated.

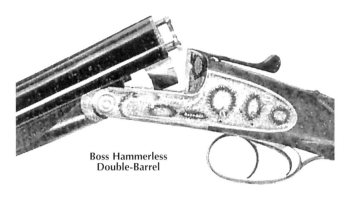

Boss Hammerless
Double-Barrel

Antares Standard Model . . . . . . .NiB $543 Ex $421 Gd $336
Argus Model . . . . NiB $521 Ex $390 Gd $266
Aries Model . . . . NiB $521 Ex $390 Gd $266

STANDARD GRADE GOLD SERIES . . . NiB $377 Ex $290 Gd $245
12 ga. 2.75-inch chamber. Recoil operated. Bbl.: 25 or 27 inches. Light engraving. Disc.

GRADE 1 . . . . .NiB $644 Ex $500 Gd $336
Similar to Standard model but with fancier wood and engraving.
GRADE 2 . . . . .NiB $756 Ex $644 Gd $500
Similar to Grade 1 but with more engraving, etc.
GRADE 3 . . . . .NiB $966 Ex $771 Gd $654
Same as Grade 1 but with custom quality embellishments.

MAGNUM MODEL. . . . . .NiB $546 Ex $400 Gd $297
Similar to Standard Grade but with 3-inch chambers.

ALTAIR SPECIAL . . . . NiB $533 Ex $400 Gd $336
12 ga. 2.75-inch chamber. Gas-operated. Bbl.: 25 or 27 inches, ventilated rib standard. Alloy construction, blue or chrome receiver.

ASTRO . . . . NiB $1126 Ex $853 Gd $700
Gauges: 12 (disc. 2002) or 20. 3-inch chamber. Inertia action. Bbl.: 22 (slug), 24, 26, 28, or 30 inches; ventilated rib. Black synthetic, Advantage camo, or Circassian walnut stock and forearm. Imported 2001.
Advantage camo model, add. $125

ASTROLUX . . . . NiB $1588 Ex $1344 Gd $1033
Similar to Astro model except has two-tone receiver with engraving and deluxe checkered Circassian walnut stock and forearm. Imported 2001 to 2002.

ERMES SERIES . . . . NiB $1044 Ex $788 Gd $648
12 ga. 3-inch chamber. Semiautomatic. Inertia recoil operating system, aluminum alloy receiver, nickel-plated or blue finish on lower receiver. Bbl.: 24, 26, or 28 inches. Deluxe checkered Circassian walnut stock and forearm. Imported 2001.
Ermes Silver . . . . NiB $1287 Ex $1095 Gd $869
Ermes Gold. . . . . NiB $1452 Ex $1138 Gd $1009

MIRA. . . . . .NiB $880 Ex $622 Gd $500
12 ga. 3-inch chamber. Semiautomatic, gas-operated. Aluminum alloy receiver; black or Advantage camo finish. Bbl.: 22 (slug), 24, 26, 28, or 30 inches, ventilated rib. Circassian walnut or black synthetic stock and forearm. Imported 2001.
Sporting Clays model, add $50
Black synthetic stock & forearm, deduct .10%

ARIES 2 . . . . **NiB $879 Ex $793 Gd $649**
12 ga. 2.75-inch chamber. Semiautomatic, gas-operated. Engraved two-tone receiver. Bbl.: 20 or 30 inches, ventilated rib. Deluxe checkered Circassian walnut or black synthetic stock and forearm. Imported 2001 only.

BRETTON SHOTGUNS — St. Etienne (Cedex1), France

BABY STANDARD SPRINT O/U . . . . **NiB $1088 Ex $855 Gd $687**
Inline sliding breech action. 12 or 20 ga. 2.75-inch chambers. 27.5-inch separated bbls. w/vent rib and choke tubes. Weight: 4.8 to 5 lbs. Engraved alloy receiver. Checkered walnut buttstock and forearm w/satin oil finish. Limited import.

FAIR PLAY O/U. . . . . **NiB $1088 Ex $863 Gd $600**
Lightweight action similar to the Sprint Model except w/hinged action that pivots open and is chambered 12 or 20 ga. only. Limited import.

SPRINT DELUXE O/U. . . . .**NiB $1077 Ex $863 Gd $700**
Similar to the Standard Model except w/engraved coin-finished receiver and chambered 12, 16, and 20 ga. Limited import.

BRNO SHOTGUNS — Brno and Uherski Brod, Czech Republic (formerly Czechoslovakia)

MODEL 500 O/U SHOTGUN . . . **NiB $900 Ex $777 Gd $568**
Hammerless boxlock w/double triggers and ejectors.12 ga. 2.75-inch chambers. 27.5-inch bbls. choked M/F. 44 inches overall. Weight: 7 lbs. Etched receiver. Checkered walnut stock w/classic style cheekpiece. Imported from 1987 to 1991.

500 SERIES O/U COMBINATION GUNS
Similar to the 500 Series over/under shotgun above except w/lower bbl. chambered in rifle calibers and set trigger option. Imported from 1987 to 1995.
Model 502 12 ga./.222 or .243 (disc. 1991) . . . . .NiB $2088 Ex $1256 Gd $1077
Model 502 12 ga./.308 or .30-06 (disc. 1991). . . . . NiB $1164 Ex $1038 Gd $772
Model 571 12 ga./6x65R (disc. 1993) . . . . NiB $853 Ex $709 Gd $587
Model 572 12 ga./7x65R (imported since 1992) . . . . . . .NiB $881 Ex $733 Gd $600
Model 584 12 ga./7x57R (imported since 1992) . . . . . . .NiB $1264 Ex $1033 Gd $800
Sport Series 4-bbl. set (disc. 1991) . . . . . . NiB $3153 Ex $2571 Gd $1863

CZ 581 SOLO O/U SHOTGUN. . . . . .NiB $966 Ex $738 Gd $561
Hammerless boxlock w/double triggers, ejectors, and automatic safety. 12 ga. 2.75- or 3-inch chambers. 28-inch bbls. choked M/F. Weight: 7.5 lbs. Checkered walnut stock. Disc. 1996.

SUPER SERIES O/U SHOTGUN
Hammerless sidelock w/selective single or double triggers and ejectors. 12 ga. 2.75- or 3-inch chambers. 27.5-inch bbls. choked M/F. 44.5 inches overall. Weight: 7.25 lbs. Etched or engraved side plates. Checkered European walnut stock w/classic-style cheekpiece. Imported from 1987 to 1991.
Super Series Shotgun (disc. 1992). . . . . NiB $866 Ex $731 Gd $577
Super Series Combo (disc. 1992) . . . . NiB $2021 Ex $1190 Gd $977
Super Ser. 3-bbl. set (disc. 1990). . . . . . . NiB $1993 Ex $1578 Gd $1266
Super Series engraving, add. $1350

ZH 300 SERIES O/U SHOTGUNS
Hammerless boxlock w/double triggers. Gauge: 12 or 16. 2.75- or 3-inch chambers. Bbls.: 26, 27.5, or 30 inches; choked M/F. Weight:

7 lbs. Skip-line checkered walnut stock w/classic-style cheekpiece. Imported from 1986-93.
Model 300 (disc. 1993) . . . . NiB $786 Ex $547 Gd $408
Model 301 Field (disc. 1991) . . . . NiB $667 Ex $582 Gd $400
Model 302 Skeet (disc. 1992) . . . . NiB $745 Ex $557 Gd $442
Model 303 Trap (disc. 1992) . . . . NiB $749 Ex $566 Gd $449

ZH 300 SERIES O/U COMBINATION GUNS
Similar to the 300 Series over/under shotgun except lower bbl. chambered in rifle calibers.
Model 300 Combo
8-bbl. Set (disc. 1991) . . . . NiB $3375 Ex $2977 Gd $2500
Model 304 12 ga./7x57R (disc. 1995) . . . . . . NiB $846 Ex $698 Gd $535
Model 305 12 ga./5.6x52R (disc. 1993). . . . . . .NiB $921 Ex $769 Gd $544
Model 306 12 ga./5.6x50R (disc. 1993). . . . . . .NiB $965 Ex $798 Gd $579
Model 307 12 ga./.22 Hornet
  (Imported since 1995) . . . . NiB $843 Ex $755 Gd $507
Model 324 16 ga./7x57R (disc. 1987) . . . . . . NiB $880 Ex $742 Gd $509

ZP 149 HAMMERLESS DOUBLE
Sidelock action w/double triggers, automatic ejectors, and automatic safety. 12 ga. 2.75- or 3-inch chambers. 28.5-inch bbls. choked M/F. Weight: 7.25 lbs. Checkered walnut buttstock with cheekpiece.
Standard model . . . . NiB $669 Ex $458 Gd $388
Engraved model . . . . NiB $700 Ex $477 Gd $421

BROLIN ARMS, INC. — Pomona, California

FIELD SERIES PUMP SHOTGUN
Slide action. Gauge: 12. 3-inch chamber. 24-, 26-, 28-, or 30-inch bbl. 44 or 50 inches overall. Weight: 7.3 to 7.6 lbs. Crossbolt safety. Vent rib bbl. w/screw-in choke tube and bead sights. Non-reflective metal finish. Synthetic or oil-finished wood stock w/ swivel studs. Made from 1997 to 1998.
Synthetic stock model . . . . NiB $254 Ex $188 Gd $95
Wood stock model . . . . NiB $200 Ex $129 Gd $75

COMBO MODEL PUMP SHOTGUN
Similar to the Field Model except w/extra 18.5- or 22-inch bbl. w/ bead or rifle sight. Made from 1997 to 1998.
Synthetic stock model . . . . NiB $279 Ex $200 Gd $115
Wood stock model . . . . NiB $331 Ex $240 Gd $193

LAWMAN MODEL PUMP SHOTGUN
Similar to the Field Model except has 18.5-inch bbl. w/cylinder bore fixed choke. Weight: 7 lbs. Dual operating bars. Bead, rifle, or ghost-ring sights. Black synthetic or wood stock. Matte chrome or satin nickel finish. Made from 1997 to 1999.
Synthetic stock model . . . . .NiB $217 Ex $151 Gd $90
Wood stock model . . . . .NiB $217 Ex $151 Gd $90
Rifle sights, add. $35
Ghost ring sights, add. $50
Satin nickel finish (disc. 1997), add $50

SLUG MODEL PUMP SHOTGUN
Similar to the Field Model except has 18.5- or 22-inch bbl. w/ IC fixed choke or 4-inch extended rifled choke. Rifle, ghost-ring sights, or optional cantilevered scope mount. Black synthetic or wood stock. Matte blued finish. Made from 1998 to 1999.
Synthetic stock model . . . . .NiB $288 Ex $202 Gd $166
Wood stock model . . . . .NiB $300 Ex $221 Gd $180
Rifled bbl., add. $25
Cantilevered scope mount, add $50

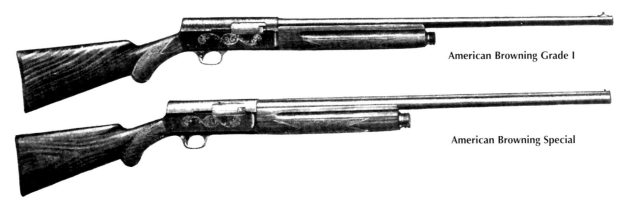

American Browning Grade I

American Browning Special

TURKEY SPECIAL PUMP SHOTGUN
Similar to the Field Model except has 22-inch vent-rib bbl. w/extended extra-full choke. Rifle, ghost-ring sights, or optional cantilevered scope mount. Black synthetic or wood stock. Matte blued finish. Made from 1998 to 1999.
Synthetic stock model . . . . NiB $266 Ex $190 Gd $125
Wood stock model . . . . NiB $305 Ex $237 Gd $154
Cantilevered scope mount, add $50

BROWNING SHOTGUNS —
Morgan (formerly Ogden), Utah

AMERICAN BROWNING SHOTGUNS

Designated American Browning because they were produced in Ilion, New York, the following Remington-made Brownings are almost identical to the Remington Model 11A, Sportsman, and the Browning Auto-5. They are the only Browning shotguns manufactured in the United States during the twentieth century and were made for Browning Arms when production was suspended in Belgium because of WWII.

NOTE: *Fabrique Nationale Herstal (formerly Fabrique Nationale d'Armes de Guerre) of Herstal, Belgium, is the longtime manufacturer of Browning shotguns dating back to 1900. Miroku Firearms Mfg. Co. of Tokyo, Japan, bought into the Browning company and has, since the early 1970s, undertaken some of the production. The following shotguns were manufactured for Browning by these two firms.*

GRADE I AUTOLOADER (AUTO-5)
Recoil-operated autoloader. Similar to the Remington Model 11A except w/different style engraving and identified w/the Browning logo. Gauges: 12, 16, or 20. Plain 26- to 32-inch bbl. w/any standard boring. 2- or 4-shell tubular magazine w/magazine cutoff. Weight: About 6.88 lbs. (20 ga.) to 8 lbs. (12 ga.). Checkered pistol-grip stock and forearm. Made from 1940 to 1949.
American Browning Grade I
Auto-5, 12 or 16 ga. . . . . NiB $856 Ex $744 Gd $400
20 ga., add 20%

SPECIAL 441
Same general specifications as Grade I except supplied w/raised matted rib or vent rib. Disc. 1949.
w/raised matted rib . . . . NiB $894 Ex $756 Gd $435
w/vent rib . . . . NiB $925 Ex $790 Gd $466
20 ga., add 20%

SPECIAL SKEET MODEL . . . . NiB $815 Ex $645 Gd $477
Same general specifications as Grade I except has 26-inch bbl. w/ vent rib and Cutts Compensator. Disc. 1949.

UTILITY FIELD GUN . . . . NiB $608 Ex $458 Gd $339
Same general specifications as Grade I except has 28-inch plain bbl. w/Poly Choke. Disc. 1949.

MODEL 12 PUMP SHOTGUN
Special limited edition Winchester Model 12. Gauge: 20 or 28. 5-round tubular magazine. 26-inch bbl., M choke. 45 inches overall. Weight: About 7 lbs. Grade I has blued receiver, checkered walnut stock w/matte finish. Grade V has engraved receiver, checkered deluxe walnut stock w/high-gloss finish. Made from 1988 to 1992. See illustration next page.
Grade I, 20 ga. 8600 prod. . . . . . . NiB $866 Ex $569 Gd $449
Grade I, 28 ga. . . . . NiB $1166 Ex $912 Gd $744
Grade V, 20 ga. 4000 prod. . . . . NiB $1455 Ex $1187 Gd $879
Grade V, 28 ga. . . . . NiB $1768 Ex $1344 Gd $961

MODEL 42 LIMITED EDITION SHOTGUN
Special limited edition Winchester Model 42 pump shotgun. Same general specifications as Model 12 except w/smaller frame in .410 ga. and 3-inch chamber. Made from 1991 to 1993.
Grade I
  (6000 produced) . . . . NiB $967 Ex $744 Gd $466
Grade V
  (6000 produced) . . . . NiB $1590 Ex $1156 Gd $863

2000 BUCK SPECIAL . . . . NiB $588 Ex $467 Gd $355
Same as Field Model except has 24-inch plain bbl. Bored for rifled slug and buckshot, fitted w/rifle sights (open rear, ramp front). 12 ga. 2.75- or 3-inch chamber; 20 ga., 2.75-inch chamber. Weight: 12 ga., 7 lbs., 8 oz.; 20 ga., 6 lbs., 10 oz. Made from 1974 to 1981 by FN.

2000 GAS AUTOMATIC SHOTGUN, FIELD MODEL
Gas-operated. Gauge: 12 or 20. 2.75-inch chamber. 4-round magazine. Bbl.: 26-, 28-, 30-inch, any standard choke plain matted bbl. (12 ga. only) or vent rib. Weight: 6 lbs., 11 oz. to 7 lbs., 12 oz. depending on ga. and bbl. length. Checkered pistol-grip stock and forearm. Made from 1974 to 1981 by FN; assembled in Portugal.
w/plain matted bbl. . . . . NiB $559 Ex $468 Gd $346

2000 MAGNUM MODEL . . . . NiB $579 Ex $377 Gd $300
Same as Field Model except chambered for 3-inch shells, 3-round magazine. Bbl.: 26- (20 ga. only), 28-, 30-, or 32-inch (latter two 12 ga. only); any standard choke; vent rib. Weight: 6 lbs., 11 oz. to 7 lbs., 13 oz. depending on ga. and bbl. Made from 1974 to 1983 by FN.

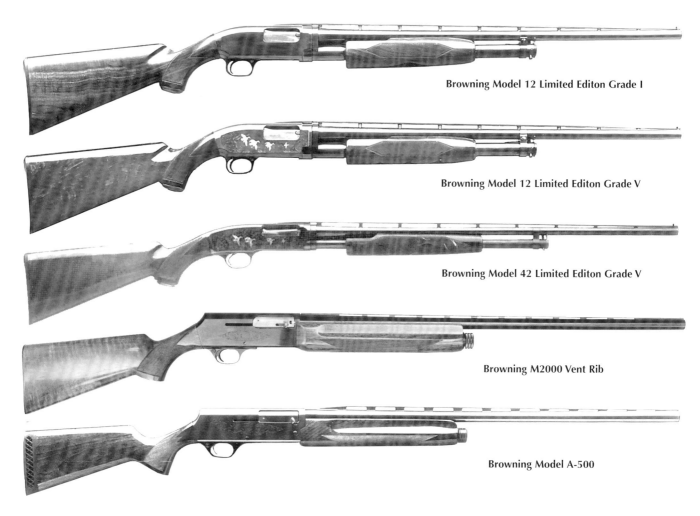

Browning Model 12 Limited Editon Grade I

Browning Model 12 Limited Editon Grade V

Browning Model 42 Limited Editon Grade V

Browning M2000 Vent Rib

Browning Model A-500

2000 SKEET MODEL . . . . **NiB $527 Ex $441 Gd $338**
Same as Field Model except has skeet-style stock w/recoil pad, 26-inch vent-rib bbl., SK choke. 12 or 20 ga. 2.75-inch chamber. Weight: 8 lbs., 1 oz. (12 ga.); 6 lbs., 12 oz. (20 ga.) Made 1974 to 1981 by FN.

2000 TRAP MODEL . . . . **NiB $527 Ex $441 Gd $338**
Same as Field Model except has Monte Carlo stock w/recoil pad, 30- or 32-inch bbl. w/high-post vent rib and receiver extension, M/I/F chokes. 12 ga. 2.75-inch chamber. Weight: About 8 lbs., 5 oz. Made 1974 to 1981 by FN.

A-500G GAS-OPERATED SEMIAUTOMATIC
Same general specifications as Browning Model A-500R except gas-operated. Made 1990 to 1993.
Buck Special . . . . **NiB $590 Ex $466 Gd $339**
Hunting model . . . . **NiB $688 Ex $491 Gd $388**

A-500G SPORTING CLAYS . . . . . . **NiB $663 Ex $490 Gd $388**
Same general specifications as Model A-500G except has matte blued receiver w/Sporting Clays logo. 28- or 30-inch bbl. w/ Invector choke tubes. Made 1992 to 1993.

A-500R SEMIAUTOMATIC
Recoil-operated. Gauge: 12. 26- to 30-inch vent-rib bbls. 24-inch Buck Special. Invector choke tube system. 2.75- or 3-inch Magnum cartridges. Weight: 7 lbs., 3 oz. to 8 lbs., 2 oz. Crossbolt

safety. Gold-plated trigger. Scroll-engraved receiver. Gloss-finished walnut stock and forend. Made by FN from 1987 to 1993.
Hunting model . . . . **NiB $677 Ex $476 Gd $388**
Buck Special . . . . **NiB $692 Ex $490 Gd $433**

A-BOLT SERIES SHOTGUN
Bolt-action repeating single-barrel shotgun. 12 ga. only. 3-inch chambers; 2-round magazine. 22- or 23-inch rifled bbl., w/ or w/o a rifled invector tube. Receiver drilled and tapped for scope mounts. Bbl. w/ or w/o open sights. Checkered walnut or graphite/fiberglass composite stock. Matte black metal finish. Imported 1995 to 1998.
Stalker model w/
  composite stock . . . . **NiB $1365 Ex $1077 Gd $867**
Hunter model w/walnut stock . . . .**NiB $1365 Ex $1077 Gd $867**
Rifled bbl., add **$200**
Open sights, add **$75**

AUTOLOADING SHOTGUNS, GRADES II, III, & IV
These higher grade models differ from the Standard or Grade I in general quality, grade of wood, checkering, engraving, etc.; otherwise specifications are the same. Grade IV guns, sometimes called Midas Grade, are inlaid w/yellow and green gold. Disc. in 1940.
Grade II, plain bbl. . . . .**NiB $1698 Ex $1390 Gd $976**
Grade III, plain bbl. . . . .**NiB $1580 Ex $1176 Gd $833**
Grade IV, plain bbl. . . . .**NiB $4469 Ex $3865 Gd $3033**
Raised, matted rib bbl., add **15%**
Vent. rib bbl., add **30%**

Browning Automatic-5
Gold Classic

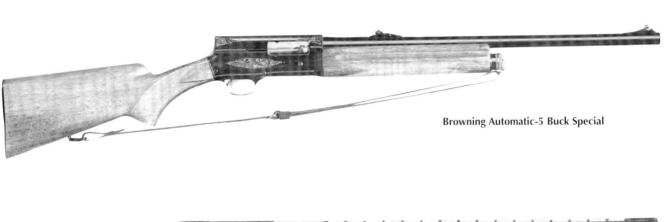

Browning Automatic-5 Buck Special

Browning Automatic-5 Classic

AUTOMATIC-5, BUCK SPECIAL MODELS

Same as Light 12, Magnum 12, Light 20, Magnum 20 in respective gauges except 24-inch plain bbl. bored for rifled slug and buckshot, fitted w/rifle sights (open rear, ramp front). Weight: 6.13 to 8.25 lbs. depending on ga. Made 1964 to 1976 by FN, since then by Miroku.

FN manu., w/plain bbl.	NiB $1276	Ex $889	Gd $567
Miroku manu.	NiB $966	Ex $843	Gd $544
3-inch mag. rec., add			.$10%

AUTOMATIC-5 CLASSIC. . . . . . NiB $1186 Ex $983 Gd $889
Gauge: 12. 5-round capacity. 28-inch vent rib bbl. M choke. 2.75-inch chamber. Engraved silver-gray receiver. Gold-plated trigger. Crossbolt safety. High-grade, hand-checkered select American walnut stock w/rounded pistol grip. 5,000 issued; made in Japan in 1984, engraved in Belgium.

AUTOMATIC-5 GOLD CLASSIC . . . . . NiB $9887 Ex $6690 Gd $4690
Same general specifications as Automatic-5 Classic except engraved receiver inlaid w/gold. Pearl border on stock and forend plus fine-line hand-checkering. Each gun numbered "One of Five Hundred," etc. 500 issued in 1984; made in Belgium.

AUTOMATIC-5, LIGHT 12

12 ga. only. Same general specifications as Standard Model except lightweight (about 7.25 lbs.), has gold-plated trigger. Guns w/rib have striped matting on top of bbl. Fixed chokes or Invector tubes. Made 1948 to 1976 by FN, since then by Miroku.

FN manu., plain bbl.	NiB $889	Ex $655	Gd $498
FN manu., w/raised matte rib	NiB $954	Ex $777	Gd $675
FN manu., vent. rib	NiB $1098	Ex $966	Gd $676
Miroku manu., vent. rib, fixed choke	NiB $889	Ex $667	Gd $487
Miroku manu., vent. rib, Invectors	NiB $1099	Ex $776	Gd $566

AUTOMATIC-5, LIGHT 20

Same general specifications as Standard Model except lightweight and 20 ga. Bbl.: 26- or 28-inch; plain or vent rib. Weight: About 6.25 to 6.5 lbs. depending on bbl. Made 1958 to 1976 by FN, since then by Miroku.

FN manu., plain bbl.	NiB $844	Ex $633	Gd $429
FN manu., vent. rib bbl.	NiB $1267	Ex $988	Gd $687
Miroku manu., vent. rib, fixed choke	NiB $965	Ex $743	Gd $846
Miroku manu., vent. rib, invectors	NiB $1065	Ex $844	Gd $600

Browning Auto-5 Sweet Sixteen (New Model)

Browning Model B-80 Upland Special

Browning BPS Hunter

Browning BPS Youth & Ladies Model

AUTOMATIC-5, MAGNUM 12 GAUGE

Same general specifications as Standard Model. Chambered for 3-inch Magnum 12-ga. shells. Bbl.: 28-inch M/F, 30- or 32-inch F/F, plain or vent rib. Weight: 8.5 to 9 lbs. depending on bbl. Buttstock has recoil pad. Made 1958 to 1976 by FN, since then by Miroku. Fixed chokes or Invector tubes.

FN manu., plain bbl. . . . . NiB $954 Ex $779 Gd $549
FN manu., vent. rib bbl. . . . . . . NiB $1288 Ex $977 Gd $765
Miroku manu., vent. rib, fixed chokes . . . . . . NiB $888 Ex $645 Gd $455
Miroku manu., vent. rib, Invectors . . . . NiB $1066 Ex $707 Gd $500

AUTOMATIC-5, MAGNUM 20 GAUGE

Same general specifications as Standard Model except chambered for 3-inch Magnum 20-ga. shell. Bbl.: 26- or 28-inch, plain or vent rib. Weight: 7 lbs., 5 oz. to 7 lbs., 7 oz. depending on bbl. Made 1967 to 1976 by FN, since then by Miroku.

FN manu., plain bbl. . . . . NiB $944 Ex $768 Gd $567
FN manu., vent. rib bbl. . . . . . . NiB $1333 Ex $989 Gd $779
Miroku manu., vent. rib, Invectors . . NiB $989 Ex $766 Gd $590

AUTOMATIC-5, SKEET MODEL

12 ga. only. Same general specifications as Light 12. Bbl.: 26- or 28-inch, plain or vent rib, SK choke. Weight: 7 lbs., 5 oz. to 7 lbs., 10 oz. depending on bbl. Made by FN prior to 1976, since then by Miroku.

FN manu., plain bbl. . . . . NiB $1177 Ex $956 Gd $654
FN manu., vent. rib bbl. . . . . . NiB $1769 Ex $1166 Gd $956
Miroku manu., vent. rib bbl. . . . . . . NiB $987 Ex $766 Gd $554

AUTOMATIC-5 STALKER

Same general specifications as Automatic-5 Light and Magnum models except w/matte blue finish and black graphite fiberglass stock and forearm. Made from 1992 to 1997.

Light model . . . . NiB $966 Ex $831 Gd $664
Magnum model . . . . NiB $1031 Ex $977 Gd $689

AUTOMATIC-5, STANDARD (GRADE I)

Recoil-operated. Gauge: 12 or 16 (16-gauge guns made prior to WWII were chambered for 2-inch shells; standard 16 disc. 1964). 4-shell magazine in 5-round model, prewar guns were also available in 3-round model. Bbls.: 26- to 32-inch; plain, raised matted or vent rib; choice of standard chokes. Weight: About 8 lbs. in 12 ga., 7.5 lbs. in 16 ga. Checkered pistol-grip stock and forearm. (Note: Browning Special, disc. about 1940.) Made from 1900 to 1973 by FN.

Grade I, plain bbl. . . . . NiB $844 Ex $677 Gd $544
Grade I (or Browning Special),
  w/raised matted rib . . . . NiB $977 Ex $778 Gd $580
Grade I (or Browning Special),
  w/ vent. rib . . . . NiB $977 Ex $778 Gd $580

AUTOMATIC-5, SWEET 16

16 ga. Same general specifications as Standard Model except light-weight (about 6.75 lbs.), has gold plated trigger. Guns w/rib have striped matting on top of bbl. Made 1937 to 1976 by FN.

w/plain bbl. . . . . NiB $1189 Ex $793 Gd $555
w/raised matted or vent. rib . . . . NiB $1769 Ex $1388 Gd $1012

AUTO-5, SWEET

SIXTEEN NEW MODEL . . . . NiB $1399 Ex $1156 Gd $922
Reissue of popular 16-gauge Hunting Model w/5-round capacity. 2.75-inch chamber. Scroll-engraved blued receiver, high-gloss French walnut stock w/rounded pistol grip. 26- or 28-inch vent-rib bbl. F choke tube. Weight: 7 lbs., 5 oz. Reintro. 1987 to 1993.

**Browning BPS
Waterfowl – Mossy Oak Shadow Grass**

Browning BPS Stalker

AUTOMATIC-5,
TRAP MODEL . . . . **NiB $1277 Ex $965 Gd $777**
12 ga. only. Same general specifications as Standard Model except has trap-style stock, 30-inch vent-rib bbl. F choke. Weight: 8.5 lbs. Disc. 1971.

MODEL B-80 GAS-OPERATED
AUTOMATIC. . . . . **NiB $699 Ex $577 Gd $400**
Gauge: 12 or 20. 2.75-inch chamber. 4-round magazine. Bbl.: 26-, 28-, or 30-inch, any standard choke, vent-rib bbl. w/fixed chokes or Invector tubes. Weight: 6 lbs., 12 oz. to 8 lbs., 1 oz. depending on ga. and bbl. Checkered pistol-grip stock and forearm. Made 1981 to 1988.

MODEL B-80 PLUS. . . . . **NiB $765 Ex $605 Gd $466**
Same general specifications as Browning Model B-80 except chambered for 3-inch shotshells. Made in 1988.

MODEL B-80 SUPERLIGHT . . . . . **NiB $689 Ex $544 Gd $432**
Same as Standard Model except weighs 1 lb. less.

MODEL B-80 UPLAND SPECIAL . . . . . . **NiB $698 Ex $566 Gd $433**
Gauge: 12 or 20. 22-inch vent-rib bbl. Invector choke tube system. 2.75-inch chambers. 42 inches overall. Weight: 5 lbs., 7 oz. (20 ga.); 6 lbs., 10 oz. (12 ga.). German nickel-silver sight bead. Crossbolt safety. Checkered walnut straight-grip stock and forend. Disc. 1988.

BPS DEER HUNTER SPECIAL. . . . . . **NiB $735 Ex $510 Gd $375**
Same general specifications as Standard BPS model except has 20.5-inch bbl. w/adj. rifle-style sights. Solid scope mounting system. Checkered walnut stock w/sling swivel studs. Made from 1992 to date.

BPS GAME GUN TURKEY SPECIAL . . . . . **NiB $498 Ex $380 Gd $295**
Same general specifications as Standard BPS model except w/ matte blue metal finish and satin-finished stock. Chambered for 12 ga. 3-inch only. 20.5-inch bbl. w/extra full Invector choke system. Receiver drilled and tapped for scope. Made from 1992 to 2001.

BPS PIGEON GRADE . . . . **NiB $699 Ex $449 Gd $354**
Same general specifications as Standard BPS model except w/select grade walnut stock and gold-trimmed receiver. Available in 12 ga. only w/26- or 28-inch vent-rib bbl. Made 1992 to 1998.

BPS PUMP INVECTOR STALKER
Same general specifications as BPS Pump Shotgun except in 10 and 12 ga. w/Invector choke system; 22-, 26-, 28-, or 30-inch bbls.; matte blue metal finish w/matte black stock. Made from 1987 to date.
12 ga. model (3-inch) . . . . **NiB $577 Ex $412 Gd $290**
10 & 12 ga. model (3.5-inch) . . . . **NiB $776 Ex $600 Gd $466**

BPS PUMP SHOTGUN
Takedown. Gauges: 10, 12 (3.5-inch chamber); 12, 20, and .410 (3-inch); and 28 ga. chambered 2.75-inch. Bbls.: 22-, 24-, 26-, 28-, 30-, or 32-inch; fixed choke or Invector tubes. Weight: 7.5 lbs. (w/28-inch bbl.). Checkered select walnut pistol-grip stock and semi-beavertail forearm, recoil pad. Introduced in 1977 by Miroku.
Magnum Hunter . . . . **NiB $690 Ex $589 Gd $477**
Magnum Stalker. . . . . **NiB $690 Ex $589 Gd $477**
Magnum Camo . . . . **NiB $779 Ex $644 Gd $546**
Hunter . . . . **NiB $690 Ex $589 Gd $477**
Upland . . . . **NiB $595 Ex $490 Gd $395**
Stalker (26, 28-, or 30-inch bbl.) . . . . **NiB $566 Ex $477 Gd $375**
Stalker 24-inch bbl. . . . . **NiB $566 Ex $477 Gd $375**
Game Gun, Turkey Special . . . . **NiB $478 Ex $390 Gd $277**
Game Gun, fully rifled bbl. . . . . **NiB $700 Ex $622 Gd $490**
Hunter 20 ga.. . . . . **NiB $600 Ex $497 Gd $400**
Upland 20 ga. . . . . **NiB $600 Ex $497 Gd $400**
Micro . . . . **NiB $488 Ex $397 Gd $300**
Hunter 28 ga.. . . . . **NiB $590 Ex $480 Gd $400**
Bore Hunter .410. . . . . **NiB $644 Ex $564 Gd $433**
Buck Spec. (10 or 12 ga., 3.5-inch) . . . . **NiB $700 Ex $566 Gd $470**
Buck Spec. (12 or 20 ga.) . . . . **NiB $455 Ex $330 Gd $229**
Waterfowl
(10 or 12 ga., 3.5-inch) . . . . **NiB $700 Ex $566 Gd $470**
Fixed choke, deduct. **$75**

BPS YOUTH AND LADIES MODEL
Lightweight (6 lbs., 11 oz.) version of BPS Pump Shotgun in 20 ga. w/22-inch bbl. and floating vent rib, F choke Invector tube. Made 1986 to 2002.
Standard Invector model (disc. 1994). . . . . . **NiB $390 Ex $288 Gd $195**
Invector Plus model. . . . . **NiB $444 Ex $300 Gd $244**

BSA 10 SEMIAUTOMATIC SHOTGUN
Gas-operated short-stroke action. 10 ga.; 3.5-inch chamber. 5-round magazine. Bbls.: 26, 28, or 30 inches w/Invector tubes and vent rib. Weight: 10.5 lbs. Checkered select walnut buttstock and forend. Blued finish. Made 1993 to date. Note: Although intro. as the BSA 10, this model is now marketed as the Gold Series. See separate listing for pricing.

B-SS SIDE-BY-SIDE
Boxlock. Automatic ejectors. Nonselective single trigger (early production) or single selective trigger (late production). Gauges: 12 or 20. 3-inch chambers. Bbls.: 26, 28, or 30 inches; IC/M, M/F, or F/F chokes; matte solid rib. Weight: 7 to 7.5 lbs. Checkered straight-grip stock and beavertail forearm. Made from 1972 to 1988 by Miroku.
Standard model (early/NSST) . . . . **NiB $1276 Ex $956 Gd $835**
Standard model (late/SST). . . . . **NiB $1276 Ex $956 Gd $835**
Grade II (antique silver receiver) . . . . . . **NiB $3365 Ex $2990 Gd $2455**
20 ga. models, add.. . . . . **$650**

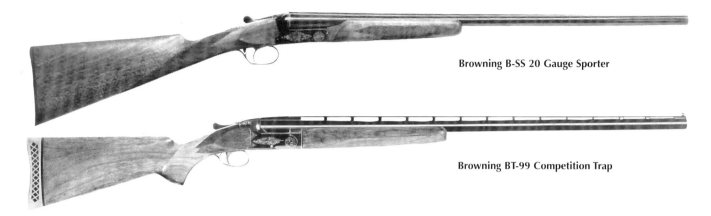

Browning B-SS 20 Gauge Sporter

Browning BT-99 Competition Trap

B-SS SIDE-BY-SIDE SIDELOCK

Same general specifications as B-SS boxlock models except sidelock version available in 26- or 28-inch bbl. lengths. 26-inch choked IC/M; 28-inch, M/F. Double triggers. Satin-grayed receiver engraved w/rosettes and scrolls. German nickel-silver sight bead. Weight: 6.25 lbs. to 6 lbs., 11 oz. 12 ga. made in 1983; 20 ga. made in 1984. Disc. 1988.

12 ga. model	NiB $3865	Ex $3077	Gd $2027
20 ga. model	NiB $5277	Ex $3388	Gd $2879

B-SS S/S 20 GAUGE SPORTER...... NiB $3241 Ex $2766 Gd $1547
Same as standard B-SS 20 ga. except has selective single trigger, straight-grip stock. Introduced 1977. Disc. 1987.

BT-99 GRADE I SINGLE BBL. TRAP .... NiB $1087 Ex $782 Gd $554
Boxlock. Automatic ejector. 12 ga. only. 32- or 34-inch vent rib bbl., M/IM/F choke. Weight: About 8 lbs. Checkered pistol-grip stock and beavertail forearm, recoil pad. Made 1971 to 1976 by Miroku.

BT-99 MAX
Boxlock. 12 ga. only w/ejector, selector, and no safety. 32- or 34-inch ported bbl. w/high post vent rib. Checkered select walnut buttstock and finger-grooved forend w/high luster finish. Engraved receiver w/blued or stainless metal finish. Made 1995 to 1996.

Blued	NiB $1398	Ex $1110	Gd $790
Stainless	NiB $1941	Ex $1590	Gd $1166

BT-99 PLUS
Similar to the BT-99 Competition except w/Browning Recoil Reduction System. Made 1989 to 1995.

Grade I	NiB $1869	Ex $1275	Gd $1013
Pigeon grade	NiB $1977	Ex $1276	Gd $912
Signature grade	NiB $1877	Ex $1233	Gd $888
Stainless model	NiB $2106	Ex $1433	Gd $1133
Golden Clays	NiB $2926	Ex $2474	Gd $2310

BT-99 PLUS MICRO .... NiB $1277 Ex $1088 Gd $872
Same general specifications as BT-99 Plus except scaled down for smaller shooters. 30-inch bbl. w/adj. rib and Browning's recoil reducer system. Made 1991 to 1996.

BT-100 COMPETITION TRAP SPECIAL
Same as BT-99 except has super-high wide rib and standard Monte Carlo or fully adj. stock. Available w/adj. choke or Invector Plus tubes w/optional porting. Made 1976 to 2000.

Grade I w/fixed choke (disc. 1992)	NiB $1867	Ex $1233	Gd $994
Grade I w/Invectors	NiB $2077	Ex $1156	Gd $1034
Grade I stainless (disc. 1994)	NiB $2366	Ex $1967	Gd $1256
Grade I Pigeon Grade (disc. 1994)	NiB $1650	Ex $1290	Gd $1072

BT-100 SINGLE-SHOT TRAP
Similar to the BT-99 Max, except w/additional stock options and removable trigger group. Made 1995 to 2002.

Grade I blued	NiB $2044	Ex $1366	Gd $1065
Stainless	NiB $2366	Ex $1998	Gd $1387
Satin finish	NiB $1490	Ex $1266	Gd $853
Adj. comb, add			$150
Thumbhole stock, add			$350
Replacement trigger assembly, add			$550
Fixed choke, deduct			$100

CITORI O/U HUNTING MODELS
Boxlock. Gauges: 12, 16 (disc. 1989), 20, 28 (disc. 1992), and .410 bore (disc. 1989). Bbl: 24, 26, 28, or 30 inch w/vent rib. Chambered 2.75-, 3-, or 3.5-inch mag. Chokes: IC/M, M/F (Fixed Chokes); Standard Invector or Invector Plus choke systems. Overall length ranges from 41 to 47 inches. 2.75-, 3-, or 3-inch Mag. loads, depending on ga. Weight: 5.75 lbs. to 7 lbs., 13 oz. Single selective, gold-plated trigger. Medium raised German nickel-silver sight bead. Checkered, rounded pistol-grip walnut stock w/beavertail forend. Invector Chokes and Invector Plus became standard in 1988 and 1995, respectively. Made from 1973 to date by Miroku.

Grade I (disc. 1994)	NiB $1076	Ex $792	Gd $566
Grade I, 3.5-inch Mag.(1989 to date)	NiB $1076	Ex $792	Gd $566
Grade II (disc. 1983)	NiB $1288	Ex $1079	Gd $721
Grade III (1985-95)	NiB $2077	Ex $1266	Gd $1091
Grade V (disc. 1984)	NiB $2888	Ex $2069	Gd $1243
Grade VI (1985-95)	NiB $2888	Ex $2069	Gd $1277
Sporting Hunter model (12 and 20 ga., 1998 to date)	NiB $1387	Ex $1176	Gd $700
Satin Hunter model (12 ga. only, 1998 to date)	NiB $1266	Ex $1006	Gd $744
w/o Invector choke system, deduct			$150
For 3.5-inch mag., add			$120
For disc. gauges (16, 28, and .410), add			15%

CITORI LIGHTNING O/U MODELS
Same general specifications as the Citori Hunting models except w/classic Browning rounded pistol-grip stock. Made from 1988 to date by Miroku.

Grade I	NiB $1059	Ex $798	Gd $612
Grade III	NiB $1969	Ex $1154	Gd $834
Grade VI	NiB $3166	Ex $2054	Gd $1152
Gran Lightning model	NiB $1998	Ex $1258	Gd $887
Feather Model (alloy receiver)	NiB $1577	Ex $1159	Gd $1013
Feather Combo model (2-bbl. set)	NiB $3500	Ex $2745	Gd $2388
Privilege model (w/engraved sideplates)	NiB $4855	Ex $3966	Gd $2767
Micro model, add			10%
w/o Invector choke system, deduct			$250
28 ga. and .410, add			15%

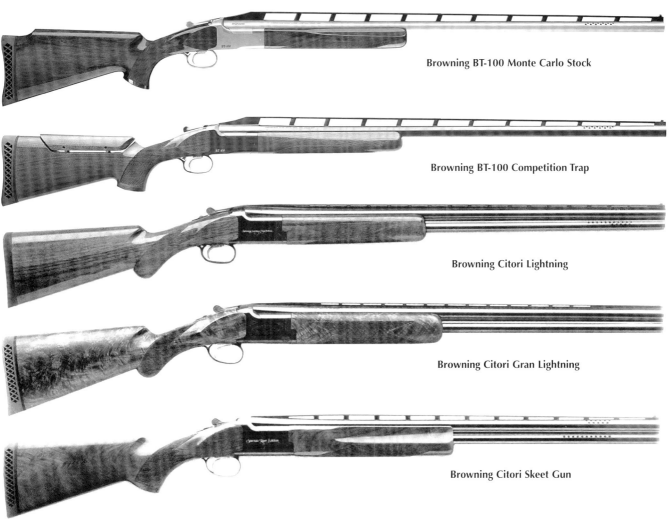

Browning BT-100 Monte Carlo Stock

Browning BT-100 Competition Trap

Browning Citori Lightning

Browning Citori Gran Lightning

Browning Citori Skeet Gun

CITORI SKEET GUN

Same as Hunting model except has skeet-style stock and forearm, 26-or 28-inch bbls., both bored SK choke. Available w/either standard vent rib or special target-type, high-post wide vent rib. Weight (w/26-inch bbls.): 12 ga., 8 lbs.; 20 ga., 7 lbs. Made 1974 to date by Miroku.

Grade I	NiB $1390	Ex $1166	Gd $990
Grade II	NiB $1690	Ex $1345	Gd $1125
Grade III	NiB $1789	Ex $1433	Gd $1093
Grade VI (disc. 1995)	NiB $2345	Ex $1765	Gd $1299
Golden Clays	NiB $2866	Ex $1889	Gd $1465
28 ga. and .410, add			15%
Grade I, 3-bbl. set (disc. 1996)	NiB $2465	Ex $2079	Gd $1500
Grade III, 3-bbl. set (disc. 1996)	NiB $3577	Ex $2260	Gd $1545
Grade VI, 3-bbl. set (disc. 1994)	NiB $3781	Ex $2477	Gd $2053
Golden Clays, 3-bbl. set (disc. 1995)	NiB $4376	Ex $3069	Gd $2210
Grade I, 4-bbl. set	NiB $3588	Ex $3066	Gd $2754
Grade III, 4-bbl. set	NiB $4361	Ex $3276	Gd $2390
Grade VI, 4-bbl. set (disc. 1994)	NiB $4733	Ex $3489	Gd $2466
Golden Clays, 4-bbl. set (disc. 1995)	NiB $5656	Ex $3892	Gd $2721

CITORI SPORTING CLAYS

Similar to the standard Citori Lightning model except Classic-style stock with rounded pistol-grip. 30-inch back-bored bbls. with Invector Plus tubes. Receiver with Lightning Sporting Clays Edition logo. Made from 1989 to date.

GTI model (disc. 1995)	NiB $1167	Ex $1058	Gd $821
GTI Golden Clays model (1993-94)	NiB $2455	Ex $1749	Gd $1256
Lightning model (intro. 1989)	NiB $1440	Ex $1102	Gd $866
Lightning Golden Clays (1993-98)	NiB $2736	Ex $1871	Gd $1319
Lightning Pigeon Grade (1993-94)	NiB $1622	Ex $1188	Gd $887
Micro Citori Lightning model (w/low rib)	NiB $1588	Ex $1266	Gd $1006
Special Sporting model (intro. 1989)	NiB $1590	Ex $1268	Gd $1010
Special Sporting Golden Clays (1993-98)	NiB $3231	Ex $3110	Gd $2127
Special Sporting Pigeon Grade (1993-94)	NiB $1454	Ex $1167	Gd $944
Ultra model (intro. 1995)	NiB $1661	Ex $1288	Gd $937
Ultra Golden Clays (intro. 1995)	NiB $2134	Ex $1822	Gd $1645
Model 325 (1993-94)	NiB $1292	Ex $1188	Gd $900
Model 325 Golden Clays (1993-94)	NiB $2545	Ex $1889	Gd $1438
Model 425 Grade I (intro. 1995)	NiB $1761	Ex $1216	Gd $1022
Model 425 Golden Clays (intro. 1995)	NiB $2665	Ex $2144	Gd $1977
Model 425 WSSF (intro. 1995)	NiB $1896	Ex $1459	Gd $1256
Model 802 Sporter (ES) Extended Swing (intro. 1996)	NiB $1488	Ex $1299	Gd $993
2 bbl. set, add			$1000
Adj. stock, add			$250
High rib, add			$125
Ported barrels, add			$100

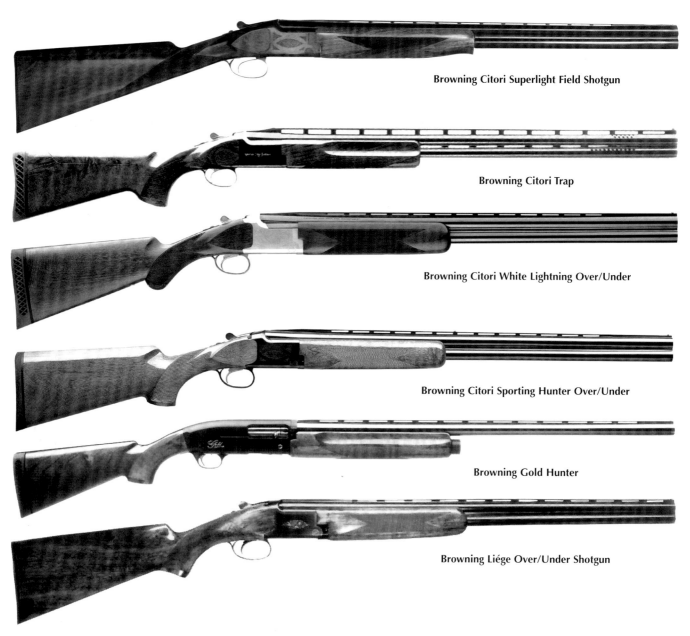

Browning Citori Superlight Field Shotgun

Browning Citori Trap

Browning Citori White Lightning Over/Under

Browning Citori Sporting Hunter Over/Under

Browning Gold Hunter

Browning Liége Over/Under Shotgun

CITORI SUPERLIGHT O/U FIELD SHOTGUNS

Similar to the Citori Hunting model except w/straight-grip stock and Schnabel forend tip. Made by Miroku 1982 to date.

Grade I . . . . NiB $1067 Ex $843 Gd $625
Grade III . . . . NiB $2066 Ex $1590 Gd $1167
Grade V (disc. 1985) . . . . NiB $3132 Ex $2398 Gd $2034
Grade VI . . . . NiB $2876 Ex $2334 Gd $1655
w/o Invectors, deduct $300
28 ga. and .410, add 10%

CITORI TRAP GUN

Same as Hunting model except 12 ga. only, has Monte Carlo or fully adjustable stock and beavertail forend, trap-style recoil pad; 20- or 32-inch bbls.; M/F, IM/F, or F/F. Available with either standard vent rib or special target-type, high-post wide vent rib. Weight: 8 lbs. Made from 1974 to 2001 by Miroku.

Grade I Trap . . . . NiB $1035 Ex $888 Gd $698

Grade I Trap Pigeon grade
  (disc. 1994) . . . . NiB $1857 Ex $1589 Gd $1134
Grade I Trap Signature grade (disc. 1994) . . . . NiB $1756 Ex $1477 Gd $1234
Grade I Plus Trap
  (disc. 1994) . . . . NiB $2878 Ex $2330 Gd $2099
Grade I Plus Trap
  w/ported bbls. (disc. 1994) . . . . . NiB $1979 Ex $1488 Gd $1253
Grade I Plus Trap
  Combo (disc. 1994) . . . . NiB $2773 Ex $2078 Gd $1760
Grade I Plus Trap
  Golden Clays (disc. 1994) . . . . NiB $3176 Ex $2465 Gd $2200
Grade II w/HP rib (disc. 1984) . . . . . . NiB $1989 Ex $1423 Gd $1166
Grade III Trap . . . . NiB $1958 Ex $1688 Gd $1290
Grade V Trap (disc. 1984) . . . . . . NiB $1890 Ex $1656 Gd $1388
Grade VI Trap (disc. 1994) . . . . . . NiB $2066 Ex $1879 Gd $1488
Grade VI Trap Golden Clays
  (disc. 1994) . . . . NiB $3000 Ex $2698 Gd $2365

CITORI UPLAND SPECIAL O/U SHOTGUN
A shortened version of the Hunting model fitted with 24-inch bbls. and straight-grip stock.
12, 20 ga. models . . . . NiB $1277 Ex $1097 Gd $900
16 ga. (disc. 1989) . . . . NiB $1426 Ex $1266 Gd $954
w/o Invector Chokes, deduct $150

CITORI WHITE LIGHTNING O/U SHOTGUN
Similar to the standard Citori Lightning model except w/silver nitride receiver w/scroll and rosette engraving. Satin wood finish w/round pistol grip. Made 1998 to 2001.
12, 20 ga. models . . . . NiB $1769 Ex $1213 Gd $879
28 ga., .410 models (Intro. 2000) . . . . . . NiB $1887 Ex $1369 Gd $1228

CITORI WHITE UPLAND SPECIAL . . . . . . NiB $1389 Ex $1168 Gd $879
Similar to the standard Citori Upland model except w/silver nitride receiver w/scroll and rosette engraving. Satin wood finish w/round pistol grip. Made 2000 to 2001.

CYNERGY SERIES
Monolock hinge system. Gauges: 12, 20, 28, or .410 bore. Bbl. lengths: 26 or 28 inch w/vent rib. 3-inch chambers. Chokes: Invector Plus choke tubes. Overall length ranges from 43 to 45 inches. Weight: 5 to 6 lbs. Single selective, gold-plated trigger. Wood or composite stock. Silver nitride finish. Made from 2004 to date.
Field grade . . . . NiB $2430 Ex $1810 Gd $930
Classic Field grade . . . . NiB $2360 Ex $1000 Gd $720
Euro Field grade . . . . NiB $2300 Ex $1500 Gd $760
Feather . . . . NiB $2530 Ex $1655 Gd $960
Sporting (made 2004-2007) . . . . NiB $1900 Ex $1410 Gd $840

DOUBLE AUTOMATIC (STEEL RECEIVER)
Short recoil system. Takedown. 12 ga. only. 2-round capacity. Bbls.: 26, 28, or 30 inches; any standard choke. Checkered pistol-grip stock and forend. Weight: About 7.75 lbs. Made 1955 to 1961.
w/plain bbl. . . . . NiB $889 Ex $679 Gd $453
w/recessed-rib bbl. . . . . NiB $1167 Ex $1090 Gd $756

GOLD DEER HUNTER AUTOLOADING SHOTGUN
Similar to the Standard Gold Hunter model except chambered 12 ga. only. 22-inch bbl. w/rifled bore or smoothbore w/5-inch rifled Invector tube. Cantilevered scope mount. Made 1997 to 2005.
w/standard finish . . . . NiB $1000 Ex $766 Gd $591
Field model (w/Mossy Oak finish) . . . . . . NiB $956 Ex $619 Gd $495

GOLD HUNTER SERIES
Self-cleaning, gas-operated, short-stroke action. Gauges: 10 or 12 (3.5-inch chamber); 12 or 20 (3-inch chamber). 26-, 28-, or 30-inch bbl. w/Invector or Invector Plus choke tubes. Checkered walnut stock. Polished or matte black metal finish. Made 1990 to date.
Gold Hunter (Light 10 ga. 3.5-inch
   w/walnut stock) . . . . NiB $1499 Ex $1277 Gd $1108
Gold Hunter (12 ga. 3.5-inch) . . . . NiB $977 Ex $790 Gd $559
Gold Hunter (12 or 20 ga. 3-inch) . . . . . . NiB $1067 Ex $880 Gd $670
Gold Hunter Classic model (12 or 20 ga., 3-inch) . . . . NiB $921 Ex $787 Gd $600
Gold Hunter High
   Grade Classic (12 or 20 ga., 3-inch) . . . . . NiB $1690 Ex $1225 Gd $1098
Gold Deer Hunter
   (12 ga. w/22-inch bbl.) . . . . NiB $1078 Ex $884 Gd $643
Gold Turkey Hunter Camo
   (12 ga. w/24-inch bbl.) . . . . NiB $987 Ex $699 Gd $534
Gold Waterfowl Hunter
   Camo (12 ga. w/24-inch bbl.) . . . . NiB $987 Ex $699 Gd $534

GOLD STALKER SERIES
Self-cleaning, gas-operated, short-stroke action. Gauges: 10 or 12 (3.5-inch chamber); 12 or 20 (3-inch chamber). 26-, 28-, or 30-inch bbl. w/Invector or Invector Plus choke tubes. Graphite/fiberglass composite stock. Polished or matte black finish. Made 1998 to 2007.

Browning Over/Under
Gold Classic

Gold Stalker Light (10 ga.,
3.5-inch w/composite stock) . . . . NiB $1487 Ex $1269 Gd $1109
Gold Stalker (12 ga. 3.5-inch) . . . . NiB $1048 Ex $911 Gd $500
Gold Stalker (12 or 20 ga., 3-inch) . . . . . NiB $898 Ex $654 Gd $521
Gold Stalker Classic Model
   (21 or 20 ga., 3-inch) . . . . NiB $1754 Ex $1228 Gd $1067
Gold Deer Stalker
   (12 ga. w/22-inch bbl.) . . . . NiB $855 Ex $529 Gd $380
Gold Turkey Stalker Camo
   (12 ga. w/24-inch bbl.) . . . . NiB $799 Ex $482 Gd $355
Gold Waterfowl Stalker
   Camo (12 ga. w/24-inch bbl.) . . . . NiB $943 Ex $667 Gd $543

GOLD SPORTING CLAYS SERIES
Similar to Gold Hunter Series except w/2.75-inch chamber and 28- or 30-inch ported bbl. w/Invector Plus chokes. Made 1996 to 2008.
Standard model . . . . NiB $1132 Ex $821 Gd $677
Sporting Clays (Youth or Ladies) . . . . . NiB $1677 Ex $1265 Gd $1071
Sporting Clays w/engraved nickel receiver . . . . NiB $1793 Ex $1277 Gd $1056

LIEGE O/U SHOTGUN (B26/27)
Boxlock. Automatic ejectors. Nonselective single trigger. 12 ga. only. Bbls.: 26.5, 28, or 30 inch; 2.75-inch chambers in 26.5- and 28-inch, 3-inch in 30-inch, IC/M, M/F, or F/F chokes; vent rib. Weight: 7 lbs., 4 oz.to 7 lbs., 14 oz., depending on bbls. Checkered pistol-grip stock and forearm. Made 1973 to 1975 by FN.
Liège (B-26 BAC production) . . . . NiB $1488 Ex $1161 Gd $988
Liège (B-27 FN prod., Standard Game model) . . . . NiB $1488 Ex $1161 Gd $988
Deluxe Game model . . . . NiB $1522 Ex $1269 Gd $1043
Grand Delux Game model . . . . NiB $1687 Ex $1438 Gd $1210
Deluxe Skeet model . . . . NiB $1488 Ex $1161 Gd $988
Deluxe Trap model . . . . NiB $1488 Ex $1161 Gd $988
NRA Sporting . . . . NiB $1067 Ex $700 Gd $5254

LIGHT SPORTING 802ES . . . . . NiB $1476 Ex $1211 Gd $989
Over/under. Invector-plus choke tubes. 12 ga. only with 28-inch bbl. Weight: 7 lbs., 5 oz.

LIGHTNING SPORTING CLAYS
Similar to the standard Citori Lightning model except Classic-style stock with rounded pistol grip. 30-inch back-bored bbls. w/Invector Plus tubes. Receiver with Lightning Sporting Clays Edition logo. Made 1989 to 1994.
Standard model . . . . NiB $1396 Ex $1178 Gd $909
Pigeon grade . . . . NiB $1378 Ex $1161 Gd $882

O/U CLASSIC . . . . NiB $2359 Ex $2091 Gd $1389
Gauge: 20. 2.75-inch chambers. 26-inch blued bbls. choked IC/M. Gold-plated, single selective trigger. Manual, top-tang mounted safety. Engraved receiver. High grade, select American walnut straight-grip stock with Schnabel forend. Fine-line checkering with pearl borders. High-gloss finish. 5,000 issued in 1986; made in Japan, engraved in Belgium.

O/U GOLD CLASSIC . . . . NiB $6245 Ex $4890 Gd $3179
Same general specifications as Over/Under Classic except more elaborate engravings, enhanced in gold, including profile of John M. Browning. Fine oil finish. 500 issued; made in 1986 in Belgium.

RECOILLESS TRAP SHOTGUN
The action and bbl. are driven forward when firing to achieve 72% less recoil. 12 ga. 2.75-inch chamber. 30-inch bbl. w/Invector Plus tubes; adjustable vent rib. 51.63 inches overall. Weight: 9 lbs. Adj. checkered walnut buttstock and forend. Blued finish. Made from 1993 to 1996.

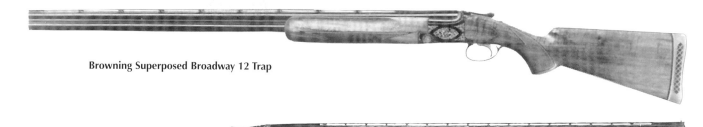

Browning Superposed Broadway 12 Trap

Browning Superposed Grade I Lightning

Left Side

Right Side

Browning Superposed Bicentennial

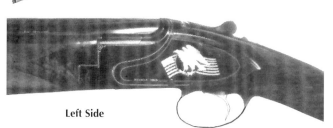

Browning Superposed Grade IV Diana (Postwar)

Browning Superposed Grade V Midas (Postwar)

Standard model.	NiB $1088	Ex $865	Gd $644
Micro model (27-inch bbl.)	NiB $1000	Ex $865	Gd $644
Signature model (27-inch bbl.)	NiB $1088	Ex $865	Gd $644

**SUPERPOSED BICENTENNIAL
COMMEMORATIVE** . . . . NiB $13,650 Ex $12,790 Gd $9779
Special limited edition issued to commemorate US Bicentennial. 51 guns, one for each state plus one for Washington, D.C. Receiver with sideplates has engraved and gold-inlaid hunter and wild turkey on right side, US flag and bald eagle on left side, together with state markings inlaid in gold on blued background. Checkered straight-grip stock and Schnabel-style forearm of highly figured American walnut. Velvet-lined wood presentation case. Made in 1976 by FN. Value shown is for gun in new, unfired condition. See illustration next page.

**SUPERPOSED
BROADWAY 12 TRAP.** . . . . . . NiB $2084 Ex $1766 Gd $1460
Same as Standard Trap Gun except has 30- or 32-inch bbls. with wider Broadway rib. Disc. 1976.

SUPERPOSED SHOTGUNS, HUNTING MODELS
O/U boxlock. Selective automatic ejectors. Selective single trigger; earlier models (worth 25% less) supplied w/double triggers, twin selective triggers, or nonselective single trigger. Gauges: 12, 20 (intro. 1949, 3-inch chambers in later production), 28, .410 (latter two ga. intro. 1960). Bbls.: 26.5, 28, 30, or 32 inch, raised matted or vent rib, prewar Lightning Model made w/ribbed bbl., postwar version supplied only w/vent rib; any combination of standard chokes. Weight (w/26.5-inch vent-rib bbls.): Standard 12, 7 lbs., 11 oz.; Lightning 12, 7 lbs., 6 oz.; Standard 20, 6 lbs., 8 oz.; Lightning 20, 6 lbs., 4 oz.; Lightning 28, 6 lbs., 7 oz.; Lightning .410, 6 lbs., 10 oz. Checkered pistol-grip stock/forearm.
Higher grades (Pigeon, Pointer, Diana, Midas, Grade VI) differ from standard Grade I models in overall quality, engraving, wood, and checkering; otherwise, specifications are the same. Midas Grade and Grade VI guns are richly gold inlaid. Made by FN 1928-1976. Prewar models may be considered as disc. in 1940 when Belgium was occupied by Germany. Grade VI offered 1955-1960. Pointer Grade disc. in 1966, Grade I Standard in 1973, Pigeon Grade in 1974. Lightning Grade I, Diana, and Midas Grades were not offered after 1976. Values shown are for models w/vent. rib.

Grade I standard weight	NiB $2390	Ex $1979	Gd $1749
Grade I Lightning	NiB $2209	Ex $1867	Gd $1428
Grade I Lightning, prewar, matted bbl., no rib.	NiB $2979	Ex $2255	Gd $1217
Grade II Pigeon.	NiB $4400	Ex $2790	Gd $1966

Browning Superposed Ltd.
Pintail Duck Issue

Grade III Pointer. . . . . NiB $5000 Ex $4155 Gd $3860
Grade IV Diana. . . . . NiB $8250 Ex $6300 Gd $3760
Grade V Midas . . . . NiB $7300 Ex $5012 Gd $3690
Grade VI . . . . NiB $10,000 Ex $8292 Gd $6659
20 ga., add 20%
28 ga., add. 75%
.410, add. 50%
Raised matted rib, deduct. 10%

SUPERPOSED LIGHTNING AND SUPERLIGHT MODELS (REISSUE B-25)
Reissue of popular 12 and 20-ga. Superposed shotguns. Lightning models available in 26.5- and 28-inch bbl. lengths. 2.75- or 3-inch chambering, full pistol grip. Superlight models available in 26.5-inch bbl. lengths w/2.75-inch chambering only and straight-grip stock w/Schnabel forend. Both have hand-engraved receivers, fine-line checkering, gold-plated single selective trigger, automatic selective ejectors, manual safety. Weight: 6 to 7.5 lbs. Reintroduced 1985.

Grade I Standard . . . . NiB $2377 Ex $1898 Gd $1344
Grade II Pigeon. . . . . NiB $5696 Ex $3863 Gd $3000
Grade III Pointer. . . . . NiB $8879 Ex $5770 Gd $3760
Grade IV Diana. . . . . NiB $8009 Ex $5679 Gd $3698
Grade V Midas . . . . .NiB $13,750 Ex $11,299 Gd $10,650
Extra bbls., add 50%

SUPERPOSED MAGNUM . . . . . .NiB $1988 Ex $1572 Gd $1189
Same as Grade I except chambered for 12-ga. 3-inch shells, 30-inch vent-rib bbls., stock w/recoil pad. Weight: About 8.25 lbs. Disc. 1976.

SUPERPOSED BLACK DUCK LTD. ISSUE. . . . . . . NiB $10,390 Ex $8977 Gd $5640
Gauge: 12. Superposed Lightning action. 28-inch vent-rib bbls. Choked M/F. 2.75-inch chambers. Weight: 7 lbs., 6 oz. Gold-inlaid receiver and trigger guard engraved w/black duck scenes. Gold-plated, single selective trigger. Top-tang mounted manual safety. Automatic selective ejectors. Front and center ivory sights. High-grade, hand-checkered, hand-oiled select walnut stock and forend. 500 issued in 1983.

SUPERPOSED MALLARD DUCK LTD. ISSUE. . . . . . . NiB $10,768 Ex $7322 Gd $5680
Same general specifications as Ltd. Black Duck issue except mallard duck scenes engraved on receiver and trigger guard, dark French walnut stock w/rounded pistol-grip. 500 issued in 1981.

SUPERPOSED PINTAIL DUCK LTD. ISSUE. . . . . . . NiB $10,766 Ex $7298 Gd $5660
Same general specifications as Ltd. Black Duck issue except pintail duck scenes engraved on receiver and trigger guard. Stock is of dark French walnut w/rounded pistol-grip. 500 issued in 1982.

SUPERPOSED, PRESENTATION GRADES
Custom versions of Superlight, Lightning Hunting, Trap, and Skeet Models, w/same general specifications as those of standard guns, but of higher overall quality. The four Presentation grades differ in receiver finish (grayed or blued), engraving gold inlays, wood and checkering. Presentation 4 has sideplates. Made by FN, these models were Intro. in 1977.
Presentation 1. . . . . NiB $3475 Ex $2770 Gd $12967
Presentation 1, gold-inlaid. . . . . . NiB $4889 Ex $3388 Gd $2491

Presentation 2. . . . . NiB $4956 Ex $3860 Gd $2709
Presentation 2, gold-inlaid. . . . . . NiB $7900 Ex $5275 Gd $4100
Presentation 3, gold-inlaid. . . . . . NiB $9975 Ex $7866 Gd $6077
Presentation 4. . . . . NiB $9106 Ex $7320 Gd $5863
Presentation 4, gold-inlaid. . . . . . .NiB $13,675 Ex $11,960 Gd $9989

SUPERPOSED SKEET GUNS, GRADE I
Same as standard Lightning 12, 20, 28, and .410 Hunting models except has skeet-style stock and forearm, 26.5- or 28-inch vent-rib bbls. w/SK choke. Available also in All Gauge Skeet Set: Lightning 12 w/removable forearm and three extra sets of bbls. in 20, 28, and .410 ga. in fitted luggage case. Disc. 1976. (For higher grades see listings for comparable Hunting models)
12 or 20 ga. . . . . NiB $2170 Ex $1690 Gd $1167
28 ga. or .410. . . . . NiB $2566 Ex $2278 Gd $1489
Combo skeet set (all gauges) . . . . . .NiB $6549 Ex $6000 Gd $5489

SUPERPOSED SUPER LIGHT MODEL . . . . NiB $7101 Ex $4877 Gd $4128
Ultralight field gun version of Standard Lightning Model has classic straight-grip stock and slimmer forearm. Available only in 12 and 20 gauges (2.75-inch chambers) w/26.5-inch vent-rib bbls. Weight: 6.5 lbs. (12 ga.), 6 lbs. (20 ga.). Made 1967 to 1976.

SUPERPOSED TRAP GUN. . . . . . NiB $5321 Ex $3867 Gd $2998
Same as Grade I except has trap-style stock, beavertail forearm, 30-inch vent-rib bbls., 12 ga. only. Disc. 1976. (For higher grades, see listings for comparable hunting models)

TWELVETTE DOUBLE AUTOMATIC
Lightweight version of Double Automatic w/same general specifications except aluminum receiver. Bbl. w/plain matted top or vent rib. Weight: 6.75 to 7 lbs. depending on bbl. Receiver is finished in black w/gold engraving; 1956-1961 receivers were also anodized in gray, brown, and green w/silver engraving. Made 1955 to 1971
w/plain bbl. . . . . NiB $900 Ex $600 Gd $380
w/vent. rib bbl. . . . . NiB $1000 Ex $750 Gd $476

CZ (CESKA ZBROJOVKA), INC. — Uhersky Brod, Czech Republic
Imported by CZ USA, Kansas City, KS

581 SOLO. . . . . NiB $730 Ex $760 Gd $360
O/U boxlock action with double triggers and ejectors. 12 ga. 2.75-inch chambers. Disc. 1995, resumed 1999 to 2005.

ARMARILLO . . . . NiB $625 Ex $430 Gd $210
Similar to Durago S/S, double triggers. Made 2005 to 2006.

BOBWHITE. . . . . NiB $778 Ex $500 Gd $260
S/S hammerless boxlock action with double trigger and extractors. 12, 16, or 20 ga. 3-inch chambers. Bbl.: 26 or 28 inch. Finish: casehardened. Stock: straight English grip, walnut. Weight: 6 to 7 lbs. Made 2005 to date.

CANVASBACK (103 D) . . . . NiB $670 Ex $460 Gd $275
O/U boxlock action with single trigger and extractors. 12, 20, or

28 ga. 3-inch chambers. Bbl.: 26 or 28 inches, vent. rib, five choke tubes, black chrome finish, light engraving. Stock: pistol grip, checkered walnut. Weight: 6.3 to 7.5 lbs. Made 2005 to 2013.
Gold (gold inlays). . . . . NiB $830 Ex $480 Gd $300
Gold (28 or .410) . . . . add 20%

DURANGO. . . . . NiB $725 Ex $530 Gd $245
S/S hammerless boxlock action with single trigger and extractors. 12 or 20 ga. 3-inch chambers. Bbl.: 20 inch. Stock: round knob pistol grip, walnut. Weight: 6 to 6.7 lbs. Made 2005 to 2006.

HAMMER COACH . . . . NiB $778 Ex $500 Gd $260
S/S boxlock action with double trigger, exposed hammers and extractors. 12 ga. 3-inch chambers. Bbl.: 20 inch., fixed choke. Finish: casehardened. Stock: pistol grip. Weight: 6.7 lbs. Made 2006 to date.
Classic (12, 30-in. bbl.,
  2010-present . . . . .NiB $963 Ex $580 Gd $300

LIMITED EDITION . . . . NiB $1980 Ex $1520 Gd $800
O/U w/engraved boxlock action, single gold trigger, and ejectors. 12 ga. 3-inch chambers. Bbl.: 28 inch., vent. rib. Stock: Cicassin walnut. 50 mfg. Made 2006 to 2009.

MALLARD. . . . . NiB $583 Ex $360 Gd $230
O/U boxlock action with dual triggers and extractors. 12 or 20 ga. 3-inch chambers. Bbl.: 28 inches, vent. rib, five choke tubes, coin-finish receiver, black chrom bbl. Stock: Prince of Wales grip, Turkish walnut. Weight: 6.5 to 7.5 lbs. Made 2005 to date.

REDHEAD PREMIER . . . . NiB $959 Ex $630 Gd $400
O/U boxlock action with single trigger and ejectors. 12 or 20 ga. 3-inch chambers. Bbl.: 26 or 28 inches, vent. rib, five choke tubes, black chrome bbl. coin-finish receiver. Stock: pistol grip, checkered walnut. Weight: 6.7 to 7.9 lbs. Made 2005 to date.
Mini (28 or .410, 2005-2013). . . . NiB $800 Ex $630 Gd $400
Target (12 ga., 30-in. bbl.) . . . . . NiB $1389 Ex $830 Gd $440

RINGNECK . . . . NiB $1022 Ex $680 Gd $360
S/S boxlock action w/engraved sideplates, single trigger, and extractors. 12, 16, or 20 ga. 3-inch chambers. Bbl.: 26 or 28 inches, five choke tubes. Finish: black chrome bbl., casehardened receiver. Stock: pistol grip, checkered walnut. Weight: 6.3 to 7.1 lbs. Made 2005 to date.
16 ga., add $200
Mini (28 or .410). . . . . NiB $1229 Ex $800 Gd $410
Target (12 ga., 30-in. bbl.) . . . . . NiB $1298 Ex $810 Gd $430
Deluxe Custom (20 ga., 28-in. bbl.,
  2006-2012) . . . . .NiB $1700 Ex $1260 Gd $630
Competition (12 ga., 28-in. ported bbl.,
  2010-2011) . . . . .NiB $2730 Ex $1830 Gd $1000

SPORTER STANDARD. . . . . NiB $3122 Ex $1630 Gd $800
O/U boxlock action with single trigger and ejectors. 12 ga. 3-inch chambers. Bbl.: 30 or 32 inches, vent. rib, six extended choke tubes, black chrome bbl., matte black receiver. Stock: pistol grip w/palm swell, adj. comb, Grade II Turkish walnut. Weight: 8.7 lbs. Made 2008 to date.

WOODCOCK DELUXE. . . . . NiB $1080 Ex $730 Gd $400
O/U boxlock action with single trigger and ejectors. 12 or 20 ga. 3-inch chambers. Bbl.: 26 or 28 inches, vent. rib, five choke tubes, black chrome bbl., casehardened receiver w/sideplates. Stock: Prince of Wales pistol grip, schnabel forend, walnut. Weight: 6.8 to 7.8 lbs. Made 2005 to 2010.
Custom (20, 2006-2010). . . . . . NiB $1900 Ex $1330 Gd $710
Target (12 ga., 30-in. bbl.) . . . . . NiB $1389 Ex $830 Gd $440

CAESAR GUERINI, s.r.l. — Marcheno, Italy

MAXUM
O/U boxlock action. 12, 20, 28, or .410 ga. Bbl.: 26 or 28 inches Coin-finish sideplates w/engraving. Checkered, oil finished Turkish walnut stock and forearm. Imported 2006 to present.
Field . . . . NiB $6175 Ex $4525 Gd $2050
Light . . . . NiB $4530 Ex $2850 Gd $2125

TEMPIO . . . . .NiB $3950 Ex $2400 Gd $2125
O/U boxlock action w/ selective single trigger. 12, 20, or 28 ga. 2.75- or 3-in. chambers. Bbl.: 26-, 28-, or 30-in. Weight: About 6.2 to 7 lbs. Checkered Prince of Wales pistol-grip stock and Schnabel forearm. Imported 2008 to present.
Light . . . . .NiB $3950 Ex $2400 Gd $2125

CENTURY ARMS formerly CENTURY INTERNATIONAL ARMS, INC. — St. Albans, VT, and Boca Raton, FL

ARTHEMIS . . . . .NiB $522 Ex $390 Gd $259
O/U boxlock action with double triggers and extractors. 12, 20, 28 ga. or .410 bore. 3-inch chambers. 28-inch bbls. Single set trigger, extractors. Checkered wood stock and forearm. Weight: 5.3 to 7.4 lbs. Mfg. in Turkey by Khan. Disc.

ARTHEMIS O/U . . . . .NiB $475 Ex $310 Gd $245
Gauge: 12, 20, 28, .410. Bbl.: 28 inches, vent. rib. 3-inch chamber. Single selective trigger, extractors. Stock: Checkered walnut. Weight: 5.3 to 7.4 lbs. Mfg. by PAR. Imported from 2002 to 2009.

CATAMOUNT FURY I. . . . . NiB $675 Ex $430 Gd $275
Gas-operated adj. piston, semiauto w/detchable 5- or 10-round magazine. Gauge: 12. Bbl.: 20.1 inches, choke tubes. Stock: Standard style checkered synthetic. Mfg. in China. Imported 2013 to date.

CATAMOUNT FURY II . . . . NiB $695 Ex $450 Gd $295
Similar specs as Fury I except synthetic thumbhole stock. Mfg. in China. Imported 2013 to date.

COACH MODEL. . . . . NiB $325 Ex $200 Gd $140
Side-by-side. Gauge: 12, 20, .410. Bbl.: 20 inches, exposed hammers, double trigger. Stock: Checkered walnut. Sling swivels. Mfg. in China.

MODEL IJ2 . . . . .NiB $220 Ex $155 Gd $100
Slide-action. Gauge: 12. 2.75- or 3-inch chamber. Bbl.: 19 inches, fixed choke. Ghost ring rear or fiber optic sights. Weight: 7 lbs. Mfg. in China.

PHANTOM . . . . .NiB $295 Ex $240 Gd $190
Semiauto. Gauge: 12. 3-inch chamber. Bbl.: 24, 26, or 28 inches; vent. rib. Three choke tubes. Stock: Black synthetic. Mfg. in Turkey. Disc.

PW87 . . . . .NiB $390 Ex $325 Gd $160
Repro. of Winchester 1887 lever-action. Gauge: 12. 2.75-inch. chamber. Bbl.: 19 inches w/brass bead M choke. Stock: Smooth hardwood. Mfg. in China. Imported from 2013 to date.

SAS-12 . . . . .NiB $250 Ex $185 Gd $100
Semiauto. Gauge: 12. 2.75-inch chamber. Bbl.: 22 or 23.5 inches. Detachable 3- or 5-round mag.
Ghost-ring rear sight, add $25

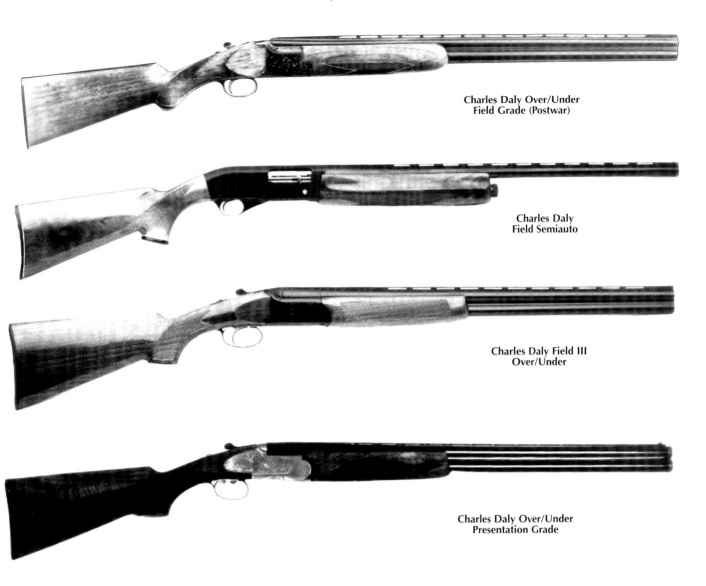

Charles Daly Over/Under
Field Grade (Postwar)

Charles Daly
Field Semiauto

Charles Daly Field III
Over/Under

Charles Daly Over/Under
Presentation Grade

ULTRA 87 .NiB $255 Ex $180 Gd $110
Slide-action. Gauge: 12. Bbl.: 19 inches. Optional heat shield and pistol grip. Side folding stock. Includes extra 28-inch bbl. Weight: 8.2 lbs.

CHARLES DALY, INC. — New York, NY

The pre-WWII Charles Daly shotguns, w/the exception of the Commander, were manufactured by various firms in Suhl, Germany. The postwar guns, except for the Novamatic series, were produced by Miroku Firearms Mfg. Co., Tokyo. Miroku ceased production in 1976 and the Daly trademark was acquired by Outdoor Sports Headquarters, in Dayton, Ohio. OSHI continued to market O/U shotguns from both Italy and Spain under the Daly logo. Automatic models were produced in Japan for distribution in the USA. In 1996, KBI, Inc. in Harrisburg, PA, acquired the Daly trademark and currently imports firearms under that logo.

COMMANDER O/U SHOTGUN
Daly-pattern Anson & Deeley system boxlock action. Automatic ejectors. Double triggers or Miller selective single trigger. Gauges: 12, 16, 20, 28, .410. Bbls.: 26 to 30 inch, IC/M or M/F choke. Weight: 5.25 to 7.25 lbs. depending on ga. and bbl. length.

Checkered stock and forend, straight or pistol grip. The two models, 100 and 200, differ in general quality, grade of wood, checkering, engraving, etc.; otherwise specs are the same. Made in Belgium c. 1939.
Model 100 . . . . .NiB $665 Ex $500 Gd $397
Model 200 . . . . NiB $866 Ex $703 Gd $511
Miller single trigger, add. $150

HAMMERLESS DOUBLE-BARREL SHOTGUN
Daly pattern Anson & Deeley system boxlock action. Automatic ejectors except Superior quality is non-ejector. Double triggers. Gauges: 10, 12, 16, 20, 28, .410. Bbls.: 26 to 32 inch, any combination of chokes. Weight: 4 to 8.5 lbs. depending on ga. and bbl. length. Checkered pistol-grip stock and forend. The four grades—Regent Diamond, Diamond, Empire, Superior—differ in general quality, grade of wood, checkering, engraving, etc.; otherwise specifications are the same. Disc. about 1933.
Diamond quality. . . . . NiB $12,677 Ex $10,445 Gd $7869
Empire quality. . . . . .NiB $6133 Ex $4632 Gd $3144
Regent Diamond quality . . . . . NiB $14,878 Ex $12,966 Gd $10,077
Superior quality . . . . .NiB $1522 Ex $1292 Gd $1000

HAMMERLESS DRILLING

Daly pattern Anson & Deeley system boxlock action. Plain extractors. Double triggers, front single set for rifle bbl. Gauges: 12, 16, 20, .25-20, .25-35, .30-30 rifle bbl. Supplied in various bbl. lengths and weights. Checkered pistol-grip stock and forend. Auto rear sight operated by rifle bbl. selector. The three grades—Regent Diamond, Diamond, Superior—differ in general quality, grade of wood, checkering, engraving, etc.; otherwise specifications are the same. Disc. 1933.

Diamond quality. . . . . NiB $7235 Ex $5530 Gd $4200
Regent Diamond quality. . . . . . .NiB $14,866 Ex $11,977 Gd $9977
Superior quality . . . . NiB $3733 Ex $2988 Gd $2036

HAMMERLESS DOUBLE

EMPIRE GRADE . . . . .NiB $1887 Ex $1352 Gd $1091
Boxlock. Plain extractors. Nonselective single trigger. Gauges: 12, 16, 20. 3-inch chambers in 12 and 20, 2.75-inch in 16 ga. Bbls.: vent rib; 26, 28, 30 inch (latter in 12 ga. only); IC/M, M/F, F/F. Weight: 6 to 7.75 lbs. depending on ga. and bbls. Checkered pistol-grip stock and beavertail forearm. Made 1968 to 1971.

1974 WILDLIFE

COMMEMORATIVE . . . . NiB $2466 Ex $2167 Gd $1477
Limited issue of 500 guns. Similar to Diamond Grade over/under. 12-ga. trap and skeet models only. Duck scene engraved on right side of receiver, fine scroll on left side. Made in 1974.

NOVAMATIC LIGHTWEIGHT AUTOLOADER

Same as Breda. Recoil-operated. Takedown.12 ga. 2.75-inch chamber. 4-round tubular magazine. Bbls.: Plain vent rib; 26-inch IC or Quick-Choke w/three interchangeable tubes, 28-inch M/F choke. Weight (w/26-inch vent-rib bbl.): 7 lbs., 6 oz. Checkered pistol-grip stock and forearm. Made 1968 by Ernesto Breda, Milan, Italy.

w/plain bbl. . . . . NiB $398 Ex $277 Gd $198
w/vent rib bbl. . . . . NiB $397 Ex $260 Gd $200
Quick-Choke, add $50

NOVAMATIC SUPER LIGHTWEIGHT

Lighter version of Novamatic Lightweight. Gauges: 12, 20. Weight (w/26-inch vent-rib bbl.): 12 ga., 6 lbs., 10 oz.; 20 ga., 6 lbs. SK choke available in 26-inch vent-rib bbl. 28-inch bbls. in 12 ga. only. Quick-Choke in 20 ga. w/plain bbl. Made 1968 by Ernesto Breda, Milan, Italy.

12 ga., plain bbl. . . . . NiB $387 Ex $288 Gd $198
12 ga., vent. rib bbl.. . . . . NiB $387 Ex $288 Gd $198
20 ga., plain bbl. . . . . NiB $543 Ex $433 Gd $315
20 ga., plain bbl. w/Quick-Choke . . . . NiB $388 Ex $335 Gd $217
20 ga., vent. rib bbl. . . . . NiB $433 Ex $290 Gd $200

NOVAMATIC SUPER LIGHTWEIGHT

20 GA. MAGNUM.. .NiB $377 Ex $296 Gd $200
Same as Novamatic Super Lightweight 2 except 3-inch chamber, has 3-round magazine, 28-inch vent-rib bbl., F choke.

NOVAMATIC

12 GA. MAGNUM.. .NiB $377 Ex $296 Gd $200
Same as Novamatic Lightweight except chambered for 12-ga. Magnum 3-inch shell. Has 3-round magazine, 30-inch vent rib bbl., F choke, and stock w/recoil pad. Weight: 7.75 lbs.

Postwar Charles Daly shotguns were imported by Sloan's Sporting Goods trading as Charles Daly in New York. In 1976, Outdoor Sports Headquarters acquired the Daly trademark and continued to import European-made shotguns under that logo. In 1996, KBI, Inc., in Harrisburg, PA, acquired the Daly trademark and currently imports firearms under that logo.

NOVAMATIC TRAP GUN . . . . . . NiB $643 Ex $500 Gd $355
Same as Novamatic Lightweight except has 30-inch vent rib bbl., F choke, and Monte Carlo stock w/recoil pad. Weight: 7.75 lbs.

O/U SHOTGUNS (PRE-WWII)

Daly pattern Anson & Deeley system boxlock action. Sideplates. Auto ejectors. Double triggers. Gauges: 12, 16, 20. Supplied in various bbl. lengths and weights. Checkered pistol-grip stock and forend. The two grades—Diamond and Empire—differ in general quality, grade of wood, checkering, engraving, etc.; otherwise specifications are the same. Disc. about 1933.

Diamond quality. . . . . NiB $6133 Ex $4965 Gd $3476
Empire quality. . . . . NiB $4771 Ex $3865 Gd $2700

O/U SHOTGUNS (POST-WWII)

Boxlock. Auto ejectors or selective auto/manual ejection. Selective single trigger. Gauges: 12, 12 Magnum (3-inch chambers), 20 (3-inch chambers), 28, .410. Bbls.: Vent rib; 26-, 28-, 30-inch; standard choke combinations. Weight: 6 to 8 lbs. depending on ga. and bbls. Select walnut stock w/pistol grip, fluted forearm check ered; Monte Carlo comb on trap guns; recoil pad on 12-ga. Mag. and trap models. The various grades differ in quality of engraving and wood. Made from 1963 to 1976.

Diamond grade. . . . . NiB $1588 Ex $1266 Gd $990
Field grade . . . . NiB $933 Ex $800 Gd $576
Superior grade . . . . NiB $1139 Ex $1008 Gd $853
Venture grade . . . . NiB $900 Ex $773 Gd $525

SEXTUPLE MODEL SINGLE-BARREL TRAP GUN

Daly pattern Anson & Deeley system boxlock action. Six locking bolts. Auto ejector. 12 ga. only. Bbls.: 30, 32, 34 inch; vent rib. Weight: 7.5 to 8.25 lbs. Checkered pistol-grip stock and forend. The two models made Empire and Regent Diamond differ in general quality, grade of wood, checkering, engraving, etc.; otherwise specifications are the same. Disc. about 1933.

Regent Diamond quality (Linder) . NiB $2788 Ex $2188 Gd $1886
Empire quality (Linder) . . . . NiB $5300 Ex $4260 Gd $3143
Regent Diamond quality (Sauer). . NiB $3921 Ex $3288 Gd $2876
Empire quality (Sauer). . . . . NiB $2966 Ex $2377 Gd $1677

SINGLE-SHOT TRAP GUN

Daly pattern Anson & Deeley system boxlock action. Auto ejector. 12 ga. only. Bbls.: 30, 32, 34 inch; vent rib. Weight: 7.5 to 8.25 lbs. Checkered pistol-grip stock and forend. This model was made in Empire Quality only. Disc. about 1933.

Empire grade (Linder) . . . . NiB $4765 Ex $3966 Gd $2960
Empire grade (Sauer) . . . . NiB $2477 Ex $2099 Gd $1776

SUPERIOR GRADE

SINGLE-SHOT TRAP . . . . NiB $954 Ex $833 Gd $700
Boxlock. Automatic ejector. 12 ga. only. 32- or 34-inch vent-rib bbl., F choke. Weight: About 8 lbs. Monte Carlo stock w/pistol grip and recoil pad, beavertail forearm, checkered. Made 1968 to 1976.

DIAMOND GRADE O/U

Boxlock. Single selective trigger. Selective automatic ejectors. Gauges: 12 and 20. 3-inch chambers (2.75 target grade). Bbls.: 26, 27, or 30 inch w/fixed chokes or screw-in tubes. Weight: 7 lbs. Checkered European walnut stock and forearm w/oil finish. Engraved antique-silver receiver and blued bbls. Made from 1984 to 1990.

Standard model . . . . NiB $1088 Ex $900 Gd $670
Skeet model . . . . NiB $1155 Ex $966 Gd $733
Trap model . . . . NiB $1155 Ex $966 Gd $733

DIAMOND GTX DL HUNTER O/U SERIES
Sidelock. Single selective trigger and selective auto ejectors. Gauges: 12, 20, 28 ga. or .410 bore. 26-, 28- and 30-inch bbls. w/3-inch chambers (2.75-inch 28 ga.). Choke tubes (12 and 20 ga.), fixed chokes (28 and 410). Weight: 5 to 8 lbs. Checkered European walnut stock w/ hand-rubbed oil finish and recoil pad. Made from 1997 to 2001.
Diamond GTX DL Hunter . . . . NiB $11,977 Ex $9478 Gd $5800
Diamond GTX EDL Hunter . . . . . . NiB $13,778 Ex $10,771 Gd $8987
Diamond GTX Sporting (12 or 20 ga.) . . . . NiB $5921 Ex $4771 Gd $3380
Diamond GTX Skeet (12 or 20 ga.) . . . . . . NiB $5540 Ex $4380 Gd $3100
Diamond GTX Trap (12 ga. only) . . . . NiB $6144 Ex $4766 Gd $3200

EMPIRE DL HUNTER O/U . . . . NiB $1456 Ex $1277 Gd $956
Boxlock. Ejectors. Single selective trigger. Gauges: 12, 20, 28 ga. and .410 bore. 26- or 28- inch bbls. w/3-inch chambers (2.75-inch 28 ga.). Choke tubes (12 and 20 ga.), fixed chokes (28 and .410). Engraved coin-silver receiver w/game scene. Imported from 1997 to 1998.

EMPIRE EDL HUNTER SERIES
Similar to Empire DL Hunter except engraved sideplates. Made 1998 to date.
Hunter model . . . . NiB $1477 Ex $1133 Gd $890
Sporting model . . . . NiB $1371 Ex $1108 Gd $870
Skeet model . . . . NiB $1388 Ex $1170 Gd $880
Trap model . . . . NiB $1366 Ex $1109 Gd $853
28 ga., add $110
.410 ga, add $150
Multi-chokes w/Monte
Carlo stock, add $175

DSS HAMMERLESS DOUBLE . . . . NiB $885 Ex $744 Gd $561
Boxlock. Single selective trigger. Selective automatic ejectors. Gauges: 12 and 20. 3-inch chambers. 26-inch bbls. w/screw-in choke tubes. Weight: 6.75 lbs. Checkered walnut pistol-grip stock and semi-beavertail forearm w/recoil pad. Engraved antique-silver receiver and blued bbls. Made from 1990. Disc.

FIELD GRADE O/U . . . . NiB $675 Ex $570 Gd $449
Boxlock. Single selective trigger. Extractors. Gauges: 12 and 20. 3-inch chambers. Bbls.: 26-inch, IC/M; 28-inch, M/F. Weight: 6.75 lbs. (12 ga.). Checkered walnut stock and forearm w/semigloss finish and recoil pad. Engraved color casehardened receiver and blued bbls. Made from 1989. Disc.

FIELD SEMIAUTO SHOTGUN . . . . . NiB $622 Ex $476 Gd $377
Recoil-operated. Takedown. 12-ga. and 12-ga. Magnum. Bbls.: 27 and 30 inch; vent rib. Made from 1982 to 1988.

FIELD III O/U SHOTGUN . . . . NiB $679 Ex $580 Gd $445
Boxlock. Plain extractors. Nonselective single trigger. Gauges: 12 or 20. Bbls.: vent rib; 26 and 28 inch; IC/M, M/F. Weight: 6 to 7.75 lbs. depending on ga. and bbls. Chrome-molybdenum steel bbls. Checkered pistol-grip stock and forearm. Made from 1982. Disc.

LUXIE O/U . . . . NiB $900 Ex $733 Gd $529
Similar to the Field Grade except w/selective automatic ejectors and choke tubes. Gauges: 12, 20, 28, and .410. Receiver w/ antique silver finish and blued bbls. Made from 1989 to 1994.

MULTI-XII SELF-LOADING SHOTGUN. . . . . . . NiB $656 Ex $490 Gd $387
Similar to the gas-operated field semiauto except w/new Multi-Action gas system designed to shoot all loads w/o adjustment. 12 ga. 3-inch chamber. 27-inch bbl. w/Invector choke tubes, vent rib. Made in Japan from 1987 to 1988.

PRESENTATION
GRADE O/U . . . . NiB $1254 Ex $1009 Gd $770
Purdey boxlock w/double cross-bolt. Gauges: 12 or 20. Engraved receiver w/single selective trigger and auto-ejectors. 27-inch chrome-molybdenum steel, rectified, honed, and internally chromed vent-rib bbls. Hand-checkered deluxe European walnut stock. Made from 1982 to 1986.

SUPERIOR II
SHOTGUN O/U . . . . NiB $1064 Ex $880 Gd $602
Boxlock. Plain extractors. Nonselective single trigger. Gauges: 12 or 20. Bbls.: chrome-molybdenum vent rib; 26, 28, 30 inch, latter in magnum only, assorted chokes. Silver engraved receiver. Checkered pistol-grip stock and forearm. Made from 1982 to 1988.

SPORTING CLAYS O/U . . . . NiB $833 Ex $644 Gd $535
Similar to the Field Grade except in 12 ga. only w/ported bbls. and internal choke tubes. Made from 1990 to 1996.

CHIAPPA FIREARMS LTD., owns Armi Sport replica firearms mfg. for Cimarron, Legacy Sports, and Taylor's and Company marketed by MKS Supply — Dayton, OH

MODEL 1887 . . . . NiB $1363 Ex $1295 Gd $400
Lever action. Gauge: 12. 18.5-, 22-, 24-, or 28-inch bbl., choke tubes. Color casehardened or chrome receiver. Weight: 6.6 lbs. Stock: oil finished smooth walnut. Made from 2009 to date.

Trophy Hunter
  (adj. sights) . . . . NiB $1260 Ex $1065 Gd $880
Mares Leg (18.5-in. barrel,
  pistol grip) . . . . NiB $1060 Ex $765 Gd $580

CHURCHILL SHOTGUNS — Italy and Spain
Imported by Ellett Brothers, Inc., Chapin, SC; previously by Kassnar Imports, Inc., Harrisburg, PA

AUTOMATIC SHOTGUN
Gas-operated. Gauge: 12, 2.75- or 3-inch chambers. 5-round magazine w/cutoff. Bbl.: 24, 25, 26, 28 inch w/ICT choke tubes. Checkered walnut stock w/satin finish. Imported from 1990 to 1994.
Standard model . . . . NiB $657 Ex $571 Gd $455
Turkey model . . . . NiB $697 Ex $586 Gd $434

MONARCH O/U SHOTGUN
Hammerless, takedown w/engraved receiver. Selective single or double triggers. Gauges: 12, 20, 28, .410. 3-inch chambers. Bbls.: 25- or 26-inch (IC/M); 28-inch (M/F). Weight: 6.5 to 7.5 lbs. Checkered European walnut buttstock and forend. Made in Italy from 1986 to 1993.
w/double triggers . . . . NiB $490 Ex $378 Gd $225
w/single trigger . . . . NiB $588 Ex $466 Gd $321

REGENT O/U SHOTGUNS
Gauges: 12 or 20. 2.75-inch chambers. 27-inch bbls. w/interchangeable choke tubes and wide vent rib. Single selective trigger, selective automatic ejectors. Checkered pistol-grip stock in fancy walnut. Imported from Italy 1984 to 1988 and 1990 to 1994.

Churchill Automatic Shotgun

Churchill Windsor Grade Side-by-Side Shotgun

Churchill Windsor Grade Flyweight Shotgun

Regent V (disc. 1988) . . . . NiB $987 Ex $680 Gd $590
Regent VII w/sideplates (disc. 1994) . . . . . .NiB $873 Ex $779 Gd $544

REGENT SKEET . . . . NiB $873 Ex $779 Gd $544
12 or 20 ga. 2.75-inch chambers. Selective automatic ejectors, singleselective trigger. 26-inch over/under bbls. w/vent rib. Weight: 7 lbs. Made in Italy from 1984 to 1988.

REGENT TRAP. . . . . NiB $876 Ex $654 Gd $490
12-ga. competition shotgun 2.75-inch chambers. 30-inch over/ under bbls. choked IM/F, vent side ribs. Weight: 8 lbs. Selective automatic ejectors, single selective trigger. Checkered Monte Carlo stock w/Supercushion recoil pad. Made in Italy 1984 to 1988.

SPORTING CLAYS O/U . . . . NiB $945 Ex $800 Gd $575
Same general specifications as Windsor IV except in 12 ga. only. 28-inch ported bbls. and choke tubes. Selective automatic ejectors. Weight: 7.5 lbs. Made from 1992 to 1994.

WINDSOR O/U SHOTGUNS
Hammerless, boxlock w/engraved receiver, selective single trigger. Extractors or ejectors. Gauges: 12, 20, 28, or .410. 3-inch chambers. Bbls.: 24 to 30 inches w/fixed chokes or choke tubes. Weight: 6 lbs., 3 oz. (Flyweight) to 7 lbs., 10 oz. (12 ga.). Checkered straight (Flyweight) or pistol-grip stock and forend of European walnut. Imported from Italy 1984 to 1993.
Windsor III w/fixed chokes. . . . . NiB $668 Ex $544 Gd $455
Windsor III w/choke tubes . . . . NiB $798 Ex $670 Gd $555
Windsor IV w/fixed chokes (disc. 1993). . . . . . .NiB $768 Ex $659 Gd $455
Windsor IV w/choke tubes . . . . NiB $833 Ex $754 Gd $500

WINDSOR SIDE-BY-SIDE SHOTGUNS
Boxlock action w/double triggers, ejectors or extractors, and automatic safety. Gauges: 10 (3.5-inch chambers), 12, 20, 28, .410 (3-inch chambers), 16 (2.75-inch chambers). Bbls.: 23 to 32 inches w/various fixed choke or choke tube combinations. Weight: 5 lbs., 12 oz. (Flyweight) to 11.5 lbs. (10 ga.). European walnut buttstock and forend. Imported from Spain 1984 to 1990.
Windsor I 10 ga. . . . . NiB $569 Ex $400 Gd $327
Windsor I 12 ga. thru .410. . . . . . NiB $569 Ex $400 Gd $327
Windsor II 12 or 20 ga. . . . . NiB $569 Ex $400 Gd $327
Windsor VI 12 or 20 ga. . . . . NiB $569 Ex $400 Gd $327

E.J. CHURCHILL, LTD. — Surrey (previously London), England
The E.J. Churchill shotguns listed below are no longer imported.

FIELD MODEL HAMMERLESS DOUBLE
Sidelock Hammerless ejector gun w/same general specifications as Premiere Model but of lower quality.
w/double triggers . . . . . . .NiB $10,667 Ex $9260 Gd $8110
Single selective trigger, add
10%

PREMIERE QUALITY HAMMERLESS DOUBLE
Sidelock. Automatic ejectors. Double triggers or selective single trigger. Gauges: 12, 16, 20, 28. Bbls.: 25, 28, 39, 32 inch; any degree of boring. Weight: 5 to 8 lbs. depending on ga. and bbl. length. Checkered stock and forend, straight or pistol grip.
w/double triggers . . . . NiB $46,775 Ex $36,950 Gd $30,000
Single selective trigger, add $10%

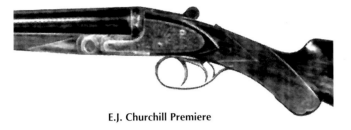

E.J. Churchill Premiere

Cogswell & Harrison
Best Quality
Hammerless Sidelock

PREMIERE QUALITY O/U SHOTGUN
Sidelock. Automatic ejectors. Double triggers or selective single trigger. Gauges: 12, 16, 20, 28. Bbls.: 25, 28, 30, 32 inch, any degree of boring. Weight: 5 to 8 lbs. depending on ga. and bbl. length. Checkered stock and forend, straight or pistol grip.
w/double triggers . . . . NiB $55,000 Ex $38,000 Gd $25,000
Selective single trigger, add 10%
Raised vent. rib, add 15%

UTILITY MODEL HAMMERLESS DOUBLE-BARREL
Anson & Deeley boxlock action. Double triggers or single trigger. Gauges: 12, 16, 20, 28, .410. Bbls.: 25, 28, 30, 32 inch, any degree of boring. Weight: 4.5 to 8 lbs. depending on ga. and bbl. length. Checkered stock and forend, straight or pistol grip.
w/double triggers . . . . NiB $7340 Ex $6077 Gd $4340
Single selective trigger, add 10%

XXV HERCULES . . . . NiB $10,750 Ex $9450 Gd $6680
Boxlock, otherwise specifications same as for XXV Premiere.

XXV IMPERIAL . . . . NiB $14,775 Ex $12,700 Gd $9775
Similar to XXV Premiere but no assisted opening feature.

XXV PREMIERE HAMMERLESS
DOUBLE . . . . NiB $47,000 Ex $40,000 Gd $35,000
Sidelock. Assisted opening. Automatic ejectors. Double triggers. Gauges: 12, 20. 25-inch bbls. w/narrow, quick-sighting rib; any standard choke combination. English-style straight-grip stock and forearm, checkered.

XXV REGAL . . . . NiB $6277 Ex $4988 Gd $3500
Similar to XXV Hercules but w/o assisted opening feature. Gauges: 12, 20, 28, .410.

CLASSIC DOUBLES — Tochigi, Japan

Imported by Classic Doubles International, St. Louis, MO, and previously by Olin as Winchester Models 101 and 23.

MODEL 101 O/U SHOTGUN
Boxlock. Engraved receiver w/single selective trigger, auto ejectors, and combination bbl. selector and safety. Gauges: 12, 20, 28, or .410. 2.75-, 3-inch chambers 25.5-, 28-, or 30-inch vent-rib bbls. Weight: 6.25 to 7.75 lbs. Checkered French walnut stock. Imported from 1987 to 1990.
Classic I Field . . . . NiB $1590 Ex $1488 Gd $1033
Classic II Field . . . . NiB $1879 Ex $1540 Gd $1133
Classic Sporter . . . . NiB $2066 Ex $1788 Gd $1233
Classic Sporter combo . . . . NiB $3475 Ex $2870 Gd $2035
Classic Trap . . . . NiB $1380 Ex $1166 Gd $990
Classic Trap Single . . . . NiB $1435 Ex $1140 Gd $1089
Classic Trap combo . . . . NiB $2560 Ex $2053 Gd $1498

Classic Skeet . . . . NiB $1765 Ex $1600 Gd $1179
Classic Skeet 2-bbl. set . . . . NiB $2867 Ex $2374 Gd $1790
Classic Skeet 4-bbl. set . . . . NiB $4488 Ex $3972 Gd $2633
ClassicWaterfowler . . . . NiB $1554 Ex $1266 Gd $1031
Grade II (28 ga.), add $900
Grade II (.410), add $300

MODEL 201 SIDE-BY-SIDE SHOTGUN
Boxlock. Single selective trigger, automatic safety, selective ejectors. Gauges: 12 or 20. 3-inch chambers. 26- or 28-inch vent-rib bbl., fixed chokes or internal tubes. Weight: 6 to 7 lbs. Checkered French walnut stock and forearm. Imported 1987 to 1990.
Field model . . . . NiB $2687 Ex $1490 Gd $1264
Skeet model . . . . NiB $2687 Ex $1490 Gd $1264
Internal choke tubes, add $100

MODEL 201
SMALL BORE SET . . . . NiB $4650 Ex $3751 Gd $2975
Same general specifications as the Classic Model 201 except w/ smaller frame in 28 ga. (IC/M) and .410 (F/M). Weight: 6 to 6.5 lbs. Imported from 1987 to 1990.

COGSWELL & HARRISON, LTD. —
London, England

AMBASSADOR HAMMERLESS
DOUBLE-BARREL SHOTGUN . . . . . . NiB $6056 Ex $4533 Gd $3718
Boxlock. Sideplates w/game scene or rose scroll engraving. Automatic ejectors. Double triggers. Gauges: 12, 16, 20. Bbls.: 26, 28, 30 inch; any choke combination. Checkered straight-grip stock and forearm. Disc.

AVANT TOUT SERIES HAMMERLESS
DOUBLE-BARREL SHOTGUNS . . . . NiB $2688 Ex $2133 Gd $1954
Boxlock. Sideplates except Avant Tout III Grade. Automatic ejectors. Double triggers or single trigger (selective or nonselective). Gauges: 12, 16, 20. Bbls.: 25, 27.5, 30 inch; any choke combination. Checkered stock and forend, straight grip standard. Made in three models (Avant Tout I or Konor, Avant Tout II or Sandhurst, Avant Tout III or Rex) which differ chiefly in overall quality of engraving, grade of wood, checkering, etc. General specifications are the same. Disc.
Avant Tout I . . . . NiB $3544 Ex $3160 Gd $2477
Avant Tout II . . . . NiB $2983 Ex $2786 Gd $1966
Avant Tout III . . . . NiB $2254 Ex $2090 Gd $1760
Nonselective single trigger, add $250
Selective single trigger, add $425

BEST QUALITY HAMMERLESS
SIDELOCK DOUBLE-BARREL SHOTGUN
Hand-detachable locks. Automatic ejectors. Double triggers or single trigger (selective or nonselective). Gauges: 12, 16, 20. Bbls.:

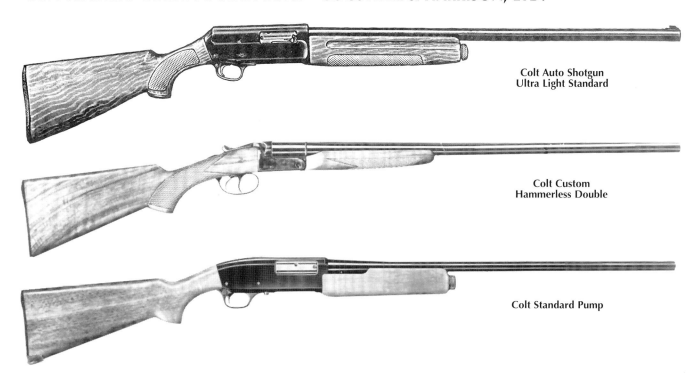

Colt Auto Shotgun
Ultra Light Standard

Colt Custom
Hammerless Double

Colt Standard Pump

25, 26, 28, 30 inch; any choke combination. Checkered stock and forend, straight grip standard.

Victor model . . . . NiB $6570 Ex $5461 Gd $4130
Primic model (disc.). . . . . NiB $6640 Ex $5521 Gd $4200
Nonselective single trigger, add. $250
Selective single trigger, add $450

HUNTIC MODEL HAMMERLESS DOUBLE
Sidelock. Automatic ejectors. Double triggers or single trigger (selective or nonselective). Gauges: 12, 16, 20. Bbls.: 25, 27.5, 30 inch; any choke combination. Checkered stock and forend, straight grip standard. Disc.

w/double triggers. . . . . NiB $4077 Ex $2986 Gd $1769
Nonselective single trigger, add $250
Selective single trigger, add $400

MARKOR HAMMERLESS DOUBLE
Boxlock. Non-ejector or ejector. Double triggers. Gauges: 12, 16, 20. Bbls.: 27.5 or 30 inch; any choke combination. Checkered stock and forend, straight grip standard. Disc.

Non-ejector . . . . NiB $1784 Ex $1599 Gd $1188
Ejector model, add 20%

REGENCY HAMMERLESS
DOUBLE. . . . . NiB $4395 Ex $3667 Gd $2971
Anson & Deeley boxlock action. Automatic ejectors. Double triggers. Gauges: 12, 16, 20. Bbls.: 26, 28, 30 inch; any choke combination. Checkered straight-grip stock and forearm. Introduced in 1970 to commemorate the firm's bicentennial, this model has deep scroll engraving and the name Regency inlaid in gold on the rib. Disc.

COLT INDUSTRIES — Hartford, Connecticut

Auto Shotguns were made by Franchi and are similar to corresponding models of that manufacturer.

AUTO SHOTGUN — MAGNUM
Same as Standard Auto except steel receiver, chambered for 3-inch Magnum shells; 30- and 32-inch bbls. in 12 ga., 28-inch in 20 ga. Weight: 12 ga., about 8.25 lbs. Made 1964 to 1966.

w/plain bbl. . . . . NiB $552 Ex $447 Gd $332
w/solid-rib bbl. . . . . NiB $622 Ex $470 Gd $356
w/vent. rib bbl.
NiB $644 Ex $500 Gd $371

AUTO SHOTGUN — MAGNUM CUSTOM
Same as Magnum except has engraved receiver, select walnut stock and forearm. Made 1964 to 66.

w/solid-rib bbl. . . . . NiB $544 Ex $422 Gd $300
w/vent. rib bbl. . . . . NiB $600 Ex $470 Gd $351

AUTO SHOTGUN — ULTRA LIGHT CUSTOM
Same as Standard Auto except has engraved receiver, select walnut stock and forearm. Made 1964 to 1966.

w/solid-rib bbl. . . . . NiB $544 Ex $470 Gd $366
w/vent. rib bbl. . . . . NiB $600 Ex $495 Gd $379

AUTO SHOTGUN — ULTRA LIGHT STANDARD
Recoil operated. Takedown. Alloy receiver. Gauges: 12, 20. Magazine. holds 4 rounds. Bbls.: plain, solid, or vent rib, chrome-lined; 26-inch IC/M choke, 28-inch M/F choke, 30-inch F choke, 32-inch F choke. Weight: 12 ga., about 6.25 lbs. Checkered pistol-grip stock and forearm. Made 1964 to 1966.

w/plain bbl. . . . . NiB $400 Ex $297 Gd $200
w/solid rib bbl. . . . . NiB $450 Ex $344 Gd $250
w/vent. rib bbl. . . . . NiB $450 Ex $344 Gd $250

CUSTOM HAMMERLESS DOUBLE . . . . . . NiB $766 Ex $509 Gd $446
Boxlock. Double triggers. Auto ejectors. Gauges: 12 Mag., 16. Bbls.: 26-inch IC/M; 28-inch M/F; 30-inch F/F. Weight: 12 ga., about 7.5 lbs. Checkered pistol-grip stock and beavertail forearm. Made in 1961.

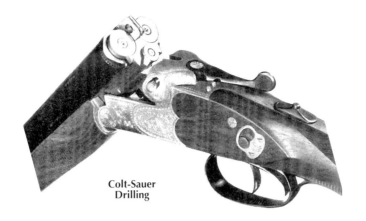

Colt-Sauer
Drilling

COLTSMAN PUMP
SHOTGUN . . . . **NiB $489 Ex $355 Gd $269**
Takedown. Gauges: 12, 16, 20. Magazine holds 4 rounds. Bbls.: 26-inch IC, 28-inch M/F choke, 30-inch F choke. Weight: About 6 lbs. Plain pistol-grip stock and forearm. Made 1961 to 1965 by Manufrance.

CUSTOM PUMP . . . . **NiB $500 Ex $377 Gd $286**
Same as Standard Pump shotgun except has checkered stock, vent-rib bbl. Weight: About 6.5 lbs. Made 1961 to 1963 by Manufrance.

SAUER DRILLING . . . . **NiB $4466 Ex $3778 Gd $2360**
3-bbl. combination gun. Boxlock. Set rifle trigger. Tang bbl. selector, automatic rear sight positioner. 12 ga. over .30-06 or .243 rifle bbl. 25-inch bbls., F/M choke. Weight: About 8 lbs. Folding leaf rear sight, blade front w/brass bead. Checkered pistol-grip stock and beavertail forearm, recoil pad. Made 1974 to 1985 by J. P. Sauer & Sohn, Eckernförde, Germany.

CONNECTICUT VALLEY CLASSICS — Westport, Connecticut

FIELD O/U
Similar to the standard Classic Sporter over/under model except w/30-inch bbls. only and nonreflective matte blued finish on both bbls. and receiver for Waterfowler; other grades w/different degrees of embellishment. Grade I the lowest and Grade III the highest. Made 1993 to 1998.
Grade I . . . . .NiB $2788 Ex $2308 Gd $1683
Grade II . . . . NiB $3166 Ex $2521 Gd $1790
Grade III . . . . NiB $3767 Ex $2866 Gd $1946
Waterfowler
NiB $2581 Ex $2264 Gd $1598

SPORTER 101 O/U
Gauge: 12. 3-inch chamber. Bbls.: 28, 30, or 32 inch w/screw-in

tubes. Weight: 7.75 lbs. Engraved stainless or nitrided receiver; blued bbls. Checkered American black walnut buttstock and forend w/low-luster satin finish. Made from 1993 to 1998.
Classic Sporter . . . . **NiB $1966 Ex $1634 Gd $1388**
Stainless Classic Sporter . . . . . **NiB $2764 Ex $2259 Gd $1744**

CONNENTO/VENTUR — Formerly imported by Ventura, Seal Beach, California

MODEL 51 . . . . .NiB $456 Ex $361 Gd $295
Gauge: 12, 16, 20, 28, and .410. Double-barrel, boxlock action. Bbls: 26, 28, 30, and 32 inches; various chokes; extractors; and double triggers. Checkered walnut stock. Introduced in 1980, disc. 1985.

MODEL 52 . . . . .NiB $610 Ex $433 Gd $329
Same as Model 51 except in 10 ga.

MODEL 53 . . . . .NiB $538 Ex $449 Gd $300
Same as Model 51 except w/scalloped receiver, automatic ejectors, and optional single selective trigger. Disc. in 1985.
Single trigger, add 25%

MODEL 62 . . . . .NiB $1132 Ex $990 Gd $760
Holland & Holland-design sidelock shotgun w/ various barrel lengths and chokes; automatic ejectors; cocking indicators. Floral engraved receiver, checkered walnut stock. Disc. in 1982.

MODEL 64 . . . . .NiB $1388 Ex $1054 Gd $877
Same as Model 62 except deluxe finish. Discontinued.

GRADE I . . . . .NiB $1259 Ex $988 Gd $844
Gauge: 12. Over/under shotgun. Barrels: 32 inches; screw-in choke tubes; high ventilated rib; automatic ejectors; single selective trigger standard. Checkered Monte Carlo walnut stock.

Davidson Model 63B
Double-Barrel Shotgun

MARK II . . . . .NiB $1569 Ex $1236 Gd $1006
Same as Mark I model but w/an extra single barrel and fitted leather case.

MARK III. . . . . .NiB $1788 Ex $1469 Gd $1100
Same as Mark I model but w/finely figured walnut stock and engraved metal.

MARK III Combo . . . . .NiB $2877 Ex $2243 Gd $2071
Same as Mark III model above but w/extra single barrel and fitted leather case.

DAKOTA ARMS, INC. — Sturgis, South Dakota

AMERICAN LEGEND
S/S SHOTGUN . . . . .NiB $16,750 Ex $15,000 Gd $11,550
Limited edition built to customer specifications. Gauge: 20 ga. 27-inch bbl. Double triggers. Selective ejectors. Fully engraved, coin-silver finished receiver w/gold inlays. Weight: 6 lbs. Hand-checkered special selection English walnut stock and forearm. Made from 1996 to 2005.

CLASSIC FIELD GRADE
S/S SHOTGUN . . . . NiB $7566 Ex $6548 Gd $4456
Boxlock. Gauge: 20 ga. 27-inch bbl. w/fixed chokes. Double triggers. Selective ejectors. Color casehardened receiver. Weight: 6 lbs. Checkered English walnut stock and splinter forearm w/hand-rubbed oil finish. Made from 1996 to 1998.

PREMIER GRADE
S/S SHOTGUN . . . . NiB $14,765 Ex $11,466 Gd $9224
Similar to Classic Field Grade model except w/50% engraving coverage. Exhibition grade English walnut stock. Made from 1996 to date.

DARNE S.A. — Saint-Etienne, France

HAMMERLESS DOUBLE-BARREL SHOTGUNS
Sliding-breech action w/fixed bbls. Auto ejectors. Double triggers. Gauges: 12, 16, 20, 28; also 12 and 20 Magnum w/3-inch chambers. Bbls.: 27.5 inch standard, 25.5- to 31.5-inch lengths available; any standard choke combination. Weight: 5.5 to 7 lbs. depending on ga. and bbl. length. Checkered straight grip or pistol-grip stock and forearm. The various models differ in grade of engraving and wood. Manufactured from 1881 to 1979.
Model R11 (Bird Hunter) . . . . NiB $7044 Ex $4698 Gd $2677
Model R15 (Pheasant
  Hunter) . . . . NiB $14,900 Ex $12,785 Gd $10,000
Model R16 (Magnum). . . . . .NiB $3775 Ex $2730 Gd $2167
Model V19
  (Quail Hunter). . . . . NiB $22,000 Ex $17,500 Gd $14,275
Model V22 . . . . NiB $31,000 Ex $26,800 Gd $22,975
Model V Hors Série No. 1. . . . . NiB $77,000 Ex $58,650 Gd $46,790

DAVIDSON GUNS — Manufactured by Fabrica de Armas ILJA, Eibar, Spain
Distributed by Davidson Firearms Co., Greensboro, NC.

MODEL 63B DOUBLE-BARREL
SHOTGUN . . . . .NiB $433 Ex $279 Gd $200
Anson & Deeley boxlock action. Frame engraved and nickel plated. Plain extractors. Auto safety. Double triggers. Gauges: 12, 16, 20, 28, .410. Bbl. lengths: 25 (.410 only), 26, 28, 30 inches (latter 12 ga. only). Chokes: IC/ M, M/F, F/F. Weight: 5 lbs., 11 oz. (.410) to 7 lbs. (12 ga.). Checkered pistol-grip stock and forearm of European walnut. Made in 1963. Disc.

MODEL 63B MAGNUM
Similar to standard Model 63B except chambered for 10 ga. 3.5-inch, 12 and 20 ga. 3-inch Magnum shells; 10 ga. has 32-inch bbls., choked F/F. Weight: 10 lb., 10 oz. Made from 1963. Disc.
12 and 20 ga. Magnum . . . . . . .NiB $455 Ex $300 Gd $210
10 ga. Magnum. . . . . NiB $477 Ex $369 Gd $230

MODEL 69SL DOUBLE-BARREL
SHOTGUN . . . . NiB $455 Ex $400 Gd $270
Sidelock action w/detachable sideplates, engraved and nickel plated. Plain extractors. Auto safety. Double triggers. 12 and 20 ga. Bbls.: 26-inch IC/M, 28-inch M/F. Weight: 12 ga; 7 lbs.; 20 ga., 6.5 lbs. Pistol-grip stock and forearm of European walnut, checkered. Made from 1963 to 1976.

MODEL 73 STAGECOACH
HAMMER DOUBLE . . . . .NiB $331 Ex $229 Gd $130
Sidelock action w/detachable sideplates and exposed hammers. Plain extractors. Double triggers. Gauges: 12, 20. 3-inch chambers. 20-inch bbls., M/F chokes. Weight: 7 lbs., 12 ga.; 6.5 lbs., 20 ga. Checkered pistol-grip stock and forearm. Made from 1976. Disc.

DIAMOND WOBURN, MA.
Currently imported by ADCO Sales, Inc., Woburn, MA.
Company established circa 1981, all guns manufactured in Turkey.

GOLD SERIES (SEMIAUTOMATIC) . . . . . . NiB $354 Ex $280 Gd $175
12 gauge, 3-inch chamber. Gas operated. Bbl. 24 (slug) or 28 inches. Ventilated rib w/three choke tubes. Semi-humpback design, anodized alloy frame, gold etching. Rotary bolt. Black synthetic or checkered Turkish walnut forearm and stock with recoil pad. Value $50 less for slug version.

IMPERIAL SERIES . . . . .NiB $475 Ex $345 Gd $265
Gauge: 12 (3.5-inch) or 20 (3-inch). Bbl.: 24 (12 ga. slug), 26 (20

Fox Model B

ga.), or 28 inches; vent. rib, rotary bilateral bolt, deluxe checkered stock and forearm. Imported 2003.

ELITE SERIES . . . . NiB $445 Ex $323 Gd $200
Gauge: 12. 3-inch chamber. Bbl.: 22 (slug), 24, 26, or 28 inches; vent. rib, deluxe checkered walnut stock and forearm. Imported 2001. Deduct $50 for slug model.

PANTHER SERIES . . . . NiB $415 Ex $338 Gd $200
Gauge: 12. 3-inch chamber. Gas operated. Black synthetic stock and forearm. Bbl.: 20 (slug or regular) or 28 inches. Imported 2002.
Walnut stock and forearm, add $75
Slug version. . . . . .deduct $50

MARINER . . . . NiB $338 Ex $198 Gd $110
Gauge: 12. 3-inch chamber. Gas operated. Bbl.: 20 (slug) or 22 inches. Vent. rib. Anodized alloy frame and receiver, satin silver finish. Checkered walnut stock and forearm. Imported 2002.
Slug model, deduct $50

GOLD ELITE SERIES
(SLIDE-ACTION) . . . . NiB $354 Ex $260 Gd $200
12 ga. 3-inch chamber. Bbl. 24 (slug with open sights) or 28 inches; vent. rib. Semi-humpback design. Anodized alloy frame, synthetic black or Turkish walnut stock and forearm. Weight: 7 lbs. Imported 2001. Value $40 less for synthetic stock.

EXCEL ARMS OF AMERICA — Gardner, MA

SERIES 100 O/U SHOTGUN
Gauge: 12. Single selective trigger. Selective auto ejectors. Hand-checkered European walnut stock w/full pistol grip, tulip forend. Black metal finish. Chambered for 2.75-inch shells (Model 103 for 3-inch). Weight: 6.88 to 7.88 lbs. Disc 1988.
Model 101 w/26-inch bbl., IC/M . . .NiB $465 Ex $367 Gd $266
Model 102 w/28-inch bbl., IC/M . . .NiB $465 Ex $367 Gd $266
Model 103 w/30-inch bbl., M/F . . . .NiB $465 Ex $367 Gd $266
Model 104 w/28-inch bbl., IC/M . . .NiB $465 Ex $367 Gd $266
Model 105, w/28-inch bbl.,
  5 choke tubes. . . . . NiB $645 Ex $480 Gd $387
Model 106, w/28-inch bbl.,
  5 choke tubes. . . . . NiB $776 Ex $689 Gd $558
Model 107 Trap, w/30-inch bbl.,
  Full or 5 tubes . . . . NiB $776 Ex $689 Gd $558

SERIES 200 SIDE-BY-SIDE
SHOTGUN . . . . .NiB $667 Ex $496 Gd $368
Gauges: 12, 20, 28, and .410. Bbls.: 26, 27, and 28 inch various choke combinations. Weight: 7 lbs. average. American or European-style stock and forend. Made from 1985 to 1987.

SERIES 300 O/U
SHOTGUN . . . . .NiB $1328 Ex $1133 Gd $1033
Gauge: 12. Bbls.: 26, 28, and 29 inch. Nonglare black-chrome

matte finish. Weight: 7 lbs. average. Selective auto ejectors, engraved receiver. Hand-checkered European walnut stock and forend. Made from 1985 to 1986.

FABARM — Brescia, Italy

Currently imported by Heckler & Koch, Inc., of Sterling, VA, previously by Ithaca Acquisition Corp., St. Lawrence Sales, Inc., and Beeman Precision Arms, Inc.

See current listings under Heckler & Koch.

FIAS — Fabrica Italiana Armi Sabatti Gardone Val Trompia, Italy

GRADE I O/U
Boxlock. Single selective trigger. Gauges: 12, 20, 28, .410. 3-inch chambers. Bbls.: 26-inch IC/M; 28-inch M/F; screw-in choke tubes. Weight: 6.5 to 7.5 lbs. Checkered European walnut stock and forearm. Engraved receiver and blued finish.
12 ga. model. . . . . NiB $587 Ex $480 Gd $355
20 ga. model. . . . . NiB $633 Ex $512 Gd $367
28 ga. and .410. . . . . NiB $800 Ex $665 Gd $457

FOX SHOTGUNS — Philadelphia, PA

Made by A. H. Fox Gun Co., 1903 to 1930, since then by Savage Arms, originally of Utica, NY, now of Westfield, MA. In 1993, Connecticut Manufacturing Co. of New Britain, CT reintroduced selected models.

Values shown are for 12- and 16-ga. doubles made by A. H. Fox. 20-ga. guns are often valued up to 75% higher. Savage-made Fox models generally bring prices 25% lower. With the exception of Model B, production of Fox shotguns was discontinued around1942.

MODEL B HAMMERLESS DOUBLE . . . . NiB $523 Ex $387 Gd $244
Boxlock. Double triggers. Plain extractor. Gauges: 12, 16, 20, .410. 24- to 30-inch bbls., vent. rib on current production; chokes: M/F, C/M, F/F (.410 only). Weight: About 7.5 lbs., 12 ga. Checkered pistol-grip stock and forend. Made about 1940 to 1985.

MODEL B-DE . . . . NiB $645 Ex $476 Gd $351
Same as Model B-ST except frame finished in satin chrome, select walnut buttstock w/checkered pistol grip, and beavertail forearm. Made from 1965 to 1966.

MODEL B-DL . . . . NiB $678 Ex $558 Gd $421
Same as Model B-ST except frame finished in satin chrome, select walnut buttstock w/checkered pistol-grip, side panels, beavertail forearm. Made from 1962 to 1966.

MODEL B-SE . . . . .NiB $922 Ex $700 Gd $531
Same as Model B except has selective ejectors and single trigger. Made from 1966 to 1989.

MODEL B-ST . . . . NiB $644 Ex $475 Gd $350
Same as Model B except has nonselective single trigger. Made from 1955-66.

HAMMERLESS DOUBLE-BARREL SHOTGUNS
The higher grades have the same general specifications as the standard Sterlingworth model w/differences chiefly in workmanship and materials. Higher grade models are stocked in fine select walnut; quantity and quality of engraving increases w/ grade and price. Except for Grade A, all others have auto ejectors.

Grade A . . . . .NiB $3160 Ex $1641 Gd $1895
Grade AE .NiB $3598 Ex $2977 Gd $2110
Grade BE .NiB $4962 Ex $3988 Gd $2860
Grade CE .NiB $6200 Ex $5110 Gd $3628
Grade DE . . . . NiB $12,779 Ex $11,360 Gd $10,475
Grade FE . . . . NiB $22,679 Ex $18,960 Gd $13,000
Grade XE .NiB $8634 Ex $7321 Gd $4208
Kautzy selective single trigger, add. $400
Vent. rib, add $500
Beavertail forearm, add $300
20 ga. model, add. 60%

SINGLE-BARREL TRAP GUNS
Boxlock. Auto ejector. 12 ga. only. 30- or 32-inch vent. rib bbl. Weight: 7.5 to 8 lbs. Trap-style stock and forearm of select walnut, checkered, recoil pad optional. The four grades differ chiefly in quality of wood and engraving; Grade M guns, built to order, have finest Circassian walnut. Stock and receiver are elaborately engraved and inlaid w/gold. Disc. 1942. Note: In 1932, the Fox Trap Gun was redesigned and those manufactured after that date have a stock w/full pistol grip and Monte Carlo comb; in the same time frame was changed to permit the rib line to extend across it to the rear.

Grade JE . . . . NiB $3990 Ex $2367 Gd $2031
Grade KE . . . . NiB $5366 Ex $4979 Gd $4000
Grade LE . . . . NiB $6778 Ex $4789 Gd $3760
Grade ME . . . . NiB $15,975 Ex $12,880 Gd $9355

SKEETER DOUBLE-BARREL
SHOTGUN . . . . NiB $4990 Ex $4078 Gd $2855
Boxlock. Gauge: 12 or 20. Bbls.: 28 inches w/full-length vent. rib. Weight: About. 7 lbs. Buttstock and beavertail forend of select American walnut, finely checkered. Soft rubber recoil pad, ivory bead sights. Made in early 1930s.

STERLINGWORTH DELUXE
Same general specifications as Sterlingworth except 32-inch bbl. also available, recoil pad, ivory bead sights.
w/extractors . . . . NiB $2187 Ex $1654 Gd $1100
w/ejectors . . . . NiB $2370 Ex $1979 Gd $1466
20 ga., add 45%

STERLINGWORTH HAMMERLESS DOUBLE
Boxlock. Double triggers (Fox-Kautzky selective single trigger extra). Plain extractors (auto ejectors extra). Gauges: 12,16, 20. Bbl. 26, 28, 30 inch; chokes F/F, M/F, C/M (any combination of C/F choke borings was available at no extra cost). Weight: 12 ga., 6.88 to 8.25 lbs.; 16 ga., 6 to 7 lbs.; 20 ga., 5.75 to 6.75 lbs. Checkered pistol-grip stock and forearm.

w/extractors . . . . NiB $1800 Ex $1489 Gd $1000
w/ejectors . . . . NiB $2170 Ex $1770 Gd $1254
Selective single trigger, add 25%

STERLINGWORTH SKEET AND UPLAND GUN
Same general specifications as the standard Sterlingworth except has 26- or 28-inch bbls. w/skeet boring only, straight-grip stock. Weight: 7 lbs. (12 ga.).
w/extractors . . . . NiB $2588 Ex $2066 Gd $1489
w/ejectors . . . . NiB $3000 Ex $2469 Gd $1785
20 ga., add 45%

SUPER HE GRADE . . . . NiB $5863 Ex $4791 Gd $3310
Long-range gun made in 12 ga. only (chambered for 3-inch shells on order), 30- or 32-inch full choke bbls., auto ejectors standard. Weight: 8.75 to 9.75 lbs. General specifications same as standard Sterlingworth.

HAMMERLESS DOUBLE-BARREL SHOTGUNS
High-grade doubles similar to the original Fox models. 20 ga. only. 26- 28- or 30-inch bbls. Double triggers, automatic safety, and ejectors. Weight: 5.5 to 7 lbs. Custom Circassian walnut stock w/hand-rubbed oil finish. Custom stock configuration: straight, semi- or full pistol-grip stock w/traditional pad, hard rubber plate, checkered or skeleton butt; Schnabel, splinter, or beavertail forend. Made 1993 to date.
CE grade . . . . NiB $9221 Ex $6855 Gd $4900
XE grade . . . . NiB $9066 Ex $7221 Gd $5054
DE grade . . . . NiB $13,788 Ex $11,650 Gd $7900
FE grade . . . . .NiB $18,977 Ex $15,220 Gd $11,760
Exhibition grade . . . . . . .NiB $27,480 Ex $22,760 Gd $14,990

LUIGI FRANCHI S.P.A. — Brescia, Italy

MODEL 48/AL ULTRA LIGHT SHOTGUN
Recoil operated, takedown, hammerless shotgun w/tubular magazine. Gauges: 12 or 20 (2.75-inch); 12-ga. Magnum (3-inch chamber). Bbls.: 24 to 32 inch w/various choke combinations. Weight: 5 lbs., 2 oz. (20 ga.) to 6.25 lbs. (12 ga.). Checkered pistol-grip walnut stock and forend w/high-gloss finish.
Standard model. . . . . NiB $779 Ex $554 Gd $430
Hunter or Magnum models . . . NiB $977 Ex $580 Gd $476

MODEL 500 STANDARD
AUTOLOADER. . . . . .NiB $400 Ex $288 Gd $190
Gas-operated. 12 gauge. Four round magazine. Bbls.: 26-, 28-inch; vent rib; IC, M, IM, F chokes. Weight: About 7 lbs. Checkered pistol-grip stock and forearm. Made from 1976 to 1980.

MODEL 520 DELUXE . . . . NiB $478 Ex $355 Gd $279
Same as Model 500 except higher grade w/engraved receiver. Made from 1975 to 1979.

MODEL 520 ELDORADO GOLD . . . . . . NiB $1088 Ex $877 Gd $743
Same as Model 520 except custom grade w/engraved and gold-inlaid receiver, finer quality wood. Intro. 1977.

MODEL 610VS SEMIAUTOMATIC SHOTGUN
Gas-operated Variopress system adj. to function w/2.75- or 3-inch shells. 12 ga. 4-round magazine. 26- or 28-inch vent. rib bbls. w/ Franchoke tubes. Weight: 7 lbs., 2 oz. 47.5 inches overall. Alloy receiver w/4-lug rotating bolt and loaded chamber indicator. Checkered European walnut buttstock and forearm w/satin finish. Imported from 1997.

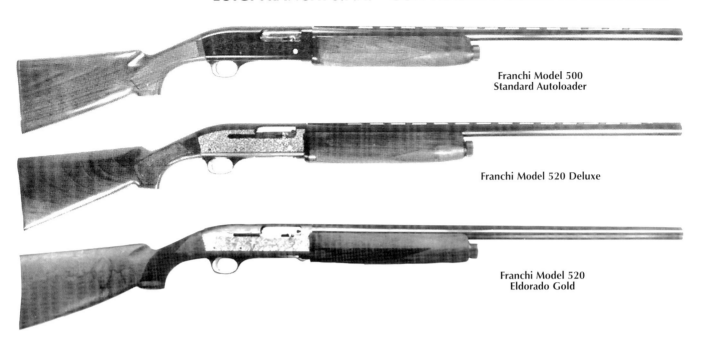

Franchi Model 500
Standard Autoloader

Franchi Model 520 Deluxe

Franchi Model 520
Eldorado Gold

Standard model. . . . . NiB $766 Ex $600 Gd $445
Engraved model . . . . NiB $800 Ex $655 Gd $500

MODEL 612 VARIOPRESS AUTOLOADING SHOTGUN
Gauge: 12 ga. only. 24- to 28-inch bbl. 45 to 49 inches overall. Weight: 6.8 to 7 lbs. 5-round magazine. Bead type sights with C, IC, M chokes. Blued, matte, or Advantage camo finish. Imported from 1999 to 2004.

w/satin walnut stock, blued finish. . . . . NiB $645 Ex $559 Gd $369
w/synthetic stock, matte finish . . . . NiB $665 Ex $590 Gd $400
w/Advantage camo finish . . . . NiB $800 Ex $645 Gd $449
Defense model. . . . . NiB $600 Ex $469 Gd $360
Sporting model. . . . . NiB $966 Ex $733 Gd $544

MODEL 620 VARIOPRESS AUTOLOADING SHOTGUN
Gauge: 20 ga. Only. 24, 26, or 28-inch bbl. 45 to 49 inches overall. Weight: 5.9 to 6.1 lbs. 5-round magazine. Bead type sights with C, IC, M chokes. Satin walnut or Advantage camo stock. Imported from 1999 to 2004.

w/satin walnut stock, matte finish. . . . . NiB $655 Ex $498 Gd $367
w/Advantage camo finish . . . . NiB $790 Ex $554 Gd $421
Youth model w/short stock . . . . NiB $615 Ex $490 Gd $379

MODEL 2003 TRAP O/U . . . . NiB $1355 Ex $1109 Gd $1005
Boxlock. Auto ejectors. Selective single trigger. 12 ga. Bbls.: 30, 32 inch (IM/F, F/F) high vent. rib. Weight (w/30-inch bbl.): 8.25 lbs. Checkered walnut beavertail forearm and stock w/straight or Monte Carlo comb, recoil pad. Luggage-type carrying case. Introduced 1976. Disc.

MODEL 2004 TRAP SINGLE
BARREL TRAP . . . . NiB $1366 Ex $1288 Gd $915
Same as Model 2003 except single bbl., 32 or 34 inch. Full choke. Weight (w/32-inch bbl.): 8.25 lbs. Introduced 1976. Disc.

MODEL 2005 COMBINATION TRAP. . . . . . . NiB $1977 Ex $1760 Gd $1233
Model 2004/2005 type gun w/two sets of bbls., single and over/under. Introduced 1976. Disc.

MODEL 2005/3 COMBINATION TRAP . . . . . . NiB $2660 Ex $2175 Gd $1648
Model 2004/2005 type gun w/three sets of bbls., any combination of single and over/under. Introduced 1976. Disc.

MODEL 3000/2 COMBINATION TRAP . . . . NiB $2876 Ex $2599 Gd $1879
Boxlock. Automatic ejectors. Selective single trigger. 12 ga. only. Bbls.: 32-inch over/under choked F/IM, 34-inch underbarrel M choke; high vent. rib. Weight (w/32-inch bbls.): 8 lbs., 6 oz. Choice of six different castoff buttstocks. Introduced 1979. Disc.

ALCIONE CLASSIC . . . . NiB $763 Ex $633 Gd $544
O/U. Boxlock. Auto ejectors. Single select trigger. 12 ga. only. 26- or 28-in. bbl. lengths, choke tubes. Weight: 7.5 lbs. Blue non-engraved receiver. Checkered stock and forearm. Made from 2004 to 2005.

ALCIONE FIELD (97-12 IBS) O/U
Similar to the Standard Alcione model except w/nickel-finished receiver. 26- or 28-inch bbls. w/Franchoke tubes. Imported from 1998 to 2005.
Standard Field model . . . . NiB $1263 Ex $1009 Gd $700
SL Field model (w/sideplates, disc.) . . . . . NiB $1296 Ex $1007 Gd $865

ALCIONE HAMMERLESS DOUBLE. . . . . . NiB $763 Ex $633 Gd $544
Boxlock. Anson & Deeley system action. Auto ejectors. Double triggers. 12 ga. Various bbl. lengths, chokes, weights. Checkered straight-grip stock and forearm. Made from 1940-50.

ALCIONE O/U SHOTGUN
Hammerless takedown shotgun w/engraved receiver. Selective single trigger and ejectors. 12 ga. 3-inch chambers. Bbls.: 26-inch (IC/M) 28-inch (M/F). Weight: 6.75 lbs. Checkered French walnut buttstock and forend. Imported from Italy. 1982 to 1989.
Standard model. . . . . NiB $755 Ex $648 Gd $479
SL model (disc. 1986) . . . . NiB $1290 Ex $1077 Gd $800

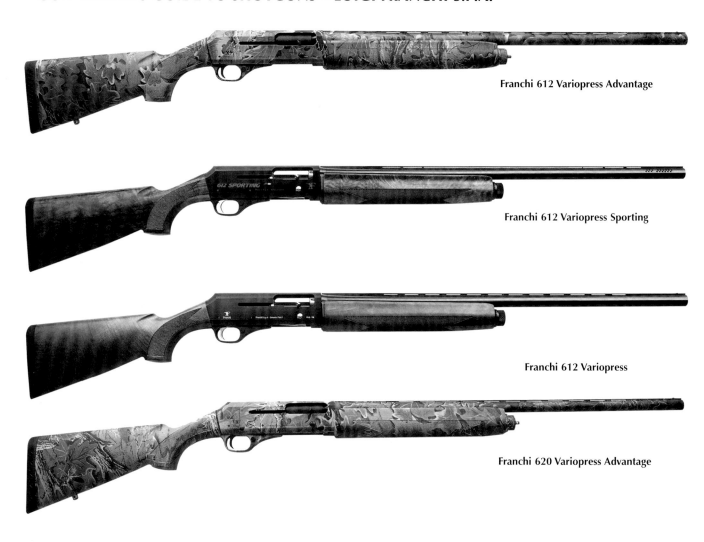

Franchi 612 Variopress Advantage

Franchi 612 Variopress Sporting

Franchi 612 Variopress

Franchi 620 Variopress Advantage

ALCIONE SPORT (SL IBS) O/U . . . . . **NiB $1567 Ex $1380 Gd $1134**
Similar to the Alcione Field model except chambered for 2.75- or 3-inch shells. Ported 29-inch bbls. w/target vent. rib and Franchoke tubes.

ALCIONE SX O/U . . . .**NiB $1540 Ex $1060 Gd $700**
Removable engraved sideplates. 12 ga. only. 26- or 28-in. vent. rib bbls. w/choke tubes. Weight: 7.4 lbs. Imported from 2001 to 2005.

ALCIONE TITANIUM O/U . . . .**NiB $1540 Ex $1060 Gd $700**
Aluminum alloy receiver w/titanium inserts. Removable sideplates. 12 or 20 ga. 26- or 28-inch. vent. rib bbls. w/choke tubes. Weight: 6.8 lbs. Imported from 2002 to 2005.

ALCIONE 2000 SX O/U SHOTGUN . . . . . . **NiB $1790 Ex $1388 Gd $1100**
Similar to the Standard Alcione model except w/silver-finished receiver, gold inlays. 28-inch bbls. w/Franchoke tubes. Weight: 7.25 lbs. Imported from 1996 to 1997.

ARISTOCRAT DELUXE AND SUPREME GRADES
Available in Field, Skeet, and Trap models w/the same general specifications as standard guns of these types. Deluxe and Supreme Grades are of higher quality w/stock and forearm of select walnut, elaborate relief engraving on receiver, trigger guard, tang, and top lever. Supreme has game birds inlaid in gold. Made from 1960 to 1966.
Deluxe grade . . . . **NiB $1077 Ex $844 Gd $657**
Supreme grade . . . . **NiB $1577 Ex $1340 Gd $1098**

ARISTOCRAT FIELD MODEL O/U . . . . . **NiB $754 Ex $600 Gd $434**
Boxlock. Selective auto ejectors. Selective single trigger. 12 ga. Bbls.: 26-inch IC/M; 28- and 30-inch M/F choke, vent. rib. Weight (w/26-inch bbls.): 7 lbs. Checkered pistol-grip stock and forearm. Made from 1960 to 1969.

ARISTOCRAT IMPERIAL AND MONTE CARLO GRADES
Custom guns made in Field, Skeet, and Trap models w/the same general specifications as standard for these types. Imperial and Monte Carlo grades are of highest quality w/stock and forearm

Franchi 620 Variopress

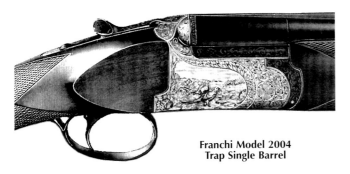

**Franchi Model 2004
Trap Single Barrel**

of select walnut, fine engraving—elaborate on latter grade. Made 1967 to 1969.
Imperial grade . . . . NiB $4134 Ex $2570 Gd $2160
Monte Carlo grade . . . . NiB $3677 Ex $2920 Gd $2100

ARISTOCRAT MAGNUM MODEL. . . . . . NiB $765 Ex $557 Gd $469
Same as Field Model except chambered for 3-inch shells, has 32-inch bbls. choked F/F; stock has recoil pad. Weight: About 8 lbs. Made from 1962 to 1965.

ARISTOCRAT SILVER KING . . . . . NiB $888 Ex $712 Gd $559
Available in Field, Magnum, Meet, and Trap models w/the same general specifications as standard guns of these types. Silver King has stock and forearm of select walnut, more elaborately engraved silver-finished receiver. Made 1962 to 1969.

ARISTOCRAT SKEET MODEL . . . . NiB $866 Ex $754 Gd $544
Same general specifications as Field Model except made only w/26-inch vent. rib bbls. w/SK chokes No. 1 and No. 2, skeet-style stock and forearm. Weight: About 7.5 lbs. Later production had wider (10mm) rib. Made from 1960 to 1969.

ARISTOCRAT TRAP MODEL . . . . . NiB $877 Ex $754 Gd $561
Same general specifications as Field Model except made only w/30-inch vent. rib bbls., M/F choke, trap-style stock w/recoil pad, beavertail forearm. Later production had Monte Carlo comb, 10mm rib. Made from 1960 to 1969.

ASTORE HAMMERLESS DOUBLE . . . . . NiB $1032 Ex $866 Gd $713
Boxlock. Anson & Deeley system action. Plain extractors. Double triggers. 12 ga. Various bbl. lengths, chokes, weights. Checkered straight-grip stock and forearm. Made 1937 to 1960.

ASTORE II . . . . NiB $1389 Ex $1166 Gd $876
Similar to Astore S but not as high grade. Furnished w/either plain

extractors or auto ejectors, double triggers, pistol-grip stock. Bbls.: 27-inch IC/IM; 28-inch M/F chokes. Currently manufactured for Franchi in Spain.

ASTORE 5 . . . . NiB $2458 Ex $1987 Gd $1466
Same as Astore except has higher grade wood, fine engraving. Automatic ejectors, single trigger, 28-inch bbl. M/F or IM/F chokes are standard on current production. Disc.

DE LUXE MODEL PRITI O/U . . . . NiB $400 Ex $320 Gd $210
Boxlock. 12 or 20 ga. only. 26- or 28-in. vent. rib bbls. w/choke tubes. Single trigger. Weight: 7.4 lbs. Imported from 1988 to 1989.

RENAISSANCE FIELD O/U . . . . NiB $1430 Ex $1240 Gd $680
Boxlock. Blued receiver. 12, 20, or 28 ga. 26- or 28-inch. vent. rib. bbls. w/choke tubes. Oil finish walnut stock w/Twin Shock recoil pad. Weight: 5.5 to 6.2 lbs. Imported from 2006 to 2010.
Classic (gold trigger, inlays). . . . . NiB $1560 Ex $1230 Gd $800
Classic Combo (two bbl. set) . . NiB $2330 Ex $1700 Gd $1200
Elite (engraved w/gold inlays) . . . NiB $2000 Ex $1500 Gd $830
Sporting (30-in. ported bbls.) . . . NiB $1930 Ex $1460 Gd $830

VELOCE O/U . . . . NiB $1250 Ex $1000 Gd $740
Aluminum engraved receiver w/gold inlays. 20 or 28 ga. 26- or 28-in. vent. rib bbls. w/choke tubes. Pistol or straight deluxe oil finish stock. Weight: 5.5 to 5.8 lbs. Imported from 2001 to 2005.
Grade II (semi-pistol grip). . . . NiB $1760 Ex $1240 Gd $900
Squire (two bbl. set) . . . . NiB $2070 Ex $1500 Gd $910

STANDARD MODEL AUTOLOADER
Recoil operated. Light alloy receiver. Gauges: 12, 20. 4-round magazine. Bbls.: 26, 28, 30 inch; plain, solid, or vent. rib, IC/M/F chokes. Weight: 12 ga., about 6.25 lbs.; 20 ga., 5.13 lbs. Checkered pistol-grip stock and forearm. Made from 1950. Disc.
w/plain bbl. . . . . NiB $490 Ex $335 Gd $260
w/solid rib . . . . NiB $550 Ex $512 Gd $339
w/vent rib . . . . NiB $560 Ex $489 Gd $368

CROWN, DIAMOND, AND IMPERIAL GRADE
Same general specifications as Standard Model except these are custom guns of the highest quality. Crown grade has hunting scene engraving, Diamond grade has silver-inlaid scroll engraving, Imperial grade has elaborately engraved hunting scenes w/figures inlaid in gold. Stock and forearm of fancy walnut. Made 1954 to 1975.
Crown grade . . . . NiB $1670 Ex $1496 Gd $1212
Diamond grade . . . . NiB $2044 Ex $1760 Gd $1233
Imperial grade . . . . NiB $2480 Ex $2239 Gd $1799

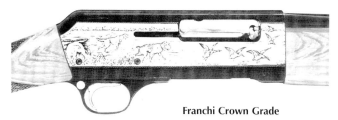

Franchi Crown Grade

Franchi Diamond Grade

Franchi Eldorado

Franchi Astore 5

STANDARD MODEL MAGNUM
Same general specifications as Standard model except has 3-inch chamber, 32-inch (12 ga.) or 28-inch (20 ga.) F choke bbl., recoil pad. Weight: 12 ga., 8.25 lbs.; 20 ga., 6 lbs. Formerly designated Superange Model. Made from 1954 to 1988.
w/plain bbl. . . . . .NiB $500 Ex $412 Gd $286
w/vent. rib . . . . NiB $577 Ex $468 Gd $360

DYNAMIC-12
Same general specifications and appearance as Standard Model except 12 ga. only, has heavier steel receiver. Weight: About 7.25 lbs. Made from 1965 to 1972.
w/plain bbl. . . . . NiB $522 Ex $430 Gd $331
w/vent. rib . . . . NiB $550 Ex $433 Gd $330

DYNAMIC-12 SLUG GUN . . . . . . NiB $578 Ex $490 Gd $354
Same as standard gun except 12 ga. only, has heavier steel receiver. Made 1965 to 1972.

DYNAMIC-12 SKEET GUN . . . . . . NiB $677 Ex $549 Gd $456
Same general specifications and appearance as Standard model except has heavier steel receiver, made only in 12 ga. w/26-inch vent. rib bbl., SK choke, stock and forearm of extra fancy walnut. Made from 1965 to 1972.

ELDORADO MODEL . . . . NiB $588 Ex $370 Gd $355
Same general specifications as Standard model except highest grade w/gold-filled engraving, stock and forearm of select walnut, vent. rib bbl. only. Made from 1954 to 1975.

FALCONET INTERNATIONAL
SKEET MODEL . . . . NiB $1163 Ex $977 Gd $800
Similar to Standard Skeet model but higher grade. Made 1970 to 1974.

FALCONET INTERNATIONAL
TRAP MODEL . . . . NiB $1165 Ex $980 Gd $803
Similar to Standard model but higher grade; w/straight or Monte Carlo comb stock. Made from 1970 to 1974.

FALCONET O/U FIELD MODELS
Boxlock. Auto ejectors. Selective single trigger. Gauges: 12, 16, 20, 28, .410. Bbls.: 24, 26, 28, 30 inch; vent. rib. Chokes: C/IC, IC/M, M/F. Weight: About 6 lbs. Engraved lightweight alloy receiver, light-colored in Buckskin model, blued in Ebony model, pickled silver in Silver model. Checkered walnut stock and forearm. Made from 1968 to 1975.
Buckskin or Ebony model . . . . . . NiB $655 Ex $460 Gd $449
Silver model . . . . NiB $655 Ex $460 Gd $449

FALCONET STANDARD SKEET MODEL . . . . NiB $1055 Ex $876 Gd $690
Same general specifications as Field models except made only w/26-inch bbls. w/SK chokes No. 1 and No. 2, wide vent. rib, color casehardened receiver, skeet-style stock and forearm. Weight: 12 ga., about 7.75 lbs. Made from 1970 to 1974.

FALCONET STANDARD TRAP MODEL . . . . NiB $1366 Ex $965 Gd $744
Same general specifications as Field models except made only in 12 ga. w/30-inch bbls., choked M/F, wide vent. rib, color casehardened receiver, Monte Carlo trap style stock and forearm, recoil pad. Weight: About 8 lbs. Made from 1970 to 1974.

GAS-OPERATED SEMIAUTOMATIC SHOTGUN
Gas-operated, takedown, hammerless shotgun w/tubular magazine. 12 ga. w/2.75-inch chamber. 5-round magazine. Bbls.: 24 to 30 inches w/vent. rib. Weight: 7.5 lbs. Gold-plated trigger. Checkered pistol-grip stock and forend of European walnut. Imported from Italy 1985 to 1990.
Prestige model . . . . NiB $677 Ex $456 Gd $449
Elite model . . . . NiB $688 Ex $571 Gd $388

HAMMERLESS SIDELOCK DOUBLES
Hand-detachable locks. Self-opening action. Auto ejectors. Double triggers or single trigger. Gauges: 12, 16, 20. Bbl. lengths, chokes, weights according to customer specifications. Checkered stock and forend, straight or pistol grip. Made in six grades—Condor, Imperiale, Imperiale S, Imperiale Montecarlo No. 5, Imperiale

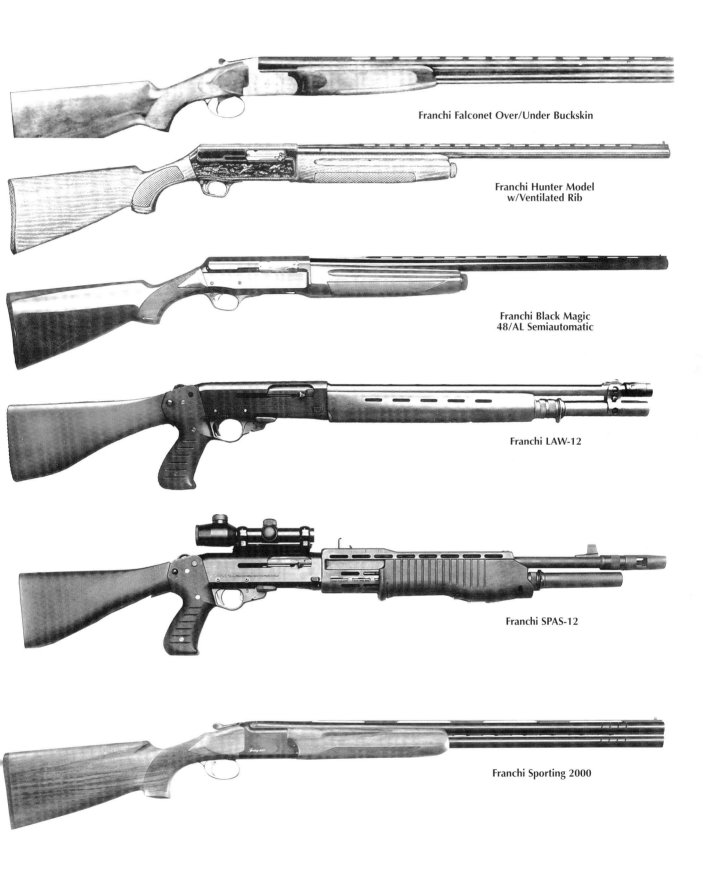

Franchi Falconet Over/Under Buckskin

Franchi Hunter Model
w/Ventilated Rib

Franchi Black Magic
48/AL Semiautomatic

Franchi LAW-12

Franchi SPAS-12

Franchi Sporting 2000

Montecarlo No. 11, Imperiale Montecarlo Extra—which differ chiefly in overall quality, engraving, grade of wood, checkering, etc.; general specifications are the same. Only the Imperial Montecarlo Extra Grade is currently manufactured.

Condor grade . . . . NiB $7897 Ex $6200 Gd $4978
Imperiale, Imperiales grades . . . . NiB $11,776 Ex $9899 Gd $7217
Imperiale Monte Carlo
   grades No. 5, 11 . . . . NiB $32,766 Ex $25,777 Gd $21,989
Imperiale Monte Carlo Extra grade . . . . . Custom only. Prices start at $110,000

HUNTER MODEL
Same general specifications as Standard model except higher grade w/engraved receiver; w/ribbed bbl. only. Made from 1950 to 1990.

w/solid rib . . . . NiB $500 Ex $390 Gd $322
w/vent rib . . . . NiB $616 Ex $488 Gd $400

HUNTER MODEL MAGNUM . . . . NiB $544 Ex $454 Gd $330
Same as Standard Model Magnum except higher grade w/engraved receiver, vent rib bbl. only. Formerly designated Wildfowler Model. Made from 1954 to 1973.

PEREGRINE MODEL 400 . . . . NiB $733 Ex $544 Gd $400
Same general specifications as Model 451 except has steel receiver. Weight (w/26.5-inch bbl.): 6 lbs., 15 oz. Made from 1975 to 1978.

PEREGRINE MODEL 451 O/U . . . NiB $605 Ex $451 Gd $267
Boxlock. Lightweight alloy receiver. Automatic ejectors. Selective single trigger. 12 ga. Bbls.: 26.5, 28 inch; choked C/IC, IC/M, M/F; vent. rib. Weight (w/26.5-inch bbls.): 6 lbs., 1 oz. Checkered pistol-grip stock and forearm. Made from 1975 to 1978.

SKEET GUN . . . . NiB $450 Ex $320 Gd $228
Same general specifications and appearance as Standard model except made only w/26-inch vent. rib bbl., SK choke. Stock and forearm of extra fancy walnut. Made from 1972 to 1974.

SLUG GUN . . . . NiB $435 Ex $288 Gd $190
Same as Standard model except has 22-inch plain bbl., Cyl. bore, folding leaf open rear sight, gold bead front sight. Made 1960 to 1990. Disc.

TURKEY GUN . . . . NiB $556 Ex $377 Gd $298
Same as Standard Model Magnum except higher grade w/turkey scene engraved receiver, 12 ga. only, 36-inch matted rib bbl., Extra Full choke. Made from 1963 to 1965.

BLACK MAGIC 48/AL SEMIAUTOMATIC
Similar to the Franchi Model 48/AL except w/Franchoke screw-in tubes and matte black receiver w/Black Magic logo. Gauge: 12 or 20. 2.75-inch chamber. Bbls.: 24, 26, 28 inch; vent. rib; 24-inch rifled slug w/sights. Weight: 5.2 lbs. (20 ga.). Checkered walnut buttstock and forend. Blued finish.

Standard model. . . . . NiB $657 Ex $543 Gd $466
Trap model . . . . NiB $722 Ex $596 Gd $500

FALCONET 2000 O/U . . . . NiB $1355 Ex $1121 Gd $967
Boxlock. Single selective trigger. Selective automatic ejectors. Gauge: 12. 2.75-inch chambers. Bbls.: 26-inch w/Franchoke tubes; IC/M/F. Weight: 6 lbs. Checkered walnut stock and forearm. Engraved silver receiver w/gold-plated game scene. Imported from 1992 to 1993.

LAW-12 SHOTGUN . . . . NiB $689 Ex $454 Gd $377
Similar to the SPAS-12 Model except gas-operated semiautomatic

action only, ambidextrous safety, decocking lever, and adj. sights. Made from 1983 to 1994.

SPAS-12 SHOTGUN
Selective operating system functions as a gas-operated semi-automatic or pump action. Gauge: 12. 2.75-inch chamber. 7-round magazine. Bbl.: 21.5 inches w/cylinder bore and muzzle protector or optional screw-in choke tubes, matte finish. 41 inches overall w/fixed stock. Weight: 8.75 lbs. Blade front sight, aperture rear sight. Folding or black nylon buttstock w/pistol grip and forend, nonreflective anodized finish. Made from 1983 to 1994. Limited importation.

Fixed stock model . . . . NiB $5000 Ex $4500 Gd $2390
Folding stock model . . . . NiB $7000 Ex $6500 Gd $3390
Choke tubes, add $150

SPORTING 2000 O/U . . . . NiB $1376 Ex $1125 Gd $966
Similar to the Franchi Falconet 2000. Boxlock. Single selective trigger. Selective automatic ejectors. Gauge: 12. 2.75-inch chambers. Ported (1992-93) or unported 28-inch bbls. w/vent. rib. Weight: 7.75 lbs. Blued receiver. Bead front sight. Checkered walnut stock and forearm; plastic composition buttplate. Imported from 1992 to 1993 and 1997 to 1998.

AUGUSTE FRANCOTTE & CIE., S.A. — Liège, Belgium

Francotte shotguns for many years were distributed in the US by Abercrombie & Fitch of New York City. This firm has used a series of model designations for Francotte guns that do not correspond to those of the manufacturer. Because so many Francotte owners refer to their guns by the A & F model names and numbers, the A & F series is included in a listing separate from that of the standard Francotte numbers.

BOXLOCK HAMMERLESS DOUBLES
Anson & Deeley system. Side clips. Greener crossbolt on models 6886, 8446, 4996, and 9261; square crossbolt on Model 6930, Greener-Scott crossbolt on Model 8537, Purdey bolt on Models 11/18E and 10/18E/628. Auto ejectors. Double triggers. Made in all standard gauges, barrel lengths, chokes, weights. Checkered stock and forend, straight or pistol grip. The eight models listed vary chiefly in fastenings as described above, finish and engraving, etc.; custom options increase value. Disc.

Model 6886 . . . . NiB $14,688 Ex $13,879 Gd $11,776
Model 8446 (Francotte Special),
   6930, 4996 . . . . NiB $15,889 Ex $14,799 Gd $14,776
Model 8537, 9261
   (Francotte Original), 11/18E . NiB $17,345 Ex $16,221 Gd $14,998
Model 10/18E/628 . . . . NiB $17,998 Ex $16,789 Gd $15,900

BOXLOCK HAMMERLESS DOUBLES – A & F SERIES
Boxlock, Anson & Deeley type. Crossbolt. Sideplate on all except Knockabout Model. Side clips. Auto ejectors. Double triggers. Gauges: 12, 16, 20, 28, .410. Bbls.: 26 to 32 inch in 12 ga., 26 and 28 inch in other ga.; any boring. Weight: 4.75 to 8 lbs. depending on gauge and barrel length. Checkered stock and forend; straight, half, or full pistol grip. The seven grades differ chiefly in overall quality, engraving, grade of wood, checkering, etc.; general specifications are the same. Disc.

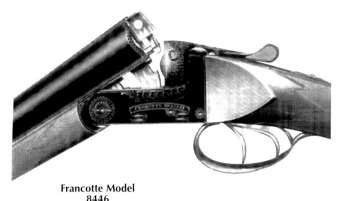

Francotte Model
8446

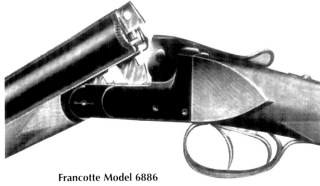

Francotte Model 6886

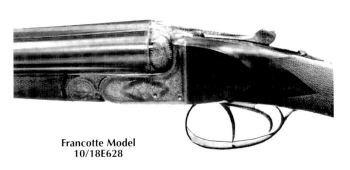

Francotte Model
10/18E628

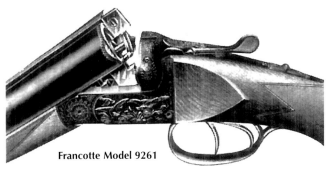

Francotte Model 9261

Jubilee model
No. 14 . . . . NiB $4200 Ex $2633 Gd $1470
Jubilee model
No. 18 . . . . NiB $4687 Ex $3577 Gd $1890
Jubilee model
No. 20 . . . . NiB $5670 Ex $4122 Gd $2250
Jubilee model
No. 25 . . . . NiB $6245 Ex $4738 Gd $2290
Jubilee model
No. 30 . . . . NiB $7832 Ex $6110 Gd $3580
Eagle grade
No. 45 . . . . .NiB $11,100 Ex $8854 Gd $5220
Knockabout
model. . . . . NiB $3377 Ex $2688 Gd $1769
20 ga., add 125%
28 ga. or .410, add 300%

BOXLOCK HAMMERLESS DOUBLES (W/SIDEPLATES)
Anson & Deeley system. Reinforced frame w/side clips.
Purdey-type bolt except on Model 8535, which has Greener
crossbolt. Auto ejectors. Double triggers. Made in all standard
gauges; bbl. lengths, chokes, weights. Checkered stock and
forend, straight or pistol grip. Models 10594, 8535, and 6982
are of equal quality, differing chiefly in style of engraving;
Model 9/40E/38321 is a higher grade gun in all details and has
fine English-style engraving. Built to customer specifications.
Models 10594, 8535, 6982. . . . . . . NiB $6044 Ex $4566 Gd $3177
Model 9/40E/3831 . . . . NiB $6588 Ex $5344 Gd $3889

FINE O/U SHOTGUN . . . . . NiB $10,566 Ex $8978 Gd $6450
Model 9/40.SE. Boxlock, Anson & Deeley system. Auto ejectors.
Double triggers. Made in all standard gauges; bbl. length, boring to
order. Weight: About 6.75 lbs. 12 ga. Checkered stock and forend,
straight or pistol grip. Manufactured to customer specifications. Disc
1990.

FINE SIDELOCK
HAMMERLESS DOUBLE . . . NiB $26,350 Ex $21,789 Gd $15,680
Model 120.HE/328. Automatic ejectors. Double triggers. Made in
all standard ga.; bbl. length, boring, weight to order. Checkered
stock and forend, straight or pistol grip. Manufactured to customer
specifications. Disc. 1990.

HALF-FINE O/U SHOTGUN . . . . NiB $11,656 Ex $9377 Gd $6275
Model SOB.E/11082. Boxlock, Anson & Deeley system. Auto ejectors.
Double triggers. Made in all standard gauges; barrel length, boring to
order. Checkered stock and forend, straight or pistol grip. Note: This model
is similar to No. 9/40.SE except general quality lower. Disc. 1990.

GALEF SHOTGUNS — Manufactured for J. L. Galef & Son, Inc., New York, NY, by M. A. V. I., Gardone F. T., Italy; by Zabala Hermanos, Eiquetta, Spain; and by Antonio Zoli, Gardone V. T., Italy

SILVER SNIPE OVER/UNDER SHOTGUN . . . . . . NiB $699 Ex $598 Gd $445
Boxlock. Plain extractors. Single trigger. Gauges: 12, 20. 3-inch chambers.
Bbls. 26, 28, 30 inch (latter in 12 ga. only); IC/M, M/F chokes; vent. rib.
Weight: (12 ga. w/28-inch bbls.) 6.5 lbs. Checkered walnut pistol-grip
stock and forearm. Introduced by Antonio Zoli in 1968. Disc.

GOLDEN SNIPE . . . . NiB $689 Ex $570 Gd $455
Same as Silver Snipe except has selective automatic ejectors. Made
by Antonio Zoli 1968 to date.

MONTE CARLO TRAP
SINGLE-BARREL SHOTGUN. . . . . .NiB $356 Ex $221 Gd $177
Hammerless. Underlever. Plain extractor. 12 ga. 32-inch bbl., F choke, vent. rib.

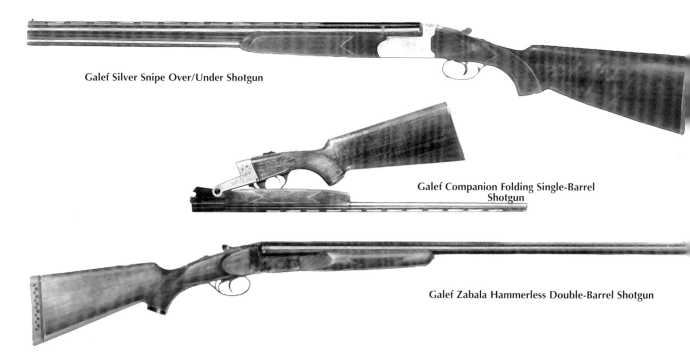

Galef Silver Snipe Over/Under Shotgun

Galef Companion Folding Single-Barrel Shotgun

Galef Zabala Hammerless Double-Barrel Shotgun

Weight: About 8.25 lbs. Checkered pistol-grip stock w/Monte Carlo comb and recoil pad, beavertail forearm. Introduced by M. A. V. I. in 1968. Disc.

SILVER HAWK HAMMERLESS DOUBLE........ NiB $565 Ex $455 Gd $300
Boxlock. Plain extractors. Double triggers. Gauges: 12, 20. 3-inch chambers. Bbls.: 26, 28, 30 inch (latter in 12 ga. only); IC/M, M/F chokes. Weight: (12 ga. w/26-inch bbls.) 6 lbs., 6 oz. Checkered walnut pistol-grip stock and beavertail forearm. Made by Angelo Zoli 1968 to 1972.

COMPANION FOLDING SINGLE-BARREL SHOTGUN
Hammerless. Underlever. Gauges: 12 Mag., 16, 20 Mag., 28, .410. Bbls.: 26 inch (.410 only), 28 inch (12, 16, 20, 28), 30 inch (12 only); F choke; plain or vent. rib. Weight: 4.5 lbs. for .410; 5 lbs., 9 oz. for 12 ga. Checkered pistol-grip stock and forearm. Made by M. A. V. I. from 1968-83.
w/plain bbl. .... NiB $245 Ex $179 Gd $95
w/ventilated rib .... NiB $270 Ex $196 Gd $110

ZABALA HAMMERLESS DOUBLE-BARREL SHOTGUN
Boxlock. Plain extractors. Double triggers. Gauges: 10 Mag., 12 Mag., 16, 20 Mag., 28, .410. Bbls.: 22, 26, 28, 30, 32 inch IC/IC, IC/M, M/F chokes. Weight: (12 ga. w/28-inch bbls.) 7.75 lbs. Checkered walnut pistol-grip stock and beavertail forearm, recoil pad. Made by Zabala from 1972-83.
10 ga. .... NiB $355 Ex $270 Gd $200
Other ga. .... NiB $244 Ex $179 Gd $115

GAMBA — Gardone V. T. (Brescia), Italy

DAYTONA COMPETITION O/U
Boxlock w/Boss-style locking system. Anatomical single trigger; optional adj. single-selective release trigger. Selective automatic ejectors. Gauge: 12 or 20. 2.75- or 3-inch chambers. Bbls.: 26.75-, 28-, 30-, or 32-inch choked SK/SK, IM/F, or M/F. Weight: 7.5 to 8.5 lbs. Black or chrome receiver w/blued bbls. Checkered select walnut stock and forearm w/oil finish. Imported by Heckler & Koch until 1992.
American Trap model............... NiB $2240 Ex $1680 Gd $1021

Pigeon, Skeet, Trap models .... NiB $1323 Ex $1078 Gd $877
Sporting model .... NiB $5678 Ex $4498 Gd $3123
Sideplate model ....NiB $11,789 Ex $9809 Gd $5977
Engraved models........ NiB $13,788 Ex $10,666 Gd $7477
Sidelock model .... .NiB $28,560 Ex $23,778 Gd $19,580

GARBI SHOTGUNS — Eibar, Spain

MODEL 100
SIDELOCK SHOTGUN ...... NiB $5700 Ex $3433 Gd $2433
Gauges: 12, 16, 20, and 28. Bbls.: 25, 28, 30 inch. Action: Holland & Holland pattern sidelock; automatic ejectors and double trigger. Weight: 5 lbs., 6 oz. to 7 lbs., 7 oz. English-style straight-grip stock w/fine-line hand-checkered butt; classic forend. Made from 1985 to date.
MODEL 101
SIDELOCK SHOTGUN ...... NiB $6788 Ex $4331 Gd $3000
Same general specifications as Model 100 above except the sidelocks are handcrafted w/hand-engraved receiver; select walnut straight-grip stock.

MODEL 102
SIDELOCK SHOTGUN ...... NiB $7175 Ex $4576 Gd $3177
Similar to the Model 101 except w/large scroll engraving. Made from 1985 to 1993.

MODEL 103
HAMMERLESS DOUBLE
Similar to Model 100 except w/Purdey-type, higher grade engraving.
Model 103A Standard ...... NiB $14,675 Ex $11,650 Gd $9967
Model 103A Royal Deluxe....... NiB $11,870 Ex $9443 Gd $7655
Model 103B ....NiB $21,660 Ex $17,707 Gd $15,990
Model 103B Royal Deluxe....... NiB $25,677 Ex $22,770 Gd $18,989

MODEL 200
HAMMERLESS DOUBLE........ NiB $17,766 Ex $15,221 Gd $11,488
Similar to Model 100 except w/double heavy-duty locks. Continental-style floral and scroll engraving. Checkered deluxe walnut stock and

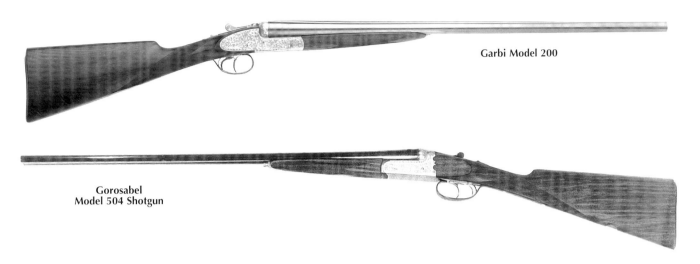

Garbi Model 200

Gorosabel
Model 504 Shotgun

forearm.

GARCIA CORPORATION — Teaneck, NJ

BRONCO 22/.410 O/U COMBO. . . . . . **NiB $300 Ex $197 Gd $100**
Swing-out action. Takedown. 18.5-inch bbls.; .22 LR over, .410 ga. under. Weight: 4.5 lbs. One-piece stock and receiver, crackle finish. Intro. In 1976. Disc.

BRONCO .410 SINGLE SHOT . . . . **NiB $233 Ex $120 Gd $90**
Swing-out action. Takedown. .410 ga. 18.5-inch bbl. Weight: 3.5 lbs. One-piece stock and receiver, crackle finish. Intro. in 1967. Disc.

GOLDEN EAGLE FIREARMS INC. — Houston, TX
Manufactured by Nikko Firearms Ltd., Tochigi, Japan.

**EAGLE MODEL 5000
GRADE I FIELD O/U** . . . .**NiB $989 Ex $844 Gd $659**
Receiver engraved and inlaid w/gold eagle head. Boxlock. Auto ejectors. Selective single trigger. 12, 20 ga. 2.75- or 3-inch chambers, 12 ga.; 3-inch, 20 ga. Bbls.: 26, 28, 30 inch (latter only in 12-ga. 3-inch Mag.); IC/M, M/F chokes; vent. rib. Weight: 6.25 lbs., 20 ga.; 7.25 lbs., 12 ga.; 8 lbs., 12-ga. Mag. Checkered pistol-grip stock and semi-beavertail forearm. Imported 1975 to 1982. Note: Guns marketed 1975 to 1976 under the Nikko brand name have white receivers; guns made since 1976 are blued.

**EAGLE MODEL 5000
GRADE I SKEET.** . . . .**NiB $954 Ex $743 Gd $522**
Same as Field model except has 26- or 28-inch bbls. w/wide (11 mm) vent. rib, SK choked. Imported from 1975 to 1982.

**EAGLE MODEL 5000
GRADE I TRAP** . . . .**NiB $954 Ex $755 Gd $569**
Same as Field model except has 30-, or 32-inch bbls. w/wide (11 mm) vent. rib (M/F, IM/F, F/F chokes), trap-style stock w/recoil pad. Imported from 1975 to 1982.

**EAGLE MODEL 5000
GRADE II FIELD** . . . . **NiB $1077 Ex $890 Gd $776**
Same as Grade I Field model except higher grade w/fancier wood, more elaborate engraving, and screaming eagle inlaid in gold. Imported from 1975 to 1982.

**EAGLE MODEL 5000
GRADE II SKEET** . . . . **NiB $1100 Ex $940 Gd $800**
Same as Grade I Skeet model except higher grade w/fancier wood, more elaborate engraving, and screaming eagle inlaid in gold; inertia trigger, vent side ribs. Imported from 1975 to 1982.

**EAGLE MODEL 5000
GRADE II TRAP.** . . . .**NiB $1100 Ex $940 Gd $800**
Same as Grade I Trap model except higher grade w/fancier wood, more elaborate engraving, and screaming eagle inlaid in gold; inertia trigger, vent side ribs. Imported from 1975 to 1982.

**EAGLE MODEL 5000
GRADE III GRANDEE** . . . . **NiB $2760 Ex $2255 Gd $1798**
Best grade, available in Field, Skeet, and Trap models w/same general specifications as lower grades. Has sideplates w/game scene engraving, scroll on frame and bbls., fancy wood (Monte Carlo comb, full pistol-grip, and recoil pad on Trap model). Made from 1976 to 1982.

GOROSABEL SHOTGUNS — Spain

MODEL 503 SHOTGUN. . . . . . . **NiB $1088 Ex $866 Gd $735**
Gauges: 12, 16, 20, and .410. Action: Anson & Deely-style boxlock. Bbls.: 26, 27, and 28 inch. Select European walnut, English or pistol grip, sliver or beavertail forend, hand-checkering. Scalloped frame and scroll engraving. Intro. 1985; disc.

MODEL 504 SHOTGUN. . . . . . . **NiB $1167 Ex $953 Gd $655**
Gauge: 12 or 20. Action: Holland & Holland-style sidelock. Bbl.: 26, 27, or 28 inch. Select European walnut, English or pistol grip, sliver or beavertail forend, hand-checkering. Holland-style large scroll engraving. Intro. 1985; disc.

MODEL 505 SHOTGUN. . . . . . . **NiB $1590 Ex $1266 Gd $965**
Gauge: 12 or 20. Action: Holland & Holland-style sidelock. Bbls.: 26, 27, or 28 inch. Select European walnut, English or pistol grip, silver or beavertail forend, hand-checkering. Purdey-style fine scroll and rose engraving. Intro. 1985; disc.

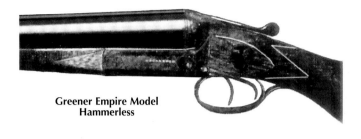

Greener Empire Model
Hammerless

Greener
Far-Killer

STEPHEN GRANT — Hertfordshire, England

**BEST QUALITY SELF-OPENER DOUBLE-BARREL
SHOTGUN** . . . . NiB $19,870 Ex $16,920 Gd $12,612
Sidelock, self-opener. Gauges: 12, 16, and 20. Bbls.: 25 to 30 inches standard. Highest grade English or European walnut straight-grip buttstock and forearm w/Greener-type lever. Imported by Stoeger in the 1950s.

**BEST QUALITY SIDE-LEVER DOUBLE-BARREL
SHOTGUN** . . . . NiB $13,657 Ex $11,770 Gd $9879
Sidelock, self-lever. Gauges: 12, 16, and 20. Bbls.: 25 to 30 inches standard. Highest-grade English or European walnut straight-grip buttstock and forearm w/Greener-type lever. Imported by Stoeger in the 1950s.

W. W. GREENER, LTD. — Birmingham, England

EMPIRE MODEL HAMMERLESS DOUBLES
Boxlock. Non-ejector or w/automatic ejectors. Double triggers. 12 ga. only (2.75- or 3-inch chamber). Bbls.: 28 to 32 inch; any choke combination. Weight: 7.25 to 7.75 lbs. depending on bbl. length. Checkered stock and forend, straight or half-pistol grip. Also furnished in Empire Deluxe Grade, this model has same general specs, but deluxe finish.
w/non-ejector . . . . NiB $1887 Ex $1671 Gd $1388
w/ejector . . . . NiB $1955 Ex $1771 Gd $1480
Deluxe model, non-ejector . . . . NiB $2088 Ex $1933 Gd $1387
Deluxe model, ejector . . . . NiB $2677 Ex $2200 Gd $1588

FARKILLER MODEL GRADE F35
HAMMERLESS DOUBLE-BARREL SHOTGUN
Boxlock. Non-ejector or w/automatic ejectors. Double triggers. Gauges: 12 (2.75-inch or 3-inch), 10, 8. Bbls.: 28, 30, or 32 inch Weight: 7.5 to 9 lbs. in 12 ga. Checkered stock, forend; straight or half-pistol grip.
Non-ejector, 12 ga. . . . . NiB $1577 Ex $1122 Gd $909
Ejector, 12 ga. . . . . NiB $3897 Ex $3138 Gd $2217
Non-ejector, 10 or 8 ga. . . . . . NiB $2886 Ex $2231 Gd $1977
Ejector, 10 or 8 ga. . . . . NiB $5500 Ex $4230 Gd $3110

G. P. (GENERAL PURPOSE)
SINGLE BARREL . . . . NiB $444 Ex $358 Gd $229
Greener Improved Martini Lever Action. Takedown. Ejector. 12 ga. only. Bbl. lengths: 26, 30, 32 inch. M/F choke. Weight: 6.25 to 6.75 lbs. depending on bbl. length. Checkered straight-grip stock and forearm.

HAMMERLESS EJECTOR DOUBLE-BARREL SHOTGUNS
Boxlock. Auto ejectors. Double triggers, nonselective or selective single trigger. Gauges: 12, 16, 20, 28, .410 (two latter

gauges not supplied in Grades DH40 and DH35). Bbls.: 26, 28, 30 inch; any choke combination. Weight: 4.75 to 8 lbs. depending on ga. and bbl. length. Checkered stock and forend, straight or half-pistol grip. The Royal, Crown, Sovereign, and Jubilee models differ in quality, engraving, grade of wood, checkering, etc. General specifications are the same.
Royal Model Grade DH75 . . . . . NiB $4170 Ex $3008 Gd $2166
Crown Model Grade DH55 . . . . NiB $5166 Ex $3188 Gd $2270
Sovereign Model Grade DH40 . . . NiB $5277 Ex $4866 Gd $3900
Jubilee Model Grade DH35 . . . . . NiB $4197 Ex $3145 Gd $2176
Selective single trigger, add $400
Nonselective single trigger, add $300
Vent. rib, add. $425
Single trigger, add. $455

GREIFELT & COMPANY — Suhl, Germany

GRADE NO. 1 O/U SHOTGUN
Anson & Deeley boxlock, Kersten fastening. Auto ejectors. Double triggers or single trigger. Elaborately engraved. Gauges: 12, 16, 20, 28, .410. Bbls.: 26 to 32 inch, any combination of chokes, vent. or solid matted rib. Weight: 4.25 to 8.25 lbs. depending on ga. and bbl. length. Straight or pistol-grip stock, Purdey-type forend, both checkered. Manufactured prior to WWII.
w/solid matted-rib bbl.,
except .410 and 28 ga. . . . . . . NiB $3797 Ex $3166 Gd $2280
w/solid matted-rib bbl.,
.410 and 28 ga. . . . . NiB $3844 Ex $3208 Gd $2300
Ventilated rib, add $125
Single trigger, add. $550

GRADE NO. 3 O/U SHOTGUN
Same general specifications as Grade No. 1 except less fancy engraving. Manufactured prior to WWII.
w/solid matted-rib bbl.,
except .410 and 28 ga. . . . . NiB $2987 Ex $2379 Gd $1979
w/solid matted-rib bbl.,
.410 and 28 ga. . . . . NiB $5187 Ex $4156 Gd $3110
Ventilated rib, add $125
Single trigger, add. $450

MODEL 22
HAMMERLESS DOUBLE . . . . NiB $2288 Ex $1843 Gd $1244
Anson & Deeley boxlock. Plain extractors. Double triggers. Gauges: 12 and 16. Bbls.: 28 or 30 inch, M/F choke. Checkered stock and forend, pistol grip and cheekpiece standard, English-style stock also supplied. Manufactured since WWII.

MODEL 22E
HAMMERLESS DOUBLE . . . . . . NiB $2866 Ex $2430 Gd $1832
Same as Model 22 except has automatic ejectors.

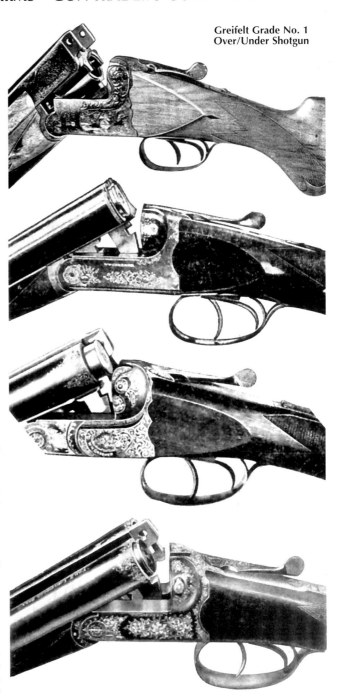

Greifelt Grade No. 1
Over/Under Shotgun

MODEL 103
HAMMLERLESS DOUBLE . . . . . .NiB $2100 Ex $1821 Gd $1292
Anson & Deeley boxlock. Plain extractors. Double triggers. Gauges: 12 and 16. Bbls.: 28 or 30 inch, M/F choke. Checkered stock and forend, pistol grip and cheekpiece standard, English-style stock also supplied. Manufactured since WWII.

MODEL 103E
HAMMERLESS DOUBLE. . . . . . NiB $2200 Ex $1727 Gd $1224
Same as Model 103 except has automatic ejectors.

MODEL 143E O/U SHOTGUN
General specifications same as prewar Grade No. 1 Over/Under except this model is not supplied in 28 and .410 ga. or w/32-inch bbls. Model 143E is not as high quality as the Grade No. 1 gun. Mfd. since WWII.
w/raised matted rib,
   double triggers. . . . . NiB $2571 Ex $2068 Gd $1563
w/vent. rib, single
   selective trigger . . . . NiB $2860 Ex $2276 Gd $1865

HAMMERLESS DRILLING (THREE-BARREL
COMBINATION GUN). . . . . . NiB $3677 Ex $3220 Gd $2179
Boxlock. Plain extractors. Double triggers, front single set for rifle bbl. Gauges: 12, 16, 20. Rifle bbl. in any caliber adapted to this type of gun. 26-inch bbls. Weight: About 7.5 lbs. Auto rear sight operated by rifle bbl. selector. Checkered stock and forearm, pistol-grip and cheekpiece standard. Manufactured prior to WWII. Note: Value shown is for guns chambered for cartridges readily obtainable. If rifle bbl. is an odd foreign caliber, value will be considerably less.

O/U COMBINATION GUN
Similar in design to this maker's over/under shotguns. Gauges: 12, 16, 20, 28, .410. Rifle bbl. in any caliber adapted to this type of gun. Bbls.: 24 or 26 inch, solid matted rib. Weight: 4.75 to 7.25 lbs. Folding rear sight. Manufactured prior to WWII. Note: Values shown are for gauges other than .410 w/rifle bbl. Chambered for a cartridge readily obtainable; if in an odd foreign caliber, value will be considerably less. .410 ga. increases in value by about 50%.
w/non-automatic ejector. . . . . NiB $5477 Ex $4651 Gd $3822
w/automatic ejector . . . . NiB $6055 Ex $5310 Gd $4430

HARRINGTON & RICHARDSON ARMS COMPANY — Gardner, MA
now H&R 1871, Inc.

Formerly Harrington & Richardson Arms Co. of Worcester, MA. One of the oldest and most distinguished manufacturers of handguns, rifles, and shotguns, H&R suspended operations on January 24, 1986. In 1987, New England Firearms was established as an independent company producing selected H&R models under the NEF logo. In 1991, H&R 1871, Inc. was formed from the residual of the parent company and then took over the New England Firearms facility. H&R 1871 produced firearms under both their logo and the NEF brand name until 1999, when the Marlin Firearms Company acquired the assets of H&R 1871.

NO. 3 HAMMERLESS
SINGLE-SHOT SHOTGUN. . . . . . NiB $230 Ex $115 Gd $85
Takedown. Automatic ejector. Gauges: 12, 16, 20, .410. Bbls.: Plain 26 to 32 inch, F choke. Weight: 6.5 to 7.25 lbs. depending on ga. and bbl. length. Plain pistol-grip stock and forend. Disc. 1942.

NO. 5 STANDARD LIGHTWEIGHT
HAMMER SINGLE. . . . . .NiB $227 Ex $120 Gd $90
Takedown. Auto ejector. Gauges: 24, 28, .410. Bbls.: 26 or 28 inch, F choke. Weight: 4 to 4.75 lbs. Plain pistol-grip stock and forend. Disc. 1942.

NO. 6 HEAVY BREECH SINGLE-SHOT
HAMMER SHOTGUN . . . . NiB $244 Ex $135 Gd $90
Takedown. Automatic ejector. Gauges: 10, 12, 16, 20. Bbls.: Plain 28 to 36 inch, F choke. Weight: 7 to 7.25 lbs. Plain stock and forend. Disc. 1942.

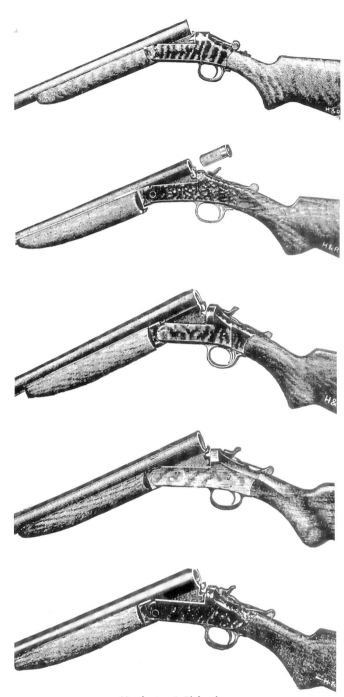

Harrington & Richardson
No. 3, 5, 6, 7, and 8 Shotguns

NO. 7 & 9 BAY STATE SINGLE-SHOT
HAMMER SHOTGUN . . . . NiB $235 Ex $140 Gd $95
Takedown. Automatic ejector. Gauges: 12, 16, 20, .410. Bbls.: Plain 26 to 32 inch, F choke. Weight: 5.5 to 6.5 lbs. depending on ga. and bbl. length. Plain pistol-grip stock and forend. Disc. 1942.

NO. 8 STANDARD SINGLE-SHOT
HAMMER SHOTGUN . . . . NiB $255 Ex $145 Gd $98
Takedown. Automatic ejector. Gauges: 12, 16, 20, 24, 28, .410. Bbl.: Plain 26 to 32 inch, F choke. Weight: 5.5 to 6.5 lbs. depending on ga. and bbl. length. Plain pistol-grip stock and forend. Made from 1908 to 1942.

MODEL 348 GAMESTER
BOLT-ACTION SHOTGUN . . . . . .NiB $217 Ex $117 Gd $88
Takedown. 12 and 16 ga. 2-round tubular magazine, 28-inch bbl., F choke. Plain pistol-grip stock. Weight: About 7.5 lbs. Made from 1949 to 1954.

MODEL 349 GAMESTER DELUXE . . . . .NiB $220 Ex $115 Gd $85
Same as Model 348 except has 26-inch bbl. w/adj. choke device, recoil pad. Made from 1953 to 1955.

MODEL 351 HUNTSMAN
BOLT-ACTION SHOTGUN . . . . . NiB $239 Ex $200 Gd $125
Takedown. 12 and 16 ga. 2-round tubular magazine. Pushbutton safety. 26-inch bbl. w/H&R variable choke. Weight: About 6.75 lbs. Monte Carlo stock w/recoil pad. Made from 1956 to 1958.

MODEL 400 PUMP . . . . .NiB $335 Ex $254 Gd $180
Hammerless. Gauges: 12, 16, 20. Tubular magazine holds 4 shells. 28-inch bbl., F choke. Weight: About 7.25 lbs. Plain pistol-grip stock (recoil pad in 12 and 16 ga.), grooved slide handle. Made from 1955 to 1967.MODEL 401 . . NiB $335   Ex $240 Gd $190
Same as Model 400 on previous page except has H&R variable choke. Made from 1956 to 1963.

MODEL 402 . . . . NiB $315 Ex $220 Gd $170
Similar to Model 400 except .410 ga. Weight: About 5.5 lbs. Made from 1959 to 1967.

MODEL 403 AUTOLOADING
SHOTGUN . . . . .NiB $338 Ex $300 Gd $210
Takedown. .410 ga. Tubular magazine holds 4 shells. 26-inch bbl., F choke. Weight: About 5.75 lbs. Plain pistol-grip stock and forearm. Made in 1964.

MODEL 404/404C PUMP
SHOTGUN . . . . NiB $366 Ex $275 Gd $209
Boxlock. Plain extractors. Double triggers. Gauges: 12, 20, .410. Bbls.: 28 inch in 12 ga. (M/F choke), 26 inch in 20 ga. (IC/M), and .410 (F/F). Weight: 5.5 to 7.25 lbs. Plain walnut-finished hardwood stock and forend on Model 404; 404C checkered. Made in Brazil by Amadeo Rossi from 1969 to 1972.

MODEL 440 PUMP SHOTGUN . . . . . .NiB $255 Ex $194 Gd $145
Hammerless. Gauges: 12, 16, 20. 2.75-inch chamber in 16 ga.; 3-inch in 12 and 20 ga. 3-round magazine. Bbls.: 26, 28, 30 inch; IC/M/F choke. Weight: 6.25 lbs. Plain pistol-grip stock and slide handle, recoil pad. Made from 1968 to 1973.

MODEL 442 PUMP SHOTGUN . . . . . .NiB $320 Ex $254 Gd $188
Same as Model 440 except has vent. rib bbl., checkered stock and forearm. Weight: 6.75 lbs. Made from 1969 to 1973.

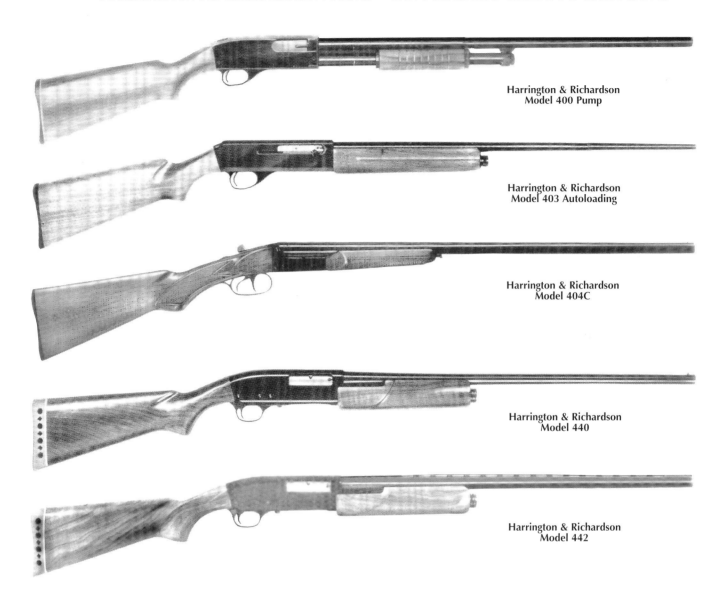

Harrington & Richardson
Model 400 Pump

Harrington & Richardson
Model 403 Autoloading

Harrington & Richardson
Model 404C

Harrington & Richardson
Model 440

Harrington & Richardson
Model 442

ULTRA SLUG SERIES. . . . . NiB $287 Ex $220 Gd $175
Single-shot 12 or 20 ga. 3-inch chamber w/heavy-wall 24-inch
fully rifled bbl. w/scope. Weight: 9 lbs. Walnut-stained Monte
Carlo stock, sling swivels, black nylon sling. Made from 1995 to
date.

MODEL 1212 FIELD . . . . NiB $435 Ex $321 Gd $250
Boxlock. Plain extractors. Selective single trigger. 12 ga., 2.75-inch
chambers. 28-inch bbls., IC/IM, vent. rib. Weight: 7 lbs. Checkered
walnut pistol-grip stock and fluted forearm. Made 1976 to 1980 by
Lanber Arms S. A., Zaldibar (Vizcaya), Spain.

MODEL 1212
WATERFOWL GUN . . . . NiB $544 Ex $368 Gd $277
Same as Field Gun except chambered for 12 ga. 3-inch Mag.
shells, has 30-inch bbls., M/F chokes, stock and recoil pad.
Weight: 7.5 lbs. Made from 1976 to 1980.

MODEL 1908
SINGLE-SHOT SHOTGUN . . . . . . NiB $244 Ex $177 Gd $100
Takedown. Automatic ejector. Gauges: 12, 16, 24, and 28. Bbls.:
26 to 32 inch, F choke. Weight: 5.25 to 6.5 lbs. depending on ga.
and bbl. length. Casehardened receiver. Plain pistol-grip stock.
Bead front sight. Made from 1908 to 1934.

MODEL 1908 .410 (12MM)
SINGLE-SHOT SHOTGUN . . . . . . NiB $233 Ex $177 Gd $120
Same general specifications as standard Model 1908 except
chambered for .410 or 12mm shot cartridge w/bbl. milled down at
receiver to give a more pleasing contour.

MODEL 1915 SINGLE-SHOT SHOTGUN
Takedown. Both nonauto and auto-ejectors available. Gauges:
24, 28, .410, 14mm, and 12mm. Bbls.: 26 or 28 inch, F choke.
Weight: 4 to 4.75 lbs. depending on ga. and bbl. length. Plain
black walnut stock w/semi-pistol grip.
24 ga. . . . . NiB $390 Ex $275 Gd $190
28, .410 ga.. . . . . NiB $390 Ex $275 Gd $190

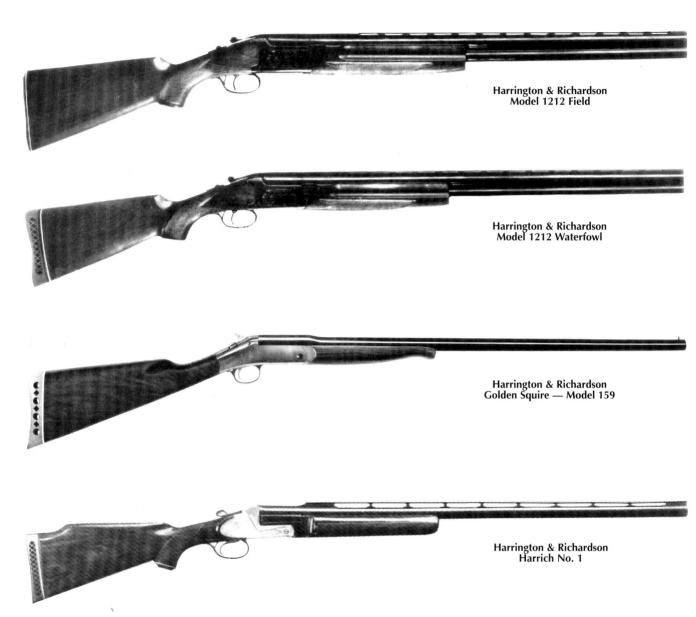

Harrington & Richardson
Model 1212 Field

Harrington & Richardson
Model 1212 Waterfowl

Harrington & Richardson
Golden Squire — Model 159

Harrington & Richardson
Harrich No. 1

FOLDING GUN . . . . **NiB $320 Ex $210 Gd $165**
Single bbl. hammer shotgun hinged at the front of the frame, the bbl. folds down against the stock. Light Frame model: Gauges: 28, 14mm, .410. 22-inch bbl. Weight: About 4.5 lbs. Heavy Frame model: Gauges: 12, 16, 20, 28, .410. 26-inch bbl. Weight: 5.75 to 6.5 lbs. Plain pistol-grip stock and forend. Disc. 1942.

GOLDEN SQUIRE MODEL 159 SINGLE-BARREL
HAMMER SHOTGUN . . . . **NiB $265 Ex $170 Gd $121**
Hammerless. Side lever. Automatic ejection. Gauges: 12, 20. Bbls: 30 inch in 12 ga., 28 inch in 20 ga., both F choke. Weight: About 6.5 lbs. Straight-grip stock w/recoil pad, forearm w/Schnabel. Made from 1964 to 1966.

GOLDEN SQUIRE JR.
MODEL 459 . . . . **NiB $255 Ex $170 Gd $125**
Same as Model 159 except gauges 20 and .410, 26-inch bbl., youth stock. Made in 1964.

HARRICH NO. 1 SINGLE-BARREL
TRAP GUN . . . . **NiB $1733 Ex $1456 Gd $974**
Anson & Deeley-type locking system w/Kersten top locks and double underlocking lugs. Sideplates engraved w/hunting scenes. 12 ga. Bbls.: 32, 34 inch; F choke; high vent. rib. Weight: 8.5 lbs. Checkered Monte Carlo stock w/pistol grip and recoil pad, beavertail forearm of select walnut. Made in Austria 1971 to 1975.

TOP RIB
SINGLE-BARREL SHOTGUN . . . . **NiB $335 Ex $265 Gd $190**
Takedown. Auto ejector. Gauges: 12, 16, and 20. Bbls.: 28 to 30 inch, F choke w/full-length matted top rib. Weight: 6.5 to 7 lbs. depending on ga. and bbl. length. Black walnut pistol-grip stock (capped) and forend; both checkered. Flexible rubber buttplate. Made during 1930s.

TOPPER NO. 48 SINGLE-BARREL
HAMMER SHOTGUN . . . . **NiB $280 Ex $195 Gd $145**
Similar to old Model 8 Standard. Takedown. Top lever. Auto ejec-

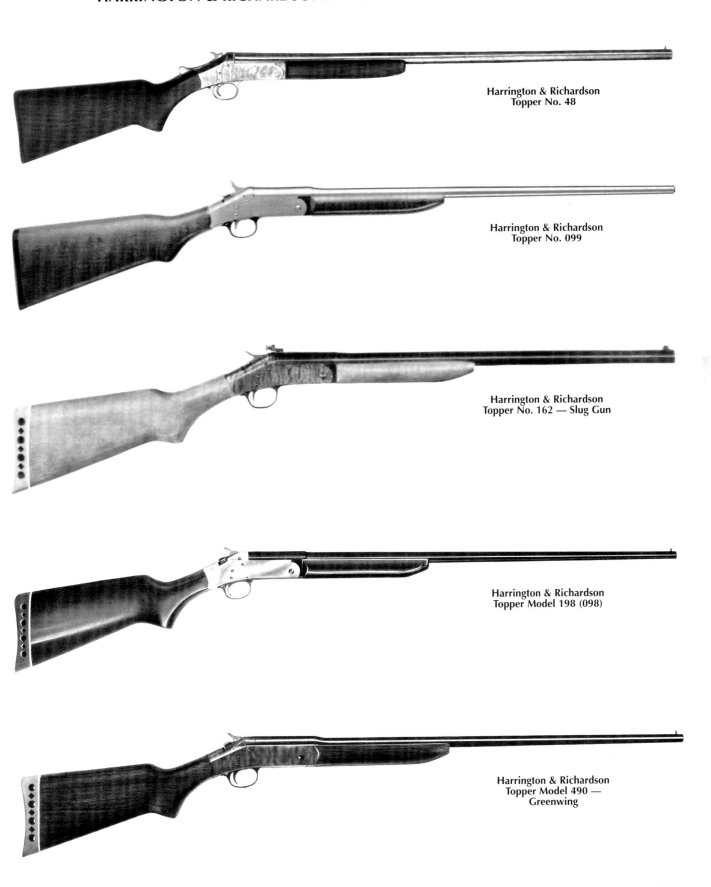

Harrington & Richardson
Topper No. 48

Harrington & Richardson
Topper No. 099

Harrington & Richardson
Topper No. 162 — Slug Gun

Harrington & Richardson
Topper Model 198 (098)

Harrington & Richardson
Topper Model 490 —
Greenwing

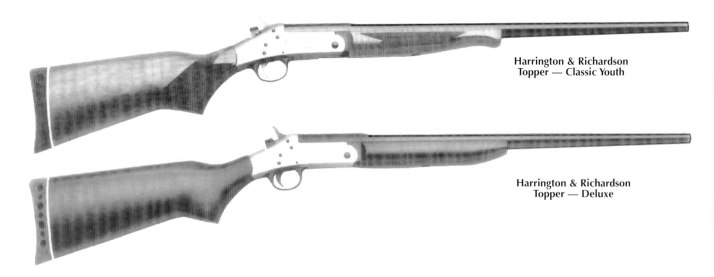

Harrington & Richardson Topper — Classic Youth

Harrington & Richardson Topper — Deluxe

tor. Gauges: 12, 16, 20, .410. Bbls.: Plain 26 to 30 inch; M/F choke. Weight: 5.5 to 6.5 lbs. depending on ga. and bbl. length. Plain pistol-grip stock and forend. Made from 1946 to 1957.

TOPPER MODEL 099 DELUXE . . . . . NiB $244 Ex $155 Gd $110
Same as Model 158 except has matte nickel finish, semi-pistol grip walnut-finished American hardwood stock; semi-beavertail forearm; 12, 16, 20, and .410 ga. Made from 1982 to 1986.

TOPPER MODEL 148 SINGLE-SHOT
HAMMER SHOTGUN . . . . NiB $200 Ex $177 Gd $120
Takedown. Side lever. Auto-ejection. Gauges: 12, 16, 20, .410. Bbls.: 12 ga., 30, 32, and 36 inch; 16 ga., 28 and 30 inch; 20 and .410 ga., 28 inch; F choke. Weight: 5 to 6.5 lbs. Plain pistol-grip stock and forend, recoil pad. Made from 1958 to 1961.

TOPPER MODEL 158 (058) SINGLE-SHOT
HAMMER SHOTGUN . . . . NiB $245 Ex $165 Gd $120
Takedown. Side lever. Automatic ejection. Gauges: 12, 20, .410 (2.75 and 3-inch shells), 16 (2.75-inch). Bbl. length and choke combinations: 12 ga., 36-inch/F, 32-inch/F, 30-inch/F, 28-inch/ F/M; .410, 28-inch/F. Weight: About 5.5 lbs. Plain pistol-grip stock and forend, recoil pad. Made from 1962 to 1981. Note: Designation changed to 058 in 1974.

TOPPER MODEL 162
SLUG GUN . . . . NiB $300 Ex $221 Gd $165
Same as Topper Model 158 except has 24-inch bbl., Cyl. bore, w/ rifle sights. Made from 1968 to 1986.

TOPPER MODEL 176 10 GA.
MAGNUM . . . . NiB $280 Ex $185 Gd $145
Similar to Model 158 but has 36-inch heavy bbl. chambered for 3.5-inch 10-ga. Mag. shells. Weight: 10 lbs.; stock w/Monte Carlo comb and recoil pad, longer and fuller forearm. Made from 1977 to 1986.

TOPPER MODEL 188 DELUXE . . . . NiB $265 Ex $200 Gd $145
Same as standard Topper Model 148 except has chromed frame, stock, and forend in black, red, yellow, blue, green, pink, or purple colored finish. .410 ga. only. Made from 1958 to 1961.

TOPPER MODEL 198 (098) DELUXE . . . . . NiB $244 Ex $180 Gd $130
Same as Model 158 except has chrome-plated frame, black finished stock and forend. 12, 20, and .410 ga. Made 1962 to 1981. Note: Designation changed to 098 in 1974.

TOPPER JR. MODEL 480 . . . . . . NiB $236 Ex $165 Gd $100
Similar to No. 48 Topper except has youth-size stock, 26-inch bbl., .410 ga. only. Made from 1958 to 1961.

TOPPER NO. 488 DELUXE . . . . . NiB $254 Ex $179 Gd $115
Same as standard No. 48 Topper except chrome-plated frame, black lacquered stock and forend, recoil pad. Disc. 1957.

TOPPER MODEL 490 . . . . NiB $245 Ex $185 Gd $135
Same as Model 158 except has youth-size stock (3 inches shorter), 26-inch bbl.; 20 and 28 ga. (M choke), .410 (F). Made 1962 to 1986.

TOPPER MODEL 490 GREENWING . . . . . NiB $266 Ex $190 Gd $140
Same as the Model 490 except has a special high-polished finish. Made from 1981 to 1986.

TOPPER JR. MODEL 580 . . . . . . NiB $210 Ex $166 Gd $100
Same as Model 480 except has colored stocks as on Model 188. Made from 1958 to 1961.

TOPPER MODEL 590 . . . . NiB $210 Ex $166 Gd $100
Same as Model 490 except has chrome-plated frame, black finished stock and forend. Made from 1962 to 1963.

The following models are manufactured and distributed by the reorganized company of H&R 1871, Inc.

MODEL 098 TOPPER
CLASSIC YOUTH . . . . NiB $200 Ex $155 Gd $100
Same as Topper Junior except also available in 28 ga. and has checkered American black walnut stock and forend w/satin finish and recoil pad. Made from 1991 to date.

MODEL 098 TOPPER DELUXE . . . . . NiB $200 Ex $155 Gd $100
Same as Model 098 Single-Shot Hammer except in 12 ga. 3-inch chamber only. 28-inch bbl.; M choke tube. Made from 1992 to date.

MODEL 098 TOPPER
DELUXE RIFLED SLUG GUN . . . . . NiB $217 Ex $125 Gd $95
Same as Topper Deluxe Shotgun except has compensated 24-inch rifled slug bbl. Nickel-plated receiver and blued bbl. Black finished hardwood stock. Made from 1996 to date.

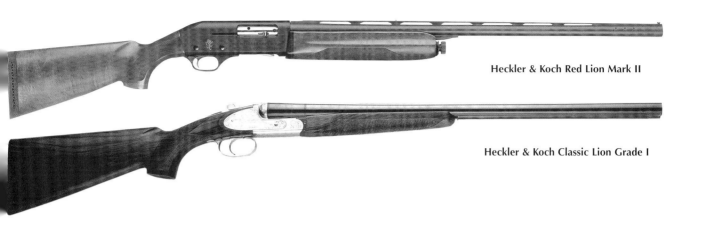

Heckler & Koch Red Lion Mark II

Heckler & Koch Classic Lion Grade I

MODEL 098 TOPPER HAMMER
SINGLE-SHOT SHOTGUN . . . . **NiB $165 Ex $115 Gd $88**
Side lever. Automatic ejector. Gauges: 12, 20, and .410. 3-inch
chamber. Bbls.: 28 inch (12 ga./M), 26 inch (20 ga./M), 26 inch
(.410/F). Weight: 5 to 6 lbs. Satin nickel receiver, blued bbl. Plain
pistol-grip stock and semi-beavertail forend w/black finish. Reintro.
1992.

MODEL 098 TOPPER JUNIOR . . . . . . **NiB $200 Ex $129 Gd $90**
Same as Model 098 except has youth-size stock and 22-inch bbl.
20 or .410 ga. only. Made 1991 to date.

MODEL .410
TAMER SHOTGUN . . . . **NiB $200 Ex $145 Gd $100**
Takedown. Topper-style single-shot, side-lever action w/auto
ejector. Gauge: .410. 3-inch chamber. 19.5-inch bbl. 33 inches
overall. Weight: 5.75 lbs. Black polymer thumbhole stock
designed to hold 4 extra shotshells. Matte nickel finish. Made
from 1994 to date.

MODEL NWTF TURKEY MAG
Same as Model 098 Single-Shot Hammer except has 24-inch bbl.
chambered 10 or 12 ga. 3.5-inch chamber w/screw-in choke tube.
Weight: 6 lbs. American hardwood stock, Mossy Oak camo finish.
Made from 1991 to 1996.
NWTF 10 ga. Turkey Mag (Made 1996) . . . . . . .NiB $200 Ex $125 Gd $90
NWTF 12 ga. Turkey Mag (Made 1991-95) . . . . . . .NiB $200 Ex $125 Gd $90

MODEL NWTF
YOUTH TURKEY GUN. . . . . **NiB $195 Ex $115 Gd $88**
Same as Model NWTF Turkey Mag except has 22-inch bbl. chambered in 20 ga. 3-inch chamber, fixed full choke. Realtree camo
finish. Made from 1994 to 1995.

MODEL SB1-920
ULTRA SLUG HUNTER. . . . . **NiB $275 Ex $198 Gd $155**
Special 12 ga. action w/12-ga. bbl. blank underbored to 20 ga. to
form a fully rifled slug bbl. Gauge: 20. 3-inch chamber. 24-inch
bbl. Weight: 8.5 lbs. Satin nickel receiver, blued bbl. Walnut
finished hardwood Monte Carlo stock. Made from 1996 to 1998.

ULTRA SLUG HUNTER . . . . **NiB $275 Ex $219 Gd $175**
12 or 20 ga. 3-inch chamber. 22- or 24-inch rifled bbl. Weight:

9 lbs. Matte black receiver and bbl. Walnut finished hardwood
Monte Carlo stock. Made from 1997 to date.

ULTRA SLUG HUNTER DELUXE. . . . .**NiB $335 Ex $210 Gd $155**
Similar to Ultra Slug Hunter model except with compensated bbl.
Made from 1997 to date.

HECKLER & KOCH FABARM SHOTGUNS —
Oberndorf am Neckar, Germany, and Sterling, VA

CLASSIC LION SIDE-BY-SIDE SHOTGUN
12 ga. only. 28- or 30-inch non-ported Tribor bbl. w/3-inch chamber. 46.5 to 48.5 inches overall. Weight: 7 to 7.2 lbs. 5 choke
tubes, C/IC/M/IM/F. Traditional boxlock design. Oil-finished walnut forearms and stocks w/diamond-cut checkering. Imported from
1999 to date.
Grade I . . . . NiB $1456 Ex $1288 Gd $890
Grade II . . . . NiB $2177 Ex $1766 Gd $1292

CAMO LION SEMIAUTO SHOTGUN . . . . . . .NiB $988 Ex $853 Gd $679
12 ga. only. 24 to 28-inch Tribor bbl. 44.25 to 48.25 inches
overall. Weight: 7 to 7.2 lbs. 3-inch chamber w/5 choke tubes,
C/IC/M/IM/F. 2-round mag. Camo-covered walnut stock w/rear
front bar sights. Imported 1999 to date.

MAX LION O/U SHOTGUN. . . . . . . **NiB $1977 Ex $1660 Gd $1000**
12 or 20 ga. 26-, 28-, or 30-inch TriBore system bbls. 42.5 to 47.25
inches overall. Weight: 6.8 to 7.8 lbs. 3-inch chamber w/5 choke
tubes (C/IC/M/IM/F). Single selective adj. trigger and auto ejectors.
Side plates w/high-grade stock and rubber recoil pad. Made from
1999 to date.

RED LION MARK II SEMIAUTO
SHOTGUN . . . . **NiB $954 Ex $700 Gd $544**
12 ga. only. 24-, 26-, or 28-inch TriBore system bbls. 44.25 to 48.25
inches overall. Weight: 7 to 7.2 lbs. 3-inch chamber w/5 choke tubes
(C/IC/M/IM/F). 2-round magazine. Matte finish w/walnut wood stock.
Rubber vented recoil pad w/leather cover. Made from 1999 to date.

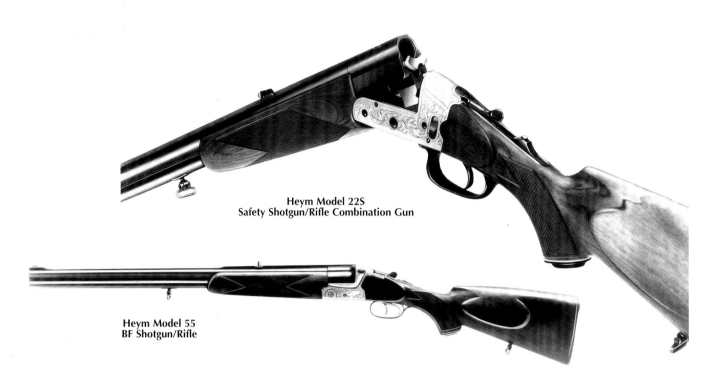

Heym Model 22S
Safety Shotgun/Rifle Combination Gun

Heym Model 55
BF Shotgun/Rifle

SILVER LION O/U SHOTGUN . . . . . . **NiB $1388 Ex $1097 Gd $766**
12 or 20 ga. 26-, 28-, or 30-inch TriBore system bbls. 43.25 to 47.25 inches overall. 3-inch chamber w/5 choke tubes (C/IC/M/IM/F). Single selective trig. and auto ejectors. Walnut stock w/rubber recoil pad. Made from 1999 to date.

SPORTING CLAY LION
SEMIAUTO SHOTGUN. . . . . . . **NiB $1087 Ex $944 Gd $644**
12 ga. only. 28- or 30-inch bbl. 3-inch chamber and ported Tribore system barrel. Matte finish w/gold plated trigger and carrier release button. Made from 1999 to date.

HERCULES SHOTGUNS

See Listings under "W" for Montgomery Ward.

HEYM SHOTGUNS — Münnerstadt, Germany

MODEL 22S SAFETY SHOTGUN/
RIFLE COMBINATION . . . . **NiB $3798 Ex $2889 Gd $2250**
16 and 20 ga. Calibers: .22 Mag., .22 Hornet, .222 Rem., .222 Rem. Mag., 5.6x50R Mag., 6.5x57R, 7x57R, .243 Win. 24-inch bbls. 40 inches overall. Weight: About 5.5 lbs. Single-set trigger. Left-side bbl. selector. Integral dovetail base for scope mounting. Arabesque engraving. Walnut stock. Disc. 1993.

MODEL 55 BF SHOTGUN/
RIFLE COMBO . . . . **NiB $7045 Ex $5370 Gd $4398**
12, 16, and 20 ga. Calibers: 5.6x50R Mag., 6.5x57R, 7x57R, 7x65R, .243 Win., .308 Win., .30-06. 25-inch bbls., 42 inches overall. Weight: About 6.75 lbs. Black satin finished, corrosion-resistant bbls. of Krupp special steel. Hand-checkered walnut stock w/long pistol-grip. Hand-engraved leaf scroll. German cheekpiece. Disc. 1988.

J. C. HIGGINS

See Sears, Roebuck & Company.

HUGLU HUNTING FIREARMS — Huglu, Turkey

Imported by Turkish Firearms Corp.

MODEL 101 B 12 AT-DT
COMBO O/U TRAP . . . . **NiB $2387 Ex $1885 Gd $1444**
Over/Under boxlock. 12 ga. 3-inch chambers. Combination 30- or 32-inch top single & O/U bbls. w/fixed chokes or choke tubes. Weight: 8 lbs. Automatic ejectors or extractors. Single selective trigger. Manual safety. Circassian walnut Monte Carlo trap stock w/palm-swell grip and recoil pad. Silvered frame w/engraving. Imported from 1993 to 1997.

MODEL 101 B 12 ST O/U TRAP . . . . . . **NiB $1577 Ex $1377 Gd $937**
Same as Model 101 AT-DT except in 32-inch O/U configuration only. Imported from 1994 to 1996.

MODEL 103 B 12 ST O/U
Boxlock. Gauges: 12, 16, 20, 28, or .410. 28-inch bbls. w/fixed chokes. Engraved action w/inlaid game scene and dummy sideplates. Double triggers, extractors, and manual safety. Weight: 7.5 lbs. Circassian walnut stock. Imported 1995 to 1996.
Model 103B w/extractors . . . . **NiB $954 Ex $733 Gd $496**
28 ga. and .410, add **$125**

MODEL 103 C 12 ST O/U
Same general specs as Model 103 B 12 S except w/extractors or ejectors. 12 or 20 ga. 3-inch chambers. Black receiver w/50% engraving coverage. Imported from 1995 to 1097.

Model 103C w/extractors . . . . . . NiB $920 Ex $733 Gd $578
Model 103C w/ejectors . . . . NiB $979 Ex $766 Gd $634

MODEL 103 D 12 ST O/U
Same gen. specs as Model 103 B 12 ST except stand. Boxlock. Extractors or ejectors. 12 or 20 ga. 3-inch chambers. 80% engraving coverage. Imported from 1995 to 1997.
Model 103D w/extractors . . . . . . NiB $920 Ex $733 Gd $578
Model 103D w/ejectors . . . . NiB $979 Ex $766 Gd $634

MODEL 103 F 12 ST O/U
Same as Model 103 B except extractors or ejectors. 12 or 20 ga. only. 100% engraving coverage. Imported from 1996 to 1997.
Model 103F w/extractors . . . . . NiB $1000 Ex $835 Gd $657
Model 103F w/ejectors . . . . . . NiB $1154 Ex $1010 Gd $745

MODEL 104 A 12 ST O/U
Boxlock. Gauges: 12, 20, 28, or .410. 28-inch bbls. Fixed chokes or choke tubes. Silvered, engraved receiver w/15% engraving coverage. Double triggers, manual safety, and extractors or ejectors. Weight: 7.5 lbs. Circassian walnut stock w/field dimensions. Imported from 1995 to 1997.
Model 104A w/extractors . . . . NiB $777 Ex $688 Gd $545
Model 104A w/ejectors . . . . NiB $790 Ex $700 Gd $600
28 ga. and .410, add $150
Choke Tubes, add $75

MODEL 200 SERIES DOUBLE
Boxlock. Gauges: 12, 20, 28, or .410. 3-inch chambers. 28-inch bbls. Fixed chokes. Silvered, engraved receiver. Extractors, manual safety, single selective trigger or double triggers. Weight: 7.5 lbs. Circassion walnut stock. Imported from 1995 to 1997.
Model 200 (w/15%
   engraving coverage, SST) . . . . NiB $1033 Ex $878 Gd $633
Model 201 (w/30%
   engraving coverage, SST) . . . . NiB $1277 Ex $1100 Gd $955
Model 202 (w/Greener
   crossbolt, DT) . . . . NiB $888 Ex $645 Gd $469
28 ga. and .410, add $125

HIGH STANDARD SPORTING ARMS — East Hartford, CT; formerly High Standard Mfg. Corp. of Hamden, CT

In 1966, High Standard introduced a new series of Flite-King Pumps and Supermatic autoloaders, both readily identifiable by the damascened bolt and restyled checkering. To avoid confusion, these models are designated Series II in this text. This is not an official factory designation. Operation of this firm was discontinued in 1984.

FLITE-KING FIELD
PUMP—12 GA. . . . . NiB $256 Ex $180 Gd $110
Hammerless. Magazine holds five rounds. Bbls.: 26-inch IC, 28-inch M or F, 30-inch F choke. Weight: 7.25 lbs. Plain pistol-grip stock and slide handle. Made from 1960 to 1966.

FLITE-KING BRUSH—12 GA. . . . . . NiB $285 Ex $245 Gd $170
Same as Flite-King Field 2 except has 18- or 20-inch bbl. (Cyl. bore) w/rifle sights. Made from 1962 to 1964.

FLITE-KING BRUSH DELUXE . . . . . . NiB $275 Ex $190 Gd $120
Same as Flite-King Brush except has adj. peep rear sight, checkered pistol grip, recoil pad, fluted slide handle, swivels, and sling. Not available w/18-inch bbl. Made from 1964 to 1966.

FLITE-KING BRUSH (SERIES II) . . . . . NiB $275 Ex $190 Gd $120
Same as Flite-King Deluxe 12 (II) except has 20-inch bbl., Cyl. bore, w/rifle sights. Weight: 7 lbs. Made from 1966 to 1975.

FLITE-KING BRUSH DELUXE (II) . . . . . NiB $290 Ex $200 Gd $135
Same as Flite-King Brush (II) except has adj. peep rear sight, swivels, and sling. Made from 1966 to 1975.

FLITE-KING DELUXE 12 GA. (SERIES II)
Hammerless. 5-round magazine. 27-inch plain bbls.w/adj. choke. 26-inch IC, 28-inch M/F, 30-inch F choke. Weight: About 7.25 lbs. Checkered pistol-grip stock and forearm, recoil pad. Made from 1966 to 1975.
w/adj. choke . . . . NiB $245 Ex $170 Gd $110
w/fixed choke . . . . NiB $245 Ex $170 Gd $110

FLITE-KING DELUXE
20, 28, .410 GA. (SERIES II) . . . . . NiB $255 Ex $178 Gd $120
Same as Flite-King Deluxe 12 (II) except chambered for 20 and .410 ga., 3-inch shell; 28 ga., 2.75-inch shell. 20- or 28-inch plain bbl. Weight: About 6 lbs. Made from 1966 to 1975.

FLITE-KING DELUXE RIB 12 GA. . . . . NiB $280 Ex $200 Gd $155
Same as Flite-King Field 12 except vent. rib bbl. (28-inch M/F, 30-inch F). Checkered stock and forearm. Made from 1961 to 1966.

FLITE-KING DELUXE RIB 12 GA. (II)
Same as Flite-King Deluxe 12 (II) except has vent. rib bbl., available in 27-inch w/adj. choke, 28-inch M/F, 30-inch F choke. Made from 1966 to 1975.
w/adj. choke . . . . NiB $292 Ex $217 Gd $175
w/fixed choke . . . . NiB $292 Ex $217 Gd $175

FLITE-KING DELUXE RIB 20 GA. . . . NiB $265 Ex $198 Gd $125
Same as Flite-King Field 20 except vent. rib bbl. (28-inch M/F), checkered stock and slide handle. Made from 1962 to 1966.

FLITE-KING DELUXE RIB 20, 28, .410 GA. (SERIES II)
Same as Flite-King Deluxe 20, 28, .410 (II) except 20 ga. available w/27-inch adj. choke, 28-inch M/F choke. Weight: About 6.25 lbs. Made from 1966 to 1975.
w/adj. choke . . . . NiB $265 Ex $198 Gd $125
w/I adj. choke . . . . NiB $265 Ex $198 Gd $125

FLITE-KING DELUXE SKEET GUN
12 GA. (SERIES II) . . . . NiB $544 Ex $423 Gd $318
Same as Flite-King Deluxe Rib 12 (II) except available only w/26-inch vent. rib bbl., SK choke, recoil pad optional. Made from 1966 to 1975.

FLITE-KING DELUXE SKEET GUN
20, 28, .410 GA. (SERIES II) . . . . . . NiB $454 Ex $39 Gd $243
Same as Flite-King Deluxe Rib 20, 28, .410 (II) except available only w/26-inch vent. rib bbl., SK choke. Made 1966 to 1975.

FLITE-KING DELUXE TRAP
GUN (SERIES II) . . . . NiB $338 Ex $265 Gd $129
Same as Flite-King Deluxe Rib 12 (II) except available only w/30-inch vent. rib bbl., F choke; trap-style stock. Made 1966 to 1975.

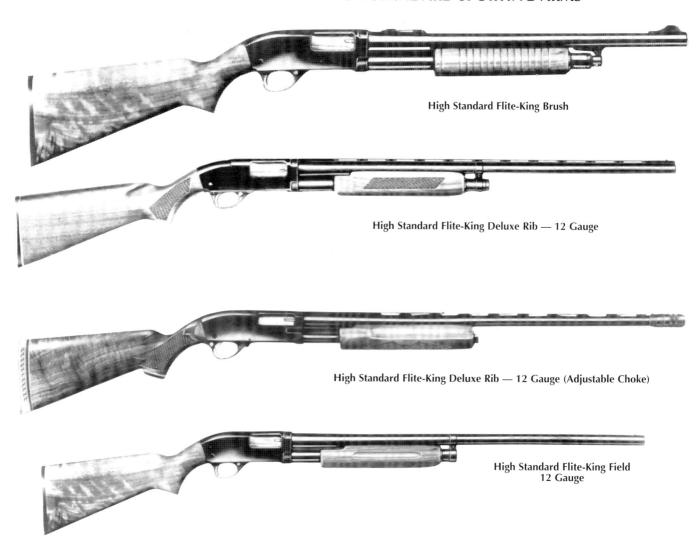

High Standard Flite-King Brush

High Standard Flite-King Deluxe Rib — 12 Gauge

High Standard Flite-King Deluxe Rib — 12 Gauge (Adjustable Choke)

High Standard Flite-King Field
12 Gauge

FLITE-KING FIELD PUMP
SHOTGUN 16 GA . . . . **NiB $250 Ex $175 Gd $135**
Same general specifications as Flite-King 12 except not available in Brush, Skeet, and Trap models or 30-inch bbl. Values same as for 12-ga. guns. Made from 1961 to 1965.

FLITE-KING FIELD PUMP 20 GA. . . . . . **NiB $250 Ex $175 Gd $135**
Hammerless. Chambered for 3-inch Mag. shells, also handles 2.75-inch. Magazine holds 4 rounds. Bbls.: 26-inch IC, 28-inch M/F choke. Weight: About 6 lbs. Plain pistol-grip stock and slide handle. Made from 1961 to 1966.

FLITE-KING PUMP
SHOTGUN (.410) . . . .**NiB $350 Ex $275 Gd $235**
Same general specifications as Flite-King 20 except not available in Special and Trophy models, or w/other than 26-inch choke bbl.
Add $100 to 20-ga. price.. . . . .
Made from 1962 to 1966.

FLITE-KING SKEET 12 GA. . . . . . . **NiB $330 Ex $225 Gd $170**
Same as Flite-King Deluxe Rib except 26-inch vent. rib bbl., w/SK choke. Made from 1962 to 1966.

FLITE-KING SPECIAL 12 GA. . . . . . . **NiB $250 Ex $175 Gd $135**
Same as Flite-King Field 12 except has 27-inch bbl. w/adj. choke. Made from 1960 to 1966.

FLITE-KING SPECIAL 20 GA. . . . . . . **NiB $250 Ex $175 Gd $135**
Same as Flite-King Field 20 except has 27-inch bbl. w/adj. choke. Made from 1961 to 1966.

FLITE-KING TRAP 12 GA. . . . . **NiB $330 Ex $225 Gd $140**
Same as Flite-King Deluxe Rib 12 except 30-inch vent. rib bbl., F choke, special trap stock w/recoil pad. Made from 1962 to 1966.

FLITE-KING TROPHY 12 GA. . . . . . **NiB $290 Ex $200 Gd $105**
Same as Flite-King Deluxe Rib 12 except has 27-inch vent. rib bbl. w/adj. choke. Made from 1960 to 1966.

FLITE-KING TROPHY 20 GA. . . . . . **NiB $290 Ex $200 Gd $105**
Same as Flite-King Deluxe Rib 20 except has 27-inch vent. rib bbl. w/adj. choke. Made from 1962 to 1966.

SUPERMATIC DEER GUN. . . . . . . **NiB $345 Ex $165 Gd $100**
Same as Supermatic Field 12 except has 22-inch bbl. (Cyl. bore) w/ rifle sights, checkered stock and forearm, recoil pad. Weight: 7.75 lbs. Made in 1965.

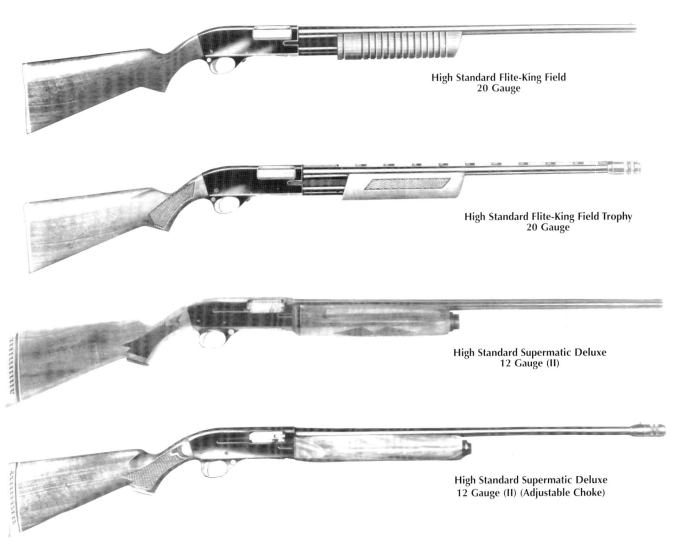

High Standard Flite-King Field
20 Gauge

High Standard Flite-King Field Trophy
20 Gauge

High Standard Supermatic Deluxe
12 Gauge (II)

High Standard Supermatic Deluxe
12 Gauge (II) (Adjustable Choke)

SUPERMATIC DELUXE 12 GA. (SERIES II)
Gas-operated autoloader. 4-round magazine. Bbls.: Plain 27-inch w/adj. choke (disc. about 1970); 26-inch IC, 28-inch M/F; 30-inch F choke. Weight: About 7.5 lbs. Checkered pistol-grip stock and forearm, recoil pad. Made from 1966 to 1975.
w/adj. choke . . . . NiB $375 Ex $195 Gd $120
Vent. rib, add $40

SUPERMATIC DELUXE 20 GA. (SERIES II)
Same as Supermatic Deluxe 12 (II) except chambered for 20 ga. 3-inch shell; bbls. available in 27-inch w/adj. choke (disc. about 1970), 26-inch IC, 28-inch M/F choke. Weight: About 7 lbs. Made from 1966 to 1975.
w/adj. choke . . . . NiB $315 Ex $199 Gd $99
Vent. Rib, add $20

SUPERMATIC DELUXE DEER GUN
(SERIES II). . . . . NiB $345 Ex $165 Gd $100
Same as Supermatic Deluxe 12 (II) except has 22-inch bbl., Cyl. bore, rifle sights. Weight: 7.75 lbs. Made from 1966 to 1974.

SUPERMATIC DELUXE DUCK
12 GA. MAGNUM (SERIES II) . . . . . . NiB $335 Ex $227 Gd $140
Same as Supermatic Deluxe 12 (II) except chambered for 3-inch Mag. shells, 3-round magazine, 30-inch plain bbl., F choke. Weight: 8 lbs. Made from 1966 to 1974.

SUPERMATIC DELUXE
RIB 12 GA. . . . . NiB $335 Ex $227 Gd $140
Same as Supermatic Field 12 except vent. rib bbl. (28-inch M/F, 30-inch F), checkered stock and forearm. Made from 1961 to 1966.

SUPERMATIC DELUXE RIB 12 GA. (II)
Same as Supermatic Deluxe 12 (II) except has vent. rib bbl.; available in 27-inch w/adj. choke, 28-inch M/F, 30-inch F choke. Made from 1966 to 1975.
w/adj. choke . . . . NiB $335 Ex $227 Gd $140
Vent. rib, add $50

SUPERMATIC DELUXE RIB
20 GA. . . . . NiB $377 Ex $265 Gd $180
Same as Supermatic Field 20 except vent. rib bbl. 28-inch M/F. Checkered stock and forearm. Made from 1963 to 1966.

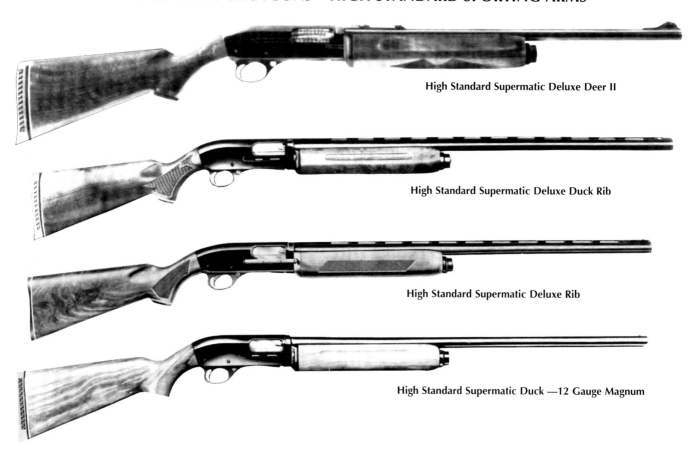

High Standard Supermatic Deluxe Deer II

High Standard Supermatic Deluxe Duck Rib

High Standard Supermatic Deluxe Rib

High Standard Supermatic Duck —12 Gauge Magnum

SUPERMATIC DELUXE RIB 20 GA. (II)
Same as Supermatic Deluxe 20 (II) except has vent. rib bbl. Made from 1966 to 1975.
w/adj. choke . . . . **NiB $377 Ex $265 Gd $180**
Vent. rib, add **$50**

SUPERMATIC DELUXE SKEET GUN
12 GA. (SERIES II) . . . . **NiB $380 Ex $275 Gd $190**
Same as Supermatic Deluxe Rib 12 (II) except available only w/26-inch vent. rib bbl., SK choke. Made from 1966 to 1975.

SUPERMATIC DELUXE SKEET GUN
20 GA. (SERIES II) . . . . **NiB $370 Ex $285 Gd $200**
Same as Supermatic Deluxe Rib 20 (II) except available only w/26-inch vent. rib bbl., SK choke. Made from 1966 to 1975.

SUPERMATIC DELUXE
TRAP GUN (SERIES II) . . . . **NiB $315 Ex $239 Gd $177**
Same as Supermatic Deluxe Rib 12 (II) except available only w/30-inch vent. rib bbl., full choke; trap-style stock. Made 1966 to 1975.

SUPERMATIC DELUXE DUCK RIB
12 GA. MAG. (SERIES II) . . . . . . **NiB $375 Ex $265 Gd $180**
Same as Supermatic Deluxe Rib 12 (II) except chambered for 3-inch Mag. shells, 3-round magazine; 30-inch vent. rib bbl., F choke. Weight: 8 lbs. Made from 1966 to 1975.

SUPERMATIC DUCK 12 GA. MAG. . . . . . **NiB $355 Ex $241 Gd $188**
Same as Supermatic Field 12 except chambered for 3-inch Mag. shell, 30-inch F choke bbl., recoil pad. Made from 1961 to 1966.

SUPERMATIC TROPHY 12 GA. . . . . . .NiB $300 Ex $198 Gd $140
Same as Supermatic Deluxe Rib 12 except has 27-inch vent. rib bbl. w/adj. choke. Made from 1961 to 1966.

SUPERMATIC DUCK RIB 12 GA. MAG.. . . . . . .NiB $355 Ex $241 Gd $188
Same as Supermatic Duck 12 Mag. except has vent. rib bbl., checkered stock and forearm. Made from 1961 to 1966.

SUPERMATIC FIELD AUTOLOADING
SHOTGUN 12 GA. . . . . **NiB $270 Ex $197 Gd $110**
Gas operated. Magazine holds 4 rounds. Bbls.: 26-inch IC, 28-inch M/F choke, 30-inch F choke. Weight: About 7.5 lbs. Plain pistol-grip stock and forearm. Made from 1960 to 1966.

SUPERMATIC FIELD AUTOLOADING
SHOTGUN 20 GA.. . . . . **NiB $290 Ex $217 Gd $156**
Gas operated. Chambered for 3-inch Mag. shells, also handles 2.75-inch. Magazine holds 3 rounds. Bbls.: 26-inch IC, 28-inch M/F choke. Weight: About 7 lbs. Plain pistol-grip stock and forearm. Made from 1963 to 1966.

SUPERMATIC SHADOW AUTOMATIC . . . . .NiB $455 Ex $265 Gd $200
Gas operated. Ga.: 12, 20. 2.75- or 3-inch chamber in 12 ga., 3-inch in 20 ga. Holds four 2.75-inch shells, three 3-inch. Bbls.: Full-size airflow rib; 26-inch (IC/SK choke), 28-inch (M/IM/F), 30-inch (trap or F choke), 12-ga. 3-inch Mag. available only in 30-inch F choke; 20 ga. not available in 30-inch. Weight: (12 ga.) 7 lbs. Checkered walnut stock and forearm. Made 1974 to 1975 by Caspoll Int'l., Inc., Tokyo.

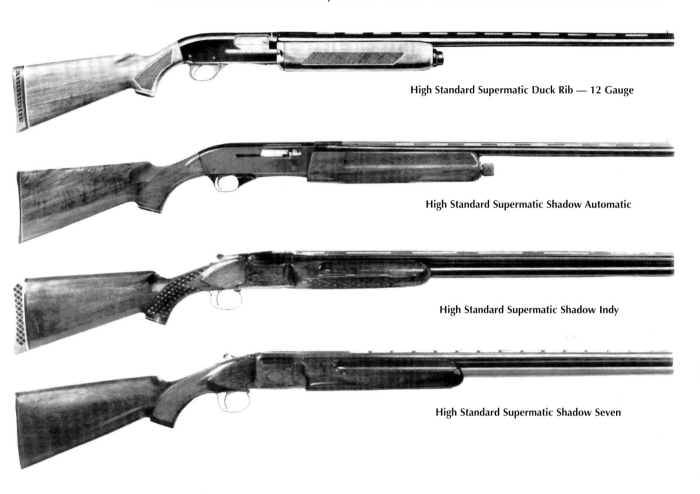

High Standard Supermatic Duck Rib — 12 Gauge

High Standard Supermatic Shadow Automatic

High Standard Supermatic Shadow Indy

High Standard Supermatic Shadow Seven

SUPERMATIC SHADOW
INDY O/U. . . . . NiB $935 Ex $770 Gd $500
Boxlock. Fully engraved receiver. Selective auto ejectors. Selective single trigger. 12 ga. 2.75-inch chambers. Bbls.: Full-size airflow rib; 27.5-inch both SK choke, 29.75-inch IM/F or F/F. Weight: (29.75-inch bbls.) 8 lbs., 2 oz. Pistol-grip stock w/recoil pad, ventilated forearm, skip checkering. Made 1974 to 1975 by Caspoll Int'l., Inc., Tokyo.

SUPERMATIC SHADOW SEVEN. . . . . . NiB $755 Ex $533 Gd $400
Same general specifications as Shadow Indy except has conventional vent. rib, less elaborate engraving, standard checkering forearm is not vented, no recoil pad. 27.5-inch bbls.; also available in IC/M, M/F choke. Made from 1974 to 1975.

SUPERMATIC SKEET 12 GA. . . . . . NiB $344 Ex $245 Gd $177
Same as Supermatic Deluxe Rib 12 except 26-inch vent. rib bbl. w/SK choke. Made from 1962 to 1966.

SUPERMATIC SKEET 20 GA. . . . . . NiB $390 Ex $277 Gd $217
Same as Supermatic Deluxe Rib 20 except 26-inch vent. rib bbl. w/SK choke. Made from 1964 to 1966.

SUPERMATIC SPECIAL 12 GA. . . . . .NiB $290 Ex $190 Gd $145
Same as Supermatic Field 12 except has 27-inch bbl. w/adj. choke. Made from 1960 to 1966.

SUPERMATIC SPECIAL 20 GA. . . . . .NiB $315 Ex $220 Gd $145
Same as Supermatic Field 20 except has 27-inch bbl. w/adj. choke. Made from 1963 to 1966.

SUPERMATIC TRAP 12 GA. . . . . . NiB $330 Ex $245 Gd $170
Same as Supermatic Deluxe Rib 12 except 30-inch vent. rib bbl., F choke, special trap stock w/recoil pad. Made from 1962 to 1966.

SUPERMATIC TROPHY 20 GA.. . . . . .NiB $360 Ex $275 Gd $190
Same as Supermatic Deluxe Rib 20 except has 27-inch vent. rib bbl. w/adj. choke. Made from 1963 to 1966.

HOLLAND & HOLLAND, LTD. —
London, England

BADMINTON HAMMERLESS DOUBLE-BARREL SHOTGUN, ORIGINAL NO. 2 GRADE
General specifications same as Royal Model except without self-opening action. Made as a game gun or pigeon and wildfowl gun. Introduced in 1902. Disc.
w/double triggers . . . . . .NiB $27,875 Ex $22,500 Gd $18,975
w/single trigger. . . . . . . .NiB $28,875 Ex $24,000 Gd $19,600
20 ga., add 25%
28 ga., add 40%
.410, add. 65%

CENTENARY MODEL HAMMERLESS DOUBLE-BARREL SHOTGUN
Lightweight (5.5 lbs.). 12 ga. game gun designed for 2-inch shell. Made in four grades—Model Deluxe, Royal, Badminton, Dominion. Values: Add 35% to prices shown for standard guns in those grades. Disc. 1962.

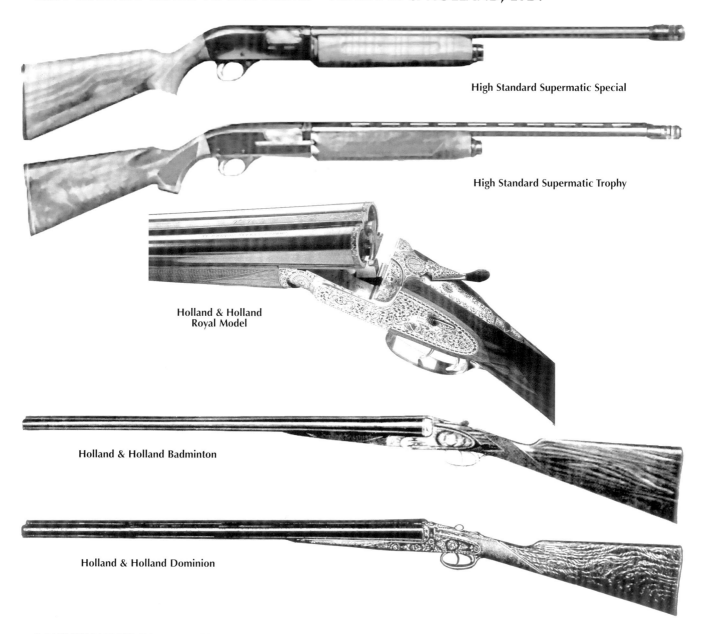

High Standard Supermatic Special

High Standard Supermatic Trophy

Holland & Holland
Royal Model

Holland & Holland Badminton

Holland & Holland Dominion

DOMINION MODEL HAMMERLESS
DOUBLE-BARREL SHOTGUN ... NiB $7355 Ex $6121 Gd $3896
Game Gun. Sidelock. Auto ejectors. Double triggers. Gauges: 12, 16, 20. Bbls. 25 to 30 inch, any standard boring. Checkered stock and forend, straight grip standard. Disc. 1967.

DELUXE HAMMERLESS DOUBLE
Same as Royal Model except has special engraving and exhibition grade stock and forearm. Currently manufactured.
w/double triggers ..... NiB $44,579 Ex $41,960 Gd $34,590
w/single trigger ...... NiB $66,800 Ex $53,980 Gd $40,676

NORTHWOOD MODEL HAMMERLESS
DOUBLE-BARREL SHOTGUN....... NiB $6154 Ex $4944 Gd $4000
Anson & Deeley-system boxlock. Auto ejectors. Double triggers. Gauges: 12, 16, 20, 28 in Game Model; 28 ga. not offered in Pigeon Model; Wildfowl Model in 12 ga. only (3-inch chambers available). Bbls.: 28 inch standard in Game and Pigeon Models, 30 inch in

Wildfowl Model; other lengths, any standard choke combination available. Weight: 5 to 7.75 lbs. depending on ga. and bbls. Checkered straight-grip or pistol-grip stock and forearm. Disc. 1990.

RIVIERA MODEL
PIGEON GUN .... NiB $32,877 Ex $25,788 Gd $19,900
Same as Badminton Model but supplied w/two sets of bbls., double triggers. Disc. 1967.

ROYAL MODEL HAMMERLESS DOUBLE
Self-opening. Sidelocks hand-detachable. Auto ejectors. Double triggers or single trigger. Gauges: 12, 16, 20, 28, .410. Built to customer specifications as to bbl. length, chokes, etc. Made as a Game Gun or Pigeon and Wildfowl Gun, the latter having treble-grip action and side clips. Checkered stock and forend, straight grip standard. Made from 1885, disc. 1951.
w/double triggers ...... NiB $39,900 Ex $31,676 Gd $28,800
w/single trigger ....NiB $44,980 Ex $42,600 Gd $36,700

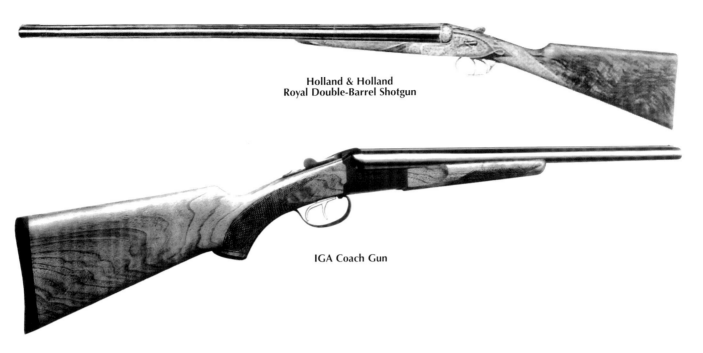

Holland & Holland
Royal Double-Barrel Shotgun

IGA Coach Gun

ROYAL MODEL O/U

Sidelocks, hand-detachable. Auto-ejectors. Double triggers or single trigger. 12 ga. Built to customer specifications as to bbl. length, chokes, etc. Made as a Game Gun or Pigeon and Wildfowl Gun. Checkered stock and forend, straight grip standard. Note: In 1951 Holland & Holland introduced its New Model Over/Under w/an improved, narrower action body. Disc. 1960.

New model
  (double triggers) . . . . . NiB $40,770 Ex $32,550 Gd $21,900
New model
  (single trigger) . . . . NiB $41,800 Ex $33,750 Gd $22,500
Old model
  (double triggers) . . . . . NiB $33,970 Ex $27,600 Gd $20,550
Old model
  (single trigger) . . . . NiB $36,975 Ex $29,500 Gd $21,880

SINGLE-SHOT SUPER TRAP GUN

Anson & Deeley-system boxlock. Auto-ejector. No safety. 12 ga. Bbls.: Wide vent. rib, 30 or 32 inch. Extra Full choke. Weight: About 8.75 lbs. Monte Carlo stock w/pistol grip and recoil pad, full beavertail forearm. Models differ in grade of engraving and wood used. Disc.

Standard grade . . . . NiB $4890 Ex $2988 Gd $1598
Deluxe grade . . . . NiB $7355 Ex $6355 Gd $3559
Exhibition grade . . . . NiB $9677 Ex $7355 Gd $4977

SPORTING O/U . . . . . . NiB $31,750 Ex $24,776 Gd $17,870

Blitz action. Auto ejectors; single selective trigger. Gauges: 12 or 20. 2.75-inch chambers. Barrels: 28 to 32 inch w/screw-in choke tubes. Hand-checkered European walnut straight-grip or pistol grip stock, forearm. Made from 1993 to 2003.

SPORTING O/U

DELUXE . . . . NiB $38,875 Ex $32,669 Gd $23,670

Same general specs as Sporting O/U except better engraving and select wood. Made from 1993 to date.

HUNTER ARMS COMPANY — Fulton, NY

FULTON HAMMERLESS DOUBLE-BARREL SHOTGUN

Boxlock. Plain extractors. Double triggers or nonselective single trigger. Gauges: 12, 16, 20. Bbls.: 26 to 32 inch, various choke combinations. Weight: About 7 lbs. Checkered pistol-grip stock and forearm. Disc. 1948.

w/double triggers . . . . NiB $775 Ex $450 Gd $375
w/single trigger . . . . NiB $990 Ex $700 Gd $555

SPECIAL HAMMERLESS DOUBLE-BARREL SHOTGUN

Boxlock. Plain extractors. Double triggers or nonselective single trigger. Gauges: 12,16, 20. Bbls.: 26 to 30 inch various choke combinations. Weight: 6.5 to 7.25 lbs. depending on bbl. length and ga. Checkered full pistol-grip stock and forearm. Disc. 1948.

w/double triggers . . . . NiB $933 Ex $655 Gd $500
w/single trigger . . . . NiB $1155 Ex $820 Gd $600

IGA — Veranopolis, Brazil.

Imported by Stoeger Industries, Inc., Accokeek, MD

STANDARD COACH GUN

Side-by-side double. Gauges: 12, 20, and .410. 20-inch bbls. 3-inch chambers. Fixed chokes (standard model) or screw-in tubes (Deluxe model). Weight: 6.5 lbs. Double triggers. Ejector and automatic safety. Blued or nickel finish. Hand-rubbed oil-finished pistol grip stock and forend w/hand checkering—hardwood on standard model or Brazilian walnut (Deluxe). Imported 1983 to 2000.

Blued finish. . . . . NiB $400 Ex $295 Gd $200
Nickel finish . . . . NiB $465 Ex $377 Gd $259
Engraved stock . . . . NiB $445 Ex $335 Gd $225
Deluxe Coach Gun (intro. 1997) . . . . . . NiB $400 Ex $290 Gd $195
Choke tubes, add $75

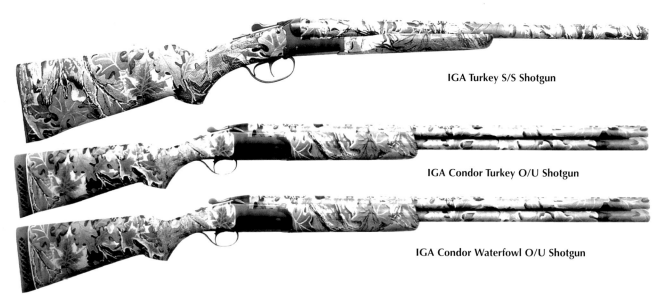

IGA Turkey S/S Shotgun

IGA Condor Turkey O/U Shotgun

IGA Condor Waterfowl O/U Shotgun

CONDOR I
O/U, single trigger. Gauges: 12 or 20. 26- or 28-inch bbls. of chrome-molybdenum steel. Chokes: Fixed (M/F or IC/M), screw-in choke tubes (12 and 20 ga.). 3-inch chambers. Weight: 6.75 to 7 lbs. Sighting rib w/anti-glare surface. Hand-checkered hardwood pistol-grip stock and forend. Imported from 1983 to 1985.
w/fixed choke . . . . NiB $420 Ex $377 Gd $210
w/screw-in tubes . . . . NiB $499 Ex $441 Gd $350

CONDOR II . . . . NiB $477 Ex $365 Gd $290
Same general specifications as the Condor I O/U except w/double triggers and fixed chokes only; 26-inch bbls., IC/M; 28-inch bbls., M/F.

CONDOR OUTBACK . . . . NiB $499 Ex $370 Gd $290
Same general specifications as the Condor I O/U except w/20-inch bbls., IC/M choke tubes, rifle-style sights. Made 2007 to date.

CONDOR SUPREME. . . . . NiB $655 Ex $545 Gd $477
Same general specifications as Condor I except upgraded w/fine-checkered Brazilian walnut buttstock and forend, matte-laquered finish, and massive monoblock that joins the bbls. in a solid one-piece assembly at the breech end. Bbls. w/recessed interchangeable choke tubes formulated for use w/steel shot. Automatic ejectors. Imported from 1995 to 2000.

CONDOR TURKEY MODEL . . . . . NiB $755 Ex $600 Gd $445
12 ga. only. 26-inch vent. rib bbls. 3-inch chambers fitted w/ recessed interchangeable choke tubes. Weight: 8 lbs. Mechanical single trigger. Ejectors and automatic safety. Advantage camouflage on stock and bbls. Made from 1997 to 2000.

CONDOR WATERFOWL MODEL . . . . . . NiB $770 Ex $605 Gd $475
Similar to Condor Turkey-Advantage camo model except w/30-inch bbls. Made from 1998 to 2000.

DELUXE HUNTER CLAYS . . . . NiB $700 Ex $552 Gd $435
Same general specifications and values as IGA Condor Supreme. Imported from 1997 to 1999.

DOUBLE DEFENSE . . . . NiB $499 Ex $280 Gd $135
Similar to Coach S/S boxlock. Gauges: 12 or 20. 20-inch ported bbls. w/Picatinny rails. Fixed IC choke. 3-inch chambers. Weight: 6.4 to 7.1 lbs. Single trigger. Matte black finish receiver and pistol-grip wood stock. Imported from 2009 to date.
Non-ported bbl.. . . . . NiB $479 Ex $275 Gd $120

ERA MODEL 2000 . . . . NiB $500 Ex $379 Gd $290
Gauge: 12. 3-inch chambers. 26- or 28-inch bbls. of chrome-molybdenum steel w/screw-in choke tubes. Extractors. Manual safety. (Mechanical triggers.) Weight: 7 lbs. Checkered Brazilian hardwood stock w/oil finish. Imported from 1992 to 1995.

REUNA SINGLE-SHOT
Visible hammer. Under-lever release. Gauges: 12, 20, and .410. 3-inch chambers. w/fixed chokes or screw-in choke tubes (12 ga. only). Extractors. Weight: 5.25 to 6.5 lbs. Plain Brazilian hardwood stock and semi-beavertail forend. Imported from 1992 to1998.
w/fixed choke . . . . NiB $210 Ex $155 Gd $90
w/choke tubes. . . . . NiB $275 Ex $190 Gd $145

UPLANDER
S/S boxlock. Gauges: 12, 20, 28, and .410. 26- or 28-inch bbls. of chrome-molybdenum steel. Various fixed-choke combinations; screw-in choke tubes (12 and 20 ga.). 3-inch chambers (2.75-inch in 28 ga.). Weight: 6.25 to 7 lbs. Double triggers. Automatic safety. Matte-finished solid sighting rib. Hand checkered pistol-grip or straight stock and forend w/hand-rubbed oil finish. Imported from 1997 to 2000.
Upland w/fixed chokes. . . . . NiB $390 Ex $275 Gd $225
Upland w/screw-in tubes . . . . NiB $420 Ex $345 Gd $290
English model (straight grip) . . . . . NiB $500 Ex $395 Gd $290
Ladies model. . . . . NiB $477 Ex $365 Gd $300
Supreme model. . . . . NiB $610 Ex $477 Gd $325
Youth model . . . . NiB $477 Ex $345 Gd $270

UPLANDER TURKEY MODEL . . . . . . NiB $588 Ex $440 Gd $379
12 ga. only. 24-inch solid rib bbls. 3-inch chambers choked F/F. Weight: 6.75 lbs. Double triggers. Automatic safety. Advantage camo on stock and bbls. Made from 1997 to 2000.

ITHACA GUN COMPANY — King Ferry (formerly Ithaca), NY; Ithaca Acquisition Corp./Ithaca Gun Co.

MODEL 37 BICENTENNIAL
COMMEMORATIVE . . . . NiB $645 Ex $553 Gd $445
Limited to issue of 1976. Similar to Model 37 Supreme except has special Bicentennial design etched on receiver, fancy walnut stock and slide handle. Serial numbers U.S.A. 0001 to U.S.A. 1976. Originally issued w/presentation case w/cast-pewter belt buckle. Made in 1976. Best value is for gun in new unfired condition.

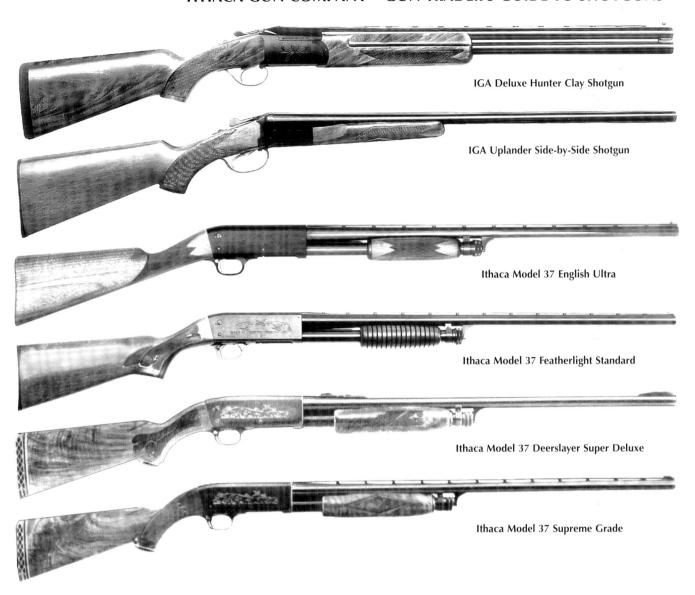

IGA Deluxe Hunter Clay Shotgun

IGA Uplander Side-by-Side Shotgun

Ithaca Model 37 English Ultra

Ithaca Model 37 Featherlight Standard

Ithaca Model 37 Deerslayer Super Deluxe

Ithaca Model 37 Supreme Grade

MODEL 37 DEERSLAYER DELUXE
Formerly Model 87 Deerslayer Deluxe, reintroduced under the original Model 37 designation w/same specifications. Available w/ smoothbore or rifled bbl. Reintroduced 1996. Disc.
Deluxe model (smooth bore) .... NiB $575 Ex $490 Gd $335
Deluxe model (rifled bbl.)........ NiB $608 Ex $522 Gd $370

MODEL 37 DEERSLAYER II...... NiB $608 Ex $522 Gd $370
Gauges: 12 or 20. 5-round capacity. 20- or 25-inch rifled bbl. Weight: 7 lbs. Monte Carlo checkered walnut stock and forearm. Receiver drilled and tapped for scope mount. Made 1996 to 2000.

MODEL 37 DEERSLAYER STANDARD........NiB $355 Ex $280 Gd $225
Same as Model 37 Standard except has 20- or 26-inch bbl. bored for rifled slugs, rifle-type open rear sight, and ramp front sight. Weight: 5.75 to 6.5 lbs. depending on ga. and bbl. length. Made from 1959 to 1986.

MODEL 37 DEERSLAYER
SUPER DELUXE .... NiB $465 Ex $344 Gd $220
Formerly Deluxe Deerslayer. Same as Model 37 Standard Deerslayer except has stock and slide handle of fancy walnut. Made 1962 to 1986.

MODEL 37 ENGLISH ULTRALIGHT........ NiB $635 Ex $500 Gd $400
Same general specifications as Model 37 Ultralite except straight buttstock, 25-inch Hot Forged vent. rib bbl. Made 1984 to 1987.

MODEL 37 FEATHERLIGHT STANDARD GRADE
SLIDE-ACTION REPEATING SHOTGUN
Adaptation of the earlier Remington Model 17, a Browning design patented in 1915. Hammerless. Takedown. Gauges: 12, 16 (disc. 1973), 20. 4-round magazine. Bbl. lengths: 26, 28, 30 inch (the latter in 12 ga. only); standard chokes. Weight: 5.75 to 7.5 lbs. depending on ga. and bbl. length. Checkered pistol-grip stock and slide handle. Some guns made in the 1950s and 1960s have grooved slide handle; plain or checkered pistol-grip. Made 1937 to 1984.
Standard model w/checkered
pistol grip .... NiB $675 Ex $390 Gd $300
w/plain stock .... NiB $325 Ex $229 Gd $190
Mdl 37D Deluxe (1954-77) ..... NiB $675 Ex $390 Gd $300
Mdl 37DV Deluxe vent. rib (1962-84) ...... NiB $675 Ex $390 Gd $300
Mdl 37R Deluxe
solid rib (1955-61)........... NiB $675 Ex $390 Gd $300
Mdl 37V Standard
vent. rib (1962-84).......... NiB $315 Ex $244 Gd $148

**Ithaca Model 51
Deluxe Trap**

MODEL 37 FIELD GRADE
MAG. W/TUBES . . . . **NiB $355 Ex $298 Gd $199**
Same general specifications as Model 37 Featherlight except 32-inch bbl. and detachable choke tubes. Vent. rib bbl. Made 1984 to 1987.

MODEL 37 CLASSIC . . . . **NiB $755 Ex $555 Gd $465**
Gauges: 12 or 20. 20- or 28-inch vent. rib bbl. w/choke tubes. Knuckle-cut receiver and original-style ring-tail forend. Limited prod. Made from 1998 to 2005.

MODEL 37 $1000 GRADE
Custom built, elaborately engraved, and inlaid w/gold, hand-finished working parts. Stock and forend of select figured walnut. General specifications same as standard Model 37. Note: Designated The $1000 Grade prior to WWII. Made 1937 to 1967.
$1000 grade . . . . **NiB $5988 Ex $4776 Gd $3987**
$5000 grade . . . . **NiB $5588 Ex $4487 Gd $3960**

MODEL 37 SUPREME GRADE . . . . . . **NiB $955 Ex $588 Gd $535**
Available in Skeet or Trap Gun, similar to Model 37T. Made 1967 to 1986 and 1997. Subtract $225 for newer models.

MODEL 37 ULTRALITE
Same general specifications as Model 37 Featherlight except streamlined forend, gold trigger, Sid Bell grip cap and vent. rib. Weight: 5 to 5.75 lbs. Made from 1984 to 1987.
Standard . . . . **NiB $559 Ex $400 Gd $363**
Choke tubes, add **$150**

MODEL 37R SOLID RIB GRADE
Same general specifications as the Model 37 Featherlight except has a raised solid rib, adding about .25 lbs. of weight. Made 1937 to 1967.
**w/checkered grip
  and slide handle.** . . . . **NiB $400 Ex $310 Gd $200**
w/plain stock . . . . **NiB $292 Ex $195 Gd $145**

MODEL 37S SKEET GRADE . . . . **NiB $565 Ex $455 Gd $335**
Same general specifications as the Model 37 Featherlight except has vent. rib and large extension-type forend. Weight: About .5 lb. more. Made from 1937 to 1955.

MODEL 37T TARGET GRADE . . . . . . **NiB $545 Ex $376 Gd $255**
Same general specifications as Model 37 Featherlight except has vent. rib bbl., checkered stock and slide handle of fancy walnut (choice of skeet- or trap-style stock). Note: This model replaced Model 37S Skeet and Model 37T Trap. Made from 1955 to 1961.

MODEL 37T TRAP GRADE . . . . . . **NiB $545 Ex $376 Gd $255**
Same general specifications as Model 37S except has straighter trap-style stock of select walnut, recoil pad. Weight: About .5 lb. more. Made from 1937 to 1955.

MODEL 37 TURKEYSLAYER
Gauges: 12 ga. (Standard) or 20 ga. (Youth). Slide action. 22-inch bbl. Extended choke tube. Weight: 7 lbs. Advantage camo or Realtree pattern. Made from 1996 to 2005.
Standard model . . . . **NiB $425 Ex $260 Gd $190**
Youth model (intro. 1998). . . . . **NiB $555 Ex $456 Gd $345**

MODEL 37 WATERFOWLER. . . . . . **NiB $490 Ex $375 Gd $260**
12 ga. only. 28-inch bbl. Wetlands camo. Made 1998 to 2005.

MODEL 51 DEERSLAYER . . . . . . **NiB $400 Ex $279 Gd $200**
Same as Model 51 Standard except has 24-inch plain bbl. w/slug boring, rifle sights, recoil pad. Weight: About 7.25 lbs. Made from 1972 to 1984.

MODEL 51 SUPREME SKEET GRADE . . . . . . **NiB $525 Ex $390 Gd $270**
Same as Model 51 Standard except 26-inch vent. rib bbl. only, SK choke, skeet-style stock, semi-fancy wood. Weight: About 8 lbs. Made from 1970 to 1987.

MODEL 51 SUPREME TRAP
Same as Model 51 Standard except 12 ga. only. 30-inch bbl. w/ broad floating rib, F choke, trap-style stock w/straight or Monte Carlo comb, semi-fancy wood, recoil pad. Weight: About 8 lbs. Made from 1970 to 1987.
w/straight stock . . . . **NiB $544 Ex $390 Gd $295**
Monte Carlo stock, add **$75**

MODEL 51 FEATHERLITE STANDARD
Gas operated. Gauges: 12, 20. 3-round. Bbls.: Plain or vent. rib, 30-inch F choke (12 ga. only), 28-inch F/M, 26-inch IC. Weight: 7.25 to 7.75 lbs. depending on ga. and bbl. Checkered pistol-grip stock, forearm. Made 1970 to 1980. Available in 12 and 20 ga., 28-inch M choke only.
w/plain barrel . . . . **NiB $300 Ex $197 Gd $121**
Vent rib, add **$65**

MODEL 51A STANDARD MAGNUM
Same as Model 51 Standard except has 3-inch chamber, handles Mag. shells only; 30-inch bbl. in 12 ga., 28-inch in 20 ga. F/M choke, stock w/recoil pad. Weight: 7.75 to 8 lbs. Made 1972 to 1982.
w/plain bbl. (disc. 1976). . . . . **NiB $375 Ex $290 Gd $200**
Camo finish, add. **$65**

MODEL 51A TURKEY GUN . . . . . **NiB $455 Ex $300 Gd $217**
Same general specifications as standard Model 51 Mag. except 26-inch bbl. and matte finish. Disc. 1986.

MODEL 66 LONG TOM . . . . **NiB $210 Ex $155 Gd $100**
Same as Model 66 Standard except has 36-inch F choke bbl., 12 ga. only, checkered stock and recoil pad standard. Made 1969 to 1974.

MODEL 66 STANDARD SUPER SINGLE LEVER
Single shot. Hand-cocked hammer. Gauges: 12 (disc. 1974), 20, .410. 3-inch chambers. Bbls.: 12 ga., 30-inch F choke, 28-inch F/M; 20 ga., 28-inch F/M; .410, 26-inch F. Weight: About 7 lbs. Plain or checkered straight-grip stock, plain forend. Made from 1963 to 1978.
Standard model . . . . **NiB $220 Ex $115 Gd $90**
Vent. rib model (20 ga., 1969-74) . . . . . . **NiB $225 Ex $159 Gd $135**
Youth model (1965-78) . . . . **NiB $250 Ex $179 Gd $130**

MODEL 66RS BUCKBUSTER . . . . . **NiB $279 Ex $200 Gd $155**
Same as Model 66 Standard except has 22-inch bbl. Cyl. bore w/rifle sights, later version has recoil pad. Originally offered in 12 and 20 ga.; the former was disc. in 1970. Made from 1967 to 1978.

Ithaca
Model 66RS
Buckbuster

Previously issued as the Ithaca Model 37, the Model 87 guns listed below were made available through the Ithaca Acquisition Corp. from 1986 to 1995. Production of the Model 37 resumed under the original logo in 1996.

MODEL 87 DEERLSLAYER SHOTGUN
Gauges: 12 or 20. 3-inch chamber. Bbls.: 18.5, 20, or 25 inch (w/special or rifled bore). Weight: 6 to 6.75 lbs. Ramp blade front sight, adj. rear. Receiver grooved for scope. Checkered American walnut pistol-grip stock and forearm. Made from 1988 to 1996.
Basic model . . . . NiB $445 Ex $355 Gd $225
Basic Field Combo
  (w/extra 28-inch bbl.). . . . . . NiB $475 Ex $390 Gd $280
Deluxe model . . . . NiB $480 Ex $395 Gd $290
Deluxe Combo
  (w/extra 28-inch bbl.). . . . . . NiB $635 Ex $460 Gd $339
DSPS (8-round model) . . . . . . NiB $554 Ex $400 Gd $290
Field model . . . . NiB $433 Ex $330 Gd $287
Monte Carlo model . . . . NiB $448 Ex $356 Gd $255
Ultra model (disc. 1991) . . . . . NiB $500 Ex $398 Gd $325

MODEL 87 DEERSLAYER II
RIFLED SHOTGUN . . . . NiB $600 Ex $433 Gd $310
Similar to Standard Deerslayer except w/solid frame construction and 25-inch rifled bbl. Monte Carlo stock. Made 1988 to 1996.

MODEL 87 FIELD GRADE
Gauge: 12 or 20. 3-inch chamber. 5-round magazine. Fixed chokes or screw-in choke tubes (IC/M/F). Bbls.: 18.5 inch (M&P); 20 and 25 inch (Combo); 26-, 28-, 30-inch vent. rib. Weight: 5 to 7 lbs. Made from 1988 to 1996.
Basic field model (disc. 1993) . . . . NiB $446 Ex $270 Gd $210
Camo model . . . . NiB $490 Ex $339 Gd $260
Deluxe model . . . . NiB $505 Ex $340 Gd $280
Deluxe Combo model . . . . NiB $590 Ex $493 Gd $377
English model . . . . NiB $490 Ex $339 Gd $260
Hand grip model
  (w/polymer pistol-grip). . . . . . NiB $533 Ex $425 Gd $315
M&P model (disc. 1995) . . . . . NiB $466 Ex $380 Gd $279
Supreme model . . . . NiB $720 Ex $589 Gd $400
Turkey model. . . . . NiB $445 Ex $365 Gd $256
Ultra Deluxe model (disc. 1992) . . . . . . NiB $400 Ex $356 Gd $260

MODEL 87 ULTRALITE
FIELD PUMP SHOTGUN . . . . . . NiB $490 Ex $387 Gd $260
Gauges: 12 and 20. 2.75-inch chambers. 25-inch bbl. w/choke tube. Weight: 5 to 6 lbs. Made from 1988 to 1990.

HAMMERLESS DOUBLE-BARREL SHOTGUNS
Boxlock. Plain extractors, auto ejectors standard on the E grades. Double triggers, nonselective or selective single trigger extra.

Gauges: Mag. 10, 12; 12, 16, 20, 28, .410. Bbls.: 26 to 32 inch, any standard boring. Weight: 5.75 (.410) to 10.5 lbs. (Mag. 10). Checkered pistol-grip stock and forearm standard. Higher grades differ from Field Grade in quality of workmanship, grade of wood, checkering, engraving, etc.; general specifications are the same. Ithaca doubles made before 1925 (serial number 425,000) the rotary bolt and a stronger frame were adopted. Values shown are for this latter type; earlier models valued about 50% lower. Smaller gauge guns may command up to 75% higher. Disc. 1948.
Field grade . . . . NiB $1088 Ex $900 Gd $677
No. 1 grade . . . . NiB $1377 Ex $1099 Gd $890
No. 2 grade . . . . NiB $2480 Ex $2077 Gd $1100
No. 3 grade . . . . NiB $2456 Ex $1866 Gd $1376
No. 4E grade (ejector) . . . . NiB $6225 Ex $3688 Gd $2977
No. 5E grade (ejector) . . . . NiB $5235 Ex $3767 Gd $4400

EXTRAS:
Magnum 10 or 12 ga.
(in other than the four highest grades), add. 20%
Automatic ejectors (grades No. 1, 2, 3, w/ejectors
  designated No. 1E, 2E, 3E), add. 35%
Selective single trigger, add. $250
Nonselective single trigger, add. $200
Beavertail forend (Field No. 1 or 2), add. $200
Beavertail forend (No. 3 or 4), add $200
Beavertail forend (No. 5, 7, or $2000 grade), add. $200
Ventilated rib (No. 4, 5, 7, or $2000 grade), add. $400
Ventilated rib (lower grades), add $250

LSA-55 TURKEY GUN . . . . NiB $935 Ex $700 Gd $590
Over/under shotgun/rifle combination. Boxlock. Exposed hammer. Plain extractor. Single trigger. 12 ga./222 Rem. 24.5-inch rib bbls. (rifle bbl. has muzzle brake). Weight: About 7 lbs. Folding leaf rear sight, bead front sight. Checkered Monte Carlo stock and forearm. Made 1970 to 1977 by Oy Tikkakoski AB, Finland.

MAG-10 AUTOMATIC SHOTGUN
Gas operated. 10 ga. 3.5-inch Mag. 3-round capacity. 32-inch plain (Standard Grade only) or vent. rib bbl. F choke. Weight: 11 lbs., plain bbl.; 11.5 lbs., vent. rib. Standard grade has plain stock and forearm. Deluxe and Supreme grades have checkering, semi-fancy and fancy wood respectively, and stud swivel. All have recoil pad. Deluxe and Supreme grades made 1974 to 1982. Standard Grade intro. in 1977. All grades disc. 1986.
Camo model . . . . NiB $735 Ex $555 Gd $379
Deluxe grade. . . . . NiB $890 Ex $774 Gd $522
Roadblocker . . . . NiB $855 Ex $740 Gd $533
Standard grade, plain bbl. . . . . . NiB $744 Ex $610 Gd $477
Standard grade
  w/vent. rib . . . . NiB $844 Ex $633 Gd $530
Standard grade, w/choke tubes. . . . . NiB $988 Ex $755 Gd $544
Supreme grade . . . . NiB $1044 Ex $856 Gd $600

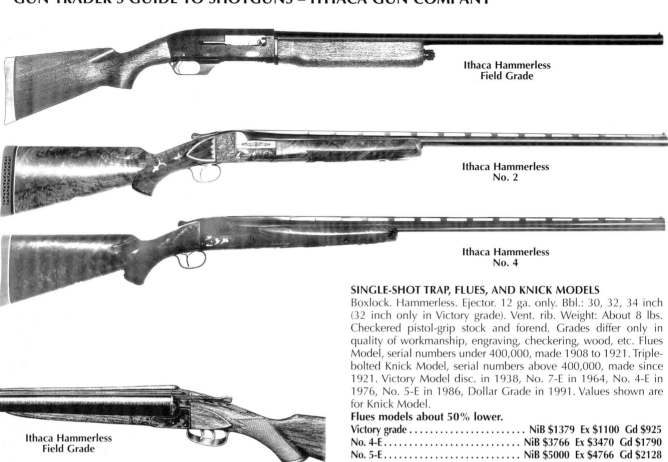

Ithaca Hammerless
Field Grade

Ithaca Hammerless
No. 2

Ithaca Hammerless
No. 4

Ithaca Hammerless
Field Grade

Ithaca Model 5-E

Ithaca Single-Shot Trap
Dollar Grade

SINGLE-SHOT TRAP, FLUES, AND KNICK MODELS

Boxlock. Hammerless. Ejector. 12 ga. only. Bbl.: 30, 32, 34 inch (32 inch only in Victory grade). Vent. rib. Weight: About 8 lbs. Checkered pistol-grip stock and forend. Grades differ only in quality of workmanship, engraving, checkering, wood, etc. Flues Model, serial numbers under 400,000, made 1908 to 1921. Triple-bolted Knick Model, serial numbers above 400,000, made since 1921. Victory Model disc. in 1938, No. 7-E in 1964, No. 4-E in 1976, No. 5-E in 1986, Dollar Grade in 1991. Values shown are for Knick Model.

Flues models about 50% lower.

Victory grade . . . . NiB $1379 Ex $1100 Gd $925
No. 4-E . . . . NiB $3766 Ex $3470 Gd $1790
No. 5-E . . . . NiB $5000 Ex $4766 Gd $2128
No. 6-E (rare) . . . . NiB $16,980 Ex $14,700 Gd $10,000
No. 7-E (rare) . . . . NiB $7445 Ex $6000 Gd $4655
$2,000 grade . . . . NiB $9,500 Ex $8500 Gd $6650
Prewar $1000 grade . . . . NiB $10,000 Ex $9577 Gd $6650
Sousa grade (rare) . . . . NiB $14,500+ Ex $12,700+ Gd $9000+

NOTE: *The following Ithaca-Perazzi shotguns were manufactured by Manifattura Armi Perazzi, Brescia, Italy. See also separate Perazzi listings.*

PERAZZI COMPETITION I SKEET . . . . NiB $14,877 Ex $13,900 Gd $11,270
Boxlock. Auto ejectors. Single trigger. 12 ga. 26.75-inch vent. rib bbls. SK choke w/integral muzzle brake. Weight: About 7.75 lbs. Checkered skeet-style pistol-grip buttstock and forearm; recoil pad. Made from 1969 to 1974.

PERAZZI COMPETITION
TRAP I O/U . . . . NiB $14,889 Ex $13,679 Gd $11,650
Boxlock. Auto ejectors. Single trigger. 12 ga. 30- or 32-inch vent. rib bbls. IM/F choke. Weight: About 8.5 lbs. Checkered pistol-grip stock, forearm; recoil pad. Made from 1969 to 1974.

PERAZZI COMPETITION I
TRAP SINGLE BARREL . . . . NiB $11,770 Ex $9455 Gd $7655
Boxlock. Auto ejection. 12 ga. 32- or 34-inch bbl., vent. rib, F choke. Weight: 8.5 lbs. Checkered Monte Carlo stock and beavertail forearm, recoil pad. Made from 1973 to 1978.

PERAZZI COMPETITION IV
TRAP GUN . . . . NiB $13,890 Ex $11,870 Gd $10,000
Boxlock. Auto ejection. 12 ga. 32- or 34-inch bbl. With high, wide vent. rib, four interchangeable choke tubes (Extra Full/F/IM/M). Weight: About 8.75 lbs. Checkered Monte Carlo stock and beavertail forearm, recoil pad. Fitted case. Made from 1977 to 1978.

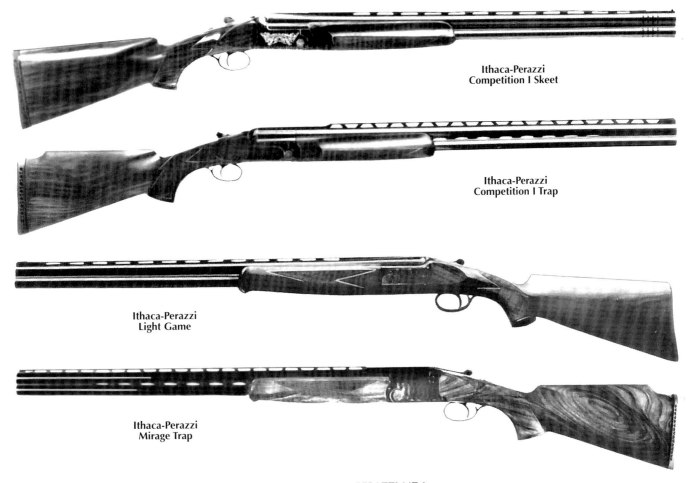

Ithaca-Perazzi
Competition I Skeet

Ithaca-Perazzi
Competition I Trap

Ithaca-Perazzi
Light Game

Ithaca-Perazzi
Mirage Trap

PERAZZI LIGHT GAME
O/U FIELD . . . . NiB $15,800 Ex $14,790 Gd $13,955
Boxlock. Auto ejectors. Single trigger. 12 ga. 27.5-inch vent. rib
bbls., M/F or IC/M choke. Weight: 6.75 lbs. Checkered field-style
stock and forearm. Made from 1972 to 1974.

PERAZZI MIRAGE . . . . NiB $6987 Ex $4677 Gd $2700
Same as Mirage Trap except has 28-inch bbls., M/Extra Full choke,
special stock and forearm for live bird shooting. Weight: About 8
lbs. Made from 1973 to 1978.

PERAZZI MIRAGE SKEET . . . . NiB $4350 Ex $3866 Gd $2789
Same as Mirage Trap except has 28-inch bbls. w/integral muzzle
brakes, SK choke, skeet-stype stock and forearm. Weight: About 8
lbs. Made from 1973 to 1978.

PERAZZI MIRAGE TRAP . . . . . . NiB $4365 Ex $3900 Gd $2820
Same general specifications as MX-8 Trap except has tapered rib.
Made from 1973 to 1978.

PERAZZI MT-6 SKEET . . . . NiB $4233 Ex $3380 Gd $2770
Same as MT-6 Trap except has 28-inch bbls. w/two skeet choke
tubes instead of Extra Full/F, skeet-style stock and forearm. Weight:
About 8 lbs. Made from 1976 to 1978.

PERAZZI MT-6 TRAP COMBO . . . . . . NiB $5377 Ex $4260 Gd $3100
MT-6 w/extra single under bbl. w/high-rise aluminum vent. rib, 32
or 34 inch; seven interchangeable choke tubes (IC through Extra
Full). Fitted case. Made from 1977 to 1978.

PERAZZI MT-6
TRAP O/U . . . . NiB $3700 Ex $2566 Gd $2044
Boxlock. Auto selective ejectors. Nonselective single trigger. 12
ga. Barrels separated, wide vent. rib, 30 or 32 inch, five interchangeable choke tubes (Extra Full/F/IM/M/IC). Weight: About 8.5
lbs. Checkered pistol-grip stock and forearm, recoil pad. Fitted
case. Made from 1976 to 1978.

PERAZZI MX 8 TRAP COMBO . . . NiB $5688 Ex $4355 Gd $2460
MX-8 w/extra single bbl., vent. rib, 32 or 34 inch, F choke, forearm; two trigger groups included. Made from 1973 to 1978.

PERAZZI MX-8 TRAP O/U . . . NiB $4356 Ex $3879 Gd $2889
Boxlock. Auto selective ejectors. Non-selective single trigger. 12
ga. Bbls.: High vent. rib; 30 or 32 inch, IM/F choke. Weight: 8.25
to 8.5 lbs. Checkered Monte Carlo stock and forearm, recoil pad.
Made from 1969 to 1978.

PERAZZI SINGLE-BARREL
TRAP GUN . . . . NiB $3350 Ex $2459 Gd $2000
Boxlock. Auto ejection. 12 ga. 34-inch vent. rib bbl., F choke.
Weight: About 8.5 lbs. Checkered pistol-grip stock, forearm; recoil
pad. Made from 1971 to 1972.

*The following Ithaca-SKB shotguns, manufactured by SKB Arms
Company, Tokyo, Japan, were distributed in the US by Ithaca Gun
Company from 1966 to 1976. See also listings under SKB.*

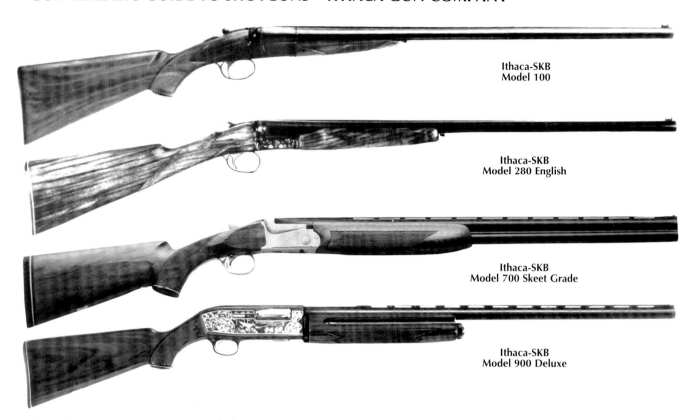

Ithaca-SKB
Model 100

Ithaca-SKB
Model 280 English

Ithaca-SKB
Model 700 Skeet Grade

Ithaca-SKB
Model 900 Deluxe

SKB MODEL 100 SIDE-BY-SIDE. . . . . . NiB $779 Ex $580 Gd $490
Boxlock. Plain extractors. Selective single trigger. Auto safety. Gauges: 12 and 20. 2.75-inch and 3-inch chambers, respectively. Bbls.: 30-inch F/F (12 ga. only), 28-inch F/M, 26-inch IC/M (12 ga. only), 25-inch IC/M (20 ga. only). Weight: 12 ga., about 7 lbs.; 20 ga., about 6 lbs. Checkered stock and forend. Made 1966 to 1976.

SKB MODEL 150 FIELD GRADE. . . . . . NiB $770 Ex $600 Gd $488
Same as Model 100 except has fancier scroll engraving, beavertail forearm. Made from 1972 to 1974.

SKB 200E FIELD GRADE S/S . . . . . . NiB $1077 Ex $767 Gd $580
Same as Model 100 except auto selective ejectors, engraved and silver-plated frame, gold-plated nameplate and trigger, beavertail forearm. Made from 1966 to 1976.

SKB MODEL 200E SKEET GUN . . . . . . NiB $995 Ex $687 Gd $485
Same as Model 200E Field Grade except 26-inch (12 ga.) and 25-inch (20 ga./2.75-inch chambers) bbls., SK choke; nonautomatic safety and recoil pad. Made from 1966 to 1976.

SKB MODEL 200 ENGLISH . . . . . NiB $1154 Ex $990 Gd $759
Same as Model 200E except has scrolled game scene engraving on frame, English-style straight-grip stock. 30-inch bbls. not available; special quail gun in 20 ga. has 25-inch bbls., both bored IC. Made from 1971 to 1976.

SKB MODEL 300 STANDARD AUTOMATIC SHOTGUN
Recoil-operated. Gauges: 12, 20 (3 inch). 5-round capacity. Bbls.: Plain or vent. rib; 30-inch F choke (12 ga. only), 28-inch F/M, 26-inch IC. Weight: About 7 lbs. Checkered pistol-grip stock and forearm. Made from 1968 to 1972.
w/plain barrel. . . . . NiB $1088 Ex $765 Gd $490
20 ga., add 30%

SKB MODEL 500
FIELD GRADE O/U. . . . . NiB $665 Ex $455 Gd $323
Boxlock. Auto selective ejectors. Selective single trigger. Nonautomatic safety. Gauges: 12 and 20. 2.75-inch and 3-inch chambers, respectively. Vent. rib bbls.: 30-inch M/F (12 ga. only); 28-inch M/F; 26-inch IC/M. Weight: 12 ga., about 7.5 lbs; 20 ga., about 6.5 lbs. Checkered stock and forearm. Made from 1966 to 1976.

SKB MODEL 500 MAGNUM. . . . . . NiB $639 Ex $455 Gd $344
Same as Model 500 Field Grade except chambered for 3-inch 12 ga. shells, has 30-inch bbls., IM/F choke. Weight: About 8 lbs. Made 1973 to 1976.

SKB MODEL 600 DOUBLES GUN . . . . . . NiB $1096 Ex $766 Gd $500
Same as Model 600 Trap Grade except specially choked for 21-yard first target, 30-yard second. Made from 1973 to 1975.

SKB MODEL 600 FIELD GRADE . . . . . . NiB $1100 Ex $775 Gd $525
Same as Model 500 except has silver-plated frame, higher grade wood. Made from 1969 to 1976.

SKB MODEL 600 MAGNUM . . . . . . NiB $1125 Ex $800 Gd $550
Same as Model 600 Field Grade except chambered for 3-inch 12 ga. shells; has 30-inch bbls., IM/F choke. Weight: 8.5 lbs. Made from 1969 to 1972.

SKB MODEL 600 SKEET GRADE
Same as Model 500 except also available in 28 and .410 ga., has silver-plated frame, higher grade wood, recoil pad, 26- or 28-inch bbls. (28-inch only in 28 and .410), SK choke. Weight: 7 to 7.75 lbs. depending on ga. and bbl. length. Made from 1966 to 1976.
12 or 20 ga. . . . . NiB $1155 Ex $830 Gd $575
28 ga. or .410. . . . . NiB $1500 Ex $1266 Gd $1077

SKB MODEL 600 SKEET SET . . . . . . NiB $2866 Ex $2249 Gd $1545
Model 600 Skeet Grade w/matched set of 20, 28, and .410 ga. bbls., 28-inch, fitted case. Made from 1970 to 1976.

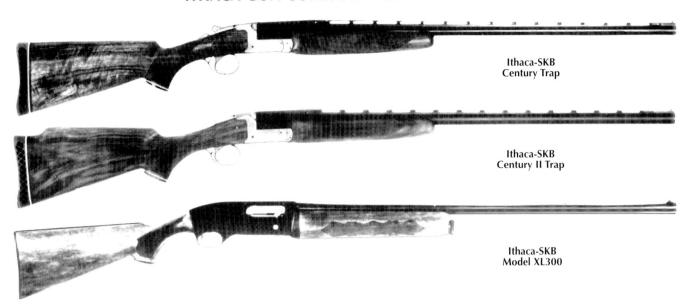

Ithaca-SKB
Century Trap

Ithaca-SKB
Century II Trap

Ithaca-SKB
Model XL300

SKB MODEL 600
TRAP GRADE O/U . . . . **NiB $1055 Ex $700 Gd $533**
Same as Model 500 except 12 ga. only, has silver-plated frame, 30- or 32-inch bbls. choked F/F or F/IM, choice of Monte Carlo or straight stock of higher grade wood, recoil pad. Weight: About 8 lbs. Made from 1966 to 1976.

SKB MODEL 600 ENGLISH . . . NiB $1388 Ex $1055 Gd $775
Same as Model 600 Field Grade except has intricate scroll engraving, English-style straight-grip stock, forearm of extra-fine walnut. 30-inch bbls. not available. Made from 1973 to 1976.

SKB MODEL 700
DOUBLES GUN . . . . **NiB $866 Ex $744 Gd $559**
Same as Model 700 Trap Grade except choked for 21-yard first target, 30-yard second target. Made from 1973 to 1975.

SKB MODEL 700
SKEET COMBO SET . . . . **NiB $3988 Ex $2970 Gd $2175**
Model 700 Skeet Grade w/matched set of 20, 28, and .410 ga. bbls., 28-inch fitted case. Made from 1970 to 1971.

SKB MODEL 700 SKEET GRADE . . . . . NiB $955 Ex $779 Gd $575
Same as Model 600 Skeet Grade except not available in 28 and .410 ga., has more elaborate scroll engraving, extra-wide rib, higher grade wood. Made from 1969 to 1975.

SKB MODEL 700 TRAP GRADE . . . . . NiB $945 Ex $665 Gd $544
Same as Model 600 Trap Grade except has more elaborate scroll engraving, extra-wide rib, higher grade wood. Made from 1969 to 1975.

SKB MODEL 900
DELUXE AUTOMATIC. . . . . **NiB $475 Ex $359 Gd $255**
Same as Model 30 except has game scene etched and gold-filled on receiver, vent. rib standard. Made 1968 to 1972.

SKB MODEL 900 SLUG GUN . . . . . . .NiB $350 Ex $264 Gd $190
Same as Model 900 Deluxe except has 24-inch plain bbl. w/slug boring, rifle sights. Weight: About 6.5 lbs. Made 1970 to 1972.

SKB CENTURY SINGLE-SHOT
TRAP GUN . . . . **NiB $689 Ex $500 Gd $356**
Boxlock. Auto ejector. 12 ga. Bbls.: 32 or 34 inch, vent. rib, F choke.

Weight: About 8 lbs. Checkered walnut stock w/pistol grip, straight, or Monte Carlo comb, recoil pad, beavertail forearm. Made 1973 to 1974.

SKB CENTURY II TRAP . . . . NiB $700 Ex $495 Gd $400
Boxlock. Auto ejector. 12 ga. Bbls: 32 or 34 inch, vent. rib, F choke. Weight: 8.25 lbs. Improved version of Century. Same general specifications except has higher comb on checkered stock, reverse-taper beavertail forearm w/redesigned locking iron. Made from 1975 to 1976.

SKB MODEL XL300 STANDARD AUTOMATIC
Gas operated. Gauges: 12, 20 (3-inch). 5-round capacity. Bbls.: Plain or vent. rib; 30-inch F choke (12 ga. only), 28-inch F/M, 26-inch IC. Weight: 6 to 7.5 lbs. depending on ga. and bbl. Checkered pistol-grip stock, forearm. Made from 1972 to 1976.
w/plain barrel . . . . **NiB $389 Ex $296 Gd $210**
w/ventilated rib . . . . **NiB $365 Ex $283 Gd $205**

SKB MODEL XL900
DELUXE AUTOMATIC. . . . . **NiB $379 Ex $335 Gd $260**
Same as Model XL300 except has game scene finished in silver on receiver, vent. rib standard. Made from 1972 to 1976.

SKB MODEL XL900 SKEET GRADE. . . NiB $490 Ex $377 Gd $315
Gas operated. Gauges: 12, 20 (3-inch). 5-round tubular magazine. Same as Model XL900 Deluxe except has scrolled receiver finished in black chrome, 26-inch bbl. only, SK choke, skeet-style stock. Weight: 7 or 7.5 lbs. depending on ga. Made from 1972 to 1976.

SKB MODEL XL900 SLUG GUN. . . NiB $445 Ex $377 Gd $290
Same as Model XL900 Deluxe except has 24-inch plain bbl. w/ slug boring, rifle sights. Weight: 6.5 or 7 lbs. depending on ga. Made from 1972 to 1976.

SKB MODEL XL900 TRAP GRADE. . . NiB $488 Ex $358 Gd $290
Same as Model XL900 Deluxe except 12 ga. only, has scrolled receiver finished in black chrome, 30-inch bbl. only, IM/F choke, trap style w/straight or Monte Carlo comb, recoil pad. Weight: About 7.75 lbs. Made from 1972 to 1976.

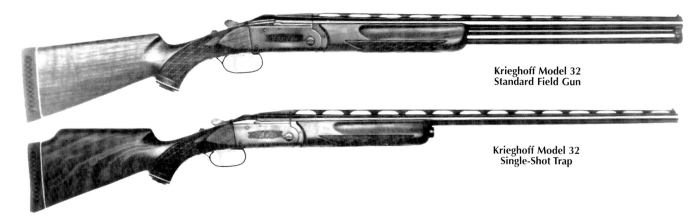

Krieghoff Model 32
Standard Field Gun

Krieghoff Model 32
Single-Shot Trap

IVER JOHNSON ARMS & CYCLE WORKS — Fitchburg, MA

Currently a division of the American Military Arms Corp., Jacksonville, AR.

CHAMPION GRADE TOP SNAP
Auto ejector. Gauges: 12,16, 20, 28, and .410. Bbls.: 26 to 36 inch, F choke. Weight: 5.75 to 7.5 lbs. depending on ga. and bbl. length. Plain pistol-grip stock and forend. Extras include checkered stock and forend, pistol-grip cap, and knob forend. Known as Model 36. Also made in Semi-Octagon Breech, Top Matted, and Jacketed Breech (extra heavy) models. Made in Champion Lightweight as Model 39 in gauges 24, 28, 32, and .410, .44, and .45 caliber, 12 and 14mm w/same extras. $200; add $100 in the smaller and obsolete gauges. Made from 1909 to 1973.

Standard model. . . . . NiB $377 Ex $290 Gd $100
Semi-Octagon Breech . . . . NiB $466 Ex $351 Gd $229
Top Matted Rib (disc. 1948) . . . . . NiB $398 Ex $297 Gd $195

HERCULES GRADE HAMMERLESS DOUBLE
Boxlock. (Some made w/false sideplates.) Plain extractors and auto ejectors. Double or Miller single triggers (both selective or nonselective). Gauges: 12, 16, 20, and .410. Bbl.: 26 to 32 inch, all chokes. Weight: 5.75 to 7.75 lbs. depending on ga. and bbl. length. Checkered stock and forend. Straight grip in .410 ga. w/both 2.5- and 3-inch chambers. Extras include Miller single trigger, Jostam Anti-Flinch recoil pad and Lyman ivory sights at extra cost. Disc. 1946.

w/double triggers, extractors . . . . . . NiB $1166 Ex $955 Gd $760
Double triggers, ejectors, add. 30%
Nonselective single trigger, add $50
Selective single trigger, add $50
.410 ga., add 100%

MATTED RIB SINGLE-SHOT HAMMER SHOTGUN
IN SMALLER GAUGES. . . . . NiB $400 Ex $355 Gd $210
Same general specifications as Champion Grade except has solid matted top rib, checkered stock and forend. Weight: 6 to 6.75 lbs. Disc. 1948.

MODEL 412/422 SILVER SHADOW O/U SHOTGUN
Boxlock. Plain extractors. Double triggers or nonselective single trigger. 12 ga. 3-inch chambers. Bbls.: 26-inch IC/M; 28-inch IC/M, 28-inch M/F; 30-inch F/F choke; vent. rib. Weight: 28-inch bbls., 7.5 lbs. Checkered pistol-grip stock and forearm. Made by F. Marocchi, Brescia, Italy, from 1973 to 1977.

Model 412 w/double triggers . . . . . NiB $590 Ex $455 Gd $387
Model 422 w/single trigger . . . . NiB $754 Ex $600 Gd $445

SKEETER MODEL HAMMERLESS DOUBLE
Boxlock. Plain extractors or selective auto ejectors. Double triggers or Miller single trigger (selective or nonselective). Gauges: 12, 16, 20, 28, and .410. 26- or 28-inch bbls., skeet boring standard. Weight: About 7.5 lbs, less in smaller gauges. Pistol- or straight-grip stock and beavertail forend, both checkered, of select fancy-figured black walnut. Extras include Miller single trigger, selective or nonselective, Jostam Anti-Flinch recoil pad, and Lyman ivory rear sight at additional cost. Disc. 1942.

w/double triggers,
  plain extractors . . . . NiB $2298 Ex $1987 Gd $1133
Double triggers, automatic ejectors, add 20%
Nonselective single trigger, add 20%
Selective single trigger, add 50%
20 ga, add 30%
28 ga., add 90%
.410 ga., add 100%

SPECIAL TRAP SINGLE-SHOT
HAMMER SHOTGUN . . . . NiB $500 Ex $365 Gd $298
Auto ejector. 12 ga. only. 32-inch bbl. w/vent. rib, F choke. Checkered pistol-grip stock and forend. Weight: About 7.5 lbs. Disc. 1942.

SUPER TRAP HAMMERLESS DOUBLE
Boxlock. Plain extractors. Double trigger or Miller single trigger (selective or nonselective), 12 ga. only, F choke 32-inch bbl., vent. rib. Weight: 8.5 lbs. Checkered pistol-grip stock and beavertail forend, recoil pad. Disc. 1942.

w/double triggers . . . . NiB $1756 Ex $1170 Gd $990
Nonselective single trigger, add $150
Selective single trigger, add $150

KBI INC.

See listings under Armscor, Baikal, Charles Daly, Fias, and Omega.

KESSLER ARMS CORP. — Deggendorf, Germany

LEVER-MATIC REPEATING
SHOTGUN . . . . NiB $335 Ex $227 Gd $179
Lever action. Takedown. Gauges: 12, 16, 20; 3-round magazine. Bbls.: 26, 28, 30 inch; F choke. Plain pistol-grip stock, recoil pad. Weight: 7 to 7.75 lbs. Disc. 1953.

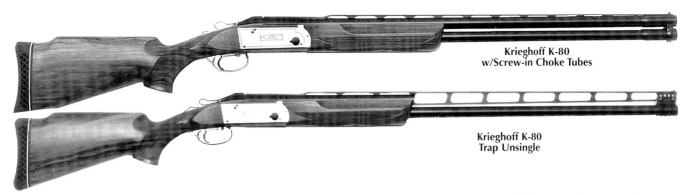

Krieghoff K-80
w/Screw-in Choke Tubes

Krieghoff K-80
Trap Unsingle

THREE-SHOT BOLT-ACTION REPEATER...NiB $200 Ex $138 Gd $90
Takedown. Gauges: 12, 16, 20. 2-round detachable box magazine. Bbls.: 28-inch in 12 and 16 ga.; 26-inch in 20 ga. F choke.
Weight: 6.25 to 7.25 lbs. depending on ga. and bbl. length. Plain
one-piece pistol-grip stock recoil pad. Made from 1951 to 1953.

H. KRIEGHOFF JAGD UND SPORTWAFFENFABRIK — Ulm (Donau), Germany

MODEL 32 FOUR-BARREL SKEET SET
Over/under w/four sets of matched bbls.: 12, 20, 28, and .410
ga. in fitted case. Available in six grades that differ in quality of
engraving and wood. Disc. 1979.
Standard grade . . . . NiB $9344 Ex $7120 Gd $4688
München grade. . . . . .NiB $10,077 Ex $8767 Gd $6233
San Remo grade . . . . .NiB $13,876 Ex $11,990 Gd $10,550
Monte Carlo grade . . . . .NiB $20,000 Ex $17,890 Gd $14,650
Crown grade. . . . . .NiB $27,700 Ex $22,800 Gd $15,660
Super Crown grade. . . . .NiB $29,000 Ex $24,770 Gd $17,600
Exhibition grade . . . . . . .NiB $32,000 Ex $28,900 Gd $23,750

MODEL 32 STANDARD GRADE O/U
Similar to prewar Remington Model 23. Boxlock. Auto ejector. Single
trigger. Gauges: 12, 20, 28, .410. Bbls.: Vent. rib, 26.5 to 32 inch,
any chokes. Weight: 12 ga. Field gun w/28-inch bbls., about 7.5 lbs.
Checkered pistol-grip stock and forearm of select walnut; available in
field, skeet, and trap styles. Made from 1958 to 1981.
w/one set of bbls. . . . . NiB $3125 Ex $2460 Gd $2099
Low-rib two-bbl. trap combo . . . . . .NiB $4166 Ex $3550 Gd $2779
Vandalia (high-rib)
  two-bbl. trap combo . . . . NiB $5355 Ex $4288 Gd $3150

MODEL 32 STANDARD GRADE
SINGLE-SHOT TRAP GUN . . . . . NiB $4160 Ex $3277 Gd $3080
Same action as over/under. 28 ga. or .410 bore w/low vent. rib
on bbl.; M/IM/F choke. Checkered Monte Carlo buttstock w/thick
cushioned recoil pad, beavertail forearm. Disc. 1979.

MODEL K-80
Refined and enhanced version of the Mdl. 32. Single selective
mech. trig., adj. for position; release trigger optional. Fixed chokes
or screw-in choke tubes. Interchangeable front bbl. Hangers to
adjust point of impact. Quick-removable stock. Color casehardened or satin grey finish rec.; aluminum alloy rec. on lightweight
models. Available in standard plus five engraved grades. Made
from 1980 to date. Standard grade shown except where noted.

SKEET MODELS
Skeet International . . . . NiB $9160 Ex $5375 Gd $3853
Skeet Special. . . . . NiB $9277 Ex $6659 Gd $4390

Skeet standard model . . . . NiB $9000 Ex $4788 Gd $3360
Skeet w/choke tubes. . . . . . . .NiB $12,776 Ex $9879 Gd $5780

SKEET SETS—Disc. 1999.
Standard grade 2-bbl. set. . . . . . . .NiB $12,769 Ex $10,000 Gd $6690
Standard grade 4-bbl. set. . . . . . . .NiB $14,879 Ex $11,890 Gd $9877
Bavaria grade 4-bbl. set . . . . . . NiB $11,900 Ex $9388 Gd $7710
Danube grade 4-bbl. set . . . . . . NiB $23,998 Ex $20,600 Gd $17,000
Gold Target grade 4-bbl. set . . . . NiB $31,800 Ex $24,800 Gd $17,955

SPORTING MODELS
Pigeon. . . . . NiB $9980 Ex $6654 Gd $4135
Sporting Clays. . . . . NiB $9566 Ex $5760 Gd $4400

TRAP MODELS
Trap Combo, add 30%
Trap Single, add $600
Trap Standard . . . . .NiB $10,550 Ex $7677 Gd $4612
Trap Unsingle . . . . .NiB $11,880 Ex $9678 Gd $6389
RT models (removable trigger), add $1500

KRIEGHOFF MODEL KS-5 SINGLE-BARREL TRAP
Boxlock w/no sliding top latch. Adjustable or optional release
trigger. Gauge: 12. 2.75-inch chamber. Bbl.: 32, 34 inch w/fixed
choke or screw-in tubes. Weight: 8.5 lbs. Adjustable or Monte
Carlo European walnut stock. Blued or nickel receiver. Made from
1985 to 1999. Redesigned and streamlined in 1993.
Standard model w/fixed chokes . . NiB $2650 Ex $1887 Gd $1109
Standard model w/tubes, add. $250
Special model w/adj. rib & stock, add $250
Special model w/adj. rib
  & stock, choke tubes, add $500

TRUMPF DRILLING. . . . . . .NiB $14,987 Ex $13,677 Gd $10,880
Boxlock. Steel or Dural receiver. Split extractor or ejector for
shotgun bbls. Double triggers. Gauges: 12, 16, 20; latter w/either
2.75- or 3-inch chambers. Calibers: .243, 6.5x57r5, 7x57r5,
7x65r5, .30-06; other calibers available. 25-inch bbls. w/solid
rib, folding leaf rear sight, post or bead front sight. Rifle bbl.
soldered or free floating. Weight: 6.6 to 7.5 lbs. depending on
type of receiver, ga., and caliber. Checkered pistol-grip stock w/
cheekpiece and forearm of figured walnut, sling swivels. Made
from 1953 to 2003.

NEPTUN DRILLING . . . . . NiB $14,988 Ex $11,987 Gd $9000
Same general specifications as Trumpf model except has sidelocks
w/hunting scene engraving. Disc. 2003.

NEPTUN-PRIMUS
DRILLING . . . . NiB $19,800 Ex $16,779 Gd $13,980
Deluxe version of Neptun model; has detachable sidelocks, higher
grade engraving, and fancier wood. Disc. 2003.

**Krieghoff
Neptun Drilling**

**Krieghoff ULM
Over/Under**

TECK O/U
RIFLE-SHOTGUN . . . . NiB $9788 Ex $5780 Gd $4466
Boxlock. Kersten double crossbolt system. Steel or Dural receiver. Split extractor or eject. for shotgun bbl. Single or double triggers. Gauges: 12, 16, 20; latter w/either 2.75- or 3-inch chamber. Cal: .22 Hornet, .222 Rem., .222 Rem. Mag., 7x57r5, 7x64, 7x65r5, .30-30, .300 Win. Mag., .30-06, .308, 9.3x74R. 25-inch bbls. w/solid rib, folding leaf rear sight, post or bead front sight. Over bbl. is shotgun, under bbl. rifle (fixed or interchangeable; ext. rifle bbl., $175). Weight: 7.9 to 9.5 lbs. depending on type of rec. and caliber. Checkered pistol-grip stock w/cheekpiece and semi-beavertail forearm of figured walnut, sling swivels. Made from 1967 to 2004. Note: This combination gun is similar in appearance to the same model shotgun.

TECK O/U SHOTGUN . . . . . . NiB $7354 Ex $5678 Gd $4000
Boxlock. Kersten double crossbolt system. Auto ejector. Single or double triggers. Gauges: 12, 16, 20; latter w/either 2.75- or 3-inch chambers. 28-inch vent. rib bbl., M/F choke. Weight: About 7 lbs. Checkered walnut pistol-grip stock and forearm. Made 1967 to 1989.

ULM O/U
RIFLE-SHOTGUN . . . . . . NiB $16,228 Ex $12,876 Gd $10,336
Same general specifications as Teck model except has sidelocks w/ leaf Arabesque engraving. Made from 1963 to 2004. Note: This combination gun is similar in appearance to the same model shotgun.

ULM O/U SHOTGUN. . . . . . NiB $13,899 Ex $11,679 Gd $8445
Same general specifications as Teck model except has sidelocks w/ leaf Arabesque engraving. Made from 1958 to 2004.

ULM-P LIVE PIGEON GUN
Sidelock. Gauge: 12. 28- and 30-inch bbls. Chokes: F/IM. Weight: 8 lbs. Oil-finished, fancy English walnut stock w/semi-beavertail forearm. Light scrollwork engraving. Tapered, vent. rib. Made from 1983 to 2004.
Standard . . . . NiB $19,577 Ex $15,890 Gd $11,088

Dural. . . . . NiB $13,776 Ex $11,087 Gd $9459

ULM-PRIMUS O/U . . . . . NiB $19,779 Ex $17,888 Gd $13,090
Deluxe version of Ulm model; detachable sidelocks, higher grade engraving, and fancier wood. Made from 1958 to 2004.

ULM-PRIMUS O/U
RIFLE-SHOTGUN . . . . . . NiB $21,870 Ex $18,744 Gd $15,877
Deluxe version of Ulm model; has detachable sidelocks, higher grade engraving, and fancier wood. Made 1963 to 2004. Note: This combination gun is similar in appearance to the same model shotgun.

ULM-S SKEET GUN
Sidelock. Gauge: 12. Bbl.: 28-inch. Chokes: SK/SK. Other specifications similar to the Model ULM-P. Made from 1983 to 1986.
Bavaria . . . . NiB $13,789 Ex $11,132 Gd $9000
Standard . . . . NiB $1188 Ex $9131 Gd $7330

ULM-P O/U LIVE TRAP GUN
Over/under sidelock. Gauge: 12. 30-inch bbl. Tapered vent. rib. Chokes: IM/F; optional screw-in choke. Custom grade versions command a higher price. Disc. 1986.
Bavaria . . . . NiB $18,966 Ex $15,980 Gd $12,776
Standard . . . . NiB $15,660 Ex $13,000 Gd $10,100

ULTRA TS RIFLE-SHOTGUN
Deluxe Over/Under combination w/25-inch vent. rib bbls. Chambered 12 ga. only and various rifle calibers for lower bbl. Kickspanner design permits cocking w/thumb safety. Satin receiver. Weight: 6 lbs. Made from 1985 to 1995. Disc.
Ultra O/U combination . . . . . NiB $4220 Ex $3670 Gd $2800
Ultra B w/selective front trigger . . . . . . NiB $5589 Ex $4498 Gd $4000

LANBER — Zaldibar, Spain

MODEL 82 O/U SHOTGUN . . . . . NiB $577 Ex $459 Gd $390
Boxlock. Gauge: 12 or 20. 3-inch chambers. 26- or 28-inch vent. rib bbls. w/ejectors and fixed chokes. Weight: 7 lbs., 2 oz. Double or single selective trigger. Engraved silvered receiver. Checkered European walnut stock and forearm. Imported 1994.

MODEL 87 DELUXE . . . . NiB $875 Ex $760 Gd $555
Over/Under; boxlock. Single selective trigger. 12 or 20 ga. 3-inch chambers. Bbls: 26 or 28-inch w/choke tubes. Silvered engraved receiver. Imported 1994 only.

MODEL 97 SPORTING CLAYS . . . . . . NiB $998 Ex $790 Gd $566
Over/Under; boxlock. Single selective trigger. 12 ga. 2.75-inch chambers. Bbls: 28-inch w/choke tubes. European walnut stock, forend. Engraved receiver. Imported 1994 only.

MODEL 844 MST MAGNUM O/U . . . . . NiB $533 Ex $448 Gd $360
Field grade. Gauge: 12. 3-inch Mag. chambers. 30-inch flat vent. rib bbls. Chokes: M/F. Weight: 7 lbs., 7 oz. Single selective trigger. Blued bbls. and engraved receiver. European walnut stock w/hand-checkered pistol grip and forend. Imported from 1984 to 1986.

MODEL 2004 LCH O/U . . . . NiB $669 Ex $490 Gd $370
Field grade. Gauge: 12. 2.75-inch chambers. 28-inch flat vent. rib bbls. Five interchangeable choke tubes (C/IC/M/IM/F). Weight: About 7 lbs. Single selective trigger. Engraved silver receiver w/ fine-line scroll. Walnut stock w/checkered pistol grip and forend. Rubber recoil pad. Imported from 1984 to 1986.

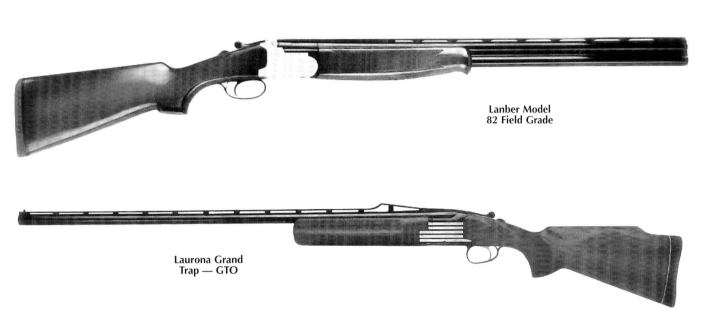

Lanber Model
82 Field Grade

Laurona Grand
Trap — GTO

MODEL 2004 LCH O/U SKEET . . . . . . NiB $855 Ex $659 Gd $544
Same as Model 2004 LCH except 28-inch bbls. w/five interchangeable choke tubes. Imported from 1984 to 1986.MODEL 2004 LCH O/U TRAP . . . . .NiB $764 Ex $520 Gd $413
Gauge: 12. 30-inch vent. rib bbls. Three interchangeable choke tubes (M/IM/F). Manual safety. Other specifications same as Model 2004 LCH O/U. Imported from 1984 to 1986.

CHARLES LANCASTER — London, England

TWELVE-TWENTY DOUBLE-BARREL
SHOTGUN . . . . NiB $16,788 Ex $14,990 Gd $10,880
Sidelock, self-opener. Gauge: 12. Bbls.: 24 to 30 inches standard. Weight: About 5.75 lbs. Elaborate metal engraving. Highest quality English or French walnut buttstock and forearm. Imported by Stoeger in the 1950s.

JOSEPH LANG & SONS — London, England

HIGHEST QUALITY
O/U SHOTGUN . . . . NiB $31,900 Ex $27,678 Gd $20,980
Sidelock. Gauges: 12, 16, 20, 28, and .410. Bbls.: 25 to 30 inches standard. Highest grade English or French walnut buttstock and forearm. Selective single trigger. Imported by Stoeger in 1950s.

LAURONA SHOTGUNS — Eibar, Spain

MODEL 300 SERIES
Same general specifications as Model 300 Super Series except supplied w/29-inch over/under bbls. and beavertail forearms. Disc. 1992.
Trap model . . . . NiB $1377 Ex $1190 Gd $921
Sporting Clays model . . . . NiB $1389 Ex $1440 Gd $1000

SILHOUETTE 300 O/U
Boxlock. Single selective trigger. Selective automatic ejectors. Gauge: 12. 2.75-, 3-, or 3.5-inch chambers. 28- or 29-inch vent. rib bbls. w/ flush or knurled choke tubes. Weight: 7.75 to 8 lbs. Checkered pistol-grip European walnut stock and beavertail forend. Engraved receiver w/silvered finish and black chrome bbls. Made from 1988 to 1992.
Model 300 Sporting Clays. . . . . NiB $1498 Ex $1277 Gd $900
Model 300 Trap, single . . . . .NiB $1577 Ex $1264 Gd $900
Model 300 Ultra-Magnum . . . NiB $1599 Ex $1300 Gd $1055

SUPER MODEL O/U SHOTGUNS
Boxlock. Single selective or twin single triggers. Selective automatic ejectors. Gauges: 12 or 20. 2.75- or 3-inch chambers. 26-, 28-, or 29-inch vent. rib bbls. w/fixed chokes or screw-in choke tubes. Weight: 7 to 7.25 lbs. Checkered pistol-grip European walnut stock. Engraved receiver w/silvered finish and black chrome bbls. Made from 1985 to 1989.
Model 82 Super Game (disc.) . . . . NiB $688 Ex $500 Gd $395
Model 83 MG Super Game. . . . . NiB $1090 Ex $800 Gd $707
Model 84 S Super Trap . . . . NiB $1366 Ex $1150 Gd $986
Model 85 MS Super Game . . . . . NiB $1098 Ex $833 Gd $727
Model 85 MS 2-bbl. set. . . . . . . NiB $2200 Ex $1789 Gd $1340
Model 85 MS Special Sporting (disc.). . . . . NiB $1390 Ex $1173 Gd $999
Model 85 MS Super Trap. . . . . . NiB $1386 Ex $1160 Gd $974
Model 85 MS Pigeon. . . . . NiB $1409 Ex $1190 Gd $1034
Model 85 MS Super Skeet. . . . . NiB $1409 Ex $1190 Gd $1034

LEBEAU-COURALLY — Belgium

BOXLOCK SIDE-BY-SIDE
SHOTGUNS . . . . .NiB $19,000 Ex $15,870 Gd $10,477
Gauges: 12, 16, 20, and 28. 26- to 30-inch bbls. Weight: 6.5 lbs. average. Checkered, hand-rubbed, oil-finished, straight-grip stock of French walnut. Classic forend. Made from 1986 to 1988 and 1993.

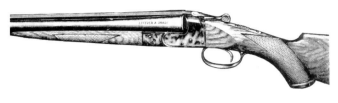

**Lefever A Grade
Hammerless Double-Barrel Shotgun**

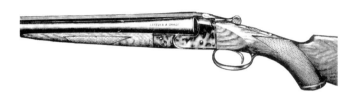

LEFEVER ARMS COMPANY —
Syracuse and Ithaca, NY

Lefever sidelock hammerless double-barrel shotguns were made by Lefever Arms Company of Syracuse, New York from about 1885 to 1915 (serial numbers 1 to 70,000) when the firm was sold to Ithaca Gun Company of Ithaca, New York. Production of these models was continued at the Ithaca plant until 1919 (serial numbers 70,001 to 72,000). Grades listed are those that appear in the last catalog of the Lefever Gun Company, Syracuse. In 1921, Ithaca introduced the boxlock Lefever Nitro Special double, followed in 1934 by the Lefever Grade A; there were also two single-barrel Lefevers made from 1927 to 1942. Manufacture of Lefever brand shotguns was disc. in 1948. Note: New Lefever boxlock shotguns made circa 1904 to 1906 by D. M. Lefever Company, Bowling Green, Ohio, are included in a separate listing.

GRADE A HAMMERLESS DOUBLE-BARREL SHOTGUN
Boxlock. Plain extractors or auto ejector. Single or double triggers. Gauges: 12, 16, 20, .410. Bbls.: 26 to 32 inches, standard chokes. Weight: About 7 lbs. in 12 ga. Checkered pistol-grip stock and forearm. Made from 1934 to 1942.
w/plain extractors,
double triggers . . . . NiB $1198 Ex $955 Gd $773
Automatic ejector, add 33%
Single trigger, add 10%
Beavertail Forearm, add $100
16 ga., add 25%
20 ga., add 80%
.410 ga., add 200%

GRADE A SKEET MODEL
Same as Grade A except standard features include auto ejector, single trigger, beavertail forearm; 26-inch bbls., skeet boring. Disc. 1942.
Grade A Skeet model, 12 ga. . . . . NiB $1699 Ex $1188 Gd $880
16 ga., add 40%
20 ga., add 80%
.410 ga., add 200%

HAMMERLESS SINGLE-SHOT
TRAP GUN . . . . NiB $766 Ex $600 Gd $477
Boxlock. Ejector. 12 ga. only. 26- or 32-inch bbl. Full choke. Weight: About 8 lbs. Checkered pistol-grip stock. Made from 1904 to 1906. Rare.

LONG-RANGE HAMMERLESS
SINGLE-BARREL FIELD GUN . . . . ..NiB $500 Ex $394 Gd $277
Boxlock. Plain extractor. Gauges: 12, 16, 20, .410. Bbl: 26 to 32 inches. Weight: 5.5 to 7 lbs. depending on ga. and bbl. length. Checkered pistol-grip stock and forend. Made from 1927 to 1942.

NITRO SPECIAL HAMMERLESS DOUBLE
Boxlock. Plain extractors. Single or double triggers. Gauges: 12, 16, 20, .410. Bbls.: 26 to 32 inch, standard chokes. Weight: About 7 lbs. in 12 ga. Checkered pistol-grip stock and forend. Made 1921 to 1948.
Nitro Special w/
   double triggers . . . . NiB $855 Ex $522 Gd $377
Nitro Special w/
   single trigger . . . . NiB $933 Ex $654 Gd $433
16 ga., add 25%
20 ga., add 50%
.410 ga., add 200%

SIDELOCK HAMMERLESS DOUBLES
Plain extractors or auto ejectors. Boxlock. Double triggers or selective single trigger. Gauges: 10, 12, 16, 20. Bbls.: 26 to 32 inches; standard choke combinations. Weight: 5.75 to 10.5 lbs. depending on ga. and bbl. length. Checkered walnut straight-grip or pistol-grip stock and forearm. Grades differ chiefly in quality of workmanship, engraving, wood, checkering, etc.; general specifications are the same. DS and DSE grade guns lack the cocking indicators found on all other models. Suffix E means model has auto ejector; also standard on A, AA, Optimus, and Thousand Dollar grade guns.
H grade. . . . . NiB $2266 Ex $1770 Gd $1480
HE grade . . . . NiB $3270 Ex $2266 Gd $1780
G grade . . . . NiB $2288 Ex $1998 Gd $1440
GE grade . . . . NiB $3388 Ex $2771 Gd $1880
F grade . . . . NiB $2566 Ex $1966 Gd $1276
FE grade . . . . NiB $3360 Ex $2770 Gd $1866
E grade . . . . NiB $3790 Ex $2690 Gd $2210
EE grade . . . . NiB $5750 Ex $3880 Gd $2547
D grade. . . . . NiB $4980 Ex $3777 Gd $2869
DE grade. . . . . NiB $7132 Ex $4971 Gd $4111
DS grade. . . . . NiB $1754 Ex $1530 Gd $1129
DSE grade . . . . NiB $2184 Ex $1788 Gd $1290
C grade . . . . NiB $7443 Ex $4270 Gd $2988
CE grade . . . . NiB $9112 Ex $8445 Gd $6110
B grade . . . . .NiB $10,500 Ex $8667 Gd $6330
BE grade . . . . .NiB $10,580 Ex $8777 Gd $6580
A grade . . . . .NiB $19,880 Ex $17,900 Gd $16,888
AA grade. . . . . .NiB $28,566 Ex $23,667 Gd $21,876
Optimus grade . . . . . . .NiB $47,900 Ex $42,870 Gd $37,980
Thousand Dollar grade . . . . .NiB $78,980 Ex $46,888 Gd $36,890
Single trigger, add. 10%
10 ga., add 15%
16 ga., add 45%
20 ga., add 90%

D. M. LEFEVER COMPANY —
Bowling Green, OH

In 1901, D. M. "Uncle Dan" Lefever, founder of the Lefever Arms Company, withdrew from that firm to organize D. M. Lefever, Sons & Company (later D. M. Lefever Company) to manufacture the New Lefever boxlock double- and single-barrel shotguns. These were produced at Bowling Green, Ohio, from about 1904 to 1906, when Dan Lefever died and the factory closed permanently. Grades listed are those that appear in the last catalog of D. M. Lefever Co.

HAMMERLESS DOUBLE-BARREL SHOTGUNS

New Lefever. Boxlock. Auto ejector standard on all grades except O Excelsior, which was regularly supplied w/plain extractors (auto ejector offered as an extra). Double triggers or selective single trigger (latter standard on Uncle Dan Grade, extra on all others). Gauges: 12, 16, 20. Bbls.: Any length and choke combination. Weight: 5.5 to 8 lbs. depending on ga. and bbl. length. Checkered walnut straight-grip or pistol-grip stock and forearm. Grades differ chiefly in quality of workmanship, engraving, wood, checkering, etc. General specifications are the same.

O Excelsior grade
   w/plain extractors . . . . NiB $2889 Ex $2255 Gd $1989
O Excelsior grade
   w/automatic ejectors . . . . . . NiB $3244 Ex $2990 Gd $2469
No. 9, F grade. . . . . NiB $3277 Ex $2929 Gd $2240
No. 8, E grade. . . . . NiB $4240 Ex $3888 Gd $2377
No. 7, D grade . . . . NiB $5277 Ex $4766 Gd $3698
No. 6, C grade . . . . NiB $7000 Ex $4590 Gd $3667
No. 5, B grade . . . . NiB $6722 Ex $4588 Gd $3292
No. 4, AA grade . . . . .NiB $10,770 Ex $8857 Gd $5497
Uncle Dan grade (very rare). . . . .$165,000+
Single trigger, add. 10%
16 ga., add 45%
20 ga., add 15%

D. M. LEFEVER SINGLE-BARREL TRAP GUN

Boxlock. Auto ejector. 12 ga. only. Bbls.: 26 to 32 inches, F choke. Weight: 6.5 to 8 lbs. depending on bbl. length. Checkered walnut pistol-grip stock and forearm. Made 1904 to 1906. Extremely rare.

MAGTECH SHOTGUNS — San Antonio, TX

Manufactured by CBC in Brazil.

MODEL 586-2 SLIDE-ACTION SHOTGUN

Gauge: 12. 3-inch chamber. 19-, 26-, or 28-inch bbl.; fixed chokes or integral tubes. 46.5 inches overall. Weight: 8.5 lbs. Double-action slide bars. Brazilian hardwood stock. Polished blued finish. Imported 1992 to 1995.

Model 586.2F
   (28-inch bbl., fixed choke). . . . . NiB $288 Ex $147 Gd $100
Model 586.2P
   (19-inch plain bbl., Cyl. bore) . . . NiB $244 Ex $165 Gd $99
Model 586.2 S
   (24-inch bbl., rifle sights, Cyl. bore) . . . . . . NiB $290 Ex $155 Gd $125
Model 586.2 VR
   (vent. rib w/tubes) . . . . NiB $275 Ex $198 Gd $135

MARLIN FIREARMS CO. — Madison, NC

Formerly North Haven, CT, and New Haven, CT. Acquired by the Freedom Group in 2007.

MODEL 16 VISIBLE HAMMER SLIDE-ACTION REPEATER

Takedown. 16 ga. 5-round tubular magazine. Bbls.: 26 or 28 inch, standard chokes. Weight: About 6.25 lbs. Pistol-grip stock, grooved slide handle; checkering on higher grades. Difference among grades is in quality of wood, engraving on Grades C and D. Made from 1904 to 1910.

Grade A . . . . NiB $400 Ex $322 Gd $297
Grade B . . . . NiB $590 Ex $477 Gd $388
Grade C . . . . NiB $722 Ex $466 Gd $388
Grade D . . . . NiB $1496 Ex $1377 Gd $947

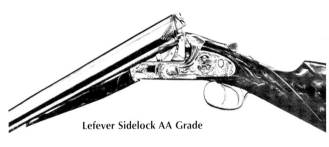

Lefever Sidelock AA Grade

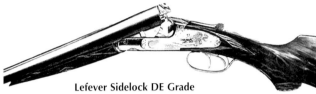

Lefever Sidelock DE Grade

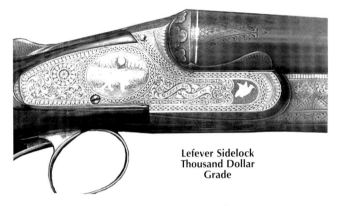

Lefever Sidelock
Thousand Dollar
Grade

Lefever Sidelock Sideplate BE Grade

Lefever Sidelock Sideplate CE Grade

Lefever Sidelock Optimus Grade

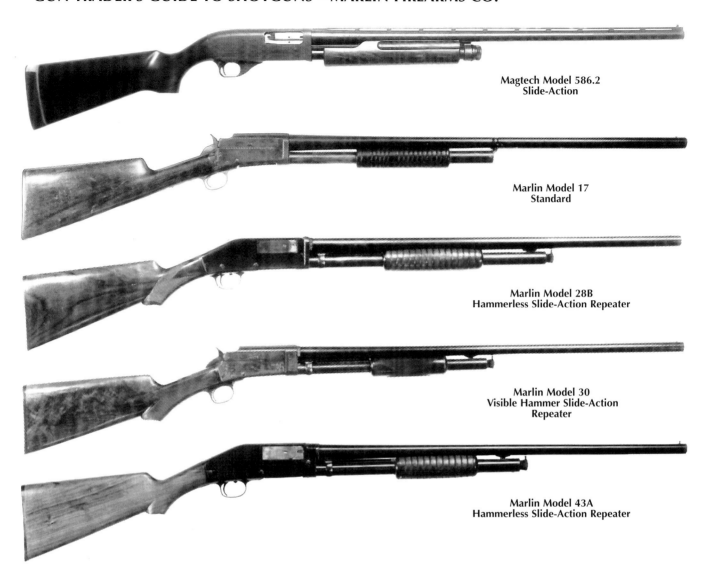

Magtech Model 586.2
Slide-Action

Marlin Model 17
Standard

Marlin Model 28B
Hammerless Slide-Action Repeater

Marlin Model 30
Visible Hammer Slide-Action
Repeater

Marlin Model 43A
Hammerless Slide-Action Repeater

MODEL 17 BRUSH GUN . . . . **NiB $389 Ex $297 Gd $190**
Same as Model 17 Standard except has 26-inch bbl., Cyl. bore.
Weight: About 7 lbs. Made from 1906 to 1908.

MODEL 17 RIOT GUN. . . . . **NiB $480 Ex $308 Gd $200**
Same as Model 17 Standard except has 20-inch bbl., Cyl. bore.
Weight: About 6.88 lbs. Made from 1906 to 1908.

MODEL 17 STANDARD VISIBLE HAMMER
SLIDE-ACTION REPEATER. . . . . **NiB $422 Ex $290 Gd $188**
Solid frame. 12 ga. 5-round tubular magazine. Bbls.: 30 or 32 inch,
F choke. Weight: About 7.5 lbs. Straight-grip stock, grooved slide
handle. Made from 1906 to 1908.

MODEL 19 VISIBLE HAMMER SLIDE-ACTION REPEATER
Similar to Model 1898 but improved, lighter weight, w/two extrac-
tors, matted sighting groove on receiver top. Weight: About 7 lbs.
Made from 1906 to 1907.
Grade A . . . . NiB $466 Ex $390 Gd $277
Grade B . . . . NiB $566 Ex $448 Gd $339
Grade C . . . . NiB $744 Ex $390 Gd $244
Grade D . . . . NiB $1396 Ex $1087 Gd $944

MODEL 21 TRAP VISIBLE HAMMER
SLIDE-ACTION REPEATER
Similar to Model 19 w/same general specifications except has
straight-grip stock. Made from 1907 to 1909.
Grade A . . . . NiB $433 Ex $290 Gd $197
Grade B . . . . NiB $580 Ex $450 Gd $344
Grade C . . . . NiB $788 Ex $590 Gd $445
Grade D . . . . NiB $1488 Ex $1116 Gd $977

MODEL 24 VISIBLE HAMMER SLIDE-ACTION REPEATER
Similar to Model 19 but has improved takedown system and auto
recoil safety lock, solid matted rib on frame. Weight: About 7.5 lbs.
Made from 1908 to 1915.
Grade A . . . . NiB $376 Ex $190 Gd $112
Grade B . . . . NiB $448 Ex $277 Gd $156
Grade C . . . . NiB $766 Ex $500 Gd $410
Grade D . . . . NiB $1500 Ex $1399 Gd $1177

MODEL 26
BRUSH GUN . . . . **NiB $388 Ex $270 Gd $135**
Same as Model 26 Standard except has 26-inch bbl., Cyl. bore.
Weight: About 7 lbs. Made from 1909 to 1915.

Marlin Model 43T
Hammerless Slide-Action
Repeater

Marlin Model 53
Hammerless Slide-Action

Marlin Model 55
Goose Gun

Marlin Model 55
Humter Bolt-Action Repeater

Marlin Model 55
Swap Gun

MODEL 26 RIOT GUN . . . . **NiB $360 Ex $266 Gd $131**
Same as Model 26 Standard except has 20-inch bbl., Cyl. bore.
Weight: About 6.88 lbs. Made from 1909 to 1915.

**MODEL 26 STANDARD VISIBLE HAMMER
SLIDE-ACTION REPEATER** . . . . . . **NiB $366 Ex $298 Gd $199**
Similar to Model 24 Grade A except solid frame and straight-grip
stock. 30- or 32-inch Full choke bbl. Weight: About 7.13 lbs.
Made from 1909 to 1915.

MODEL 28 HAMMERLESS SLIDE-ACTION REPEATER
Takedown. 12 ga. 5-round tubular magazine. Bbls.: 26, 28, 30,
32 inch, standard chokes; matted-top bbl. except on Model 28D,
which has solid matted rib. Weight: About 8 lbs. Pistol-grip stock,
grooved slide handle; checkering on higher grades. Grades differ
in quality of wood, engraving on Models 28C and 28D. Made
1913 to 1922; all but Model 28A disc. in 1915.
Model 28A . . . . NiB $433 Ex $288 Gd $165
Model 28B . . . . NiB $577 Ex $458 Gd $313
Model 28C . . . . NiB $755 Ex $544 Gd $340
Model 28D . . . . NiB $1480 Ex $1198 Gd $955

MODEL 28T TRAP GUN . . . . **NiB $789 Ex $566 Gd $449**
Same as Model 28 except has 30-inch matted-rib bbl., Full choke,
straight-grip stock w/high-fluted comb of fancy walnut, checkered.
Made in 1915.

MODEL 28TS
TRAP GUN . . . . **NiB $588 Ex $400 Gd $378**
Same as Model 28T except has matted-top bbl., plainer stock.
Made in 1915.

MODEL 30 FIELD GUN . . . . **NiB $466 Ex $355 Gd $245**
Same as Model 30 Grade B except has 25-inch bbl., M choke,
straight-grip stock. Made from 1913 to 1914.

MODEL 30 VISIBLE HAMMER SLIDE-ACTION REPEATER
Similar to Model 16 but w/Model 24 improvements. Made from
1910 to 1914.
Grade A . . . . NiB $460 Ex $388 Gd $210
Grade B . . . . NiB $660 Ex $433 Gd $309
Grade C . . . . NiB $777 Ex $566 Gd $363
Grade D . . . . NiB $1488 Ex $1177 Gd $1065

MODELS 30A, 30B, 30C, 30D
Same as Model 30; designations were changed in 1915. Also
available in 20 ga. w/25- or 28-inch bbl., matted-top bbl. on all
grades. Suffixes A, B, C, and D correspond to former grades. Made
in 1915.
Model 30A . . . . NiB $412 Ex $290 Gd $188
Model 30B . . . . NiB $576 Ex $445 Gd $310
Model 30C . . . . NiB $756 Ex $554 Gd $39
Model 30D . . . . NiB $1421 Ex $1131 Gd $1070

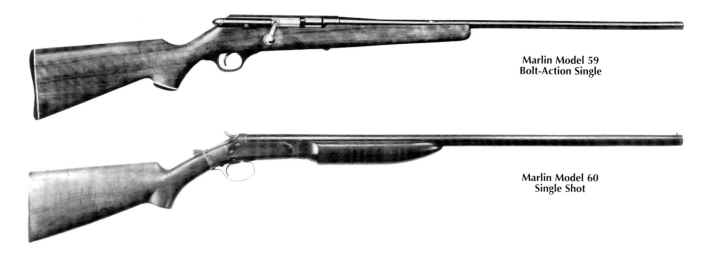

Marlin Model 59
Bolt-Action Single

Marlin Model 60
Single Shot

MODEL 31 HAMMERLESS SLIDE-ACTION REPEATER
Similar to Model 28 except scaled down for 16 and 20 ga. Bbls.:
25 inch (20 ga. only), 26 inch (16 ga. only), 28 inch, all w/matted top, standard chokes. Weight: 16 ga., about 6.75 lbs.; 20 ga.,
about 6 lbs. Pistol-grip stock, grooved slide handle; checkering on
higher grades; straight-grip stock optional on Model 31D. Made
from 1915 to 1917; Model 31A until 1922.

Model 31A . . . . NiB $476 Ex $355 Gd $254
Model 31B . . . . NiB $598 Ex $455 Gd $389
Model 31C . . . . NiB $766 Ex $644 Gd $490
Model 31D . . . . NiB $1498 Ex $1154 Gd $990

MODEL 31F FIELD GUN . . . . . . NiB $488 Ex $366 Gd $271
Same as Model 31B except has 25-inch bbl., M choke, straight- or
pistol-grip stock. Made from 1915 to 1917.

MODEL 42A VISIBLE HAMMER
SLIDE-ACTION REPEATER . . . . . . NiB $498 Ex $366 Gd $288
Similar to pre-WWI Model 24 Grade A w/same general specifications but not as high quality. Made from 1922 to 1934.

MODEL 43 HAMMERLESS SLIDE-ACTION REPEATER
Similar to pre-WWI Models 28A, 28T, and 28TS w/same general
specifications but not as high quality. Made from 1923 to 1930.

Model 43A . . . . NiB $355 Ex $200 Gd $144
Model 43TS . . . . NiB $665 Ex $400 Gd $228

MODEL 44 HAMMERLESS SLIDE-ACTION REPEATER
Similar to pre-WWI Model 31A w/same general specifications but
not as high quality. 20 ga. only. Model 44A is a standard grade
field gun. Model 44S Special Grade has checkered stock and slide
handle of fancy walnut. Made from 1923 to 1935.

Model 44A . . . . NiB $466 Ex $381 Gd $222
Model 44S . . . . NiB $622 Ex $476 Gd $338

MODEL 49 VISIBLE HAMMER SLIDE-ACTION REPEATING
SHOTGUN . . . . NiB $566 Ex $449 Gd $367
Economy version of Model 42A, offered as a bonus on the purchase
of four shares of Marlin stock. About 3000 made 1925 to 1928.

MODEL 50DL BOLT-
ACTION SHOTGUN. . . . . NiB $388 Ex $229 Gd $131
Gauge: 12. 3-inch chamber. 2-round magazine. 28-inch bbl. w/
modified choke. 48.75 inches overall. Weight: 7.5 lbs. Checkered
black synthetic stocks w/ventilated rubber recoil pad. Made 1997
to 1999.

MODEL 53 HAMMERLESS
SLIDE-ACTION REPEATER . . . . . NiB $480 Ex $200 Gd $144
Similar to Model 43A w/same general specifications. Made 1929 to 1930.

MODEL 55 GOOSE GUN
Same as Model 55 Hunter except chambered for 12-ga. 3-inch Mag.
shell, has 36-inch bbl., F choke, swivels and sling. Weight: About 8 lbs.
Walnut stock (standard model) or checkered black synthetic stock w/
ventilated rubber recoil pad (GDL model). Made from 1962 to 1996.

Model 55 Goose Gun . . . . NiB $335 Ex $266 Gd $195
Model 55GDL Goose Gun
(intro. 1997) . . . . NiB $398 Ex $297 Gd $239

MODEL 55 HUNTER BOLT-ACTION REPEATER
Takedown. Gauges: 12, 16, 20. 2-round clip magazine. 28-inch bbl.
(26-inch in 20 ga.), F or adj. choke. Plain pistol-grip stock; 12 ga. has
recoil pad. Weight: About 7.25 lbs.; 20 ga., 6.5 lbs. Made 1954 to 1965.

w/plain bbl. . . . . NiB $120 Ex $70 Gd $50
w/adj. choke . . . . NiB $155 Ex $99 Gd $75

MODEL 55 SWAMP GUN . . . . . . NiB $225 Ex $179 Gd $90
Same as Model 55 Hunter except chambered for 12 ga. 3-inch
Mag. shell, has shorter 20.5-inch bbl. w/adj. choke, sling swivels,
and slightly better quality stock. Weight: About 6.5 lbs. Made from
1963 to 1965.

MODEL 55S SLUG GUN . . . . NiB $200 Ex $99 Gd $75
Same as Model 55 Goose Gun except has 24-inch bbl., Cyl. bore,
rifle sights. Weight: About 7.5 lbs. Made from 1974 to 1979.

MODEL 59 AUTO-SAFE
BOLT-ACTION SINGLE . . . . NiB $244 Ex $176 Gd $95
Takedown. Auto thumb safety, .410 ga. 24-inch bbl., F choke.
Weight: About 5 lbs. Plain pistol-grip stock. Made 1959 to 1961.

MODEL 60 SINGLE-SHOT
SHOTGUN . . . . NiB $210 Ex $145 Gd $95
Visible hammer. Takedown. Boxlock. Automatic ejector. 12 ga. 30-
or 32-inch bbl., F choke. Weight: About 6.5 lbs. Pistol-grip stock,
beavertail forearm. Note: Only about 600 were produced in 1923.

MODEL 63 HAMMERLESS SLIDE-ACTION REPEATER
Similar to Models 43A and 43T w/same general specifications.
Model 63TS Trap Special is same as Model 63T Trap Gun except
stock style and dimensions to order. Made from 1931 to 1935.

Model 63A . . . . NiB $466 Ex $355 Gd $200
Model 63T or 63TS . . . . NiB $484 Ex $355 Gd $241

Marlin Model 90
Standard Over-and-Under

Marlin Model 120
Magnum Slide-Action Repeater

Marlin Model 410
Lever-Action Repeater

Marlin Model 512
Slugmaster

Marlin Model 55-10
Super Goose 10

Marlin Premier Mark I
Slide-Action Repeater

Marlin Premier Mark IV

Marlin-Glenfield
Model 50 Bolt-Action Repeater

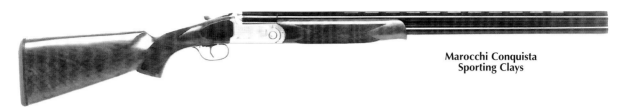

**Marocchi Conquista
Sporting Clays**

MODEL 90 STANDARD O/U SHOTGUN
Hammerless. Boxlock. Double triggers; nonselective single trigger was available as an extra on prewar guns except .410. Gauges: 12, 16, 20, .410. Bbls.: Plain 26, 28, or 30 inch; chokes IC/M or M/F; bbl. design changed in 1949 eliminating full-length rib between bbls. Weight: 12 ga., about 7.5 lbs.; 16 and 20 ga., about 6.25 lbs. Checkered pistol-grip stock and forearm, recoil pad standard on prewar guns. Postwar production: Model 90-DT (double trigger), Model 90-ST (single trigger). Made from 1937 to 1958.

w/double triggers	NiB $566	Ex $400	Gd $245
w/single trigger	NiB $670	Ex $555	Gd $435
Combination model	NiB $2879	Ex $1976	Gd $1777
16 ga., deduct			10%
20 ga., add			15%
.410, add			30%

MODEL 120 MAGNUM
SLIDE-ACTION REPEATER . . . . . . **NiB $354 Ex $230 Gd $155**
Hammerless. Takedown. 12 ga. (3-inch). 4-round tubular magazine. Bbls.: 26-inch vent. rib, IC; 28-inch vent. rib M choke; 30-inch vent. rib, F choke; 38-inch plain, F choke; 40-inch plain, F choke; 26-inch slug bbl. w/rifle sights, IC. Weight: About 7.75 lbs. Checkered pistol-grip stock and forearm, recoil pad. Made from 1971 to 1985.

MODEL 120 SLUG GUN . . . . NiB $344 Ex $265 Gd $175
Same general specifications as Model 120 Mag. except w/20-inch bbl. and about .5 lb. lighter in weight. No vent. rib. Adj. rear rifle sights; hooded front sight. Disc. 1990.

MODEL 410 LEVER-ACTION REPEATER
Action similar to that of Marlin Model 93 rifle. Visible hammer. Solid frame. .410 ga. (2.5-inch shell). 5-round tubular magazine. 22- or 26-inch bbl., F choke. Weight: About 6 lbs. Plain pistol-grip stock and grooved beavertail forearm. Made from 1929 to 1932.

Model 410 w/22-in. bbl.	NiB $1546	Ex $1463	Gd $1320
Model 410 w/26-in. bbl.	NiB $1470	Ex $1355	Gd $1110
Deluxe model, add			30%

MODEL 512 SLUGMASTER SHOTGUN
Bolt-action repeater. Gauge: 12. 3-inch chamber, 2-round magazine. 21-inch rifled bbl. w/adj. open sight. Weight: 8 lbs. Walnut-finished birch stock (standard model) or checkered black synthetic stock w/ventilated rubber recoil pad (GDL model). Made from 1994 to 1999.

Model 512 Slugmaster	NiB $466	Ex $338	Gd $243
Model 512DL Slugmaster (intro. 1998)	NiB $390	Ex $278	Gd $176
Model 512P Slugmaster w/ported bbl. (intro. 1999)	NiB $447	Ex $366	Gd $260

MODEL 1898 VISIBLE HAMMER SLIDE-ACTION REPEATER
Takedown. 12 ga. 5-shell tubular magazine. Bbls.: 26, 28, 30, 32 inch; standard chokes. Weight: About 7.25 lbs. Pistol-grip stock, grooved slide handle; checkering on higher grades. Difference among grades is in quality of wood, engraving on Grades C and D. Made 1898 to 1905. Note: This was the first Marlin shotgun.

Grade A (Field)	NiB $387	Ex $270	Gd $190
Grade B	NiB $558	Ex $400	Gd $294
Grade C	NiB $700	Ex $554	Gd $449
Grade D	NiB $2170	Ex $1799	Gd $954

MODEL 5510 SUPER GOOSE . . . . .NiB $292 Ex $225 Gd $179
Similar to Model 55 Goose Gun except chambered for 10 ga. 3.5-inch Mag. shell, has 34-inch heavy bbl., F choke. Weight: About 10.5 lbs. Made from 1976 to 1985.

PREMIER MARK I
SLIDE-ACTION REPEATER . . . . . . **NiB $255 Ex $198 Gd $110**
Hammerless. Takedown. 12 ga. Magazine holds 3 shells. Bbls.: 30-inch F choke, 28-inch M, 26-inch IC or SK choke. Weight: About 6 lbs. Plain pistol grip stock and forearm. Made in France from 1960 to 1963.

PREMIER MARK II & IV
Same action and mechanism as Premier Mark except engraved receiver (Mark IV is more elaborate), checkered stock and forearm, fancier wood, vent. rib, and similar refinements. Made 1960 to 1963.

Premier Mark II	NiB $356	Ex $265	Gd $200
Premier Mark IV (plain barrel)	NiB $389	Ex $339	Gd $233
Premier Mark IV (vent. rib barrel)	NiB $400	Ex $370	Gd $280

GLENFIELD MODEL 50
BOLT-ACTION REPEATER . . . . **NiB $320 Ex $255 Gd $175**
Similar to Model 55 Hunter except chambered for 12 or 20 ga. 3-inch Mag. shell; 28-inch bbl. in 12 ga., 26-inch in 20 ga., F choke. Made from 1966 to 1974.

GLENFIELD 778 SLIDE-ACTION
REPEATER . . . . **NiB $325 Ex $255 Gd $180**
Hammerless. 12 ga. 2.75 or 3 inch. 4-round tubular magazine. Bbls.: 26-inch IC, 28-inch M, 30-inch F, 38-inch MXR, 20-inch slug bbl. Weight: 7.75 lbs. Checkered pistol-grip. Made from 1979 to 1984.

MAROCCHI — Brescia, Italy
Imported by Precision Sales International of Westfield, MA.

CONQUISTA MODEL O/U SHOTGUN
Boxlock. Gauge: 12. 2.75-inch chambers. 28-, 30-, or 32-inch vent. rib bbl. Fixed choke or internal tubes. 44.38 to 48 inches overall. Weight: 7.5 to 8.25 lbs. Adj. single selective trigger. Checkered American walnut stock w/recoil pad. Imported 1994 to 2003.

Lady Sport Grade I	NiB $1978	Ex $1754	Gd $1288
Lady Sport Grade II	NiB $2144	Ex $1788	Gd $1488
Lady Sport Grade III	NiB $3577	Ex $2875	Gd $2290
Skeet Model Grade I	NiB $1895	Ex $1544	Gd $1154
Skeet Model Grade II	NiB $2250	Ex $1863	Gd $1455
Skeet Model Grade III	NiB $3598	Ex $3210	Gd $2240
Sporting Clays Grade I	NiB $1890	Ex $1669	Gd $1275
Sporting Clays Grade II	NiB $2200	Ex $1790	Gd $1376
Sporting Clays Grade III	NiB $3550	Ex $2977	Gd $2169
Trap Model Grade I	NiB $1890	Ex $1588	Gd $1300
Trap Model Grade II	NiB $2170	Ex $1877	Gd $1470
Trap Model Grade III	NiB $3588	Ex $3120	Gd $2260
Left-handed model, add			10%

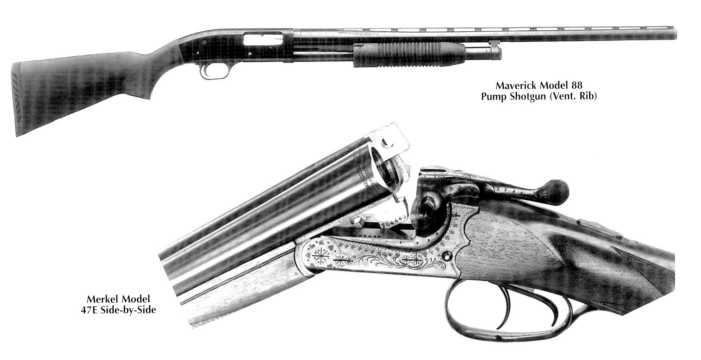

Maverick Model 88
Pump Shotgun (Vent. Rib)

Merkel Model
47E Side-by-Side

MAVERICK ARMS, INC. — Eagle Pass, TX

Distributed by O.F. Mossberg.

MODEL 88 BULLPUP . . . . **NiB $265 Ex $190 Gd $110**
Gauge: 12. 3-inch chamber. Bbl.: 18.5-inch w/fixed choke, blued. Weight: 9.5 lbs. Dual safeties: Grip style and crossbolt. Fixed sights in carrying handle. High-impact black synthetic stock; trigger-forward bullpup configuration w/twin pistol-grip design. Made 1990 to 1995.

MODEL 88 DEER GUN . . . . **NiB $377 Ex $241 Gd $176**
Crossbolt safety and dual slide bars. Cyl. bore choke. Gauge: 12 only. 3-inch chamber. Bbl.: 24 inch. Weight: 7 lbs. Synthetic stock and forearm. Disc. 1995.

MODEL 88 PUMP SHOTGUN
Gauge: 12. 2.75- or 3-inch chamber. Bbl.: 28-inch M or 30-inch F w/fixed choke or screw-in integral tubes; plain or vent. rib, blued. Weight: 7.25 lbs. Bead front sight. Black synthetic or wood buttstock and forend; forend grooved. Made from 1989 to date.
Synthetic stock w/plain bbl. . . . . . **NiB $287 Ex $228 Gd $175**
Synthetic stock w/vent. rib bbl.. . . . **NiB $300 Ex $238 Gd $195**
Synthetic Combo w/18.5-in. bbl. . . . .**NiB $321 Ex $220 Gd $184**
Wood stock w/vent. rib bbl./tubes.. . . . **NiB $300 Ex $225 Gd $179**
Wood Combo w/vent. rib bbl./tubes . . . .**NiB $255 Ex $200 Gd $162**

MODEL 88 SECURITY . . . . **NiB $275 Ex $190 Gd $145**
Crossbolt safety and dual slide bars. Optional heat shield. Cyl. bore choke. Gauge: 12 only. 3-inch chamber. Bbl.: 18.5 inch. Weight: 6 lbs., 8 oz. Synthetic stock and forearm. Made from 1993 to date.

MODEL 91 PUMP SHOTGUN
Same as Model 88, except w/2.75-, 3-, or 3.5-inch chamber; 28-inch bbl. w/ACCU-F choke, crossbolt safety, and synthetic stock only. Made from 1991 to 1995.
Synthetic stock w/plain bbl. . . . . . **NiB $330 Ex $256 Gd $180**
Synthetic stock w/vent. rib bbl. . . **NiB $335 Ex $270 Gd $195**

MODEL 95 BOLT-ACTION . . . . . **NiB $255 Ex $190 Gd $140**
Fixed M choke. Built-in 2-round magazine. Gauge: 12 only. Bbl.: 25 inch. Weight: 6.75 lbs. Bead sight. Synthetic stock and rubber recoil pad. Made from 1995 to 1997.

MODEL HS12 TACTICAL . . . . **NiB $582 Ex $350 Gd $150**
O/U boxlock. C/IM choke. Single trigger w/extractors. Gauge: 12 only. Bbl.: 18.5 inch. Weight: 6.25 lbs. Fiber optic sight. Synthetic stock w/rubber recoil pad. Picatinny rails. Made from 2011 to date.
Thunder Ranch.. . . . . **NiB $583 Ex $360 Gd $160**

MODEL HUNTER FIELD . . . . **NiB $518 Ex $275 Gd $130**
O/U boxlock. C/IM choke. Single trigger w/extractors. Gauge: 12 only. Bbl.: 28 inch. Weight: 7 lbs. Front bead sight. Synthetic stock w/rubber recoil pad. Made from 2010 to date.

GEBRÜDER MERKEL — Suhl, Germany

Manufactured by Suhler Jagd-und Sportwaffen GmbH; Imported by GSI, Inc., Trussville, AL, previously by Armes de Chasse.

MODEL 8 HAMMERLESS
DOUBLE . . . . **NiB $1522 Ex $1190 Gd $955**
Anson & Deeley boxlock action w/Greener double-bbl. hook lock. Double triggers. Extractors. Automatic safety. Gauges: 12, 16, 20. 2.75- or 3-inch chambers. 26- or 28-inch bbls. w/fixed standard chokes. Checkered European walnut stock, pistol-grip or English-style w/ or w/o cheekpiece. Scroll-engraved receiver w/tinted marble finish.

SIDE-BY-SIDE MODEL 47E . . . . **NiB $4000 Ex $3200 Gd $1890**
Hammerless boxlock similar to Model 8 except w/automatic ejectors and cocking indicators. Double hook bolting. Single selective or double triggers. 12, 16, or 20 ga. 2.75-inch chambers. Standard bbl. lengths, choke combos. Hand-checkered European walnut stock, forearm; pistol grip and cheekpiece or straight English style; sling swivels.

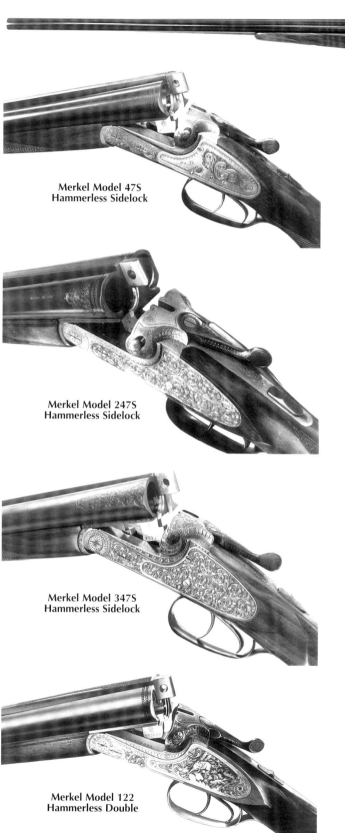

Merkel Model 47S
Hammerless Sidelock

Merkel Model 247S
Hammerless Sidelock

Merkel Model 347S
Hammerless Sidelock

Merkel Model 122
Hammerless Double

Merkel Model 47LSC
Sporting Clay

MODEL 47LSC
SPORTING CLAYS S/S . . . . . NiB $3100 Ex $2500 Gd $1789
Anson & Deeley boxlock action w/single selective adj. trigger, cocking indicators, and manual safety. Gauge: 12. 3-inch chambers. 28-inch bbls. w/Briley choke tubes and H&H-style ejectors. Weight: 7.25 lbs. Color casehardened receiver w/Arabesque engraving. Checkered select grade walnut stock, beavertail forearm. Imported from 1993 to 1994.

MODELS 47SL, 147SL, 247SL, 347SL, 447SL
HAMMERLESS SIDELOCKS
Same general specifications as Model 147E except has sidelocks engraved w/Arabesques, borders, scrolls, or game scenes in varying degrees of elaborateness.

Model 47SL . . . . .NiB $8350 Ex $5780 Gd $4200
Model 147SL . . . . NiB $10,099 Ex $7988 Gd $6754
Model 147SSL . . . . .NiB $9655 Ex $6130 Gd $4200
Model 247SL . . . . .NiB $8360 Ex $5110 Gd $3966
Model 347SL . . . . .NiB $7229 Ex $5263 Gd $3800
Model 447SL . . . . NiB $10,450 Ex $8550 Gd $5110
28 ga., .410, add 20%

NOTE: *Merkel over/under guns were often supplied with accessory barrels that were interchangeable to convert the gun into an arm of another type; for example, a set might consist of one pair each of shotgun, rifle, and combination gun barrels. Each pair of interchangeable barrels has a value of approximately one-third that of the gun with which they are supplied.*

MODEL 100 O/U SHOTGUN
Hammerless. Boxlock. Greener crossbolt. Plain extractor. Double triggers. Gauges: 12, 16, 20. Made w/plain or ribbed bbls. in various lengths and chokes. Plain finish, no engraving. Checkered forend and stock w/pistol grip and cheekpiece or English-style. Made prior to WWII.
w/plain bbl. . . . . .NiB $1964 Ex $1771 Gd $1333
w/ribbed bbl. . . . . .NiB $2175 Ex $1890 Gd $1377

MODELS 101 AND 101E O/U
Same as Model 100 except ribbed bbl. standard, has separate extractors (ejectors on Model 101E), English engraving. Made prior to WWII.
Model 101 . . . . .NiB $2210 Ex $1879 Gd $1360
Model 101E . . . . .NiB $2330 Ex $1968 Gd $1466

MODEL 122
HAMMERLESS DOUBLE . . . ..NiB $3965 Ex $3177 Gd $2300
Similar to the Model 147S except w/nonremovable sidelocks in gauges 12, 16, or 20. Imported since 1993.

MODEL 122E
HAMMERLESS SIDELOCK . . . . NiB $4865 Ex $3850 Gd $2700
Similar to the Model 122 except w/removable sidelocks and cocking indicators. Importation disc. 1992.

MODEL 126E
HAMMERLESS SIDELOCK . . . . NiB $25,788 Ex $22,650 Gd $18,700
Holland & Holland system, hand-detachable locks. Auto ejectors. Double triggers. 12, 16, or 20 gauge w/standard bbl. lengths and chokes. Checkered forend and pistol-grip stock; available w/cheekpiece or English-style buttstock. Elaborate game scenes and engraving. Made prior to WWII.

MODEL 127E
HAMMERLESS SIDELOCK . . . . NiB $24,849 Ex $21,939 Gd $16,374
Similar to the Model 126E except w/elaborate scroll engraving on removable sidelocks w/cocking indicators. Made prior to WWII.

MODEL 128E HAMMERLESS
BOXLOCK DOUBLE . . . . NiB $28,679 Ex $22,167 Gd $16,954
Scalloped Anson & Deeley action w/hinged floorplate and removable sideplates. Auto-ejectors. Double triggers. Elaborate hunting scene or Arabesque engraving. 12, 16, or 20 gauge w/various bbl. lengths and chokes. Checkered forend and stock w/pistol grip and cheekpiece or English-style. Made prior to WWII.

MODEL 130 HAMMERLESS
BOXLOCK DOUBLE . . . . NiB $21,400 Ex $18,560 Gd $16,450
Similar to Model 128E except w/fixed sideplates. Auto ejectors. Double triggers. Elaborate hunting scene or Arabesque engraving. Made prior to WWII.

MODELS 147 & 147E HAMMERLESS
BOXLOCK DOUBLE-BARREL SHOTGUN
Anson & Deeley system w/extractors or auto ejectors. Single selective or double triggers. Gauges: 12, 16, 20, or 28. (3-inch chambers available in 12 and 20 ga.). Bbls.: 26 inch standard, other lengths available w/any standard choke combination. Weight: 6.5 lbs. Checkered straight-grip stock and forearm. Disc. 1998.
Model 147 w/extractors . . . . . NiB $2588 Ex $2254 Gd $1899
Model 147E w/ejectors . . . . . . NiB $5540 Ex $3770 Gd $2840

MODELS 200, 200E, 201, 201E, 202, 202E, AND 202EL O/U SHOTGUNS
Hammerless. Boxlock. Kersten double crossbolt. Scalloped frame. Sideplates on Models 202 and 202E. Arabesque or hunting engraving supplied on all except Models 200 and 200E. E models have ejectors, others have separate extractors, signal pins, double triggers. Gauges: 12, 16, 20, 24, 28, 32 (last three not available in postwar guns). Ribbed bbls. in various lengths and chokes. Weight: 5.75 to 7.5 lbs. depending on bbl. length and gauge. Checkered forend and stock w/pistol grip and cheekpiece or English-style. The 200, 201, and 202 differ in overall quality, engraving, wood, checkering, etc.; aside from the faux sideplates on Models 202 and 202E, general specifications are the same. Models 200, 201, 202, and 202E, all made before WWII, are disc. Models 201E and 202E in production w/revised 2000 series nomenclature.
Model 200 . . . . NiB $2920 Ex $2255 Gd $1730
Model 200E . . . . NiB $3688 Ex $2987 Gd $2116
Model 200 ES Skeet . . . . NiB $4760 Ex $4200 Gd $2977
Model 200ET Trap . . . . NiB $4660 Ex $4189 Gd $3255
Model 200 SC Sporting Clays . . . . NiB $6930 Ex $4599 Gd $3238
Model 201 (disc.) . . . . NiB $3400 Ex $2566 Gd $1888
Model 201E (Pre-WWII) . . . . NiB $7335 Ex $4990 Gd $3288
Model 201E (Post-WWII) . . . . NiB $5100 Ex $3991 Gd $2977
Model 201 ES Skeet . . . . NiB $8100 Ex $6655 Gd $5133
Model 201 ET Trap . . . . NiB $7661 Ex $6255 Gd $4409
Model 202 (disc.) . . . . NiB $8255 Ex $5588 Gd $3577
Model 202E (Pre-WWII) . . . . NiB $8255 Ex $4967 Gd $3886
Model 202E (Post-WWII & 202EL) . . . . . NiB $7091 Ex $5897 Gd $3994

Merkel Model 147E
Hammerless Boxlock Double-Barrel Shotgun

Merkel Model 200E
O/U Shotgun

Merkel Model 203E
Sidelock O/U Shotgun

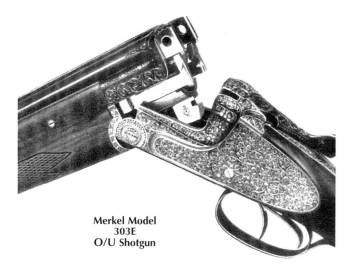

Merkel Model
303E
O/U Shotgun

MODEL 203E SIDELOCK O/U SHOTGUNS
Hammerless action w/hand-detachable sidelocks. Kersten double crossbolt, auto ejectors, and double triggers. Gauges: 12 or 20 (16, 24, 28, and 32 disc.). 26.75- or 28-inch vent. rib bbls. Arabesque engraving standard or hunting engraving optional on coin-finished receiver. Checkered English or pistol-grip stock and forend.
Model 203E sidelock
  (disc. 1998) . . . . NiB $10,335 Ex $8556 Gd $5830
Model 203ES skeet
  (imported 1993-97) . . . . NiB $12,450 Ex $12,330 Gd $10,245
Model 203ET trap
  (disc. 1997) . . . . NiB $13,770 Ex $12,560 Gd $10,665

MODEL 204E
O/U SHOTGUN . . . . NiB $8843 Ex $6751 Gd $4766
Similar to Model 203E; has Merkel sidelocks, fine English engraving. Made prior to WWII.

MODEL 210E
SIDELOCK O/U SHOTGUN . . . . NiB $7239 Ex $5340 Gd $3882
Kersten double crossbolt, scroll-engraved, casehardened receiver. 12, 16, or 20 ga. Double triggers; pistol-grip stock w/cheekpiece.

MODEL 211E
SIDELOCK O/U SHOTGUN . . . . NiB $6865 Ex $5388 Gd $4488
Same specifications as Model 210E except w/engraved hunting scenes on silver-gray receiver.

MODELS 300, 300E, 301, 301E, AND 302 O/U
Merkel-Anson system boxlock. Kersten double crossbolt, two underlugs, scalloped frame, sideplates on Model 302. Arabesque or hunting engraving. E models and Model 302 have auto ejectors, others have separate extractors. Signal pins. Double triggers. Gauges: 12, 16, 20, 24, 28, 32. Ribbed bbls. in various lengths and chokes. Checkered forend and stock w/pistol grip and cheekpiece or English-style. Grades 300, 301, and 302 differ in overall quality, engraving, wood, checkering, etc.; aside from the dummy sideplates on Model 302, general specifications are the same. Manufactured prior to WWII.
Model 300 . . . . NiB $5865 Ex $3579 Gd $2988
Model 300E . . . . NiB $8155 Ex $6888 Gd $5224
Model 301 . . . . NiB $6960 Ex $4977 Gd $3200
Model 301E . . . . NiB $8235 Ex $6276 Gd $5004
Model 302 . . . . NiB $14,998 Ex $12,688 Gd $10,097

MODEL 303EL O/U
SHOTGUN . . . . NiB $29,880 Ex $25,609 Gd $21,223
Similar to Model 203E. Has Kersten crossbolt, double underlugs, Holland & Holland-type hand-detachable sidelocks, auto-ejectors. This is a finer gun than Model 203E. Currently manufactured. Special order items.

MODEL 304E O/U
SHOTGUN . . . . NiB $24,770 Ex $19,760 Gd $13,010
Special version of the Model 303E type, but higher quality throughout. This is the top grade Merkel over/under. Currently manufactured. Special order items.

MODELS 400, 400E, 401, 401E O/U
Similar to Model 101 except have Kersten double crossbolt, Arabesque engraving on Models 400 and 400E, hunting engraving on Models 401 and 401E, finer general quality. E models have Merkel ejectors, others have separate extractors. Made prior to WWII.
Model 400 . . . . NiB $2190 Ex $1993 Gd $1465
Model 400E . . . . NiB $2433 Ex $2254 Gd $1934
Model 401 . . . . NiB $2798 Ex $2170 Gd $1588
Model 401E . . . . NiB $4366 Ex $3757 Gd $2486

O/U COMBINATION GUNS (BOCKBÜCHSFLINTEN)
Shotgun bbl. over, rifle bbl. under. Gauges: 12, 16, 20; calibers: 5.6x35 Vierling, 7x57r5, 8x57JR, 8x60R Mag., 9.3x53r5, 9.3x72r5, 9.3x74R, and others including domestic calibers from .22 Hornet to .375 H&H. Various bbl. lengths, chokes, and weights. Other specifications and values correspond to those of Merkel over/under shotguns listed below. Currently manufactured. Model 210 and 211 series disc. 1992.
Models 410, 410E, 411E (see shotgun models 400, 400E, 401, 401E)
Models 210, 210E, 211, 211E, 212, 212E
  (see shotgun models 200, 200E, 201, 201E, 202, 202E)

MODEL 2000EL O/U SHOTGUNS
Kersten double crossbolt. Gauges: 12 and 20. 26.75- or 28-inch bbls. Weight: 6.4 to 7.28 lbs. Scroll-engraved silver-gray receiver. Automatic ejectors and single selective or double triggers. Checkered forend and stock w/pistol grip and cheekpiece or English-style stock w/luxury grade wood. Imported from 1998 to 2005.
Model 2000EL Standard . . . . . . NiB $5733 Ex $4560 Gd $3288
Model 2000EL Sporter . . . . . . NiB $5980 Ex $4677 Gd $3455

MODEL 2001EL O/U SHOTGUNS
Gauges: 12, 16, 20, and 28; Kersten double crossbolt lock receiver. 26.75- or 28-inch IC/M, M/F bbls. Weight: 6.4 to 7.28 lbs. 3-piece forearm, automatic ejectors, and single selective or double triggers. Imported from 1993 to 2005.
Model 2001EL 12 ga. . . . . NiB $6566 Ex $5270 Gd $3880
Model 2001EL 16 ga.
  (disc. 1997) . . . . NiB $6400 Ex $5277 Gd $3760
Model 2001EL 20 ga. . . . . NiB $6400 Ex $5277 Gd $3760
Model 2001EL 28 ga.
  (made 1995) . . . . NiB $7200 Ex $5933 Gd $4200

MODEL 2002EL . . . . NiB $11,990 Ex $8530 Gd $6177
Same specifications as Model 2000EL except hunting scenes w/ Arabesque engraving.

ANSON DRILLINGS
Three bbl. combination guns usually made w/double shotgun bbls. over rifle bbl., although Doppelbüchsdrillingen were made w/two rifle bbls. over a shotgun bbl. Hammerless.

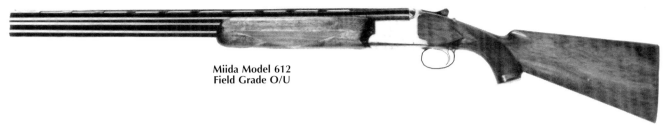

Miida Model 612
Field Grade O/U

Boxlock. Anson & Deeley system. Side clips. Plain extractors. Double triggers. Gauges: 12, 16, 20; rifle calibers: 7x57r5, 8x57JR, and 9.3x74R are most common, but other calibers from 5.6mm to 10.75mm available. Bbls.: Standard drilling 25.6 inches; short drilling, 21.6 inches. Checkered pistol-grip stock and forend. The three models listed differ chiefly in overall quality, grade of wood, etc.; general specifications are the same. Made prior to WWII.
Model 142 Engraved . . . . NiB $5698 Ex $4887 Gd $3366
Model 142 Standard . . . . . . NiB $4880 Ex $3688 Gd $2588
Model 145 Field . . . . NiB $3865 Ex $3200 Gd $2365

MIIDA — Manufactured for Marubeni America Corp., New York, by Olin-Kodensha Co., Tochigi, Japan

MODEL 612 FIELD GRADE O/U . . . NiB $863 Ex $665 Gd $400
Boxlock. Auto ejectors. Selective single trigger. 12 ga. Bbls.: Vent. rib; 26-inch, IC/M; 28-inch, M/F choke. Weight: (w/26-inch bbl) 6 lbs., 11 oz. Checkered pistol-grip stock and forearm. Made 1972 to 1974.

MODEL 2100 SKEET GUN . . . . . . NiB $954 Ex $749 Gd $488
Similar to Model 612 except has more elaborate engraving on frame (50% coverage), skeet-style stock and forearm of select grade wood; 27-inch vent. rib bbls., SK choke. Weight: 7 lbs., 11 oz. Made from 1972 to 1974.

MODEL 2200T TRAP GUN,
MODEL 2200S SKEET GUN . . . . . NiB $925 Ex $691 Gd $541
Similar to Model 612 except more elaborate engraving on frame (60% coverage), trap- or skeet-style stock and semi-beavertail forearm of fancy walnut, recoil pad on trap stock. Bbls.: Wide vent. rib; 29.75-inch, IM/F choke on Trap Gun; 27-inch, SK choke on Skeet Gun. Weight: Trap, 7 lbs., 14 oz.; Skeet, 7 lbs., 11 oz. Made 1972 to 1974.

MODEL 2200 TRAP
AND SKEET MODELS. . . . . .NiB $1088 Ex $766 Gd $594
Same as models 2200T and 2200S except more elaborate engraving on frame (70% coverage). Made from 1972 to 1974.

GRANDEE MODEL GRT/IRS
TRAP/SKEET GUN . . . . NiB $2655 Ex $2390 Gd $1866
Boxlock w/sideplates. Frame, breech ends of bbls., trigger guard, and locking lever fully engraved and gold inlaid. Auto ejectors. Selective single trigger. 12 ga. Bbls.: Wide vent. rib; 29-inch, F choke on Trap Gun; 27-inch, SK choke on Skeet Gun. Weight: Trap, 7 lbs., 14 oz.; Skeet, 7 lbs., 11 oz. Trap- or skeet-style stock and semi-beavertail forearm of extra fancy wood, recoil pad on trap stock. Made 1972 to 1974.

MITCHELL ARMS — Santa Ana, CA

MODEL 9104/9105 PUMP SHOTGUNS
Slide action in Field/Riot configuration. Gauge: 12.5-round tubular magazine. 20-inch bbl.; fixed choke or screw-in tubes. Weight: 6.5 lbs. Plain walnut stock. Made from 1994 to 1996.
Model 9104 (w/plain bbl.) . . . . . . .NiB $299 Ex $288 Gd $188
Model 9105 (w/rifle sight) . . . . . . .NiB $299 Ex $288 Gd $188

Choke tubes, add $40

MODEL 9108/9109 PUMP SHOTGUN
Slide action in Military/Police/Riot configuration. Gauge: 12.7-round tubular magazine. 20-inch bbl.; fixed choke or screw-in tubes. Weight: 6.5 lbs. Plain walnut stock and grooved slide handle w/ brown, green, or black finish. Blued metal. Made from 1994 to 1996.
Model 9108 (w/plain bbl.) . . . . . . NiB $292 Ex $225 Gd $196
Model 9109 (w/rifle sights) . . . . . NiB $292 Ex $225 Gd $196
Choke tubes, add $40

MODEL 9111/9113 PUMP SHOTGUN
Slide action in Military/Police/Riot configuration. Gauge: 12. 6-round tubular magazine. 18.5-inch bbl.; fixed choke or screw-in tubes. Weight: 6.5 lbs. Synthetic or plain walnut stock and grooved slide handle w/brown, green, or black finish. Blued metal. Made from 1994 to 1996.
Model 9111 (w/plain bbl.) . . . . . . NiB $292 Ex $225 Gd $196
Model 9113 (w/rifle sights) . . . . . NiB $292 Ex $225 Gd $196
Choke tubes, add $40

MODEL 9114/9114FS
Slide action in Military/Police/Riot configuration. Gauge: 12. 7-round tubular magazine. 20-inch bbl.; fixed choke or screw-in tubes. Weight: 6.5 to 7 lbs. Synthetic pistol-grip or folding stock. Blued metal. Made from 1994 to 1996.
Model 9114 . . . . NiB $345 Ex $245 Gd $169
Model 9114FS . . . . NiB $345 Ex $245 Gd $169

MODEL 9115/9115FS
PUMP SHOTGUN. . . . . NiB $366 Ex $240 Gd $159
Slide action in Military/Police/Riot configuration. Gauge: 12. 6-round tubular magazine. 18.5-inch bbl. w/heat shield handguard. Weight: 7 lbs. Gray synthetic stock and slide handle. Parkerized metal. Made from 1994 to 1996.

MONTGOMERY WARD — Chicago, IL, Western Field and Hercules Models

Although they do not correspond to specific models below, the names Western Field and Hercules have been used to designate various Montgomery Ward shotguns at various times.

MODEL 25 SLIDE-ACTION REPEATER . . . . .NiB $337 Ex $228 Gd $178
Solid frame. 12 ga. only. 2- or 5-round tubular magazine. 28-inch bbl., various chokes. Weight: About 7.5 lbs. Plain pistol-grip stock, grooved slide handle.

MODEL 40 O/U SHOTGUN. . . . . . NiB $866 Ex $700 Gd $522
Hammerless. Boxlock. Double triggers. Gauges: 12, l6, 20, .410. Bbls.: Plain, 26 to 30 inch, various chokes. Checkered pistol-grip stock and forearm.

Ward Western Field Model 50

Ward Western Field Model 52

Mossberg Model 83D

Mossberg Model 85D
Bolt-Action Repeating Shotgun

Mossberg Model 183K

Mossberg Model 185K

MODEL 40N
SLIDE-ACTION REPEATER . . . . . . **NiB $329   Ex $233   Gd $179**
Same general specifications as Model 25.

(WESTERN FIELD) MODEL 50
PUMPGUN . . . . **NiB $300   Ex $244   Gd $178**
Solid frame. Gauges: 12 and 16. 2- and 5-round magazine. 26-, 28-,
or 30-inch bbl. 48 inches overall w/28-inch bbl. Weight: 7.25 to
7.75 lbs. Metal bead front sight. Walnut stock and grooved forend.

(WESTERN FIELD) MODEL 52
DOUBLE-BARREL SHOTGUN. . . . . **NiB $388   Ex $277   Gd $191**
Hammerless coil-spring action. Gauges: 12, 16, 20, and .410. 26-, 28-,
or 30-inch bbls. 42 to 46 inches overall depending upon bbl. length.
Weight: 6 lbs. (.410 ga. w/26-inch bbl.) to 7.25 lbs. (12 ga. w/30-inch
bbls.) depending upon gauge and bbl. length. Casehardened receiver;
blued bbls. Plain buttstock and forend. Made circa 1954.

MODEL 172 BOLT-ACTION
SHOTGUN . . . . **NiB $217   Ex $139   Gd $95**
Takedown. 2-round detachable clip magazine. 12 ga. 28-inch

bbl. w/variable choke. Weight: About 7.5 lbs. Monte Carlo stock
w/recoil pad.

MODEL 550A SLIDE-ACTION
REPEATER . . . . **NiB $367   Ex $265   Gd $190**
Takedown. Gauges: 12, 16, 20, .410. 5-round tubular magazine.
Bbls.: Plain, 26 to 30 inch, various chokes. Weight: 6 lbs. (.410 ga.
w/26-inch bbl.) to 8 lbs. (12 ga. w/30-inch bbls.). Plain pistol-grip
stock and grooved slide handle.

MODEL SB300 DOUBLE-BARREL
SHOTGUN. . . . . **NiB $376   Ex $298   Gd $220**
Same general specifications as Model SD52A.

MODEL SB312 DOUBLE-BARREL
SHOTGUN . . . . **NiB $421   Ex $337   Gd $244**
Boxlock. Double triggers. Plain extractors. Gauges: 12, 16, 20, .410.
Bbls.: 24 to 30 inch. Various chokes. Weight: About 7.5 lbs. in 12
ga.; 6.5 lbs in .410 ga. Checkered pistol-grip stock and forearm.

MODEL SD52A DOUBLE-BARREL
SHOTGUN . . . . **NiB $344   Ex $255   Gd $200**
Boxlock. Double triggers. Plain extractors. Gauges: 12, 16, 20,
.410. Bbls.: 26 to 32 inch various chokes. Plain forend and pistol-
grip buttstock. Weight: 6 lbs. (.410 ga., 26-inch bbls.) to 7.5 lbs.
(12 ga., 32-inch bbls.).

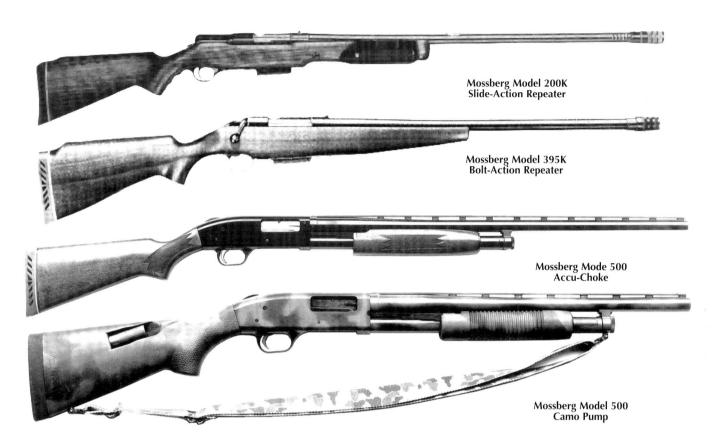

Mossberg Model 200K
Slide-Action Repeater

Mossberg Model 395K
Bolt-Action Repeater

Mossberg Mode 500
Accu-Choke

Mossberg Model 500
Camo Pump

MORRONE SHOTGUN — Manufactured by Rhode Island Arms Company, Hope Valley, RI

STANDARD MODEL 46 O/U . . . NiB $1366 Ex $890 Gd $677
Boxlock. Plain extractors. Nonselective single trigger. Gauges: 12, 20. Bbls.: Plain, vent. rib; 26-inch IC/M, 28-inch M/F choke. Weight: About 7 lbs., 12 ga.; 6 lbs., 20 ga. Checkered straight- or pistol-grip stock and forearm. Made 1949 to 1953. Note: Fewer than 500 of these guns were produced, about 50 in 20 ga. A few had vent. rib bbls. Value shown is for 12 ga. w/plain bbls. The rare 20 ga. and vent. rib types should bring considerably more.

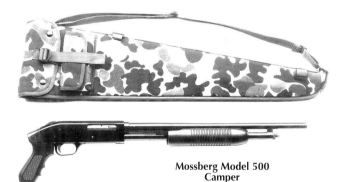

Mossberg Model 500
Camper

O.F. MOSSBERG & SONS, INC. — North Haven (formerly New Haven), CT

MODEL G4, 70, 73, 73B. . . . . NiB $150 Ex $85 Gd $50
Single shot. .410 ga. only. Made from 1932 to 1940.

MODEL 83D, 183D . . . . NiB $217 Ex $121 Gd $95
Bolt action, 3-round. Takedown. .410 ga. only. 2-shell fixed top-loading magazine. 23-inch bbl. w/two interchangeable choke tubes (M/F). Later production had 24-inch bbl. Plain one-piece pistol-grip stock. Weight: About 5.5 lbs. Originally designated Model 83D, changed in 1947 to Model 183D. Made from 1940 to 1971.

MODEL 85D, 185D BOLT-ACTION
REPEATING SHOTGUN . . . . NiB $217 Ex $121 Gd $95
Bolt action. Takedown. 3-round. 20 ga. only. 2-shell detachable box magazine. 25-inch bbl., three interchangeable choke tubes (F/M/IC). Later production had 26-inch bbl. w/F/IC choke tubes. Weight: About 6.25 lbs. Plain one-piece, pistol-grip stock. Originally designated Model 85D, changed in 1947 to Model 185D. Made from 1940 to 1971.

MODEL 183K . . . . NiB $240 Ex $131 Gd $100
Same as Model 183D except has 25-inch bbl. w/variable C-Lect choke instead of interchangeable choke tubes. Made 1953 to 1986.

MODEL 185K . . . . NiB $240 Ex $131 Gd $100
Same as Model 185D except has variable C-Lect choke instead of interchangeable choke tubes. Made from 1950 to 1963.

**Mossberg Model 500
Persuader Law Enforcement**

**Mossberg Model 500
Mariner**

MODEL 190D . . . . **NiB $240 Ex $131 Gd $100**
Same as Model 185D except in 16 ga. Weight: About 6 lbs. Made from 1955 to 1971.

MODEL 190K . . . . **NiB $240 Ex $131 Gd $100**
Same as Model 185K except in 16 ga. Takedown. 3-round capacity; 2-round magazine. Weight: About 6.75 lbs. Made 1956 to 1963.

MODEL 195D . . . . **NiB $240 Ex $131 Gd $100**
Same as Model 185D except in 12 ga. Takedown. 3-round capacity; 2-round magazine. Weight: About 6.75 lbs. Made 1955 to 1971.

MODEL 195K . . . . **NiB $240 Ex $131 Gd $100**
Same as Model 185K except in 12 ga. Takedown. 3-round capacity; 2-round magazine. Weight: About 7.5 lbs. Made 1956 to 1963.

MODEL 200D . . . . **NiB $355 Ex $240 Gd $125**
Same as Model 200K except w/two interchangeable choke tubes instead of C-Lect choke. Made from 1955 to 1959.

MODEL 200K SLIDE-ACTION REPEATER . . . . **NiB $355 Ex $190 Gd $120**
12 ga. 3-round detachable box magazine. 28-inch bbl. C-Lect choke. Plain pistol-grip stock. Black nylon slide handle. Weight: About 7.5 lbs. Made from 1955 to 1959.

MODEL 395K BOLT-ACTION REPEATER . . . . **NiB $255 Ex $155 Gd $120**
Takedown. 3-round; detachable clip magazine holds two rounds. 12 ga. 3-inch chamber. 28-inch bbl. w/C-Lect choke. Weight: About 7.5 lbs. Monte Carlo stock w/recoil pad. Made 1963 to 1983.

MODEL 385K . . . . **NiB $240 Ex $131 Gd $100**
Same as Model 395K except 20 ga. (3-inch), 26-inch bbl. w/C-Lect choke. Weight: About 6.25 lbs.

MODEL 390K . . . . **NiB $240 Ex $131 Gd $100**
Same as Model 395K except 16 ga. (2.75-inch). Made 1963 to 1974.

MODEL 395S SLUGSTER . . . . **NiB $240 Ex $131 Gd $100**
Same as Model 395K except has 24-inch bbl., Cyl. bore, rifle sights, swivels, and web sling. Weight: About 7 lbs. Made from 1968 to 1981.

MODEL 500 ACCU-CHOKE SHOTGUN . . . . **NiB $290 Ex $231 Gd $125**
Pump-action. Gauge: 12. 24- or 28-inch bbl. Weight: 7.25 lbs. Checkered walnut-finished wood stock w/ventilated recoil pad. Available w/synthetic field or Speed-Feed stocks. Drilled and tapped receivers, swivels and camo sling on camo models. Made from 1987 to date.

MODEL 500 BANTAM SHOTGUN
Same as Model 500 Sporting Pump except 20 or .410 ga. only. 22-inch w/Accu-Choke tubes or 24-inch w/F choke; vent. rib. Scaled-down checkered hardwood or synthetic stock w/standard or Realtree camo finish. Made from 1990 to 1996 and 1998 to 1999.
Bantam Model (hardwood stock) . . . .**NiB $255 Ex $198 Gd $130**
Bantam Model (synthetic stock) . . . .**NiB $330 Ex $229 Gd $165**
Bantam Model (Realtree camo), add **$75**

MODEL 500 BULLPUP SHOTGUN . . . . . **NiB $722 Ex $486 Gd $344**
Pump. Gauge: 12. 6- or 8-round capacity. Bbl.: 18.5 to 20 inches. 26.5 and 28.5 inches overall. Weight: About 9.5 lbs. Multiple independent safety systems. Dual pistol grips, rubber recoil pad. Fully enclosed rifle-type sights. Synthetic stock. Ventilated bbl. heat shield. Made from 1987 to 1990.

MODEL 500 CAMO PUMP
Same as Model 500 Sporting Pump except 12 ga. only. Receiver drilled and tapped. QD swivels and camo sling. Special camouflage finish.
Standard model . . . . **NiB $390 Ex $255 Gd $200**
Combo model (w/ext. Slugster bbl.) . . .**NiB $409 Ex $270 Gd $220**

MODEL 500 CAMPER . . . . **NiB $290 Ex $210 Gd $175**
Same general specifications as Model 500 Field Grade except .410 bore, 6-round magazine, 18.5-inch plain Cyl. bore bbl. Synthetic pistol grip and camo carrying case. Made 1986 to 1990.

**MODEL 500 FIELD GRADE HAMMERLESS
SLIDE-ACTION REPEATER**
Pre-1977 type. Takedown. Gauges: 12, 16, 20, .410. 3-inch chamber (2.75-inch in 16 ga.). Tubular magazine holds five 2.75-inch rounds or four 3-inch. Bbls.: Plain 30-inch, regular or heavy Mag. F choke (12 ga. only); 28-inch, M/F; 26-inch, IC or adj. C-Lect-choke; 24-inch Slugster, Cyl. bore, w/rifle sights. Weight: 5.75 lbs. Plain pistol-grip stock w/recoil pad, grooved slide handle. After 1973, these guns have checkered stock and slide handles; Models 500AM and 500AS have receivers etched w/ game scenes. The latter has swivels and sling. Made from 1962 to 1976.
Model 500A, 12 ga. . . . .**NiB $310 Ex $225 Gd $170**
Model 500AM, 12 ga., hvy. Mag. bbl. . . . . . .**NiB $310 Ex $225 Gd $170**
Model 500AK, 12 ga., C-Lect choke . . . . .**NiB $335 Ex $250 Gd $190**
Model 500AS, 12 ga., Slugster . . . .**NiB $359 Ex $250 Gd $195**
Model 500B 16 ga. . . . .**NiB $369 Ex $275 Gd $205**
Model 500BK, 16 ga., C-Lect choke . . . .**NiB $300 Ex $220 Gd $145**
Model 500BS, 16 ga., Slugster . . . .**NiB $359 Ex $250 Gd $195**
Model 500C 20 ga. . . . .**NiB $360 Ex $275 Gd $160**
Model 500CK, 20 ga., C-Lect choke . . . .**NiB $335 Ex $250 Gd $190**
Model 500CS, 20 ga., Slugster . . . .**NiB $330 Ex $239 Gd $180**
Model 500E, .410 ga. . . . .**NiB $300 Ex $220 Gd $140**
Model 500EK, .410 ga., C-Lect choke . . . . .**NiB $350 Ex $275 Gd $165**

MODEL 500 L SERIES
L in model designation. Same as pre-1977 Model 500 Field Grade except not available in 16 ga., has receiver etched w/different game scenes. Accu-Choke w/three interchangeable tubes (IC/M/F) standard, restyled stock and slide handle. Bbls.: Plain or vent. rib; 30 or 32 inch, heavy, F choke (12 ga. Mag. and vent. rib only); 28-inch, Accu-Choke (12 and 20 ga.); 26-inch F choke (.410 bore); 18.5-inch (12 ga. only); 24-inch (12 and 20 ga.) Slugster w/rifle sights, Cyl. bore. Weight: 6 to 8.5 lbs. Intro. 1977.
**Model 500ALD, 12 ga.,
plain bbl. (disc. 1980)** . . . . **NiB $275 Ex $195 Gd $110**
Model 500ALDR, 12 ga., vent. rib . . . . . .**NiB $300 Ex $220 Gd $131**

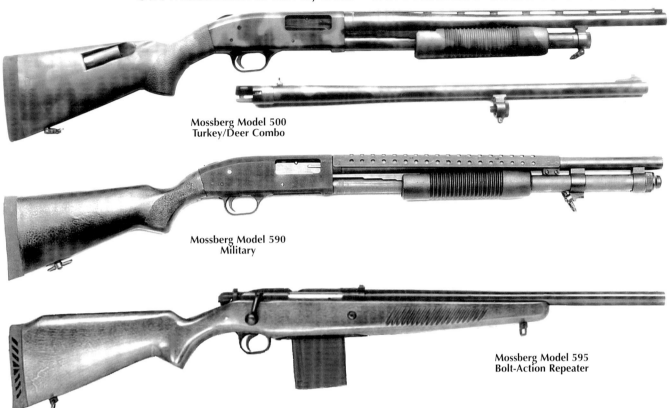

Mossberg Model 500
Turkey/Deer Combo

Mossberg Model 590
Military

Mossberg Model 595
Bolt-Action Repeater

Model 500ALMR, 12 ga.,
Heavy Duck Gun (disc. 1980) . . . . NiB $325 Ex $240 Gd $165
Model 500CLD, 20 ga.,
plain bbl. (disc. 1980) . . . . NiB $355 Ex $265 Gd $185
Model 500CLDR, 20 ga., vent. rib . . . . . . NiB $310 Ex $235 Gd $135
Model 500CLS, 20 ga.,
Slugster (disc. 1980) . . . . NiB $355 Ex $265 Gd $185
Model 500EL, .410 ga.,
plain bbl. (disc. 1980) . . . . NiB $295 Ex $200 Gd $125
Model 500ELR, .410 ga., vent. rib. . . . . . NiB $325 Ex $240 Gd $135

MODEL 500 MARINER SHOTGUN . . . . . NiB $500 Ex $390 Gd $277
Slide action. Gauge: 12. 18.5- or 20-inch bbl. 6-round and 8-round,
respectively. Weight: 7.25 lbs. High-strength synthetic buttstock and
forend. Available in extra round-carrying Speed Feed synthetic buttstock.
All metal treated for protection against saltwater corrosion. Intro. 1987.

MODEL 500 MUZZLELOADER COMBO. . . . . . NiB $390 Ex $275 Gd $190
Same as Model 500 Sporting Pump except w/extra 24-inch rifled
.50-caliber muzzleloading bbl. w/ramrod. Made 1991 to 1996.

MODEL 500 PERSUADER LAW ENFORCEMENT
Similar to pre-1977 Model 500 Field Grade except 12 ga. only,
6- or 8-round capacity, has 18.5- or 20-inch plain bbl., Cyl. bore,
either shotgun or rifle sights, plain pistol-grip stock and grooved
slide handle, sling swivels. Special Model 500ATP8-SP has bayonet lug. Parkerized finish. Intro. 1995.
Model 500ATP6, 6-round, 18.5-inch
bbl., shotgun sights . . . . NiB $410 Ex $275 Gd $190
Model 500ATP6CN, 6-round,
nickle finish Cruiser pistol-grip. . . . . . NiB $440 Ex $300 Gd $225
Model 500ATP6N, 6-round, nickel
finish, 2.75- or 3-inch Mag. shells . . . NiB $410 Ex $275 Gd $190
Model 500ATP6S, 6-round,
18.5-inch bbl., rifle sights . . . . NiB $410 Ex $275 Gd $190

Model 500ATP8, 8-round,
20-inch bbl., shotgun sights . . . . NiB $440 Ex $300 Gd $225
Model 500ATP8S, 8-round,
20-inch bbl., rifle sights . . . . NiB $450 Ex $315 Gd $240
Model 500ATP8-SP Spec. Enforcement . . . . NiB $391 Ex $313 Gd $226
Model 500 Bullpup . . . . NiB $690 Ex $500 Gd $345
Model 500 Intimidator w/laser sight, blued . . . . NiB $644 Ex $470 Gd $329
Model 500 Intimidator w/laser sight,
Parkerized . . . . NiB $425 Ex $320 Gd $190
Model 500 Security combo pack . . . . NiB $345 Ex $270 Gd $185
Model 500 Cruiser w/pistol grip . . . . NiB $440 Ex $325 Gd $220

MODEL 500 PIGEON GRADE
Same as Model 500 Super Grade except higher quality w/fancy
wood, floating vent. rib; field guns have hunting dog etching, trap
and skeet guns have scroll etching. Bbls.: 30-inch, F choke (12
ga. only); 28-inch, M choke; 26-inch, SK choke or C-Lect choke.
Made from 1971 to 1975.
Model 500APR, 12 ga., field, trap, or skeet . . . . . NiB $510 Ex $409 Gd $320
Model 500APKR, 12 ga. field gun, C-Lect choke . . NiB $455 Ex $279 Gd $144
Model 500 APTR, 12 ga.,
trap gun, Monte Carlo stock . . . . NiB $475 Ex $300 Gd $165
Model 500CPR, 20 ga., field or skeet gun . . . . . NiB $365 Ex $279 Gd $180
Model 500EPR, .410 ga.
field or skeet gun . . . . NiB $345 Ex $292 Gd $190

MODEL 500 CAMO COMBO SHOTGUN . . . . . . NiB $440 Ex $335 Gd $255
Gauges: 12 and 20. 24- and 28-inch bbl. w/adj. rifle sights. Weight: 7 to 7.25
lbs. Available w/blued or camo finish. Drilled and tapped receiver w/sling
swivels and camo web sling. Made from 1987 to 1998.

MODEL 500 PUMP SLUGSTER SHOTGUN
Gauges: 12 or 20. 3-inch chamber. 24-inch smoothbore or rifled bbl. w/adj.
rifle sights or intregral scope mount and optional muzzle break (1997 porting
became standard). Weight: 7 to 7.25 lbs. Wood or synthetic stock w/ standard

**Mossberg Model 1000
Junior Autoloading**

**Mossberg Model 5500
Guardian**

or Woodland Camo finish. Blued, matte black, or Marinecote metal finish. Drilled and tapped receiver w/camo sling and swivels. Made 1987 to date.

Slugster (w/Cyl. bore, rifle sights)	NiB $335	Ex $245	Gd $190
Slugster (w/rifled bore, ported)	NiB $415	Ex $335	Gd $240
Slugster (w/rifled bore, unported)	NiB $320	Ex $219	Gd $190
Slugster (w/rifled bore, ported, integral scope mount)	NiB $320	Ex $219	Gd $190
Slugster (w/Marinecote and synthetic stock), add			$100
Slugster (w/Truglo fiber optics), add			$50

MODEL 500 REGAL SLIDE-ACTION REPEATER
Similar to regular Model 500 except higher quality workmanship throughout. Gauges: 12 and 20. Bbls.: 26 and 28 inch w/various chokes or Accu-Choke. Weight: 6.75 to 7.5 lbs. Checkered walnut stock and forearm. Made from 1985 to 1987.

Model 500 w/Accu-Choke	NiB $320	Ex $219	Gd $190
Model 500 w/fixed choke	NiB $300	Ex $200	Gd $165

MODEL 500 SPORTING PUMP
Gauges: 12, 20, or .410. 2.75- or 3-inch chamber. Bbls.: 22 to 28 inches w/fixed choke or screw-in tubes; plain or vent. rib. Weight: 6.25 to 7.25 lbs. White bead front sight, brass mid-bead. Checkered hardwood buttstock and forend w/walnut finish.

Standard model	NiB $345	Ex $275	Gd $190
Field combo (w/extra Slugster bbl.)	NiB $440	Ex $325	Gd $240

MODEL 500 SUPER GRADE
Same as pre-1977 Model 500 Field Grade except not made in 16 ga., has vent. rib bbl., checkered pistol grip and slide handle. Made from 1965 to 1976.

Model 500AR, 12 ga.	NiB $400	Ex $299	Gd $221
Model 500AMR, 12 ga., heavy Magnum bbl.	NiB $400	Ex $299	Gd $221
Model 500AKR, 12 ga., C-Lect choke	NiB $425	Ex $315	Gd $235
Model 500CR 20 ga.	NiB $400	Ex $299	Gd $221
Model 500CKk, 20 ga., C-Lect choke	NiB $425	Ex $315	Gd $235
Model 500ER, .410 ga.	NiB $400	Ex $299	Gd $221
Model 500EKR, .410 ga., C-Lect choke	NiB $425	Ex $315	Gd $235

MODEL 500 TURKEY/DEER COMBO
NiB $425 Ex $315 Gd $235
Pump (slide action). Gauge: 12. 20- and 24-inch bbls. Weight: 7.25 lbs. Drilled and tapped receiver, camo sling and swivels. Adj. rifle sights and camo finish. Vent. rib. Made from 1987 to 1997.

MODEL 500 TURKEY GUN
NiB $465 Ex $325 Gd $254
Same as Model 500 Camo Pump except w/24-inch Accu-Choke bbl. w/extra F choke tube and ghost-ring sights. Made 1992 to 1997.

MODEL 500 VIKING PUMP SHOTGUN
Gauges: 12 or 20. 3-inch chamber. 24-, 26- or 28-inch bbls. available in smoothbore w/Accu-Choke and vent. rib or rifled bore w/iron sights and optional muzzle brake (1997 porting became standard). Optional

optics: Slug Shooting System (SSS). Weight: 6.9 to 7.2 lbs. Moss-green synthetic stock. Matte black metal finish. Made from 1996 to 1998.

Mdl. 500 Viking (w/VR & choke tubes, unported)	NiB $300	Ex $225	Gd $144
Mdl. 500 Viking (w/rifled bore, ported)	NiB $390	Ex $295	Gd $240
Mdl. 500 Viking (w/rifled bore, SSS & ported)	NiB $390	Ex $295	Gd $240
Mdl. 500 Viking (w/rifled bore, unported)	NiB $300	Ex $225	Gd $144
Mdl. 500 Viking Turkey (w/VR, tubes, ported)	NiB $300	Ex $225	Gd $144

MODEL 500 WATERFOWL/DEER COMBO
NiB $455 Ex $350 Gd $285
Same general specifications as the Turkey/Deer combo except w/either 28- or 30-inch bbl. along w/the 24-inch bbl. Made 1987 to date.

MODEL 500 ATR SUPER GRADE TRAP
NiB $400 Ex $310 Gd $225
Same as pre-1977 Model 500 Field Grade except 12 ga. only w/ vent. rib bbl.; 30-inch F choke, checkered Monte Carlo stock w/ recoil pad, beavertail slide handle. Made from 1968 to 1971.

MODEL 500DSPR DUCK STAMP COMMEMORATIVE
NiB $600 Ex $465 Gd $300
Limited edition of 1000 to commemorate the Migratory Bird Hunting Stamp program. Same as Model 500DSPR Pigeon Grade 12-ga. Mag. Heavy Duck Gun w/heavy 30-inch vent. rib bbl., F choke. Receiver has special wood duck etching. Gun accompanied by a special wall plaque. Made in 1975.

MODEL 590 BULLPUP
NiB $745 Ex $449 Gd $335
Same general specifications as the Model 500 Bullpup except 20-inch bbl. and 9-round magazine. Made from 1989 to 1990.

MODEL 590 MARINER PUMP
Same general specifications as the Model 590 Military Security except has Marinecote metal finish and field configuration synthetic stock w/pistol-grip conversion included. Made 1989 to 1999.

Model 590 Mariner (w/18.5-inch bbl.)	NiB $645	Ex $554	Gd $470
Model 590 Mariner (w/20-inch bbl.)	NiB $645	Ex $554	Gd $470
Model 590 Mariner (w/grip conversion), add			$40
Model 590 Mariner (w/ghost ring sight), add			$75

MODEL 590 MILITARY SECURITY
NiB $544 Ex $389 Gd $290
Same general specifications as the Model 590 Military except there is no heat shield and gun has short pistol-grip style instead of buttstock. Weight: About 6.75 lbs. Made from 1987 to 1993.

MODEL 590 MILITARY SHOTGUN
Slide action. Gauge: 12. 9-round capacity. 20-inch bbl. Weight: About 7 lbs. Synthetic or hardwood buttstock and forend. Ventilated bbl. heat shields. Equipped w/bayonet lug. Blued or Parkerized finish. Made from 1987 to date.

Synthetic model, blued . . . . NiB $465 Ex $377 Gd $260
Synthetic model, Parkerized . . . . NiB $490 Ex $400 Gd $280
Speedfeed model, blued . . . . NiB $475 Ex $380 Gd $285
Speedfeed model, Parkerized . . . . NiB $475 Ex $ 380 Gd $285
Intimidator model
   w/laser sight, blued . . . . NiB $640 Ex $500 Gd $365
Intimidator model
   w/laser sight, Parkerized . . . . . . NiB $665 Ex $515 Gd $380
Ghost-ring sight, add $100

MODEL 595/595K
BOLT-ACTION REPEATER . . . . NiB $425 Ex $260 Gd $159
12 ga. only. 4-round detachable magazine. 18.5-inch bbl. Weight: About 7 lbs. Walnut finished stock w/recoil pad and sling swivels. Made 1985 to 1986.

MODEL 695 BOLT-ACTION SLUGSTER
Gauge: 12. 3-inch chamber. 2-round detachable magazine. 22-inch fully rifled and ported bbl. w/blade front and folding leaf rear sights. Receiver drilled and tapped for Weaver-style scope bases. Available w/1.5x to 4.5x scope or fiber optics installed. Weight: 7.5 lbs. Black synthetic stock w/swivel studs and recoil pad. Made 1996 to 2002.
Model 695 (w/Accu-Choke bbl.) . . . . NiB $300 Ex $220 Gd $175
Model 695
  (w/open sights) . . . . NiB $380 Ex $296 Gd $207
Model 695
  (w/1.5x-4.5x Bushnell scope). . . NiB $390 Ex $310 Gd $219
Model 695 (w/Truglo fiber optics) . . . NiB $385 Ex $305 Gd $210
Model 695 OFM Camo . . . . NiB $355 Ex $280 Gd $196

MODEL 695 BOLT-ACTION
TURKEY GUN . . . . NiB $375 Ex $265 Gd $195
Similar to 695 Slugster Model except has smoothbore 22-inch bbl. w/extra-full turkey Accu-Choke tube. Bead front and U-notch rear sights. Full OFM camo finish. Made from 1996 to 2002.

MODEL 712 AUTOLOADING SHOTGUN
Gas-operated, takedown, hammerless shotgun w/5-round (4-round w/3-inch chamber) tubular magazine. 12 ga. Bbls.: 28-inch vent. rib or 24-inch plain bbl. Slugster w/rifle sights. Fixed choke or Accu-Choke tube system. Weight: 7.5 lbs. Plain alloy receiver w/top-mounted ambidextrous safety. Checkered stained hardwood stock w/recoil pad. Imported from Japan 1986 to 1990.
Model 712 w/fixed chokes. . . . . NiB $369 Ex $237 Gd $185
Model 712 w/Accu-Choke tube system . . . NiB $390 Ex $275 Gd $219
Model 712 Regal
  w/Accu-Choke tube system. . . . . NiB $390 Ex $275 Gd $219
Model 712 Regal
  w/Accu-Choke II tube system . . . NiB $390 Ex $275 Gd $219

MODEL 835 FIELD PUMP SHOTGUN
Similar to the Model 9600 Regal except has walnut-stained hardwood stock and one Accu-Choke tube only.
Standard model . . . . NiB $365 Ex $220 Gd $154
Turkey model . . . . NiB $365 Ex $220 Gd $154
Combo model (24- and 28-inch bbls.) . NiB $390 Ex $250 Gd $180

MODEL 835 NWTF ULTI-MAG SHOTGUN
National Wild Turkey Federation pump action. Gauge: 12. 3.5-inch chamber. 24-inch vent. rib bbl. w/four Accu-Mag chokes. Realtree camo finish. QD swivel and post. Made from 1989 to 1993.
Limited Edition model . . . . NiB $470 Ex $366 Gd $239
Special Edition model . . . . NiB $400 Ex $325 Gd $225

MODEL 835 REGAL ULTI-MAG PUMP
Gauge: 12. 3.5-inch chamber. Bbls.: 24- or 28-inch vent. rib w/Accu-Choke screw-in tubes. Weight: 7.75 lbs. White bead front, brass mid-bead. Checkered hardwood or synthetic stock w/camo finish. Made 1991 to 1996.

Special model . . . . NiB $400 Ex $350 Gd $235
Standard model . . . . NiB $509 Ex $377 Gd $295
Camo Synthetic model . . . . NiB $490 Ex $375 Gd $299
Combo model . . . . NiB $528 Ex $420 Gd $310

MODEL 835 VIKING PUMP SHOTGUN
Gauge: 12. 3-inch chamber. 28-inch smoothbore bbl. w/Accu-Choke, vent. rib and optional muzzle brake (in 1997 porting became standard). Weight: 7.7 lbs. Green synthetic stock. Matte black metal finish. Made from 1996 to 1998.
Model 835 Viking (w/VR and
  choke tubes, ported) . . . . NiB $300 Ex $217 Gd $175
Model 835 Viking (w/VR
  and choke tubes, unported) . . . . . . NiB $445 Ex $270 Gd $210

MODEL 1000 AUTOLOADING SHOTGUN
Gas-operated, takedown, hammerless shotgun w/tubular magazine. Gauges: 12, 20. 2.75- or 3-inch chamber. Bbls.: 22- to 30-inch vent. rib w/fixed choke or Accu-Choke tubes; 22-inch plain bbl., Slugster w/rifle sights. Weight: 6.5 to 7.5 lbs. Scroll-engraved alloy receiver, crossbolt-type safety. Checkered walnut buttstock and forend. Imported from Japan 1986 to 1987.
Junior model, 20 ga., 22-inch bbl. . NiB $555 Ex $435 Gd $320
Standard model w/fixed choke . NiB $555 Ex $435 Gd $320
Standard model w/choke tubes . . NiB $555 Ex $435 Gd $320

MODEL 1000 SUPER AUTOLOADING SHOTGUN
Similar to Model 1000, but in 12 ga. only. 3-inch chamber and new gas metering system. Bbls.: 26-, 28-, or 30-inch vent. rib w/ Accu-Choke tubes.
Standard model w/choke tubes . . . . NiB $555 Ex $435 Gd $320
Waterfowler model (Parkerized) . . . . NiB $590 Ex $466 Gd $380

MODEL 1000S SUPER SKEET . . . . NiB $655 Ex $500 Gd $422
Similar to Model 1000 in 12 or 20 ga. except w/all-steel receiver and vented jug-type choke for reduced muzzle jump. Bright-point front sight and brass mid-bead. 1 and 2 oz. forend cap weights.

MODEL 5500 AUTOLOADING SHOTGUN
Gas operated. Takedown. 12 ga. only. 4-round magazine (3-round w/3-inch shells). Bbls.: 18.5 to 30 inch; various chokes. Checkered walnut finished hardwood. Made from 1985 to 1986.
Model 5500 w/Accu-Choke . . . . . NiB $300 Ex $210 Gd $148
Model 5500 modified junior . . . . NiB $300 Ex $210 Gd $148
Model 5500 Slugster. . . . . NiB $355 Ex $209 Gd $155
Model 5500 12 ga. Mag . . . . NiB $335 Ex $254 Gd $190
Model 5500 Guardian . . . . NiB $330 Ex $250 Gd $180

MODEL 5500 MKII AUTOLOADING SHOTGUN
Same as Model 5500 except equipped w/two Accu-Choke bbls.: 26-inch ported for non-Mag. 2.75-inch shells; 28-inch for Mag. loads. Made from 1988 to 1993.
Standard model . . . . NiB $330 Ex $209 Gd $135
Camo model . . . . NiB $366 Ex $270 Gd $198
NWTF Mossy Oak model . . . . NiB $415 Ex $330 Gd $225
USST model (1991-92) . . . . NiB $370 Ex $292 Gd $217

MODEL 6000 AUTO SHOTGUN . . . . NiB $320 Ex $231 Gd $198
Similar to the Model 9200 Regal except has 28-inch vent. rib bbl. w/mod. Accu-Choke tube only. Made 1993 only.

MODEL 9200 CAMO SHOTGUN
Similar to the Model 9200 Regal except has synthetic stock and forend and is completely finished in camouflage pattern (including bbl.). Made from 1993 to date.
Standard model (OFM camo) . . . . NiB $500 Ex $415 Gd $306
Turkey model (Mossy Oak camo) . . . . NiB $475 Ex $429 Gd $360
Turkey model (Shadow Branch camo) . . . . NiB $615 Ex $490 Gd $376
Comb. model (24 and 28-inch bbls.
  w/OFM camo) . . . . NiB $635 Ex $515 Gd $390

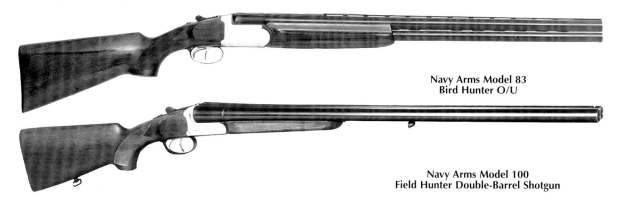

**Navy Arms Model 83
Bird Hunter O/U**

**Navy Arms Model 100
Field Hunter Double-Barrel Shotgun**

MODEL 9200 CROWN (REGAL) AUTOLOADER
Gauge: 12. 3-inch chamber. Bbls.: 18.5- to 28-inch w/Accu-Choke tubes; plain or vent. rib. Weight: 7.25 to 7.5 lbs. Checkered hardwood buttstock and forend w/walnut finish. Made from 1992 to 2001.
Model 9200 Bantam (w/1 inch shorter stock) .... NiB $500 Ex $433 Gd $329
Model 9200 w/Accu-Choke .... NiB $500 Ex $433 Gd $329
Model 9200 w/rifled bbl. .... NiB $500 Ex $433 Gd $329
Model 9200 Combo (w/extra Slugster bbl.).... NiB $550 Ex $493 Gd $379
Model 9200 SP (w/matte blue finish,
   18.5-inch bbl.)................... NiB $500 Ex $433 Gd $329

MODEL 9200 PERSUADER...... NiB $500 Ex $443 Gd $329
Similar to the Model 9200 Regal except has 18.5-inch plain bbl. w/fixed M choke. Parkerized finish. Black synthetic stock w/sling swivels. Made from 1996 to 2001.

MODEL 9200 A1 JUNGLE GUN.... NiB $665 Ex $533 Gd $347
Similar to the Model 9200 Persuader except has mil-spec heavy wall 18.5-inch plain bbl. w/Cyl. bore designed for 00 Buck shot. 12 ga. 2.75-inch chamber. 5-round magazine. 38.5 inches overall. Weight: 7 lbs. Black synthetic stock. Parkerized finish. Made from 1998 to 2001.

MODEL 9200 SPECIAL HUNTER ....NiB $555 Ex $435 Gd $365
Similar to the Model 9200 Regal except has 28-inch vent. rib bbl. Accu-Choke tubes. Parkerized finish. Black synthetic stock. Made from 1998 to 2001.

MODEL 9200 TROPHY
Similar to the Model 9200 Regal except w/24-inch rifled bbl. or 24- or 28-inch vent. rib bbl. w/Accu-Choke tubes. Checkered walnut stock w/sling swivels. Made from 1992 to 1998.
Trophy (w/vent. rib bbl.)........ NiB $650 Ex $583 Gd $479
Trophy (w/rifled bbl. & cantilever
   scope mount) . ...NiB $675 Ex $609 Gd $495
Trophy (w/rifled bbl.
   & rifle sights) ....NiB $635 Ex $570 Gd $460

MODEL 9200 USST AUTOLOADER ....NiB $525 Ex $390 Gd $295
Similar to the Model 9200 Regal except has 26-inch vent. rib bbl. w/Accu-Choke tubes. "United States Shooting Team" engraved on receiver. Made from 1993 to date.

MODEL 9200 VIKING AUTOLOADER .... NiB $425 Ex $330 Gd $290
Gauge: 12. 3-inch chamber. 28-inch smoothbore bbl. w/Accu-Choke and vent. rib. Weight: 7.7 lbs. Green synthetic stock. Matte black metal finish. Made from 1996 to 1998.

MODEL HS410 HOME SECURITY PUMP SHOTGUN
Gauge: .410. 3-inch chamber. Bbl.: 18.5-inch w/muzzle brake; blued. Weight: 6.25 lbs. Synthetic stock and pistol-grip slide. Optional laser

sight. Made from 1990 to date. A similar version of this gun is marketed by Maverick Arms under the same model designation.
Standard model .... NiB $345 Ex $270 Gd $195
Laser model .... NiB $544 Ex $396 Gd $277

LINE LAUNCHER .... NiB $1066 Ex $833 Gd $545
Gauge: 12 w/blank cartridge. Projectile travels from 250 to 275 feet.

NEW HAVEN BRAND SHOTGUNS
Promotional models, similar to their standard guns but plainer in finish, are marketed by Mossberg under the New Haven brand name. Values generally are about 20 percent lower than for corresponding standard models.

ONYX RESERVE SPORTING ..... NiB $760 Ex $580 Gd $370
O/U boxlock, blued engraved receiver. Gauges: 12 only. 3-inch chambers. Bbls.: 28-inch ported vent. rib. Checkered walnut stock and forearm. Made 2010 to 2012.

SILVER RESERVE FIELD .... NiB $600 Ex $460 Gd $340
O/U boxlock, gold inlay, silver receiver. Gauges: 12, 20, 28, or .410. Bbls.: 26- or 28-inch. vent. rib Checkered walnut stock and forearm. Extractors. Manufactured in Turkey. Imported from 2005 to 2012.
Sporting .... NiB $755 Ex $585 Gd $400

SILVER RESERVE II FIELD ...... NiB $736 Ex $470 Gd $300
O/U boxlock, silver receiver w/engraving. Gauges: 12, 20, 28, or .410. Bbls.: 26- or 28-inch vent. rib. Checkered black walnut stock and forearm. Extractors or ejectors. Imported from 2012 to date.
Sporting (ported 28-inch bbl.) .. NiB $1253 Ex $580 Gd $350
Super Sport (ported 30- or
   32-inch bbl.) .... NiB $1253 Ex $580 Gd $350

SILVER RESERVE FIELD .... NiB $860 Ex $640 Gd $370
S/S boxlock, blued or silver w/scroll-engraved receiver, extractors. Gauges: 12, 20, 28, or .410. Bbls.: 26 or 28 inch. Checkered black walnut stock and forearm. Extractors. Made from 2008 to 2012.
Onyx (12 ga., onyx finish) ...... NiB $860 Ex $640 Gd $380

SILVER RESERVE II FIELD ...... NiB $1100 Ex $690 Gd $420
S/S boxlock, blued or silver w/scroll-engraved receiver. Gauges: 12, 20, or 28. Bbls.: 26 or 28 inch. Checkered black walnut stock and forearm. Weight: 6.5 to 7.5 lbs. Made from 2012 to date.

NAVY ARMS — Ridgefield, NJ

MODEL 83/93 BIRD HUNTER O/U
Hammerless. Boxlock, engraved receiver. Gauges: 12 and 20. 3-inch chambers. Bbls.: 28-inch chrome lined w/double vent. rib

construction. Checkered European walnut stock and forearm. Gold plated triggers. Imported 1984 to 1990.
Model 83 w/extractors .... NiB $355 Ex $285 Gd $200
Model 93 w/ejectors .... NiB $379 Ex $339 Gd $255

MODEL 95/96 O/U SHOTGUN
Same as the Model 83/93 except w/five interchangeable choke tubes. Imported 1984 to 1990.
Model 95 w/extractors .... NiB $448 Ex $355 Gd $210
Model 96 w/ejectors .... NiB $555 Ex $376 Gd $280

MODEL 100/150 FIELD HUNTER DOUBLE-BARREL SHOTGUN
Boxlock. Gauges: 12 and 20. Bbls.: 28-inch chrome lined. Checkered European walnut stock and forearm. Imported 1984 to 1990.
Model 100 .... NiB $460 Ex $390 Gd $288
Model 150 (auto ejectors) ..... NiB $510 Ex $355 Gd $290

MODEL 100 O/U SHOTGUN.... NiB $277 Ex $169 Gd $109
Hammerless, takedown shotgun w/engraved chrome receiver. Single trigger. 12, 20, 28, or .410 ga. 3-inch chambers. Bbls.: 26 inch (F/F or SK/SK); vent. rib. Weight: 6.25 lbs. Checkered European walnut buttstock and forend. Imported 1986 to 1990.

NEW ENGLAND FIREARMS —
Gardner, MA

In 1987, New England Firearms was established as an independent company producing selected H&R models under the NEF logo after Harrington & Richardson suspended operations on January 24, 1986. In 1991, H&R 1871, Inc. was formed from the residual of the parent H&R company and then took over the New England Firearms facility. H&R 1871 produced firearms under both their logo and the NEF brand name until 1999, when the Marlin Firearms Company acquired the assets of H&R 1871.

NEW ENGLAND FIREARMS NWTF TURKEY SPECIAL
Similar to Turkey and Goose models except 10 or 20 gauge w/22- or 24-inch plain bbl. w/screw-in F choke tube. Mossy Oak camo finish on entire gun. Made from 1992 to 1996.
Turkey Special 10 ga. .... NiB $265 Ex $177 Gd $98
Turkey Special 20 ga. .... NiB $335 Ex $219 Gd $189

NRA FOUNDATION YOUTH .... NiB $190 Ex $155 Gd $100
Smaller scale version of Pardner Model chambered for 20, 28, or .410. 22-inch plain bbl. High luster blue finish. NRA Foundation logo laser etched on stock. Made from 1999 to 2002.

PARDNER SHOTGUN
Takedown. Side lever. Single bbl. Gauges: 12, 20, and .410 w/3-inch chamber; 16 and 28 w/2.75-inch chamber. 26-, 28-, or 32-inch plain bbl. fixed choke. Weight: 5 to 6 lbs. Bead front sight. Pistol grip-style hardwood stock w/walnut finish. Made from 1988 to date.
Standard model .... NiB $255 Ex $185 Gd $99
Youth model .... NiB $255 Ex $185 Gd $99
Turkey model .... NiB $323 Ex $217 Gd $110
32-inch bbl., add. $40

PARDNER SPECIAL PURPOSE 10-GA. SHOTGUN
Similar to the standard Pardner model except chambered 10 ga. only. 3.5-inch chamber. 24- or 28-inch plain bbl. w/F choke tube or fixed choke. Weight: 9.5 lbs. Bead front sight. Pistol-grip-style hardwood stock w/camo or matte black finish. Made from 1989 to date.
Special Purpose model w/fixed choke .... NiB $315 Ex $220 Gd $125
Camo finish, add $40

Choke tube, add $25
24-inch bbl. turkey option, add $50

PARDNER SPECIAL PURPOSE
WATERFOWL SINGLE-SHOT .... NiB $255 Ex $190 Gd $129
Similar to Special Purpose 10 ga. model except w/32-inch bbl. Mossy Oak camo stock w/swivel and sling. Made from 1988 to date.

PARDNER TURKEY GUN
Similar to Pardner model except chambered in 12 ga. w/3- or 3.5-inch chamber. 24-inch plain bbl. w/turkey F choke tube or fixed choke. Weight: 9.5 lbs. American hardwood stock w/camo or matte black finish. Made from 1999 to date.
Standard Turkey model .... NiB $200 Ex $110 Gd $85
Camo Turkey model .... NiB $200 Ex $110 Gd $85

SURVIVOR SERIES
Takedown single bbl. shotgun w/side lever release, automatic ejector, and patented transfer-bar safety. Gauges: 12, 20, and .410/.45 ACP. 3-inch chamber. 22-inch bbl. w/M choke and bead sight. Weight: 6 lbs. Polymer stock and forend w/hollow cavity for storage. Made 1992 to 1993 and 1995 to date.
12 or 20 ga. w/blued finish. ...... NiB $220 Ex $144 Gd $98
12 or 20 ga. w/nickel finish ..... NiB $260 Ex $177 Gd $120
.410/.45 LC add $75

TRACKER SLUG GUN
Similar to Pardner model except in 10, 12, or 20 ga. 24-inch w/Cyl. choke or rifled slug bbl. (Tracker II). Weight: 6 lbs. American hardwood stock w/walnut or camo finish, Schnabel forend, sling swivel studs. Made from 1992 to 2001.
Tracker Slug (10 ga.) .... NiB $180 Ex $110 Gd $79
Tracker Slug (12 or 20 ga.) ...... NiB $219 Ex $120 Gd $85
Tracker II (rifled bore) .... NiB $219 Ex $120 Gd $85

NIKKO FIREARMS LTD. — Tochigi, Japan

See listings under Golden Eagle Firearms, Inc.

NOBLE MANUFACTURING COMPANY —
Haydenville, MA

Series 602 and 70 are similar in appearance to the corresponding Model 66 guns.

MODEL 40 HAMMERLESS SLIDE-ACTION
REPEATING SHOTGUN .... NiB $255 Ex $190 Gd $130
Solid frame. 12 ga. only. 5-round tubular magazine. 28-inch bbl. w/ventilated multi-choke. Weight: About 7.5 lbs. Plain pistol-grip stock, grooved slide handle. Made from 1950 to 1955.

MODEL 50 SLIDE-ACTION ..... NiB $266 Ex $190 Gd $125
Same as Model 40 except w/o multi-choke. M/F choke bbl. Made from 1953 to 1955.

MODEL 60 HAMMERLESS SLIDE-ACTION
REPEATING SHOTGUN .... NiB $325 Ex $255 Gd $159
Solid frame. 12 and 16 ga. 5-round tubular magazine. 28-inch bbl. w/adj. choke. Plain pistol-grip stock w/recoil pad, grooved slide handle. Weight: About 7.5 lbs. Made from 1955 to 1966.

MODEL 65 .... NiB $300 Ex $225 Gd $165
Same as Model 60 except without adj. choke and recoil pad. M/F choke bbl. Made from 1955 to 1966.

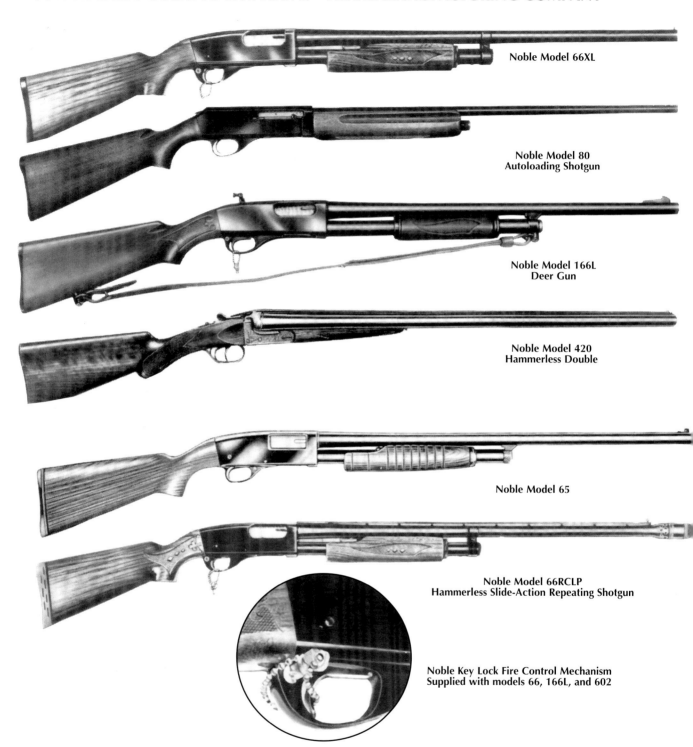

Noble Model 66XL

Noble Model 80
Autoloading Shotgun

Noble Model 166L
Deer Gun

Noble Model 420
Hammerless Double

Noble Model 65

Noble Model 66RCLP
Hammerless Slide-Action Repeating Shotgun

Noble Key Lock Fire Control Mechanism
Supplied with models 66, 166L, and 602

MODEL 66CLP . . . . **NiB $235 Ex $185 Gd $135**
Same as Model 66RCLP except has plain bbl. Introduced in 1967. Disc.

**MODEL 66RCLP HAMMERLESS SLIDE-ACTION
REPEATING SHOTGUN** . . . . **NiB $339 Ex $235 Gd $176**
Solid frame. Key lock fire control mechanism. Gauges: 12, 16.
3-inch chamber in 12 ga. 5-round tubular magazine. 28-inch bbl.,
vent. rib, adj. choke. Weight: About 7.5 lbs. Checkered pistol-grip
stock and slide handle, recoil pad. Made from 1967 to 1970.

MODEL 66RLP . . . . **NiB $329 Ex $225 Gd $165**

Same as Model 66RCLP except w/F/M choke. Made 1967 to 1970.

MODEL 66XL . . . . **NiB $245 Ex $185 Gd $129**
Same as Model 66RCL except has plain bbl., F/M choke, slide
handle only checkered, no recoil pad. Made from 1967 to 1970.

**MODEL 70CLP HAMMERLESS SLIDE-ACTION
REPEATING SHOTGUN** . . . . **NiB $277 Ex $198 Gd $145**
Solid frame. .410 gauge. Magazine holds 5 rounds. 26-inch bbl. w/
adj. choke. Weight: About 6 lbs. Checkered buttstock and forearm,
recoil pad. Made from 1958 to 1970.

178

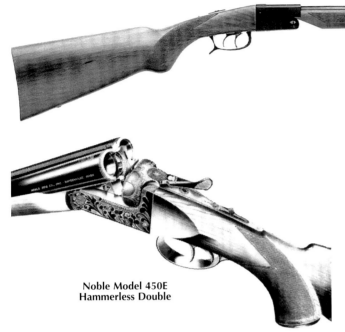

Omega Deluxe Side-by-Side Shotgun

MODEL 602CLP . . . . **NiB $366 Ex $255 Gd $235**
Same as Model 602RCLP except has plain barrel. Made from 1958 to 1970.

MODEL 602RCLP HAMMERLESS SLIDE-ACTION
REPEATING SHOTGUN . . . . **NiB $355 Ex $255 Gd $190**
Solid frame. Key lock fire control mechanism. 20 ga. 3-inch chamber. 5-round tubular magazine. 28-inch bbl., vent. rib, adj. choke. Weight: About 6.5 lbs. Checkered pistol-grip stock and slide handle, recoil pad. Made from 1967 to 1970.

MODEL 602RLP . . . . **NiB $315 Ex $233 Gd $157**
Same as Model 602RCLP except without adj. choke, bored F/M choke. Made from 1967 to 1970.

MODEL 602XL . . . . **NiB $285 Ex $177 Gd $145**
Same as Model 602RCL except has plain bbl., F/M choke, slide handle only checkered, no recoil pad. Made from 1958 to 1970.

MODEL 662 . . . . **NiB $308 Ex $244 Gd $165**
Same as Model 602CLP except has aluminum receiver and bbl. Weight: About 4.5 lbs. Made from 1966 to 1970.

Noble Model 450E
Hammerless Double

MODEL 70RCLP . . . . **NiB $280 Ex $199 Gd $149**
Same as Model 70CLP except has vent. rib. Made 1967 to 1970.

MODEL 70RLP . . . . **NiB $278 Ex $199 Gd $145**
Same as Model 70CLP except has vent. rib and no adj. choke. Made from 1967 to 1970.

MODEL 70XL . . . . **NiB $255 Ex $160 Gd $110**
Same as Model 70CLP except without adj. choke and checkering on buttstock. Made from 1958 to 1970.

MODEL 80
AUTOLOADING SHOTGUN . . . . **NiB $344 Ex $265 Gd $196**
Recoil operated. .410 ga. Magazine holds three 3-inch shells, four 2.5-inch shells. 26-inch bbl., full choke. Weight: About 6 lbs. Plain pistol-grip stock and fluted forearm. Made from 1964 to 1966.

MODEL 166L DEER GUN . . . . . . **NiB $355 Ex $270 Gd $199**
Solid frame. Key lock fire control mechanism. 12 ga. 2.75-inch chamber. 5-round tubular magazine. 24-inch plain bbl., specially bored for rifled slug. Lyman peep rear sight, post ramp front sight.
Receiver dovetailed for scope mounting. Weight: About 7.25 lbs. Checkered pistol-grip stock and slide handle, swivels, and carrying strap. Made from 1967 to 1970.

MODEL 420
HAMMERLESS DOUBLE . . . . **NiB $466 Ex $361 Gd $255**
Boxlock. Plain extractors. Double triggers. Gauges: 12 ga. 3-inch Mag.; 16 ga.; 20 ga. 3-inch Mag.; .410 ga. Bbls.: 28-inch, except .410 in 26-inch, M/F choke. Weight: About 6.75 lbs. Engraved frame. Checkered walnut stock and forearm. Made from 1958 to 1970.

MODEL 450E
HAMMERLESS DOUBLE . . . . **NiB $490 Ex $376 Gd $290**
Boxlock. Engraved frame. Selective auto ejectors. Double triggers. Gauges: 12, 16, 20. 3-inch chambers in 12 and 20 ga. 28-inch bbls., M/F choke. Weight: About 6 lbs., 14 oz. in 12 ga. Checkered pistol-grip stock and beavertail forearm, recoil pad. Made from 1967 to 1970.

OMEGA SHOTGUNS — Brescia, Italy, and Korea

FOLDING OVER/UNDER STANDARD SHOTGUN
Hammerless Boxlock. Gauges: 12, 20, 28. 2.75-inch chambers or .410 w/3-inch chambers. Bbls.: 26- or 28-inch vent. rib w/fixed chokes (IC/M, M/F, or F/F .410). Automatic safety. Single trigger. 40.5 inches overall (42.5 inches, 20 ga., 28-inch bbl.). Weight: 6 to 7.5 lbs. Checkered European walnut stock and forearm. Imported from 1984 to 1994.
Standard model (12 ga.) . . . . **NiB $475 Ex $355 Gd $298**
Standard model (20 ga.) . . . . **NiB $475 Ex $355 Gd $298**
Standard model (28 ga. and .410) . . . . . . **NiB $475 Ex $355 Gd $298**

O/U DELUXE SHOTGUN . . . . **NiB $390 Ex $287 Gd $200**
Gauges: 20, 28, and .410. 26- or 28-inch vent. rib bbls. 40.5 inches overall (42.5 inches, 20 ga., 28-inch bbl.). Chokes: IC/M, M/F, or F/F (.410). Weight: About 5.5 to 6 lbs. Single trigger. Automatic safety. European walnut stock w/checkered pistol grip and tulip forend. Imported from Italy 1984 to 1990.

DELUXE SIDE-BY-SIDE SHOTGUN . . . . . **NiB $290 Ex $225 Gd $165**
Same general specifications as the Standard Side-by-Side except has checkered European walnut stock and low bbl. rib. Made in Italy from 1984 to 1989.

STANDARD SIDE-BY-SIDE SHOTGUN . . . . . . **NiB $245 Ex $135 Gd $90**
Gauge: .410. 26-inch bbl. 40.5 inches overall. Choked F/F. Weight: 5.5 lbs. Double trigger. Manual safety. Checkered beechwood stock and semi-pistol grip. Imported from Italy 1984 to 1989.

STANDARD SINGLE-SHOT SHOTGUN
Gauges: 12, 16, 20, 28, and .410. Bbls.: 26, 28, or 30 inch. Weight: 5 lbs., 4 oz. to 5 lbs., 11 oz. Indonesian walnut stock. Matte-chromed receiver and top lever break. Imported from 1984 to 1987.
Standard fixed . . . . **NiB $155 Ex $90 Gd $65**
Standard folding . . . . **NiB $175 Ex $110 Gd $75**
Deluxe folding . . . . **NiB $255 Ex $185 Gd $95**

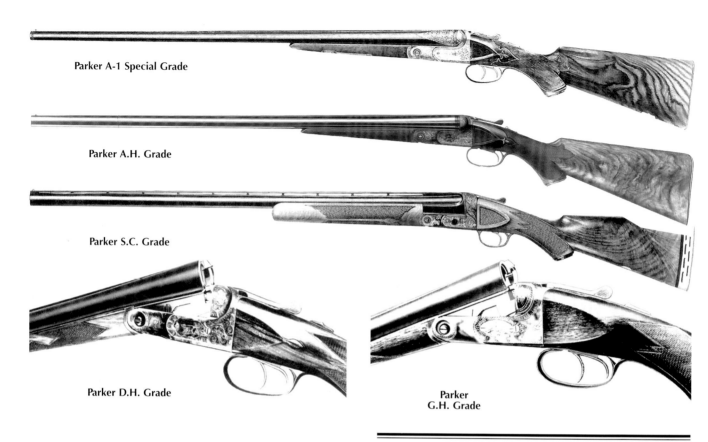

Parker A-1 Special Grade

Parker A.H. Grade

Parker S.C. Grade

Parker D.H. Grade

Parker
G.H. Grade

Parker B.H.
Grade

Parker C.H.
Grade

DELUXE SINGLE-SHOT SHOTGUN ..... NiB $229 Ex $145 Gd $99
Same general specifications as the Standard Single bbl. except has
checkered walnut stock, top lever break, fully-blued receiver, vent.
rib. Imported from Korea 1984 to 1987.

PARKER BROTHERS — Meriden, CT

*This firm was taken over by Remington Arms Company in 1934
and its production facilities moved to Remington's Ilion, New
York, plant. In 1984, Winchester took over production until
1999.*

HAMMERLESS DOUBLE-BARREL SHOTGUNS
Grades V.H. through A-1 Special. Boxlock. Auto ejectors. Double
triggers or selective single trigger. Gauges: 10, 12, 16, 20, 28,
.410. Bbls.: 26 to 32 inch, any standard boring. Weight: 6.88 to
8.5 lbs.,12 ga. Stock and forearm of select walnut, checkered;
straight, half or full-pistol grip. Grades differ only in quality of
workmanship, grade of wood, engraving, checkering, etc. General
specifications are the same for all. Disc. about 1940.

V.H. grade, 12 or 16 ga. . . . . NiB $5733 Ex $4187 Gd $2266
V.H. grade, 20 ga. . . . . NiB $9455 Ex $6077 Gd $3145
V.H. grade, 28 ga. . . . . NiB $28,998 Ex $27,966 Gd $26,778
V.H. grade, .410 . . . . NiB $34,669 Ex $25,766 Gd $21,560
G.H. grade, 12 ga. . . . . NiB $7566 Ex $3998 Gd $2779
G.H. grade, 16 ga. . . . . NiB $8120 Ex $4233 Gd $2988
G.H. grade, 20 ga. . . . . NiB $12,960 Ex $10,679 Gd $7789
G.H. grade, 28 ga. . . . . NiB $33,790 Ex $29,645 Gd $27,889
G.H. grade, .410. . . . . NiB $45,890 Ex $39,955 Gd $27,987
D.H. grade, 12 or 16 ga. . . . . NiB $10,440 Ex $7866 Gd $4350
D.H. grade, 20 ga. . . . . NiB $16,777 Ex $13,790 Gd $11,556
D.H. grade, 28 ga. . . . . NiB $43,088 Ex $39,655 Gd $32,200
D.H. grade, .410. . . . . NiB $72,799 Ex $48,950 Gd $37,788
C.H. grade, 12 or 16 ga. . . . . NiB $17,300 Ex $13,988 Gd $10,996
C.H. grade, 20 ga. . . . . NiB $25,779 Ex $20,099 Gd $17,376
C.H. grade, 28 ga. . . . . NiB $73,588 Ex $60,977 Gd $52,411
B.H. grade, 12 or 16 ga. . . . . NiB $21,689 Ex $18,933 Gd $16,900

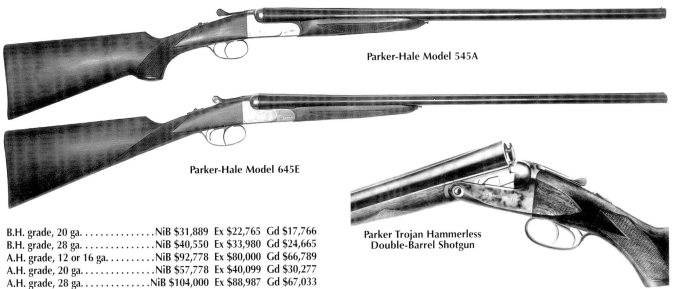

Parker-Hale Model 545A

Parker-Hale Model 645E

Parker Trojan Hammerless
Double-Barrel Shotgun

B.H. grade, 20 ga. . . . . .NiB $31,889 Ex $22,765 Gd $17,766
B.H. grade, 28 ga. . . . . .NiB $40,550 Ex $33,980 Gd $24,665
A.H. grade, 12 or 16 ga. . . . . .NiB $92,778 Ex $80,000 Gd $66,789
A.H. grade, 20 ga. . . . . .NiB $57,778 Ex $40,099 Gd $30,277
A.H. grade, 28 ga. . . . . .NiB $104,000 Ex $88,987 Gd $67,033
A.A.H. grade, 12 or 16 ga. . . . . . .NiB $57,980 Ex $52,077 Gd $37,773
A.A.H. grade, 20 ga. . . . . .NiB $83,672 Ex $62,955 Gd $43,900
A.A.H. grade, 28 ga. . . . . .NiB $200,000 Ex $175,000 Gd $155,000
A-1 Special grade,
    12 or 16 ga. . . . . .NiB $100,000 Ex $80,000 Gd $60,000
A-1 Special grade, 20 ga. . . . . . .NiB $82,000 Ex $65,000 Gd $45,000
A-1 Special grade, 28 ga. . . . .NiB $200,000 Ex $165,000 Gd $110,000
Selective single trigger, add 20%
Vent. rib, add 35%
Non-ejector models, deduct 30%

SINGLE-SHOT TRAP GUNS
Hammerless. Boxlock. Ejector. 12 ga. only. Bbl: 30, 32, 34 inch, any boring, vent. rib. Weight: 7.5 to 8.5 lbs. Stock and forearm of select walnut, checkered; straight, half or full-pistol grip. The five grades differ only in quality of workmanship, grade of wood, checkering, engraving, etc. General specifications same for all. Disc. about 1940.
S.C. grade . . . . NiB $9355   Ex $7088   Gd $5167
S.B. grade . . . . .NiB $11,870 Ex $7279   Gd $6344
S.A. grade . . . . .NiB $17,500 Ex $14,223 Gd $11,989
S.A.1 Special (rare) . . . . . NiB $42,000 Ex $31,000 Gd $27,000

SKEET GUN
Same as other Parker doubles from Grade V.H.E. up except selective single trigger and beavertail forearm are standard on this model, as are 26-inch bbls., SK choke. Disc. about 1940. Values are 35% higher.

TROJAN HAMMERLESS DOUBLE-BARREL SHOTGUN
Boxlock. Plain extractors. Double trigger or single trigger. Gauges: 12, 16, 20. Bbls.: 30-inch F/F choke (12 ga. only), 26- or 28-inch M/F choke. Weight: 6.25 to 7.75 lbs. Checkered pistol-grip stock and forearm. Disc. 1939.
12 ga. . . . . NiB $5444   Ex $4249   Gd $2677
16 ga. . . . . NiB $6077   Ex $4488   Gd $3210
20 ga. . . . . NiB $6898   Ex $4539   Gd $3556

PARKER REPRODUCTIONS — Middlesex, NJ

HAMMERLESS DOUBLE-BARREL SHOTGUNS
Reproduction of the original Parker boxlock. Single selective trigger or double triggers. Selective automatic ejectors. Automatic safety. Gauges: 12, 16, 20, 28, or .410. 2.75- or 3-inch chambers. Bbls.: 26- or 28-inch w/fixed or internal screw choke tubes SK/SK, IC/M, M/F. Weight: 5.5 to 7 lbs. Checkered English-style or pistol-grip

American walnut stock w/beavertail or splinter forend and checkered skeleton buttplate. Color casehardened receiver with game scenes and scroll engraving. Produced in Japan by Olin Kodensha from 1984 to 1988.
DHE grade, 12 ga. . . . . NiB $4250   Ex $3288   Gd $1366
DHE grade, 12 ga Sporting Clays. . . . . . NiB $4466   Ex $3890   Gd $2877
DHE grade, 20 ga. . . . . NiB $4866   Ex $3989   Gd $2977
DHE grade, 28 ga. . . . . NiB $5433   Ex $3200   Gd $2366
DHE grade 2-barrel set (16 & 20 ga.). . . . NiB $6590   Ex $4880   Gd $3588
DHE grade 2-barrel set (28 & .410) . . . . NiB $7377   Ex $5433   Gd $3980
DHE grade 3-barrel set . . . . .NiB $10,000 Ex $6566   Gd $5080
B grade Bank Note Lim. Ed., 12 ga. . . . NiB $5799   Ex $4765   Gd $3499
B grade Bank Note Lim. Ed., 20 ga. . . . NiB $7352   Ex $6088   Gd $4139
B grade Bank Note Lim. Ed., 28 ga. . . . . . .NiB $12,000 Ex $9898   Gd $7455
B grade Bank Note Lim. Ed., .410 ga. . . . . . .NiB $13,900 Ex $10,000 Gd $8894
A-1 Special grade, 12 ga. . . . . .NiB $10,877 Ex $8871   Gd $6000
A-1 Special grade, 16 ga. . . . . .NiB $12,433 Ex $10,770 Gd $7379
A-1 Special grade, 20 ga. . . . . .NiB $10,665 Ex $8932   Gd $6281
A-1 Special grade, 28 ga. . . . . NiB $14,933 Ex $12,966 Gd $9855
A-1 Special gr. 2-barrel set . . . . NiB $13,770 Ex $10,433 Gd $7791
A-1 Special gr. 3-barrel set . . . . . . .NiB $29,650 Ex $23,991 Gd $17,498
A-1 Special gr. custom engraved . . . . . NiB $17,888 Ex $14,699 Gd $10,000
A-1 Special gr. custom 2-barrel set . . . . .NiB $14,600 Ex $10,553 Gd $7699
Extra bbl. set, add $500

PARKER-HALE — Manufactured by Ignacio Ugartechea, Spain

MODEL 645A (AMERICAN)
SIDE-BY-SIDE SHOTGUN . . . . .NiB $1344 Ex $1116 Gd $844
Gauges: 12, 16, and 20. Boxlock action. 26- and 28-inch bbls. Chokes: IC/M, M/F. Weight: 6 lbs. average. Single nonselective trigger. Automatic safety. Hand-checkered pistol grip walnut stock w/beavertail forend. Raised matted rib. English scroll-engraved receiver. Disc. 1990.

MODEL 645E (ENGLISH) SIDE-BY-SIDE SHOTGUN
Same general specifications as the Model 645A except double triggers, straight grip, splinter forend, checkered butt, and concave rib. Disc. 1990.
12, 16, 20 ga. w/26- or 28-inch bbl. . . . . . NiB $1388 Ex $1166 Gd $898
28, .410 ga. w/27-inch bbl. . . . . NiB $1800 Ex $1490 Gd $1128

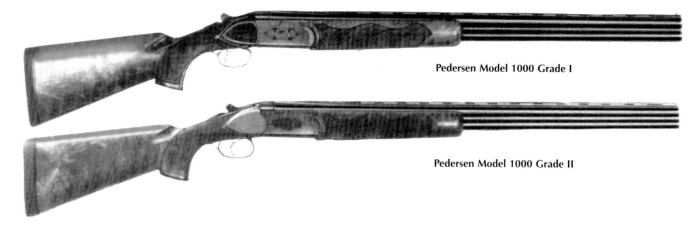

Pedersen Model 1000 Grade I

Pedersen Model 1000 Grade II

MODEL 645E-XXV
12, 16, 20 ga. w/25-inch bbl. . . . . NiB $1288 Ex $1189 Gd $900
28, .410 ga. w/25-inch bbl. . . . . NiB $1698 Ex $1377 Gd $1110

PEDERSEN CUSTOM GUNS — North Haven, CT; division of O.F. Mossberg & Sons, Inc.

MODEL 1000 O/U HUNTING SHOTGUN
Boxlock. Auto ejectors. Selective single trigger. Gauges: 12, 20. 2.75-inch chambers in 12 ga., 3-inch in 20 ga. Bbls.: Vent. rib; 30-inch M/F (12 ga. only); 28-inch IC/M (12 ga. only), M/F; 26-inch IC/M. Checkered pistol-grip stock and forearm. Grade I is the higher quality gun with custom stock dimensions, fancier wood, more elaborate engraving, silver inlays. Made from 1973 to 1975.
Grade I . . . . NiB $2366 Ex $1969 Gd $1449
Grade II . . . . NiB $2210 Ex $1781 Gd $1290

MODEL 1000 MAGNUM
Same as Model 1000 Hunting Gun except chambered for 12-ga. Mag. 3-inch shells, 30-inch bbls., IM/F choke. Made 1973 to 1975.
Grade I . . . . NiB $2809 Ex $2277 Gd $1677
Grade II . . . . NiB $2400 Ex $1900 Gd $1378

MODEL 1000 SKEET GUN
Same as Model 1000 Hunting Gun except has skeet-style stock; 26- and 28-inch bbls. (12 ga. only), SK choke. Made from 1973 to 1975.
Grade I . . . . NiB $2433 Ex $1977 Gd $1698
Grade II . . . . NiB $1998 Ex $1569 Gd $1062

MODEL 1000 TRAP GUN
Same as Model 1000 Hunting Gun except 12 ga. only, has Monte Carlo trap-style stock, 30- or 32-inch bbls., M/F or IM/F choke. Made from 1973 to 1975.
Grade I . . . . NiB $2287 Ex $1862 Gd $1300
Grade II . . . . NiB $1844 Ex $1477 Gd $1106

MODEL 1500 O/U
HUNTING SHOTGUN . . . . NiB $790 Ex $676 Gd $478
Boxlock. Auto ejectors. Selective single trigger. 12 ga. 2.75- or 3-inch chambers. Bbls.: Vent. rib; 26-inch IC/M; 28-inch M/F; Mag. has 30-inch IM/F choke. Weight: 7 to 7.5 lbs. depending on bbl. length. Checkered pistol-grip stock and forearm. Made from 1973 to 1975.

MODEL 1500 SKEET GUN . . . . . . NiB $833 Ex $690 Gd $569

Same as Model 1500 Hunting Gun except has skeet-style stock, 27-inch bbls., SK choke. Made from 1973 to 1975.

MODEL 1500 TRAP GUN . . . . . . NiB $788 Ex $648 Gd $520
Same as Model 1500 Hunting Gun except has Monte Carlo trap-style stock, 30- or 32-inch bbls., M/F or IM/F chokes. Made 1973 to 1975.

MODEL 2000 HAMMERLESS DOUBLE
Boxlock. Auto ejectors. Selective single trigger. Gauges: 12, 20. 2.75-inch chambers in 12 ga., 3-inch in 20 ga. Bbls.: Vent. rib; 30-inch M/F; (12 ga. only); 28-inch M/F; 26-inch IC/M choke. Checkered pistol-grip stock and forearm. Grade I is the higher quality gun w/custom dimensions, fancier wood, more elaborate engraving, silver inlays. Made from 1973 to 1974.
Grade I . . . . NiB $2887 Ex $2260 Gd $1740
Grade II . . . . NiB $2389 Ex $2276 Gd $1578

MODEL 2500
HAMMERLESS DOUBLE . . . . NiB $780 Ex $655 Gd $356
Boxlock. Auto ejectors. Selective single trigger. Gauges: 12, 20. 2.75-inch chambers in 12 ga., 3-inch in 20 ga. Bbls.: Vent. rib; 28-inch M/F; 26-inch IC/M choke. Checkered pistol-grip stock and forearm. Made 1973 to 1974.

MODEL 4000 HAMMERLESS SLIDE-ACTION
REPEATING SHOTGUN . . . . NiB $597 Ex $440 Gd $375
Custom version of Mossberg Model 500. Full-coverage floral engraving on receiver. Gauges: 12, 20, .410. 3-inch chamber. Bbls.: Vent. rib; 26-inch IC/SK choke; 28-inch F/M; 30-inch F. Weight: 6 to 8 lbs. depending on ga. and bbl. Checkered stock and slide handle of select wood. Made in 1975.

MODEL 4000 TRAP GUN . . . . . . NiB $590 Ex $466 Gd $265
Same as standard Model 4000 except 12 ga. only, has 30-inch F choke bbl., Monte Carlo trap-style stock w/recoil pad. Made in 1975.

MODEL 4500 . . . . NiB $500 Ex $390 Gd $335
Same as Model 4000 except has simpler scroll engraving. Made in 1975.

MODEL 4500 TRAP GUN . . . . . . NiB $525 Ex $420 Gd $366
Same as Model 4000 Trap Gun except has simpler scroll engraving. Made in 1975.

J. C. PENNEY CO., INC. — Dallas, TX

MODEL 4011
AUTOLOADING SHOTGUN . . . . NiB $377 Ex $290 Gd $197
Hammerless. 5-round magazine. Bbls.: 26-inch IC; 28-inch M/F; 30-inch

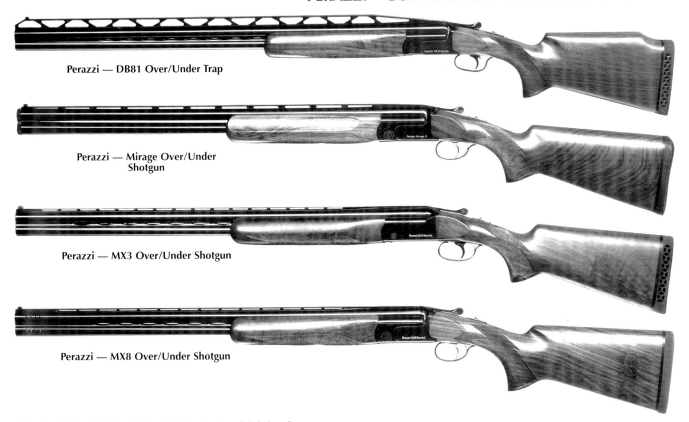

Perazzi — DB81 Over/Under Trap

Perazzi — Mirage Over/Under Shotgun

Perazzi — MX3 Over/Under Shotgun

Perazzi — MX8 Over/Under Shotgun

F choke. Weight: 7.25 lbs. Plain pistol-grip stock and slide handle.
MODEL 6610
SINGLE-SHOT SHOTGUN . . . . . . NiB $205 Ex $100 Gd $75
Hammerless. Takedown. Auto ejector. Gauges: 12, 16, 20, and
.410. Bbl.: 28 to 36 inches. Weight: About 6 lbs. Plain pistol-grip
stock and forearm.

MODEL 6630
BOLT-ACTION SHOTGUN . . . . . NiB $254 Ex $179 Gd $115
Takedown. Gauges: 12, 16, 20. 2-round clip magazine. 26- and
28-inch bbl.; w/ or w/o adj. choke. Plain pistol-grip stock. Weight:
About 7.25 lbs.

MODEL 6670
SLIDE-ACTION SHOTGUN . . . . . NiB $260 Ex $188 Gd $140
Hammerless. Gauges: 12, 16, 20, and .410. 3-round tubular magazine. Bbls.: 26 to 30-inch; various chokes. Weight: 6.25 to 7.25
lbs. Walnut finished hardwood stock.

MODEL 6870 SLIDE-ACTION
SHOTGUN . . . . NiB $315 Ex $225 Gd $178
Hammerless. Gauges: 12, 16, 20, .410. 4-round magazine. Bbls.:
Vent. rib; 26 to 30 inch, various chokes. Weight: Average 6.5 lbs.
Plain pistol-grip stock.

PERAZZI — Manufactured by Manifattura Armi Perazzi, Brescia, Italy
See also listings under Ithaca-Perazzi.

DB81 O/U TRAP. . . . . NiB $5266 Ex $4300 Gd $3450
Gauge: 12. 2.75-inch chambers. 29.5- or 31.5-inch bbls. w/
wide vent. rib; M/F chokes. Weight: 8 lbs., 6 oz. Detachable
and interchangeable trigger with flat V-springs. Bead front sight.
Interchangeable and custom-made checkered stock; beavertail
forend. Imported 1988 to 1994.

DB81 SINGLE-SHOT TRAP . . . . NiB $5300 Ex $4277 Gd $3389
Same general specifications as the DB81 over/under except in
single bbl. version w/32- or 34-inch wide vent. rib bbl., F choke.
Imported 1988 to 1994.

GRAND AMERICAN 88 SPECIAL SINGLE TRAP
Same general specifications as MX-8 Special Single Trap except w/
high ramped rib. Fixed choke or screw-in choke tubes.
Model 88 standard . . . . NiB $4988 Ex $3988 Gd $2777
Model 88 w/interchangeable
  choke tubes . . . . NiB $4990 Ex $4100 Gd $3099

MIRAGE O/U SHOTGUN
Gauge: 12. 2.75-inch chambers. Bbls.: 27.63-, 29.5-, or 31.5-inch
vent. rib w/fixed chokes or screw-in choke tubes. Single selective
trigger. Weight: 7 to 7.75 lbs. Interchangeable and custom-made
checkered buttstock and forend.
Competition Trap,
Skeet, Pigeon, Sporting . . . . . NiB $6400 Ex $5440 Gd $3200
Skeet 4-bb. sets . . . . NiB $14,680 Ex $12,890 Gd $9800
Competition Special (w/adj. 4-position trigger), add $500

MX-1 O/U SHOTGUN
Similar to Model MX-8 except w/ramp-style, tapered rib, and
modified stock configuration.
Competition Trap, Skeet,
Pigeon, Sporting . . . . NiB $6799 Ex $5240 Gd $3390
MX-IC (w/choke tubes) . . . . . NiB $3698 Ex $3288 Gd $2298
MX-IB (w/flat low rib) . . . . . . NiB $3467 Ex $2980 Gd $2098

MX-2 O/U SHOTGUN
Similar to Model MX-8 except w/broad high-ramped competition rib.
Competition Trap, Skeet,
  Pigeon, Sporting . . . . NiB $6780 Ex $3544 Gd $3589
MX-2C (w/choke tubes) . . . . . NiB $4988 Ex $3998 Gd $2766
MX-3 O/U SHOTGUN

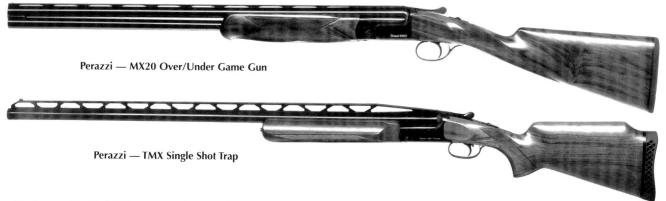

Perazzi — MX20 Over/Under Game Gun

Perazzi — TMX Single Shot Trap

Similar to Model MX-8 except w/ramp-style, tapered rib, and modified stock configuration.

Competition Trap, Skeet,
Pigeon, Sporting . . . . NiB $48,988 Ex $42,998 Gd $35,999
Competition Special (w/adj. 4-position trigger), add . . . $400
Game models . . . . NiB $4478 Ex $3659 Gd $2699
Combo O/U plus SB . . . . NiB $5563 Ex $4478 Gd $3380
SB Trap 32- or 34-inch . . . . . NiB $3987 Ex $3166 Gd $2267
Skeet 4-bbl. sets . . . . NiB $12,888 Ex $10,099 Gd $7789
Skeet Special 4-bbl. sets . . . . NiB $13,066 Ex $11,288 Gd $8,996

MX-3 SPECIAL PIGEON SHOTGUN . . . . NiB $5344 Ex $4276 Gd $3110
Gauge: 12. 2.75-inch chambers. 29.5- or 31.5-inch vent. rib bbl.; IC/M and extra full chokes. Weight: 8 lbs., 6 oz. Detachable and interchangeable trigger group w/flat V-springs. Bead front sight. Interchangeable and custom-made checkered stock for live pigeon shoots; splinter forend. Imported 1991 to 1992.

MX-4 O/U SHOTGUN
Similar to Model MX-3 in appearance and shares the MX-8 locking system. Detachable, adj. 4-position trigger standard. Interchangeable choke tubes optional.
Competition Trap, Skeet,
Pigeon, Sporting. . . . . NiB $4487 Ex $4089 Gd $3124
MX-4C (w/choke tubes) . . . . . NiB $5388 Ex $4500 Gd $3787

MX-5 O/U GAME GUN
Similar to Model MX-8 except in hunting configuration, chambered in 12 or 20 ga. Nondetachable single selective trigger.
MX-5 Standard . . . . NiB $3977 Ex $2886 Gd $2066
MX-5C (w/choke tubes) . . . . . NiB $4264 Ex $3188 Gd $2200

MX-6 AMERICAN
TRAP SINGLE-BARREL . . . . NiB $4302 Ex $2677 Gd $1988
Single shot. Removable trigger group. 12 ga. Barrels: 32- or 34-inch with fixed or choke tubes. Raised vent. rib. Checkered European walnut Monte Carlo stock, beavertail forend. Imported 1995 to 1998.

MX-6 SKEET O/U . . . . NiB $4277 Ex $3100 Gd $2250
Same general specs as MX-6 American Trap single barrel except over/under; boxlock. Barrels: 26.75 or 27.5 inch. Imported 1995 to 1998.

MX-6 SPORTING O/U . . . . . . NiB $4277 Ex $3100 Gd $2250
Same specs as MX-6 American Trap single barrel except over/under; boxlock. Single selective trigger; external selector. Barrels: 28.38, 29.5, or 31.5 inch. Imported 1995 to 1998.

MX-6 TRAP O/U . . . . NiB $4350 Ex $2929 Gd $1877
Same general specs as MX-6 American Trap single barrel except over/under; boxlock. Barrels: 29.5, 30.75, or 31.5 inch. Imported 1995 to 1998.
MX-7 O/U SHOTGUN . . . . . . NiB $4188 Ex $3755 Gd $2690

Similar to Model MX-12 except w/MX-3-style receiver and top-mounted trigger selector. Bbls.: 28.73-, 31.5-inch w/vent. rib; screw-in choke tubes. Imported 1992 to 1998.

MX-8 O/U SHOTGUN
Gauge: 12. 2.75-inch chambers. Bbls.: 27.63-, 29.5-, or 31.5-inch vent. rib w/fixed chokes or screw-in choke tubes. Weight: 7 to 8.5 lbs. Interchangeable and custom-made checkered stock; beavertail forend. Special models have detachable and interchangeable 4-position trigger group w/flat V-springs. Imported 1968 to date.
MX-8 Standard . . . . NiB $8099 Ex $4133 Gd $2377
MX-8 Special
(adj. 4-position trigger) . . . . NiB $4229 Ex $3378 Gd $2490
MX-8 Special single
(32- or 34-inch bbl.) . . . . . . NiB $8380 Ex $7121 Gd $4365
MX-8 Special combo . . . . . . NiB $8009 Ex $6355 Gd $4682

MX-8/20 O/U SHOTGUN . . . NiB $4155 Ex $3370 Gd $2499
Similar to the Model MX-8 except w/smaller frame and custom stock. Available in sporting or game configurations w/fixed chokes or screw-in tubes. Imported 1993 to date.

MX-9 O/U SHOTGUN . . . . . . NiB $6880 Ex $5672 Gd $4200
Gauge: 12. 2.75-inch chambers. Bbls.: 29.5- or 30.5-inch w/ choke tubes and vent. side rib. Selective trigger. Checkered walnut stock w/adj. cheekpiece. Available in single bbl., combo, O/U trap, skeet, pigeon, and sporting models. Imported 1993 to 1994.

MX-10 O/U SHOTGUN . . . . NiB $8293 Ex $5760 Gd $34,105
Similar to the Model MX-9 except w/fixed chokes and different rib configuration. Imported 1993.

MX-10 PIGEON-ELECTROCIBLES . . . . NiB $8996 Ex $6133 Gd $4400
Over/Under; boxlock. Removable trigger group; external selector. 12 ga. Bbls. 27.50 or 29.50 inch. Checkered European walnut adjustable stock, beavertail forend. Imported 1995 to date.

MX-11 AMERICAN TRAP COMBO . . . . NiB $5440 Ex $4688 Gd $3277
Over/Under; boxlock. External selector. Removable trigger group; single selective trigger. 12 ga. Bbls.: 29.5- to 34-inch w/fixed choke tubes; vent. rib. European walnut Monte Carlo adj. stock, beavertail forend. Imported 1995 to date.

MX-11 AMERICAN TRAP
SINGLE BARREL . . . . NiB $5155 Ex $4309 Gd $2879
Same general specs as MX-11 American Trap combo except 32- or 34-inch single bbl. Imported 1995 to 1996.

MX-11 PIGEON-ELECTROCIBLES O/U . . . . NiB $5331 Ex $4277 Gd $3100
Same specs as MX-11 American Trap combo except 27.5-inch O/U bbls. Checkered European walnut pistol-grip adj. stock, beavertail

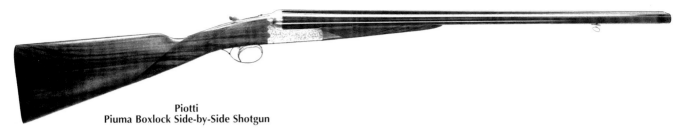

**Piotti
Piuma Boxlock Side-by-Side Shotgun**

forend. Imported 1995 to 1996.

MX-11 SKEET O/U . . . . **NiB $5390 Ex $4369 Gd $3122**
Same general specs as MX-11 American Trap combo except 26.75-
or 27.5-inch O/U bbls. Checkered European walnut pistol-grip adj.
stock, beavertail forend. Imported 1995 to 1996.

MX-11 SPORTING O/U . . . . . **NiB $5344 Ex $4766 Gd $3409**
Same general specs as MX-11 American Trap combo except 28.38,
29.5-, or 31.5-inch O/U bbls. Checkered European walnut pistol-
grip adj. stock, beavertail forend. Imported 1995 to 1996.

MX-11 TRAP O/U . . . . **NiB $5293 Ex $4266 Gd $3109**
Same general specs as MX-11 American Trap combo except 29.5-,
30.75, or 31.5-inch O/U bbls. Checkered European walnut pistol-
grip adj. stock, beavertail forend. Imported 1995 to 1996.

MX-12 O/U GAME GUN
Gauge: 12. 2.75-inch chambers. Bbls.: 26, 27.63, 28.38, or 29.5
inch, vent. rib, fixed chokes or screw-in choke tubes. Nondetachable
single selective trigger group w/coil springs. Weight: 7.25 lbs.
Interchangeable and custom-made checkered stock; Schnabel forend.
MX-12 Standard . . . . **NiB $7966 Ex $4312 Gd $3100**
MX-12C (w/choke tubes) . . . . **NiB $7994 Ex $4366 Gd $3180**

**MX-14 AMERICAN TRAP
SINGLE-BARREL** . . . . **NiB $6892 Ex $3677 Gd $2573**
Single shot. Removable trigger group; unsingle configuration. 12
ga. Bbl: 34-inch w/fixed or choke tubes; vent. rib. Checkered
European walnut Monte Carlo adj. stock, beavertail forend.
Imported 1995 to 1996.

**MX-15 AMERICAN TRAP
SINGLE-BARREL** . . . . **NiB $6654 Ex $4138 Gd $2998**
Full choke. Detachable trigger group. Gauge: 12 only. 2.75-inch
chamber. Bbls.: 32 and 34 inch. Weight: 8 lbs., 6 oz.

MX-20 O/U GAME GUN
Gauges: 20, 28, and .410; 2.75- or 3-inch chambers. 26-inch vent.
rib bbls., M/F chokes or screw-in chokes. Auto selective ejectors.
Selective single trigger. Weight: 6 lbs., 6 oz. Nondetachable coil-
spring trigger. Bead front sight. Interchangeable and custom-made
checkered stock w/Schnabel forend. Imported from 1988 to date.
Standard grade . . . . **NiB $5311 Ex $4255 Gd $2987**
**Standard grade
  w/gold outline** . . . . **NiB $8991 Ex $7200 Gd $5102**
MX-20C w/choke tubes . . . . . **NiB $5886 Ex $4480 Gd $3171**
SC3 grade . . . . **NiB $9766 Ex $7764 Gd $5433**
SCO grade . . . . **NiB $13,978 Ex $11,888 Gd $9166**

MX-28 O/U GAME GUN. . .**NiB $15,660 Ex $12,987 Gd $9821**
Similar to the Model MX-12 except chambered in 28 ga. 26-inch
bbls. fitted to smaller frame. Imported from 1993 to date.

MX-410 O/U GAME GUN . . .**NiB $15,890 Ex $13,298 Gd $10,350**
Similar to the Model MX-12 except in .410 bore. 3-inch chambers,
26-inch bbls. fitted to smaller frame. Imported from 1993 to date.

**TM1 SPECIAL
SINGLE-SHOT TRAP** . . . . **NiB $3150 Ex $2770 Gd $2000**
Gauge: 12. 2.75-inch chambers. 32- or 34-inch bbl. w/wide vent.
rib; F choke. Weight: 8 lbs., 6 oz. Detachable and interchangeable
trigger group with coil springs. Bead front sight. Interchangeable
and custom-made stock w/checkered pistol grip and beavertail
forend. Imported from 1988 to 1995.

**TMX SPECIAL
SINGLE-SHOT TRAP** . . . . **NiB $3890 Ex $2553 Gd $1966**
Same general specifications as Model TM1 Special except w/ultra-
high rib. Interchangeable choke tubes optional.

PIOTTI — Brescia, Italy

BOSS O/U . . . . **NiB $58,998 Ex $50,000 Gd $35,965**
Over/Under; sidelock. Gauges: 12 or 20. Barrels: 26 to 32 inch.
Standard chokes. Best quality walnut. Custom-made to customer
specifications. Imported from 1993 to date.

KING NO. 1 SIDELOCK . . . **NiB $35,866 Ex $29,821 Gd $19,670**
Gauges: 10, 12, 16, 20, 28, and .410. 25- to 30-inch bbls. (12 ga.),
25- to 28-inch (other ga.). Weight: About 5 lbs. (.410) to 8 lbs. (12
ga.) Holland & Holland pattern sidelock. Double triggers standard.
Coin finish or color casehardened. Level file-cut rib. Full-coverage
scroll engraving, gold inlays. Hand-rubbed, oil-finished, straight-
grip stock w/checkered butt, splinter forend.

**KING EXTRA SIDE-BY-SIDE
SHOTGUN** . . . . **NiB $77,850 Ex $52,290 Gd $42,777**
Same general specifications as the Piotti King No. 1 except has choice
of engraving, gold inlays, plus stock is exhibition-grade wood.

**LUNIK SIDELOCK
SHOTGUN** . . . . **NiB $35,660 Ex $31,299 Gd $26,000**
Same general specifications as the Monte Carlo model except has
level, file-cut rib. Renaissance-style large scroll engraving in relief,
gold crown in top lever, gold name, and gold crest in forearm;
finely figured wood.

**MONTE CARLO
SIDELOCK SHOTGUN** . . . . . **NiB $11,488 Ex $9889 Gd $7577**
Gauges: 10, 12, 16, 20, 28, or .410. Bbls.: 25 to 30 inch. Holland
& Holland pattern sidelock. Weight: 5 to 8 lbs. Automatic ejec-
tors. Double triggers. Hand-rubbed, oil-finished, straight-grip stock
w/checkered butt. Choice of Purdey-style scroll and rosette or
Holland & Holland-style large scroll engraving.

**PIUMA BOXLOCK SIDE-BY-SIDE
SHOTGUN.** . . . . **NiB $18,667 Ex $12,933 Gd $10,011**
Same general specifications as the Monte Carlo model except
has Anson & Deeley boxlock action w/demi-bloc bbls., scalloped
frame. Standard scroll and rosette engraving. Hand-rubbed, oil-
finished, straight-grip stock.

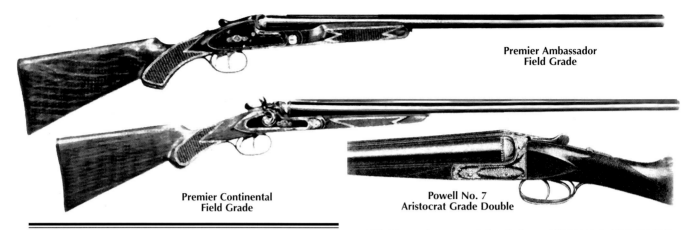

Premier Ambassador
Field Grade

Premier Continental
Field Grade

Powell No. 7
Aristocrat Grade Double

WILLIAM POWELL & SON, LTD. —
Birmingham, England

NO. 1 BEST GRADE DOUBLE-BARREL
SHOTGUN . . . . NiB $42,777 Ex $38,698 Gd $31,033
Sidelock. Gauges: Made to order w/12, 16, and 20 the most common. Bbls.: Made to order in any length but 28 inches was recommended. Highest grade French walnut buttstock and forearm w/ fine checkering. Metal elaborately engraved. Imported by Stoeger from about 1938 to 1951.

NO. 2 BEST GRADE
DOUBLE-BARREL . . . . . NiB $29,766 Ex $24,761 Gd $16,888
Same general specifications as the Powell No. 1 except plain finish w/o engraving. Imported by Stoeger from about 1938 to 1951.

NO. 6 CROWN GRADE
DOUBLE-BARREL . . . . . NiB $15,999 Ex $12,733 Gd $10,111
Boxlock. Gauges: Made to order w/12, 16, and 20 the most common. Bbls.: Made to order, but 28 inches was recommended. Highest grade French walnut buttstock and forearm w/fine checkering. Metal elaborately engraved. Uses Anson & Deeley locks. Imported by Stoeger from about 1938 to 1951.

NO. 7 ARISTOCRAT GRADE DOUBLE-BARREL
SHOTGUN . . . . NiB $9022 Ex $6988 Gd $4766
Same general specifications as the Powell No. 6 Crown Grade Double-Barrel above except w/lower quality wood and metal engraving.

PRECISION SPORTS SHOTGUNS —
Cortland, NY
Manufactured by Ignacio Ugartechea, Spain.

600 SERIES AMERICAN HAMMERLESS DOUBLES
Boxlock. Single selective trigger. Selective automatic ejectors. Automatic safety. Gauges: 12, 16, 20, 28, .410. 2.75- or 3-inch chambers. Bbls.: 26-, 27-, or 28-inch w/raised matte rib; choked IC/M or M/F. Weight: 5.75 to 7 lbs. Checkered pistol-grip walnut buttstock with beavertail forend. Engraved silvered receiver w/blued bbls. Imported from 1986 to 1994.
640A (12, 16, 20 ga. w/extractors) . . . . NiB $1177 Ex $909 Gd $677
640A (28 ga., .410 w/extractors) . . . . . NiB $1288 Ex $1067 Gd $779
640 Slug Gun (12 ga. w/extractors) . . . .NiB $1277 Ex $1059 Gd $723
645A (12, 16, 20 ga. w/ejectors) . . . . . .NiB $1177 Ex $909 Gd $677
645A (28 ga., .410, two-bbl. set) . . . . .NiB $1488 Ex $1176 Gd $877
645A (20/28 ga. 2-bbl. set) . . . . .NiB $1563 Ex $1253 Gd $919

650A (12 ga. w/extractors, choke tubes) . . . . NiB $1165 Ex $977 Gd $710
655A (12 ga. w/ejectors, choke tubes) . . . . NiB $1288 Ex $1022 Gd $766

600 SERIES ENGLISH HAMMERLESS DOUBLES
Boxlock. Same general specifications as American 600 series except w/double triggers and concave rib. Checkered English-style walnut stock w/splinter forend, straight grip, and oil finish.
640E (12, 16, 20 ga. w/extractors) . . . . .NiB $956 Ex $790 Gd $622
640E (28 ga., .410 w/extractors) . . . . . .NiB $1088 Ex $900 Gd $644
640 Slug Gun (12 ga. w/extractors) . . . .NiB $1297 Ex $1044 Gd $780
645E (12, 16, 20 ga. w/ejectors) . . . . . .NiB $1300 Ex $1066 Gd $800
645E (28 ga., .410 w/ejectors) . . . . . . .NiB $1266 Ex $1022 Gd $776
645E (20/28 ga. 2-bbl. set) . . . . .NiB $1545 Ex $1296 Gd $1000
650E (12 ga. w/extractors, choke tubes) . . . . NiB $1178 Ex $938 Gd $715
655E (12 ga. w/ejectors, choke tubes) . . . . NiB $1190 Ex $980 Gd $750

MODEL 640M MAGNUM 10 HAMMERLESS DOUBLE
Similar to Model 640E except in 10 ga. w/3.5-inch Mag. chambers. Bbls.: 26, 30, 32 inch, choked F/F.
Model 640M Big Ten, Turkey . . . . .NiB $1106 Ex $933 Gd $700
Model 640M Goose Gun . . . . . . NiB $1133 Ex $955 Gd $735

MODEL 645E-XXV HAMMERLESS DOUBLE
Similar to Model 645E except w/25-inch bbl. and Churchill-style rib.
645E-XXV (12, 16, 20 ga. w/ejectors) . . . NiB $1160 Ex $982 Gd $755
645E-XXV (28, .410 ga. w/ejectors) . . . .NiB $1366 Ex $1093 Gd $835

PREMIER
Premier shotguns have been produced by various gunmakers in Europe.

AMBASSADOR MODEL FIELD GRADE HAMMERLESS
DOUBLE-BARREL SHOTGUN. . . . NiB $544 Ex $466 Gd $377
Sidelock. Plain extractors. Double triggers. Gauges: 12, 16, 20, .410. 3-inch chambers in 20 and .410 ga., 2.75-inch in 12 and 16 ga. Bbls.: 26-inch in .410 ga., 28-inch in other ga.; choked M/F. Weight: 6 lbs., 3 oz. to 7 lbs., 3 oz. depending on ga. Checkered pistol-grip stock and beavertail forearm. Intro. in 1957; disc.

BRUSH KING . . . . NiB $440 Ex $330 Gd $255
Same as standard Regent model except chambered for 12 (2.75-inch) and 20 ga. (3-inch) only; has 22-inch bbls., IC/M choke, straight-grip stock. Weight: 6 lbs., 3 oz. in 12 ga.; 5 lbs., 12 oz. in 20 ga. Introduced in 1959; disc.

CONTINENTAL MODEL FIELD GRADE HAMMER
DOUBLE-BARREL SHOTGUN. . . . NiB $577 Ex $426 Gd $300
Sidelock. Exposed hammers. Plain extractors. Double triggers. Gauges: 12, 16, 20, .410. 3-inch chambers in 20 and .410 ga., 2.75-inch in 12 and 16 ga. Bbls.: 26-inch in .410 ga.; 28-inch in other ga.; choked M/F. Weight: 6 lbs., 3 oz to 7 lbs., 3 oz. depending on gauge. Checkered

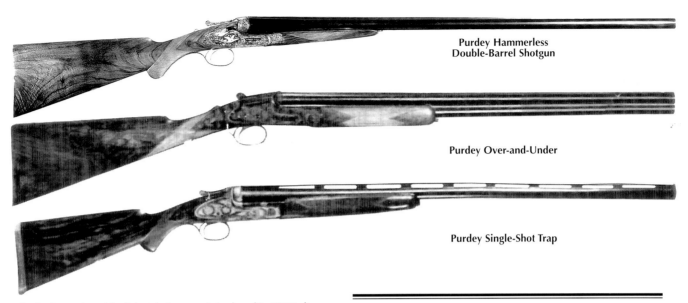

Purdey Hammerless
Double-Barrel Shotgun

Purdey Over-and-Under

Purdey Single-Shot Trap

pistol-grip stock and English-style forearm. Introduced in 1957; disc.

MONARCH SUPREME GRADE HAMMERLESS
DOUBLE-BARREL SHOTGUN. . . . NiB $667 Ex $487 Gd $367
Boxlock. Auto ejectors. Double triggers. Gauges: 12, 20. 2.75-inch chambers in 12 ga., 3-inch in 20 ga. Bbls.: 28-inch M/F; 26-inch IC/M choke. Weight: 6 lbs., 6 oz to 7 lbs., 2 oz. depending on ga. and bbl. Checkered pistol-grip stock and beavertail forearm of fancy walnut. Introduced in 1959; disc.

PRESENTATION
CUSTOM GRADE . . . . NiB $1488 Ex $1109 Gd $856
Similar to Monarch model but made to order of higher quality with hunting scene engraving, gold and silver inlay, fancier wood. Introduced in 1959; disc.

REGENT 10 GA.
MAGNUM EXPRESS . . . . NiB $665 Ex $431 Gd $345
Same as standard Regent model except chambered for 10 ga. Mag. 3.5-inch shells, has heavier construction, 32-inch bbls. choked F/F, stock w/recoil pad. Weight: 11.25 lbs. Introduced in 1957; disc.

REGENT 12 GA.
MAGNUM EXPRESS . . . . NiB $465 Ex $388 Gd $290
Same as standard Regent model except chambered for 12 ga. Mag. 3-inch shells, has 30-inch bbls. choked F/F, stock w/recoil pad. Weight: 7.25 lbs. Introduced in 1957; disc.

REGENT FIELD GRADE HAMMERLESS
DOUBLE-BARREL SHOTGUN. . . . NiB $477 Ex $355 Gd $271
Boxlock. Plain extractors. Double triggers. Gauges: 12,16, 20, 28, .410. 3-inch chambers in 20 and .410 ga., 2.75-inch in other ga. Bbls.: 26-inch IC/M, M/F (28 and .410 ga. only); 28-inch M/F; 30-inch M/F (12 ga. only). Weight: 6 lbs., 2 oz. to 7 lbs., 4 oz. depending on ga. and bbl. Checkered pistol-grip stock and beavertail forearm. Introduced in 1955; disc.

PUMA — Italy
Manufactured in Italy by Chiappa Firearms.

M-87 . . . . .NiB $1180 Ex $830 Gd $555
Lever action. 12 ga. only. 5-shell tubular magazine. Bbls.: Plain; 22 or 28 inch; choke tubes. Weight: About 9 lbs. Smooth walnut pistol-grip stock and forend. Made from 2009 to present.

JAMES PURDEY & SONS, LTD. — London, England

HAMMERLESS DOUBLE-BARREL SHOTGUN
Sidelock. Auto ejectors. Single or double triggers. Gauges: 12, 16, 20. Bbls.: 26, 27, 28, 30 inch (latter in 12 ga. only); any boring, any shape or style of rib. Weight: 5.25 to 5.5 lbs. depending on model, ga., and bbl. Checkered stock and forearm, straight grip standard, pistol grip also available. Purdey guns of this type have been made from about 1880 to date. Models include: Game Gun, Featherweight Game Gun, Two-Inch Gun (chambered for 12 ga. 2-inch shells), Pigeon Gun (w/ third fastening and side clips); values of all models are the same.
w/double triggers . . . . . . .NiB $62,700 Ex $54,890 Gd $44,782
Single trigger, add $1000

OVER/UNDER SHOTGUN
Sidelock. Auto ejectors. Single or double triggers. Gauges: 12, 16, 20. Bbls.: 26, 27, 28, 30 inch (latter in 12 ga. only); any boring, any style rib. Weight: 6 to 7.5 pounds depending on ga. and bbl. Checkered stock and forend, straight or pistol grip. Prior to WWII, the Purdey Over/Under Gun was made w/ Purdey action; since the war James Purdey & Sons have acquired the business of James Woodward & Sons, and all Purdey over/under guns are now built on the Woodward principle. General specifications of both types are the same.
w/Purdey action,
double triggers . . . . .NiB $78,880 Ex $52,609 Gd $24,655
Woodward action,
double triggers, add $3000
Single trigger, add 10%

SINGLE-BARREL TRAP
GUN . . . . NiB $12,775 Ex $10,560 Gd $8,300
Sidelock. Mechanical features similar to those of the over/under model w/Purdey action. 12 ga. only. Built to customer specifications. Made prior to WWII.

REMINGTON ARMS CO. — Ilion, NY

Eliphalet Remington Jr. began making long arms with his father in 1816. In 1828 they moved their facility to Ilion, NY, where it remained a family-run business for decades. As the family began to diminish, other people bought controlling interests. Today, still a successful gunmaking

**Remington Model 11-87
Premier Autoloader**

company, it is a subsidiary of the DuPont Corporation.

MODEL 10A STANDARD GRADE SLIDE-ACTION REPEATING
SHOTGUN . . . . .NiB $420 Ex $335 Gd $255
Hammerless. Takedown. 6-round capacity. 12 ga. only. 5-shell tubular magazine. Bbls.: Plain; 26 to 32-inch; choked F/M/C. Weight: About 7.5 lbs. Plain pistol-grip stock, grooved slide handle. Made from 1907 to 1929.

MODEL 11 SPECIAL, TOURNAMENT, EXPERT, AND PREMIER GRADE GUNS
These higher grade models differ from the Model 11A in general quality, grade of wood, checkering, engraving, etc. General specifications are the same.
Model 11B Special grade . . . . .NiB $788 Ex $609 Gd $466
Model 11D Tournament grade . . . . NiB $1388 Ex $1122 Gd $866
Model 11E Expert grade . . . . . . .NiB $1880 Ex $1455 Gd $1090
Model 11F Premier grade . . . . .NiB $2998 Ex $2356 Gd $1800

MODEL 11A STANDARD GRADE AUTOLOADER
Hammerless Browning type. 5-round capacity. Takedown. Gauges: 12, 16, 20. Tubular magazine holds four rounds. Bbls.: Plain, solid or vent. rib, lengths from 26 to 32 inches, F/M/IC/C/SK chokes. Weight: About 8 lbs., 12 ga.; 7.5 lbs., 16 ga.; 7.25 lbs., 20 ga. Checkered pistol grip and forend. Made from 1905 to 1949.
w/plain barrel . . . . NiB $355 Ex $260 Gd $229
w/solid rib barrel . . . . .NiB $477 Ex $339 Gd $366
w/vent. rib barrel . . . . .NiB $544 Ex $420 Gd $367

MODEL 11R RIOT GUN. . . . . . . NiB $445 Ex $300 Gd $195
Same as Model 11A Standard grade except has 20-inch plain barrel, 12 ga. only. Remington Model 11-48. (See Remington Sportsman-48 Series.)

NOTE: *Model 11-87 bbls. are not interchangable w/Model 1100 bbls.*

MODEL 11-87 PREMIER AUTOLOADER
Gas operated. Gauge: 12. 3-inch chamber. Bbl.: 26-, 28- or 30-inch w/REMChoke. Weight: 8.13 to 8.38 lbs. depending on bbl. length. Checkered walnut w/satin finish. Made from 1987 to 2006.
Deer Gun w/cant. scope mount. . . . . .NiB $855 Ex $654 Gd $477
Premier Skeet (1987-99) . . . . .NiB $740 Ex $535 Gd $420
Premier Standard . . . . .NiB $766 Ex $598 Gd $455
Premier Trap (1987-99). . . . . .NiB $844 Ex $707 Gd $510
Left-hand models, add $125

MODEL 11-87 PREMIER SUPER MAGNUM
Gas operated. Gauge: 12 only. 3.5-inch chamber. Bbl.: 28-inch only w/extended REMChoke. Weight: 8.4 lbs. Checkered gloss finish, walnut stock and forend. Made from 2001 to 2006.
Standard . . . . NiB $760 Ex $622 Gd $479
Camo (disc. 2004) . . . . NiB $836 Ex $684 Gd $489

MODEL 11-87 SP (SPECIAL PURPOSE)
Same general specifications as Model 11-87 Premier except w/nonreflective wood finish and Parkerized metal. 26-, 28-, or 30-inch vent. rib bbl. w/REMChoke tubes. Made from 1987 to 1993.
Standard . . . . .NiB $600 Ex $400 Gd $280
Deer Gun (21-in. bbl., rifle sights) . . . . NiB $690 Ex $445 Gd $295
Magnum (3.5-in. chamber) . . . . NiB $730 Ex $450 Gd $300

MODEL 11-87 SPS (SPECIAL PURPOSE SYNTHETIC)
Same general specifications as Model 11-87 SP except w/synthetic buttstock and forend. 21-, 26-, or 28-inch vent. rib bbl. w/ REMChoke tubes. Matte black or Mossy Oak camo finish except NWTF turkey gun. Made from 1990 to 2007.
Deer Gun (21-in. bbl., rifle sights) . . . . . NiB $696 Ex $494 Gd $358
Magnum (3-in., matte black, disc. 2004) . . . .NiB $733 Ex $643 Gd $471
Mossy Oak camo . . . . NiB $760 Ex $622 Gd $479
Deer Gun w/cant. scope mount. (1987-2005) . . NiB $859 Ex $633 Gd $490
NWTF Turkey Gun
 (Brown Treebark, disc. 1993) . . . . .NiB $775 Ex $690 Gd $510
NWTF Turkey Gun
 (Greenleaf, disc. 1996) . . . . .NiB $725 Ex $650 Gd $479
NWTF Turkey
 Gun (Mossy Oak, disc. 1996) . . . . . . .NiB $730 Ex $655 Gd $485
NWTF Turkey Gun (Mossy
 Oak Breakup, introduced 1999) . . . . . .NiB $730 Ex $655 Gd $485
NWTF 20 ga. Turkey Gun
 (Mossy Oak Breakup, 1998 only) . . . . .NiB $730 Ex $655 Gd $485
Thumbhole Deer Gun (2006-07) . . . . NiB $730 Ex $655 Gd $485
SPST Turkey Gun (matte bbl.) . . . . NiB $730 Ex $655 Gd $485
Super Magnum
 (3.5-in., matte black, disc. 2007) . . . . .NiB $950 Ex $730 Gd $300
Super Magnum Turkey Camo
 (3.5-in., Mossy Oak Breakup, disc. 2007) . . . . .NiB $950 Ex $730 Gd $300
Waterfowl (Mossy Oak
 Shadow Grass) . . . . NiB $1010 Ex $780 Gd $530

MODEL 11-87 SPORTING CLAYS . . . . . NiB $866 Ex $700 Gd $509
Gas operated. Gauge: 12 only. Bbl.: 26-inch only w/extended REMChoke. Weight: 7.5 lbs. Checkered satin finish, walnut stock and forend. Made from 1929 to 1999.
NP (nickel-plated receiver). . . . . NiB $890 Ex $735 Gd $533

MODEL 11-87 SPORTSMAN
Same general specifications as Model 11-87 Premier except w/ matte metal finish. 12 or 20 ga. Bbl.: 20- or 21-inch rifled, or 26- or 28-inch w/REMChoke. Weight: 7.3 to 8.3 lbs. Made from 2005 to date.
Camo (Mossy Oak New Breakup) . . . . NiB $915 Ex $570 Gd $370
Field (wood stock) . . . . NiB $845 Ex $470 Gd $270
ShurShot (synthetic thumbhole stock, cantilever
 scope mount). NiB $1012 Ex $680 Gd $430
Synthetic (synthetic stock) . . . . NiB $804 Ex $460 Gd $260
Synthetic Deer (synthetic stock, cantilever
 scope mount). NiB $929 Ex $585 Gd $385

MODEL 11-96 EURO LIGHTWEIGHT
AUTOLOADING SHOTGUN . . . . NiB $800 Ex $644 Gd $500

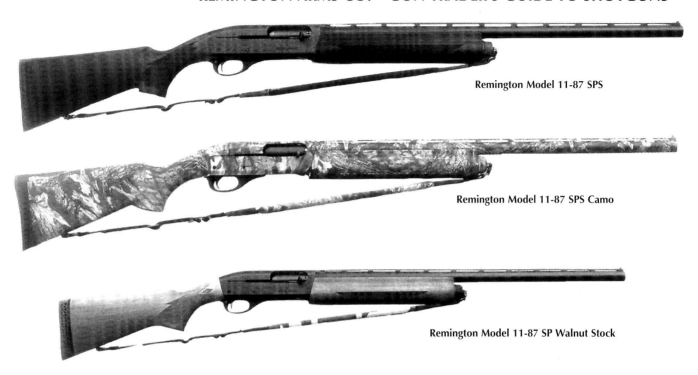

Remington Model 11-87 SPS

Remington Model 11-87 SPS Camo

Remington Model 11-87 SP Walnut Stock

Lightweight version of Model 11-87 w/reprofiled receiver. 12 ga. only. 3-inch chamber. 26- or 28-inch bbl. w/6mm vent. rib and REMChoke tubes. Semi-fancy Monte Carlo walnut buttstock and forearm. Weight: 6.8 lbs. w/26-inch bbl. Made in 1996 only.

MODEL 17A STANDARD GRADE SLIDE-ACTION REPEATING SHOTGUN
Hammerless. Takedown. 5-round capacity. 20 ga. only. 4-round tubular magazine. Bbls.: Plain; 26 to 32 inch; choked F/M/C. Weight: About 5.75 lbs. Plain pistol-grip stock, grooved slide handle. Made 1921 to 1933. Note: The present Ithaca Model 37 is an adaptation of this Browning design.
Plain barrel . . . . NiB $422 Ex $292 Gd $190
Solid rib . . . . NiB $490 Ex $400 Gd $290

MODEL 29A STANDARD GRADE
SLIDE-ACTION REPEATING SHOTGUN . . . . . . NiB $390 Ex $300 Gd $287
Hammerless. Takedown. 6-round capacity. 12 ga. only. 5-round tubular magazine. Bbls.: Plain, 26 to 32 inch, choked F/M/C. Weight: About 7.5 lbs. Checkered pistol-grip stock and slide handle. Made from 1929 to 1933.

MODEL 29T TARGET GRADE. . . . NiB $600 Ex $490 Gd $377
Same general specifications as Model 29A except has trap-style stock w/ straight grip, extension slide handle, vent. rib bbl. Disc. 1933.

MODEL 31/31L SKEET GRADE
Same general specifications as Model 31A except has 26-inch bbl. w/ raised solid or vent. rib, SK choke, checkered pistol-grip stock, and beavertail forend. Weight: About 8 lbs. 12 ga. Made from 1932 to 1939.
Model 31 Standard w/raised solid rib . . . . . NiB $477 Ex $290 Gd $200
Model 31 Standard w/vent. rib . . . . NiB $566 Ex $408 Gd $335
Model 31L Lightweight w/raised solid rib . . . . . NiB $455 Ex $330 Gd $245
Model 31L Lightweight w/vent. rib . . . . NiB $555 Ex $350 Gd $287
MODEL 31D SPECIAL, TOURNAMENT, EXPERT, AND PREMIER GRADE GUNS
These higher grade models differ from the Model 31A in quality,

grade of wood, checkering, engraving, etc. General specifications are the same.
Model 31B Special grade . . . . NiB $745 Ex $600 Gd $477
Model 31D Tournament grade . . . . NiB $1688 Ex $1099 Gd $722
Model 31E Expert grade . . . . . . NiB $1890 Ex $1266 Gd $977
Model 31F Premier grade . . . . . NiB $3100 Ex $2013 Gd $1544

MODEL 31A SLIDE-ACTION REPEATER
Hammerless. Takedown. 3- or 5-round capacity. Gauges: 12, 16, 20. Tubular magazine. Bbls.: Plain, solid or vent. rib; 26 to 32 inches; F/M/IC/C/SK choke. Weight: About 7.5 lbs., 12 ga.; 6.75 lbs., 16 ga.; 6.5 lbs., 20 ga. Earlier models have checkered pistol-grip stock and slide handle; later models have plain stock and grooved slide handle. Made from 1931 to 1949.
Model 31A w/plain barrel . . . . . . NiB $479 Ex $366 Gd $244
Model 31A w/solid rib barrel . . . . . . NiB $565 Ex $443 Gd $300
Model 31A w/vent. rib barrel . . . . . NiB $580 Ex $465 Gd $335
Model 31H Hunter
  w/sporting-style stock . . . . NiB $440 Ex $292 Gd $222
Model 31R Riot Gun w/20-
  inch plain bbl., 12 ga. . . . . NiB $509 Ex $388 Gd $287

MODEL 31S TRAP SPECIAL/31TC TRAP GRADE
Same general specifications as Model 31A except 12 ga. only, has 30- or 32-inch vent. rib bbl., F choke, checkered trap stock w/full pistol grip and recoil pad, checkered extension beavertail forend. Weight: About 8 lbs. (Trap Special has solid rib bbl., half pistol-grip stock w/standard walnut forend).
Model 31S Trap Special . . . . NiB $655 Ex $490 Gd $423
Model 31TC Trap grade . . . . NiB $955 Ex $677 Gd $590

MODEL 32A STANDARD GRADE O/U
Hammerless. Takedown. Auto ejectors. Early model had double triggers, later built w/selective single trigger only. 12 ga. only. Bbls.: Plain, raised matted solid or vent. rib; 26, 28, 30, 32 inch; F/M choke standard, option of any combination of F/M/IC/C/SK choke. Weight: About 7.75 lbs. Checkered pistol-grip stock and forend. Made from 1932 to 1942.

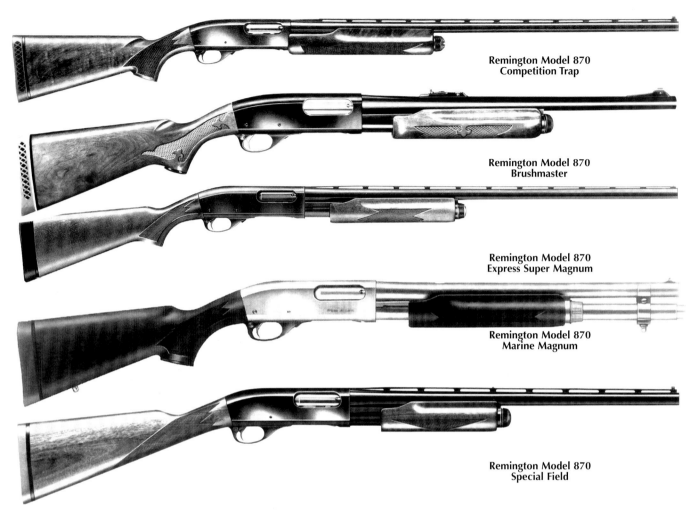

**Remington Model 870
Competition Trap**

**Remington Model 870
Brushmaster**

**Remington Model 870
Express Super Magnum**

**Remington Model 870
Marine Magnum**

**Remington Model 870
Special Field**

w/double triggers . . . . NiB $2165 Ex $1800 Gd $1287
w/selective single trigger . . . . .NiB $2466 Ex $2100 Gd $1533
Raised solid rib, add 10%
Vent. rib, add 20%

MODEL 32 TOURNAMENT, EXPERT, AND PREMIER GRADE GUNS
These higher-grade models differ from the Model 32A in general quality, grade of wood, checkering, engraving, etc. General specifications are the same. Made from 1932 to 1942.
Model 32D Tournament grade . . . . . .NiB $4377 Ex $3310 Gd $2560
Model 32E Expert grade . . . . . NiB $4598 Ex $4166 Gd $3000
Model 32F Premier grade . . . NiB $6986 Ex $5809 Gd $3976

MODEL 32 SKEET GRADE . . . . . NiB $2200 Ex $1798 Gd $1433
Same general specifications as Model 32A except 26- or 28-inch bbl., SK choke, beavertail forend, selective single trigger only. Weight: About 7.5 lbs. Made from 1932 to 1942.

MODEL 32TC
TARGET (TRAP) GRADE . . . . .NiB $3233 Ex $2866 Gd $1974
Same general specifications as Model 32A except 30- or 32-inch vent. rib bbl., F choke, trap-style stock w/checkered pistol grip and beavertail forend. Weight: About 8 lbs. Made from l932 to 1942.

MODEL 89 (1889) . . . . NiB $2133 Ex $1788 Gd $1141
Hammers. Circular action. Gauges: 10, 12, 16. 28- to 32-inch bls.; steel or Damascus twist. Weight 7 to 10 lbs. Made from 1889 to 1908.

MODEL 90-T SINGLE-SHOT TRAP . . . .NiB $1988 Ex $1790 Gd $1377
Gauge: 12. 2.75-inch chambers. 30-, 32-, or 34-inch vent. rib bbl. w/fixed chokes or screw-in REMChokes; ported or non-ported. Weight: 8.25 lbs. Checkered American walnut standard or Monte Carlo stock w/low-luster finish. Engraved sideplates and drop-out trigger group optional. Made from 1990 to 1997.

MODEL 105 CTI . . . . NiB $1230 Ex $880 Gd $600
Gas-operated semiautomatic. Titanium and carbon fiber receiver. Gauge: 12. 3-inch chamber. Bbl.: 26- or 28-inch w/REMChoke. Weight: 7 lbs. depending on bbl. Checkered walnut stock and forend in satin finish. Made from 2006 to 2008.
105 CTi-II (2009 only) . . . . .NiB $1230 Ex $880 Gd $600

MODEL 396 O/U
Boxlock. 12 ga. only. 2.75-inch chamber. 28- and 30-inch blued bbls. w/REMChoke. Weight: 7.5 lbs. Nitride-grayed engraved receiver, trigger guard, tang, hinge pins, and forend metal. Engraved sideplates. Checkered satin-finished American walnut stock w/target style forend. Made from 1996 to 1998.
Sporting Clays . . . . NiB $1933 Ex $1658 Gd $1277
396 Skeet . . . . NiB $1855 Ex $1544 Gd $1153

MODEL 870 ALL AMERICAN
TRAP GUN . . . . NiB $1277 Ex $1073 Gd $777
Same as Model 870TB except custom grade w/engraved receiver, trigger guard, and bbl.; Monte Carlo or straight-comb stock and forend of fancy walnut; available only w/30-inch F choke bbl.

**Remington Model 870
Wingmaster Field Gun**

Made from 1972 to 1977.

MODEL 870 COMPETITION TRAP . . . . . NiB $766 Ex $555 Gd $439
Based on standard Model 870 receiver except is single-shot w/ gas-assisted recoil-reducing system, new choke design, a high step-up vent. rib and redesigned stock, forend w/cut checkering and satin finish. Weight: 8.5 lbs. Made from 1981 to 1987.

MODEL 870 STANDARD . . . . NiB $566 Ex $444 Gd $339
Same as Model 870 Wingmaster Riot Gun except has rifle-type sights.

MODEL 870 BRUSHMASTER DELUXE
Same as Model 870 Standard except available in 12 and 20 ga.; has cut-checkered, satin-finished American walnut stock and forend, recoil pad.
Right-hand model . . . . NiB $559 Ex $477 Gd $366
Left-hand model . . . . NiB $659 Ex $490 Gd $380

MODEL 870 EXPRESS
Same general specifications Model 870 Wingmaster except has low-luster walnut-finished hardwood stock w/pressed checkering and black recoil pad. Gauges: 12, 20, or .410. 3-inch chambers. Bbls.: 26- or 28-inch vent. rib w/REMChoke; 25-inch vent. rib w/ fixed choke (.410 only). Black oxide metal finish. Made from 1987 to date.
12 or 20 ga. . . . . NiB $355 Ex $290 Gd $200
.410 (w/fixed choke). . . . . NiB $455 Ex $300 Gd $225
Combo (w/extra 20-inch deer bbl.) . . . . NiB $465 Ex $387 Gd $290

MODEL 870 EXPRESS DEER GUN
Same general specifications as Model 870 Express except in 12 ga. only. 20-inch bbl. w/fixed IC choke, adj. rifle sights, and Monte Carlo stock. Made from 1991 to date.
w/standard barrel . . . . NiB $433 Ex $297 Gd $200
w/rifled barrel . . . . NiB $450 Ex $310 Gd $220

MODEL 870 ESM (EXPRESS MAGNUM)
Similar to Model 870 Express except chambered for 12 ga. Mag. 3.5-inch chamber. Bbls.: 23-, 26-, or 28-inch vent. rib w/REMChoke. Checkered low-luster walnut-finished hardwood, black synthetic or camo buttstock and forearm. Matte black oxide metal finish or full camo finish. Made from 1998 to date.
w/hardwood stock . . . . NiB $455 Ex $310 Gd $225
w/black synthetic stock . . . . NiB $455 Ex $310 Gd $225
w/camo synthetic stock . . . . NiB $488 Ex $395 Gd $259
Turkey (w/synthetic stock) . . . . . . NiB $488 Ex $395 Gd $259
Turkey (w/full camo) . . . . NiB $488 Ex $395 Gd $259
w/full camo, extra bbl. . . . . NiB $509 Ex $400 Gd $323

**MODEL 870 EXPRESS
SYNTHETIC HOME DEFENSE. . . . NiB $422 Ex $300 Gd $200**
Slide action, hammerless, takedown. 12 ga. only. 18-inch bbl. w/Cyl. choke and bead front sight. Positive checkered synthetic stock and forend with nonreflective black finish. Made from 1995 to date.

MODEL 870 EXPRESS TURKEY . . . . . . NiB $448 Ex $290 Gd $210
Same general specifications as Model 870 Express except has 21-inch vent. rib bbl. and Turkey extra-full REMChoke. Made from 1991 to date.

MODEL 870 EXPRESS YOUTH . . . . . . NiB $391 Ex $248 Gd $181
Same general specifications as Model 870 Express except has scaled-down stock w/12.5-inch pull and 21-inch vent. rib bbl. w/ REMChoke. Made from 1991 to date.

MODEL 870 LIGHTWEIGHT
Same as standard Model 870 but w/scaled-down receiver and lightweight mahogany stock; 20 ga. only. 2.75-inch chamber. Bbls.: Plain or vent. rib; 26-inch IC; 28-inch M/F choke. REMChoke available from 1987. Weight 5.75 lbs. w/26-inch plain bbl. American walnut stock and forend w/satin or high-gloss finish. Made from 1972 to 1994.
w/plain barrel . . . . NiB $477 Ex $366 Gd $290
w/vent. rib bbl. . . . . NiB $490 Ex $380 Gd $315
w/REMChoke bbl. . . . . NiB $566 Ex $435 Gd $335

MODEL 870 LIGHTWEIGHT MAGNUM
Same as Model 870 Lightweight but chambered for 20 ga. Mag. 3-inch shell. 28-inch bbl., plain or vent. rib, F choke. Weight: 6 lbs. w/plain bbl. Made from 1972 to 1994.
w/plain bbl. . . . . NiB $477 Ex $377 Gd $292
w/vent. rib bbl. . . . . NiB $580 Ex $455 Gd $422

MODEL 870 MAGNUM DUCK GUN
Same as Model 870 Field Gun except has 3-inch chamber. 12 and 20 ga. Mag. only. 28- or 30-inch bbl., plain or vent. rib, M/F choke, recoil pad. Weight: 7 or 6.75 lbs. Made from 1964 to date.
w/plain bbl. . . . . NiB $310 Ex $225 Gd $179
w/vent. rib bbl. . . . . NiB $655 Ex $430 Gd $335

**MODEL 870
MARINE MAGNUM . . . . NiB $735 Ex $496 Gd $359**
Same general specifications as Model 870 Wingmaster except w/7-round magazine. 18-inch plain bbl. w/fixed IC choke, bead front sight and nickel finish. Made from 1992 to date.

**MODEL 870 MISSISSIPPI
MAGNUM DUCK GUN . . . . NiB $865 Ex $667 Gd $520**
Same as Remington Model 870 Mag. duck gun except has 32-inch bbl. "Ducks Unlimited" engraved receiver, Made in 1983.

**MODEL 870
SA SKEET GUN, SMALL GAUGE . . . . . . .NiB $875 Ex $677 Gd $529**
Similar to Wingmaster Model 870SA except chambered for 28 and .410 ga. (2.5-inch chamber for latter); 25-inch vent. rib bbl., SK choke. Weight: 6 lbs., 28 ga.; 6.5 lbs., .410. Made from 1969 to 1982.

**MODEL 870
SPECIAL FIELD SHOTGUN. . . . . .NiB $466 Ex $322 Gd $245**
Pump action. Hammerless. Gauge: 12 or 20. 21-inch vent. rib bbl. w/REMChoke. 41.5 inches overall. Weight: 6 to 7 lbs. Straight-grip

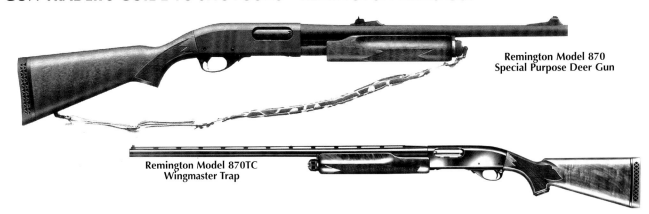

Remington Model 870
Special Purpose Deer Gun

Remington Model 870TC
Wingmaster Trap

checkered walnut stock and forend. Made from 1987 to 1995.

MODEL 870 SPECIAL PURPOSE DEER GUN
Similar to Special Purpose Mag. except w/20-inch IC choke, rifle sights. Matte black oxide and Parkerized finish. Oil-finished, checkered buttstock and forend w/recoil pad. Made from 1986 to date.
Model 870 SP Deer Gun . . . . NiB $744 Ex $488 Gd $333
w/cant. scope mount. . . . . NiB $800 Ex $523 Gd $366

MODEL 870 SPECIAL
PURPOSE MAGNUM. . . . . NiB $735 Ex $555 Gd $467
Similar to the 870 Mag. duck gun except w/26-, 28-, or 30-inch vent. rib REMChoke bbl. 12 ga. only. 3-inch chamber. Oil-finished field-grade stock w/recoil pad, QD swivels, and Cordura sling. Made from 1985 to date.

MODEL 870SPS MAGNUM
Same general specifications Model 870 Special Purpose Mag. except w/ synthetic stock and forend. 26- or 28-inch vent. rib bbl. w/REMChoke tubes. Matte black or Mossy Oak camo finish. Made from 1991 to date.
70 SPS Mag. (black syn. stock) . . . NiB $688 Ex $455 Gd $325
870 SPS-T Camo (Mossy Oak camo). . . . . NiB $866 Ex $533 Gd $400

MODEL 870 WINGMASTER FIELD GUN
Same general specifications as Model 870AP except checkered stock and forend. Later models have REMChoke systems in 12 ga. Made from 1964 to date.
w/plain bbl. . . . . NiB $366 Ex $264 Gd $155
w/vent. rib bbl. . . . . NiB $665 Ex $439 Gd $266

MODEL 870 WINGMASTER FIELD GUN, SMALL GAUGE
Same as standard Model 870 except w/scaled-down lightweight receivers. Gauges: 28 and .410. Plain or vent. rib 25-inch bbl. choked IC/M/F. Weight: 5.5 to 6.25 lbs. depending on ga. and bbl. Made 1969 to 1994.
w/plain bbl . . . . NiB $775 Ex $600 Gd $445
w/vent. rib bbl . . . . NiB $808 Ex $625 Gd $465

MODEL 870 WINGMASTER
MAGNUM DELUXE GRADE. . . . . NiB $667 Ex $559 Gd $400
Same as Model 870 Mag. standard grade except has checkered stock and extension beavertail forearm, bbl. w/matted top surface. Disc. 1963.

MODEL 870 WINGMASTER MAGNUM STANDARD
GRADE . . . . NiB $633 Ex $479 Gd $365
Same as Model 870AP except chambered for 12 ga. 3-inch Mag., 30-inch F choke bbl., recoil pad. Weight: About 8.25 lbs. Made 1955 to 1963.

MODEL 870 WINGMASTER REMCHOKE SERIES
Slide action, hammerless, takedown w/blued all-steel receiver. Gauges: 12, 20. 3-inch chamber. Tubular magazine. Bbls.: 21-, 26-,

28-inch vent. rib w/REMChoke. Weight: 7.5 lbs. (12 ga.) Satin-finished, checkered walnut buttstock and forend w/recoil pad. Right- or left-hand models. Made from 1986 to date.
Standard model, 12 ga. . . . . NiB $500 Ex $377 Gd $266
Standard model, 20 ga. . . . . NiB $535 Ex $400 Gd $288
Youth model, 21-inch bbl . . . . NiB $500 Ex $377 Gd $321

MODEL 870ADL WINGMASTER DELUXE GRADE
Same general specifications as Wingmaster Model 870AP except has pistol-grip stock and extension beavertail forend, both finely checkered; matted top surface or vent. rib bbl. Made 1950 to 1963.
w/matted top surface bbl. . . . . . . NiB $488 Ex $365 Gd $288
w/vent. rib bbl. . . . . NiB $509 Ex $412 Gd $300

MODEL 870AP WINGMASTER STANDARD GRADE
Hammerless. Takedown. Gauges: 12, 16, 20. Tubular magazine holds four rounds. Bbls.: Plain, matted top surface or vent. rib; 26-inch IC, 28-inch M/F choke, 30-inch F choke (12 ga. only). Weight: About 7 lbs., 12 ga.; 6.75 lbs., 16 ga.; 6.5 lbs., 20 ga. Plain pistol-grip stock, grooved forend. Made 1950 to 1963.
w/plain bbl. . . . . NiB $359 Ex $300 Gd $209
w/matted surface bbl. . . . . NiB $435 Ex $335 Gd $225
w/vent. rib bbl. . . . . NiB $466 Ex $372 Gd $260
Left-hand model . . . . NiB $489 Ex $400 Gd $265

MODEL 870DL WINGMASTER DELUXE SPECIAL
Same as Model 870ADL except select American walnut stock and forend. Made from 1950 to 1963.
w/matted surface bbl. . . . . NiB $665 Ex $445 Gd $310
w/vent. rib bbl. . . . . NiB $715 Ex $477 Gd $349

MODEL 870D, 870F WINGMASTER
TOURNAMENT AND PREMIER GRADE GUNS
These higher-grade models differ from the Model 870AP in general quality, grade of wood, checkering, engraving, etc. General operating specifications are essentially the same. Made from 1950 to date.
Model 870D Tournament grade . . . . . NiB $3139 Ex $2288 Gd $1660
Model 870F Premier grade . . . . NiB $6445 Ex $4753 Gd $3465
Model 870F Premier gr. w/gold inlay . . . . . NiB $10,098 Ex $7517 Gd $5237

MODEL 870R WINGMASTER RIOT GUN . . . NiB $375 Ex $280
Gd $210
Same as Model 870AP except 20-inch bbl., IC choke. 12 ga. only.

MODEL 870 SA WINGMASTER SKEET GUN
Same general specifications as Model 870AP except has 26-inch vent. rib bbl., SK choke, ivory bead front sight, metal bead rear sight, pistol-grip stock and extension beavertail forend. Weight: 6.75 to 7.5 lbs. depending on ga. Made 1950 to 1982.
Model 870SA Skeet grade (disc. 1982) . . . . . NiB $677 Ex $395 Gd $288
Model 870SC Skeet Target
grade (disc. 1980) . . . . NiB $795 Ex $549 Gd $400

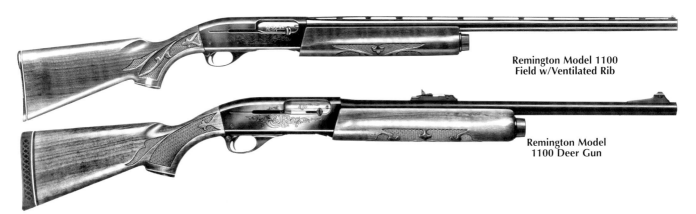

Remington Model 1100
Field w/Ventilated Rib

Remington Model
1100 Deer Gun

MODEL 870TB WINGMASTER

TRAP SPECIAL . . . . **NiB $633 Ex $500 Gd $388**
Same general specifications as Model 870AP Wingmaster except-trear sight. Special grade trap-style stock and forend, both checkered, recoil pad. Weight: About 8 lbs. Made from 1950 to 1981.

MODEL 870TC TRAP GRADE. . . . **NiB $795 Ex $554 Gd $400**
Same as Model 870 Wingmaster TC except has tournament-grade walnut stock and forend w/satin finish. Over-bored 30-inch vent. rib bbl. w/2.75-inch chamber and REMChoke tubes. Reissued in 1996. See separate listing for earlier model.

MODEL 870TC WINGMASTER TRAP GRADE
Same as Model 870TB except higher-grade walnut stock and forend, has both front and rear sights. Made 1950 to 1979. Model 870 TC reissued in 1996. See separate listing for later model.
Model 870 TC Trap (Standard) . . . **NiB $515 Ex $466 Gd $325**
Model 870 TC Trap (Monte Carlo) . . . . **NiB $545 Ex $480 Gd $366**

MODEL 878A AUTOMASTER. . . . **NiB $376 Ex $266 Gd $195**
Gas-operated autoloader. 12 ga. 3-round magazine. Bbls.: 26-inch IC, 28-inch M, 30-inch F choke. Weight: About 7 lbs. Plain pistol-grip stock and forearm. Made from 1959 to 1962.

MODEL 887 NITRO MAG . . . . . . **NiB $445 Ex $285 Gd $200**
Based on Model 870 except has Armorlokt overmolding on metal. 26- or 28-inch bbl. Finish: matte black. Stock: black synthetic. Made from 2009 to date.
Camo Combo . . . . **NiB $728 Ex $700 Gd $300**
Tactical (extended magazine, Picatinny rail, ported
    extended choke tube) . . . . **NiB $534 Ex $340 Gd $230**
Waterfowl Camo (Real tree Advantage
    Max-4 finish) . . . . **NiB $594 Ex $370 Gd $270**

NOTE: *New stock checkering patterns and receiver scroll markings were incorporated on all standard Model 1100 field, Magnum, skeet, and trap models in 1979.*

MODEL 1100 FIELD
Gas operated. Hammerless. Takedown. Gauges: 12, 16, 20. Bbls.: Plain or vent. rib; 30-inch F, 28-inch M/F, 26-inch IC, or REMChoke tubes. Weight: Average 7.25 to 7.5 lbs. depending on ga. and bbl. length. Checkered walnut pistol-grip stock and forearm in high-gloss finish. Made 1963 to 1988. 16 ga. disc. 1980.
w/plain bbl. . . . . **NiB $380 Ex $291 Gd $200**
w/vent. rib bbl. . . . . **NiB $422 Ex $356 Gd $239**
REMChoke model . . . . **NiB $466 Ex $390 Gd $292**
REMChoke, Left-hand action . . . **NiB $744 Ex $544 Gd $356**

MODEL 1100 CLASSIC FIELD . . . **NiB $675 Ex $480 Gd $310**

Similar to Model 1100 Field except 12, 16, 20, or .410 w/light contoured REMchoke bbl. Non-engraved receiver. Made from 2003 to 2006.

MODEL 1100 DEER GUN. . . . . . **NiB $515 Ex $386 Gd $265**
Same as Model 1100 Field Gun except has 22-inch barrel, IC, w/ rifle-type sights. 12 and 20 ga. only; recoil pad. Weight: About 7.25 lbs. Made from 1963 to 1998.

MODEL 1100 DUCKS UNLIMITED
ATLANTIC COMMEMORATIVE. . . . . **NiB $1188 Ex $987 Gd $766**
Limited production for one year. Similar specifications to Model 1100 Field except w/32-inch F choke, vent. rib bbl. 12 ga. Mag. only. Made in 1982.

MODEL 1100 DUCKS UNLIMITED "THE CHESAPEAKE"
COMMEMORATIVE . . . . **NiB $878 Ex $753 Gd $555**
Limited edition 1 to 2400. Same general specifications as Model 1100 Field except sequentially numbered w/markings "The Chesapeake." 12 ga. Mag. w/30-inch F choke, vent. rib bbl. Made in 1981.

MODEL 1100 FIELD GRADE, SMALL BORE
Same as standard Model 1100 but scaled down. Gauges: 28, .410. 25-inch bbl., plain or vent. rib; IC/M/F choke. Weight: 6.25 to 7 lbs. depending on gauge and bbl. Made from 1969 to 1994.
w/plain bbl. . . . . **NiB $669 Ex $533 Gd $435**
w/vent. rib . . . . **NiB $866 Ex $677 Gd $480**

MODEL 1100 G3 . . . . **NiB $1050 Ex $800 Gd $500**
Similar to Model 1100 Field except satin finish steel receiver w/ titanium PVD coating. 12 or 20 ga.; 3-inch chamber. Bbls.: 26- or 28-inch vent. rib w/ProBore choke tubes. Weight: 6.7 to 7.6 lbs. depending on bbl. Stock: RealWood fiber laminate w/ high-gloss finish and checkering. Made from 2006 to 2008.

MODEL 1100 LIGHTWEIGHT
Same as standard Model 1100 but scaled-down receiver and light-weight mahogany stock. 20 ga. only. 2.75-inch chamber. Bbls.: Plain or vent. rib; 26-inch IC, 28-inch M/F choke. Weight: 6.25 lbs. Made from 1970 to 1976.
w/plain bbl. . . . . **NiB $654 Ex $500 Gd $390**
w/vent. rib . . . . **NiB $735 Ex $566 Gd $408**

MODEL 1100 LIGHTWEIGHT MAGNUM
Same as Model 1100 Lightweight but chambered for 20 ga. Mag. 3-inch shell. 28-inch bbl., plain or vent. rib, F choke. Weight: 6.5 lbs. Made from 1977 to 1998.
w/plain bbl. . . . . **NiB $688 Ex $544 Gd $422**
w/vent. rib . . . . **NiB $788 Ex $590 Gd $466**
w/choke tubes . . . . **NiB $855 Ex $598 Gd $466**

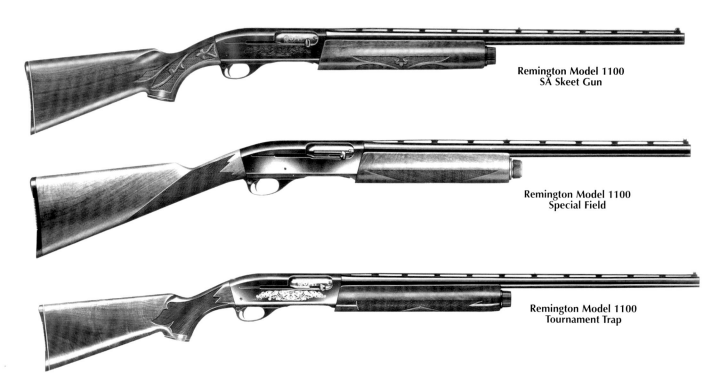

Remington Model 1100
SA Skeet Gun

Remington Model 1100
Special Field

Remington Model 1100
Tournament Trap

MODEL 1100 LT-20 DUCKS UNLIMITED SPECIAL
COMMEMORATIVE . . . . **NiB $1486 Ex $1156 Gd $844**
Limited edition 1 to 2400. Same general specifications as Model 1100 Field except sequentially numbered w/markings, "The Chesapeake." 20 ga. only. 26-inch IC, vent. rib bbl. Made in 1981.

MODEL 1100 LT-20 SERIES
Same as Model 1100 Field Gun except in 20 ga. w/shorter 23-inch vent. rib bbl., straight-grip stock. REMChoke series has 21-inch vent. rib bbl., choke tubes. Weight: 6.25 lbs. Checkered grip and forearm. Made from 1977 to 1995.
LT-20 Special. . . . . NiB $588 Ex $498 Gd $377
LT-20 Deer Gun . . . . NiB $490 Ex $399 Gd $295
LT-20 Youth . . . . NiB $585 Ex $444 Gd $300

MODEL 1100 MAGNUM . . . . NiB $598 Ex $499 Gd $378
Limited production. Similar to the Model 1100 Field except w/26-inch F choke, vent. rib bbl., and 3-inch chamber. Made in 1981.

MODEL 1100 MAGNUM DUCK GUN
Same as Model 1100 Field Gun except has 3-inch chamber. 12 and 20 ga. Mag. only. 30-inch plain or vent. rib bbl. in 12 ga., 28-inch in 20 ga.; M/F choke. Recoil pad. Weight: About 7.75 lbs. Made from 1963 to 1988.
w/plain bbl. . . . . NiB $555 Ex $399 Gd $324
w/vent. rib bbl. . . . . NiB $575 Ex $435 Gd $355

MODEL 1100
ONE OF 3000 FIELD . . . . **NiB $1210 Ex $966 Gd $790**
Limited edition, numbered 1 to 3000. Similar to Model 1100 Field except w/fancy wood and gold-trimmed etched hunting scenes on receiver. 12 ga. w/28-inch M, vent. rib bbl. Made in 1980.

MODEL 1100 SA SKEET GUN
Same as Model 1100 Field Gun 12 and 20 ga. except has 26-inch vent. rib bbl., SK choke, or w/Cutts Compensator. Weight: 7.25 to 7.5 lbs. Made from 1963 to 1994.
w/skeet-choked
  bbl. . . . . **NiB $977 Ex $644 Gd $388**
Cutts Comp, add. $200
Left-hand action, add $75

MODEL 1100 SA
LIGHTWEIGHT SKEET . . . . **NiB $655 Ex $497 Gd $366**
Same as Model 1100 Lightweight except has skeet-style stock and forearm, 26-inch vent. rib bbl., SK choke. Made from 1971 to 1997.

MODEL 1100 SA
SKEET SMALL BORE . . . . **NiB $625 Ex $443 Gd $311**
Similar to standard Model 1100SA except chambered for 28 and .410 ga. (2.5-inch chamber for latter) 25-inch vent. rib bbl., SK choke. Weight: 6.75 lbs., 28 ga.; 7.25 lbs., .410. Made from 1969 to 1994.

MODEL 1100 SB
LIGHTWEIGHT SKEET . . . . **NiB $644 Ex $433 Gd $310**
Same as Model 1100SA Lightweight except has select wood. Introduced in 1977.

MODEL 1100
SB SKEET GUN . . . . **NiB $654 Ex $443 Gd $319**
Same specifications as Model 1100SA except has select wood. Made from 1963 to 1997.

MODEL 1100
SPECIAL FIELD SHOTGUN. . . . . . . **NiB $600 Ex $492 Gd $388**
Gas operated. 5-round capacity. Hammerless. Gauges: 12, 20, or

Remington Model 3200
One of 1000 Skeet

.410. 21- or 23-inch. vent. rib bbl. w/REMChoke. Weight: 6.5 to 7.25 lbs. Straight-grip checkered walnut stock and forend. Note: .410 Made from 1983 to 1999.

MODEL 1100 SP MAGNUM
Same as Model 1100 Field except 12 ga. only. 3-inch chambers. Bbls.: 26- or 30-inch F choke; 26-inch w/REMChoke tubes; vent. rib. Nonreflective matte black, Parkerized bbl. and receiver. Satin-finished stock and forend. Made 1986.
w/fixed choke . . . . NiB $475 Ex $397 Gd $321
w/REMChoke . . . . NiB $490 Ex $417 Gd $344

MODEL 1100 SPECIAL FIELD
Similar to Model 1100 Field except 12, 20, or .410. Bbls.: 21- and 23-inch vent. rib w/REMChoke tubes (intro. 1987). Weight: Average 7.25 to 7.5 lbs. depending on ga. and bbl. High-gloss checkered walnut straight-grip stock and forearm. Made 1983 to 1999.
12 ga. . . . . NiB $525 Ex $350 Gd $200
20 ga. . . . . NiB $690 Ex $540 Gd $400
.410 . . . . NiB $840 Ex $710 Gd $480

MODEL 1100 SYNTHETIC . . . . . . NiB $435 Ex $280 Gd $170
Similar to Model 1100 Field except 12, 16, or 20 ga. Bbls.: 26- or 28-inch vent. rib w/REMChoke tubes. Weight: Average 7 to 7.5 lbs. depending on ga. and bbl. Sythentic stock and forearm. Made 1996 to 2004.
Deer . . . . NiB $500 Ex $280 Gd $170
LT 20 Youth . . . . NiB $440 Ex $270 Gd $160

MODEL 1100 TAC-2 . . . . NiB $800 Ex $580 Gd $400
Similar to Model 1100 Field except 12 ga. only. 2.75-inch chamber. Bbls.: 18- or 22-inch. vent. rib w/REMChoke tubes, HiViz sights. Weight: 7.5 lbs. depending on bbl. Stock: black sythentic SFIV. 6- or 8-round capacity. Made 2006 to date.
Tac-4 (pistol grip) . . . . NiB $870 Ex $650 Gd $240

MODEL 1100 TACTICAL . . . . NiB $435 Ex $280 Gd $170
Similar to Model 1100 Field except 12 ga. only. 3-inch chamber. Bbls.: 18- or 22-inch vent. rib w/REMChoke tubes, HiViz sights. Weight: 7.5 lbs. depending on bbl. Sythentic pistol-grip or standard stock and forearm. 6- or 8-round capacity. Disc. 2006.

MODEL 1100 TOURNAMENT/PREMIER
These higher grade guns differ from standard models in overall quality, grade of wood, checkering, engraving, gold inlays, etc. General specs are the same. Made 1963 to 1994, 1997 to 1999,

2003.
1100D Tournament . . . . NiB $966 Ex $633 Gd $577
1100F Premier . . . . NiB $1266 Ex $1059 Gd $833
1100F Premier w/gold inlay . . . . NiB $10,332 Ex $7833 Gd $4460

MODEL 1100
TOURNAMENT SKEET . . . . NiB $977 Ex $738 Gd $490
Similar to Model 1100 Field except w/26-inch bbl. SK choke. Gauges: 12, LT-20, 28, and .410. Features select walnut stocks and new cut-checkering patterns. Made from 1979 to 1999.

MODEL 1100TA TRAP GUN . . . . . NiB $529 Ex $417 Gd $330
Similar to Model 1100TB Trap Gun except w/regular-grade stocks. Available in both left- and right-hand versions. Made 1979 to 1986.

MODEL 1100TB TRAP GUN
Same as Model 1100 Field Gun except has special trap stock, straight or Monte Carlo comb, recoil pad. 30-inch vent. rib bbl., F/M trap choke; 12 ga. only. Weight: 8.25 lbs. Made 1963 to 1979.
w/straight stock . . . . NiB $588 Ex $460 Gd $339
w/Monte Carlo stock . . . . NiB $599 Ex $443 Gd $360

MODEL 1900
HAMMERLESS DOUBLE . . . . . NiB $1889 Ex $1366 Gd $1177
Improved version of Model 1894. Boxlock. Auto ejector. Double triggers. Gauges: 10, 12, 16. Bbls.: 28 to 32 inch. Value shown is for standard grade w/ordnance steel bbls. Made 1900 to 1910.

MODEL 3200 FIELD GRADE . . . . . NiB $1388 Ex $1178 Gd $900
O/U, boxlock. Auto ejectors. Selective single trigger. 12 ga. 2.75-inch chambers. Bbls.: Vent. rib, 26- and 28-inch M/F; 30-inch IC/M. Weight: About 7.75 lbs. w/26-inch bbls. Checkered pistol-grip stock and forearm. Made from 1973 to 1978.

MODEL 3200 COMPETITION
SKEET GUN . . . . NiB $1799 Ex $1588 Gd $1165
Same as Model 3200 Skeet Gun except has gilded scrollwork on frame, engraved forend, latch plate, and trigger guard, select fancy wood. Made from 1973 to 1984.

MODEL 3200 COMPETITION
SKEET SET . . . . NiB $5733 Ex $4790 Gd $3300
Similar specifications to Model 3200 Field. 12 ga. O/U w/additional, interchangeable bbls. in 20, 28, and .410 ga. Cased. Made from 1980 to 1984.

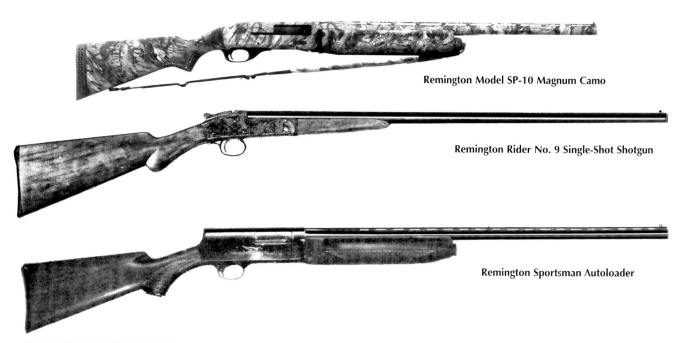

Remington Model SP-10 Magnum Camo

Remington Rider No. 9 Single-Shot Shotgun

Remington Sportsman Autoloader

MODEL 3200 COMPETITION
TRAP GUN . . . . NiB $1598 Ex $1266 Gd $1177
Same as Model 3200 Trap Gun except has gilded scrollwork on frame, engraved forend, latch plate, and trigger guard, select fancy wood. Made from 1973 to 1984.

MODEL 3200
FIELD GRADE MAGNUM. . . . NiB $1766 Ex $1588 Gd $1177
Same as Model 3200 Field except chambered for 12 ga. Mag. 3-inch shells, 30-inch bbls., M/F or F/F choke. Made 1975 to 1984.

MODEL 3200
ONE OF 1000 SKEET . . . . . . NiB $2088 Ex $1577 Gd $1288
Same as Model 3200 One of 1000 Trap except has 26- or 28-inch bbls., SK choke, skeet-style stock and forearm. Made in 1974.

MODEL 3200
ONE OF 1000 TRAP . . . . NiB $2170 Ex $1660 Gd $1375
Limited edition numbered 1 to 1000. Same general specifications as Model 3200 Trap Gun but has frame, trigger guard, and forend latch elaborately engraved (designation "One of 1,000" on frame side), stock and forearm of high grade walnut. Supplied in carrying case. Made in 1973.

MODEL 3200 SKEET GUN . . . NiB $1779 Ex $1398 Gd $1055
Same as Model 3200 Field Grade except skeet-style stock and full beavertail forearm, 26- or 28-inch bbls., SK choke. Made from 1973 to 1980.

MODEL 3200
SPECIAL TRAP GUN . . . . NiB $1598 Ex $1366 Gd $988
Same as Model 3200 Trap Gun except has select fancy-grade wood and other minor refinements. Made from 1973 to 1984.

MODEL 3200 TRAP GUN. . . . NiB $1499 Ex $1262 Gd $1077
Same as Model 3200 Field Grade except trap-style stock w/Monte Carlo or straight comb, select wood, beavertail forearm, 30- or 32-inch bbls. w/vent. rib, IM/F or F/F chokes. Made 1973 to 1977.

RIDER NO. 9 SINGLE-SHOT . . . . NiB $555 Ex $433 Gd $335
Improved version of No. 3 Single-Barrel Shotgun made in the late 1800s. Semi-hammerless. Gauges: 10, 12, 16, 20, 24, 28. 30- to 32-inch plain bbl. Weight: About 6 lbs. Plain pistol-grip stock and forearm. Auto ejector. Made from 1902 to 1910.

SP-10. NiB $1480 Ex $1050 Gd $730
Autoloader. Takedown. Gas operated w/stainless steel piston. 10 ga. 3.5-inch chamber. Bbls.: 30-inch vent. rib w/REMChoke screw-in tubes. Weight: 11 lbs. Metal bead front. Checkered walnut stock w/satin finish. QD swivels and camo sling. Made from 1989 to 2010.

SP-10 MAGNUM CAMO . . . . . NiB $1560 Ex $1000 Gd $710
Same general specifications as Model SP-10 except has 23- or 26-inch bbl. Finish: Mossy Oak, Mossy Oak break up, Mossy Oak Obession, Bottomland, or Duck Blind. Stock: standard or thumbhole. Made from 1993 to 2010.
Synthetic (matte finish). . . . . NiB $990 Ex $800 Gd $560
Turkey
  (Mossy Oak Obession) . . . . . NiB $1660 Ex $1100 Gd $810
Turkey Combo
  (turkey bbl. and deer bbl.) . . . NiB $1300 Ex $930 Gd $660
Waterfowl
  (Mossy Oak Duck Blind) . . . . NiB $1570 Ex $1010 Gd $350

SP-10 TURKEY CAMO
NWTF 25TH ANNIVERSARY . . . NiB $1050 Ex $775 Gd $710
Same general specifications as Model SP-10 except limited manufacture for NWTF 25th Anniversary in 1998. Made 1998 only.

PEERLESS O/U . . . . NiB $1165 Ex $966 Gd $788
Boxlock action and removable, engraved sideplates. Gauge: 12 only. 3-inch chambers. Barrels: 26-, 28-, or 30-inch w/vent. rib and REMChoke system. Automatic safety and single selective trigger. Weight: 7.25 lbs. to 7.5 lbs. Blued receiver and bbls. Checkered American walnut stock. Made from 1993 to 1998.

Remington Sportsman — 48A

SPORTSMAN A STANDARD GRADE AUTOLOADER
Same general specifications as Model 11A except magazine holds two shells. Also available in B Special Grade, D Tournament Grade, E Expert Grade, F Premier Grade. Made from 1931 to 1948. Same values as for Model 11A.
48D . . . . **NiB $445 Ex $321 Gd $226**

VERSA MAX
Gas-operated semiauto. 12 ga. 3.5 in. chambers only. Bbls.: 26- or 28-inch w/vent. rib, HiViz bead, and ProBore choke tubes. Finish: Matte black. Stock: Black synthetic w/gray checkered insert panels. Made from 2010 to date.
Synthetic . . . . **NiB $1427 Ex $900 Gd $530**
Synthetic Left Hand . . . . **NiB $1497 Ex $970 Gd $600**
Waterfowl Camo . . . . **NiB $1630 Ex $1100 Gd $660**
Waterfowl Pro . . . . **NiB $1730 Ex $1120 Gd $670**
Wood Tech . . . . **NiB $1630 Ex $1100 Gd $660**

VERSA MAX
COMPETITION TACTICAL . . . . **NiB $1699 Ex $1100 Gd $660**
Same general specs as Versa Max except has 22-inch bbl. and 8-round capacity. Finish: Green cerakote. Made from 2014 to date.

VERSA MAX SPORTSMAN . . . . . **NiB $1045 Ex $700 Gd $500**
Same general specs as Versa Max except w/26- or 28-inch bbl. w/ one choke tube, black synthetic stock, matte blue finish. Made from 2013 to date.
Camo . . . . **NiB $1199 Ex $730 Gd $500**
Turkey Model . . . . **NiB $1199 Ex $730 Gd $500**

VERSA MAX TACTICAL . . . . . . **NiB $1699 Ex $1100 Gd $660**
Same general specs as Versa Max except has 22-inch vent. rib bbl. w/HiViz sights, magazine extension, and Picatinny rail. Finish: Black. Made from 2012 to date.
Zombie Gargoyle Green . . . . . . **NiB $1627 Ex $1100 Gd $730**
Zombie Pink Explosion finish
(2013 only) . . . . **NiB $1627 Ex $1100 Gd $730**

SPORTSMAN SKEET GUN
Same general specifications as the Sportsman A except has 26-inch bbl. (plain, solid, or vent. rib), SK choke, beavertail forend. Disc. in 1949.
w/plain bbl. . . . . **NiB $408 Ex $320 Gd $255**
w/solid rib bbl. . . . . **NiB $408 Ex $320 Gd $255**
w/vent. rib bbl. . . . . **NiB $475 Ex $355 Gd $290**

MODEL 48 MOHAWK SPORTSMAN AUTO
Streamlined receiver. Hammerless. Takedown. Gauges: 12, 16, 20. Tubular magazine holds two rounds. Bbls.: Plain, matted top surface, or vent. rib; 26-inch IC, 28-inch M/F, 30-inch F choke (12 ga. only). Weight: About 7.5 lbs., 12 ga.; 6.25 lbs., 16 ga.; 6.5 lbs., 20 ga. Pistol-grip stock, grooved forend, both check-

ered. Made from 1949 to 1959.
w/plain bbl . . . . **NiB $376 Ex $270 Gd $198**
w/matted top surface bbl.. . . . . . . **NiB $466 Ex $355 Gd $290**
w/vent rib bbl. . . . . **NiB $566 Ex $477 Gd $379**

SPORTSMAN MODEL 48 B, D, F, SELECT, TOURNAMENT, AND PREMIER GRADE GUNS
These higher grade models differ from the Sportsman-48A in general quality, grade of wood, checkering, engraving, etc. General specifications are the same. Made from 1949 to 1959.
Sportsman-48B Select grade . . . . **NiB $490 Ex $330 Gd $225**
Sportsman-48D Tournament
grade . . . . **NiB $1688 Ex $1178 Gd $988**
Sportsman-48F Premier grade . . . **NiB $6355 Ex $3988 Gd $2500**

MODEL 48SA SPORTSMAN SKEET GUN
Same general specifications as Sportsman-48A except has 26-inch bbl. w/matted top surface or vent. rib, SK choke, ivory bead front sight, metal bead rear sight. Made from 1949 to 1960.
w/plain bbl. . . . . **NiB $377 Ex $279 Gd $200**
w/vent. rib bbl. . . . . **NiB $466 Ex $344 Gd $229**
Sportsman-48SC Skeet . . . . **NiB $577 Ex $466 Gd $355**
Tournament grade . . . . **NiB $1688 Ex $1299 Gd $1100**
Sportsman-48SF Skeet
Premier grade . . . . **NiB $6220 Ex $4014 Gd $2444**

MODEL 11-48A RIOT GUN . . . . . **NiB $420 Ex $322 Gd $276**
Same as Model 11-48A except 20-inch plain bbl. and 12 ga. only. Disc. in 1969.

MODEL 11-48A STANDARD GRADE 4-ROUND AUTOLOADER .410 & 28 GAUGE
Same general specifications as Sportsman-48A except ga. 3-round magazine. 25-inch bbl. Weight: About 6.25 lbs. 28 ga. introduced 1952, .410 in 1954. Disc. in 1969. Values same as shown for Sportsman-48A.

MODEL 11-48A STANDARD GRADE AUTOLOADER
Same general specifications as Sportsman-48A except magazine holds four rounds, forend not grooved. Also available in Special Grade (11-48B), Tournament Grade (11-48D), and Premier Grade (11-48F). Made 1949 to 1969. Values same as for Sportsman-48A.

MODEL 11-48SA SKEET
28 GA. AND .410 . . . . **NiB $398 Ex $300 Gd $233**
Same general specifications as Model 11-48A 28 gauge except has 25-inch vent. rib bbl., SK choke. 28 ga. introduced 1952, .410 in 1954.

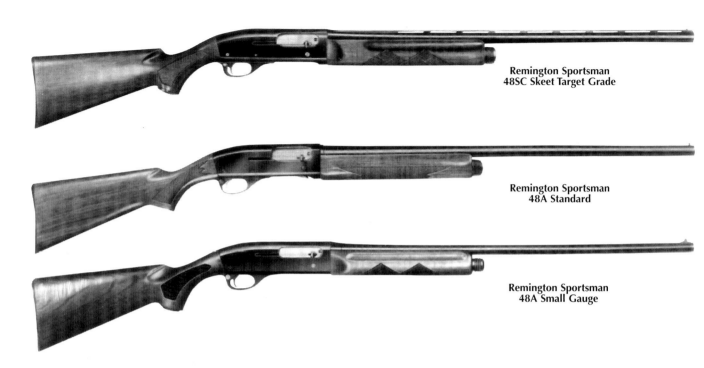

Remington Sportsman
48SC Skeet Target Grade

Remington Sportsman
48A Standard

Remington Sportsman
48A Small Gauge

SPORTSMAN-58 SKEET, TARGET, TOURNAMENT, AND PREMIER GRADES

These higher grade models differ from the Sportsman-58SA in general quality, grade of wood, checkering, engraving, and other refinements. General operating and physical specifications are the same.
Sportsman-58C Skeet Gun . . . . . . NiB $544 Ex $397 Gd $322
Sportsman-58D Tournament . . . . . NiB $1656 Ex $1267 Gd $1100
Sportsman-58SF Premier. . . . . NiB $6222 Ex $3566 Gd $2924

SPORTSMAN-58 TOURNAMENT AND PREMIER

These higher grade models differ from the Sportsman-58ADL w/vent. rib bbl. in general quality, grade of wood, checkering, engraving, etc. General specifications are the same.
Sportsman-58D Tournament . . . . NiB $1099 Ex $824 Gd $590
Sportsman-58F Premier . . . . . NiB $1889 Ex $1488 Gd $1051

MODEL 58ADL AUTOLOADER

Deluxe grade. Gas operated. 12 ga. 3-round magazine. Bbls.: Plain or vent. rib; 26, 28, or 30 inch; IC/M/F choke or Remington Special Skeet choke. Weight: About 7 lbs. Checkered pistol-grip stock and forearm. Made from 1956 to 1964.
w/plain bbl. . . . . NiB $366 Ex $267 Gd $188
w/vent. rib bbl. . . . . NiB $433 Ex $320 Gd $221

MODEL 58BDL DELUXE SPECIAL GRADE

Same as Model 58ADL except select grade wood.
w/plain bbl. . . . . NiB $544 Ex $422 Gd $338
w/vent. rib bbl. . . . . NiB $577 Ex $476 Gd $390

MODEL 58SADL

SKEET GRADE. . . . . NiB $588 Ex $432 Gd $338
Same general specifications as Model 58ADL w/vent. rib bbl. except special skeet stock and forearm.

REVELATION SHOTGUNS

See Western Auto listings.

RICHLAND ARMS COMPANY — Blissfield, MI

Manufactured in Italy and Spain.

MODEL 200
FIELD GRADE DOUBLE . . . . NiB $400 Ex $294 Gd $179
Hammerless, boxlock, Anson & Deeley-type. Plain extractors. Double triggers. Gauges: 12, 16, 20, 28, .410. 3-inch chambers in 20 and .410; others have 2.75-inch. Bbls.: 28-inch M/F choke, 26-inch IC/M; .410 w/26-inch M/F only; 22-inch IC/M in 20 ga. only. Weight: 6 lbs., 2 oz. to 7 lbs., 4 oz. Checkered walnut stock w/cheekpiece, pistol grip, recoil pad; beavertail forend. Made in Spain from 1963 to 1985.

MODEL 202
ALL PURPOSE FIELD GUN. . . . . . NiB $554 Ex $348 Gd $245
Hammerless, boxlock, Anson & Deeley-type. Same as Model 200 except has two sets of barrels same gauge. 12 ga.: 30-inch bbls. F/F, 3-inch chambers; 26-inch bbls. IC/M, 2.75-inch chambers. 20 gauge: 28-inch bbls. M/F; 22-inch bbls. IC/M, 3-inch chambers. Made from 1963. Disc.

MODEL 707
DELUXE FIELD GUN . . . . NiB $433 Ex $266 Gd $180
Hammerless, boxlock, triple bolting system. Plain extractors. Double triggers. Gauges: 12, 2.75-inch chambers; 20, 3-inch chambers. Bbls.: 12 ga., 28-inch M/F, 26-inch IC/M; 20 ga., 30-inch F/F, 28-inch M/F, 26-inch IC/M. Weight: 6 lbs., 4 oz. to 6 lbs., 15 oz. Checkered walnut stock and forend, recoil pad. Made from 1963 to 1972.

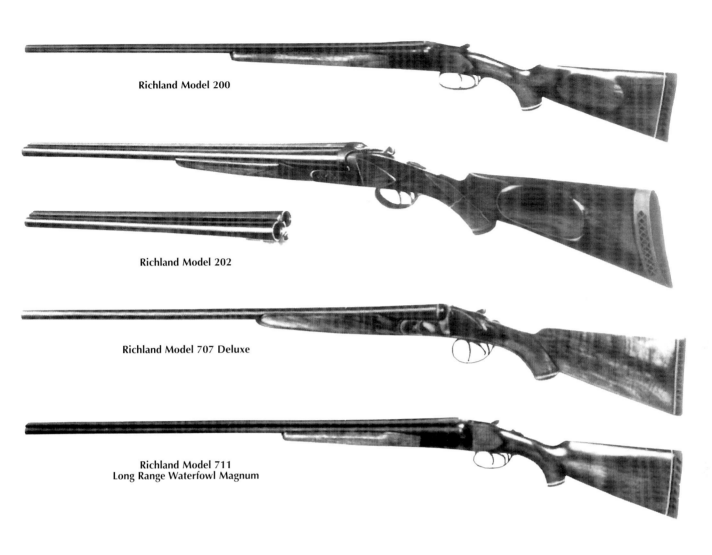

Richland Model 200

Richland Model 202

Richland Model 707 Deluxe

Richland Model 711
Long Range Waterfowl Magnum

MODEL 711 LONG-RANGE WATERFOWL MAGNUM DOUBLE-BARREL SHOTGUN
Hammerless, boxlock, Anson & Deeley-type, Purdey triple lock. Plain extractors. Double triggers. Auto safety. Gauges: 10, 3.5-inch chambers; 12, 3-inch chambers. Bbls.: 10 ga., 32-inch; 12 ga., 30-inch; F/F. Weight: 10 ga., 11 pounds; 12 ga., 7.75 lbs. Checkered walnut stock and beavertail forend; recoil pad. Made in Spain from 1963 to 1985.
10 ga. Mag. . . . . NiB $545 Ex $356 Gd $280
12 ga. Mag. . . . . NiB $566 Ex $377 Gd $300

MODEL 808
O/U SHOTGUN . . . . NiB $559 Ex $394 Gd $290
Boxlock. Plain extractors. Nonselective single trigger. 12 ga. only. Bbls. (Vickers steel): 30-inch F/F, 28-inch M/F, 26-inch IC/M. Weight: 6 lbs., 12 oz. to 7 lbs., 3 oz. Checkered walnut stock and forend. Made in Italy from 1963 to 1968.

JOHN RIGBY & CO. — London, England

HAMMERLESS BOXLOCK DOUBLE-BARREL SHOTGUN
Auto ejectors. Double triggers. Made in all ga., bbls., and chokes.

Rigby Regal
Side Lock

Checkered stock and forend, straight grip standard. Made in two grades: Sackville and Chatsworth. These guns differ in general quality, engraving, etc.; specifications are the same.
Sackville grade . . . . NiB $6450 Ex $4255 Gd $3790
Chatsworth grade . . . . NiB $4779 Ex $4109 Gd $3200

HAMMERLESS SIDELOCK DOUBLE-BARREL SHOTGUN
Auto ejectors. Double triggers. Made in all ga., bbls., and chokes. Checkered stock and forend, straight grip standard.

Made in two grades: Regal (best quality) and Sandringham; these guns differ in general quality, engraving, etc., specifications are the same.

Regal grade . . . .**NiB $13,677 Ex $11,773 Gd $9892**
Sandringham grade . . . . . .**NiB $11,088 Ex $9000 Gd $5698**

RIZZINI, BATTISTA — Marcheno, Italy

Rizzini was purchased by San Swiss AG IN 2002. Imported in the US by SIB Arms, Exeter, NH; William Larkin Moore & Co., Scottsdale, AZ; and New England Arms Co., Kittery, ME

AURUM O/U . . . .**NiB $2770 Ex $2243 Gd $2016**
Gauge: 12, 16, and 20. Boxlock action, light engraving. Case included. Introduced 1996.

AURUM LIGHT . . . .**NiB $4088 Ex $2867 Gd $2390**
Similaar to Aurum but 16 ga. only. Imported beginning in 2000.

ARTEMIS . . . .**NiB $2733 Ex $2270 Gd $1966**
Similar to Aurum but w/improved engraving and gold inlays.

ARTEMIS DELUXE . . . .**NiB $6777 Ex $3861 Gd $3223**
Similar to Artemis but w/detailed game scene engraving. Available in all ga.

ARTEMIS EL . . . .**NiB $17,776 Ex $14,600 Gd $12,980**
Same as Artemis Deluxe. Custom gun w/superior quality wood and detailed hand engraving. Disc. 2000.

MODEL 780 FIELD . . . .**NiB $2140 Ex $1088 Gd $977**
Gauge: 10, 12, or 16. Boxlock action, double triggers, extractors, walnut stock and forearm. Disc. 2000.
10 ga., add **$625**
Ejector model (S780EL), add **$200**
Single selective trigger w/ejectors, add **$250**
SST, ejectors, and upgraded stock, add **$425**

MODEL S780 EMEL . . . .**NiB $14,900 Ex $13,655 Gd $11,330**
Same as Model 780 Field but w/special engraving and hand finished.

MODEL 780 COMPETITION . . . .**NiB $1488 Ex $1276 Gd $1099**
Same as Model 780 Field but w/skeet, trap, or sporting clays features. Disc.1998.

MODEL 780
SMALL GAUGE SERIES . . . .**NiB $1388 Ex $1164 Gd $889**
Same as Model 780 Field but in 20, 28, or 36 ga. Double triggers, ejectors. Disc. 1998.

MODEL 782 EM FIELD . . . .**NiB $1566 Ex $1275 Gd $1074**
Gauge: 12 or 16. Boxlock action w/sideplates, single selective trigger, ejectors and extractors, walnut stock and forearm. Disc. 1998.
Model 782 EM Slug, add **$550**
Model 782 EML, add **$450**

MODEL S782 EMEL . . . .**NiB $14,990 Ex $11,860 Gd $10,066**
Same as Model 782 EM Field but specially engraved and hand finished.

MODEL S782 EMEL DELUXE . . . . .**NiB $13,899 Ex $11,776 Gd $10,066**
Gauge: 10, 12, 16, 20, 28, 36, and .410. Bbl.: 28-inch vent. rib w/ choke tubes (except .410); coin-finish engraving; gold inlays; fine scroll borders; deluxe English walnut stock. Imported 1994.

MODEL 790 COMPETITION . . . .**NiB $1877 Ex $1687 Gd $1261**
Gauge: 12 or 20. Available in trap, skeet, or sporting clays models. Black frame outlined w/gold line engraving. Disc. 1999.
20 ga. Sporting (sideplates and QD stock), add **$1200**
Trap model, 20 gauge, deduct **$200**

MODEL 790 SMALL GAUGE . . . .**NiB $1499 Ex $1179 Gd $1088**
Similar to Model 790 Competition but in 20, 29, or 36 ga. Single selective trigger, ejectors. Disc. 2000.

MODEL 790 EL . . . .**NiB $7088 Ex $4977 Gd $3766**
Same as Model 790 but hand finished w/18k gold inlays, hand engraving.

MODEL 790 EL . . . .**NiB $7132 Ex $4460 Gd $3477**
Same as Model 790 but w/multiple chokes, fitted case. Disc. 2000.

MODEL S790 EMEL DELUXE . . . .**NiB $12,970 Ex $10,088 Gd $8990**
Gauges: All. Custom gun w/27.5-inch vent. rib bbls. choke tubes (except .410); color casehardened or coin-finished receiver; ornate engraving w/Rizzini crest. Stock is deluxe English walnut; leather case included.

MODEL 792 SMALL GAUGE MAGNUM   **NiB $1791 Ex $1476 Gd $1199**
Gauge: 20, 28, or 36. Mag. chambers. Single selective trigger, ejectors, engraved sideplates. Disc. 1998.

MODEL 792 EMEL DELUXE . . . .**NiB $9133 Ex $8093 Gd $6166**
Same as Model 793 but hand finished w/18k gold inlays and hand engraving.

MODEL S792 EMEL . . . .**NiB $14,000 EX $11,980 GD $10,760**
Gauges: All. Custom gun w/27.5-inch vent. rib bbls. choke tubes (except .410); coin-finished receiver; sideplates w/fine game scene engraving and scroll borders; deluxe English walnut stock; leather case included. Imported 1994.

MODEL 2000 TRAP . . . .**NiB $1798 Ex $1448 Gd $1190**
Gauge: 12 only. Nickel-finished receiver; sideplates; gold trigger; vent. rib bbls. Disc 1998.

MODEL 2000 TRAP EL . . . .**NiB $5477 Ex $4100 Gd $3110**
Same as Model 2000 Trap but hand finished w/18k gold inlays and ornate hand engraving.

MODEL 2000-SP . . . .**NiB $3210 Ex $2976 Gd $2241**
Gauge: 12 only. Bbls.: 26, 29.5, or 32 inches. Over-bored barrels w/ choke tubes. Engraved sideplates, semi-fancy select QD stock. Case included. Imported 1994 to 1998.

PREMIER SPORTING. . . . .**NiB $2669 Ex $2280 Gd $1881**
Gauges: 12 or 20. Bbls.: 28, 29.5, or 32 inches. Five chokes per bbl. Custom built on request. Imported 1994

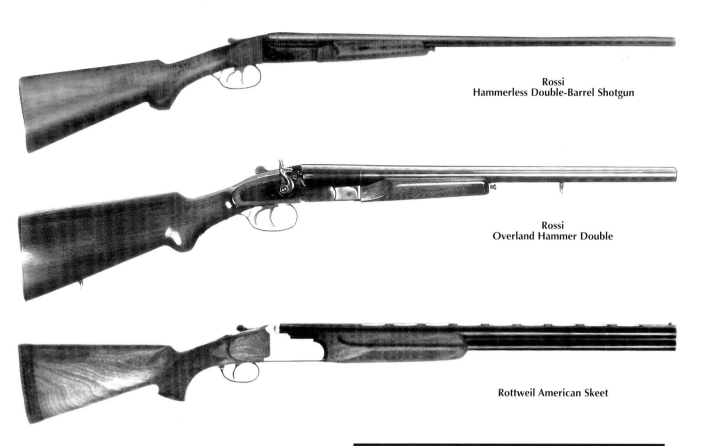

Rossi
Hammerless Double-Barrel Shotgun

Rossi
Overland Hammer Double

Rottweil American Skeet

SPORTING EL .NiB $3126 Ex $2390 Gd $2177
Same as Premier model but includes multiple chokes and fitted
case. Disc. 2000.

UPLAND EL .NiB $2793 Ex $2277 Gd $1965
Gauges: All. Custom gun w/27.5-inch vent. rib bbls. choke tubes
(except .410); casehardened receiver; deluxe walnut stock. Hard
case included. Imported 1994.

AMADEO ROSSI, S.A. — Sao Leopoldo, Brazil

**SQUIRE HAMMERLESS DOUBLE-
BARREL SHOTGUN**. . . . . .NiB $435 Ex $333 Gd $245
Boxlock. Plain extractors. Double triggers. 12 and 20 ga., .410.
3-inch chambers. Bbls.: 20-, 26-inch IC/M; 28-inch M/F choke.
Weight: 7 to 7.5 lbs. Pistol-grip hardwood stock and beavertail
forearm, uncheckered. Made 1985 to 1990.

**OVERLAND
HAMMER DOUBLE** . . . . NiB $380 Ex $244 Gd $179
Sidelock. Plain extractors. Double triggers. Gauges: 12, .410;
3-inch chambers. Bbls.: 20-inch, IC/M in 12 ga.; 26-inch, F/F
choke in .410. Weight: 7 lbs. (12 ga.); 6 lbs. (.410). Pistol-grip
stock and beavertail forearm, uncheckered. Note: Because of
its resemblance to the short-barreled doubles carried by guards
riding shotgun on 19th-century stagecoaches, the 12 ga. version originally was called the Coach Gun. Made 1968 to 1989.

ROTTWEIL — Germany

MODEL 72 O/U SHOTGUN. . . . . .NiB $1988 Ex $1687 Gd $1277
Hammerless, takedown w/engraved receiver. 12 ga. 2.75-
inch chambers. 26.75-inch bbls. w/SK/SK chokes. Weight:
7.5 lbs. Interchangeable trigger groups and buttstocks.
Checkered French walnut buttstock and forend. Imported
from Germany.

MODEL 650 FIELD O/U SHOTGUN . . . . . . .NiB $888 Ex $675 Gd $544
Breech action. Gauge: 12. 28-inch bbls. Six screw-in choke tubes.
Automatic ejectors. Engraved receiver. Checkered pistol grip stock.
Made from 1984 to 1986.

AMERICAN SKEET . . . . NiB $2010 Ex $1798 Gd $1288
Boxlock action. Gauge: 12. 27-inch vent. rib bbls. 44.5 inches
overall. SK chokes. Weight: 7.5 lbs. Designed for tube sets.
Hand-checkered European walnut stock w/modified forend.
Made from 1984 to 1987.

**INTERNATIONAL
TRAP SHOTGUN**. . . . . NiB $2066 Ex $1799 Gd $1263
Box lock action. Gauge: 12. 30-inch bbls. 48.5 inches overall.
Weight: 8 lbs. Choked IM/F. Selective single trigger. Metal bead
front sight. Checkered European walnut stock w/pistol grip.
Engraved action. Made from 1984 to 1987.

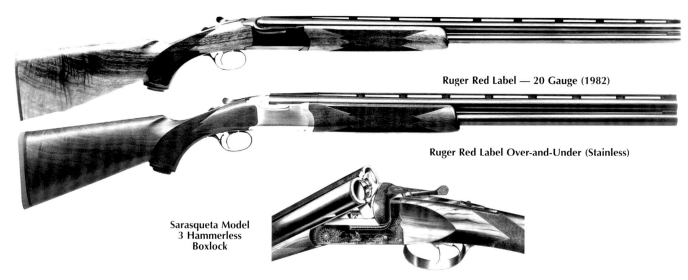

Ruger Red Label — 20 Gauge (1982)

Ruger Red Label Over-and-Under (Stainless)

Sarasqueta Model
3 Hammerless
Boxlock

SAIGA — Manufactured by Izhmash in Izhevsk, Russia

Last imported by RWC Group, Tullytown, PA, in 2015; currently manufactured by RWC Group under license from Izhmash.

SAIGA-12
AK-style action, gas-operated piston, semiauto w/detachable 5-round magazine. 12 or 20 ga. 3-inch chamber. Bbl.: 19- or 22-inch w/ choke tubes (12 ga. only). Stock: Black synthetic. Finish: Matte black. Weight: 6.7 to 10 lbs. Imported 2002 to 2004, reintroduced 2006 to 2014. Importation banned since 2014 due to US sanctions.
12 or 20 ga. . . . . NiB $780 Ex $500 Gd $300
.410 . . . . NiB $646 Ex $415 Gd $250
Hunting Model (Monte Carlo-style stock
  in wood or synthetic). . . . . NiB $885 Ex $580 Gd $360
Skeletonized stock . . . . NiB $994 Ex $660 Gd $400
Tactical (AR15 style stock,
  10 round magazine). . . . . NiB $1239 Ex $1115 Gd $734

STURM, RUGER & COMPANY, INC. — Southport, CT

RED LABEL STANDARD GRADE
O/U boxlock. Auto ejectors. Selective single trigger. 12, 20, or 28 ga. 2.75- or 3-inch chambers. 26-inch vent. rib bbl., IC/M or SK choke. Single selective trigger. Selective automatic ejectors. Automatic top safety. Standard gold bead front sight. Pistol-grip or English-style American walnut stock and forearm w/hand-cut checkering. The 20 ga. model was introduced in 1977, 12 ga. version in 1982, and the stainless receiver became standard in 1985. Choke tubes were optional in 1988 and standard in 1990. Weight: 7 to 7.5 lbs.
w/fixed chokes . . . . NiB $1733 Ex $1388 Gd $1077
w/screw-in tubes . . . . NiB $1760 Ex $1410 Gd $1100
w/grade 1 engraving. . . . . NiB $1893 Ex $1421 Gd $1107
w/grade 2 engraving . . . . NiB $2298 Ex $2100 Gd $1733
w/grade 3 engraving . . . . NiB $2798 Ex $2255 Gd $2100

RED LABEL O/U ALL-WEATHER STAINLESS
Gauges: 12 ga. only. Bbls.: 26, 28, or 30-inch w/various chokes, fixed or screw-in tubes. Stainless receiver and barrel. Checkered black synthetic stock and forearm. Weight: 7.5 lbs. Made 1999 to 2006.
All-weather stainless model . . . NiB $1387 Ex $1189 Gd $900
w/30-inch bbl., add $200

RED LABEL WOODSIDE
Similar to the Red Label O/U Stainless except in 12 ga. only w/ wood sideplate extensions. Made from 1995 to 2002. Disc.
Standard . . . . NiB $1687 Ex $1445 Gd $1110
Engraved . . . . NiB $2389 Ex $1955 Gd $1533

RED LABEL SPORTING CLAYS
Similar to the standard Red Label model except chambered 12 or 20 ga. only. 30-inch vent. rib bbls., no side ribs; back-bored w/ screw-in choke tubes (not interchangeable w/other Red Label O/U models). Brass front and mid-rib beads. Made from 1992 to date.
Standard . . . . NiB $1766 Ex $1288 Gd $998
Engraved . . . . NiB $2680 Ex $2110 Gd $1590

RED LABEL WILDLIFE FOREVER SPECIAL EDITION
Limited edition commemorating the 50th Wildlife Forever anniversary. Similar to the standard Red Label model except chambered 12 ga. only. Engraved receiver enhanced w/gold mallard and pheasant inlays. 300 produced in 1993.
Special edition . . . . NiB $1690 Ex $1655 Gd $1299
Special edition w/hard case, add $200

GOLD LABEL . . . . NiB $3650 Ex $2288 Gd $1060
S/S boxlock. Auto ejectors. Selective single trigger. 12 ga. 3-inch chambers. 28-inch solid rib bbl., choke tubes. Top safety. Pistol-grip or English-style American walnut stock and forearm w/hand-cut checkering. Stainless receiver. Made from 2002 to 2008.

VICTOR SARASQUETA, S. A. — Eibar, Spain

MODEL 3 HAMMERLESS
BOXLOCK DOUBLE-BARREL SHOTGUN
Plain extractors or auto ejectors. Double triggers. Gauges: 12, 16, 20. Made in various bbl., chokes, and weights. Checkered stock and forend, straight grip standard. Imported from 1985 to 1987.
Model 3, plain extractors . . . . NiB $599 Ex $445 Gd $329
Model 3E, automatic ejectors . . . NiB $655 Ex $500 Gd $435

HAMMERLESS SIDELOCK DOUBLES
Automatic ejectors except on Models 4 and 203, which have plain extractors. Double triggers. Gauges: 12, 16, 20. Bbls., chokes, and weights made to order. Checkered stock and forend, straight grip standard. Models differ chiefly in overall quality, engraving, grade of wood, checkering, etc.; general specifications are the same. Imported from 1985 to 1987.

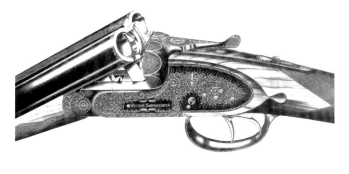

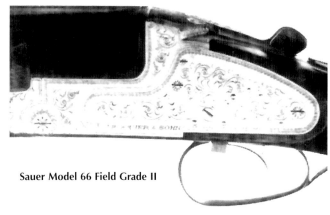

Sauer Model 66 Field Grade II

Sauer Model 66 Field Grade III

Sarasqueta Models 6E, 11E, and 12E

Model 4	NiB $779	Ex $643	Gd $441
Model 4E	NiB $879	Ex $754	Gd $570
Model 203	NiB $744	Ex $600	Gd $435
Model 203E	NiB $800	Ex $632	Gd $544
Model 6E	NiB $1388	Ex $1108	Gd $700
Model 7E	NiB $1443	Ex $1156	Gd $965
Model 10E	NiB $2588	Ex $2188	Gd $1966
Model 11E	NiB $2800	Ex $2577	Gd $2234
Model 12E	NiB $3110	Ex $2770	Gd $2369

J. P. SAUER & SOHN — Eckernförde (formerly Suhl), Germany

MODEL 66 O/U FIELD GUN

Purdey-system action w/Holland & Holland-type sidelocks. Selective single trigger. Selective auto ejectors. Automatic safety. Available in three grades of engraving. 12 ga. only. Krupp special steel bbls. w/vent. rib 28-inch, M/F choke. Weight: About 7.25 lbs. Checkered walnut stock and forend; recoil pad. Made from 1966 to 1975.

Grade I	NiB $2377	Ex $2120	Gd $1798
Grade II	NiB $3256	Ex $2460	Gd $2190
Grade III	NiB $4100	Ex $3712	Gd $2644

MODEL 66 O/U SKEET GUN

Same as Model 66 Field Gun except 26-inch bbls. w/wide vent. rib, SK choked skeet-style stock and vent. beavertail forearm; nonautomatic safety. Made from 1966 to 1975.

Grade I	NiB $2312	Ex $2198	Gd $1655
Grade II	NiB $3270	Ex $2980	Gd $2110
Grade III	NiB $3988	Ex $3655	Gd $2980

MODEL 66 O/U TRAP GUN

Same as Model 66 Skeet Gun except has 30-inch bbls. choked F/F or M/F; trap-style stock. Values same as for Skeet model. Made from 1966 to 1975.

MODEL 3000E DRILLING

Combination rifle and double bbl. shotgun. Blitz action w/Greener crossbolt, double underlugs, separate rifle cartridge extractor, front set trigger, firing pin indicators. Greener side safety, sear slide selector locks right shotgun bbl. for firing rifle bbl. Gauge/calibers: 12 ga. (2.75-inch chambers); .222, .243, .30-06, 7x65R. 25-inch Krupp special steel bbls.; M/F choke automatic folding leaf rear rifle sight. Weight: 6.5 to 7.25 lbs. depending on rifle caliber. Checkered walnut stock and forend; pistol grip, Monte Carlo comb, and cheekpiece, sling swivels. Standard model w/Arabesque engraving; Deluxe model w/hunting scenes engraved on action. Currently manufactured. Note: Also see listing under Colt.

Standard model	NiB $4490	Ex $3891	Gd $2776
Deluxe model	NiB $5782	Ex $4669	Gd $3533

ARTEMIS DOUBLE-BARREL SHOTGUN
Holland & Holland-type sidelock with Greener crossbolt, double underlugs, double sear safeties, selective single trigger, selective auto ejectors. Grade I w/fine-line engraving, Grade II w/full English Arabesque engraving. 12 ga. (2.75-inch chambers). Krupp special steel bbls., 28-inch, M/F choke. Weight: About 6.5 lbs. Checkered walnut pistol-grip stock and beavertail forend; recoil pad. Made from1966 to 1977.

Grade I . . . . NiB $5698 Ex $4766 Gd $4133
Grade II . . . . NiB $6880 Ex $5744 Gd $4500

BBF 54 O/U COMBINATION RIFLE/SHOTGUN
Blitz action w/Kersten lock, front set trigger fires rifle bbl., slide-operated sear safety. Gauge/calibers: 16 ga., .30-30, .30-06, 7x65R. 25-inch Krupp special steel bbls.; shotgun bbl. F choke, folding-leaf rear sight. Weight: About 6 lbs. Checkered walnut stock and forend; pistol grip, mod. Monte Carlo comb and cheekpiece, sling swivels. Standard model w/Arabesque engraving; Deluxe model w/hunting scenes engraved on action. Currently manufactured.

Standard model . . . . NiB $2977 Ex $2455 Gd $1766
Deluxe model . . . . NiB $3566 Ex $3088 Gd $2655

ROYAL DOUBLE-BARREL SHOTGUNS
Anson & Deeley action (boxlock) w/Greener crossbolt, double underlugs, signal pins, selective single trigger, selective auto ejectors, auto safety. Scalloped frame w/Arabesque engraving. Krupp special steel bbls. Gauges: 12, 2.75-inch chambers; 20, 3-inch chambers. Bbls.: 30-inch (12 ga. only); 28-inch, M/F; 26-inch (20 ga. only), IC/M. Weight: 12 ga., about 6.5 lbs.; 20 ga., 6 lbs. Checkered walnut pistol-grip stock and beavertail forend; recoil pad. Made from 1955 to 1977.

Standard model . . . . NiB $1790 Ex $1533 Gd $1206
20 ga., add 20%

SAVAGE ARMS — Westfield, MA

Formerly located in Utica, NY

MODEL 24C .22/.410 O/U
COMBINATION . . . . NiB $570 Ex $388 Gd $245
Same as Stevens No. 22-.410 w/walnut stock and forearm. Made from 1950 to 1965.

MODEL 24C
CAMPER'S COMPANION . . . . NiB $675 Ex $466 Gd $290
Same as Model 24FG except made in .22 Magnum/20 ga. only; has 20-inch bbls., shotgun tube Cyl. bore. Weight: 5.75 lbs. Trap in butt provides ammunition storage; comes with carrying case. Made 1972 to 1989.

MODEL 24 FIELD . . . . NiB $498 Ex $277 Gd $190
Same as Models 24DL and 24MDL except frame has black or casehardened finish. Game scene decoration of frame eliminated in 1974; forearm uncheckered after 1976. Made from 1970 to 1989.

MODEL 24DL . . . . NiB $400 Ex $366 Gd $243
Same general specifications as Model 24S except top-lever opening; satin-chrome-finished frame decorated w/game scenes, checkered Monte Carlo stock and forearm. Made from 1962 to 1965.

MODEL 24F-12T TURKEY GUN . . . . NiB $700 Ex $488 Gd $337
12- or 20-ga. shotgun bbl./.22 Hornet, .223, or .30-30 caliber rifle. 24-inch blued bbls. 3-inch chambers, extra removable F choke tube. Hammer block safety. Color casehardened frame. DuPont Rynite camo stock. Swivel studs. Made from 1989 to 2007.

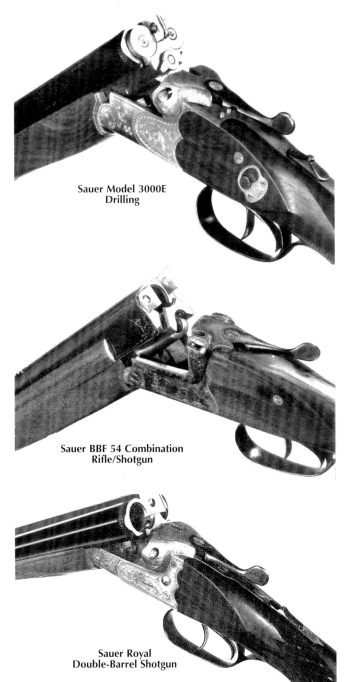

Sauer Model 3000E
Drilling

Sauer BBF 54 Combination
Rifle/Shotgun

Sauer Royal
Double-Barrel Shotgun

MODEL 24FG FIELD GRADE . . . . NiB $525 Ex $433 Gd $276
Same general specifications as Model 24S except top lever opening. Made 1972. Disc.

MODEL 24MDL . . . . NiB $577 Ex $400 Gd $229
Same as Model 24DL except rifle bbl. chambered for 22 WMR. Made from 1962 to 1969.

MODEL 24MS . . . . NiB $690 Ex $535 Gd $389
Same as Model 24S except rifle bbl. chambered for 22 WMR. Made from 1964 to 1971.

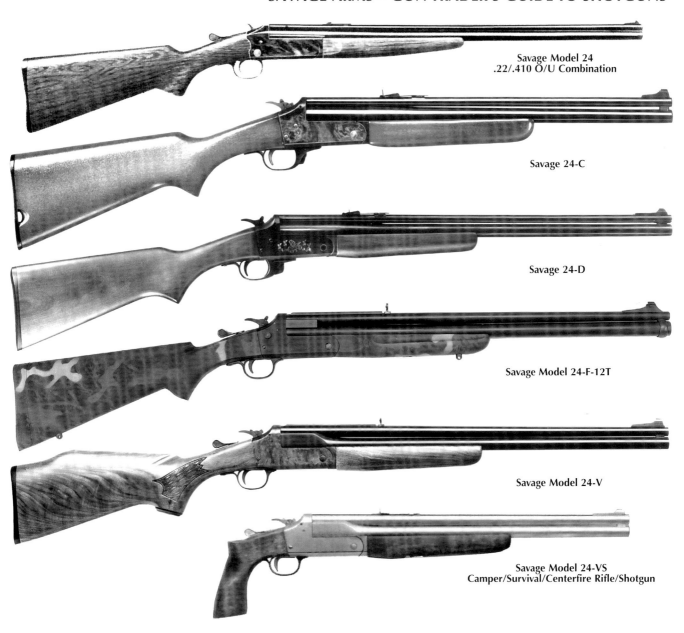

Savage Model 24
.22/.410 O/U Combination

Savage 24-C

Savage 24-D

Savage Model 24-F-12T

Savage Model 24-V

Savage Model 24-VS
Camper/Survival/Centerfire Rifle/Shotgun

MODEL 24S O/U
COMBINATION . . . . **NiB $477 Ex $339 Gd $225**
Boxlock. Visible hammer. Side lever opening. Plain extractors. Single trigger. 20 ga. or .410 bore shotgun bbl. under 22 LR bbl., 24-inch. Open rear sight, ramp front, dovetail for scope mounting. Weight: About 6.75 lbs. Plain pistol-grip stock and forearm. Made from 1964 to 1971.

MODEL 24V . . . . **NiB $588 Ex $379 Gd $298**
Similar to Model 24D except 20 ga. under .222 Rem., .22 Rem., .357 Mag., .22 Hornet, or .30-30 rifle bbl. Made 1967 to 1989.

MODEL 24-CS CAMPER'S COMPANION
CENTERFIRE RIFLE/SHOTGUN . . . **NiB $680 Ex $389 Gd $319**
Caliber: .22 LR over 20 ga. Nickel finish full-length stock, accessory pistol-grip stock. Overall length: 36 inches w/full stock; 26 inches w/pistol grip. Weight: About 5.75 lbs. Made 1972 to 1988.
.357 Mag./20 ga., add. **$50**

MODEL 28A STANDARD GRADE SLIDE-ACTION REPEATING
SHOTGUN. . . . . **NiB $445 Ex $398 Gd $300**
Hammerless. Takedown. 12 ga. 5-round tubular magazine. Plain bbl., lengths: 26, 28, 30, 32 inch, choked C/M/F. Weight: About 7.5 lbs. w/30-inch bbl. Plain pistol-grip stock, grooved slide handle. Made from 1928 to 1931.

MODEL 28B . . . . **NiB $366 Ex $287 Gd $245**
Raised matted rib; otherwise the same as Model 28A.

MODEL 28D TRAP GRADE. . . . . . . **NiB $366 Ex $287 Gd $245**
Same general specifications as Model 28A except has 30-inch F choke bbl. w/matted rib, trap-style stock w/checkered pistol grip, checkered slide handle of select walnut.

MODEL 30 SOLID FRAME HAMMERLESS
SLIDE-ACTION SHOTGUN . . . . . **NiB $290 Ex $221 Gd $175**
Gauges: 12, 16, 20, .410. 2.75-inch chamber in 16 ga., 3-inch in other ga. Magazine holds four 2.75-inch shells or three 3-inch

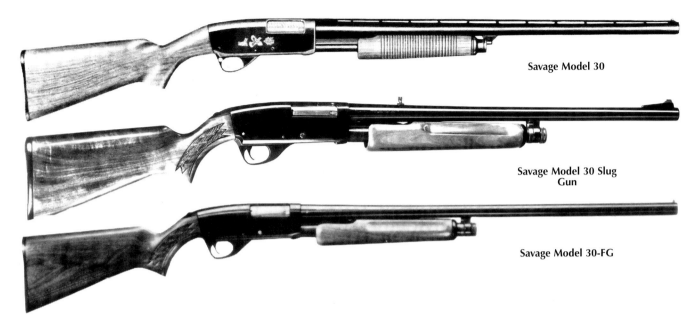

Savage Model 30

Savage Model 30 Slug Gun

Savage Model 30-FG

shells. Bbls.: Vent. rib; 26, 28, 30 inch; IC/M/F choke. Weight: Average 6.25 to 6.75 lbs. depending on ga. Plain pistol-grip stock (checkered on later production), grooved slide handle. Made from 1958 to 1970.

MODEL 30 TAKEDOWN SLUG GUN. . . NiB $255 Ex $175 Gd $125
Same as Model 30FG except 21-inch Cyl. bore bbl. w/rifle sights. Made from 1971 to 1979.

MODEL 30AC SOLID FRAME. . . . NiB $379 Ex $288 Gd $179
Same as Model 30 Solid Frame except has 26-inch bbl. w/adj. choke; 12 ga. only. Made from 1959 to 1970.

MODEL 30AC TAKEDOWN . . . . . NiB $366 Ex $265 Gd $160
Same as Model 30FG except has 26-inch bbl. w/adj. choke; 12 and 20 ga. only. Made from 1971 to 1972.

MODEL 30D TAKEDOWN . . . . . . NiB $277 Ex $200 Gd $167
Deluxe Grade. Same as Model 30FG except has receiver engraved w/game scene, vent. rib bbl., recoil pad. Made from 1971. Disc.

MODEL 30FG TAKEDOWN HAMMERLESS
SLIDE-ACTION SHOTGUN . . . . . . NiB $265 Ex $180 Gd $95
Field Grade. Gauges: 12, 20, .410. 3-inch chamber. Magazine holds four 2.75-inch shells or three 3-inch shells. Bbls.: Plain; 26-inch F choke (.410 ga. only); 28-inch M/F choke; 30-inch F choke (12 ga. only). Weight: Average 7 to 7.75 lbs. depending on ga. Checkered pistol-grip stock, fluted slide handle. Made 1970 to 1979.

MODEL 30L SOLID FRAME . . . . . NiB $300 Ex $241 Gd $176
Same as Model 30 Solid Frame except left-handed model w/ejection port and safety on left side; 12 ga. only. Made 1959 to 1970.

MODEL 30T SOLID FRAME
TRAP AND DUCK . . . . NiB $377 Ex $288 Gd $190
Same as Model 30 Solid Frame except only in 12 ga. w/30-inch F choke bbl.; has Monte Carlo stock w/recoil pad. Weight: About 8 lbs. Made from 1963 to 1970.

MODEL 30T TAKEDOWN
TRAP GUN . . . . NiB $335 Ex $292 Gd $197
Same as Model 30D except only in 12 ga. w/30-inch F choke bbl. Monte Carlo stock w/recoil pad. Made from 1970 to 1973.

MODEL 69-RXL SLIDE-ACTION
SHOTGUN . . . . NiB $366 Ex $256 Gd $190
Similar to Model 67 (law enforcement configuration). Hammerless, side ejection top tang safe for left- or right-hand use. 12 ga. chambered for 2.75- and 3-inch Mag. shells. 18.25-inch bbl. Tubular magazine holds six rounds (one fewer for 3-inch Mag.). Walnut finish hardwood stock w/recoil pad and grooved operating handle. Weight: About 6.5 lbs. Made from 1982 to 1989.

MODEL 210F BOLT-ACTION
SLUG GUN. . . . . NiB $490 Ex $377 Gd $290
Built on Savage 110 action. Gauge: 12. 3-inch chamber. 2-round detachable magazine. 24-inch fully rifled bbl. Receiver drilled and tapped for scope mounts w/no sights. Weight: 7.5 lbs. Checkered black synthetic stock w/swivel studs and recoil pad. Made from 1997 to 2000.

MODEL 210FT BOLT-ACTION SHOTGUN. . . NiB $599 Ex $459 Gd $335
Similar to Model 210F except has smoothbore 24-inch bbl. w/ choke tubes. Bead front and U-notch rear sights. Advantage Camo finish. Made from 1997 to 2000. MODEL 220 SINGLE-BARREL SHOTGUN . . . . NiB $590 Ex $386 Gd $265
Hammerless. Takedown. Auto ejector. Gauges: 12,16, 20 .410. Single shot. Bbl.: 12 ga., 28- to 36-inch; 16 ga., 28- to 32-inch; 20 ga., 26- to 32-inch; .410 bore, 26- to 28-inch. F choke. Weight: About 6 lbs. Plain pistol-grip stock and wide forearm. Made 1938 to 1965.

MODEL 220AC. . . . . NiB $490 Ex $255 Gd $190
Same as Model 220 except has Savage adj. choke.
MODEL 220L . . . . NiB $490 Ex $388 Gd $229
Same general specifications as Model 220 except has side lever opening instead of top lever. Made from 1965 to 1972.

MODEL 220P . . . . NiB $490 Ex $388 Gd $229
Same as Model 220 except has PolyChoke bbl., made in 12 ga. with 30-inch bbl., 16 and 20 ga. w/28-inch bbl., no .410 bore; recoil pad.

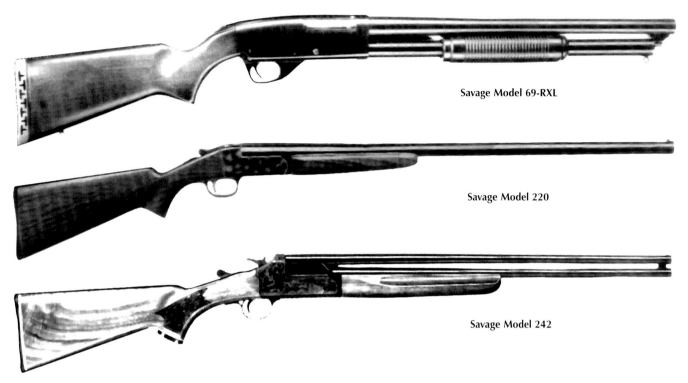

Savage Model 69-RXL

Savage Model 220

Savage Model 242

MODEL 242 O/U SHOTGUN. . . . NiB $498 Ex $376 Gd $292
Similar to Model 24D except both bbls. .410 bore, F choke.
Weight: About 7 lbs. Made from 1977 to 1980.

MODEL 312 FIELD GRADE O/U . . . . NiB $688 Ex $554 Gd $400
Gauge: 12. 2.75- or 3-inch chambers. 26- or 28-inch bbls. w/vent.
rib; F/M/IC chokes. 43 or 45 inches overall. Weight: 7 lbs. Internal
hammers. Top tang safety. American walnut stock w/checkered
pistol grip and recoil pad. Made from 1990 to 1993.

MODEL 312 SPORTING CLAYS O/U . . . . NiB $688 Ex $578 Gd $445
Same as Model 312 Field Grade except furnished w/number 1
and number 2 Skeet tubes and 28-inch bbls. only. Made 1990
to 1993.

MODEL 312 TRAP O/U . . . . NiB $756 Ex $600 Gd $477
Same as Model 312 Field Grade except w/30-inch bbls. only,
Monte Carlo buttstock. Weight: 7.5 lbs. Made from 1990 to 1993.

MODEL 330 O/U SHOTGUN. . . . NiB $589 Ex $477 Gd $398
Boxlock. Plain extractors. Selective single trigger. Gauges: 12, 20.
2.75-inch chambers in 12 ga., 3-inch in 20 gauge. Bbls.: 26-inch
IC/M; 28-inch M/F; 30-inch M/F choke (12 ga. only). Weight: 6.25
to 7.25 lbs. depending on ga. Checkered pistol-grip stock and
forearm. Made from 1969 to 1978.

MODEL 333 O/U SHOTGUN
Boxlock. Auto ejectors. Selective single trigger. Gauges: 12, 20.
2.75-inch chambers in 12 ga., 3-inch in 20 ga. Bbls.: vent. rib;
26-inch SK choke, IC/M; 28-inch M/F; 30-inch M/F choke (12 ga.
only). Weight: Average 6.25 to 7.25 lbs. Checkered pistol-grip
stock and forearm. Made from 1973 to 1979.
12 ga. . . . . NiB $598 Ex $467 Gd $366
20 ga., add 30%

MODEL 333T TRAP GUN. . . . . . . NiB $654 Ex $498 Gd $396
Similar to Model 330 except only in 12 ga. w/30-inch vent. rib

bbls., IM/F choke; Monte Carlo stock w/recoil pad. Weight: 7.75
lbs. Made from 1972 to 1979.

MODEL 420 O/U SHOTGUN
Boxlock. Hammerless. Takedown. Automatic safety. Double triggers or nonselective single trigger. Gauges: 12, 16, 20. Bbls.:
Plain, 26 to 30 inch (the latter in 12 ga. only); choked M/F, C/
IC. Weight w/28-inch bbls.: 12 ga., 7.75 lbs.; 16 ga., 7.5 lbs.;
20 ga., 6.75 lbs. Plain pistol-grip stock and forearm. Made from
1938 to 1942.
w/double triggers . . . . NiB $589 Ex $477 Gd $300
w/single trigger . . . . NiB $633 Ex $498 Gd $376

MODEL 430
Same as Model 420 except has matted top bbl., checkered
stock of select walnut w/recoil pad, checkered forearm. Made
from 1938 to 1942.
w/double triggers . . . . NiB $677 Ex $544 Gd $390
w/single trigger . . . . NiB $677 Ex $559 Gd $443

MODEL 440 O/U SHOTGUN. . . . NiB $635 Ex $490 Gd $387
Boxlock. Plain extractors. Selective single trigger. Gauges: 12,
20. 2.75-inch chambers in 12 ga., 3-inch in 20 ga. Bbls.: Vent.
rib; 26-inch SK choke, IC/M; 28-inch M/F; 30-inch M/F choke
(12 ga. only). Weight: Average 6 to 6.5 lbs. depending on ga.
Made from 1968 to 1972.

MODEL 440T TRAP GUN. . . . . . . NiB $598 Ex $488 Gd $392
Similar to Model 440 except only in 12 ga. w/30-inch bbls.,
extra-wide vent. rib, IM/F choke. Trap-style Monte Carlo stock and
semibeavertail forearm of select walnut, recoil pad. Weight: 7.5
lbs. Made from 1969 to 1972.

**MODEL 444 DELUXE
O/U SHOTGUN . . . . NiB $687 Ex $500 Gd $369**
Similar to Model 440 except has auto ejectors, select walnut
stock, and semi-beavertail forearm. Made from 1969 to 1972.

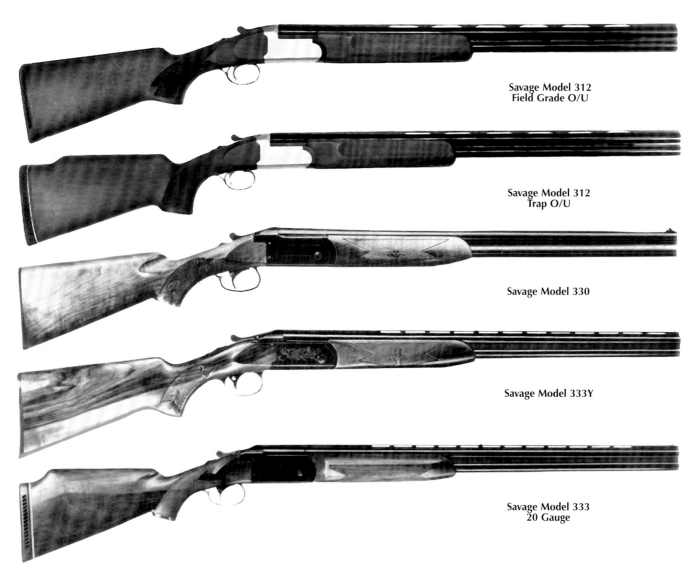

Savage Model 312
Field Grade O/U

Savage Model 312
Trap O/U

Savage Model 330

Savage Model 333Y

Savage Model 333
20 Gauge

MODEL 550

HAMMERLESS DOUBLE . . . . **NiB $355 Ex $290 Gd $200**
Boxlock. Auto ejectors. Nonselective single trigger. Gauges: 12, 20. 2.75-inch chamber in 12 ga., 3-inch in 20 ga. Bbls.: Vent. rib; 26-inch IC/M; 28-inch M/F; 30-inch M/F choke (12 ga. only). Weight: 7 to 8 lbs. Checkered pistol-grip stock and semi-beavertail forearm. Made 1971 to 1973.

MODEL 720 STANDARD GRADE 5-SHOT AUTOLOADING

SHOTGUN . . . . **NiB $335 Ex $269 Gd $200**
Browning type. Takedown. 12 and 16 ga. 4-round tubular magazine. Bbl.: Plain; 26- to 32-inch (the latter in 12 ga. only); choked IC/M/F. Weight: About 8.25 lbs., 12 ga. w/30-inch bbl.; 16 ga., about .5 lb. lighter. Checkered pistol-grip stock and forearm. Made from 1930 to 1949.

MODEL 726 UPLAND SPORTER AUTO

SHOTGUN . . . . **NiB $377 Ex $292 Gd $233**
Same as Model 720 except has 2-round magazine capacity. Made from 1931 to 1949.

MODEL 740C SKEET GUN . . . . . **NiB $410 Ex $300 Gd $237**
Same as Model 726 except has special skeet stock and full beavertail forearm, equipped w/Cutts Compensator. Bbl. length overall w/spreader tube is about 24.5 inches. Made from 1936 to 1949.

MODEL 745 LIGHTWEIGHT

AUTOLOADER . . . . **NiB $377 Ex $266 Gd $198**
3- or 5-round models. Same general specifications as Model 720 except has lightweight alloy receiver, 12 ga. only. 28-inch plain bbl. Weight: About 6.75 lbs. Made from 1940 to 1949.

MODEL 750

AUTO SHOTGUN. . . . . **NiB $355 Ex $287 Gd $239**
Browning-type autoloader. Takedown. 12 ga. 4-round tubular magazine. Bbls.: 28-inch F/M choke; 26-inch IC. Weight: About 7.25 lbs. Checkered walnut pistol-grip stock and grooved forearm. Made from 1960 to 1967.

MODEL 750-AC . . . . **NiB $377 Ex $280 Gd $210**
Same as Model 750 except has 26-inch bbl. w/adj. choke. Made from 1964 to 1967.

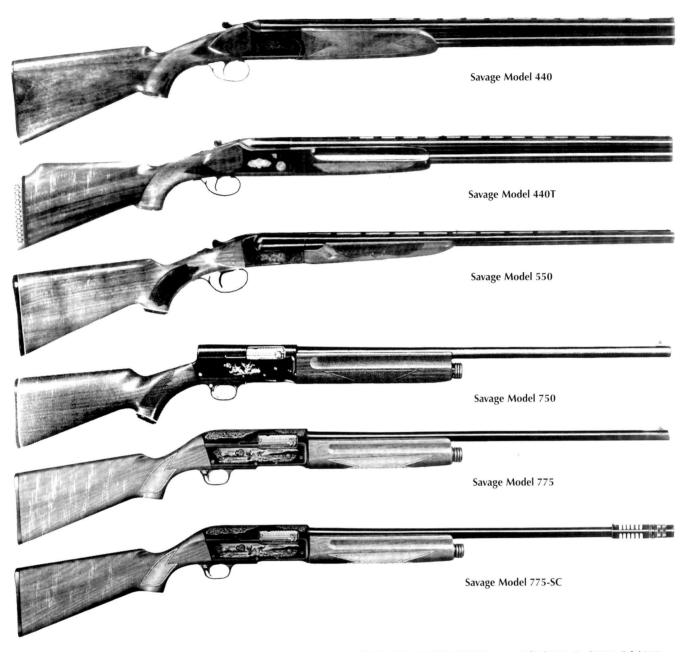

Savage Model 440

Savage Model 440T

Savage Model 550

Savage Model 750

Savage Model 775

Savage Model 775-SC

MODEL 750-SC . . . . **NiB $368 Ex $267 Gd $198**
Same as Model 750 except has 26-inch bbl. w/Savage Super Choke. Made from 1962 to 1963.

MODEL 755 STANDARD
GRADE AUTOLOADER. . . . . **NiB $389 Ex $297 Gd $245**
Streamlined receiver. Takedown.12 and 16 ga. 4-round tubular magazine (a 3-round model w/magazine capacity of two rounds was also produced until 1951). Bbl.: Plain, 30-inch F choke (12 ga. only), 28-inch F/M, 26-inch IC. Weight: About 8.25 lbs., 12 ga. Checkered pistol-grip stock and forearm. Made from 1949 to 1958.

MODEL 755-SC . . . . **NiB $389 Ex $297 Gd $245**
Same as Model 755 except has 26-inch bbl. w/recoil-reducing adj. Savage Super Choke.

MODEL 775 LIGHTWEIGHT . . . . **NiB $389 Ex $297 Gd $245**
Same general specifications as Model 755 except has lightweight alloy receiver. Weight: About 6.73 lbs. Made from 1950 to 1965.

MODEL 775-SC . . . . **NiB $410 Ex $300 Gd $255**
Same as Model 775 except has 26-inch bbl. w/Savage Super Choke.

MODEL 2400 O/U
COMBINATION . . . . **NiB $775 Ex $577 Gd $450**
Boxlock action similar to that of Model 330. Plain extractors. Selective single trigger. 12-ga. (2.75-inch chamber) shotgun bbl., F choke over .308 Win. or .222 Rem. rifle bbl.; 23.5-inch; solid matted rib with blade front sight and folding leaf rear, dovetail for scope mounting. Weight: About 7.5 lbs. Monte Carlo stock w/pistol grip and recoil pad, semibeavertail forearm, checkered. Made 1975 to 1979 by Valmet.

**Savage Model 2400
O/U Combination Gun**

SEARS, ROEBUCK & COMPANY — Chicago, IL

J. C. Higgins and Ted Williams Models

Although they do not correspond to specific models below, the names Ted Williams and J. C. Higgins have been used to designate various Sears shotguns at various times.

MODEL 18
BOLT-ACTION REPEATER . . . . **NiB $200 Ex $125 Gd $90**
Takedown. 3-round top-loading magazine. Gauge: .410 only. Bbl.: 25 inch w/variable choke. Weight: About 5.75 lbs.

MODEL 20 SLIDE-ACTION REPEATER. . . . **NiB $300 Ex $210 Gd $155**
Hammerless. 5-round magazine. Bbls.: 26 to 30 inch w/various chokes. Weight: 7.25 lbs. Plain pistol-grip stock and slide handle.

MODEL 21 SLIDE-ACTION REPEATER . . . . . **NiB $320 Ex $235 Gd $190**
Same general specifications as the Model 20 except vent. rib and adj. choke.

MODEL 30 SLIDE-ACTION REPEATER . . . . . **NiB $305 Ex $220 Gd $175**
Hammerless. Gauges: 12, 16, 20, and .410. 4-round magazine. Bbls.: 26 to 30 inch, various chokes. Weight: 6.5 lbs. Plain pistol-grip stock, grooved slide handle.

MODEL 97 SINGLE-SHOT SHOTGUN. . . . **NiB $165 Ex $100 Gd $79**
Takedown. Visible hammer. Automatic ejector. Gauges: 12, 16, 20, and .410. Bbls.: 26 to 36 inch, F choke. Weight: Average 6 lbs. Plain pistol-grip stock and forearm.

MODEL 97-AC SINGLE-SHOT SHOTGUN . . . . . **NiB $190 Ex $121 Gd $89**
Same general specifications as Model 97 except fancier stock and forearm.

MODEL 101.7 DOUBLE-BARREL
SHOTGUN . . . . **NiB $335 Ex $229 Gd $175**
Boxlock. Double triggers. Gauges: 12, 16, 20, .410. Bbls.: 26 to 32 inch, choked M/F. Weight: From 6 to 7.5 lbs. Plain stock and forend.

MODEL 101.7C DOUBLE-BARREL
SHOTGUN . . . . **NiB $345 Ex $239 Gd $185**
Same general specifications as Model 101.7 except checkered stock and forearm.

MODEL 101.25 BOLT-ACTION SHOTGUN . . . . . **NiB $220 Ex $125 Gd $90**
Takedown. .410 gauge. 5-round tubular magazine. 24-inch bbl., F choke. Weight: About 6 lbs. Plain, one-piece pistol-grip stock.

MODEL 101.40 SINGLE-SHOT SHOTGUN . . . . . **NiB $175 Ex $105 Gd $80**
Takedown. Visible hammer. Automatic ejector. Gauges: 12, 16, 20, and .410. Bbls.: 26 to 36 inch, F choke. Weight: Average 6 lbs. Plain pistol-grip stock and forearm.

MODEL 101.1120 BOLT-ACTION REPEATER . . . . . . **NiB $170 Ex $119 Gd $88**
Takedown. .410 ga. 24-inch bbl., F choke. Weight: About 5 lbs. Plain one-piece pistol-grip stock.

MODEL 101.1380
BOLT-ACTION REPEATER . . . . **NiB $195 Ex $130 Gd $95**
Takedown. Gauges: 12, 16, 20. 2-round detachable box magazine. 26-inch bbl., F choke. Weight: About 7 lbs. Plain one-piece pistol-grip stock.

MODEL 101.1610 DOUBLE-BARREL
SHOTGUN . . . . **NiB $495 Ex $322 Gd $275**
Boxlock. Double triggers. Plain extractors. Gauges: 12, 16, 20, and .410. Bbls.: 24 to 30 inch. Various chokes, but mostly M/F. Weight: About 7.5 lbs, 12 ga. Checkered pistol-grip stock and forearm.

MODEL 101.1701 DOUBLE-BARREL
SHOTGUN . . . . **NiB $420 Ex $335 Gd $240**
Same general specifications as Model 101.1610 except satin chrome frame and select walnut stock and forearm.

MODEL 101.5350-D
BOLT-ACTION REPEATER . . . . **NiB $229 Ex $120 Gd $89**
Takedown. Gauges: 12, 16, 20. 2-round detachable box magazine. 26-inch bbl., F choke. Weight: About 7.25 lbs. Plain one-piece pistol-grip stock.

MODEL 101.5410
BOLT-ACTION REPEATER . . . . **NiB $200 Ex $115 Gd $90**
Same general specifications as Model 101.5350-D.

SKB ARMS COMPANY — Tokyo, Japan

Imported by G.U. Inc., Omaha, NE

MODELS 300 AND 400 SIDE-BY-SIDE SHOTGUNS
Similar to Model 200E except higher grade. Models 300 and 400 differ in that the latter has more elaborate engraving and fancier wood.
Model 300 . . . . **NiB $1077 Ex $900 Gd $635**
Model 400 . . . . **NiB $1566 Ex $1309 Gd $1187**

MODEL 385 SIDE-BY-SIDE . . . **NiB $2200 Ex $1790 Gd $1176**
Boxlock action w/double locking lugs. Gauges: 12, 20, and 28. 2.75- and 3-inch chambers. 26- or 28-inch bbls. w/Inter-Choke tube system. Single selective trigger. Selective automatic ejectors and automatic safety. Weight: 6 lbs., 10 oz. Silver nitride receiver w/engraved scroll and game scene. Solid rib w/flat matte finish and metal front bead sight. Checkered American walnut English or pistol-grip stock. Imported from 1992.

MODEL 400 SKEET . . . . **NiB $1566 Ex $1309 Gd $1187**
Similar to Model 200E Skeet except higher grade w/more elaborate engraving and full fancy wood.

MODEL 480 ENGLISH . . . . . . **NiB $1766 Ex $1510 Gd $1377**
Similar to Model 280 English except higher grade w/more elaborate engraving and full fancy wood.

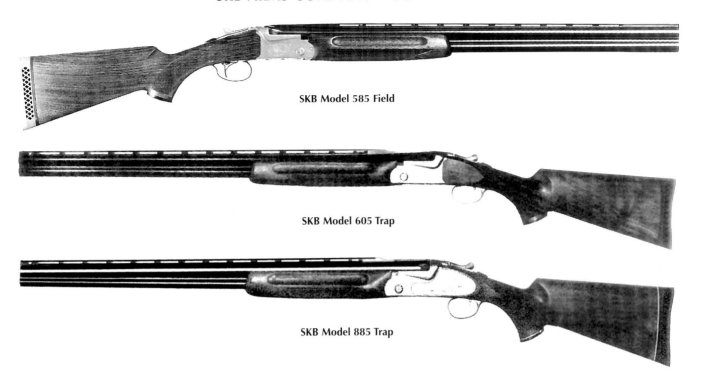

SKB Model 585 Field

SKB Model 605 Trap

SKB Model 885 Trap

MODEL 500 SERIES O/U SHOTGUN
Boxlock. Gauges: 12 and 20. 2.75- or 3-inch chambers. Bbls.: 26-, 28- or 30-inch w/vent. rib; fixed chokes. Weight: 7.5 to 8.5 lbs. Single selective trigger. Selective automatic ejectors. Manual safety. Checkered walnut stock. Blue finish w/scroll engraving. Imported 1967 to 1980.

500 Field, 12 ga. . . . . NiB $1000 Ex $750 Gd $415
500 Field, 20 ga, add. 20%
500 Magnum, 12 ga, add. 25%

MODEL 500 SMALL
GAUGE O/U SHOTGUN . . . . NiB $884 Ex $652 Gd $466
Similar to Model 500 except ga. 28 and .410; has 28-inch vent. rib bbls., M/F chokes. Weight: About 6.5 lbs.

MODEL 505 O/U SHOTGUN
Blued boxlock action. Gauge: 12, 20, 28, and .410. Bbls.: 26, 28, 30 inch; IC/M, M/F, or inner choke tubes. 45.19 inches overall. Weight: 6.6 to 7.4 lbs. Hand checkered walnut stock. Metal bead front sight, ejectors, single selective trigger. Introduced 1988.

Standard Field, Skeet, or Trap grade . . NiB $1365 Ex $1188 Gd $765
Standard 2-bbl. Field set. . . . . . .NiB $1590 Ex $1277 Gd $1006
Skeet grade, 3-bbl. set . . . . . . NiB $1904 Ex $1888 Gd $1301
Sporting Clays . . . . NiB $1189 Ex $977 Gd $668
Trap grade 2-bbl. set . . . . NiB $965 Ex $800 Gd $652

MODEL 585 O/U SHOTGUN
Boxlock. Gauges: 12, 20, 28, and .410. 2.75- or 3-inch chambers. Bbls.: 26-, 28-, 30-, 32-, or 34-inch w/vent. rib; fixed chokes or Inter-Choke tubes. Weight: 6.5 to 8.5 lbs. Single selective trigger. Selective automatic ejectors. Manual safety. Checkered walnut stock in standard or Monte Carlo style. Silver nitride finish w/engraved game scenes. Made from 1992 to 2008.

Field, Skeet, Trap grades . . . . . NiB $1477 Ex $1211 Gd $933
Field grade, 2-bbl. set . . . . . . NiB $2376 Ex $1969 Gd $1387
Skeet set (20, 28, .410 ga.) . . . NiB $2933 Ex $2460 Gd $1977
Sporting Clays . . . . NiB $1700 Ex $1390 Gd $1054
Trap Combo (2-bbl. set) . . . . . NiB $2433 Ex $1976 Gd $1366

MODEL 600 SERIES O/U SHOTGUN
Similar to 500 Series except w/silver nitride receiver. Checkered deluxe walnut stock in both Field and Target Grade configurations. Imported from 1969 to 1980.

600 Field, 12 ga. . . . . NiB $1093 Ex $773 Gd $540
600 Field, 20 ga. . . . . NiB $1100 Ex $977 Gd $650
600 Magnum, 12 ga.
   3-inch chambers . . . . NiB $1100 Ex $977 Gd $650
600 Skeet or Trap grade . . . . . . NiB $1154 Ex $1008 Gd $690
600 Trap Doubles model . . . . . . NiB $1154 Ex $1008 Gd $690

MODEL 600 SMALL GAUGE. . . . NiB $1210 Ex $945 Gd $650
Same as Model 500 Small Gauge except higher grade w/more elaborate engraving and fancier wood.

MODEL 605 SERIES O/U SHOTGUN
Similar to the Model 505 except w/engraved silver nitride receiver and deluxe wood. Introduced 1988.

Field, Skeet, Trap grade . . . . . . NiB $1233 Ex $1026 Gd $779
Skeet 3-bbl. set . . . . NiB $2290 Ex $2003 Gd $1544
Sporting Clays . . . . NiB $1266 Ex $1033 Gd $780

MODEL 680 ENGLISH O/U SHOTGUN
Similar to 600 Series except w/English style select walnut stock and fine scroll engraving. Imported from 1973 to 1977.

680 English, 12 ga. . . . . NiB $1477 Ex $1179 Gd $993
680 English, 20 ga. . . . . NiB $1788 Ex $1165 Gd $1055

MODEL 685 DELUXE O/U
Similar to the 585 Deluxe except w/semi-fancy American walnut stock. Gold trigger and jeweled barrel block. Silvered receiver w/fine engraving.

Field, Skeet, Trap grade . . . . . NiB $1477 Ex $1319 Gd $1066
Field grade, 2-bbl. set . . . . . . NiB $1977 Ex $1819 Gd $1566
Skeet set . . . . NiB $1977 Ex $1819 Gd $1566
Sporting Clays . . . . NiB $1477 Ex $1319 Gd $1066
Trap Combo, 2-bbl. set. . . . . . NiB $2189 Ex $1844 Gd $1360

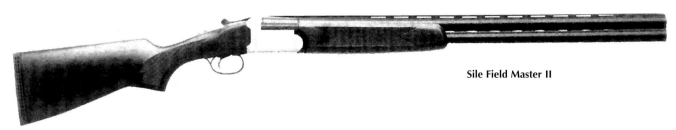

Sile Field Master II

MODEL 800 SKEET/TRAP O/U
Similar to Model 700 Skeet and Trap except higher grade w/more elaborate engraving and fancier wood.
Skeet model . . . . NiB $1329 Ex $1166 Gd $973
Trap model . . . . NiB $1266 Ex $1090 Gd $945

MODEL 880 SKEET/TRAP
Similar to Model 800 Skeet except has sideplates.
Skeet model . . . . NiB $1688 Ex $1470 Gd $1137
Trap model . . . . NiB $1859 Ex $1466 Gd $1123

MODEL 885 DELUXE O/U
Similar to the 685 Deluxe except w/engraved sideplates.
Field, Skeet, Trap grade . . . . . NiB $1779 Ex $1456 Gd $1160
Field grade, 2-bbl. set . . . . . . NiB $2665 Ex $2167 Gd $1800
Skeet Set . . . . NiB $1782 Ex $1693 Gd $1366
Sporting Clays . . . . NiB $1834 Ex $1500 Gd $1220
Trap Combo . . . . NiB $2591 Ex $2277 Gd $1989

The following SKB shotguns were distributed by Ithaca Gun Co. from 1966 to 1976. For specific data, see corresponding listings under Ithaca.

CENTURY SINGLE-BARREL TRAP GUN
The SKB catalog does not differentiate between Century and Century II; however, specifications of current Century are those of Ithaca-SKB Century II.
Century (505) . . . . NiB $966 Ex $831 Gd $634
Century II (605) . . . . NiB $1190 Ex $1006 Gd $798

GAS-OPERATED AUTOMATIC SHOTGUNS
Model XL300 w/plain bbl. . . . . . . NiB $365 Ex $247 Gd $180
Model XL300 w/vent. rib . . . . NiB $400 Ex $365 Gd $217
Model XL900 . . . . NiB $449 Ex $300 Gd $198
Model XL900 Trap. . . . . NiB $487 Ex $376 Gd $221
Model XL900 Skeet. . . . . NiB $510 Ex $375 Gd $266
Model XL900 Slug. . . . . NiB $488 Ex $370 Gd $259
Model 1300 Upland, Slug. . . . . . . NiB $598 Ex $455 Gd $290
Model 1900 Field, Trap, Slug . . . . NiB $588 Ex $443 Gd $376

SKB OVER/UNDER SHOTGUNS
Model 500 Field. . . . . NiB $677 Ex $489 Gd $389
Model 500 Magnum. . . . . NiB $690 Ex $500 Gd $421
Model 600 Field. . . . . NiB $1070 Ex $883 Gd $600
Model 600 Magnum. . . . . NiB $1165 Ex $955 Gd $690
Model 600 Trap . . . . NiB $1190 Ex $975 Gd $710
Model 600 Doubles . . . . NiB $1190 Ex $975 Gd $710
Model 600 Skeet, 12 or 20 ga. . . . . NiB $1190 Ex $975 Gd $710
Model 600 Skeet, 28 or .410. . . . . NiB $1595 Ex $1266 Gd $1065
Model 600 Skeet Combo . . . . NiB $2651 Ex $2210 Gd $2085
Model 600 English . . . . NiB $1190 Ex $975 Gd $710
Model 700 Trap . . . . NiB $950 Ex $844 Gd $630
Model 700 Doubles . . . . NiB $877 Ex $600 Gd $490
Model 700 Skeet . . . . NiB $988 Ex $765 Gd $633
Model 700 Skeet Combo . . . . NiB $2690 Ex $2166 Gd $1650

SKB RECOIL-OPERATED AUTOMATIC SHOTGUNS
Model 300 w/plain bbl. . . . . NiB $477 Ex $370 Gd $269
Model 300 w/vent. rib . . . . NiB $554 Ex $425 Gd $335
Model 900 . . . . NiB $559 Ex $400 Gd $298
Model 900 Slug . . . . NiB $573 Ex $455 Gd $360

SKB SIDE-BY-SIDE DOUBLE-BARREL SHOTGUNS
Model 100 . . . . NiB $795 Ex $650 Gd $425
Model 150 . . . . NiB $795 Ex $650 Gd $425
Model 200E. . . . . NiB $1179 Ex $900 Gd $808
Model 200E Skeet . . . . NiB $1179 Ex $900 Gd $808
Model 280 English . . . . NiB $1280 Ex $1006 Gd $922

SIG SAUER — (SIG) Schweizerische Industrie-Gesellschaft, Neuhausen, Switzerland

MODEL SA3 O/U SHOTGUN
Monobloc boxlock action. Single selective trigger. Automatic ejectors. Gauges: 12 or 20. 3-inch chambers. 26-, 28- or 30-inch vent. rib bbls. w/choke tubes. Weight: 6.8 to 7.1 lbs. Checkered select walnut stock and forearm. Satin nickel-finished receiver w/game scene and blued bbls. Imported from 1997-98.
Field model . . . . NiB $1294 Ex $1126 Gd $966
Sporting Clays model . . . . . . NiB $1500 Ex $1398 Gd $1225

MODEL SA5 O/U SHOTGUN
Similar to SA3 Model except w/detachable sideplates. Gauges: 12 or 20. 3-inch chambers. 26.5-, 28-, or 30-inch vent. rib bbls. w/ choke tubes. Imported from 1997 to 1999.
Field model . . . . NiB $2288 Ex $2055 Gd $1530
Sporting Clays model . . . . . . NiB $2455 Ex $2160 Gd $1880

SILE — Sile Distributors, New York, NY

FIELD MASTER II O/U SHOTGUN. . . . . NiB $735 Ex $615 Gd $479
Gauge: 12. 3-inch chambers. 28-inch bbl., IC/M/IM/F choke tubes. 45.25 inches overall. Weight: 7.25 lbs. Satin-finished walnut, checkered stock and forend. Introduced 1989.

L. C. SMITH — Made 1890 to 1945 by Hunter Arms Company, Fulton, NY 1946 to 1951 and 1968 to 1973 and 2004 by Marlin Firearms Company, New Haven, CT

L. C. SMITH DOUBLE-BARREL SHOTGUNS
Values shown are for L. C. Smith doubles made by Hunter. Those of 1946 to 1951 Marlin manufacture generally bring prices about 1/3 lower. Smaller gauge models, especially in the higher grades, command premium prices—up to 50 percent more for 20 gauge, up to 400 percent for .410.

L.C. Smith Crown

L.C. Smith Field

Crown grade, double triggers,
 automatic ejectors . . . . . .NiB $11,650 Ex $9000 Gd $7750
Crown grade, selective single trigger,
 automatic ejectors . . . . NiB $12,275 Ex $10,200 Gd $9976
Deluxe grade, selective single trigger,
 automatic ejectors . . . .NiB $80,000 Ex $65,000 Gd $44,000
Eagle grade, double triggers,
 automatic ejectors . . . . NiB $7450 Ex $6600 Gd $3540
Eagle grade, selective
 single trigger . . . . NiB $8433 Ex $7210 Gd $4450
Field grade, double trigger
 plain extractors . . . . NiB $1877 Ex $1659 Gd $1200
Field grade, double triggers
 automatic ejectors. . . . . . . NiB $2400 Ex $2175 Gd $1765
Field grade, nonselective single trigger,
 plain extractors . . . . NiB $1788 Ex $1489 Gd $1016
Field grade, selective single trigger,
 automatic ejectors . . . . . . NiB $2276 Ex $1998 Gd $1688
Ideal grade, double triggers,
 plain extractors . . . . NiB $2698 Ex $2100 Gd $1933
Ideal grade, double triggers,
 automatic ejectors. . . . . . . NiB $3355 Ex $2288 Gd $1987
Ideal grade, selective single trigger,
 automatic ejectors . . . . . . NiB $2979 Ex $2466 Gd $2132
Monogram grade, selective single trigger,
 automatic ejectors . . . NiB $17,800 Ex $15,888 Gd $11,880
Olympic grade, selective single trigger,
 automatic ejectors . . . . . . NiB $7225 Ex $5179 Gd $3889
Premier grade, selective single trigger
 automatic ejectors . . . NiB $42,975 Ex $33,670 Gd $25,000
Skeet Special, nonselective single trigger,
 automatic ejectors . . . . . . NiB $4055 Ex $3329 Gd $2165
Skeet Special, selective single trigger,
 automatic ejectors. . . . . . . NiB $4070 Ex $3360 Gd $2185
.410 ga. . . . . NiB $14,887 Ex $11,965 Gd $9865
Specialty grade, double triggers,
 automatic ejectors . . . . NiB $4177 Ex $3688 Gd $3245
Specialty grade, selective single trigger,
 automatic ejectors. . . . . . . NiB $3866 Ex $3390 Gd $2788
Trap grade, selective single trigger,
 automatic ejectors. . . . . . . NiB $3687 Ex $3255 Gd $2877

L. C. SMITH HAMMERLESS DOUBLE-BARREL SHOTGUNS

Sidelock. Auto ejectors standard on higher grades, extra on Field and Ideal Grades. Double triggers or Hunter single trigger (non-selective or selective). Gauges: 12, 16, 20, .410. Bbls.: 26 to 32 inch, any standard boring. Weight: 6.5 to 8.25 lbs., 12 ga. Checkered stock and forend; choice of straight, half-, or full-pistol grip, beavertail or standard-type forend. Grades differ only in quality of workmanship, wood, checkering, engraving, etc. Same general specifications apply to all. Manufacture of these L. C. Smith guns was disc. in 1951. Production of Field Grade 12 ga. was resumed 1968 to 1973. Note: L. C. Smith Shotguns manufactured by the Hunter Arms Co. 1890 to 1913 were designated by numerals to indicate grade w/the exception of Pigeon and Monogram.

00 grade . . . . NiB $1577 Ex $1369 Gd $1100
0 grade . . . . NiB $1735 Ex $1575 Gd $1244
1 grade . . . . NiB $2170 Ex $1876 Gd $1390
2 grade . . . . NiB $3533 Ex $2177 Gd $1566
3 grade . . . . NiB $4480 Ex $3066 Gd $2200
Pigeon . . . . NiB $5250 Ex $3688 Gd $2531
4 grade . . . . NiB $6244 Ex $5187 Gd $4966
5 grade . . . . .NiB $10,300 Ex $8879 Gd $6610
Monogram . . . . .NiB $13,975 Ex $11,755 Gd $10,000
A1 . . . . NiB $7225 Ex $4488 Gd $3240
A2. . . . . .NiB $14,779 Ex $11,960 Gd $10,066
A3 . . . . .NiB $42,600 Ex $37,988 Gd $32,776

HAMMERLESS DOUBLE
MODEL 1968 FIELD GRADE . . . NiB $1165 Ex $980 Gd $644
Re-creation of the original L. C. Smith double. Sidelock. Plain extractors. Double triggers. 12 ga. 28-inch vent. rib bbls., M/F choke. Weight: About 6.75 lbs. Checkered pistol-grip stock and forearm. Made from 1968 to 1973.

HAMMERLESS DOUBLE
MODEL 1968 DELUXE . . . . . . NiB $1688 Ex $1076 Gd $884
Same as 1968 Field Grade except has Simmons floating vent. rib, beavertail forearm. Made from 1971 to 1973.

SINGLE-SHOT TRAP GUNS
Boxlock. Hammerless. Auto ejector.12 ga. only. Bbl.: 32- or 34-inch vent. rib. Weight: 8 to 8.25 lbs. Checkered pistol-grip stock and forend, recoil pad. Grades vary in quality of workmanship, wood, engraving, etc.; general specifications are the same. Disc. 1951. Note: Values shown are for L. C. Smith single-barrel trap guns made by Hunter. Those of Marlin manufacture generally bring prices about 1/3 lower.
Olympic grade . . . . NiB $3188 Ex $2677 Gd $2190
Specialty grade . . . . NiB $3598 Ex $3200 Gd $2560
Crown grade. . . . . NiB $4488 Ex $3900 Gd $2677
Monogram grade. . . . . NiB $8865 Ex $6231 Gd $4997
Premier grade . . . . Very rare (three or fewer manufactured)
Deluxe grade . . . . Very rare (four or fewer manufactured)

Marlin resurrected the L.C. Smith brand from 2005 to 2009 importing O/U and S/S models from manufacturers in Italy and Spain.

MODEL LC12 . . . . NiB $860 Ex $800 Gd $560
O/U boxlock. Ejectors. 12 ga. only. 28-inch bbl., vent. rib, choke tubes. Stock: Fluer-de-lis checkered walnut w/pistol grip.
LC20 (20 ga.) . . . . NiB $1000 Ex $875 Gd $580

MODEL LC12 DB . . . . NiB $1400 Ex $1280 Gd $900
S/S boxlock. Ejectors. Detachable side plates. 12 ga. only. 28-inch bbl., vent. rib, choke tubes. Stock: Fluer-de-lis checkered walnut w/ pistol grip, beavertail forend.
LC20 DB (20 ga.) . . . . NiB $1600 Ex $1480 Gd $1200
LC28 DB (28 ga.) . . . . NiB $1900 Ex $1695 Gd $1395
LC410 DB (.410). . . . . NiB $1900 Ex $1695 Gd $1395

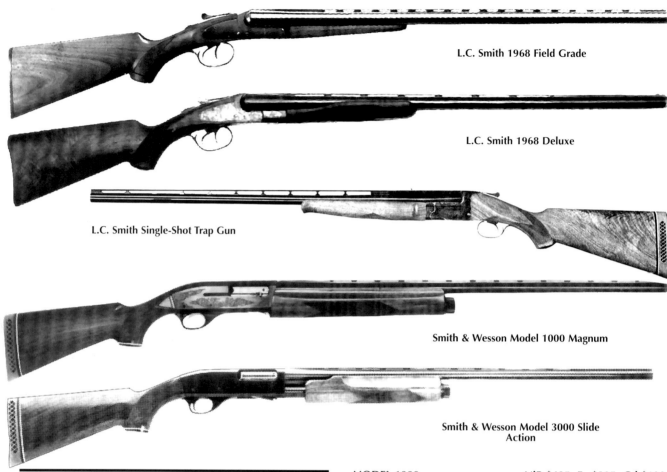

L.C. Smith 1968 Field Grade

L.C. Smith 1968 Deluxe

L.C. Smith Single-Shot Trap Gun

Smith & Wesson Model 1000 Magnum

Smith & Wesson Model 3000 Slide Action

SMITH & WESSON — Springfield, MA

Sold several times, currently Saf-T-Hammer.

MDEL 916 SLIDE-ACTION REPEATER
Hammerless. Solid frame. Gauges: 12, 16, 20. 3-inch chamber in 12 and 20 ga. 5-round tubular magazine. Bbls.: Plain or vent. rib; 20-inch C (12 ga., plain only); 26-inch IC; 28-inch M/F; 30-inch F choke (12 ga. only). Weight: w/28-inch plain bbl., 7.25 lbs. Plain pistol-grip stock, fluted slide handle. Made 1972 to 1981.
w/plain bbl. . . . . NiB $225 Ex $170 Gd $110
w/vent. rib bbl. . . . . NiB $255 Ex $185 Gd $120

MODEL 916T
Same as Model 916 except takedown. 12 ga. only. Not available w/20-inch bbl. Made from 1976 to 1981.
w/plain bbl. . . . . NiB $250 Ex $180 Gd $115
w/vent. rib bbl. . . . . NiB $275 Ex $200 Gd $140

MODEL 1000 AUTOLOADER. . . . NiB $433 Ex $355 Gd $240
Gas operated. Takedown. Gauges: 12, 20. 2.75-inch chamber in 12 ga., 3-inch in 20 ga. 4-round magazine. Bbls.: Vent. rib, 26-inch SK choke, IC; 28-inch M/F; 30-inch F choke (12 ga. only). Weight: w/28-inch bbl., 6.5 lbs. in 20 ga., 7.5 lbs. in 12 ga. Checkered pistol-grip stock and forearm. Made from 1972. Disc.

MODEL 3000 SLIDE ACTION. . . . NiB $425 Ex $295 Gd $190
Hammerless. 20-ga. Bbls.: 26-inch IC; 28-inch M/F. Chambered for 3-inch Mag. and 2.75-inch loads. American walnut stock and forearm. Checkered pistol grip and forearm. Introduced 1982.

MODEL 1000 . . . . NiB $425 Ex $295 Gd $190
Same as Model 3000 but an earlier version.

MODEL 1000 MAGNUM . . . . . . NiB $595 Ex $445 Gd $398
Same as standard Model 1000 except chambered for 12 ga. Mag., 3-inch shells. 30-inch bbl. only, M/F choke; stock w/recoil pad. Weight: About 8 lbs. Introduced in 1977.

SPRINGFIELD ARMS — Built by Savage Arms Company, Utica, NY

SPRINGFIELD DOUBLE-BARREL
HAMMER SHOTGUN . . . . NiB $588 Ex $439 Gd $366
Gauges: 12 and 16. Bbls.: 28 to 32 inches. In 12 ga., 32-inch model, F/F choke. All other ga. and barrel lengths are F/M. Weight: 7.25 to 8.25 lbs. depending on ga. and bbl. length. Black walnut checkered buttstock and forend. Disc. 1934.

SQUIRES BINGHAM CO., INC. — Makati, Rizal, Philippines

MODEL 30
PUMP SHOTGUN. . . . . NiB $366 Ex $255 Gd $175
Hammerless. 12 ga. 5-round magazine. Bbl.: 20-inch Cyl.; 28-inch M; 30-inch F choke. Weight: About 7 lbs. Pulong Dalaga stock and slide handle. Currently manufactured.

Squires Bingham Model 30 Pump Shotgun

J. STEVENS ARMS COMPANY — Chicopee Falls, MA

Division of Savage Arms Corporation.

NO. 20 FAVORITE SHOTGUN. . . . . .NiB $325 Ex $217 Gd $140
Calibers: .22 and .32 shot. Smoothbore bbl. Blade front sight; no rear. Made from 1893 to 1939.

NO. 22-.410 O/U COMBINATION GUN
.22 caliber rifle barrel over .410 ga. shotgun barrel. Visible hammer. Takedown. Single trigger. 24-inch bbls., shotgun bbl. F choke. Weight: About 6 lbs. Open rear sight and ramp front sight of sporting rifle type. Plain pistol-grip stock and forearm; originally supplied w/walnut stock and forearm. Tenite (plastic) was used in later production. Made 1939 to 1950. Note: This gun is now manufactured as the Savage Model 24.
w/wood stock and forearm . . . . . NiB $545 Ex $435 Gd $300
w/Tenite stock and forearm . . . . . . NiB $525 Ex $460 Gd $345

NO. 39 NEW MODEL
POCKET SHOTGUN . . . . NiB $800 Ex $605 Gd $490
Gauge: .410. Calibers: .38-40 shot, .44-40 shot. Bbls.: 10, 12, 15, or 18 inches, half-octagonal smoothbore. Shotgun sights. Made 1895 to 1906.

MODEL 51 BOLT-ACTION
SHOTGUN . . . . NiB $235 Ex $154 Gd $95
Single shot. Takedown. .410 ga. 24-inch bbl., F choke. Weight: About 4.75 lbs. Plain one-piece pistol-grip stock. Checkered on later models. Made from 1962 to 1971.

MODEL 58 BOLT-ACTION
REPEATER . . . . NiB $254 Ex $165 Gd $120
Takedown. Gauges: 12, 16, 20. 2-round detachable box magazine. 26-inch bbl., F choke. Weight: About 7.25 lbs. Plain one-piece pistol-grip stock on early models w/takedown screw on bottom of forend. Made 1933 to 1981. Note: Later production models have 3-inch chamber in 20 ga., checkered stock w/recoil pad.

MODEL 58-.410 BOLT-ACTION
REPEATER . . . . .NiB $225 Ex $130 Gd $95
Takedown. .410 ga. 3-round detachable box magazine. 24-inch bbl., F choke. Weight: About 5.5 lbs. Plain one-piece pistol-grip stock, checkered on later production. Made from 1937 to 1981.

MODEL 59 BOLT-ACTION
REPEATER . . . . NiB $255 Ex $190 Gd $135
Takedown. .410 ga. 5-round tubular magazine. 24-inch bbl., F choke. Weight: About 6 lbs. Plain one-piece pistol-grip stock, checkered on later production. Made from 1934 to 1973.

MODEL 67 PUMP SHOTGUN
Hammerless, side-ejection solid-steel receiver. Gauges: 12, 20, and .410. 2.75- or 3-inch shells. Bbls.: 21-, 26-, 28-, 30-inch w/fixed chokes or interchangeable choke tubes, plain or vent. rib. Weight: 6.25 to 7.5 lbs. Optional rifle sights. Walnut-finished hardwood stock with corncob-style forend.

Standard model, plain bbl. . . . . . .NiB $245 Ex $195 Gd $120
Standard model, vent. rib . . . . . . NiB $255 Ex $205 Gd $125
Standard model, w/choke tubes . . NiB $275 Ex $220 Gd $155
Slug model w/rifle sights . . . . . . .NiB $255 Ex $205 Gd $125
Lobo model, matte finish . . . . . . NiB $255 Ex $205 Gd $125
Youth model, 20 ga. . . . . NiB $260 Ex $210 Gd $130
Camo model w/choke tubes . . . . NiB $275 Ex $220 Gd $155

MODEL 67 WATERFOWL SHOTGUN . . . . NiB $335 Ex $200 Gd $135
Hammerless. Gauge: 12. 3-round tubular magazine. Walnut finished hardwood stock. Weight: About 7.5 lbs. Made 1972 to 1989.

MODEL 77 SLIDE-ACTION REPEATER . . . . NiB $225 Ex $130 Gd $95
Solid frame. Gauges: 12, 16, 20. 5-round tubular magazine. Bbls.: 26-inch IC, 28-inch M/F choke. Weight: About 7.5 lbs. Plain pistol-grip stock w/recoil pad, grooved slide handle. Made from 1954 to 1971.

MODEL 77-AC . . . . NiB $217 Ex $125 Gd $95
Same as Model 77 except has Savage Super Choke.

MODEL 79-VR SUPER VALUE. . . . . NiB $355 Ex $265 Gd $190
Hammerless, side ejection. Bbl.: Chambered for 2.75-inch and 3-inch Mag. shells. 12, 20, and .410 ga. Vent. rib. Walnut finished hardwood stock w/checkering on grip. Weight: 6.75 to 7 lbs. Made 1979 to 1990.

MODEL 94 SINGLE-SHOT SHOTGUN . . . NiB $165 Ex $95 Gd $70
Takedown. Visible hammer. Auto ejector. Gauges: 12, 16, 20, 28, .410. Bbls.: 26, 28, 30, 32, 36 inch, F choke. Weight: About 6 lbs. depending on ga. and bbl. Plain pistol-grip stock and forearm. Made from 1939 to 1961.

MODEL 94C . . . . NiB $165 Ex $95 Gd $70
Same as Model 94 except has checkered stock, fluted forearm on late production. Made from 1965 to 1990.

MODEL 94Y YOUTH GUN. . . . . NiB $165 Ex $95 Gd $70
Same as Model 94 except made in 20 and .410 ga. only. 26-inch F choke bbl., 12.5-inch buttstock w/recoil pad; checkered pistol grip and fluted forend on late production. Made from 1959 to 1990.

MODEL 95 SINGLE-SHOT SHOTGUN. . . . . NiB $200 Ex $140 Gd $95
Solid frame. Visible hammer. Plain extractor. 12 ga. 3-inch chamber. Bbls.: 28-inch M; 30-inch F choke. Weight: About 7.25 lbs. Plain pistol-grip stock, grooved forearm. Made 1965 to 1969.

MODEL 107 SINGLE-SHOT
HAMMER SHOTGUN. . . . . NiB $217 Ex $129 Gd $95
Takedown. Auto ejector. Gauges: 12, 16, 20, .410. Bbl.: 28 and 30 inch (12 and 16 ga.), 28 inch (20 ga.), 26 inch (.410); F choke only. Weight: About 6 lbs., 12 ga. Plain pistol-grip stock and forearm. Made from about 1937 to 1953.

MODEL 124
BOLT-ACTION REPEATER . . . . NiB $265 Ex $198 Gd $155
Hammerless. Solid frame. 12 ga. only. 2-round tubular magazine. 28-inch bbl.; IC/M/F choke. Weight: About 7 lbs. Tenite stock and forearm. Made from 1947 to 1952.

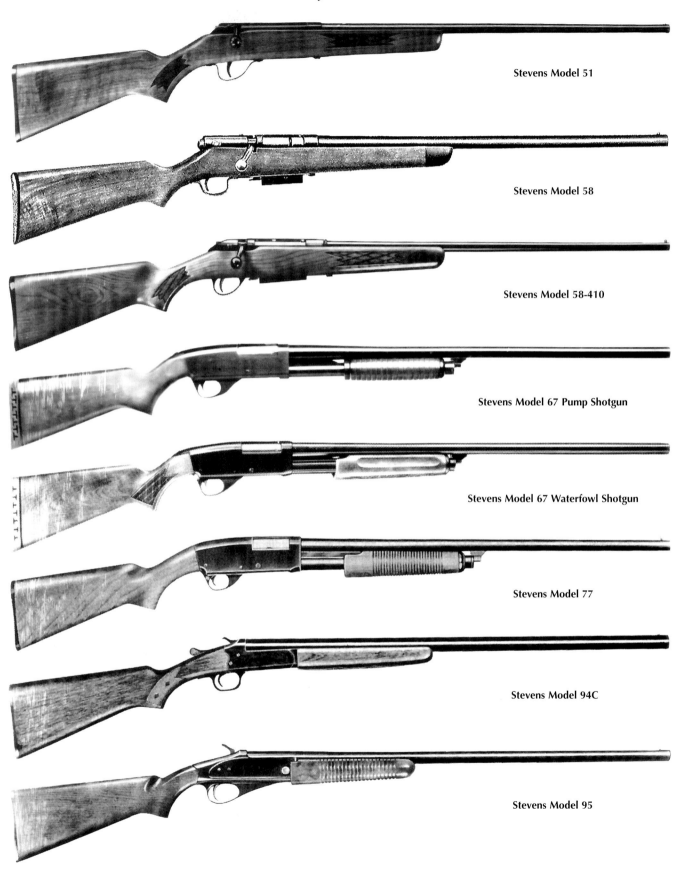

Stevens Model 51

Stevens Model 58

Stevens Model 58-410

Stevens Model 67 Pump Shotgun

Stevens Model 67 Waterfowl Shotgun

Stevens Model 77

Stevens Model 94C

Stevens Model 95

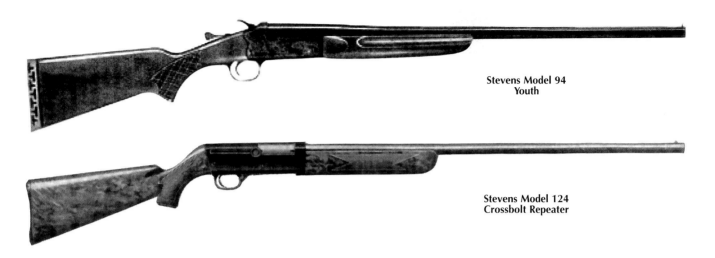

Stevens Model 94
Youth

Stevens Model 124
Crossbolt Repeater

MODEL 240 O/U SHOTGUN. . . . NiB $448 Ex $375 Gd $270
Visible hammer. Takedown. Double triggers. .410 ga. 26-inch bbls., F choke. Weight: 6 lbs. Tenite (plastic) pistol-grip stock and forearm. Made from 1940 to 1949.

**MODEL 258 BOLT-ACTION
REPEATER . . . . NiB $290 Ex $174 Gd $100**
Takedown. 20-ga. 2-round detachable box magazine. 26-inch bbl., F choke. Weight: About 6.25 lbs. Plain one-piece pistol-grip stock. Made from 1937 to 1965.

MODEL 311 SPRINGFIELD HAMMERLESS DOUBLE
Same general specifications as Stevens Model 530 except earlier production has plain stock and forearm; checkered on current guns. Originally produced as a Springfield gun, this model became a part of the Stevens line in 1948 when the Springfield brand name was disc. Made from 1931 to 1989.
Pre-WWII . . . . NiB $675 Ex $450 Gd $325
Post-WWII . . . . NiB $335 Ex $200 Gd $125

**MODEL 311-R
HAMMERLESS DOUBLE . . . . NiB $300 Ex $225 Gd $145**
Same general specifications as Stevens Model 311 except compact design for law enforcement use. Bbls.: 18.25 inch. 12 ga. w/solid rib, chambered for 2.75- and 3-inch Mag. shells. Double triggers and auto top tang safety. Walnut finished hardwood stock w/recoil pad and semi-beavertail forend. Weight: About 6.75 lbs. Made from 1982 to 1989.

**MODEL 530
HAMMERLESS DOUBLE . . . . NiB $335 Ex $245 Gd $200**
Boxlock. Double triggers. Gauges: 12, 16, 20, .410. Bbl.: 26 to 32 inch; choked M/F, C/M, F/F. Weight: 6 to 7.5 lbs. depending on ga. and bbl. length. Checkered pistol-grip stock and forearm; some early models w/recoil pad. Made from 1936 to 1954.

MODEL 530M. . . . . NiB $339 Ex $255 Gd $210
Same as Model 530 except has Tenite (plastic) stock and forearm. Disc. about 1947.

MODEL 530ST DOUBLE GUN . . . NiB $339 Ex $255 Gd $210
Same as Model 530 except has nonselective single trigger. Disc.

**MODEL 620 HAMMERLESS SLIDE-ACTION
REPEATING SHOTGUN . . . . NiB $400 Ex $255 Gd $180**
Takedown. Gauges: 12, 16, 20. 5-round tubular magazine. Bbl.: 26, 28, 30, 32 inch; choked F/M/IC/C. Weight: About 7.75 lbs., 12 ga.; 7.25 lbs., 16 ga.; 6 lbs., 20 ga. Checkered pistol-grip stock and slide handle. Made from 1927 to 1953.

MODEL 620-C . . . . NiB $365 Ex $255 Gd $160
Same specifications as Model 620 except equipped w/Cutts Compensator and two choke tubes.

MODEL 620-P. . . . . NiB $288 Ex $200 Gd $155
Same specifications as Model 620 equipped w/Aero-Dyne PolyChoke and 27-inch bbl.

MODEL 620-PV . . . . NiB $280 Ex $190 Gd $155
Same specifications as Model 620 except equipped w/vent. PolyChoke and 27-inch bbl.

MODEL 621 . . . . NiB $359 Ex $210 Gd $155
Same as Model 620 except has raised solid matted rib barrel. Disc.

**MODEL 820 HAMMERLESS
REPEATING SHOTGUN . . . . NiB $388 Ex $266 Gd $190**
Solid frame. 12 ga. only. 5-round tubular magazine. 28-inch bbl.; IC/M/F choke. Weight: About 7.5 lbs. Plain pistol-grip stock, grooved slide handle. Early models furnished w/Tenite buttstock and forend. Made from 1949 to 1954.

MODEL 820-SC . . . . NiB $400 Ex $330 Gd $217
Same as Model 820 except has Savage Super Choke.

**MODEL 940 SINGLE-
SHOT SHOTGUN. . . . . NiB $256 Ex $138 Gd $110**
Same general specifications as Model 94 except has side lever opening instead of top lever. Made from 1961 to 1970.

MODEL 940Y YOUTH GUN. . . . . NiB $265 Ex $155 Gd $115
Same general specifications as Model 94Y except has side lever opening instead of top lever. Made from 1961 to 1970.

Stevens Model 258

Stevens Model 311

Stevens Model 530

Stevens Model 620

Stevens Model 620-P

Stevens Model 820

MODEL 9478 . . . . **NiB $145   Ex $90   Gd $65**
Takedown. Visible hammer. Automatic ejector. Gauges: 12, 20, .410. Bbls.: 26, 28, 30, 36 inch; F choke. Weight: Average 6 lbs. depending on ga. and bbl. Plain pistol-grip stock and forearm. Made from 1978 to 1985.

MODEL 5151 SPRINGFIELD. . . . . **NiB $556   Ex $435   Gd $300**
Same specifications as the Stevens Model 311 except w/checkered grip and forend; equipped w/recoil pad and two ivory sights.

STOEGER SHOTGUNS

See IGA and Tikka.

TAR-HUNT CUSTOM RIFLES, INC. — Bloomsburg, PA

MODEL RSG-12 MATCHLESS
BOLT-ACTION SLUG GUN . . . . **NiB $2366   Ex $2165   Gd $1590**
Similar to Professional model except has McMillan Fibergrain stock and deluxe blue finish. Made from 1995 to 2004.

MODEL RSG-12 PEERLESS
BOLT-ACTION SLUG GUN . . . . **NiB $2944   Ex $2577   Gd $2320**
Similar to Professional model except has McMillan Fibergrain stock and deluxe NP-3 (Nickel/Teflon) metal finish. Made from 1995 to 2004.

MODEL RSG-12 PROFESSIONAL
BOLT-ACTION SLUG GUN
Bolt-action 12 ga. 2.75-inch chamber. 2-round detachable magazine, 21.5-inch fully rifled bbl. w/ or w/o muzzle brake. Receiver drilled and tapped for scope mounts w/no sights. Weight: 7.75 lbs. 41.5 inches overall. Checkered black McMillan fiberglass stock w/swivel studs and Pachmayr Deacelerator pad. Made from 1991 to 2004.
w/o muzzle brake (disc. 1993) ... NiB $2688 Ex $2320 Gd $1997
w/muzzle brake .... NiB $2700 Ex $2375 Gd $2044

MODEL RSG-20 MOUNTAINEER
BOLT-ACTION SLUG GUN .... NiB $2276 Ex $1966 Gd $1433
Similar to Professional model except 20 ga. 2.75-inch chamber. Black McMillan synthetic stock w/blind magazine. Weight: 6.5 lbs. Made from 1997 to 2004.

TECNI-MEC SHOTGUNS — Italy

Imported by RAHN Gun Work, Inc., Hastings, MI.

MODEL SPL 640 FOLDING SHOTGUN
Gauges: 12, 16, 20, 24, 28, 32, and .410 bore. 26-inch bbl. Chokes: IC/IM. Weight: 6.5 lbs. Checkered walnut pistol-grip stock and forend. Engraved receiver. Available w/single or double triggers. Imported from 1988 to 1994.
w/single trigger.............. NiB $596 Ex $477 Gd $369
w/double trigger............. NiB $655 Ex $498 Gd $388

THOMPSON/CENTER ARMS — Rochester, NH, and Springfield, MA

Purchased by Smith & Wesson in 2006.

CONTENDER
.410 CARBINE............... NiB $500 Ex $387 Gd $279
Gauge: .410 smoothbore. 21-inch vent. rib bbl. 34.75 inches overall. Weight: About 5.25 lbs. Bead front sight. Rynite stock and forend. Made 1991 to date.

ENCORE 20 GA. SHOTGUN
Gauge: 20 smoothbore w/rifled slug bbl. or 26-inch vent. rib bbl. w/three internal screw choke tubes. 38 to 40.5 inches overall. Weight: About 5.25 to 6 lbs. Bead or fiber optic sights. Walnut stock and forend. Made from 1998 to date.
w/vent. rib .... NiB $485 Ex $390 Gd $275
w/rifled slug bbl.............. NiB $522 Ex $421 Gd $300
Extra bbl., add................................ $325

HUNTER SHOTGUN MODEL.... NiB $580 Ex $466 Gd $355
Single shot. Gauge: 10 or 12. 3.5-inch chamber, 25-inch field bbl. w/F choke. Weight: 8 lbs. Bead front sight. American black walnut stock w/recoil pad. Made from 1987 to 1992.

HUNTER SLUG MODEL....... NiB $580 Ex $466 Gd $355
Gauge: 10 (3.5-inch chamber) or 12 (3-inch chamber). Same general specifications as Model '87 Hunter Shotgun except w/22-inch slug (rifled) bbl. and rifle sights. Made from 1987 to 1992.

TIKKA — Manufactured by Sako, Ltd. in Armi Marocchi, Italy

M 07 SHOTGUN/
RIFLE COMBINATION ...... NiB $1287 Ex $1009 Gd $766
Gauge/caliber: 12/.222 Rem. Shotgun bbl.: About 25 inches; rifled bbl.: About 22.75 inches. 40.66 inches overall. Weight: About 7 lbs. Dovetailed for telescopic sight mounts. Single trigger w/selector between the bbls. Vent. rib. Monte Carlo-style walnut stock w/checkered pistol grip and forend. Made from 1965 to 1987.

M 77 O/U SHOTGUN ...... NiB $1345 Ex $1265 Gd $950
Gauge: 12. 27-inch vent. rib bbls. Approx. 44 inches overall. Weight: About 7.25 lbs. Bbl. selector. Ejectors. Monte Carlo-style walnut stock w/checkered pistol grip and forend; rollover cheekpiece. Made from 1977 to 1987.

M 77K SHOTGUN/ RIFLE
COMBINATION....................NiB $1733 Ex $1388 Gd $1009
Gauge: 12/70. Calibers: .222 Rem., 5.6x52r5, 6.5x55, 7x57r5, 7x65r5, .308 Win. Vent. rib bbls.: About 25 inches (shotgun), 23 inches (rifle); 42.3 inches overall. Weight: About 7.5 lbs. Double triggers. Monte Carlo-style walnut stock w/checkered pistol grip and forend; rollover cheekpiece. Made from 1977 to 1986.

412S/512S SHOOTING SYSTEM
Boxlock action w/both under lug and sliding top latch locking mechanism designed to accept interchangeable monobloc barrels, including O/U shotgun, combination, and double rifle configurations. Blued or satin nickel receiver w/cocking indicators. Selective single trigger design w/barrel selector incorporated into the trigger (double triggers available). Blued barrels assemblies w/extractors or auto ejectors as required. Select American walnut stock with checkered pistol grip and forend. Previously produced in Finland (same as the former Valmet Model 412) but currently manufactured in Italy by joint venture arrangement with Armi Marocchi. From 1990 to 1993, Stoeger Industries imported this model as the 412/S. In 1993 the nomenclature of this shooting system was changed to 512/S. Disc. 1997. Note: For double rifle values, see Tikka Rifles.

MODEL 412S/512S O/U SHOTGUN
Gauge: 12. 3-inch chambers. 24-, 26-, 28-, or 30-inch chrome-lined bbls. w/blued finish and integral stainless steel choke tubes. Weight: 7.25 to 7.5 lbs. Blue or matte nickel receiver. Select American walnut from stock w/checkered pistol grip and forend. Imported 1990 to 1997.
Standard Field model .... NiB $1145 Ex $989 Gd $766
Standard Trap model .... NiB $1277 Ex $1050 Gd $766
Premium Field model .... NiB $1688 Ex $1279 Gd $1100
Premium Trap model .... NiB $1688 Ex $1279 Gd $1100
Sporting Clays model .... NiB $1233 Ex $1054 Gd $866
Extra O/U shotgun bbl., add................................. $700
Extra O/U combo bbl., add................................. $800
Extra O/U rifle bbl., add $1025

MODEL 412S/512S OVER/UNDER COMBINATION
Gauge: 12. 3-inch chamber. Calibers: .222 Rem., .30-06, or .308 Win. Blue or matte nickel receiver, 24-inch chrome-lined bbls. w/extractors and blued finish. Weight: 7.25 to 7.5 lbs. Select American walnut stock w/checkered pistol grip and forend. Imported from 1990 to 1997.
Standard Combination model ......NiB $1598 Ex $1335 Gd $1109
Premium Combination model ......NiB $1622 Ex $1365 Gd $1135
Extra bbl. options, add $800

TRADITIONS PERFORMANCE FIREARMS

Importers of shotguns produced by Fausti Stefano of Brescia, Italy, and ATA Firearms, Turkey.

FIELD HUNTER MODEL . . . . **NiB $825 Ex $630 Gd $535**
Same as Field I except 12 and 20 ga. 3-inch chambers, screw-in chokes, and extractors.

CLASSIC SERIES, FIELD I O/U . . . . . **NiB $853 Ex $677 Gd $545**
Available in 12, 20, 28 (2.75-inch chamber), and .410 gauge, 26- or 28-inch vent. rib bbls. w/fixed chokes and extractors. Weight: 6.75 to 7.25 lbs. Blued finish, silver receiver engraved w/game birds. Single selective trigger. Brass bead front sight. European walnut stock. Overall length 43 to 45 inches. Intro. 2000.

FIELD II MODEL . . . .**NiB $945 Ex $679 Gd $555**
Same as Field I except w/screw-in chokes and automatic ejectors.

FIELD III GOLD MODEL . . . . **NiB $1217 Ex $1109 Gd $998**
Same as Field I model except 12 ga. only, high-grade, oil-finish walnut, coin-finish receiver w/engraved pheasants and woodcock, deep blue finish on barrels, automatic ejectors, and nonslip recoil pad.

SPORTING CLAY II MODEL. . . . . .**NiB $1165 Ex $977 Gd $620**
Same as Sporting Clay III model but w/European walnut stocks, cut checkering, and extended choke tubes. Overall length: 47 inches. Weight: 7.75 lbs.

CLASSIC SERIES O/U
SPORTING CLAY III . . . . **NiB $1200 Ex $1095 Gd $985**
Available in 12 and 20 ga. 3-inch chambers, high grade walnut stock, oil-satin finish, palm swell Schnabel forend. 28- and 30-inch bbls. w/3/8-inch top and middle vent. rib, red target front bead sight. Automatic ejectors, extended choke tubes. Weight: 8.25 lbs. Intro. 2000.

UPLAND II MODEL . . . . **NiB $1065 Ex $775 Gd $546**
Same as Upland III model except w/English walnut straight-grip stock and Schnabel forend. 24- and 26-inch vent. rib bbls., floral engraving on blued receiver, automatic ejectors.

UPLAND III MODEL. . . . . **NiB $1187 Ex $977 Gd $755**
Same as Sporting Clay III model but round pistol grip and Schnabel forend, blued receiver w/engraved upland scene. Weight: 7.5 lbs.

MAG 350 SERIES TURKEY II O/U. . . . . . .**NiB $1144 Ex $942 Gd $700**
Magnum 3.5-inch chambers in 12 ga. only. 24- and 26-inch bbls., screw-in flush fitting chokes: F/XF. Matte finish, engraved receiver, Mossy Oak or Realtree camo. Intro. 2000.

WATERFOWL II MODEL. . . . . **NiB $1159 Ex $910 Gd $715**
Same as Turkey II model except w/Advantage Wetlands camo stock and barrels. Weight: 8 lbs., overall length 45 inches. Waterfowl model has 28-inch bbls.

MAG HUNTER II. . . . . **NiB $1159 Ex $910 Gd $715**
Same as Turkey II model except blued engraved receiver and matte finish walnut stocks. 3.5-inch chambers, 28-inch bbls. w/screw-in chokes.

ELITE HUNTER . . . . **NiB $1256 Ex $1044 Gd $770**
Same as Elite Field model except 12 and 20 ga. European walnut stock, beavertail forend, screw-in choke tubes, extractors, 3-inch chambers.   Blued finish. Vent. rib, tang safety. Weight: 6.5 pounds.

ELITE FIELD I DT. . . . .**NiB $1006 Ex $853 Gd $600**
Same as Elite Field I except w/double triggers, fixed chokes, extractors. Available in 12, 20, 28 (2.75-inch chambers) and .410. Bbls: 26 inches, fixed IC/M chokes. Weight: 5.5 to 6.25 lbs.

ELITE FIELD I ST . . . . **NiB $1118 Ex $1065 Gd $790**
Same as Elite Field III except single trigger, fixed chokes, extractors; European walnut stock. Available in 12, 20, 28 (2.75-inch chambers), and .410 ga. fixed IC/M chokes. Weight: 5.75 to 6.5 lbs.

ELITE FIELD III ST . . . . **NiB $1967 Ex $1689 Gd $1333**
Checkered English walnut straight stock, splinter forend, fixed chokes. Available in 28 and .410 ga. 26-inch chrome-lined bbls., C/M chokes. Silver trigger guard and receiver w/hand-finished engraving of upland game scenes w/gold inlays. Automatic ejectors. Brass front sight bead. Weight: About 6.5 lbs. Intro. 2000.

ALS 2100 SEMIAUTO SHOTGUNS
FIELD SERIES, WALNUT MODEL . . . .**NiB $366 Ex $245 Gd $190**
Gas operated. 12 and 20 ga. 3-inch chambers. Cut-checkered Turkish walnut stock and forend, blued 26- and 28-inch vent. rib bbls., multi-choke system, chrome bore lining. Weight: About 6 lbs. Rifled barrel w/cantilever mount available Intro. 2001.

SYNTHETIC STOCK MODEL . . . . . . **NiB $350 Ex $290 Gd $225**
Same as the ALS 2100 Walnut model except w/synthetic stock, matted finish on receiver and bbl. Weight: About 6 lbs.

YOUTH MODEL . . . . **NiB $344 Ex $229 Gd $175**
Same as ALS 2100 Walnut model except w/shorter walnut stock (length of pull: 13.5 inches). Available in 12 or 20 ga. w/24-inch vent. rib barrel. Weight: 5.5 to 6 lbs.

HUNTER COMBO MODEL
Same as ALS 2100 Walnut model except comes w/two bbls. (28-inch vent. rib and 24-inch slug), TruGlo adjustable sights, and cantilever mount. Available w/Turkish walnut or synthetic stock w/ matte barrel finish. Weight: 6.5 lbs.
w/walnut stock. . . . .**NiB $500 Ex $377 Gd $210**
w/synthetic stock . . . .**NiB $475 Ex $339 Gd $220**

SLUG HUNTER MODEL. . . . . **NiB $355 Ex $245 Gd $190**
Same as ALS 2100 Walnut except w/fully-rifled barrel, choice of walnut or synthetic stocks, matte or blue finish; rifle or TruGlo adjustable sights. Weight: About 6.25 lbs.

TURKEY HUNTER/WATERFOWL
MODEL . . . . **NiB $375 Ex $265 Gd $220**
Same as ALS 2100 Walnut except w/synthetic stock. 3-inch chambers. 26-inch vent. rib bbl., screw-in chokes, Mossy Oak or Realtree camo stocks.

HOME SECURITY MODEL . . . . **NiB $335 Ex $260 Gd $190**
Same as ALS 2100 Walnut but w/20-inch cylinder-bore bbl., synthetic stock. 3-inch chambers, 6-round capacity w/2.75-inch shells. Weight: About 6 lbs.

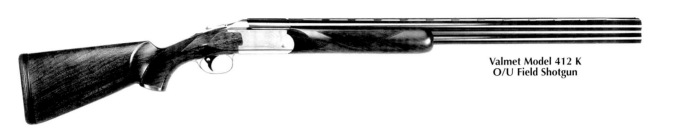

Valmet Model 412 K
O/U Field Shotgun

TRISTAR SPORTING ARMS — North Kansas City, MO

MODEL 1887 LEVER-ACTION REPEATER . . . . . . NiB $765 Ex $580 Gd $445
Copy of John Browning's Winchester Model 1887 lever-action shotgun. 12 ga. only. 30-inch bbl., which may be cut down to any desired length of 18 inches or more. Version shown has 20-inch bbl. Imported from 1997 to 1999.

MODEL 300 O/U SHOTGUN. . . . . NiB $465 Ex $335 Gd $199
Similar to the Model 333 except 12 ga. only. 3-inch chambers. 26- or 28-inch vent. rib bbls. w/extractors and fixed chokes. Etched receiver w/double triggers and standard walnut stock. Imported 1994 to 1998.

MODEL 311 SIDE-BY-SIDE SHOTGUN
Boxlock action w/underlug and Greener crossbolt. 12 or 20 ga. 3-inch chambers. 20-, 28-, or 30-inch bbls. w/choke tubes or fixed chokes (311R). Double triggers. Extractors. Black chrome finish. Checkered Turkish walnut buttstock and forend. Weight: 6.9 to 7.2 lbs. Imported from 1994 to 1997.
w/extractors and choke tubes . . . . NiB $575 Ex $476 Gd $390
311R (w/20-inch bbls. and fixed chokes) . . . . NiB $445 Ex $355 Gd $235

MODEL 330 O/U SHOTGUN
Similar to the Model 333 except 12 ga. only. 3-inch chambers. 26-, 28-, or 30-inch vent. rib bbls w/extractors or ejectors and fixed chokes or choke tubes. Etched receiver and standard walnut stock. Imported from 1994 to 1999.
330 model (w/extractor and fixed chokes). . . . .NiB $545 Ex $420 Gd $300
330 D model (w/ejectors and choke tubes) . . . . .NiB $733 Ex $567 Gd $488

MODEL 333 O/U SHOTGUN
Boxlock action. 12 or 20 ga. 3-inch chambers. 26-, 28-, or 30-inch vent. rib bbls. w/choke tubes. Single selective trigger. Selective automatic ejectors. Engraved receiver w/satin nickel finish. Checkered Turkish fancy walnut buttstock and forend. Weight: 7.5 to 7.75 lbs. Imported from 1994 to 1998.

Field model . . . . NiB $844 Ex $700 Gd $545
Sporting Clays model (1994-97) . . . . . . .NiB $900 Ex $755 Gd $580
TRL Ladies Field model . . . . .NiB $800 Ex $675 Gd $550
SCL Ladies Sporting Clays model
(1994-97) . . . . .NiB $900 Ex $755 Gd $580

SHOTGUNS OF ULM — Ulm, Germany

See listings under Krieghoff.

U.S. REPEATING ARMS CO. — New Haven, CT

See also Winchester.

VALMET — Jyväskylä, Finland

NOTE: *In 1987, Valmet and Sako merged and the Valmet production facilities were moved to Riihimaki, Finland. In 1989 a joint venture agreement was made with Armi Marocchi, and when production began in Italy, the Valmet name was changed to Tikka (Oy Tikkakoski Ab).*

See also Savage Models 330, 333T, 333, and 2400, which were produced by Valmet.

VALMET LION O/U SHOTGUN . . . . . . NiB $475 Ex $388 Gd $293
Boxlock. Selective single trigger. Plain extractors. 12 ga. only. Bbls.: 26-inch IC/M; 28-inch M/F, 30-inch M/F, F/F. Weight: About 7 lbs. Checkered pistol-grip stock and forearm. Imported 1947 to 1968.

MODEL 412 S O/U FIELD SHOTGUN . . . NiB $955 Ex $744 Gd $535
Hammerless. 12-ga. 3-inch chamber. 36-inch bbl., F/F chokes. American walnut Monte Carlo stock. Disc 1989.

Weatherby Model 82
Autoloading Shotgun

MODEL 412 S SHOTGUN RIFLE
COMBINATION . . . . **NiB $1135 Ex $956 Gd $745**
Similar to model 412 K except bottom bbl. chambered for .222 Rem., .223 Rem., .243 Win., .308 Win., or .30-06. 12-ga. shotgun bbl. w/IM choke. Monte Carlo American walnut stock, recoil pad.

MODEL 412 O/U
FIELD SHOTGUN . . . . **NiB $866 Ex $723 Gd $587**
12-ga. Chambered for 2.75-inch shells. 26-inch bbl., IC/M chokes; 28-inch bbl., M/F chokes. 12-ga. chambered for 3-inch shells, 30-inch bbl., M/F chokes. 20-ga. (3-inch shells), 26-inch bbl., IC/M chokes; 28-inch bbl., M/F chokes. American walnut Monte Carlo stock.

MODEL 412 ST SKEET . . . . **NiB $1176 Ex $922 Gd $766**
Similar to Model 412 K except skeet stock and chokes. 12 and 20 ga. Disc. 1989.

MODEL 412 SE TRAP . . . . **NiB $1176 Ex $922 Gd $766**
Similar to Model 412 K Field except trap stock, recoil pad. 30-inch bbls., IM/F chokes. Disc. 1989.
Extra bbl., add. $500

WEATHERBY, INC. — Pasa Robles, CA

MODEL 82 AUTOLOADING
SHOTGUN . . . .**NiB $556 Ex $435 Gd $332**
Hammerless, gas operated. 12 ga. only. Bbls.: 22- to 30-inch, various integral or fixed chokes. Weight: 7.5 lbs. Checkered walnut stock and forearm. Imported from 1982 to 1989.
BuckMaster Auto Slug
w/rifle sights (1986-90) . . . . **NiB $570 Ex $455 Gd $355**
Fixed choke, deduct. $50

MODEL 92 SLIDE-ACTION
SHOTGUN . . . . **NiB $390 Ex $288 Gd $217**
Hammerless, short-stroke action. 12 ga. 3-inch chamber. Tubular magazine. Bbls.: 22-, 26-, 28-, 30-inch w/fixed choke or IMC choke tubes; plain or vent. rib w/rifle sights. Weight: 7.5 lbs. Engraved, matte black receiver and blued barrel. Checkered high-gloss buttstock and forend. Imported from Japan since 1982.
Standard Model 92 . . . . **NiB $330 Ex $261 Gd $195**
BuckMaster Pump Slug
   w/rifle sights, (intro. 1986) . . . . **NiB $420 Ex $315 Gd $235**

ATHENA O/U SHOTGUN
Engraved boxlock action w/Greener crossbolt and sideplates. Gauges: 12, 20, 28, and .410. 2.75- or 3.5-inch chambers. Bbls.: 26-, 28-, 30-, or 32-inch w/fixed or IMC multi-choke tubes. Weight: 6.75 to 7.38 lbs. Single selective trigger. Selective auto ejectors. Top tang safety. Checkered Claro walnut stock and forearm w/high-luster finish. Imported from 1982 to 2002.
Field Model w/IMC multi-chokes,
   12 or 20 ga. . . . . .NiB $2177 Ex $1898 Gd $1635
Field Model w/fixed chokes, 28 ga. or .410. . . . . . NiB $1976 Ex $1645 Gd $1389
Skeet Model w/fixed chokes, 12 or 20 ga. . . . . . NiB $1766 Ex $1432 Gd $1255
Skeet Model w/fixed chokes, 28 ga. or .410 . . . . . NiB $3320 Ex $2808 Gd $2366
Master Skeet tube set. . . . . .NiB $3155 Ex $2776 Gd $2388
Trap Model w/IC tubes . . . . .NiB $2388 Ex $1977 Gd $1677
Grade V (1993 to date) . . . . .NiB $3566 Ex $3100 Gd $2665

CENTURION AUTOMATIC SHOTGUN
Gas operated. Takedown. 12 ga. 2.75-inch chamber. 3-round magazine. Bbls.: Vent. ribs; 26-inch SK/IC/M, 28-inch M/F, 30-inch F choke. Weight: w/28-inch bbl., 7 lbs., 10.5 oz. Checkered pistol-grip stock and forearm, recoil pad. Made in Japan from 1972 to 1981.
Field Grade . . . . **NiB $398 Ex $288 Gd $219**
Trap Gun (30-inch
   full-choke bbl.) . . . . .NiB $435 Ex $377 Gd $235

Deluxe model (etched receiver,
   fancy wood stock) . . . . **NiB $525 Ex $425 Gd $265**

OLYMPIAN O/U SHOTGUN
Gauges: 12 and 20. 2.75- (12 ga.) and 3-inch (20 ga.) chambers. Bbls.: 26, 28, 30, and 32 inch. Weight: 6.75 to 8.75 lbs. American walnut stock and forend.
Field Model. . . . . **NiB $988 Ex $700 Gd $577**
Skeet Model . . . . **NiB $1033 Ex $800 Gd $690**
Trap Model . . . . **NiB $995 Ex $745 Gd $650**

ORION O/U SHOTGUN
Boxlock w/Greener crossbolt. Gauges: 12, 20, 28, and .410; 2.75- or 3-inch chambers. Bbls.: 26-, 28-, 30-, 32-, or 34-inch w/fixed or IMC multi-choke tubes. Weight: 6.5 to 9 lbs. Single selective trigger. Selective auto ejectors. Top tang safety. Checkered, high-gloss pistol-grip. Claro walnut stock and forearm. Finish: Grade I, plain blued receiver; Grade II, engraved blued receiver; Grade III, silver gray receiver. Imported from 1982 and 2002.
Orion I Field w/IC (12 or 20 ga.) . . . . **NiB $1456 Ex $1188 Gd $975**
Orion II Field w/IC (12 or 20 ga.) . . . . **NiB $1155 Ex $965 Gd $743**
Orion II Classic w/IC (12, 20, or 28 ga.) . . . . **NiB $1644 Ex $1388 Gd $1166**
Orion II Sporting Clays w/IC (12 ga.) . . . . **NiB $1997 Ex $1688 Gd $1388**
Orion III Field w/IC (12 or 20 ga.) . . . . . **NiB $1688 Ex $1397 Gd $1188**
Orion III Classic w/IC (12 or
   20 ga.) . . . . **NiB $1988 Ex $1669 Gd $1367**
Orion III English Field w/IC (12 or 20 ga.). . . . . .NiB $1733 Ex $1448 Gd $1244
Orion Upland w/IC (12 or 20 ga.) . . . . . . **NiB $1376 Ex $1133 Gd $976**
Skeet II w/fixed chokes . . . . **NiB $1355 Ex $1125 Gd $950**
Super Sporting Clays . . . . **NiB $1988 Ex $1743 Gd $1129**

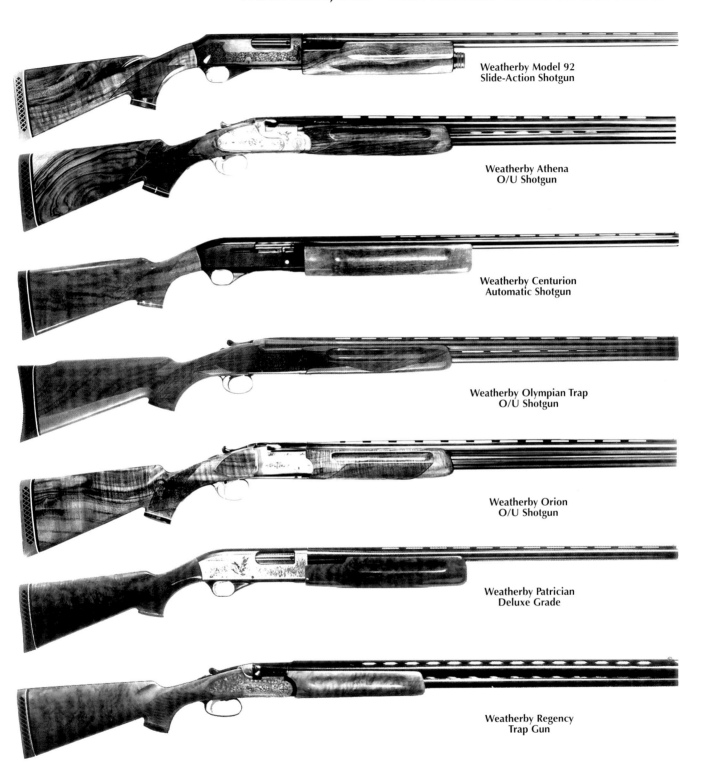

Weatherby Model 92
Slide-Action Shotgun

Weatherby Athena
O/U Shotgun

Weatherby Centurion
Automatic Shotgun

Weatherby Olympian Trap
O/U Shotgun

Weatherby Orion
O/U Shotgun

Weatherby Patrician
Deluxe Grade

Weatherby Regency
Trap Gun

PATRICIAN SLIDE-ACTION SHOTGUN

Hammerless. Takedown. 12 ga. 2.75-inch chamber. 4-round tubular magazine. Bbls.: Vent. rib; 26-inch, SK/IC/M; 28-inch, M/F; 30-inch, F choke. Weight: w/28-inch bbl., 7 lbs., 7 oz. Checkered pistol-grip stock and slide handle, recoil pad. Made in Japan from 1972 to 1982.

Field Grade.	NiB $369	Ex $248	Gd $125
Deluxe model (etched receiver, fancy grade stock)	NiB $455	Ex $329	Gd $260
Trap Gun (w/30-inch full-choke bbl.)	NiB $399	Ex $255	Gd $190

REGENCY FIELD GRADE O/U SHOTGUN..... NiB $1387 Ex $1266 Gd $885
Boxlock w/sideplates, elaborately engraved. Auto ejectors. Selective single trigger. Gauges: 12, 20. 2.75-inch chamber in 12 ga., 3-inch in 20 ga. Bbls.: Vent. rib; 26-inch SK, IC/M, M/F (20 ga. only); 28-inch SK, IC/M, M/F; 30-inch M/F (12 ga only). Weight: w/28-inch bbls., 7 lbs., 6 oz. in 12 ga.; 6 lbs., 14 oz. in 20 ga. Checkered pistol-grip stock and forearm of fancy walnut. Made in Italy from 1965 to 1982.

REGENCY TRAP GUN.......... NiB $990 Ex $823 Gd $688
Similar to Regency Field Grade except has trap-style stock w/straight or Monte Carlo comb. Bbls. have vent. side ribs and high, wide vent. top rib. 30 or 32 inch, M/F, IM/F, or F/F chokes. Weight: w/32-inch bbls., 8 lbs. Made in Italy from 1965 to 1982.

WESTERN ARMS CORP. — Ithaca, NY, division of Ithaca Gun Company

LONG-RANGE HAMMERLESS DOUBLE
Boxlock. Plain extractors. Single or double triggers. Gauges: 12, 16, 20, .410. Bbls.: 26 to 32 inch, M/F choke standard. Weight: 7.5 lbs., 12 ga. Plain pistol-grip stock and forend. Made 1929 to 1946.
w/double triggers .... NiB $398 Ex $244 Gd $165
w/single trigger .... NiB $400 Ex $295 Gd $188

WESTERN AUTO SHOTGUNS — Kansas City, MO

MODEL 300H SLIDE-ACTION REPEATER .... NiB $435 Ex $300 Gd $255
Gauges: 12,16, 20, .410. 4-round tubular magazine. Bbls.: 26 to 30 inch, various chokes. Weight: About 7 lbs. Plain pistol-grip stock, grooved slide handle.

MODEL 310A SLIDE-ACTION REPEATER..... NiB $366 Ex $270 Gd $200
Takedown. 12 ga. 5-round tubular magazine. Bbls.: 28 and 30 inch. Weight: About 7.5 lbs. Plain pistol-grip stock.

MODEL 310B SLIDE-ACTION REPEATER..... NiB $377 Ex $245 Gd $190
Same general specifications as Model 310A except chambered for 16 ga.

MODEL 310C SLIDE-ACTION REPEATER..... NiB $365 Ex $269 Gd $180
Same general specifications as Model 310A except chambered for 20 ga.

MODEL 310E SLIDE-ACTION REPEATER .... NiB $425 Ex $366 Gd $229
Same general specifications as Model 310A except chambered for .410 bore.

MODEL 325BK BOLT-ACTION REPEATER ..... NiB $276 Ex $190 Gd $125
Takedown. 2-round detachable clip magazine. 20 ga. 26-inch bbl. w/variable choke. Weight: 6.25 lbs.

WESTERN FIELD SHOTGUNS

See also "W" for listings under Montgomery Ward.

WESTLEY RICHARDS & CO., LTD. — Birmingham, England

The Pigeon and Wildfowl gun, available in all of the Westley Richards models except the Ovundo, has the same general specifications as the corresponding standard field gun except has

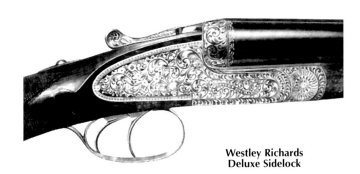

**Westley Richards
Deluxe Sidelock**

Magnum action of extra strength and treble bolting, chambered for 12 ga. only (2.75- or 3-inch); 30-inch F choke barrels standard. Weight: About 8 lbs. The manufacturer warns that 12 ga. Mag. shells should not be used in their standard weight double-barrel shotguns.

BEST QUALITY BOXLOCK HAMMERLESS DOUBLE-BARREL SHOTGUN
Boxlock. Hand-detachable locks and hinged cover plate. Selective ejectors. Double triggers or selective single trigger. Gauges: 12, 16, 20. Bbl. lengths and boring to order. Weight: 5.5 to 6.25 lbs. depending on ga. and bbl. length. Checkered stock and forend, straight or half-pistol grip. Also supplied in Pigeon and Wildfowl models w/same values. Made from 1899 to date.
w/double triggers.............. NiB $22,975 Ex $18,990 Gd $14,270
w/selective single trigger........ NiB $26,790 Ex $21,998 Gd $14,880

BEST QUALITY SIDELOCK HAMMERLESS DOUBLE-BARREL SHOTGUN
Hand-detachable sidelocks. Selective ejectors. Double triggers or selective single trigger. Gauges: 12, 16, 20, 28, .410. Bbl. lengths and boring to order. Weight: 4.75 to 6.75 lbs. depending on ga. and bbl. length. Checkered stock and forend, straight or half-pistol grip. Also supplied in Pigeon and Wildfowl models w/same values. Currently manufactured.
w/double triggers.............. NiB $29,669 Ex $26,766 Gd $22,880
w/selective single trigger........ NiB $30,000 Ex $27,898 Gd $24,550

DELUXE MODEL BOXLOCK HAMMERLESS DOUBLE-BARREL SHOTGUN
Same general specifications as standard Best Quality gun except higher quality throughout. Has Westley Richards top-projection and treble-bite lever-work, hand-detachable locks. Also supplied in Pigeon and Wildfowl models w/same values. Currently manufactured.
w/double trigger .... NiB $12,767 Ex $10,433 Gd $8998
w/selective
single trigger.................. NiB $32,880 Ex $30,880 Gd $13,990

DELUXE MODEL SIDELOCK
Same as Best Quality Sidelock except higher grade engraving and wood. Currently manufactured.
w/double triggers ...... NiB $27,889 Ex $22,999 Gd $14,887
w/single trigger........ NiB $31,998 Ex $26,999 Gd $18,998

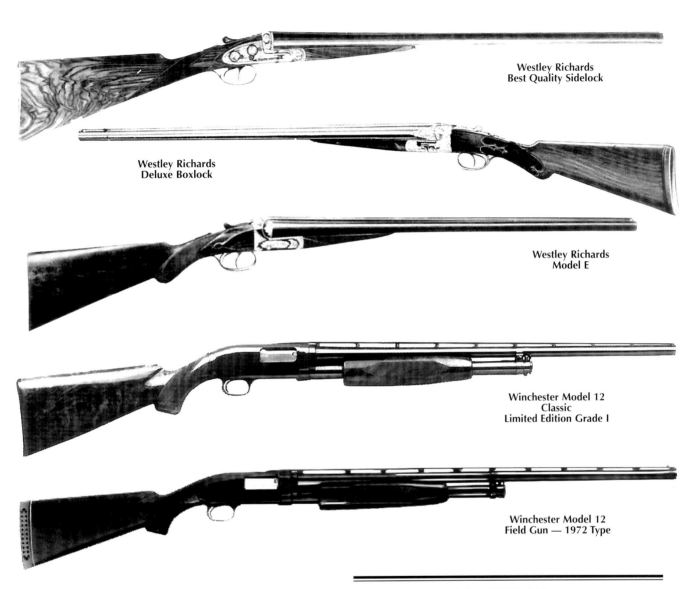

Westley Richards
Best Quality Sidelock

Westley Richards
Deluxe Boxlock

Westley Richards
Model E

Winchester Model 12
Classic
Limited Edition Grade I

Winchester Model 12
Field Gun — 1972 Type

MODEL E HAMMERLESS DOUBLE

Anson & Deeley-type boxlock action. Selective ejector or non-ejector. Double triggers. Gauges: 12, 16, 20. Bbl. lengths and boring to order. Weight: 5.5 to 7.25 lbs. depending on type, ga., and bbl. length. Checkered stock and forend, straight or half-pistol grip. Also supplied in Pigeon and Wildfowl models w/same values. Currently manufactured.

Ejector model . . . . NiB $5388 Ex $4378 Gd $2990
Non-ejector model . . . . NiB $4998 Ex $3788 Gd $3277

OVUNDO (O/U) . . . . NiB $19,677 Ex $16,999 Gd $12,998
Hammerless. Boxlock. Hand-detachable locks. Dummy sideplates. Selective ejectors. Selective single trigger. 12 ga. Bbl.lengths and boring to order. Checkered stock and forend, straight or half-pistol grip. Manufactured before WWII.

TED WILLIAMS SHOTGUNS

See also Sears, Roebuck & Company

WINCHESTER — New Haven, CT

Formerly Winchester Repeating Arms Co., and then manufactured by Winchester-Western Div., Olin Corp., later by U.S. Repeating Arms Company. In 1999, production rights were acquired by Browning Arms Company.

MODEL 12 CLASSIC LIMITED EDITION

Gauge: 20. 2.75-inch chamber. Bbl.: 26-inch vent. rib; IC. Weight: 7 lbs. Checkered walnut buttstock and forend. Polished blue finish (Grade I) or engraved w/gold inlays (Grade IV). Made from 1993 to 1995.

Grade I (4000) . . . . NiB $1100 Ex $889 Gd $656
Grade IV (1000) . . . . NiB $1700 Ex $1308 Gd $998

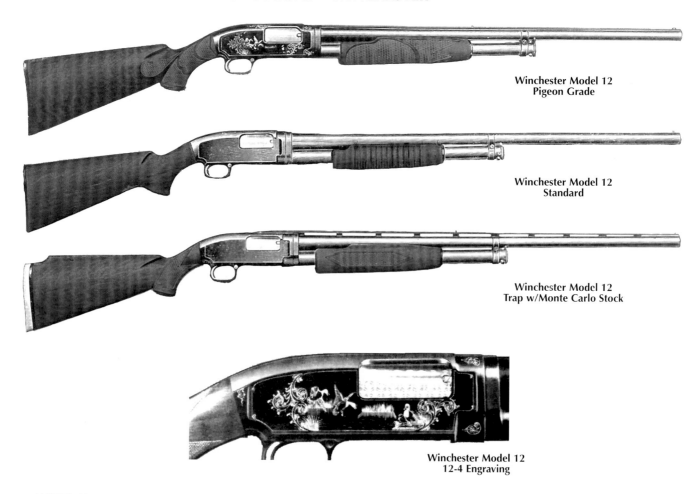

Winchester Model 12
Pigeon Grade

Winchester Model 12
Standard

Winchester Model 12
Trap w/Monte Carlo Stock

Winchester Model 12
12-4 Engraving

MODEL 12

FEATHERWEIGHT............ **NiB $688 Ex $577 Gd $555**
Same as Model 12 Standard w/plain barrel except has alloy trigger guard. Modified takedown w/redesigned magazine tube, cap and slide handle. 12 ga. only. Bbls.: 26-inch IC; 28-inch M/F; 30-inch F choke. Serial numbers with F prefix. Weight: About 6.75 lbs. Made from 1959 to 1962.

MODEL 12 FIELD GUN, 1972 TYPE..... **NiB $800 Ex $685 Gd $522**
Same general specifications as Standard Model 12 but 12 ga. only, 26-, 28-, or 30-inch vent. rib bbl., standard chokes. Engine-turned bolt and carrier. Hand-checkered stock and slide handle of semi-fancy walnut. Made from 1972 to 1975.

MODEL 12 HEAVY DUCK GUN

Same general specifications as Standard Grade except 12 ga. only chambered for 3-inch shells. 30- or 32-inch plain, solid, or vent. rib bbl. w/F choke only. 3-round magazine. Checkered slide handle and pistol-grip walnut buttstock w/recoil pad. Weight: 8.5 to 8.75 lbs. Made from 1935 to 1963.

w/plain bbl. `........................ **NiB $1366 Ex $890 Gd $644**
w/solid rib (disc. 1959) .... **NiB $1977 Ex $1288 Gd $876**
w/vent. rib .... **NiB $3288 Ex $2810 Gd $2466**

MODEL 12 PIGEON GRADE

Deluxe versions of the regular Model 12 Standard or Field Gun; Duck Gun, Skeet Gun, and Trap Gun made on special order. This grade has finer finish throughout, hand-smoothed action, engine-turned breech bolt and carrier, stock and extension slide handle of high grade walnut, fancy checkering, stock dimensions to individual specifications. Engraving and carving available at extra cost ranging from about $135 to more than $1000. Disc. 1965.

Field Gun, plain bbl.	NiB $4233	Ex $3698	Gd $3166
Field Gun, vent. rib	NiB $2255	Ex $1987	Gd $1459
Skeet Gun, matted rib	NiB $2255	Ex $1987	Gd $1459
Skeet Gun, vent. rib...............	NiB $3889	Ex $3350	Gd $3180
Skeet Gun, Cutts Compensator	NiB $1755	Ex $1398	Gd $1100
Trap Gun, matted rib...............	NiB $2233	Ex $1966	Gd $1399
Trap Gun, vent. rib................	NiB $2288	Ex $2190	Gd $2008
16 ga. (Field), add			100%
16 ga. (Skeet), add			100%
20 ga. (Field), add			175%
20 ga. (Skeet), add			175%
28 ga. (Skeet), add			550%

MODEL 12 RIOT GUN........ **NiB $977 Ex $844 Gd $600**
Same general specifications as plain barrel Model 12 Standard except has 20-inch Cyl. bore bbl.,12 ga. only. Made from 1918 to 1963.

MODEL 12 SKEET GUN ..... **NiB $2200 Ex $1977 Gd $1488**
Gauges: 12, 16, 20, 28. 5-round tubular magazine. 26-inch matted rib bbl., SK choke. Weight: About 7.75 lbs., 12 ga.; 6.75 lbs. other ga. Bradley red or ivory bead front sight. Winchester 94B middle sight. Checkered pistol-grip stock and extension slide handle. Disc. after WWII.

Winchester Model 21
Custom Grade

Winchester Model 21
Pigeon Grade

MODEL 12 SKEET GUN, CUTTS COMPENSATOR . . . . NiB $1233 Ex $1000 Gd $766
Same general specifications as standard Model 12 Skeet Gun except has plain bbl. fitted w/Cutts Compensator, 26 inches overall. Disc. 1954.

MODEL 12 SKEET GUN, PLAIN-BARREL . . . . . . NiB $2099 Ex $1887 Gd $1650
Same general specifications as standard Model 12 Skeet except w/no rib.

MODEL 12 SKEET GUN, VENT. RIB . . . . . NiB $4288 Ex $3760 Gd $3290
Same general specifications as standard Model 12 Skeet Gun except has 26-inch bbl. w/vent. rib, 12 and 20 ga. Disc. in 1965.

MODEL 12 SKEET GUN, 1972 TYPE. . . . . . . NiB $1288 Ex $909 Gd $663
Same general specifications as Standard Model 12 but 12 ga. only. 26-inch vent. rib bbl., SK choke. Engine-turned bolt and carrier. Hand-checkered skeet-style stock and slide handle of choice walnut, recoil pad. Made from 1972 to 1975.

MODEL 12 STANDARD GR., MATTED RIB . . . . . NiB $835 Ex $579 Gd $443
Same general specifications as plain bbl. Model 12 Standard except has solid raised matted rib. Disc. after WWII.

MODEL 12 STANDARD GR., VENT RIB. . . . . NiB $866 Ex $571 Gd $400
Same general specifications as plain barrel Model 12 Standard except has vent. rib. 26.75- or 30-inch bbl.,12 ga. only. Disc. after WWII.

MODEL 12 STANDARD SLIDE-ACTION REPEATER
Hammerless. Takedown. Gauges: 12, 16, 20, 28. 6-round tubular magazine. Plain bbl. Lengths: 26 to 32 inch; choked F/C. Weight: About 7.5 lbs., 12 ga. 30-inch; 6.5 lbs. in other ga. w/28-inch bbl. Plain pistol-grip stock, grooved slide handle. Made from 1912 to 1964.

12 ga., 28-inch bbl., F choke	NiB $870	Ex $733	Gd $534
16 ga.	NiB $966	Ex $881	Gd $533
20 ga.	NiB $1277	Ex $855	Gd $633
28 ga.	NiB $5767	Ex $3488	Gd $2499

MODEL 12 SUPER PIGEON GRADE . . . . NiB $4329 Ex $3887 Gd $3176
Custom version of Model 12 w/same general specifications as standard models. 12 ga. only. 26-, 28-, or 30-inch vent. rib bbl., any standard choke. Engraved receiver. Hand-smoothed and fitted action. Full fancy walnut stock and forearm made to individual order. Made from 1965 to 1972.

MODEL 12 TRAP GUN
Same general specifications as Standard Model 12 except has straighter stock, checkered pistol grip and extension slide handle, recoil pad, 30-inch matted rib bbl., F choke, 12 ga. only. Disc. after WWII; vent. rib model disc. 1965.

Matted rib bbl.	NiB $2210	Ex $1966	Gd $1544
w/straight stock, vent. rib	NiB $2299	Ex $2178	Gd $1933
w/Monte Carlo stock, vent. rib	NiB $2175	Ex $2000	Gd $1865

MODEL 12 TRAP GUN, 1972 TYPE . . . . . NiB $1299 Ex $1077 Gd $669
Same general specifications as Standard Model 12 but 12 ga. only. 30-inch vent. rib bbl., F choke. Engine-turned bolt and carrier. Hand-checkered trap-style stock (straight or Monte Carlo comb) and slide handle of select walnut, recoil pad. Intro. in 1972. Disc.

MODEL 20 SINGLE-SHOT HAMMER GUN. . . . . . NiB $1577 Ex $1266 Gd $1008
Takedown. .410 bore. 2.5-inch chamber. 26-inch bbl., F choke. Checkered pistol-grip stock and forearm. Weight: About 6 lbs. Made from 1919 to 1924.

ORIGINAL MODEL 21 DOUBLE-BARREL SHOTGUNS (ORIGINAL PRODUCTION SERIES, 1930 to 1959)
Hammerless. Boxlock. Automatic safety. Double triggers or selective single trigger, selective or nonselective ejection (all postwar Model 21 shotguns have selective single trigger and selective ejection). Gauges: 12, 16, 20, 28, and .410 bore. Bbls.: Raised matted rib or vent. rib; 26, 28, 30, 32 inch, the latter in 12 ga. only; F/IM/M/IC/SK chokes. Weight: 7.5 lbs., 12 ga. w/30-inch bbl.; about 6.5 lbs. 16 or 20 ga. w/28-inch bbl. Checkered pistol- or straight-grip stock, regular or beavertail forend. Made from 1930 to 1959.

Standard Grade, 12 ga.	NiB $7344	Ex $6100	Gd $4350
Standard Grade, 16. Ga.	NiB $9000	Ex $5466	Gd $4000
Standard Grade, 20 ga.	NiB $10,008	Ex $6355	Gd $3988
Tournament Grade, 12 ga. (1933-34)	NiB $5733	Ex $5000	Gd $3889
Tournament Grade, 16 ga. (1933-34)	NiB $6893	Ex $6324	Gd $4388
Tournament Grade, 20 ga. (1933-34)	NiB $8244	Ex $6887	Gd $4632
Trap Grade, 12 ga. (1940-59).	NiB $5689	Ex $5000	Gd $4277
Trap Grade, 16 ga. (1940-59).	NiB $6044	Ex $4988	Gd $3776
Trap Grade, 20 ga. (1940-59).	NiB $7768	Ex $6322	Gd $3200
Skeet Grade, 12 ga. (1936-59).	NiB $5463	Ex $4465	Gd $3100
Skeet Grade, 16 ga. (1936-59).	NiB $6200	Ex $4988	Gd $3677
Skeet Grade, 20 ga. (1936-59).	NiB $7100	Ex $5998	Gd $4325
Duck Gun, 12 ga., 3-inch (1940-52).	NiB $5980	Ex $4966	Gd $3544
Magnum, 12 ga., 3-inch (1953-59)	NiB $5688	Ex $4765	Gd $3300
Magnum, 20 ga., 3-inch (1953-59)	NiB $6900	Ex $5779	Gd $4200
Cust. Deluxe grade, 12 ga. (1993-59)	NiB $8634	Ex $6892	Gd $4855
Cust. Deluxe grade, 16 ga., (1933-59)	NiB $10,339	Ex $8833	Gd $6450
Cust. Deluxe grade, 20 ga. (1933-59)	NiB $11,880	Ex $9893	Gd $6588
Cust. Deluxe grade, 28 ga. (1933-59) Very Rare.	NiB $30,000+		
Cust. Deluxe grade, .410 (1933-59) Very Rare. . . .	NiB $35,000+		

Fewer than 100 small bore models (28 ga. and .410) were built, which precludes accurate pricing, but projected values could exceed $30,000. Such rare specimens should be authenticated by factory letter and/or independent appraisals.

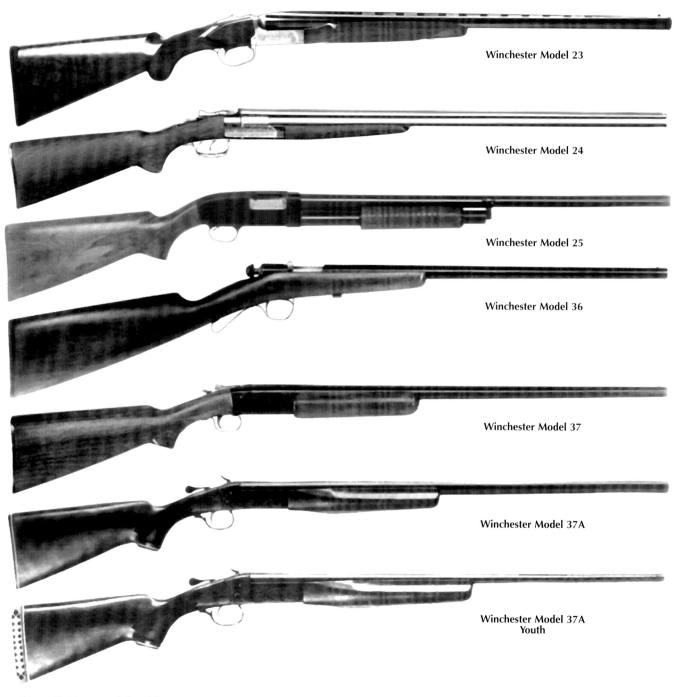

Winchester Model 23

Winchester Model 24

Winchester Model 25

Winchester Model 36

Winchester Model 37

Winchester Model 37A

Winchester Model 37A
Youth

Vent. rib,12 ga. models, add $900
Vent. rib, 16 ga. models, add $1825
Vent. rib, 20 ga. models, add $1375
Double triggers & extractors, deduct 30%
Double triggers, selective ejection, deduct 20%
Custom engraving:
  No. 1 pattern, add 25%
  No. 2 pattern, add 35%
  No. 3 pattern, add 50%
  No. 4 pattern, add 35%
  No. 5 pattern, add 65%
  No. 6 pattern, add 75%

MODEL 21 CUSTOM, PIGEON, GRAND AMERICAN (CUSTOM SHOP SERIES, PRODUCTION 1959 TO 1981)

Since 1959 the Model 21 has been offered through the Custom Shop in deluxe models. Custom, Pigeon, Grand American on special order. General specifications same as for Model 21 standard models except these custom guns have full fancy American walnut stock and forearm with fancy checkering, finely polished and hand-smoothed working parts, etc.; engraving inlays, carved stocks, and other extras are available at additional cost. Made 1959 to 1981.
Custom grade, 12 ga. . . . . NiB $11,980 Ex $9876 Gd $6759
Custom grade, 16 ga. . . . . NiB $17,544 Ex $13,977 Gd $10,655
Custom grade, 20 ga. . . . . NiB $14,677 Ex $11,877 Gd $8321

Winchester
Model 40 Skeet

Pigeon grade, 12 ga. . . . . .NiB $17,889 Ex $14,670 Gd $10,300
Pigeon grade, 16 ga. . . . . NiB $22,889 Ex $18,987 Gd $13,770
Pigeon grade, 20 ga. . . . . .NiB $21,800 Ex $19,880 Gd $14,800
Grand American, 12 ga. . . . . .NiB $25,700 Ex $19,900 Gd $14,600
Grand American, 16 ga. . . . . .NiB $39,600 Ex $31,877 Gd $22,955
Grand American, 20 ga. . . . . .NiB $30,888 Ex $27,888 Gd $20,556
Grand American 3-bbl. Set . . . . . .NiB $42,750 Ex $35,799 Gd $25,799
Small Bore Models
28 ga. and .410 (fewer than 20 made) . . . . $35,000+

NOTE: *Fewer than 20 small bore models (28 ga. and .410) were built during this period, which precludes accurate pricing, but projected values could exceed $35,000. Such rare specimens should be authenticated by factory letter and/or independent appraisals.*
For Custom Shop Engraving from this period:
No. 1 Pattern, add 10%
No. 2 Pattern, add 15%
No. 3 Pattern, add 25%
No. 4 Pattern, add 35%
No. 5 Pattern, add 45%
No. 6 Pattern, add 50%

MODEL 21 U.S.R.A. CUSTOM SERIES
(CUSTOM SHOP PRODUCTION 1982 TO DATE)
Individual model designations for the Model 21 (made from 1931 to 1982) were changed when U.S. Repeating Arms Company assumed production. The new model nomenclature for the custom-built catagory includes: Standard Custom, Special Custom, and Grand American—all of which are available on special order through the Custom Shop. General specifications remained the same on these consolidated model variations and included the addition of a small bore 2-bbl. set (28/.410) and a 3-bbl. set (20/28/.410). Made 1982 to date.
Standard custom model. . . . . NiB $6988 Ex $5570 Gd $4000
Special Custom model. . . . . NiB $8000 Ex $6500 Gd $4666
Grand American model . . . . NiB $14,880 Ex $12,980 Gd $9660
Grand American model, 2-bbl. set . . . . .NiB $48,900 Ex $38,790 Gd $26,998
Grand American, 3-bbl. set . . . . . .NiB $72,877 Ex $59,988 Gd $26,800

The values shown above represent the basic model in each catagory. Since many customers took advantage of the custom options, individual gun appointments vary, and values will need to be adjusted accordingly. For this reason, individual appraisals should be obtained on all subject firearms.

MODEL 23 SIDE-BY-SIDE SHOTGUN
Boxlock. Single trigger. Automatic safety. Gauges: 12, 20, 28, .410. Bbls.: 25.5-, 26-, 28-inch w/fixed chokes or Winchoke tubes.

Weight: 5.88 to 7 lbs. Checkered American walnut buttstock and forend. Made in 1979 for Olin at its Olin-Kodensha facility, Japan.
Classic 23 (gold inlay, engraved) . . . . NiB $2779 Ex $2466 Gd $2365
Custom 23 (plain receiver, Winchoke). . . . . NiB $1477 Ex $1155 Gd $966
Heavy Duck 23, Standard . . . . NiB $2768 Ex $2398 Gd $2077
Lightweight 23, Classic . . . . NiB $2188 Ex $1808 Gd $1266
Light Duck 23, Standard . . . . NiB $2987 Ex $2665 Gd $2240

Light Duck 23, 12 ga. Golden Quail . . . . .NiB $2877 Ex $2549 Gd $2266
Light Duck 23, .410 Golden Quail . . . . . NiB $4577 Ex $4328 Gd $3972
Custom Set 23, 20, and 28 ga. . . . . NiB $6988 Ex $5100 Gd $3766

MODEL 24 HAMMERLESS DOUBLE
Boxlock. Double triggers. Plain extractors. Auto safety. Gauges: 12, 16, 20. Bbls.: 26-inch IC/M; 28-inch M/F (also IC/M in 12 ga. only); 30-inch M/F in 12 ga. only. Weight: About 7.5 lbs., 12 ga. Metal bead front sight. Plain pistol-grip stock, semi-beavertail forearm. Made from 1939 to 1957.
12 ga. model. . . . . NiB $966 Ex $733 Gd $544
16 ga. model. . . . . NiB $1088 Ex $800 Gd $623
20 ga. model. . . . . NiB $1221 Ex $945 Gd $711

MODEL 25 RIOT GUN . . . . NiB $677 Ex $455 Gd $390
Same as Model 25 Standard except has 20-inch Cyl. bore bbl., 12 ga. only. Made from 1949 to 1955.

MODEL 25 7550 . . . . Ex $404 Gd $358
Hammerless. Solid frame. 12 ga. only. 4-round tubular magazine. 28-inch plain bbl.; IC/M/F choke. Weight: About 7.5 lbs. Metal bead front sight. Plain pistol-grip stock, grooved slide handle. Made from 1949 to 1955.

MODEL 36 SINGLE-SHOT
BOLT ACTION . . . . NiB $1893 Ex $1688 Gd $1477
Takedown. Uses 9mm Short or Long shot or ball cartridges interchangeably. 18-inch bbl. Plain stock. Weight: About 3 lbs. Made from 1920 to 1927.

MODEL 37 SINGLE-SHOT SHOTGUN
Semi-hammerless. Auto ejection. Takedown. Gauges: 12, 16, 20, 28, .410. Bbl.: 28, 30, 32 inch in all ga. except .410; 26 or 28 inch in .410; all barrels plain w/F choke. Weight: About 6.5 lbs., 12 ga. Made from 1937 to 1963.
12, 16, 20 ga. models . . . . NiB $559 Ex $438 Gd $315
Youth model (20 ga. w/red dot indicator) . . . . NiB $559 Ex $438 Gd $315
.410 model. . . . . NiB $769 Ex $588 Gd $437
28 ga. model (Red Letter version). . . . . NiB $2687 Ex $2531 Gd $2033
Other Red Letter models, add. 20%
32-inch bbl., add 15%

MODEL 37A SINGLE-SHOT SHOTGUN
Similar to Model 370 except has engraved receiver and gold trigger, checkered pistol-grip stock, fluted forearm; 16 ga. available w/30-inch bbl. only. Made from 1973 to 1980.
12, 16, or 20 ga. models. . . . . NiB $579 Ex $300 Gd $219
28 ga. model. . . . . NiB $2590 Ex $2331 Gd $2268
.410 model . . . . NiB $754 Ex $559 Gd $366
32-inch bbl., add. $50

MODEL 37A YOUTH . . . . NiB $566 Ex $397 Gd $244
Similar to Model 370 Youth except has engraved receiver and gold trigger, checkered pistol-grip stock, fluted forearm. Made 1973 to 1980.

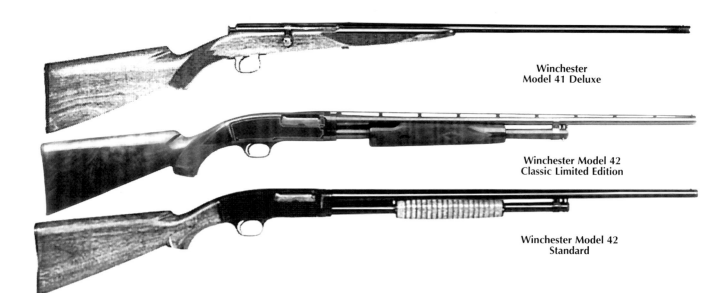

Winchester
Model 41 Deluxe

Winchester Model 42
Classic Limited Edition

Winchester Model 42
Standard

MODEL 40 SKEET GUN . . . . . . NiB $1188 Ex $966 Gd $700
Same general specifications as Model 40 Standard except has
24-inch plain bbl. w/Cutts Compensator and screw-in choke
tube, checkered forearm and pistol grip, grip cap. Made 1940
to 1941.

MODEL 40 STANDARD AUTOLOADER . . . . .NiB $977 Ex $721 Gd $533
Streamlined receiver. Hammerless. Takedown. 12 ga. only. 4-round
tubular magazine. 28- or 30-inch bbl.; M/F choke. Weight: About
8 lbs. Bead sight on ramp. Plain pistol-grip stock, semi-beavertail
forearm. Made from 1940 to 1941.

MODEL 41 SINGLE-SHOT BOLT ACTION
Takedown. .410 bore. 2.5-inch chamber (chambered for 3-inch
shells after 1932). 24-inch bbl., F choke. Plain straight stock stan-
dard. Also made in deluxe version. Made from 1920 to 1934.
Standard model. . . . . NiB $800 Ex $618 Gd $509
Deluxe model . . . . NiB $954 Ex $732 Gd $600

MODEL 42 STANDARD GRADE
Hammerless. Takedown. .410 bore (3- or 2.5-inch shell). Tubular
magazine holds five 3-inch or six 2.5-inch shells. 26- or 28-inch
plain or solid rib bbl.; Cyl. bore, M/F choke. Weight: 5.8 to 6.5
lbs. Plain pistol-grip stock; grooved slide handle. Made from
1933 to 1963.
w/plain bbl. . . . . Nib $2675 Ex $2143 Gd $1609
w/solid rib . . . . .NiB $3750 Ex $3396 Gd $3184

MODEL 42 CLASSIC LTD. EDITION . . . . . . NiB $1886 Ex $1599 Gd $1179
Gauge: .410. 2.75-inch chamber. Bbl.: 26-inch vent. rib; F
choke. Weight: 7 lbs. Checkered walnut buttstock and forend.
Engraved blue w/gold inlays. Limited production of 850. Made
from 1993.

MODEL 42 DELUXE . . . . NiB $22,700 Ex $19,745 Gd $17,998
Same general specifications as the Model 42 Trap Grade except
available w/vent. rib after 1955. Finer finish throughout w/hand-
smoothed action, engine-turned breech bolt and carrier, stock and
extension slide handle of high grade walnut, fancy checkering,
stock dimensions to individual specifications. Engraving and carving were offered at extra cost. Made 1940 to 1963. **NOTE:** *Exercise
caution on VR models not marked DELUXE on the bottom of the
receiver. A factory letter will ensure that the rib was installed during*

*the initial manufacturing process. Unfortunately, factory authenti-
cation is not always possible due to missing or destroyed records.
To further complicate this matter, not all VR ribs were installed by
Winchester. From 1955 to 1963, both Deluxe and Skeet Grade
models were available with Simmons-style ribs. Aftermarket rib
installations are common.*

MODEL 42 PIGEON GRADE
This higher-grade designation is similar to the Deluxe grade and
is available in all configurations. May be identified by engraved
pigeon located at the base of the magazine tube. Most production
occurred in the late 1940s. **NOTE:** *To determine the value of any
Model 42 Pigeon Grade, add 50% to value listed under the specified Model 42 configuration.*

MODEL 42 SKEET GUN
Same general specifications as Model 42 Standard except has
checkered straight or pistol-grip stock and extension slide handle.
26- or 28-inch plain, solid rib, or vent. rib bbl. May be choked
F/M/IC/SK. Note: Some Model 42 Skeet Guns are chambered for
2.5-inch shells only. Made from 1933 to 1963.
w/plain bbl. . . . . NiB $6277 Ex $4500 Gd $3769
w/solid rib . . . . NiB $6277 Ex $4500 Gd $3769
w/vent. rib . . . . NiB $6833 Ex $5971 Gd $4948
2.5-inch chamber, add 35%

MODEL 42 TRAP GRADE
This higher grade designation was available in both field and skeet
configurations and is fitted w/deluxe wood w/trap grade checkering pattern and marked TRAP on bottom of receiver. Made 1934 to
1939. Superseded by the Deluxe model in 1940.
w/plain bbl. . . . . .NiB $27,977 Ex $24,770 Gd $22,665
w/solid rib . . . . .NiB $27,977 Ex $24,770 Gd $22,665
w/vent. rib . . . . .NiB $27,855 Ex $25,693 Gd $23,449

MODEL 50 FIELD GUN, VENT. RIB . . . . NiB $766 Ex $541 Gd $396
Same as Model 50 Standard except has vent. rib.

MODEL 50 SKEET GUN . . . . . NiB $1422 Ex $1269 Gd $1031
Same as Model 50 Standard except has 26-inch vent. rib bbl. w/SK
choke, skeet-style stock of select walnut.

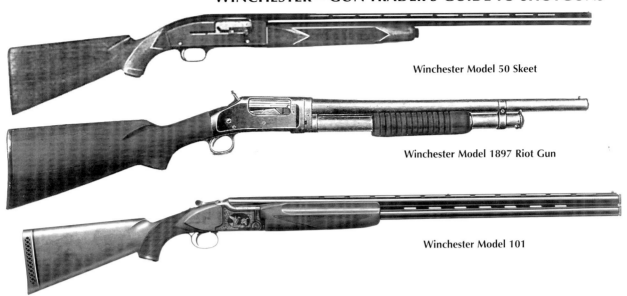

Winchester Model 50 Skeet

Winchester Model 1897 Riot Gun

Winchester Model 101

MODEL 50 STANDARD GRADE.... NiB $779 Ex $500 Gd $388
Non-recoiling bbl. and independent chamber. Gauges: 12 and 20. 2-round tubular magazine. Bbl.: 12 ga., 26, 28, 30 inch; 20 ga., 26, 28 inch; IC/SK/M/F choke. Checkered pistol-grip stock and forearm. Weight: About 7.75 lbs. Made from 1954 to 1961.

MODEL 50 TRAP GUN...... NiB $1466 Ex $1284 Gd $1066
Same as Model 50 Standard except 12 ga. only, has 30-inch vent. rib bbl. w/F choke, Monte Carlo stock of select walnut.

MODEL 59 SEMIAUTOMATIC ....NiB $878 Ex $655 Gd $555
Gauge: 12. Magazine holds two rounds. Alloy receiver. Win-Lite steel and fiberglass bbl.: 26-inch IC, 28-inch M/F choke, 30-inch F choke; also furnished w/26-inch bbl. w/Versalite choke (interchangeable F/M/IC tubes; one supplied w/gun). Weight: About 6.5 lbs. Checkered pistol-grip stock and forearm. Made 1959 to 1965.

MODEL 1893 .... NiB $1100 Ex $930 Gd $600
First pump-action shotgun manufactured by Winchester. Standard Grade. Solid frame. Gauges: 12. Black powder shells only. 5-round tubular magazine. Bbl.: Plain; 30 or 32 inches, F choke. Plain pistol-grip stock, grooved slide handle. Appox. 34,000 manufactured. Made from 1893 to 1897.

MODEL 1897 BUSH GUN
Takedown or solid frame. Same general specifications as standard Model 1897 except w/26-inch Cyl. bore bbl. Made 1897 to 1931.
w/solid frame .... NiB $995 Ex $700 Gd $554
Takedown model........... NiB $1299 Ex $1056 Gd $800

MODEL 1897 RIOT GUN
Takedown or solid frame. Same general specifications as standard Model 1897 except 12 ga. only. 20-inch Cyl. bore bbl. Made from 1898 to 1935.
w/solid frame ....NiB $1544 Ex $1187 Gd $900
Takedown model..............NiB $1390 Ex $1055 Gd $773

MODEL 1897 TRAP, TOURNAMENT, AND PIGEON GRADES
These higher grade models offer higher overall quality than the standard grade. Made from 1897 to 1939.
Standard Trap grade .... NiB $2600 Ex $2208 Gd $1188
Special Trap grade......... NiB $1794 Ex $1566 Gd $1180
Tournament grade
(Black Diamond)........... NiB $2971 Ex $2387 Gd $1698
Pigeon grade.............NiB $11,000 Ex $9533 Gd $3000

MODEL 1897 TRENCH GUN.... NiB $4800 Ex $3693 Gd $2138
Solid frame. Same as Model 1897 Riot Gun except has handguard and is equipped w/a bayonet. WWI government issue from 1917 to 1918.
Military markings, add 20%

MODEL 1897 SLIDE-ACTION REPEATER
Standard Grade. Takedown or solid frame. Gauges: 12 and 16. 5-round tubular magazine. Bbl.: Plain; 26 to 32 inches, the latter in 12 ga. only; choked F/C. Weight: About 7.75 lbs. (12 ga. w/28-inch barrel). Plain pistol-grip stock, grooved slide handle. Made from 1897 to 1957.
12 ga. w/solid frame.......... NiB $1110 Ex $855 Gd $675
16 ga. w/solid frame.......... NiB $1110 Ex $855 Gd $675
12 ga., takedown model ..... NiB $1356 Ex $1108 Gd $888
16 ga., takedown model ..... NiB $1356 Ex $1108 Gd $888

Note: All Winchester Model 101s are manufactured for Olin Corp. at its Olin-Kodensha facility in Tochigi, Japan. Production for Olin Corp. stopped in Nov. 1987. Importation of Model 101s was continued by Classic Doubles under that logo until 1990. See separate heading for additional data.

MODEL 101
COMBINATION GUN ...... NiB $2983 Ex $2777 Gd $2369
12-ga. Winchoke bbl. on top and rifle bbl. chambered for .30-06 on bottom (over/under). 25-inch bbls. Engraved receiver. Hand checkered walnut stock and forend. Weight: 8.5 lbs. Manufactured for Olin Corp. in Japan.

MODEL 101 DIAMOND
GRADE TARGET .... NiB $1978 Ex $1596 Gd $1180
Similar to Model 101 Standard except silvered frame and Winchoke interchangeable choke tubes. Made from 1981 to 1990.

MODEL 101 O/U FIELD GUN
Boxlock. Engraved receiver. Auto ejectors. Single selective trigger. Combination bbl. selector and safety. Gauges: 12 and 28, 2.75-inch chambers; 20 and .410, 3-inch chambers. Vent. rib bbls.: 30 (12 ga. only) and 26.5 inch, IC/M. Weight: 6.25 to 7.75 lbs. depending on gauge and bbl. length. Hand-checkered French walnut and forearm. Made from 1963 to 1981. Ga. other than 12 introduced 1966.
12 and 20 ga. .... NiB $1099 Ex $882 Gd $723
28 and .410 ga.............. NiB $1622 Ex $1244 Gd $977
12 and 20 ga. Mag.......... NiB $1288 Ex $1077 Gd $766

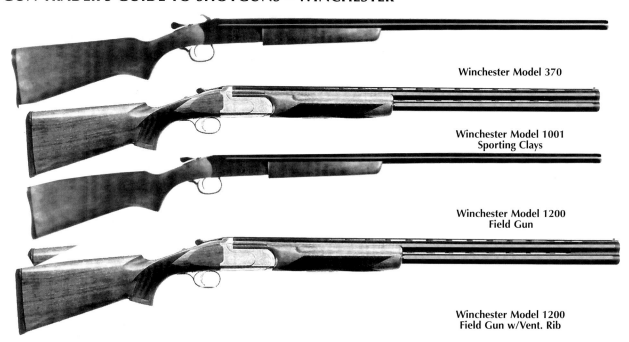

Winchester Model 370

Winchester Model 1001
Sporting Clays

Winchester Model 1200
Field Gun

Winchester Model 1200
Field Gun w/Vent. Rib

MODEL 101 MAGNUM . . . . . . NiB $1300 Ex $1000 Gd $520
Same specifications as Model 101 Field except w/ 30-in. bbl. 12
or 20 ga. w/3-inch chambers. 25.5-inch bbls. w/F/M or F/F choke.
Made 1966 to 1981.

MODEL 101 PIGEON GRADE
Similar to Model 101 Standard except engraved silvered frame and
select wood. Winchoke tubes. Made from 1974 to 1987.
12 ga. model. . . . . NiB $2200 Ex $1820 Gd $1150
20 ga. model. . . . . NiB $2700 Ex $2000 Gd $1500
28 ga. model. . . . . NiB $3760 Ex $2920 Gd $1700
.410 model . . . . NiB $3530 Ex $2925 Gd $1700

MODEL 101 PIGEON GRADE LIGHTWEIGHT
Similar to Model 101 Standard except 20 ga. only. 27-inch bbl.
Receiver engraved w/gold. Limited production. Made 1995 to 1996.
2-bbl. set. . . . . NiB $3600 Ex $2960 Gd $1900

MODEL 101 PIGEON GRADE
SPORTING . . . . NiB $2275 Ex $1630 Gd $900
Similar to Model 101 Standard except 12 ga. only w/30- or
32-inch ported, wide rib bbl. Silver nitride receiver. Stock: adj.
comb, high grade walnut. Made 2009 to 2010.

MODEL 101 QUAIL SPECIAL
Same specifications as small-frame Model 101 except in 28 and
.410 ga. w/3-inch chambers. 25.5-inch bbls. w/choke tubes (28 ga.)
or M/F chokes (.410). Imported from Japan in 1984 to 1987.
12 ga. model. . . . . NiB $3155 Ex $2926 Gd $2554
20 ga. . . . . NiB $3599 Ex $3466 Gd $3200
28 ga. model. . . . . NiB $5799 Ex $4933 Gd $4200
.410 model . . . . NiB $4733 Ex $4122 Gd $3888

MODEL 101 SKEET . . . . NiB $1200 Ex $830 Gd $600
Same specifications as Model 101 Field except w/26.5-inch
bbl., 12 or 20 ga.; 28-in. bbl., 28 ga. or .410. Made 1966 to
1984.
3-ga. set
 (1974 to 1984). . . . . NiB $3800 Ex $3100 Gd $2000

MODEL 101 TRAP . . . . .NiB $1330 Ex $950 Gd $620
Same specifications as Model 101 Field except w/30 or 32-inch
bbl., 12 ga. only. Standard or wide vent. rib. Made 1966 to 1984.

MODEL 370
SINGLE-SHOT SHOTGUN . . . . . . NiB $245 Ex $200 Gd $99
Visible hammer. Auto ejector. Takedown. Gauges: 12, 16, 20, 28,
.410. 2.75-inch chambers in 16 and 28 ga., 3-inch in other ga.
Bbls.: 12 ga., 30, 32, or 36 inch; 16 ga., 30 or 32 inch; 20 and 28
ga., 28 inch; .410 bore, 26 inch; all F choke. Weight: 5.5 to 6.25
lbs. Plain pistol-grip stock and forearm. Made from 1968 to 1973.

MODEL 370 YOUTH MODEL
Same as standard Model 370 except has 26-inch bbl. and 12.5-
inch stock w/recoil pad. 20 ga. w/IM choke, .410 bore w/F choke.
Made from 1968 to 1973.
12, 16, or 20 ga. models. . . . . . . NiB $244 Ex $190 Gd $121
20 ga. model. . . . . NiB $300 Ex $221 Gd $165
.410 model . . . . NiB $355 Ex $220 Gd $175

MODEL 1001 O/U SHOTGUN
Boxlock. 12 ga. 2.75- or 3-inch chambers. Bbls.: 28- or 30-inch
vent. rib; WinPlus choke tubes. Weight: 7 to 7.75 lbs. Checkered
walnut buttstock and forend. Blued finish w/scroll engraved
receiver. Made from 1993 to 1998.
Field model
 (28-inch bbl., 3-inch) . . . . NiB $1133 Ex $978 Gd $726
Sporting Clays model . . . . NiB $1166 Ex $1044 Gd $863
Sporting Clays Lite model. . . . . . NiB $1187 Ex $990 Gd $734

MODEL 1200 DEER GUN. . . . . . . NiB $398 Ex $221 Gd $155
Same as standard Model 1200 except has special 22-inch bbl.
w/rifle-type sights for rifled slug or buckshot. 12 ga. only. Weight:
6.5 lbs. Made from 1965 to 1974.

MODEL 1200 DEFENDER SERIES
SLIDE-ACTION SECURITY SHOTGUNS
Hammerless. 12 ga. 3-inch chamber. 18-inch bbl. w/Cyl. bore
and metal front bead or rifle sights. 4- or 7-round magazine.
Weight: 5.5 to 6.75 lbs. 25.6 inches (PG Model) or 38.6 inches overall. Matte blue finish. Synthetic pistol grip or walnut
finished hardwood buttstock w/grooved synthetic or

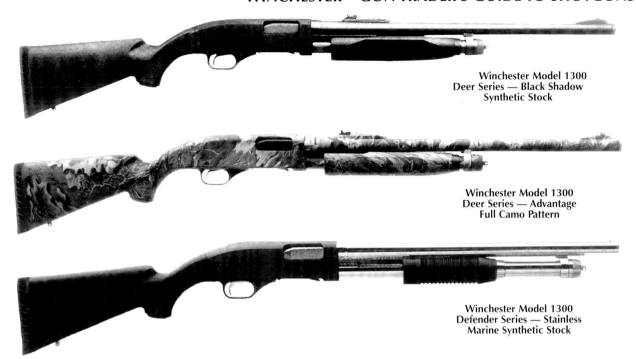

Winchester Model 1300
Deer Series — Black Shadow
Synthetic Stock

Winchester Model 1300
Deer Series — Advantage
Full Camo Pattern

Winchester Model 1300
Defender Series — Stainless
Marine Synthetic Stock

hardwood slide handle. Note: Even though the 1200 series was introduced in 1964 and was supplanted by the Model 1300 in 1978, the Security series (including the Defender model) was marketed under 1200 series alpha-numeric product codes (G1200DM2R) until 1989. In 1990, the same Defender model was marketed under a 4-digit code (7715) and was then advertised in the 1300 series.

w/hardwood stock, bead sight . . . NiB $325 Ex $233 Gd $188
w/hardwood stock, rifle sights . . . NiB $325 Ex $233 Gd $188
w/pistol-grip stock . . . . NiB $325 Ex $233 Gd $188
Combo model
  w/extra 28-inch plain bbl. . . . . . NiB $345 Ex $290 Gd $239
Defender Combo model
  w/extra 28-inch vent. rib bbl. . . . NiB $425 Ex $344 Gd $239

MODEL 1200 MAGNUM FIELD GUN
Same as standard Model 1200 except chambered for 3-inch 12 and 20 ga. Mag. shells; plain or vent. rib bbl., 28 or 30 inch, F choke. Weight: 7.38 to 7.88 lbs. Made from 1964 to 1983.
w/plain bbl. . . . . NiB $325 Ex $240 Gd $179
w/vent. rib bbl. . . . . NiB $350 Ex $265 Gd $190
Recoil reduction system, add $100

MODEL 1200 RANGER
SLIDE-ACTION SHOTGUN . . . . . NiB $400 Ex $285 Gd $195
Hammerless. 12 and 20 ga. 3-inch chambers. Walnut finished hardwood stock, ribbed forearm. 28-inch vent. rib bbl.; Winchoke system. Weight: 7.25 lbs. Made from 1982 to 1990 by U.S. Repeating Arms.

MODEL 1200 RANGER YOUTH
SLIDE-ACTION SHOTGUN . . . . . NiB $400 Ex $285 Gd $195
Same general specifications as standard Ranger Slide-Action except chambered for 20 ga. only, has 4-round magazine, recoil pad on buttstock. Weight: 6.5 lbs. Manufactured by U.S. Repeating Arms.

MODEL 1200 RANGER SLIDE-ACTION FIELD GUN
Front-locking rotary bolt. Takedown. 4-round magazine. Gauges: 12, 16, 20 (2.75-inch chamber). Bbl.: Plain or vent. rib; 26, 28, 30

inch; IC/M/F choke or w/Winchoke (interchangeable tubes IC/M/F). Weight: 6.5 to 7.25 lbs. Checkered pistol-grip stock and forearm (slide handle), recoil pad; also avail. 1966 to 1970 w/Winchester recoil reduction system (Cycolac stock). Made from 1964 to 1983.
w/plain bbl. . . . . NiB $400 Ex $285 Gd $195
w/vent. rib bbl. . . . . NiB $420 Ex $305 Gd $217
Recoil reduction system, add $100
Winchoke, add $50

MODEL 1200 STAINLESS MARINE SERIES SLIDE-ACTION SECURITY SHOTGUN
Similar to Model 1200 Defender except w/6-round magazine. 18-inch bbl. of ordnance stainless steel w/Cyl. bore and rifle sights. Weight: 7 lbs. Bright chrome finish. Synthetic pistol grip or walnut finished hardwood buttstock w/grooved synthetic or hardwood slide handle. Made from 1984 to 1990.
w/hardwood stock . . . . NiB $325 Ex $235 Gd $175
w/pistol-grip stock . . . . NiB $325 Ex $235 Gd $175

MODEL 1200 STAINLESS POLICE SERIES SLIDE-ACTION SECURITY SHOTGUN
Similar to Model 1200 Defender except w/6-round magazine. 18-inch bbl. of ordnance stainless steel w/Cyl. bore and rifle sights. Weight: 7 lbs. Matte chrome finish. Synthetic pistol grip or walnut finished hardwood buttstock w/grooved synthetic or hardwood slide handle. Made from 1984 to 1990.
Police model w/hardwood stock. . . . . NiB $255 Ex $202 Gd $125
Police model w/pistol grip stock . . . . NiB $255 Ex $202 Gd $125

MODEL 1200 TRAP GUN
Same as standard Model 1200 except 12 ga. only. Has 2-round magazine. 30-inch vent. rib bbl., F choke; 28-inch w/Winchoke. Semi-fancy walnut stock, straight. Made from 1965 to 1973 Also available 1966 to 1970 w/Winchester recoil reduction system.
w/straight trap stock . . . . NiB $425 Ex $260 Gd $180
w/Monte Carlo stock . . . . NiB $425 Ex $260 Gd $180
Recoil reduction system, add $100
Winchoke, add $50

Winchester Model 1300
Lady Defender — Synthetic Full Stock

Winchester Model 1300
Lady Defender — Synthetic Pistol Grip Stock

Winchester Model 1300
Defender 5-Shot Combo

Winchester Model 1300
Turkey Gun

Winchester Model 1300
XTR w/Winchoke

Winchester Model 1300
Magnum Waterfowl

MODEL 1200 RANGER
COMBINATION SHOTGUN . . . . . NiB $440 Ex $300 Gd $217
Same as Ranger Deer combination except has one 28-inch vent. rib bbl. w/M choke and one 18-inch Police Cyl. bore bbl. Made 1987 to 1990.

MODEL 1200 SKEET GUN . . . . . . NiB $450 Ex $310 Gd $225
Same as standard Model 1200 except 12 and 20 ga. only. 2-round magazine, specially tuned trigger, 26-inch vent. rib bbl. SK choke, semi-fancy walnut stock and forearm. Weight: 7.25 to 7.5 lbs. Made 1965 to 1973. Also available 1966 to 1970
w/Winchester recoil reduction system, add $50

MODEL 1300 CAMOPACK . . . . . . NiB $465 Ex $390 Gd $279
Gauge: 12. 3-inch Mag. 4-round magazine. Bbls.: 30- and 22-inch w/Winchoke system. Weight: 7 lbs. Laminated stock w/Win-Cam camouflage green, cut checkering, recoil pad, swivels, and sling. Made from 1987 to 1988.

MODEL 1300 DEER SERIES
Similar to standard Model 1300 except 12 or 20 ga. only. Special 22-inch Cyl. bore or rifled bbl. and rifle-type sights. Weight: 6.5 lbs. Checkered walnut or synthetic stock w/satin walnut, black, or Advantage Full Camo pattern finish. Matte blue or full-camo metal finish. Made from 1994 to 2006.
w/walnut stock (intro. 1994) . . . . NiB $425 Ex $360 Gd $265
Black Shadow Deer model
 w/synthetic stock (intro. 1994) . . . . NiB $400 Ex $298 Gd $220
Advantage Camo model (1995-98) . . . . . . NiB $445 Ex $377 Gd $280

DEER COMBO
Deer Combo w/22- and
 28-inch bbls. (1994-98) . . . . NiB $515 Ex $455 Gd $390
Rifled bbl. (intro. 1996), add $75

MODEL 1300 DEFENDER SERIES
Gauges: 12 or 20 ga. 18-, 24-, 28-inch vent. rib bbl. 3-inch chamber. 4-, 7-, or 8- round magazine. Weight: 5.6 to 7.4 lbs. Blued, chrome, or matte stainless finish. Wood or synthetic stock. Made from 1985 to 2006.
Combo model . . . . NiB $490 Ex $375 Gd $277
Hardwood stock model . . . . NiB $365 Ex $299 Gd $200
Synthetic pistol-grip model . . . . . . NiB $270 Ex $283 Gd $203
Synthetic stock model . . . . NiB $335 Ex $279 Gd $225
Lady Defender synthetic
 stock (made 1996) . . . . NiB $320 Ex $255 Gd $210
Lady Defender synthetic
 Pistol-grip (made 1996) . . . . NiB $320 Ex $255 Gd $210
Stainless marine
 model w/synthetic stock . . . . . . NiB $555 Ex $435 Gd $290

MODEL 1300 DELUXE SLIDE-ACTION
Gauges: 12 and 20. 3-inch chamber. 4-round magazine. Bbl.: 22-26-, or 28-inch vent. rib bbl. w/Winchoke tubes. Weight: 6.5 lbs. Checkered walnut buttstock and forend w/high luster finish. Polished blue metal finish w/roll-engraved receiver. Made from 1984 to 2006.
Model 1300 Deluxe
 w/high-gloss finish . . . . NiB $500 Ex $390 Gd $292
Model 1300 Ladies/Youth model
 w/22-inch bbl., (disc. 1992) . . . . NiB $455 Ex $360 Gd $258

MODEL 1300 FEATHERWEIGHT SLIDE-ACTION
SHOTGUN
Hammerless. Takedown. 4-round magazine. Gauges: 12 and 20. 3-inch chambers. Bbls.: 22-, 26-, or 28-inch w/plain or vent. rib w/Winchoke tubes. Weight: 6.38 to 7 lbs. Checkered walnut buttstock, grooved slide handle. Made from 1978 to 1994.
w/plain bbl. . . . . NiB $400 Ex $365 Gd $290
w/vent. rib . . . . NiB $400 Ex $365 Gd $290

XTR model . . . . NiB $400 Ex $365 Gd $290

MODEL 1300 RANGER SERIES
Gauges: 12 or 20 ga. 3-inch chamber. 5-round magazine. 22-(rifled), 26-, or 28-inch vent. rib bbl. w/Winchoke tubes. Weight: 7.25 lbs. Blued finish. Walnut-finished hardwood buttstock and forend. Made from 1984 to 2006.
Standard model . . . . NiB $377 Ex $366 Gd $270
Combo model . . . . NiB $465 Ex $399 Gd $280
Ranger Deer combo
 (D&T w/rings & bases) . . . . NiB $455 Ex $380 Gd $265
Ranger Ladies/Youth . . . . NiB $366 Ex $255 Gd $190

MODEL 1300 SLIDE-ACTION FIELD GUN
Takedown w/front-locking rotary bolt. Gauges: 12, 20. 3-inch chamber. 4-round magazine. Bbl.: Vent. rib; 26-, 28-, 30-inch w/ Winchoke tubes (IC/M/F). Weight: 7.25 lbs. Checkered walnut or synthetic stock w/standard, black, or Advantage Full Camo Pattern finish. Matte blue or full-camo metal finish. Made from 1994 to 2006.
Standard Field w/walnut stock . . . NiB $445 Ex $320 Gd $266
Black Shadow w/black
 synthetic stock . . . . NiB $365 Ex $275 Gd $200
Advantage Camo model . . . . NiB $455 Ex $375 Gd $290

MODEL 1300 SLUG HUNTER SERIES
Similar to standard Model 1300 except chambered 12 ga. only w/special 22-inch smoothbore w/sabot-rifled choke tube or fully rifled bbl. w/rifle-type sights. Weight: 6.5 lbs. Checkered walnut, hardwood, or laminated stock w/satin walnut or WinTuff finish. Matte blue metal finish. Made from 1988 to 1994.
w/hardwood stock . . . . NiB $465 Ex $365 Gd $250
w/laminated stock. . . . . NiB $515 Ex $400 Gd $290
w/walnut stock . . . . NiB $500 Ex $380 Gd $265
Whitetails Unlimited model
 w/beavertail forend . . . . NiB $475 Ex $396 Gd $300
Sabot-rifled choke tubes, add $50

MODEL 1300 TURKEY SERIES
Gauges: 12 or 20 ga. 22-inch bbl. 3-inch chamber. 4-round magazine. 43 inches overall. Weight: 6.4 to 6.75 lbs. Buttstock and magazine cap, sling studs w/Cordura sling. Drilled and tapped to accept scope base. Checkered walnut, synthetic, or laminated wood stock w/low luster finish. Matte blue or full camo finish. Made from 1985 to 2006.
w/Advantage camo . . . . NiB $390 Ex $285 Gd $216
w/Realtree All-Purpose camo . . . . NiB $488 Ex $369 Gd $275
w/Realtree Gray All-Purpose camo . . . . . . NiB $500 Ex $405 Gd $325
w/Realtree All-Purpose
 camo (matte finish) . . . . NiB $525 Ex $420 Gd $355
w/Black Shadow synthetic stock . . . . . . NiB $355 Ex $285 Gd $190
w/Win-Cam green laminate stock . . . . .NiB $445 Ex $365 Gd $225
Win-Cam combo
 (22- or 30-inch bbl.) . . . . NiB $465 Ex $420 Gd $350
Win-Cam NWTF model
 (22- or 30-inch bbl.) . . . . NiB $525 Ex $375 Gd $285
Win-Cam Youth/Ladies model
 (20 ga.) . . . . NiB $565 Ex $435 Gd $310
Win-Tuff model w/brown
 laminated wood stock . . . . NiB $490 Ex $388 Gd $265

MODEL 1300 WATERFOWL SLIDE-ACTION SHOTGUN
Similar to 1300 Standard model except has 28- or 30-inch vent. rib bbl. w/Winchoke tubes. Weight: 7 lbs. Matte blue metal finish. Checkered walnut finished hardwood or brown laminated Win-Tuff wood stock w/camo sling, swivels, and recoil pad. Made from 1984 to 1992.
w/hardwood stock . . . . NiB $435 Ex $300 Gd $220
w/laminated stock . . . . NiB $435 Ex $300 Gd $220

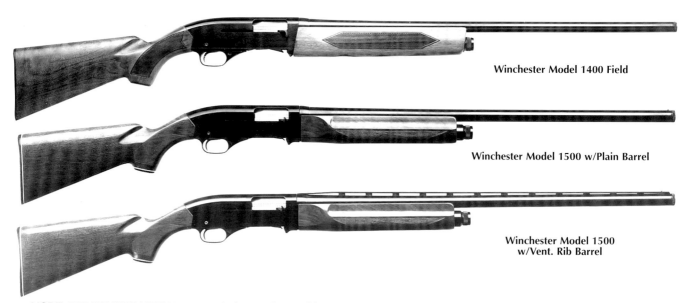

Winchester Model 1400 Field

Winchester Model 1500 w/Plain Barrel

Winchester Model 1500
w/Vent. Rib Barrel

MODEL 1300 XTR SLIDE-ACTION . . . . **NiB $550 Ex $455 Gd $3209**
Hammerless. Takedown. 4-shot magazine. Gauges: 12 and 20. 3-inch chambers. Bbl.: Plain or vent. rib; 28-inch bbls.; Winchoke interchangeable tubes IC/M/F. Weight: About 7 lbs. Disc. 2006.

MODEL 1400 AUTOMATIC FIELD GUN
Gas operated. Front-locking rotary bolt. Takedown. 2-round magazine. Gauges: 12, 16, 20. 2.75-inch chamber. Bbl.: Plain or vent. rib; 26, 28, 30 inch; IC/M/F choke or Winchoke interchangeable tubes IC/M/F. Weight: 6.5 to 7.25 lbs. Checkered pistol-grip stock and forearm, recoil pad, also available w/Winchester recoil reduction system (Cycolac stock). Made from 1964 to 1968.
w/plain bbl. . . . . NiB $355 Ex $244 Gd $190
w/vent. rib bbl. . . . . NiB $390 Ex $244 Gd $196
w/recoil reduction system, add $125
w/Winchoke, add $50

MODEL 1400 DEER GUN. . . . . . . **NiB $369 Ex $255 Gd $190**
Same as standard Model 1400 except has special 22-inch bbl. w/rifle-type sights for rifle slug or buckshot. 12 ga. only. Weight: 6.25 lbs. Made from 1965 to 1968.

MODEL 1400
MARK II DEER GUN. . . . . **NiB $460 Ex $345 Gd $290**
Same general specifications as Model 1400 Deer Gun. Made from 1968 to 1973.

MODEL 1400 MARK II FIELD GUN
Same general specifications as Model 1400 Field Gun except not chambered for 16 ga. Winchester Recoil Reduction System not available after 1970. Only 28-inch bbls. w/Winchoke offered after 1973. Made from 1968 to 1978.
w/plain bbl. . . . . NiB $450 Ex $365 Gd $287
w/plain bbl. and Winchoke. . . . . . NiB $475 Ex $388 Gd $315
w/vent. rib bbl. . . . . NiB $544 Ex $390 Gd $290
w/vent. rib bbl. and Winchoke. . . . NiB $566 Ex $445 Gd $390
w/Winchester recoil reduction system, add $150

MODEL 1400 MARK II
SKEET GUN . . . . **NiB $535 Ex $423 Gd $356**
Same general specifications as Model 1400 Skeet Gun. Made from 1968 to 1973.
MODEL 1400 MARK II TRAP GUN
Same general specifications as Model 1400 Trap Gun except also

furnished w/28-inch bbl. and Winchoke. Winchester recoil reduction system not available after 1970. Made from 1968 to 1973.
w/straight stock . . . . NiB $655 Ex $475 Gd $353
w/Monte Carlo stock . . . . NiB $657 Ex $525 Gd $400
Recoil reduction system, add $150
Winchoke, add $50

MODEL 1400 MARK II UTILITY SKEET . . . . **NiB $590 Ex $445 Gd $355**
Same general specifications as Model 1400 Mark II Skeet Gun except has stock and forearm of field grade walnut. Made 1970 to 1973.

MODEL 1400 MARK II UTILITY TRAP. . . . . **NiB $590 Ex $445 Gd $355**
Same as Model 1400 Mark II Trap Gun except has Monte Carlo stock and forearm of field grade walnut. Made from 1970 to 1973.

MODEL 1400 RANGER
SEMIAUTOMATIC SHOTGUN . . . **NiB $566 Ex $365 Gd $255**
Gauges: 12, 20. 2-round magazine. 28-inch vent. rib bbl. F choke. Overall length: 48.63 inches. Weight: 7 to 7.25 lbs. Walnut finish, hardwood stock and forearm w/cut checkering. Made from 1984 to 1990 by U. S. Repeating Arms.

MODEL 1400 RANGER SEMIAUTOMATIC
DEER SHOTGUN . . . . **NiB $500 Ex $369 Gd $255**
Same general specifications as Ranger Semiautomatic except 24.13-inch plain bbl. w/rifle sights. Manufactured by U.S. Repeating Arms.

MODEL 1400 SKEET GUN . . . . . . **NiB $525 Ex $420 Gd $375**
Same as standard Model 1400 except 12 and 20 ga. only. 26-inch vent. rib bbl., SK choke, semi-fancy walnut stock and forearm. Weight: 7.25 to 7.5 lbs. Made from 1965 to 1968.
w/Winchester recoil reduction system, add. $50

MODEL 1400 TRAP GUN
Same as standard Model 1400 except 12 ga. only. 30-inch vent. rib bbl., F choke. Semi-fancy walnut stock, straight or Monte Carlo trap style. Also available w/Winchester recoil reduction system. Weight: About 8.25 lbs. Made from 1965 to 1968.
w/straight stock . . . . NiB $435 Ex $320 Gd $220
w/Monte Carlo stock . . . . NiB $455 Ex $340 Gd $245
Recoil reduction system, add. $150

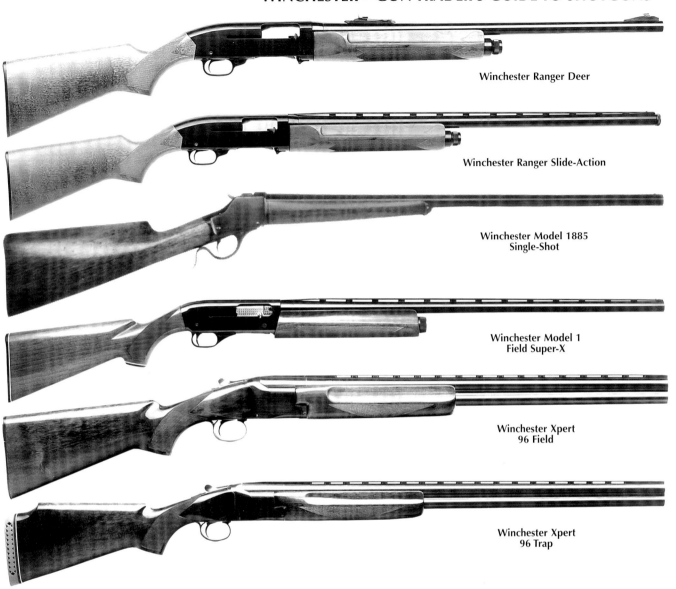

Winchester Ranger Deer

Winchester Ranger Slide-Action

Winchester Model 1885
Single-Shot

Winchester Model 1
Field Super-X

Winchester Xpert
96 Field

Winchester Xpert
96 Trap

MODEL 1500 XTR SEMIAUTOMATIC . . . . NiB $465 Ex $300 Gd $290
Gas operated. Gauges: 12 and 20. 2.75-inch chambers. Bbl.: Plain or vent. rib; 28-inch; WinChoke interchangeable tubes IC/M/F. American walnut stock and forend; checkered grip and forend. Weight: 7.25 lbs. Made from 1978 to 1982.

**MODEL 1885
SINGLE-SHOT SHOTGUN . . . NiB $4377 Ex $3554 Gd $2566**
Falling-block action, same as Model 1885 Rifle. Highwall receiver. Solid frame or takedown. 20 ga. 3-inch chamber. 26-inch bbl.; plain, matted, or matted rib; Cyl. bore, M/F choke. Weight: About 5.5 lbs. Straight-grip stock and forearm. Made from 1914 to 1916.

MODEL 1887 LEVER-ACTION SHOTGUN
First of John Browning's patent shotgun designs produced by Winchester. 10 or 12 ga. on casehardened frame fitted w/20-inch blued, Cyl. bore or F choke. 30- or 32-inch bbl. Plain or checkered walnut stock and forend. Made from 1887 to 1901.
10 or 12 ga. Standard model . . . . . . NiB $4188 Ex $3765 Gd $3287
10 or 12 ga. Deluxe model. . . . . . NiB $9233 Ex $8977 Gd $6450
10 or 12 ga. Riot Gun . . . . NiB $2770 Ex $2256 Gd $1656

w/.70-150 Ratchet rifled bbl.
.70 cal. rifle/87 produced . . . . NiB $4350 Ex $3000 Gd $2275
3 or 4 blade Del. Damascus bbl., add 20%

MODEL 1901 LEVER-ACTION SHOTGUN
Same general specifications as Model 1887, of which this is a redesigned version. 10 ga. only. Made from 1901 to 1920.
Standard model . . . . NiB $4379 Ex $3988 Gd $3500
Deluxe model . . . . NiB $6100 Ex $4988 Gd $3360

**MODEL 1911 AUTO-
LOADING SHOTGUN . . . . NiB $755 Ex $655 Gd $500**
Hammerless. Takedown. 12 ga. only. 4-round tubular magazine. Bbl.: Plain, 26 to 32 inch, standard borings. Weight: About 8.5 lbs. Plain or checkered pistol-grip stock and forearm. Made from 1911 to 1925.

RANGER DEER COMBINATION. . . . . . . NiB $455 Ex $365 Gd $245
Gauge: 12. 3-inch Mag. 3-round magazine. Bbl.: 24-inch Cyl. bore deer bbl. and 28-inch vent. rib bbl. w/WinChoke system. Weight: 7.25 lbs. Made from 1987 to 1990.

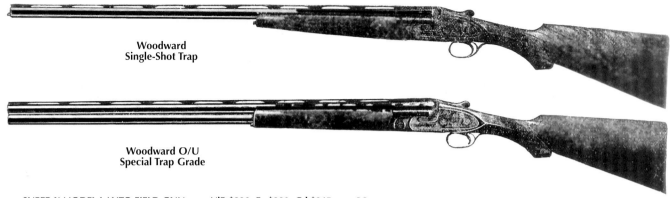

Woodward
Single-Shot Trap

Woodward O/U
Special Trap Grade

SUPER-X MODEL I AUTO FIELD GUN.....NiB $390 Ex $280 Gd $245
Gas operated. Takedown. 12 ga. 2.75-inch chamber. 4-round magazine. Bbl.: Vent. rib 26-inch IC; 28-inch M/F; 30-inch F choke. Weight: About 7 lbs. Checkered pistol-grip stock. Made 1974 to 1984.

SUPER-X MODEL I SKEET GUN.........NiB $977 Ex $755 Gd $590
Same as Super-X Field Gun except has 26-inch bbl., SK choke, skeet-style stock and forearm of select walnut. Made 1974 to 1984.

SUPER-X MODEL I TRAP GUN
Same as Super-X Field Gun except has 30-inch bbl., IM/F choke, trap-style stock (straight or Monte Carlo comb) and forearm of select walnut, recoil pad. Made from 1974 to 1984.
w/straight stock . . . . NiB $790 Ex $588 Gd $425
w/Monte Carlo stock   . . . . NiB $875 Ex $655 Gd $470

XPERT MODEL 96 O/U FIELD GUN . . . . NiB $975 Ex $770 Gd $677
Boxlock action similar to Model 101. Plain receiver. Auto ejectors. Selective single trigger. Gauges: 12, 20. 3-inch chambers. Bbl.: Vent. rib; 26-inch IC/M; 28-inch M/F, 30-inch F/F choke (12 ga. only). Weight: 6.25 to 8.25 lbs. depending on ga. and bbls. Checkered pistol-grip stock and forearm. Made from 1976 to 1981 for Olin Corp. at its Olin-Kodensha facility in Japan.

XPERT MODEL 96 SKEET GUN . . . . NiB $975 Ex $770 Gd $677
Same as Xpert Field Gun except has 2.75-inch chambers, 27-inch bbls., SK choke, skeet-style stock and forearm. Made 1976 to 1981.

XPERT MODEL 96 TRAP GUN
Same as Xpert Field Gun except 12 ga. only, 2.75-inch chambers. 30-inch bbls., IM/F or F/F choke, trap-style stock (straight or Monte Carlo comb) w/recoil pad. Made from 1976 to 1981.
w/straight stock . . . . NiB $975 Ex $770 Gd $677
w/Monte Carlo stock   . . . . NiB $1133 Ex $990 Gd $697

JAMES WOODWARD & SONS —
London, England

James Woodward & Sons was acquired by James Purdey & Sons after WWII.

BEST QUALITY HAMMERLESS DOUBLE
Sidelock. Automatic ejectors. Double triggers or single trigger. Built to order in all standard gauges, bbl. lengths, boring, and other specifications. Made as a field gun, pigeon and wildfowl gun, skeet gun, or trap gun. Manufactured prior to WWII.
12 ga.
   w/double triggers . . . . . . NiB $30,000 Ex $22,700 Gd $18,900
20 ga.
   w/double triggers . . . . . . NiB $33,000 Ex $26,890 Gd $18,700

28 ga.
   w/double triggers . . . .NiB $40,600 Ex $33,560 Gd $25,000
.410 ga.
   w/double triggers . . . . . .NiB $45,000 Ex $36,900 Gd $25,000
Selective single trigger, add 10%

BEST QUALITY O/U SHOTGUN
Sidelock. Automatic ejectors. Double triggers or single trigger. Built to order in all standard gauges, bbl. lengths, boring, and other specifications, including Special Trap Grade w/vent. rib. Woodward introduced this type of gun in 1908. Made until WWII.
12 ga.
   w/double triggers . . . . . . .NiB $31,660 Ex $25,850 Gd $20,000
20 ga.
   w/double triggers . . . . . . NiB $42,500 Ex $35,980 Gd $25,500
28 ga.
   w/double triggers . . . . . . NiB $55,000 Ex $44,900 Gd $32,000
.410 ga.
   w/double triggers . . . . NiB $63,000 Ex $49,800 Gd $35,000
Single trigger, add 10%

BEST QUALITY
SINGLE-SHOT TRAP . . . . NiB $14,860 Ex $12,790 Gd $10,000
Sidelock. Mechanical features of the O/U gun. Vent. rib bbl. 12 ga. only. Built to customer specifications and measurements, including type and amount of checkering, carving, and engraving. Made prior to WWII.

ZEPHYR — Manufactured by Victor
Sarasqueta Company, Eibar, Spain

MODEL 1
O/U SHOTGUN . . . . NiB $1341 Ex $1083 Gd $778
Same general specifications as Field Model O/U except w/more elaborate engraving, finer wood, and checkering. Imported by Stoeger 1930s to 1951.

MODEL 2
O/U SHOTGUN . . . . NiB $1746 Ex $1393 Gd $994
Sidelock. Auto ejectors. Gauges: 12, 16, 20, 28, and .410. Bbls.: 25 to 30 inches most common. Modest scroll engraving on receiver and sideplates. Checkered, straight-grain select walnut buttstock and forend. Imported by Stoeger 1930s to 1951.

MODEL 3
O/U SHOTGUN . . . . NiB $2369 Ex $1888 Gd $1337
Same general specifications as Zephyr Model 2 O/U except w/ more elaborate engraving, finer wood, and checkering. Imported by Stoeger 1930s to 1951.

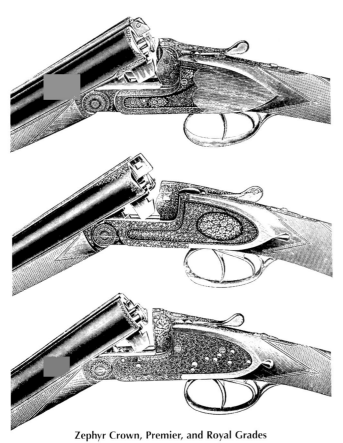

Zephyr Crown, Premier, and Royal Grades

MODEL 400E FIELD GRADE DOUBLE-BARREL SHOTGUN
Anson & Deeley boxlock system. Gauges: 12 16, 20, 28, and .410. Bbls.: 25 to 30 inches. Weight: 4.5 lbs. (.410) to 6.25 lbs. (12 ga.). Checkered French walnut buttstock and forearm. Modest scroll engraving on bbls., receiver, and trigger guard. Imported by Stoeger 1930s to 1950s.

12, 16, or 20 ga.	NiB $2166 Ex $1388 Gd $1000
28 g. or .410	NiB $1877 Ex $1497 Gd $1000
Selective single trigger, add	$250

MODEL 401 E SKEET GRADE DOUBLE-BARREL SHOTGUN
Same general specifications as Field Grade except w/beavertail forearm. Bbls.: 25 to 28 inches. Imported by Stoeger 1930s to 1950s.

12, 16, or 20 ga.	NiB $1954 Ex $1600 Gd $1216
28 ga., or .410	NiB $2144 Ex $1698 Gd $1277
Selective single trigger, add	$450
Nonselective single trigger, add	$300

MODEL 402E DELUXE
DOUBLE-BARREL SHOTGUN . . . . NiB $2455 Ex $2089 Gd $1466
Same general specifications as Model 400E Field Grade except for custom refinements. The action was carefully hand-honed for smoother operation; finer, elaborate engraving throughout, plus higher quality wood in stock and forearm. Imported by Stoeger 1930s to 1950s.

CROWN GRADE. . . . . NiB $1800 Ex $1498 Gd $1056
Boxlock. Gauges: 12, 16, 20, 28, and .410. Bbls.: 25 to 30 inches standard but any lengths could be ordered. Weight: 6 lbs., 4 oz. (.410) to 7 lbs., 4 oz. (12 ga.). Checkered Spanish walnut stock and beavertail forearm. Receiver engraved with scroll patterns. Imported by Stoeger 1938 to 1951.

FIELD MODEL
O/U SHOTGUN . . . . NiB $988 Ex $745 Gd $566
Anson & Deeley boxlock. Auto ejectors. Gauges: 12, 16, and 20. Bbls.: 25 to 30 inches standard- full-length matt rib. Double triggers. Checkered buttstock and forend. Light scroll engraving on receiver. Imported by Stoeger 1930s to 1951.

HONKER SINGLE-SHOT SHOTGUN . . . . NiB $676 Ex $580 Gd $390
Sidelock. Gauge: 10. 3.5-inch Mag. 36-inch vent. rib barrel w/F choke. Weight: 10.5 lbs. Checkered select Spanish walnut buttstock and beavertail forend; recoil pad. Imported by Stoeger 1950s to 1972.

PINEHURST DOUBLE-BARREL
SHOTGUN . . . . NiB $1388 Ex $1190 Gd $800
Boxlock. Gauges: 12, 16, 20, 28, and .410. Bbls.: 25 to 28 inches most common. Checkered, select walnut buttstock and forend. Selective single trigger and auto ejectors. Imported by Stoeger 1950s to 1972.

PREMIER GRADE
DOUBLE-BARREL SHOTGUN. . . . NiB $2870 Ex $2300 Gd $1560
Sidelock. Gauges: 12, 16, 20, 28, and .410. Bbls.: Any length, but 25 to 30 inches most popular. Weight: 4.5 lbs. (.410) to 7 lbs. (12 ga.). Checkered high-grade French walnut buttstock and forend. Imported by Stoeger 1930s to 1951.

ROYAL GRADE
DOUBLE-BARREL SHOTGUN . . . . NiB $4388 Ex $2287 Gd $2077
Same general specifications as the Premier Grade except w/more elaborate engraving, finer checkering, and wood. Imported by Stoeger 1930s to 1951.

STERLINGWORTH II
DOUBLE-BARREL SHOTGUN. . . NiB $1000 Ex $790 Gd $678
Genuine sidelocks with color casehardened sideplates. Gauges: 12, 16, 20, and .410. Bbls.: 25 to 30 inches. Weight: 6 lbs., 4 oz. (.410) to 7 lbs., 4 oz. (12 ga.). Select Spanish walnut buttstock and beavertail forearm. Light scroll engraving on receiver and sideplates. Automatic, sliding-tang safety. Imported by Stoeger 1950s to 1972.

THUNDERBIRD
DOUBLE-BARREL SHOTGUN . . . NiB $1221 Ex $900 Gd $755
Sidelock. Gauges: 12 and 10 Mag. Bbls.: 32-inch, both F choke. Weight: 8 lbs., 8 oz. (12 ga.), 12 lbs. (10 ga.). Receiver elaborately engraved w/waterfowl scenes. Checkered select Spanish walnut buttstock and beavertail forend. Plain extractors, double triggers. Imported by Stoeger 1950 to 1972.

UPLAND KING
DOUBLE-BARREL SHOTGUN . . . . NiB $1290 Ex $1066 Gd $886
Sidelock. Gauges: 12, 16, 20, 28, and .410. Bbls.: 25 to 28 inches most popular. Checkered buttstock and forend of select walnut. Selective single trigger and auto ejectors. Imported by Stoeger 1950 to 1972.

UPLANDER 4E
DOUBLE-BARREL SHOTGUN . . . NiB $900 Ex $688 Gd $525
Same general specifications as the Zephyr Sterlingworth II except w/selective auto ejectors and highly polished sideplates. Imported by Stoeger 1951 to 1972.

WOODLANDER II
DOUBLE-BARREL SHOTGUN . . . NiB $645 Ex $465 Gd $377
Boxlock. Gauges: 12, 20, and .410. Bbls.: 25 to 30 inches. Weight: 6 lbs., 4 oz. (.410) to 7 lbs., 4 oz. (12 ga.). Checkered Spanish walnut stock and beavertail forearm. Engraved receiver. Imported by Stoeger 1950 to 1972.

Appendix A: Curios and Relics

Curios and Relics (C&R) represent a segment of gun trading and collecting. Firearms designated as a C&R have slightly different classification than newly manufactured firearms. Collectors often apply for a C&R license, which allows them to collect certain firearms. The ATF website (atf.gov) has a complete list of firearms that are classified as C&R firearms. According to the ATF website: "Firearm curios or relics include firearms which have special value to collectors because they possess some qualities not ordinarily associated with firearms intended for sporting use or as offensive or defensive weapons. To be recognized as curios or relics, firearms must fall within one of the following categories:

1. Have been manufactured at least 50 years prior to the current date, but not including replicas thereof; or
2. Be certified by the curator of a municipal, State, or Federal museum which exhibits firearms to be curios or relics of museum interest; or
3. Derive a substantial part of their monetary value from the fact that they are novel, rare, bizarre, or from the fact of their association with some historical figure, period, or event.

The definition for C&R firearms found in 27 CFR § 478.11 does not specifically state that a firearm must be in its original condition to be classified as a C&R firearm. However, ATF Ruling 85-10, which discusses the importation of military C&R firearms, notes that they must be in original configuration and adds that a receiver is not a C&R item. Combining this ruling and the definition of C&R firearms, the Firearms Technology Branch (FTB) has concluded that a firearm must be in its original condition to be considered a C&R weapon.

It is also the opinion of FTB, however, that a minor change such as the addition of scope mounts, non-original sights, or sling swivels would not remove a firearm from its original condition. Moreover, we have determined that replacing particular firearms parts with new parts that are made to the original design would also be acceptable-for example, replacing a cracked M1 Grand stock with a new wooden stock of the same design, but replacing the original firearm stock with a plastic stock would change its classification as a C&R item."

Firearms automatically attain C&R status when they are fifty years old. For a list of guns classified by the ATF as Curios and Relics, go to ATF.gov.

www.skyhorsepublishing.com

Appendix B: State by State Firearms Purchase Permit Requirements

Gun laws are subject to change. This information is to be used a guide. Consult your state and local authorities for details on all gun laws in your state and local area.

PERMIT REQUIRED FOR PURCHASE

STATE	Long Guns (Rifles and Shotguns)	Handguns	Notes
Alabama	No	No	
Alaska	No	No	
Arizona	No	No	
Arkansas	No	No	
California	No	No	A valid California driver's license or California identification card and purchaser's right thumbprint required.
Colorado	No	No	
Connecticut	Yes	YEs	Long guns require a valid long gun eligibility certificate, a valid permit to carry a handgun, a valid eligibility certificate for a handgun, or a valid permit to sell at retail a handgun. Handguns require a permit to carry a handgun, a handgun eligibility certificate, or a permit to sell handguns.
Delaware	No	No	
District of Columbia	No	No	
Florida	No	No	
Georgia	No	No	Handguns require a photo ID.
Hawaii	Yes	Yes	Long guns and handguns require a local police chief to issue a permit prior to taking ownership of firearm.
Idaho	No	No	
Illinois	Yes	Yes	Long guns and handguns require FOID (Federal Owner's Identification Card).
Indiana	No	No	
Iowa	No	No	Handguns require a permit to purchase.
Kansas	No	No	
Kentucky	No	No	
Louisiana	No	No	
Maine	No	No	
Maryland	No	No	

GUN TRADER'S GUIDE TO SHOTGUNS

STATE	Long Guns (Rifles and Shotguns)	Handguns	Notes
Massachusetts	Yes	Yes	Long guns require a valid FID (Firearms Identification); Class A carry license is required for a large capacity firearm (rifle, shotgun or handgun); Class B carry license required for non-large capacity firearm (rifle, shotgun or handgun).
Michigan	No	Yes	Handguns require a license to purchase issued by a local chief of police or county sheriff.
Minnesota	No	Yes	Handguns and semiautomatic military-style assault weapons require a handgun transferee permit or a carry permit or a transfer report after a seven-day waiting period.
Mississippi	No	No	
Missouri	No	No	
Montana	No	No	
Nebraska	No	Yes	Handguns require a certificate from local sheriff or police chief.
Nevada	No	No	
New Hampshire	No	No	
New Jersey	Yes	Yes	Long guns require a valid FID (Firearms Purchasers Identification Card). Handguns require a permit to purchase issued by state police or local police chief for each handgun.
New Mexico	No	No	
New York	No	Yes	Handguns require a license to carry or possess. New York City requires a permit to purchase and possess for any firearm (rifle, shotgun or handgun).
North Carolina	No	Yes	Handguns require a permit issued by county sheriff.
North Dakota	No	No	
Ohio	No	No	
Oklahoma	No	No	
Oregon	No	No	
Pennsylvania	No	No	
Rhode Island	No	No	Long guns require a purchase of a shotgun or rifle application form. Handguns require a hunter safety course card or pistol safety course card.
South Carolina	No	No	
South Dakota	No	No	
Tennessee	No	No	All firearms (rifle, shotgun, or handgun) require an ID.
Texas	No	No	
Utah	No	No	
Vermont	No	No	
Virginia	No	No	
Washington	No	No	
West Virginia	No	No	
Wisconsin	No	No	
Wyoming	No	No	

Appendix C: Choke Tube Compatibility

Akdal MKA 1919	Interchanges with Winchester, Mossberg 500 threads
American Arms	Interchanges with Fausti/Traditions shotgun style threads
Austin & Halleck Black Powder Shotgun	Interchanges with Winchester, Mossberg 500 threads
Baikal/European American Arms	Interchanges with Standard Tru-Choke style threads
Benelli (current production square threads)	Interchanges with Beretta MobilChoke threads
Benelli Crio	Interchanges with Sport II and SuperSport and Cordoba produced prior to 2006
Benelli Crio Plus	Interchanges with Super Black Eagle 2, M-2, Ultra Light and current Sport II, Super Sport and Cordoba
Benelli M-4	Interchanges with Beretta MobilChoke/Benelli standard thread
Beretta (current production)	Interchanges with Beretta MobilChoke
Beretta (Old style no threads use muzzle cap)	No known interchange
Beretta Optima	Interchanges with Optima threads (Models 391A Extrema & 12ga. 391 Teknys) Silver Pigeon II & III
Beretta Optima Plus	Interchanges with Optima Plus threads (Models 391A Extrema and 12ga. 391 Teknys)
Bernardelli	No known interchange
Black Diamond (12ga)	Interchanges with Beretta MobilChoke/Benelli standard thread
Browning Invector	Interchanges with Winchester, Mossberg 500, Weatherby, Maverick 88, S&W, and Savage Guns-style threads
Browning Invector Plus	Interchanges with Browning Invector Plus, Winchester Super X2, and Winchester Supreme-style threads
BSA	Interchanges with Beretta MobilChoke/Benelli threads
BSA 20ga Silver Eagle	Serial #201836 or higher Beretta MobilChoke/Benelli: If serial number is below, Huglu threads
Caeser Guerini	Interchanges with Fab Arms
Century Arms/Kahn Centurion and Arthemis (12ga)	Interchanges with Berretta/Benelli
Century Arms/Kahn Centurion and Arthemis (20ga)	Interchange with Huglu-style threads
Charles Daly current production pumps, semi-autos, and Model 206	Interchanges with Remington-style threads
Charles Daly current production O/U	Interchanges with Winchester-style threads

Charles Daly S/S Field II, Model 306, and Model 106	Interchange with Beretta MobilChoke/Benelli-style threads
Churchhill (12ga)	Interchanges with Fabarm-style threads, some model American Arms-style threads
CZ USA 12ga	Interchanges with standard Beretta MobilChoke/Benelli threads
CZ USA 20ga	Interchanges with Huglu-style threads
DeHaans 12ga	Interchanges with Beretta MobilChoke/Benelli-style threads
DeHaans 20ga	Interchanges with Huglu-style threads
Fabarm 12ga	Interchanges with Fabarm-style threads
F.A.I.R. (Rizzini)	Interchanges with Verona LX threads
Franchi SxS Highlander and O/U SL series	No known interchange
Franchi (current production-square thread)	Interchanges with Beretta MobilChoke/Benelli-style threads
Franchi (old style-v threads)pre-1999 models	Interchanges with Fran Choke-style threads
H&R 1871/N.E.F. 12ga and 20ga	Interchanges with Winchester, Moss 500, etc. threads
H&R Pardner Pump	Interchanges with Winchester, Moss 500, etc. threads
H&R Excell Auto 5	Interchanges with Verona SX threads
Hastings Choke Tube 1 (old style)	Interchanges with Tru-Choke
Huglu 12ga	Interchange with Beretta MobilChoke/Benelli style threads
Huglu 20ga	Interchange with Huglu
Ithaca (old style fine threads)	Interchanges with Tru-Choke-style threads
Ithaca (new style 12ga)	Interchanges with Winchester-style threads
Ithaca (all new style 20ga)	Interchanges with Tru-Choke-style threads
Lanber 12ga	Interchanges with Lanber-style threads
Lanber imported by American Arms	Interchanges with American Arms-style threads
Laurona (O/U)	Interchanges with American Arms-style threads
LC Smith 12ga (Marlin)	Threads at top of tube are LC Smith Chokes; at bottom is American Arms
LC Smith 20ga (Marlin)	Interchanges with Fran Choke threads
Legacy Sports Escort and Pointer 12ga	Interchanges with Beretta MobilChoke/Benelli standard thread

Legacy Sports Escort 20ga	Interchanges with Huglu-style threads
Legacy Sports/Silma 12ga	No known interchange
Marrochi Golden Snip Field O/U	Interchanges with Browning Invector Plus- style threads
Maverick Model 88	Interchanges with Mossberg 500, Winchester, and Browning Invector style-threads
Miroku	Interchanges with Winchester-style threads
Mossberg 500 and 535	Interchanges with Winchester, Weatherby, Browning Invector
Mossberg 835, 935 and 9200	Interchanges with 835 Mossberg threads
Mossberg Silver Reserve 12ga	Interchanges with Benelli MobilChoke/Beretta threads
Mossberg Silver Reserve 20ga	Interchanges with Huglu style threads
Mossberg SA-20 20ga	Interchanges with Beretta MobilChoke/Benelli
New England	Interchanges with Winchester, Weatherby, Browning Invector, and Mossberg 500-style threads
Remington	Interchanges with Remington-style threads
Remington Pro Bore	Fits Model 105CTi, All Parker Models, New 1100 Competition, and Premier O/U
Remington Spartan	Interchanges with Tru-Choke threads
Renato Gambo	No known interchange
Rizzini USA, (B) & (I)	Interchanges with Verona LX-style threads
Rizzini (E)	No known interchange
Ruger older models pre-1992	Interchanges with Winchester-style threads (short chokes)
Ruger SC Newer Models	Interchanges with Ruger SC-style threads (long chokes)
Ruger (side by side) Gold Label	No known interchange
Sako/Tikka 12ga Some	Interchange with Invector Plus and some with Valmet threads
Savage	Interchanges with Winchester and Mossberg 500-style threads
Savage 411	Interchanges with Tru-Choke-style threads
Savage 512	Interchanges with Beretta MobilChoke/Benelli standard thread
SIG Arms	No known interchange
SIG Arms (Aurora)	Interchanges with Verona LX
SIG Arms (SA3)	No known interchange

SKB Short Style	Interchanges with Winchester and Mossberg 500-style threads
SKB Competition	Interchanges with SKB Competition style chokes
Smith & Wesson old version	Interchanges with Winchester, Mossberg 500, and Browning Invector-style threads
Smith & Wesson Current version 2007	Interchanges with Beretta MobilChoke/Benelli standard thread
Stevens &Savage Model 411	Interchanges with Tru-Choke or Baikal-style threads
Stoeger 2000 Semi Auto & P-350 Pump	Interchanges with Beretta MobilChoke/Benelli threads
Stoeger 2000 Condor (O/U)	Interchanges with Winchester-style threads
Stoeger Luger (O/U)	Interchanges with American Arms-style threads
Stoeger Uplander (side by side)	Interchanges with Winchester-style threads
Traditions Semi-Auto AIS2100 12-gauge	Interchanges with Beretta style-threads. The 20-gauge has no known interchange
Traditions Volo	No known interchange
Thompson Center	Interchanges with Winchester-style threads
Tri-Star Phantom 411 and TR11	Interchanges with Rizzini-style threads
Tri-Star Phantom Field and Model 380D	Interchanges with Beretta-style threads
Tri-Star Phantom HP	No known interchange
Tri-Star Silver Series	Interchanges with American Arms; Serial#4687037 or larger is Beretta MobilChoke/Benelli threads
Tri-Star Current 3 1/2 Semi Auto	Interchanges with Crio Plus system
Tri Star Fab Arms	No known interchange
Valmet	Interchanges with Valmet threads
Verona LX O/U	Interchanges with Verona LX threads
Verona 980 O/U	No known interchange
Verona SX Semi Auto Models	Interchanges with Verona SX threads
Weatherby	Interchanges with Winchester, Mossberg 500, and Weatherby-style threads
Winchester	Interchanges with Winchester, Mossberg 500 Weatherby, and Browning Invector-style threads
Winchester Select Energy	Interchanges with Browning Invector Plus
Winchester Super X2 and Supreme	Interchanges with Browning Invector Plus style threads

(Courtesy cheaperthandirt.com)

Appendix D: Choke Tube Designations

The concept of choke tubes is attributed to American gunsmith Sylvester H. Roper, who received a patent in 1866. A hundred or so years later, Winchester offered what they called the Versatile choke on the semiauto Model 59. By 1969, Winchester had redesigned and renamed the choke tube system, WinChoke, and offered it on its Model 1200 and 1400 shotguns. Other shotgun manufacturers followed. Mossberg offered the Accu-choke system in 1978, and by the 1980s shotgun manufacturers offered screw-in choke tube systems as the shooting public embraced the concept. Browning calls their system Invector and Invector-Plus. Beretta introduced its Mobilchoke first on the S687L over-and-under, and in 2000 they introduced the Optima-Choke system, which is used in conjunction with a back-bored barrel. This design features a longer internal transition taper into the choke constriction, which makes the overall length of the Optima-Choke tube longer than the original Mobilchoke tube. Many manufactures brand their choke tubes with a specific name, so when you're buying additional choke tubes for a shotgun, be sure you know the brand and model type. Just knowing the brand of shotgun is not enough to match up the correct choke tube.

Some choke tubes are compatible among manufacturers. See Appendix C for a list of compatible choke tubes. Use the charts below as a guide to help identify the specific choke constriction of a tube.

MOST COMMON SHOTGUN CHOKE DESIGNATIONS

Standard American	Constriction (12-gauge)	Choke Tube Markings (number of notches or stars)	Pattern Percentage
Cylinder	.000 inches	5 IIIII or *****	40%
Skeet	.005 inches		54%
Improved Cylinder	.010 inches	4 IIII or ****	57%
Modified	.020 inches	3 III or ***	67%
Improved Modified	.030 inches	2 II or **	73%
Full	.040 inches	1 I or *	75%

Appendix E: Shotgun Collectors Organizations

Browning Collectors Association: browningcollectors.com

AH Fox Collectors Association: foxcollectors.com

L.C. Smith Collectors Association: lcsmith.org

Marlin Collectors Association: marlin-collectors.com

National Mossberg Collectors Association: mossbergcollectors.org

Parker Gun Collectors Association: parkerguns.org

The Remington Society of America: remingtonsociety.com

Weatherby Collectors Association: weatherbycollectors.com

The Winchester Arms Collectors Association: winchestercollector.org

Index